POWER WITHOUT KNOWLEDGE

Power Without Knowledge

A CRITIQUE OF TECHNOCRACY

Jeffrey Friedman

OXFORD
UNIVERSITY PRESS

OXFORD
UNIVERSITY PRESS

Oxford University Press is a department of the University of Oxford. It furthers
the University's objective of excellence in research, scholarship, and education
by publishing worldwide. Oxford is a registered trade mark of Oxford University
Press in the UK and certain other countries.

Published in the United States of America by Oxford University Press
198 Madison Avenue, New York, NY 10016, United States of America.

CIP data is on file at the Library of Congress
ISBN 978–0–19–087717–0

9 8 7 6 5 4 3 2 1

Printed by Sheridan Books, Inc., United States of America

Contents

Preface

THIS BOOK COMES into the world at an inopportune moment. Politics in 2019 appears to be anything but technocratic, and there is a good deal of reality to the appearance. While I will suggest that populism à la Donald Trump does have surprising technocratic resonances, the struggle against him far transcends the ordinary push and pull of technocratic cost-benefit analysis. Moreover, a new style of socialist politics is arising alongside this struggle, and it is, at least arguably, not technocratic at all. A critique of technocracy, then, is anything but timely.

Nevertheless, such a critique is needed. The status quo is far more technocratic than is generally recognized, and efforts to change it are hindered by the absence of a clear understanding of what technocracy is and what it presupposes. This study is intended to bring us closer to such an understanding.

I began thinking about the issues examined here when I read Philip E. Converse's classic 1964 paper, "The Nature of Belief Systems in Mass Publics," as a first-year graduate student in the introductory statistics course at Yale in 1992. I am indebted to Edward Tufte for including Converse's statistically low-tech article in such a course. From 1995 to 2012, I was able to discuss what I saw as the implications of Converse's article, and cognate research, at occasional seminars in which some of my students at Barnard, Columbia, Dartmouth, Harvard, and Yale participated, along with other students they recommended. I am grateful to the seminar participants, who managed to change my perspective significantly over time.

Guive Assadi, Peter Beattie, Sam Bowman, Zeljka Buturovic, Zachary Caceres, Eli Davey, Samuel DeCanio, Steven DeCanio, Shterna Friedman, François Godard, Paul

Gunn, Tom Hoffman, Kai Jäger, Simon Kaye, Philip Larsen, Chris Oppermann, Richard Robb, Paul Rosenberg, Jacob Roundtree, Ilya Somin, Slavisa Tasic, Oliver Traldi, and Fengyang Zhao read the entire manuscript in various stages of its life—more than once in the cases of Steven, Shterna, Jacob, Richard, Paul, and Paul. The manuscript benefited from these readers' critical comments, and I benefited from their encouragement. Scott Althaus, Stephen Earl Bennett, Sebastian Benthall, Ryan Berg, Mark Bevir, Amar Bhidé, John Bullock, Bruce Canter, Nick Cowen, Anthony Evans, Loren Goldman, Dimitri Halikias, Colin Hay, Robert Jervis, Arnold Kling, Wladimir Kraus, Daniel Kuehn, Andrew Lamey, Russell Muirhead, Michael Murakami, Liya Nahusenay, Kyle O'Donnell, Benjamin Ogden, John E. Parsons, Mark Pennington, Paul Quirk, Julian Reiss, Lee Ross, Jochen Runde, Ivelin Sardamov, David Schraub, Rajiv Shah, Jeffrey K. Shapiro, Karl Smith, Robert Talisse, Joshua Temin, Philip E. Tetlock, Nick Weller, and Samuel Garrett Zeitlin read chapters or sections; I'm grateful for their insights. I apologize if I inadvertently left anyone off these lists. I am also indebted to David McBride and the referees for Oxford University Press; to Matt Grossman, for guiding me to the 2016 American National Election Study; and to Eli Davey for drawing a random sample from that study and analyzing it.

Richard Pious, my department chair at Barnard, was supportive when personal circumstances required that I abandon my post in New York and move to Iowa City. While writing the manuscript during two years in Iowa and ten years in rural Texas, I profited from the occasional escape to civilization, where I presented arguments and chapters from the book to the Department of Government at the University of Texas at Austin, the Political Theory Colloquium at Harvard University, and the Research Workshop in American Politics at the University of California, Berkeley. My gratitude goes to the participants in these fora for their comments, and to Tom Pangle at Texas, Jacob Roundtree at Harvard, and Gabriel Lenz at Berkeley for inviting me.

I was able to conduct research while in Texas due to a Visiting Scholar appointment with the Department of Government at the University of Texas at Austin; and then in California due to a Visiting Scholar appointment with the Charles and Louise Travers Department of Political Science at the University of California, Berkeley. I am grateful to Jeffrey Tulis and Eric Schickler, respectively, for arranging these positions.

In defending the possibility of happiness in the private sphere, I have grappled with the fact that the happiness I experience there has been available to me mainly because I was lucky enough to have met Shterna while I was in New York—a stroke of good fortune that most people may never be able to duplicate. My greatest thanks are to her and to my father, Daniel, who taught me a skeptical disposition. I dedicate this book to him and to the memory of my mother, Felice.

POWER WITHOUT KNOWLEDGE

Introduction

TECHNOCRACY AND POLITICAL EPISTEMOLOGY

In deciding who was most fit to govern, knowledge of the world was taken for granted.
The aristocrat believed that those who dealt with large affairs possessed the instinct, the
democrats asserted that all men possessed the instinct and could therefore deal with large
affairs. It was no part of political science in either case to think out how knowledge of the
world could be brought to the ruler.... What counted was a good heart, a reasoning mind, a
balanced judgment. These would ripen with age, but it was not necessary to consider how to
inform the heart and feed the reason. Men took in their facts as they took in their breath.
—WALTER LIPPMANN, *Public Opinion*

On October 31, 1958, Isaiah Berlin delivered the most influential lecture in the history of
political thought: "Two Concepts of Liberty." Berlin's remarks have, of course, become
canonical for their defense of value pluralism and their development of the contrast between positive and negative liberty. Less widely noticed has been the new spin Berlin put
on the distinction between the ends of politics and the means to those ends. "Where ends
are agreed," he pointed out, "the only questions left are those of means"; but questions of
means, he maintained, unlike questions of ends, are unworthy of political theorists' attention, for they are "not political." Rather they are "technical," and as such are "capable
of being settled by experts or machines."[1] For political theorists to study questions of
means, then, would be pointless: questions of means, as opposed to the questions raised
by plural ends, are rightly left to technocrats, for whom the answers are automatic, which
is to say self-evident.

[1] Berlin [1958] 1969, 118.

Power Without Knowledge. Jeffrey Friedman, Oxford University Press (2019). © Oxford University Press.
DOI: 10.1093/oso/9780190877170.001.0001

Ten years later, this blithe confidence in technocratic knowledge reappeared in the work of a philosopher who was otherwise poles apart from Berlin. In "The Scientization of Politics and Public Opinion," Jürgen Habermas argued that the scientific knowledge possessed by technocrats enables them to craft efficacious policy means to given political ends, just as Berlin had thought.[2] However, while Berlin was untroubled by this development, Habermas objected to it on normative grounds. Technocracy, he argued, with its obsessive focus on the efficacy of the means to given ends, emaciates the public sphere by evacuating from it discussion of what those ends should be. Lacking directives from such discussion, technocrats pursue goals that are therefore irrational[3]—like latter-day Calvinists who, in Weber's account, obsessively pursued worldly success even after having abandoned the soteriology that had once justified this pursuit.

On the other hand, regardless of the irrationality of the ends they pursued, Habermas assumed that technocrats' selection of means, being guided by science, is instrumentally rational. Therefore, he proposed yoking technocracy to a stronger form of democracy than had taken shape in the postwar West. This could be achieved by adopting John Dewey's "pragmatistic model," wherein, as Habermas put it, "scientific experts advise the decision-makers and politicians consult scientists in accordance with practical needs"— needs that are democratically determined.[4] So long as the ends of technocracy were "enlightened hermeneutically, through articulation in the discourse of citizens in a community,"[5] politicians could legitimately make use of experts' knowledge of the best policy means to those ends.

Habermas assumed, then, that the discovery of technically appropriate means to given ends is beyond the capacity of ordinary citizens, but that it is not a fundamentally challenging task. Like Berlin, he held that experts can accomplish this task, and that they do so whenever called upon. Half a century on, this view of technocracy does not seem quite so indubitable, yet it persists. Indeed, in reaction to an upsurge of populism, it may be gaining new credibility among those worried about governance by angry mobs. Whatever one's fears of populism, however, I will seek to show that technocracy is not a good alternative and, indeed, that populism can be technocratic in its own way.

My argument will take a different course than the many objections to technocracy that, like Habermas's, have been grounded in the value of democracy. Instead, I will challenge the assumption of technocratic efficacy that Habermas shared with Berlin. Technocracy, I will suggest, could be effective in achieving its ends—whether or not these ends are democratically determined—only if the human behavior that technocrats attempt to control can be reliably predicted. But the prediction of human behavior is an extremely

---

[2] Habermas [1968] 1970, 62, 65.
[3] Ibid., 64.
[4] Ibid., 66–67.
[5] Ibid., 69.

difficult task, far more so than the predictive tasks at which natural science excels. An effective technocracy, therefore, may very well be out of reach.

1.1. THE ABSENCE OF AN ARGUMENT FOR TECHNOCRATIC KNOWLEDGE

Berlin's point about technocratic efficacy was but an aside, but Habermas made the same point critical to his case for a democracy that is adapted to modern conditions. Like Berlin, however, Habermas provided no reason to think that technocracy *is* efficacious. This omission speaks volumes, so let me consider in detail his argument against an undemocratized technocracy, and the role played in the argument by the putative reliability of technocratic knowledge.

Habermas's argument proceeds in five steps.

1. Technocracy arose from the need to use public policy to compensate "for the dysfunctions of free exchange," that is, the social and economic problems caused by capitalism.
2. Technocratic experts have successfully met this need, thereby offering the masses "a guaranteed minimum level of welfare," "secure employment," "a stable income," "social security," and "the chance for individual upward mobility."
3. In exchange for these gifts, technocracy has depoliticized the recipients, "bind[ing] their loyalty" to technocratic capitalism. By offsetting the dysfunctions of capitalism and mitigating economic risks to the populace, technocracy has shifted politics "toward the solution of technical problems" and away from "communicative action," or the uncoerced democratic discussion of ends.[6]
4. Only such discussion could legitimate the ends toward which technocracy provides the means.
5. Lacking democratic legitimacy, technocracy is value-irrational, despite its instrumental rationality.

The argument does not work without its second step. For every capitalist dysfunction, Habermas seemed to suggest, there is a functional technocratic response.[7] Among these responses are not only economic stabilization and welfare policies but policy interventions to solve virtually any other economic or social problem that might arise. Habermas approvingly quoted Claus Offe: "The mass of differentiated social-scientific information that flows into the political system allows both the early identification of risk zones and the treatment of actual dangers"; the risks of capitalism can therefore be successfully "manipulated," and "preventive actions and measures" can be prescribed.[8]

---

[6] Ibid., 102–103, emphasis on the last four words removed.

[7] Ibid., 103.

[8] See ibid., 98, and Habermas [1973] 1975, 35, 53–54.

Technocrats, then, do not just attempt to solve, mitigate, or prevent social and economic problems; they succeed. This was crucial for Habermas, because technocrats' problem-solving success was, in his view, the very thing that stifles the democratic discussion of ends.

To succeed, however, technocrats must possess reliable knowledge of how to solve, mitigate, or prevent economic and social problems. Why did Habermas assume the existence of such knowledge?

It is difficult to say, for instead of explaining how technocrats could know what they need to know if they are to do what they need to do, he inserted them into a tale of the rationalization of modern life. Technocracy, in this narrative, marks "a new or second stage" of Weberian bureaucracy, and is thus *presumptively* rational, in the instrumental sense: it (somehow) produces an efficacious matching of policy means to given ends.[9] Caught up, it seems, in the Frankfurt school's vision of all things modern as instrumentally rational, Habermas failed to identify the basis for his implicit claim that technocrats' instrumental knowledge is, in fact, real.

The absence of argument here is all the more striking given the sharp line that Habermas drew between natural and social science.[10] If the two are entirely different types of enterprise, as he believed, then he cannot have been making the naturalistic assumption that reliable technocratic knowledge stems from technocrats' use of the methods—however one might define them—that are successfully deployed by physicists, chemists, biologists, and so on. A successful technocracy presupposes knowledge of a different kind, knowledge of human behavior: that is, knowledge of how to control human action effectively, hence knowledge of how to predict the outcome of manipulating it—which is what all technocratic policies do. Only by manipulating human behavior in one way or another can technocrats solve, mitigate, or prevent the social and economic problems that Habermas believed they can and do solve, mitigate, or prevent, since all such problems must stem, in one way or another, from dysfunctional human actions. But why should we believe that—setting aside their own pretensions to scientificity—social "scientists" have the necessary knowledge? If they lack it, however, then they will not be able to produce accurate forecasts of the effects of technocratic measures on the problems they are intended to solve, mitigate, or prevent. Such measures, then, far from manifesting a more advanced stage of instrumental rationality, will amount to gropings in the dark.

---

[9] Habermas [1968] 1970, 62.

[10] See Habermas [1967] 1988 and Habermas [1968] 1971. An anonymous reader suggested that Habermas may have thought that society was, in the postwar era, being treated *as if* it could be controlled in the same way that nature can be, but that Habermas believed this assumption to be false. However, this interpretation would not explain Habermas's insistence that technocracy quells discontent. To achieve this effect, technocrats' knowledge of society must be real.

I.2. TECHNOCRACY AND DISTRIBUTIVE JUSTICE

In the decades that followed Berlin's and Habermas's remarks on technocratic knowledge, political theorists' attention to the subject atrophied while technocracy itself metastasized. As a result, political theorists' chief concerns have become detached from most areas of contemporary politics and government: those that are technocratic.

Broadly speaking, the aim of technocracy is to advance social and economic welfare by addressing such problems as unemployment, inflation, failing schools, a dysfunctional health care system, drug addiction—the list begun by Habermas is potentially endless. A working definition of a technocracy, then, is: *A polity that aims to solve, mitigate, or prevent social and economic problems among its people* (henceforth, for convenience, their "social problems"). Contemporary political theory has scrutinized neither the ends nor the means of such a polity, for the technocratic project is orthogonal, at best, to contemporary political theorists' chief preoccupations: distributive justice and democracy.

While technocratic governments do redistribute a great deal of wealth, this is rarely done in the manner or for the reasons that theorists of justice recommend: by following (say) the Difference Principle, setting an income floor, or otherwise conveying primary goods to the least advantaged as a matter of right. Instead, poverty—the original "social problem"—has been disaggregated into a wide array of ills, each with at least one programmatic solution. These programs are paradigmatically technocratic because they are designed to solve, mitigate, or prevent discrete social problems—those experienced by impoverished members of the polity—*regardless* of whether their impoverishment is itself considered unjust.

In the United States, there were 92 federal poverty-related programs as of 2014, in addition to many more state and local programs.[11] Instead of giving primary goods to the poor, these programs mainly offered in-kind benefits such as housing or vouchers that, because they must be spent on specific things (such as food, education, or housing), cannot function as primary goods (means to ends chosen by the individual). Technocratic poverty-related programs take aim at specific difficulties experienced by the poor, such as the unavailability of affordable housing. Inasmuch as the programs prescribe the needs to be addressed, and often the means by which they must be addressed, rather than leaving these decisions to those being assisted, they are best described as paternalistic. Distributive justice is not their aim (although it may be their incremental side effect), so they have escaped the scrutiny of political theorists, for the most part.

Moreover, a great deal of redistributive spending—in the United States, 64 percent of it, by one estimate—is not directed toward the poor at all.[12] Social Security, Medicare, trade subsidies, agricultural subsidies, subsidies to real-estate developers, most aid to education, and a great many other redistributive programs that are not means tested have

---

[11] House Budget Committee 2014, 3.

[12] "The Poor Are Getting a Smaller Share of Government Payments," graphic, *New York Times*, February 12, 2012.

their rationales in social or economic problems that afflict citizens generally, or a subset located in the middle or upper classes. Again, because these programs are not aimed at distributive justice, political theorists have had little to say about them. Thus, they have had little to say about most of the things modern government pays for.

One might contend that in making arguments for the redistribution of primary goods to the least advantaged, Rawlsian political theorists, at least, have implicitly criticized technocracy by suggesting that redistributive spending *not* directed toward the least advantaged is illegitimate. This does not follow, though, as such spending might achieve worthwhile objectives other than distributive justice. In that case, however, the legitimacy of such spending would depend on whether the programs achieve their objectives, and the question would be, Do they?

Answering this question would require an entirely different type of inquiry than normative theorizing about distributive justice. At a minimum, what would be required is a political epistemology of technocracy: an examination of the grounds of, and the limits to, the knowledge likely to be possessed by technocratic policymakers.[13]

I.3. TECHNOCRATIC REGULATION AND THE LIMITS OF STATE AUTONOMY

The writ of technocracy extends far beyond government spending. In fact, the main form taken by government efforts to solve, mitigate, and prevent social problems is not redistribution but regulation.

Between 1993 and 2013, the ratio of new federal regulations to new congressionally enacted statutes was 223:1.[14] More than 3,000 new federal administrative rules are promulgated each year, adding more than 20,000 pages annually to the Code of Federal Regulations.[15] In 1960, the Code contained 22,877 pages; by 2016, it contained 178,277.[16] This massive expansion of public authority has flown under the radar of most political theorists, for bureaucratic authority is not democratic authority—at least not in any straightforward sense—and theorists have been preoccupied with democracy even more than with distributive justice.

Regulatory policy is made by unelected officials in scores of bureaucracies large and small, from the Federal Reserve System and the Federal Trade Commission to the Nuclear Regulatory Commission and the Office of Thrift Supervision. It is safe to say, in light of evidence regarding mass public inattention to politics and government,[17] that most citizens probably have no idea of the various regulatory agencies' responsibilities or

---

[13] For discussions of political epistemology as a general project, see Althaus et al. 2014 and Friedman 2014.

[14] Ferguson 2013.

[15] Crews 2016, fig. 13.

[16] Ibid., 21.

[17] See Chapter 6. DeCanio 2000, DeCanio 2005, DeCanio 2006, and DeCanio 2007 develop the idea of state autonomy as a function of public ignorance.

even their existence, let alone any idea of the contents—or the effects—of the countless rules these agencies produce. In this sense, regulation is outside the purview of democratic politics.

However, there is an important ambiguity in the relationship between regulatory authority and popular sovereignty, especially in the United States, where such authority is traceable to the demos through bureau heads appointed by elected presidents, governors, or mayors. In addition, concentrated media attention can arouse public indignation against whichever policies strike media personnel as worthy of sustained coverage because it is outrageous or potentially controversial (for example, the Trump administration's reversal of Obama administration policy on net neutrality).[18] This can lead regulatory bureaucracies to change course (although not always, as suggested by this example). Likewise, fear of the political effects of media attention can constrain regulators from taking actions that might draw criticism if they became known to journalists.[19] Thus, both the real power of public opinion and its latent power should, to some extent, tend to constrain the autonomy that regulators would enjoy if the only factor at work were the mass public's overall inattention to the details of public policy, particularly regulatory policy.

In light of these considerations, a political epistemology of technocracy will need to take account of not only "technocrats" in the sense referred to by Habermas (and by nearly everyone else who writes about technocracy)—trained, credentialed specialists—but also members of the general public. The most controversial aspect of this book may be its attempt to meet this need by designating as "technocrats" both trained, credentialed specialists and ordinary citizens. This is merely a matter of stipulation, but as we will soon see, it can have a significant effect on how we understand the workings of technocracy in the real world—and on our normative expectations of it.

I.4. THE TECHNOCRATIC VALUE CONSENSUS

Another reason to include ordinary citizens under the "technocratic" rubric is that, contra the Habermas of 1968, the mass public frequently does decide, in a very loose sense, on the ends to be pursued by technocratic means. To be sure, this "decision" is not made in robust, fair-minded discussions where everyone's voice is respected. Still, ever since survey research began in the 1940s, scholars of public opinion in the United States, at least, have produced findings that indicate a broad consensus around ends that can be pursued technocratically.

Thus, by 1952, Bernard Berelson, a pioneer in the academic study of public opinion, was able to state emphatically that

---

[18] See, e.g., Shepardson 2018.
[19] This is an application of V. O. Key's concept of "latent opinion" (Key 1961, ch. 11).

the *same* avowed principles underlie political positions at every point on the con-
tinuum from left to right. Full employment, a high standard of living, freedom, a
better life for one's children, peace—these are the types of answers we have now, and
we get them from persons of every political persuasion. . . . What this means . . . is
that the selection of means to reach agreed-upon ends is more likely to divide the
electorate than the selection of the ends themselves.[20]

Berelson's conclusions are not at all surprising if we consider the counterfactual. If there
were *not* a value consensus of the type he described, divisions in the electorate about
policies intended to reach the ends he named would indicate that significant numbers of
citizens thought that involuntary unemployment is good, that a high standard of living
is bad, that freedom, peace, and a better life for one's children are undesirable. This is
not logically impossible, but it is surely implausible, and I know of no evidence that
would support this interpretation of twentieth-century (or twenty-first-century) public
opinion in the United States (or elsewhere).

I recognize that in saying this, I am, to some extent, challenging Berlin's doctrine of
value pluralism, later canonized by Rawls as a "fact."[21] I do not dispute that it is indeed
a fact—sometimes, in some polities, when it comes to some issues. But it would be dogmatic to insist that it is a fact in all times and places with regard to all issues.

That it is often not a fact is suggested by the felt need of survey researchers to distinguish between "easy" or "valence" political issues, which are either symbolic issues or are
choices among ends; and "hard" or "positional" issues, which deal with means and are
difficult precisely because they are *technical*.[22] The researchers have found that, among
the citizens they poll, there tends to be broad consensus on what the researchers call the
easy issues—values issues—but dissensus, at least sometimes, about hard, technical issues
revolving around means. Most people, at least in the United States in the twentieth and
early twenty-first centuries, seem to have found it exceedingly easy to choose between
prosperity and poverty, peace and war.

To be sure, not all questions of values are thought to be easy ones—consider the social issues, often related to sexuality, that have divided many citizens since the 1970s—
but technocratic value questions, such as those listed by Berelson, *do* tend to be easy,
producing an overwhelming consensus around such objectives as low inflation and low

---

[20] Berelson 1952, 320–321.

[21] E.g., Rawls 1993, 246. However, Berlin was referring to the fact of disagreement over values as between, say,
Marxists and liberals. Mass polling would not have detected such elite disagreements. Conversely, Rawls specified that sometimes disagreement concerns means—or that is how I take his inclusion, among the "burdens
of judgment," of "conflicting and complex" evidence, "empirical and scientific," that is "hard to assess and evaluate" (Rawls 2005, 56). However, he dwelled on value pluralism (pluralism among ends), and that is primarily
how his message has been received in the subsequent literature.

[22] The easy/hard dichotomy originates in Carmines and Stimson 1980; the valence/positional dichotomy in
Stokes 1966.

unemployment (which political scientists used to call "the motherhood and apple pie of politics").[23]

The consensus around anodyne values detected by Berelson and his successors is conducive to technocracy in the following sense. As Habermas recognized, technocracy requires a consensus around ends *of some sort* if it is to devise policies that are means to those ends. Moreover, the values listed by Berelson—with the exception of freedom, which is subject to widely varying definitions—are well suited to technocratic policy-making if we assume that knowledge of the *consequences* of technocratic policies is available to technocrats. Unless a "given" end were consequentialist, a particular policy could not be a means to that end, except in the symbolic sense that adopting the policy might signify agreement with the end. But a policy adopted for symbolic reasons alone would not require, prior to its adoption, that anyone know what the actual effects of the policy will be. And in that case, there would be no role for "technocrats" under any definition of the term.

"Technocrats" are not semioticians. Nor are they trained in philosophy, as they do not purport to be Platonic knowers of the good; nor in politics, as they do not, as technocrats, purport to know how to "get things done." They purport to know what *should* get done: namely, whatever will solve social problems. Knowing which policies will be effective means to the given end of solving social problems requires, as Berlin and Habermas recognized, a type of scientific knowledge, and this has meant, for more than a century, knowledge of the sort that social scientists claim to possess: knowledge of regularities in human behavior—knowledge that can be used, inter alia, to deliver reliable predictions of how people will act in response to this or that technocratic policy initiative.

However, this type of knowledge is claimed—implicitly—not only by technocratic social scientists but by ordinary citizens when they support specific policies intended to achieve shared ends. We get a sense of this in *The Rational Public: Fifty Years of Trends in Americans' Policy Preferences* (1992), by Benjamin I. Page and Robert Y. Shapiro. Page and Shapiro reviewed polling showing that from 1940 to 1990, huge majorities of surveyed Americans consistently favored greater levels of spending on "fighting crime," on "education," on "highways and bridges," on "mass transportation,"[24] on Social Security,[25] on health care,[26] and on "the problems of big cities";[27] and that most of those surveyed consistently favored such regulatory policies as product safety regulation[28] and federal action to expand employment.[29] In 2012, Christopher Ellis and James A. Stimson used the 2008 General Social Survey to add to this list "assistance for child care," "dealing with drug

---

[23] Ellis and Stimson 2012, 15.
[24] Page and Shapiro 1992, fig. 2.2.
[25] Ibid., fig. 4.1.
[26] Ibid., fig. 4.5.
[27] Ibid., fig. 4.7.
[28] Ibid., 156.
[29] Ibid., fig. 4.2.

addiction," and "parks and recreation," for which upwards of 80 percent of the public favored greater spending.[30] It is worth noting that such high levels of agreement about means violate the expectations set up by earlier political scientists' distinction between easy and hard issues; only the easy issues, concerning ends, were supposed to generate consensus. I will attempt to explain in Chapter 6 why both ends and means might readily command consensual support. For now, the important point is that large majorities in this survey research did have opinions about public policies that were aimed at mitigating specific social conditions viewed as problematic: crime, drug addiction, poor education, decaying infrastructure, inadequate mass transit, insufficient Social Security benefits, inadequate or too-expensive health care and child care, inadequate parks and recreational opportunities, urban problems, unsafe products, and unemployment. Thus, large majorities were taking positions on technocratic issues.

A variation on this theme that brings out its epistemic side is suggested by focus groups conducted by John R. Hibbing and Elizabeth Theiss-Morse in 2002. The discussions in these groups suggested that the participants believed that "since people agree on the big goals—affordable medical care, a growing economy, a balanced budget, a secure retirement program, an adequate defense, less crime, better education, and equality of opportunity . . . a properly functioning government would just select the best way of bringing about these end goals."[31] This belief entails the tacit assumption that the government's decision-makers know which policies will bring the end goals about. On the other hand, even though they may be willing to defer to government experts, ordinary citizens pressed by survey researchers about specific technocratic policies seem willing to offer opinions about them, entailing the tacit claim that the respondents themselves know that the effect of the endorsed programs is likely to be beneficial. This is the same type of knowledge claim that would be made by "technocrats" in the standard usage: trained, credentialed specialists with expertise on the effects of such policies. To be sure, specialists would put forth more detailed proposals than the vague phrases used in polls, and they would make more explicit and fine-grained claims about the programs' effects than would most of the ordinary citizens who favor them; the specialists would likely go so far as to make quantitative estimates of costs and benefits. But however explicit or tacit, detailed or vague, quantified or not, both specialists and ordinary citizens regularly make knowledge claims about the efficacy of policies designed to further consensually valued ends: that is, technocratic knowledge claims. Even ordinary citizens, then, can be considered technocrats of a sort.

One way of parsing this is to say that technocracy is an inherently epistemic project—but not an inherently elitist one. Technocracy can be elitist because legislators and the general public often cede authority to trained, credentialed specialists who, they assume, tend to know how to solve some types of social problems. But technocracy can also be

---

[30] Ellis and Stimson 2012, table 2.4.
[31] Hibbing and Theiss-Morse 2002, 133.

populist, because members of the general public sometimes think that *they*—or their tribunes—know how to solve them.

1.5. THE POLITICS OF NEGATIVE UTILITARIANISM

To be sure, there is an alternative to taking an epistemological view of findings such as those summarized by Berelson, Page and Shapiro, Ellis and Stimson, and Hibbing and Theiss-Morse. In the alternative view, ordinary citizens' opinions about public policy stem from their perceived self-interest, not from their assumptions about which policies are likely to solve social problems. Survey respondents may, for example, favor buttressing Social Security because they worry about their own retirement needs, present or future— not the needs of others, or of society at large.

Yet the consensus view among political psychologists and survey researchers is that most citizens tend to participate in politics (when they participate at all) "sociotropi-cally," not self-interestedly. That is, they "thin[k] about most political issues, most of the time, in a disinterested frame of mind," intending to achieve the public interest.[32] They may think that the public interest includes their own self-interest; we might hazard that this is usually the case when citizens perceive their own interests to be at stake. But they may also extend the public interest beyond their own interests to include those of large sectors of the general public, or the majority, or "everyone." While some of the policies that attained overwhelming public support during the twentieth century might have been favored because they served (or were thought to serve) the self-interest of indi-vidual survey respondents, others, such as spending on big cities, mass transit, and drug addiction, along with regulatory action against unemployment, would have served the interests of substantial minorities of the US public, but minorities nonetheless. Thus, *majority* support for these policies cannot plausibly be attributed to self-interest, or at least not entirely so.

Based on the goals of the policies that command the public's support, it seems that we can make inferences not only about the sociotropic nature of the value consensus, but about how people tacitly define what counts as sociotropically significant. Most US citizens seem to assume that a social problem is important enough to justify corrective

---

[32] Sears and Funk 1990, 170. See also Kinder and Kiewiet 1979; Sears et al. 1980; Kinder and Kiewiet 1981; Kiewiet 1983; Citrin and Green 1990; Sears and Funk 1990; Blinder and Krueger 2004; Lau and Heldman 2009; Kiewiet and Lewis-Beck 2011. In Chapter 4, I suggest reasons for skepticism about social psychology, including political psychology. But this skepticism concerns reductionist approaches that, as such, are interpre-tively uncharitable. The sociotropic voting hypothesis is neither reductionist nor interpretively uncharitable. However, for a normative theorist of technocracy, the more important point is that *if* a polity is to be consid-ered technocratic, its decision-makers *must* be sociotropic (by definition). Thus, one might dispute empirical findings about sociotropic voting; this would have the effect of undermining my suggestion that, as a matter of fact, we live in a democratic technocracy. But that has no bearing on the normative legitimacy of a (sociotropic) democratic technocracy, if it were in fact to exist.

government action if it negatively affects the well-being of a large number of their fellow citizens. "Well-being," in turn, seems typically to be defined in terms that are tangible and often materialistic.[33] Suffering, squalor, major inconvenience, financial insecurity, fear— conditions of somatic and psychic discomfort—are generally considered well within the purview of public policy.[34] Indeed, pursuing the public interest is usually *equated* with solving, mitigating, or preventing problems such as these. Even political movements with symbolic, ideological, or "utopian" objectives, such as (it is said) contemporary socialism in the United States, frequently produce technocratic agendas designed to achieve mundane objectives of this sort, such as greater access to higher education or the expansion of health coverage.

The idea that government action should be directed toward sociotropic and tangible values maps remarkably well onto Karl Popper's plea, in *The Open Society and Its Enemies* (1945), for a politics aimed at "the least amount of avoidable suffering for all," a position that one of Popper's critics usefully dubbed "negative utilitarianism."[35] In pursuit of the minimization of suffering (as distinguished from the maximization of happiness), Popper recommended that we engage in "piecemeal social engineering"[36]—the case-by-case crafting of public policies in response to discrete social problems, which is to say discrete instances of suffering. This formulation was not the inspiration for any public policies of which I am aware, nor for the mass consensus in American public opinion that Berelson would describe seven years later. But Popper did put into words the presuppositions standing behind politics of a type that had already been common in Western societies for decades.[37] In the United States, for example, it had long been the case, even before the New Deal, that any proposed policy designed to prevent, mitigate, or eliminate social problems, defined in roughly negative-utilitarian terms, was widely considered legitimate

---

[33] The work of Ronald Inglehart (e.g., 1990 and 1996) suggests the emergence of a postmaterialist sensibility across the West as affluence makes materialist goals passé. The rise of postmaterialist values poses an obvious challenge to my materialistic take on the public's conception of the common good. But European and American politics in the wake of the financial crisis may serve as a reminder that postmaterialist values are secondary, in most people's minds, to affluence. When their affluence is threatened, they will vote for whichever party seems to be less of a threat to it. Only when their affluence seems secure do they have the luxury of turning in a postmaterialist direction. Moreover, postmaterialist values may problematize conditions that require technocratic solutions, such as environmental degradation.

[34] A World Public Opinion poll in 2008 found that very large majorities of Americans agreed that the government should ensure that Americans are protected from military threats, that no American should starve, that no American should be without health care, and that no American should be without an education (World Public Opinion 2008). The same was true in every one of the other 20 countries surveyed.

[35] Popper [1945] 2013, 602 n. 2; Smart 1958.

[36] Popper [1945] 2013, 148.

[37] Popper, a Viennese refugee from Hitler, wrote *The Open Society* in wartime New Zealand. His research assistant, the neoclassical economist Colin Simkin, brought to Popper's attention recent developments in economics and in the rise of the redistributive-regulatory state in Western Europe and New Zealand itself (Hacohen 2000, 370). However, Popper's biographer points out that "every progressive intellectual" in the Vienna of Popper's youth was already "familiar with *Sozialtech*" (ibid., 371).

in principle.[38] (There is evidence that similar things can be said about other technocracies, such as those in Western Europe,[39] but in the rest of the book, I will continue to focus on the United States, the country with which I am most familiar.)

Consistent with the idea of negative utilitarianism is a crucial fact about technocratic knowledge: it is knowledge of the costs and benefits of proposed or enacted public policies. (Indeed, Cass R. Sunstein's name for technocracy is "the cost-benefit state.")[40] If one is to know that a policy is serving negative-utilitarian purposes, one must tally its potential benefits against its costs. The potential benefits are clear enough: the reduction of suffering, or discomfort, through the prevention, mitigation, or solution of the discrete social problems against which the policies are directed, piecemeal. The potential costs may be less visible than the potential benefits but—from a negative-utilitarian point of view—they matter just as much. Resources wasted on ineffective policies cannot be used on effective ones; and policies may backfire, causing more distress than they relieve. In this sense, negative utilitarianism leads straight to technocracy. If one is to weigh the costs against the benefits, one must know what they are. One therefore needs "technical" knowledge in that specific sense.

Technē, to be sure, is not *epistēmē*. But *technocracy*, as the term has come to be used, refers not to a polity run by craftspeople, as suggested by the Greek, but one run by knowers or those who claim to know. What they claim to know is the costs and benefits of policies aimed at solving, mitigating, or preventing conditions that impinge on the negative-utilitarian welfare of substantial numbers of citizens.

1.6. CITIZENS AS TECHNOCRATS

Empirically oriented political scientists might scoff at the notion that ordinary citizens should be counted as technocrats—not because political scientists doubt that there is a technocratic value consensus, but because they doubt that ordinary citizens are equipped to weigh policies' costs against their benefits. The consensus view among scholars of public opinion is that ordinary citizens' political attention is sporadic at best, their political knowledge scant, and their political attitudes evanescent, so the notion that these attitudes spring from even a primitive form of cost-benefit analysis might seem incredible.[41] However, I am not claiming that ordinary citizens typically weigh the costs and benefits of particular policies in a deliberate, explicit, careful, or well-informed manner. I am suggesting only that their political decisions are heavily influenced by perceptions of whether or not public policies can be expected to "work," or are already "working,"

---

[38] See Chapter 2 and Friedman 2007 for some impressionistic evidence about the Progressive Era.
[39] On Britain, France, Germany, Italy, and Spain, see Lewis-Beck 1988, 62.
[40] Sunstein 2002. Cf. Goodin 1995, 24–25, a defense of "Government House utilitarianism."
[41] See, e.g., Achen and Bartels 2016.

in a vague but real sense; that is, a vague sense of whether they solve, mitigate, or prevent social and economic problems—and, in the process, whether they do more good
than harm.

Consider the well-established tendency of ordinary twentieth-century US citizens to
vote retrospectively: that is, on the basis of whether the incumbent candidate or party
had prevented or mitigated important social problems such as inflation, unemployment,
or war.[42] Retrospection of this sort is an all-things-considered form of cost-benefit analysis. Retrospective voters are tacitly claiming to know whether technocratic policies have
produced good economic or foreign-policy consequences overall—which would be the
upshot if the benefits of the policies outweighed the costs. Even putatively irrational
instances of retrospective voting, such as the apparent reaction of New Jersey Shore voters against President Woodrow Wilson due to shark attacks in the summer of 1916,[43] are
readily understood as rational (if perhaps misguided) if we see voters as technocratic in
orientation, but as frequently underinformed about government's technocratic actions
and capacities. The New Jersey voters may simply have faulted the Wilson administration for failing to send in the Coast Guard (which had been founded in 1914)—even if
we think that this would have been an ineffective remedy—or for failing to compensate
the Shore's tourist industry for loss of revenue due to the attacks (as it had compensated
the victims of natural disasters).[44] Even if one judges the voters to be unreasonable, then,
there are no grounds for judging them as irrational if we understand them to have been
pursuing technocratic aims.

A definition of "technocrats" that includes ordinary citizens is also supported by recent empirical evidence from conditional polls. Conditional polls (my term) attempt
to discern the assumptions behind people's policy views by asking those who support
a policy if they would continue to favor it even if it had sociotropically negative side
effects, or by asking those who oppose it if they would continue to be against it if even it
achieved sociotropically positive effects. These polls suggest that while it is unlikely that
most people carry around in their heads strong policy views based on detailed empirical
evidence (or any evidence at all), they nonetheless tend to think about public policy in
an instrumentally rational manner, that is, by weighing *perceived* costs against *perceived*
benefits. Thus, a 2012 conditional poll found that 46 percent of the respondents who favored lower taxes said they would be more likely to oppose this policy if it would "reduce

---

[42] E.g., Campbell et al. 1960, ch. 11, and Fiorina 1981.

[43] Achen and Bartels 2016, 118–128.

[44] See, for the irrationality theory, Achen and Bartels 2016, chs. 5–7; for rebuttals to it in the case of the shark
attacks, Beattie 2018, 32, and Stokes 2018, 136–137. In this case and generally speaking, the irrationality theory
begins with the theorist's conviction that nobody in her right mind could think, or vote, as people do seem
to have thought or voted in a given case. This conviction is almost always coupled with a failure to investigate what the putatively irrational political actors said, read, or heard that might have justified their beliefs
or actions in their own minds. In short, the irrationality theory displays a lack of ideational sensitivity and a
not-unrelated failure of interpretive charity, topics further discussed in Chapters 4 and 6.

government aid to the truly needy." Fifty-one percent of those who wanted to require all pharmaceuticals to be available as generics said they would be more likely to oppose this policy if "it would result in reducing the supply of new drugs by cutting drug companies' profits." And 56 percent of the respondents who opposed the decriminalization of marijuana said they would be less likely to oppose it if it would "reduce the power of organized crime."[45] A 2003 conditional poll found that "those who believe that a higher minimum wage would cause the loss of either 'a lot of' jobs (6 percent of the sample) or 'some' jobs (36 percent) are much less likely to favor raising it than are those who believe that 'hardly anyone' would lose their job (57 percent of the sample)."[46] Even in the case of what is sometimes seen as a nonconsequentialist imperative—income redistribution—a conditional poll found that 34 percent of the supporters of "higher taxes on the richest 1 percent of Americans" would have been less likely to favor this measure if they knew that "it would reduce their [the 1 percent's] investments and thus increase unemployment."[47]

This type of evidence is not dispositive; empirical evidence rarely is. But the evidence from conditional polls, and from retrospective voting, lines up with the sentiment expressed in Hibbing and Theiss-Morse's focus groups, where US citizens revealed that they tend not to care which policies are adopted so long as the policies achieve sociotropically beneficial results.[48] It stands to reason that they might be willing to revise their policy views if they learned of evidence that policies they favor would have sociotropically undesirable effects, or that policies they oppose would have sociotropically beneficial effects. This is technocratic reasoning.

Thus, as a strictly empirical matter, not only does there seem to be a technocratic value consensus, but ordinary citizens seem routinely to engage in recognizably technocratic forms of thinking about the means to shared ends. Therefore, excluding them from our definition of "technocrats" would fail to reflect contemporary realities.

I.7. DISTORTIONS CAUSED BY THE STANDARD DEFINITION OF TECHNOCRACY

Of course, one might argue that in doing political theory, our definitions should *not* reflect contemporary realities. We might want to define technocracy in a way that flies in the face of such realities because this would allow us to establish an ideal condition against which those realities should be judged. Alternatively, we might view our definitions as embodiments of ideal types in Weber's sense, that is, abstractions from empirical complications. Ideal types may allow us to analyze reality without running into the confusions thrown forth by a welter of detail.

---

[45] Buturovic 2012, tables 5, 2, and 4.
[46] Blinder and Krueger 2004, 374.
[47] Buturovic 2012, table 7.
[48] Hibbing and Theiss-Morse 2002, 9; see the discussion in Chapter 6.

However, the standard definition of technocrats as trained, credentialed specialists does not clarify reality. It creates confusion about it by excluding ordinary citizens. And normatively, the standard definition can be not only misleading but dangerous.

It can be misleading because the technocracy/democracy binary makes it all too easy for political theorists to write off technocracy as inherently illegitimate. The binary defines technocrats as members of a power-holding elite, such that technocracy is perforce anti-democratic.[49] Yet if the people set the technocratic value agenda, and if they participate in technocratic policymaking, this characterization of technocracy is unwarranted.

Moreover, the technocracy/democracy binary can lead to disastrous confusion about what is at issue when one inquires into the epistemic competence of mass electorates. This can be seen in the trajectory of survey research on the public's knowledge of politics, which began on a slightly optimistic note in the 1940s and 1950s but has gotten increasingly pessimistic ever since.[50] As one reads the more recent scholarship, it sometimes seems as if researchers have been trying to outdo each other in expressing their discouragement at the breadth and depth of the public's political ignorance. "Nothing strikes the student of public opinion and democracy more forcefully than the paucity of information most people possess about politics," John Ferejohn wrote in 1990.[51] Eight years later, Donald Kinder called the public's political ignorance "breathtaking."[52] Four years after that, Robert C. Luskin called it "jaw-dropping."[53] More recently, scholars seem to be shifting toward the even more pessimistic view that what is really disclosed by the research is not so much the public's ignorance as its irrationality.[54] The shared worry of these commentators is that, as they see it, the research calls the legitimacy of democracy into question. But this worry is misplaced. The main line of empirical research that inspires the pessimism primarily concerns knowledge of what John Zaller calls "neutral, factual public-affairs knowledge,"[55] such as the name of the chief justice of the Supreme Court, the terms of senators and representatives, and the names of widely debated bills. While it is generally recognized that testing voters for such knowledge amounts, for the most part, to the administration of "trivia quizzes,"[56] widespread ignorance of this type of trivia indicates that most members of the public, most of the time, are inattentive to politics and government. Such inattention, in turn, suggests, a fortiori, that the public

---

[49] Habermas exemplifies this standard, dismissive approach in *The Lure of Technocracy* ([2013] 2015, 3), writing of the European Union that it "legitimized itself in the eyes of its citizens primarily through the results it produced rather than by fulfilling the citizens' political will." One can see the continuity with his writings of the late 1960s, where his critique of technocracy was grounded in its undemocratic nature, despite his barbed appreciation for the material successes he ascribed to it.

[50] See Friedman 2013b for an overview of the literature.

[51] Ferejohn 1990, 3.

[52] Kinder 1998, 785.

[53] Luskin 2002, 282.

[54] A view most prominently defended in Achen and Bartels 2016.

[55] Zaller 1992, 43.

[56] Page and Shapiro 1992, 12; cf. Lupia and McCubbins 1998, 77; Landemore 2013, 200; Landemore 2014, 23.

probably lacks whatever knowledge is germane to making sound technocratic decisions, such as knowledge of the costs and benefits of programs designed to expand employment, fight crime, and solve the problems of big cities.[57] Thus, members of the public may justifiably be assumed—or so it has seemed to many empirical researchers—to have epistemically inadequate opinions about "technical" matters, as Zaller aptly describes them.[58] However, lacking the concept of democratic *technocracy*, the researchers who have established the public's technical ignorance (like the researchers who have inferred the public's technical irrationality) have frequently suggested that their findings call the legitimacy of *democracy* into question, as if the public's purported inability to make wise technocratic decisions counts against democracy tout court. The most influential recent entry in this literature goes so far as to assert that "*all* the conventional defenses of democratic government are at odds with" empirical research on voter behavior (the authors supplied the italics).[59]

This is a perilous misconception—not about the empirical research, but about conventional defenses of democratic government. If we begin with early modern Europe, Locke saw majority rule as a convenient mode of decision-making, and the people as a potentially rebellious check on tyranny and violations of rights—not as a wise judge of policy effects. Rousseau, according to a recent interpretation, wanted the people to pick a government—and then "go to sleep" while the government decides how best to pursue the people's interests.[60] In the more standard view of Rousseau, he endorsed nonstop popular political participation, but for the purpose of attaining moral autonomy by pursuing—not necessarily achieving—the common good. In turn, Rousseau inspired a line of participatory theorists who value democracy for its putative capacity to educate and elevate the participants—not for its ability to produce instrumentally rational policies.[61] Among these theorists was most notably John Stuart Mill, who held that democracy encourages moral and intellectual self-development.

Moving to the twentieth century, Joseph Schumpeter offers a particularly compelling rebuttal to the notion that all conventional defenses of democratic government conflict with the findings of empirical research. None of the great democratic theorists, with the possible exception of Mill,[62] were as aware as Schumpeter of the epistemic deficiencies of modern electorates. The section on "Human Nature in Politics" in his *Capitalism, Socialism and Democracy* (1942) anticipates almost all the unflattering empirical findings that would be produced over the subsequent decades. Nevertheless, Schumpeter endorsed mass democracy insofar as politicians' competition for votes could be coupled

---

[57] For more on this "*a fortiori* argument," see Chapter 6.
[58] Zaller 1992, 331.
[59] Achen and Bartels 2016, 306.
[60] Tuck 2015, 24–42.
[61] E.g., Pateman 1970.
[62] See especially Mill [1831] 2007.

with tolerance and civil liberty—regardless of the foolish policies that he thought were predictable outcomes in a mass democracy.[63] Popper, similarly, valued democracy not because he believed that the people will make competent piecemeal social engineers, but because majority rule allows incipient dictators to be ousted peacefully.[64] More recently, Josiah Ober, Philip Pettit, and Ian Shapiro have depicted democracy as a means of resisting domination, social hierarchy, arbitrary power, humiliation, and infantilization—not as a means of enacting cost-effective public policies.[65] Other contemporary theorists view democracy as an expression of social equality, and democratic deliberation as an expression of respect for the dignity of the deliberators, not as instruments of sound public policy (although there is some ambiguity about this in the case of deliberative democrats).[66] And voluntaristic democrats such as Michael Walzer view the will of the people as inherently self-justifying. Therefore, they explicitly object to the notion that the public's possible epistemic deficiencies matter (normatively); to accept that they matter would contradict the voluntarist premise that the people's will is *inherently* just.[67] None of these defenses of democracy are predicated on a well-informed electorate, because none of them treats democracy as primarily a device for selecting policies that produce good consequences.[68]

However, *some* democratic theorists have viewed democracy that way. For the most part, these theorists were Utilitarians or Progressives.[69] This is crucial, for Utilitarians and Progressives were proponents of democratic technocracy, not democracy per se.

Thus, Bentham's defense of democracy required that voters know which public policies will serve their (individual) interests, because this would tend to ensure that a government chosen by universal suffrage would enact policies that achieve the greatest good for the greatest number. Fortunately, according to Bentham, voters are indeed likely to know which policies will serve their interests: "On the part of the majority of the voters," he claimed, "there exists, in the breast of each, either from self-formed or from derivative

---

[63] Schumpeter 1942, ch. 22. See Cherneski 2018.

[64] Popper 1988.

[65] Ober 2015; Pettit 1997; Shapiro 1996 and 2016.

[66] Kolodny 2014; Gutmann and Thompson 1996; Waldron 1999, 158–162. See Landemore 2017 on the ambiguity.

[67] Walzer 1981. Thus, the notion that poorly informed or "nonattitudinal" voters somehow threaten the existence of "the will of the people" (Achen 1975) is mistaken. A will that is ignorant or that fluctuates from moment to moment is nonetheless, in the voluntarist view, legitimate. To impose standards of knowledgeability or constancy on such a will would replace its sovereign authority with the sovereign authority of "philosophers," as Walzer says, who dare to judge certain types of will as underinformed or irrational.

[68] Consequently, they do not judge democracy primarily by the standard of its responsiveness to people's policy preferences (Sabl 2015), an idiosyncratically technocratic legacy of Progressivism that commands widespread and unwitting support among empiricist political scientists.

[69] Achen and Bartels (2016, 2 n. 2) note the Utilitarian and Progressive roots of what they call the "folk theory of democracy," which holds that the people know what they are doing—a theory they relentlessly criticize. But they fail to register the implication that most democratic theorists, who have *not* been Utilitarians or Progressives, have not accepted the folk theory, such that criticisms of it are irrelevant to most defenses of democratic theory.

judgment, a practically adequate conception of the course dictated by his share in the universal interest."[70] Unlike Bentham, the Progressives—among whom were the founders of the modern social sciences, including political science[71]—tended to think that voters should be sociotropic, not self-interested. And in the wake of the Industrial Revolution, they were far more critical of capitalism than Bentham had been. Yet their political views were, like Bentham's, democratic and (negative-) utilitarian. They tended to think that government would be instrumental to the common good if a sociotropic majority of voters were in control, for such a majority would vote for policies that would solve, mitigate, or prevent the social problems caused by capitalism.[72] The Progressives' enthusiasm for greater popular participation in government is best understood in this technocratic light. They championed new democratic forms such as ballot initiatives, policy referenda, primary elections, and the direct election of judges, senators, and presidents largely so that the people could either solve social problems on their own, through initiatives and referenda, or by electing officials who would faithfully do so. Progressives also advocated recall elections to enable the people to cashier public officials, including judges, who failed to support problem-solving social reforms.

The epistemological assumptions undergirding this program of political reform were suggested during the course of the 1912 presidential campaign. The Progressive Party's presidential candidate, Theodore Roosevelt, explained that recall elections and other populist electoral measures were "devices" that would "make the representatives of the people more easily and certainly responsible to the people's will."[73] In response, the Republican incumbent, William Howard Taft, claimed that Roosevelt was "sowing the seeds of confusion and tyranny."[74] Roosevelt replied that Taft's argument was "really less a criticism of my proposal than a criticism of all popular government. It is wholly unfounded, unless it is founded on the belief that the people are fundamentally untrustworthy."[75] In contrast, Roosevelt continued, "I believe the majority of the plain people of the United States will, day in and day out, *make fewer mistakes* in governing themselves than any smaller class or body of men, no matter what their training."[76] This claim is quite unlike anything we find in most democratic theory, because most democratic theory does not set great store on avoiding technocratic error.

This is to the credit of most democratic theorists, for the Progressive theory places an immense epistemic burden on the people: the burden of knowing the extent and the causes of social problems, knowing what the political and policy options for dealing with them might be, and knowing which of these options are likely to pass the cost-benefit test.

---

[70] Bentham [1817] 1969, 326.

[71] See Friedman 2007, 214–225.

[72] See Chapter 2.

[73] Roosevelt 1912a, 120.

[74] Roosevelt 1912c, 156–157.

[75] Ibid., 157.

[76] Ibid., 151; my emphasis.

Political scientists' findings about political ignorance do raise doubts about whether that is more than we have a right to expect. But even if we were to conclude that no public is ever likely to know how to recognize, diagnose, and cure social problems, this conclusion would not call into question the legitimacy of democracy itself. Empirically oriented political scientists, educated in the shadow of Progressivism, have long suspected—rightly, in my view—that public-ignorance findings have troubling normative implications. But the implications are not troubling for democracy; they are troubling for the technocratic understanding of democracy, which has uncritically been picked up by empirical political scientists and equated with democracy as a whole.

Because they fail to distinguish between democracy and democratic technocracy, political scientists have assumed that their criticisms of the latter apply to the former. This has been true of certain political philosophers, too, who sometimes declare that they have been turned "against democracy" by empirical demonstrations of public ignorance.[77] This is careless and, at times like the present, reckless. But if we are to avoid the danger of erroneously condemning democracy for the shortcomings (or, rather, the potential shortcomings) of democratic technocracy, we need language that acknowledges the existence of democratic technocracy—both its existence as a normative possibility and, at least possibly, its existence in reality. We deny ourselves this language, however, if we continue to equate technocrats with trained, credentialed specialists.

There is still another problem with the conventional dichotomy between technocracy and democracy. It begs the question of the epistemic qualifications, as it were, of all technocrats, *including* trained, credentialed specialists. If we simply define those who have the needed technocratic knowledge as epistemic elites by equating the latter with "technocrats," we repeat Berlin's and Habermas's mistake: we decide by fiat, rather than by argument, the adequacy of trained, credentialed specialists' technocratic knowledge—and, by implication, the inadequacy of the general public's technocratic knowledge.

We should not ascribe adequate knowledge to technocratic elites unless we have good reason to think that they actually have it, or that they might someday acquire it. Nor should we use a mere definition to erase the possibility that the technocratic knowledge claims made by ordinary citizens are (or might someday be) warranted. This is particularly true if trained, credentialed specialists suffer from epistemic pathologies brought about by their training and their status as specialists, as I will suggest in Chapters 4 and 5. For in that case the public, even if it remains uninformed, might turn out to be better suited to technocratic decision-making than are the elites who are contrasted against the public by the technocracy/democracy dichotomy. I examine this possibility in Chapter 6.

---

[77] The title of J. Brennan 2016 (cf. G. Brennan and Lomasky 1993; Caplan 2007; Pincione and Tesón 2006; and Somin 1998, 2006, 2013, 2014, and 2015). I confess that for a long time I, too, lacking the concept of democratic technocracy, saw the problem of public ignorance as an issue of democratic theory, even though I did not think that it justified opposition to democracy, let alone an endorsement of epistocracy (e.g., Friedman 1998 and 2006).

In the meantime, let us define as "technocrats" *all* political actors who make knowledge claims (express or tacit) about the scope, causes of, and cures for social problems—whether these actors are trained, credentialed specialists or not. In turn, let us call "epistocrats" either trained, credentialed specialists (or any other political actors) who claim to have technocratic knowledge unavailable to ordinary citizens.[78] Finally, let us call "citizen-technocrats" political actors who have non-esoteric opinions—explicit or tacit—about the scope, causes of, and cures for social problems. This schema captures the elitist implications of the esoteric knowledge claims made by epistocrats, even while acknowledging that technocratic knowledge may not be esoteric, or may not be seen as esoteric, and thus may be claimed by citizens who lack specialized expertise. "Technocracy," then, as the name of a type of regime, will cover governance by putative epistocrats, by citizen-technocrats, or—as is almost always the case—by both. What distinguishes this type of regime from others is not the number of its personnel in proportion to the population being governed—"the few" versus "the many"—but the nature of the regime's mission: to solve, mitigate, and prevent social problems.

Apart from avoiding normative and empirical confusion, these new definitions have another advantage. They clarify the status of different types of critique of technocracy better than does the standard understanding of who "technocrats" are. By defining as a technocrat anyone who makes knowledge claims about social problems and how to solve, prevent, or mitigate them, we recognize technocracy as a fundamentally epistemic project, such that a critique of technocrats' knowledge claims will be an internal critique. By contrast, a critique of technocracy for being antidemocratic (because a technocracy may have elitist elements or tendencies), or for deviating from norms of distributive justice, would be external to the epistemic rationale of technocracy.

1.8. THE PUBLIC-CHOICE ALTERNATIVE

Despite the fact that technocracy can be defined as a fundamentally epistemic project, one might want to examine it critically and internally while not creating a political epistemology of it.

The clearest path to such a critique would pursue the theory of public choice, that is, the application of economic analysis to politics. If, as public-choice theorists assert, technocrats are self-interested—just like everyone else, they claim—then technocrats might

---

[78] David Estlund (2008), who coined the term *epistocracy*, meant rule by an elite with both superior knowledge of technical means, as in my usage, and superior knowledge of truly good ends. The latter type of knowledge is not at issue in my analysis, since in technocratic policymaking, the ends are taken for granted. "Epistocracy" is a more elegant term, however, than "an elite of putative experts on the costs and benefits of policies adopted to solve, mitigate, or prevent social and economic problems," so I am compelled to use "epistocracy" to cover only an elite with claims to esoteric knowledge of the latter type, and to hope that this narrowing of the term will not cause confusion.

have little incentive to solve, prevent, or mitigate social problems, and this would surely reduce the likelihood that the problems will be solved, prevented, or mitigated.

However, public-choice theory tends to be either false or only trivially true. Contrary to public-choice theory, policymakers—in the West, at least—seem, for the most part, to act on the basis of their perceptions of the public good.

Thus, as we have seen, voters tend to be sociotropic. As for legislators, bureaucrats, and other potentially epistocratic government personnel, such as judges, neither logic nor fact supports the view that their decisions are primarily motivated by self-interest.[79] It is generally considered unacceptable for public servants to favor their own interests (narrowly defined). In the West, this norm is enforced by legislation prohibiting bribes; by enforceable codes of ethics; by vigilance among journalists and public-interest groups looking for conflicts of interest; and by the inculcation of sociotropic political values in the general population, from which state personnel are drawn. There is also esprit de corps within government agencies, which reinforces public-spirited norms. For these reasons, it is illogical to extend the self-interest assumption from the economic to the political sphere merely in the interest of symmetry, as public-choice scholars advise.[80] Where there are asymmetrical norms, we should expect asymmetrical behaviors.

An acknowledgment of such asymmetries is the first step toward understanding tremendously important political phenomena such as ideological conviction, political activism, working for a cause (without pay, or for minimal pay), nationalism, and suicidal terrorism. The public-choice scholar is patently unable to explain such phenomena—as opposed to explaining them away as disguised manifestations of egoism. The public-choice scholar is therefore unable to explain *herself* and other political actors, including scholars, who attempt, as she does, to improve society despite the negligible chance that the improvements will help them personally, if they ever arrive. Public-choice theory is the ultimate manifestation of the tendency of economic imperialism to occlude knowledge, including self-knowledge.

On the other hand, a recognition of the public's political ignorance may legitimately heighten our concern about public-choice problems. After all, the public cannot resist the influence of special interests if the public does not know about it in a particular case.

---

[79] See Leif Lewin's *Self Interest and Public Interest in Western Democracies* (Lewin 1991) and the twentieth-anniversary symposium on this book in *Critical Review* 23(3) (2011). A plausible general rule is that when interest groups are able to influence legislation and regulation, it is at least under the pretext of claims about the public good. This would suggest that the motives of the political actors who are in a position to listen to interest groups tend to be properly aligned toward the public good—otherwise the pretext would be unnecessary—and that cases of corruption are scandalous exceptions to the rule. Regulatory capture, similarly (to the extent that it happens), must be caused by the putative knowledge about the public good that is conveyed to the regulators by their "clients," unless the clients are bribing the regulators; but bribery seems to be rare in the West. The "revolving door" between regulators and those they regulate is a more troubling issue, but can be addressed by bolstering ethics codes, without the input of political theorists.

[80] Buchanan and Tullock 1962, 20, 25ff.

But political theorists are not qualified to point to such cases. All they can do about the influence of special interests, then, is denounce it in general terms, but such denunciation has been a constant in political discourse since at least the Populist Era in the United States. Nearly everyone since then has been taught that corruption is intolerable, and that special interests are the chief agents of it.[81] Perhaps as a result of this teaching, the public may already exaggerate the importance of corruption and the power of special interests. This might help to explain the appeal of populism, as we will see in Chapter 6. Under the impression that corruption and special dealing are omnipresent, the people may ascribe the persistence of social problems to the influence of bad actors ("crooks—lock 'em up!") rather than to the inability of good actors to solve the problems.[82] The bad actors are widely assumed to be corrupt politicians and the special interests that control them, and one seemingly easy solution is to elect billionaires who are unlikely to need campaign contributions from those interests.[83]

Thus, if political theorists were simply to echo the public's preoccupation with special interests, they might themselves do more harm than good by bolstering the public obsession with the motives, rather than the knowledge, of those in power.

I.9. DEMOCRATIC TECHNOCRACY AND NATIONALISM

There is another possible connection between populism and technocracy. Populism often takes the form of single-minded nationalism. This may be attributable, in part, to the fact that the distinction between one's conationals and everyone else offers an accessible way for even poorly informed citizen-technocrats to organize their thinking about otherwise-complicated technocratic ("hard") questions.[84] In the eyes of an uninformed citizen-technocrat, there could hardly be a better indication of a politician's dedication to solving the problems of her conationals than bellicose, flag-waving nationalism, and she may assume that such a politician will, therefore, relentlessly pursue the interests of "the people" (defined as the citizen-technocrat's conationals). In short, nationalism can serve as a sociotropic heuristic that greatly simplifies technocratic issues.

In modern societies, the conational-versus-foreigner binary is inculcated in nearly everyone by public education, and by such quotidian aspects of mass culture as meteorological maps that display the weather only in one's own country.[85] For citizen-technocrats who pay little attention to politics and government, the primitive nationalism conveyed by such cultural devices may be the only orienting tool available in trying to understand public affairs. When these low-information citizen-technocrats hear a political candidate

---

[81] For a rare dissent, see Rauch 2015.
[82] See Friedman 2017a and Chapter 6 in this book.
[83] See Hibbing and Theiss-Morse 1995 and 2002.
[84] See Friedman 2017b.
[85] See Tyrrell 1992.

proclaim, "America first," it is unlikely that they know that this was the slogan of the opponents of US involvement in World War II.[86] Rather, it may sound like a simple commitment to solve the social problems of Americans prior to attending to the needs of "foreigners." If the candidate is running for president *of the United States*, what could be more commonsensical than that he should favor the interests of the citizens of the United States above those of everyone else?[87]

Consider the presidential campaign of Donald J. Trump, whose nationalism was motivated, in his own depiction, by a host of perceived social problems. Imposing tariffs and building a wall on the Mexican-American border were, Trump claimed, means to the end of ensuring the economic and physical security of American citizens—a fair description of a large part of the mandate of (American) "technocracy," as I am defining the term. Thus, Trump's nationalism may have appealed to voters on technocratic grounds.

Of course, one might object to this highly schematic interpretation of Trump's appeal for a number of reasons. One might contend, for example, that racism was a more significant explanatory variable than nationalism. To the extent that this was the case—and to the extent that Trump supporters' racism was directed against their conationals, rather than against the citizens of other countries, such as undocumented immigrants—then their support for him would fall outside the democratic-technocracy schema, which requires sociotropic citizen-technocrats. But if one means by racism American citizens' preference for the welfare of American citizens over, say, Mexican citizens, Trump's racist supporters would still qualify as citizen-technocrats, as this form of racism, or xenophobia, is sociotropic toward citizens of the technocracy of which they themselves are citizens. As one Trump voter told the *Wall Street Journal*, "Americans just want to feel like we're looking out for us a little more."[88] Deplorable, from a philosophical point of view, but sociotropic.

That citizen-technocrats may view technocratic problems through the lens of nationalism is also suggested by the American debate over immigration long prior to Trump's arrival on the scene. In this debate, immigration was evaluated almost entirely in terms of whether it helped or hurt American citizens, with little or no attention paid to the interests of those who wanted to live in the United States but lacked citizenship. Nearly the entire debate revolved around whether immigrants would depress the wages and employment rates of US citizens, or increase the prevalence of crime or the threat of terrorism in

---

[86] On Trump supporters as low-information voters, see Fording and Schram 2018.

[87] Donald Trump expressed this idea many times, but perhaps most clearly in his first State of the Union address: "The United States is a compassionate nation. We are proud that we do more than any other country to help the needy, the struggling, and the underprivileged all over the world. But as President *of the United States*, my highest loyalty, my greatest compassion, and my constant concern is for America's children, America's struggling workers, and America's forgotten communities" (my emphasis).

[88] Chinni 2017. Cf. a supporter of Matteo Salvini of the League party in the 2018 Italian parliamentary elections: "I like him because he puts Italians first. And I guess he's a fascist, too. What can you do?" (Brooks 2018).

the United States. Similarly, while it is thought to constitute an important social problem when a significant proportion of Americans suffers from distressing conditions, foreign aid to address the very same conditions among the residents of other countries is considered inappropriate or, at best, a low priority.

In short, sociotropic political attitudes tend to stop at the border. This is a reality we should always keep in mind in analyzing technocracy; so long as there is no global state, really existing democratic technocracies will be nationalistic, to one degree or another.

1.10. OUTLINE OF THE BOOK
Beyond Naive Technocratic Realism (Chapter 1)

Some readers may find it odd to ask, as I will, whether we have sufficient knowledge of how to solve social and economic problems. These readers may have come to think it clear that at least in some cases, technocratic questions have fairly obvious answers: namely, the answers that they themselves would give if they were asked such questions. A critical epistemology of technocracy may therefore fall on deaf ears.

If it is to gain a hearing, the reader must be willing to interrogate her own technocratic opinions, asking of them: *How do I know?* "Naive technocratic realism" stems from the failure to ask this question. It is the view that the answers to technocratic questions have self-evident answers—whether self-evident to citizen-technocrats or to epistocrats.

Chapter 1 confronts naive technocratic realism. My initial argument against it invokes *the fact of technocratic disagreement.* In policy debate, technocrats differ with one other about the nature, significance, and causes of social problems and the likely or actual effects of proposed or implemented solutions. Such disagreement shows that the truth about social problems is not self-evident: if it were, nobody would disagree about it. If there is disagreement, the truth must be counterintuitive, or the evidence must be ambivalent, such that naive technocratic realism is unsustainable.

However, the defender of naive technocratic realism might be inclined to respond to the fact of technocratic disagreement by denying the sincerity of the disagreement, and thus of policy debate itself. If, as the naive realist holds, the truth about how to solve, mitigate, or prevent social problems is self-evident, then purported differences of opinion about this truth must be disingenuous. The bulk of Chapter 1 is devoted to undermining this defense of naive realism. It does so, in part, by analyzing examples of unintended policy consequences that have been alleged in real-world policy debates. If, as is alleged, technocratic policies may produce *unintended* effects, then the truth about the policies' effects must not have been self-evident to the technocrats who designed the policies.

However, to argue that technocratic actions *may* cause unintended consequences, as I will do in Chapter 1, is not equivalent to arguing that these consequences will in fact occur; nor that, if they do, they will be adverse (rather than beneficial); nor that they will occur frequently or with significantly deleterious effects. Such an argument would amount to a critique of the reliability of technocratic knowledge, to which the rest of Parts I and II will be devoted. Chapter 1 merely sets the stage by introducing the thought that there is something about modern social problems, or modern society, that *might* make it difficult to acquire the knowledge necessary to quell technocratic disagreement. This ontological something would make modern social problems or modern society, or both, "complex" enough that solutions to the former might, counterintuitively, produce significant adverse consequences. In the presence of this type of complexity—epistemic complexity, whatever its ontological source or sources—technocrats may unintentionally do more harm than good.

The Lippmann-Dewey Debate (Chapter 2)

Chapter 2 examines the possibility of epistemic complexity through the lens of the famous debate between Walter Lippmann and John Dewey during the 1920s.

Lippmann, reflecting on the power of the media to shape political perceptions, pointed out that each of us directly perceives but a tiny corner of the society we are trying to understand; our knowledge of the rest of it is necessarily mediated to us. However, he contended that the news media are unlikely to convey to us the knowledge we need. Even avid newshounds are getting but a minuscule fraction of the relevant information. More important, this information cannot be selected or even understood—by either the journalist or the citizen—without the aid of interpretations that tend to highlight and validate the portions of the information that fit the interpretations. In Lippmann's view, epistemic complexity is (in part) a function of overabundant information, which requires interpretation if it is to become intelligible. But there is little reason to think that any given interpretation will accurately reflect the realities of a vast, unseen society, as each interpretation is itself determined by the skewed sample of information to which the interpreter happens previously to have had access. Thus, our ideas about modern society—and modern social problems—are likely to be inaccurate. Out of Lippmann's dissection of journalism, then, flows a challenging perspective on the ability of anyone to understand modern society adequately.

In Chapter 2, I contend that during the course of the debate, Dewey never took Lippmann's concerns about interpretation seriously enough to provide a plausible response to it. His appeals to a superficially improved journalism, to the knowledge possessed by those affected by social problems, and to a hoped-for social science were unresponsive to the interpretive questions Lippmann had raised. In the 1930s, however, after the debate with Lippmann had concluded, Dewey did outline two forms of technocracy that are responsive to Lippmann's concerns—but not adequately so.

An Ontology of Societal Complexity (Chapter 3)

The problem of interpretation, and the epistemic complexity to which it points, had only vague ontological underpinnings in Lippmann's writings. Therefore, his critique of technocratic knowledge would have been vulnerable to a rejoinder premised on a denial of epistemic complexity or, in other words, an affirmation of technocrats' ability to understand whatever ontological realities would otherwise produce interpretive problems. Dewey himself had such a rejoinder at his disposal, although he did not deploy it in his debate with Lippmann: his evolutionary epistemology. Dewey maintained that natural selection has given human beings the power to perceive the results of their experimental actions reliably, and that natural science is merely an extension of this power. Thus, he might have argued that experimental policy scientists, being human, are likely to master the interpretive complexities of modern society, just as natural scientists are able, through experimentation, to master the interpretive complexities of the physical environment. Such a response to Lippmann could have led to a more productive debate than the one that actually occurred, as it might, in turn, have prompted Lippmann to develop his ideas about modern society into an ontology that would undermine the reliability of even "scientific" technocracy. Thus, he could have argued that policy experiments have external validity only if we assume what Hume called "uniformity" in "the operations of nature."[89] This assumption enables natural scientists to generalize from their local experiments. However, if people in modern societies do not behave uniformly, or if technocrats are unable to gain reliable access to the uniformities that may be determining people's diverse behavior, the parallel between natural and policy science would collapse.

In Chapter 3, I contend that a variety of historical factors do indeed make the assumption of uniformity presumptively inapplicable to modern society, as a practical matter. These historical factors should, other things equal, lead to unpredictable heterogeneity in the ideas, and thus the actions, of the agents whose behavior technocracy tries to predict and manipulate. Thus, *ideational heterogeneity* should tend to produce behavioral unpredictability, such that the predictions generated by policy scientists will tend to be unreliable. Technocratic policies grounded in such predictions should, in turn, tend to produce unintended behavioral consequences.

However, this does not close the epistemological case against technocracy. For there may be homogenizing forces at work alongside heterogenizing ideational forces. It could be that in some or all cases the homogenizing forces render people's actions reliably predictable. On balance, then, technocracy might solve social problems more often than not, despite ideational heterogeneity. This outcome would depend, however, on the ability of technocrats to determine, on the whole, the extent to which the homogenizing forces of which they are aware are likely to suppress the unpredictable behavior caused by heterogeneous ideas. By exploring patterns of theorizing that seem to have been selected

---

[89] Hume [1772] 1999, 159.

for in a technocracy, and evaluating the selection pressures that would account for them, Part II (Chapters 4–6) investigates whether technocrats are likely to have such an ability.

Pathologies of Epistocracy (Chapter 4)

Chapter 4 begins with the theorizing practiced by the hegemonic epistocrats of our age: neoclassical economists. They tend to think they can derive predictions about the actions agents *will* take from an analysis of the actions they *should* take, logically, to further their self-interest. Policy design thus becomes, in the first instance, an exercise in rational-choice theory. The working assumption is that economists can predict how millions of anonymous agents will respond to policy initiatives despite the economists' ignorance about the ideas of the agents—because the one thing they think they know about *all* agents is that they will respond optimally to incentives, including the incentives created by technocratic initiatives. Thus, economists overlook the possibility of a gap between objective realities, such as incentives, and agents' subjective perceptions and interpretations of those realities. This oversight encourages the a priori policy prescriptions that have been so characteristic of economics in the twentieth and twenty-first centuries, even as it blinds economists to the ideational heterogeneity that may render their prescriptions counterproductive.

The chapter then turns to the recent trend in economics toward methodological innovations such as natural experiments and randomized controlled trials. The increasingly recognized problem of external validity plaguing this trend reveals the heterogeneity of human ideas, which may localize findings not only to each experimental venue but each experimental subject. If economists were to recognize this fact, however, it would nullify the value of economics to technocracy. This value stems from economists' putative ability to predict the behavior of masses of anonymous future agents, not merely to retrodict the behavior of the small populations "treated" in an experiment. The fact that economists, our premier epistocrats, overlook this problem suggests that technocracy may exert a selection pressure in favor of epistocrats who ignore ideational heterogeneity. A brief look at some of the interpretive problems encountered (although not recognized) by the psychologists known as behavioral economists will suggest the same type of selection pressure.

This "selection pressure" is a metaphor for the fact that if social scientists were to start paying attention to ideational heterogeneity, it would undermine their perceived ability to predict future behavior. In that case, however, we could assume that other social scientists might take these social scientists' place. Thus, the chapter closes by examining cases in which social scientists far removed from technocracy take approaches that are incompatible with an appreciation of people's idiosyncratic ideas. The fact that such an appreciation seems to be selected against in nontechnocratic social sciences suggests that it will not be easy to find adequate epistocratic replacements for economists. On the other hand, it also suggests that the selection pressures result from the ideas of technocrats—not from technocracy itself—and that the pressures may therefore, conceivably, be counteracted by better ideas.

The Spiral of Conviction (Chapter 5)

The spiral of conviction is the hypothesis that as people become better informed—that is, roughly speaking, as they move from being citizen-technocrats toward being epistocrats—they inadvertently become dogmatic.

That there is a spiral of conviction is suggested by research showing that as people gain knowledge of a topic, their opinions about it tend to rigidify. This stands to reason, as one can begin understanding a topic (as opposed to memorizing facts about it) only after hearing or generating an interpretation of it that makes certain information about it legible and coherent. In this way an interpretation clarifies part of the otherwise-mysterious world, but as Lippmann understood, this clarity comes at the price of screening out interpretation-incongruent information, which tends to remain illegible or to be dismissed as implausible. Thus, our interpretations, having identified some types of information as legible and plausible, allow us to accumulate growing heaps of confirmatory information while ignoring a much greater amount of unknown, indecipherable, or seemingly irrelevant or absurd information. In turn, we attach greater confidence to beliefs that have been repeatedly confirmed. Dogmatic confidence, then, would seem to go with the accumulation of knowledge. The more we learn, the more impermeable the interpretive bubbles in which the knowledge traps us. After a theoretical and empirical exploration of the spiral of conviction, Chapter 5 illustrates the spiral at work among economists attempting, in retrospect, to understand the financial crisis.

Political Ignorance: Radical, Not Rational (Chapter 6)

If epistocrats tend to be dogmatic, it seems possible that they might be outperformed, technocratically, by ordinary citizens. The latter may not be very knowledgeable, but they should, as a result, be relatively immune to spirals of conviction.

To see if this overlooked advantage is likely to allow citizen-technocrats to make reliably accurate predictions of policy effects, Chapter 6 reconceptualizes the political scientists' findings of mass public ignorance about public affairs. This reconceptualization requires us to reject the standard, rational-choice explanation of public ignorance. According to this view, citizens recognize that it is highly unlikely that their individual votes will matter, so they decide to save themselves pointless time and effort by deliberately choosing to underinform themselves about politics and government. Chapter 6 argues that, to the extent that voters are citizen-technocrats whose aim is to encourage the adoption of sociotropic policies, the very fact that they vote *nonrandomly* warrants rejection of the rational-ignorance analysis. The citizen-technocrat is—in theory and, apparently, in reality—motivated by the belief that her chosen candidate or party is likely to enact sociotropically desirable policies. She could not hold this belief if she had deliberately chosen to underinform herself (by her own standards) about the various candidates or parties. Had she deliberately chosen to underinform herself, she would be aware that she did not know enough to choose one candidate or party over the other, and this awareness would render her unable to vote (except by flipping a coin). Thus, if citizen-technocrats are unaware of sociotropically important information, they must be unaware of the fact that they are unaware of it. That is, they must be "radically" or inadvertently ignorant of it, not deliberately so.

In the rational-ignorance view, ignorant voters recognize that their scant political knowledge is inadequate. In the radical-ignorance view, they think their scant knowledge is adequate. What does this say about their understanding of social problems, modern society, and technocratic policy? According to Chapter 6, they tend to assume that politicians' or parties' intentions, or the intended effects of particular policies, are adequate proxies (as it were) for sociotropic consequences. Thus, the main thing they think they need to know is whether politicians, parties, or policies are or are not sociotropically motivated. In short, citizen-technocrats abstract altogether from the need to assess policy consequences, not because they think that assessing them would be a waste of their time, as in rational-ignorance theory, but because they assume that policy effects are deducible from policy intentions. A side effect of this assumption, however, is that *unintended* consequences are rarely even considered.

The Possibility of Exit (Chapter 7)

In Chapter 7, I outline an alternative to technocracy that would be less epistemically demanding than either epistocracy or democratic technocracy. This alternative is built around the exit option that Albert O. Hirschman strikingly contrasted against voice.

Chapter 7 suggests that in the private sphere, one can sometimes use the exit option as a form of quasi-controlled experimentation, with oneself as both participant and observer. This procedure reduces the need to understand or predict the behavior of others—especially those who, being anonymous, behave in ways that one is poorly positioned to understand, let alone predict. To use the exit option, one needs to know *that* one is unhappy with a given situation, but one need not know *why*: that is, one need not know what ideas caused other people to take the actions that indirectly led to one's own predicament. One simply exits from it. Exit is Dewey's experimentalism applied individually to one's own life, not collectively to the lives of millions of anonymous others. Therefore, it can succeed in the absence of the predictability that would otherwise have to be ascribed to those others, and without the predictive knowledge of their behavior that would otherwise have to be ascribed to oneself.

Chapter 7 explores the promise and the limits of personal experimentation and one of its prerequisites: wealth. Personal experimentation requires the means to exit from situations that one finds unsatisfactory, such as a bad job, and the means to give other situations a try. The purpose of wealth redistribution, then, from an internal technocratic perspective, should not be to solve particular social problems, but to enable people to exit from them.

Exit is not a panacea. But it allows a degree of problem avoidance through trial-and-error learning that can, overall, be expected to better address people's discomforts than can the use of voice, and the prediction of society-wide behavior that it demands. Hirschman intended "voice" to call democracy to mind, but his definition of voice as "any attempt at all to change, rather than escape from, an objectionable state of affairs"[90] applies to democratic and epistocratic forms of technocracy alike, both of which are committed to understanding, interpreting, and then manipulating human behavior so as to solve the problems to which it leads.

In an afterword, I suggest that "exitocracy" holds out greater promise for the political left than does either epistocracy or democratic technocracy.

---

[90] Hirschman 1970, 30, 74.

PART I

Belief, Interpretation, and Unpredictability

The truth about distant or complex matters is not self-evident.

—WALTER LIPPMANN, *Public Opinion*

I

Technocratic Naiveté

THE PRIMARY CLAIM of this study will be that modern social problems are likely to be complex enough to pose serious epistemic challenges to technocracy. Part I will explore the consequences for public policy produced by epistemic complexity, and one of the ontological reasons for it; Part II will look at how epistocrats and citizen-technocrats deal with epistemic complexity, or avoid dealing with it; Part III will consider alternative means of dealing with it.

An argument against technocracy grounded in complexity might seem immediately plausible, as few among us would deny that modern society is "complex" in some sense. Yet it is possible that the social complexity that most of us take for granted is a platitude that does not withstand scrutiny, or that it is real but does not impinge on our ability to solve social problems. Thus, social problems might, on the whole, be simple enough, epistemically, that a rational observer could use common sense or intuition to determine the causes of the problems, the likely solutions, and the likely costs of those solutions. If so, the prospects for an epistemically sound technocracy would be even more promising than Berlin and Habermas assumed. Why, after all, should technocracy require "scientific experts" if we, the people, can commonsensically diagnose social problems and prescribe effective solutions to them?

That seems to be the implicit view of many citizen-technocrats. Whatever they may think about societal complexity in the abstract, they also think that by consulting common sense, or the information accessible to any moderately informed citizen, they are able to reach sound answers to such technocratic questions as how to reduce the high

Power Without Knowledge. Jeffrey Friedman, Oxford University Press (2019). © Oxford University Press.
DOI: 10.1093/oso/9780190877170.001.0001

cost of urban housing. Thus, the *New York Times Magazine* lists confidently proposed solutions to the lack of affordable housing:

> Lots of people think they know what to do to fix housing: Stick it to the landlord with rent controls. Require developers to set aside low-cost units. Build more subsidized housing. Distribute more rent vouchers or, as San Francisco has recently done, funnel taxes and fees into a housing trust fund. For those with more faith in market forces, there is always the loosening of zoning regulations.[1]

Each of these ideas for increasing the supply of affordable housing is an obvious solution to the problem, at least in the minds of some number of citizen-technocrats. The same is true of virtually all social problems, from the high cost of health insurance to the ills of public education. Familiar, intuitively plausible theories about the causes of the latter ills include insufficient educational funding;[2] underpaid teachers;[3] too few teachers;[4] inadequate or irrelevant teacher training;[5] teachers with insufficient passion;[6] incompetent teachers;[7] incompetent principals;[8] overly large schools;[9] unmotivated students;[10] uninvolved parents;[11] teaching to the test;[12] low curricular standards;[13] too little homework;[14] too much homework;[15] too little school discipline;[16] and too much school discipline.[17] One can find a vast array of theories like these in letters to the editor published in any American newspaper, each delivered with serene confidence in the obvious truth of the author's opinion.

Thus, an education blogger writes, in a letter to the editor of the *New York Times*: "There's no question that teachers are the most important in-school factor in education."[18] However, equal certitude can be found among those who think that

---

[1] Dewan 2014.

[2] E.g., Levy 2014.

[3] E.g., Bruni 2014.

[4] E.g., Weingarten 2015, leading a half page of letter writers proposing an array of possible causes of the putative shortage.

[5] E.g., Levine 2014.

[6] E.g., Schmidt 2014.

[7] E.g., Daley 2014.

[8] E.g., Iannelli 2014.

[9] E.g., Gootman and Herzenhorn 2005.

[10] E.g., Bennett 2015.

[11] E.g., Palmer 2010.

[12] E.g., Berger 2013.

[13] E.g., Rumsey 2006.

[14] Lahey 2012.

[15] Mathews 2014.

[16] Riede 2014.

[17] Ibid.

[18] Gardner 2014.

the principal, the curriculum, or the strict enforcement of rules is the most important in-school factor; and among those who agree with the blogger about the cardinal importance of teachers but disagree among themselves about what causes teachers to perform well (motivation?[19] compensation?[20] a professional education?[21] a college education?[22]). The fact that different people's diagnoses of and prescriptions for social problems frequently contradict each other suggests that these diagnoses and prescriptions are not, in fact, drawn from intuitive perceptions of obvious realities, but that they are fallible interpretations of ambiguous realities.[23] One person infers from her personal classroom experience or that of her child that "the" problem is A. Another infers B from a now-forgotten article in the *New Yorker*. Another infers C from a movie, a novel, or a scholarly study. Another infers D from a newspaper editorial (or, indeed, a letter to the editor). Another infers E from her wider assumptions about teachers' unions, or F from her wider assumptions about learning, or G from her wider assumptions about the effects of poverty on children. Each of these wider assumptions, in turn, is predicated on narrower beliefs about particular facts or, sometimes, on even wider ideological or social-theoretic worldviews, which in turn have both theoretical and evidentiary origins. In each case, what seems to be a self-disclosing reality is actually a generalization from a partial vision of reality: the product of a fallible, contestable *interpretation*.

Charles Taylor, equating "interpretation" with the attempt to make sense of "a text, or a text-analogue," notes that the attempt would be unnecessary if the text or analogue were not "confused, incomplete, cloudy, seemingly contradictory—in one way or another unclear."[24] In this view, not only the ambiguity of the object of interpretation, but the tenuousness of the act of interpretation, are built into the interpretive situation itself. Assuming that technocracy is analogous to hermeneutics, then, citizen-technocrats who treat their perceptions of the causes of and cures for social problems as if these perceptions were revelations of self-evident truth must be unaware that they are interpreting reality rather than simply registering "the facts" about it. They must be victims of what psychologists call naive realism.

In "Naive Realism in Everyday Life: Implications for Social Conflict and Misunderstanding," Lee Ross and Andrew Ward define naive realism as the assumption that one's opinions are direct reflections of reality. The chief tenet of naive realism is "that I see things as they are, that is, that my beliefs, preferences, and resulting responses follow

---

[19] Schmidt 2014.

[20] Levy 2014.

[21] Ibid.

[22] Bruni 2014.

[23] This is not to suggest that genuinely innate, intuitive ideas about public policy would have any claim to reliability.

[24] Taylor [1971] 1985, 16.

from an essentially unmediated perception of relevant stimuli and incorporation of relevant evidence."[25] I will call this viewpoint first-person naive realism. One might also assume that *others'* beliefs are unmediated reflections of reality: second- or third-person naive realism. What is at issue is whether the relevant realities are self-evident, either to oneself or others.

Section 1.1 confronts both types of naive realism with the fact of technocratic disagreement. Where there is disagreement, the reality in question cannot be self-evident. Section 1.2 considers the possibility that technocratic disagreement is disingenuous, as the naive technocratic realist may be inclined to assert. In response, I will contend that genuine disagreement about technocratic policy effects is *always* reasonable, because in principle, *any* technocratic policy may produce unintended consequences that outweigh the good expected from the policy; and because these consequences may, contra the naive realist, be counterintuitive. In Section 1.3 I will maintain that naive realism has made significant inroads among political epistemologists and threatens to reduce their enterprise to nothing but the unwitting reaffirmation, in theoretical guise, of individual theorists' eminently contestable opinions about public policy. Section 1.4 discusses the fact that unintended consequences may be beneficial as well as harmful.

1.1. NAIVE REALISM AND THE FACT OF TECHNOCRATIC DISAGREEMENT

> Whenever we form an opinion about financial reform or healthcare policy, we are implicitly
> using our commonsense reasoning to speculate about how different rules and incentives will
> affect the various parties' behavior. And whenever we argue about politics or economics we are
> implicitly using our commonsense reasoning to reach conclusions about how society will be
> affected by whatever policy or proposal is being debated.
>
> In none of these cases are we using our common sense to reason about how we should behave
> in the here and now. Rather, we are using it to reason about how other people behaved—or will
> behave—in circumstances about which we have at best an incomplete understanding. At some
> level we understand that the world is complicated, and that everything is somehow connected to
> everything else. But when we read some story about reforming the healthcare system, or about
> the Israel-Palestine conflict, we don't try to understand how all these different problems fit
> together. We just focus on the one little piece of the huge underlying tapestry of the world that's
> being presented to us at that moment, and form our opinion accordingly. In this way, we can flip
> through the newspaper while drinking our morning cup of coffee and develop twenty different
> opinions about twenty different topics without breaking a sweat. It's all just common sense.
> —DUNCAN J. WATTS, *Everything Is Obvious*

---

[25] Ross and Ward 1996, 111.

Karl Popper called naive realism "the doctrine that truth is manifest," or "the optimistic view that truth, if put before us naked, is always recognizable as truth."[26] He held that the doctrine of manifest truth licenses intellectual complacency. If one assumes that the truth is manifest, the fallible sources of one's perceptions of the truth will go unnoticed. There will, in consequence, be little reason to question them, or to wonder if those who have different perceptions might be right.

"Complacency," however, suggests that naive realism is a psychological phenomenon, a form of laziness or self-satisfaction. Better, I think, to call it "anti-epistemological." Whenever we treat our beliefs as reflections of self-evident truth, we are failing to ask where they originated and whether that point of origin is reliable—questions asked, for example, by Plato, Descartes, Hobbes, Hume, and Kant. By contrast, whenever we wonder if there is a reasonable warrant (if not a full-fledged justification or foundation) for our beliefs, we trade naive realism for epistemology.

This is not epistemology in the sense of "theorizing about why our knowledge is reliable," but epistemology in the sense of "theorizing about the preconditions or likelihood of reliable knowledge, as opposed to inaccurate opinion." The latter definition of epistemology allows us to be agnostic about whether a given knowledge claim is, in fact, reliable. Epistemological agnosticism allows us to reject the naively assumed equivalence between reality and particular beliefs about or perceptions of reality—yet without committing ourselves to the conclusion that the beliefs and perceptions are, or tend to be, illusions. Epistemological agnosticism allows us to go wherever we are led when we investigate the reliability of opinions, presupposing neither that they tend to be true nor that they tend to be false.

Naturally, of course, one always thinks that any *particular* opinion that one holds is true. That is what it means to hold an opinion. But the epistemologist may notice reasons to doubt the general veracity of opinions in a given domain, putting meat on the bones of an otherwise emaciated fallibilism. Too often, fallibilists merely acknowledge the abstract possibility that a given opinion is false because any opinion, being a human product, may be false. Epistemological agnosticism is the result of going farther, inquiring into the general reliability of the ideas that lead us to affirm particular conclusions in a given domain.

1.1.1. The Fact of Technocratic Disagreement

Instead of resting on human fallibility in general, then, my argument will rest on our fallibility in the technocratic domain. This will mean not our ability to make errors of logic in this domain, important as that might be; but our need, as technocratic decision-makers, to rely on nonmanifest empirical knowledge of social problems and their solutions.

---

[26] Popper 1963, 7–8.

The nonmanifestness of such knowledge is entailed by the fact that technocrats disagree about the scope and causes of social problems and the costs and benefits of solving them, preventing them, and mitigating them. When two or more parties disagree about something, at least one of them must be mistaken. Insofar as we do, in fact, find technocrats disagreeing with one other about such technocratic matters as the scope and causes of social problems and the costs and benefits of solving them, naive technocratic realism must be false: the truth about such matters must not be manifest, that is, self-evident. Moreover, when we explore the claims that are often adduced in debates about such matters, it will emerge that the truth about these things is not only nonmanifest, but may be positively elusive, as these claims are frequently—yet plausibly—counterintuitive.

While the fact of technocratic disagreement, and the counterintuitiveness of many of the claims adduced in technocratic policy debate, establish that reliable technocratic knowledge *may* be elusive, this is not the same as establishing that it is *likely* to be elusive. That reliable technocratic knowledge is likely to be elusive will be my contention in the rest of the book. For now, though, I want only to establish that technocratic truths are not self-evident, justifying the inquiry to follow—an epistemological inquiry.

Epistemological inquiry can take empirical or normative forms. An empirical epistemologist of technocracy might ask such questions as these: Why do citizen-technocrats think that X is a real and significant social problem? Why do they think they know what causes X? Why do they think that policy Y is likely to solve X? Why do they think that policy Z failed to solve X? An empirical epistemologist of technocracy might also ask how epistocrats form their beliefs about these subjects, or how the opinions of certain putative experts are identified as credible by citizen-technocrats or other policymakers while the opinions of other experts, with which the first group of experts disagrees, are dismissed as unreliable. I will postpone such questions until Part II, and even then, I will only scratch the surface. By contrast, a normative epistemologist of technocracy might ask if there is reason to believe that some identifiable group of technocrats, such as ordinary citizens or trained, credentialed specialists, is likely to know what they need to know about the (empirical) causes of and solutions to social problems.[27] Depending on one's answer, the normative epistemologist might be able to reach conclusions about the desirability or legitimacy of technocracy. I will ask this type of question in Chapters 2 and 3, although the empirical political epistemology sketched in Part II will also have normative implications.

If we failed to ask such questions, we could deliver a clean normative verdict on technocracy. In answer to the question of whether it does more good than harm, we could simply weigh its successes against its failures. This would likely be the path followed by a naive technocratic realist, as it would treat one set of technocratic opinions—her own opinions about which policies have passed the cost-benefit test—as (in effect) exempt

---

[27] When I use the term *know*, I will never mean "know with certainty." I will refer only to putative knowledge that is likelier than not to be accurate.

from fallible processes of technocratic belief formation. But while all of us naturally believe that our opinions about various technocratic successes and failures are accurate—for we believe that all our opinions about everything are accurate—the same is true of those who disagree with us. They, too, think that their opinions are accurate. This fact should cause both sides in any debate, including both technocratic policy debate and debates among political epistemologists about the reliability of technocratic opinion, to reject the hypothesis that its own side in the debate has gotten hold of a *self-evident* truth.

1.1.2. Naive Political Realism, Interpretation, and Radical Ignorance

Only a universal consensus among all rational observers would be consistent with the doctrine of manifest truth and, thus, with naive realism in any domain, including the technocratic domain.[28] Of course, even a consensus among all rational observers could be wrong. People may universally err. But if they universally agree, it is at least possible that what explains the consensus is the self-evidence of their shared conclusion. If they do not agree, self-evidence is logically impossible.

Naive *political* realists, who treat their own political opinions (not merely their technocratic opinions) as self-evidently true, have failed to register the logical implications of political disagreement. Indeed, they are likely to find political disagreement mystifying. Thus, Diana Mutz points out that a central feature of American public opinion seems to be widespread perplexity about the very existence of political disagreement. Each puzzled citizen says to herself, as Mutz puts it: "The answers are obvious and we all agree on them. So what is wrong with all of those *other* people?"[29] Walter Lippmann developed a similar insight in a passage from *Public Opinion* (1922) that could be the basis for a productive research agenda in empirical political epistemology. "The opponent," Lippmann noted,

> presents himself as the man who says, evil be thou my good. He is an annoyance who does not fit into the scheme of things. Nevertheless he interferes. And since that scheme is based in our minds on incontrovertible fact fortified by irresistible logic, some place has to be found for him in the scheme. Rarely in politics or industrial disputes is a place made for him by the simple admission that he has looked upon the same reality and seen another aspect of it. That would shake the whole scheme. Thus . . . out of the opposition we make villains and conspiracies.

"He who denies my version of the facts," Lippmann points out, "is to me perverse, alien, dangerous. How shall I account for him? The opponent has always to be explained, and

---

[28] The emphasis that critics so often place on the *irrationality* of politics or democracy suggests that if only political actors or citizens were rational, the truth would be self-evident to them. Thus, the critics' focus on irrationality suggests that they are naive political realists (e.g., Schumpeter 1942, 262; Achen and Bartels 2016, *passim*).

[29] Mutz 2006, 32.

the last explanation that we ever look for is that he sees a different set of facts."[30] The *first* explanation is that the opponent is evil. The urge to demonize the opponent is, in Lippmann's view, grounded in a failure of epistemological imagination. If I fail to allow that there could be plausible interpretations of political affairs that are different from my own, a plausible explanation of my opponent will be that, seeing the same reality I see, she obtusely claims not to see this manifest reality—the better, presumably, to advance a nefarious agenda of some kind.

When I discuss "interpretations," I will be speaking more broadly than Taylor, who focused on the interpretation of texts. I will focus on *attempts to understand the implications for action of perceived information.* If one wants to know which action to take, one needs at least a tacit theory of how one's action might affect the situation, based on at least a tacit interpretation of whatever perceived information about the situation seems germane. The need for interpretation could be avoided only by an omniscient being. Knowing everything, it would not have to theorize about anything. Human beings must theorize, but theories, the products of fallible interpreters of an opaque reality, are as fallible as we are. The proliferation of competing political interpretations, like the proliferation of other types of interpretation, indicates the ubiquity of human error. If our interpretations were based on self-evident truths, we would not disagree over them. Like disagreement in general, interpretive conflicts in politics indicate that some of the interpretations (or all of them) are wrong.

The naive political realist overlooks that implication of the fact of political disagreement because she is *radically ignorant* of the plausibility of interpretations of the political situation that differ from her own. That is, plausible alternative interpretations are, to the naive political realist, unknown unknowns.[31] It is not that she denies their veridicality, or their existence. Rather, she is simply unaware (ignorant) of either their existence or the logical implication of their existence: namely, that her own interpretation may be in error. Indeed, if one is unaware that there are other interpretations that contradict one's own, one is likely to be unaware that one's own interpretation *is* an interpretation rather than a reflection of the self-evident truth.

Naive technocratic realism is a subspecies of naive political realism. Logically, the fact of technocratic disagreement should be fatal to the naive technocratic realist's assumption that her opinions about social problems are self-evidently true. When disagreement is not caused by value conflicts, as in the case of technocratic disagreement (by definition), it must be caused by a clash of interpretations about empirical realities having to do with social problems—sometimes because both parties perceive the same information about a given situation but interpret the information differently; other times because they interpret different information as being relevant to the same situation. In all cases, clashes of interpretation entail that at least some of the

---

[30] Lippmann [1922] 1997, 82–83.

[31] So far as I know, Ikeda 1996 contains the first use of "radical ignorance" along these lines.

interpretations are wrong, such that none can be self-evidently true—except in the eyes of the naive realist.

1.1.3. Naive Technocratic Realism and Policy Debate

Technocratic disagreement frequently takes the form of policy debate. Thus, the mere fact that policy debate occurs is tantamount to a falsification of naive technocratic realism.

By policy debate, I mean the expression of conflicting opinions about the definition, existence, scope, or causes of social problems; about the costs or benefits of proposed or already-implemented solutions; or about broader policy-relevant theories, such as the theory of regulatory capture, the broken-windows theory of policing, pedagogical theories applicable to education policy, or theories of the business cycle. Policy debate can occur informally among amateurs (in conversation, on social media); formally among amateurs (authors of letters to the editor, bloggers, authors of comments on proposed regulations); and, either formally or informally, among professionals such as policy wonks (policy analysts who produce policy studies for think tanks), talking heads (television commentators), opinion journalists, academic policy analysts, social scientists writing about social problems, politicians, politically appointed bureaucrats, and career civil servants.

Policy debate, and thus evidence of technocratic disagreement, can be found in abundance in any newspaper, on cable news, and on the internet. Its widespread visibility alone should alert naive technocratic realists to the interpretive nature of their ideas about social problems and policy solutions and, therefore, to the possibility that these ideas are incorrect. That should, in principle, put an end to their technocratic naiveté.

1.1.4. The Naively Cynical Rejoinder to the Fact of Technocratic Disagreement

However, a naive technocratic realist might respond to the fact of technocratic disagreement by challenging the genuineness of the disagreement. After all, she might think, if the truth is self-evident, then purported disagreement about the truth must simply be a sham. Thus, the claims advanced in policy debate—or, rather, the claims advanced in policy debate by those with whom the naive technocratic realist disagrees—must constitute "fake news."

This reaction to disagreement is but a half step removed from the phenomenon observed by Mutz and Lippmann. The citizen they describe is perplexed by the existence of political opponents because she is unaware that the opponents might be motivated by reasonable interpretations—interpretations of which she is radically ignorant. Confronted with such interpretations, however, as expressed in policy debate, the naive technocratic realist might, in all innocence, deny that they can be sincerely believed by their proponents. After all, how could any honest observer believe what is self-evidently untrue?

Ross and Ward point out that since the naive realist views her own perceptions as self-evidently true, she will be inclined to think "that other rational, reasonable people ... will share both [her] experiences and responses."[32] But when the naive realist is made aware that apparently rational, reasonable people not only oppose her point of view but adduce *reasons* for opposing it, her prime challenge becomes explaining away the reasonableness of these reasons. As Lippmann suggests, one way to do this is to appeal, tacitly or expressly, to the idea of evil, not as an evaluation of objective conditions (e.g., poverty or illness is evil), but as a causal force explaining political opinions (i.e., the reason for my opponent's political stance is that she is evil). If we favor what is self-evidently desirable, then our opponents necessarily favor what is self-evidently undesirable, and in that case, they are evil by definition. Thus, Popper maintains that naive realists have few options but to see their opponents as captives of "the most depraved wickedness." Against such wickedness, he contends, the naive realist will feel entitled to direct "almost every kind of fanaticism."[33]

One might object to this line of thought by noting that in identifying one's political opponents as evil, someone can simply be realistic—not naive. However, my point is not that there are no evil political actors, evaluatively speaking. It is, instead, that the conviction that one's political opponents *know* that they are evil (i.e., that they are in the deliberate service of evil) may be the product not of a dispassionate investigation of the opponents' motives, but of the naive political realist's incomprehension of the very possibility of sincere disagreement in the case at hand. Since the naive realist cannot fathom *real* disagreement—given the self-evidence (to her) of the truths with which her opponents disagree—she cynically dismisses their *apparent* disagreement with her as "fake." This cynicism may pass for a clear-eyed rejection of sentimentalism. But in fact, it is only as realistic as the underlying assumption: that the truth is self-evident.

In response to the radically ignorant cynicism of the naive realist, then, a political epistemologist might appeal to the notion that the objects of interpretation are complex or ambiguous, as in Taylor's view of textual interpretation. Thus, a political epistemologist of technocracy might point out that technocratic disagreement could be a sign of the epistemic complexity of modern society, which gives rise to a multitude of interpretations of the social problems we perceive. The political epistemologist would not thereby deny that some (or conceivably all) real-world policy debate is insincere, but would affirm that sincere policy debate is what we would expect among genuinely sociotropic (as opposed to evil) interpreters of an opaque reality. An *ideal policy debate*, then, would produce disagreement, not consensus, in an epistemically complex society.

---

[32] Ross and Ward 1996, 111.

[33] Popper 1963, 8.

Yet an appeal to epistemic complexity would probably leave the naive technocratic realist cold. If she recognized that modern society is complex, in the sense of being difficult to make sense of, she probably would not think that the truth about social problems is self-evident. Therefore, to insist, a priori, on the epistemic complexity of modern society would border on begging the question against her. How else, then, might we confront her naively cynical response to the (putative) fact of technocratic disagreement?

In particular cases, the best practical course might be to recommend that she "read the other side" (or sides) of a given policy debate. This would allow her to discover the reasons in which the other side claims to believe. Most of us are not policy wonks and do not know what the other side's policy wonks (or even our own) are saying about a given topic in technocratic debate. If we forced ourselves to find out, it might cure us of naive technocratic realism, and of the putatively hard-headed cynicism that may accompany it.

Consider the roiling debate over health care policy that took place in 2009, prior to the adoption of the Affordable Care Act. One eddy in the larger debate was an ongoing dispute over which countries' health care systems were examples for the United States to follow or avoid. Austria, Britain, Canada, Cuba, France, Germany, Holland, Japan, Singapore, Switzerland, and Taiwan (perhaps others, too) were all touted as models of good or bad health care systems. For the most part, this debate was technocratic: what was at issue was not the *value* of, say, more coverage, or better health care, or lower administrative costs, but various systems' efficacy in achieving these objectives.[34] Each side pointed to congenial statistics, studies, and anecdotes about the countries whose approaches they favored; all sides emphasized methodological problems in the statistics and studies cited by the other sides, and denied the representativeness of the other side's anecdotes. Social scientists familiar with the comparative method will recognize that while such debates are decidable in principle, the difficulties in interpreting society-wide evidence are so great that, in practice, sincere interpreters may disagree with each other; and that these disagreements may never come to an end, in the real world, even if it is the case that an infinite amount of policy debate, conducted under ideal conditions, might allow the unforced force of the better argument to prevail.

However, reading the other side is probably the last thing the naive realist will be inclined to do, since she believes in the self-evident truth of her own side's perspective. If her side is manifestly right, the other side must know it is wrong. In the service of its sinister objectives, the other side can be expected to dish out phony arguments. So why waste one's time reading them? Similarly, even if the naive realist could be persuaded to read the other side, she would tend to do so with bias: she would tend to assume that even

---

[34] For example, Cohn 2009 argued that while in Britain and Canada, patients might endure longer waiting periods for some medical procedures than in the United States, this was largely untrue in France and the Netherlands, and that in all other respects these two countries outperformed the US health care system. Reid 2009 compared nine countries across several value dimensions to suggest that certain systems are superior in providing all the valued outcomes.

if the other side seems to have good arguments, these arguments *must* involve twisting the truth—since the truth is manifestly not what the other side favors. Attempting, in good faith, to offset the other side's presumed bias, the naive cynic will overcompensate with a skewed response to the other side's arguments. Her convictions will therefore become unfalsifiable. (This may explain why Popper, the advocate of falsificationism, targeted the "doctrine" of manifest truth.)

Naively cynical attributions of sinister motives, no matter how groundless, may therefore be unrebuttable in practice. But these attributions can be sidestepped in principle. For what actually motivates the participants in policy debate does not affect the validity of what they say. Even if those on the other side *are* moved to oppose a given policy by venal motives or sheer malevolence, the technocratic arguments they deploy might be sound. If they are not sound, this has to be demonstrated, not merely inferred from their alleged motives. Thus, the opponent of naive technocratic realism needs only to show, in principle, that genuinely public-spirited disagreement over the need for or effects of a given policy *would be* reasonable in an ideal policy debate—regardless of whether the actual reasons adduced are reasonable ones, and regardless of whether they are badly motivated.

1.2. FOUR TYPES OF TECHNOCRATIC KNOWLEDGE AND THE POSSIBILITY OF UNINTENDED CONSEQUENCES

> Far more serious in the modern world than any difference of moral code is the difference
> in the assumptions about facts to which the code is applied. Religious, moral, and political
> formulae are nothing like so far apart as the facts assumed by their votaries. Useful
> discussion, then, instead of comparing ideals, reexamines the visions of the facts.
> —WALTER LIPPMANN, *Public Opinion*

We can begin to understand why sincere technocratic disagreement might occur by getting a handle on the categories of empirical knowledge that technocrats need. Here is a schema that divides such knowledge into four main types.

Type 1. Knowledge of which social problems are not only real but *significant*, in the sense that they affect large numbers of people—or small numbers intensely. (This amounts to knowledge of the negative-utilitarian benefits to be achieved by solving, preventing, or mitigating the problems.)

Type 2. Knowledge of what is *causing* the significant problems, and (preferably) knowledge of what might cause significant new problems in the future.

Type 3. Knowledge of which technocratic actions can *efficaciously* solve, mitigate, or prevent the significant problems.

Type 4. Knowledge of the *costs* of efficacious solutions, including not only anticipated costs but those that are not intended, and thus are not anticipated.

Let me now go into each type of knowledge in a bit of detail. Upon closer inspection, some of the types may (arguably) turn out to be optional despite their desirability, while others turn out to be more difficult to get than one might first think.

Type 1 (significance) knowledge is important insofar as problem-solving resources are scarce. If resources are scarce, the problems facing a technocracy need to be ranked so that relatively significant ones receive resources before relatively insignificant ones do. This ranking need not necessarily be precise, but technocrats have to know, in general, whether a given problem is widespread and severe for those it affects; otherwise they might spend scarce problem-solving resources on problems that are relatively unimportant, from a sociotropic perspective, instead of spending them on relatively important problems.

The *severity* component of Type 1 knowledge is the one aspect of the four types that can be garnered—to some extent—from personal experience. If one's own experience with a social problem demonstrates how severely it can affect somebody, this is important information that should be made known to technocratic decision-makers at large (whether epistocrats or citizen-technocrats). But personal experience testifying to the severity of a problem never indicates how *common* a problem is, except insofar as personal experiences are aggregated into something akin to statistics. Thus, even Type 1 knowledge has to be mediated to technocratic decision-makers—by the likes of statisticians, at the very least. One might think that much to be obvious, but it is sometimes said that personal experience with (say) unemployment or declining personal income is sufficient or nearly sufficient for adequate decision-making by citizen-technocrats. This is the theory behind defenses of "retrospective voting," which I will discuss in Chapter 6, but the theory is mistaken.[35] Statistics that establish the extent of such problems, and thus their rank order on the technocratic agenda, are essential if sociotropic objectives are to be achieved. Statistics cannot issue from unmediated personal experience.

However, statistics bring interpretive problems in a way that one's own experience does not. There is intense controversy about which unemployment statistics to use, for example, and competent statisticians would be the first to acknowledge that such controversy is reasonable in regard to any society-wide statistic.[36] Statistics can be misleading; they have to be interpreted properly.[37] Moreover, to choose which statistic to use in gauging the significance of the problem of, say, unemployment, one would need to know that a given statistical level of unemployment is *actionable*

---

[35] See Fiorina 1981, Ferejohn 1986, and Kiewiet and Rivers 2005.

[36] The most frequently reported jobless rate is based on a strict definition of unemployment that necessarily looks better than numbers that include former workers who have stopped searching for work (Levy 2011). There are also considerable measurement errors, such that virtually every unemployment report is later revised, often drastically (Goldfarb 2012). The statistical measurement of poverty is another notoriously difficult and contested technocratic project; see DeParle et al. 2011 and Dougherty 2011.

[37] See Best 2001.

(Type 3 knowledge). This leads to further interpretive problems, as statistics homogenize heterogeneous items such as "instances" of unemployment, some of which will be actionable while others are not. Knowing which problems are actionable also requires Type 2 knowledge, such as knowledge of the causes of unemployment. This calls not for personal experience but for a sound, generally applicable theory. The more capacious one's conception of the reach of economic causation, the wider technocrats' Type 2 knowledge will have to be. Thus, broad theoretical perspectives such as Keynesianism are indispensable adjuncts to—and objects of—ideal policy debate. Social theories of even greater breadth, such as Marxism, might also be looked to as sources of necessary causal knowledge, even when they lack immediate policy relevance. Clearly, however—or so I take it—no such causal theory or perspective is *self-evidently* true.

On the other hand, if one is impressed by how difficult it is to establish causal relationships in a modern society (as are a growing number of social scientists),[38] it might seem that there is an escape hatch from the need for Type 2 (causal) knowledge: the acquisition of Type 3 (efficacy) knowledge by means of randomized field tests. After all, the random testing of a multitude of pharmaceutical agents can produce knowledge of an effective cure for a medical condition even when the condition's cause is unknown, and even when the reason for the cure's efficacy is mysterious. Thus, it might seem that if we were to field test a multitude of technocratic policies, we could gain knowledge of the solutions to social problems without knowing their causes.

I will argue in Chapter 4 that this appearance is deceptive. Until then, let me forestall undue optimism about field testing by pointing to two reasons for skepticism.

First, field testing does, in fact, presuppose at least a preliminary form of causal knowledge about the problem one is trying to solve. Without guidance from such knowledge, there would be no way to produce a feasible set of *plausible* experimental treatments from the literally infinite number of possible treatments that might be tested, and thus no way to rule out treatments that could only produce a spurious correlation at best. A good analogy here is the notion that big data can spare policymakers the need to interpret the causes of social problems. The problem with this detour around causal knowledge is indicated by the multitude of spurious correlations that have been turned up by big data—that is, correlations that *im*plausibly suggest causation. If we were to act on the basis of big data without using a plausibility filter, we would attempt to reduce suicide via hanging, strangulation, and suffocation by cutting the federal science, space, and technology budget (correlation: .998); or we would try to reduce divorce rates in Maine by reducing the per capita US consumption of margarine (correlation: .993); or we would try to increase the number of biology/biomedicine doctorates awarded annually by increasing the number of lawyers in New Mexico

---

[38] See Chapter 4, Section 4.4.

(correlation: .928).[39] Big data must be tied, by a theory, to plausible causal mechanisms if the data are to be more useful than that. So, too, must be the policies tried out in field tests. Without plausible causal theories to justify the assumption that particular field tests have identified real solutions to social problems, we would implement field-tested policies that do not actually solve the problems they are intended to solve.

Second, without causal knowledge we may field effective solutions that nonetheless have deleterious effects. Aspirin may be effective against headaches, but if one does not know the cause of the headaches, prescribing aspirin may have the disastrous unintended cost of averting the treatment of an underlying condition such as brain cancer. Without knowledge of the causes of social problems, we may end up treating societal headaches by averting the treatment of societal cancers.

1.2.1. Unintended Consequences: Indirect, Direct, and Counterintuitive

Thus far, I have suggested only that technocrats will need all four types of knowledge, and that this may cause interpretive problems—not necessarily interpretive problems that cannot be solved, but interpretive problems that, as such, entail that the needed knowledge is not self-evident. A naive technocratic realist, however, could allow that it may *sometimes* be necessary to interpret evidence in order to produce the four types of knowledge, while insisting that, in the case at hand, a given statistic obviously shows that a given social problem is important, that "common sense" reveals the obvious causes of the problem, that the efficacy of a proposed treatment is equally obvious, and that so, too, are the costs of the treatment. This, in fact, is how naive technocratic realism crops up in nonideal policy debate. Few deny that, in principle, things may sometimes be complicated, but many affirm that in the case being debated, the truth is obvious (consider the assuredness of those who opined about education policy). Therefore, to establish the reasonableness of technocratic disagreement, I need to find indications that something about modern social problems, or about modern society itself, might *always* impede the acquisition of the requisite knowledge. Such indications would be the basis of a prima facie valid case for the epistemic complexity of modern social problems, or of modern society. If the problems, or the society that produces them, are epistemically complex, then naive technocratic realism would be unsustainable. (Again, this would merely establish the need for and fallibility of technocratic interpretations, not the impossibility of producing adequate technocratic interpretations.)

In an important article in the epistemic-democracy literature, Hélène Landemore and Scott Page point out that in seeking to make predictions about the effects of macroeconomic policies, various economists disagree with each other because they "make different assumptions about the world . . . use different formal constructions . . . and tend to rely on

---

[39] http://www.tylervigen.com/ provides these and other spurious big-data correlations—or presumably spurious correlations.

distinct variables and behavioral assumptions."[40] Economists would not disagree in this manner if macroeconomic problems had self-evident solutions. Let us call problems that lack self-evident solutions "epistemically complex." By contrast, Landemore and Page point out that, in response to epistemically *simple* problems, people would respond as if to an oracle ("Eureka!"). The naive realist believes, or rather assumes, that in the case or cases at hand she has had a Eureka moment—not just in the sense that she may think she has hit upon self-evident truths, but in the sense that she really has. Therefore, the naive realist finds disagreement unreasonable.

I will soon start listing examples of claims drawn from real-world technocratic debate to suggest that technocratic problems may always be epistemically complex, in that they may always produce unintended consequences. Nothing will depend on the truth value of the particular claims; everything will depend on their initial *plausibility*, that is, on the reasonable *possibility* that they are true. Before producing these examples, however, let me use the fourfold schema of technocratic knowledge to create a typology of possible unintended consequences to which the ensuing discussion can refer.

1. If a failure in our Type 1 knowledge leads us to adopt a policy to solve a problem that is relatively insignificant, an unintended consequence will be that resources devoted to that policy cannot be devoted to relatively significant problems (assuming that we have finite problem-solving resources). We can label this type of unintended consequence "indirect." An indirect unintended consequence stems from an action that we forgo because of an action that we take. In contrast, a direct unintended consequence would follow from the action we take, regardless of the foregone actions that indirectly result.

2. A second variant of indirect unintended consequence may follow from a lack of causal knowledge (Type 2), on the analogy of treating a headache with aspirin in the absence of knowledge that the cause of the headache is brain cancer. If we treat the symptoms of a problem without addressing its cause, it may lead to worse problems than the one treated, because of the actions (akin to brain surgery) that we forego.

3. Similarly, if we lack efficacy (Type 3) knowledge, we may devote scarce problem-solving resources to inefficacious solutions, indirectly causing unintended problems by reducing our ability to implement efficacious solutions.

4. The most important type of indirect unintended consequence, from the perspective of dispelling naive technocratic realism, is *counterintuitive*. (Although all unintended consequences are, by definition, *unanticipated* by the policymaker, this need not be due to their counterintuitiveness.) An indirect, counterintuitive unanticipated consequence would bespeak inadequate Type 4 knowledge.

However, a naive realist would object to any counterintuitive claim by saying that its counterintuitiveness shows that it must be wrong, since the naive realist treats the truth

---

[40] Landemore and Page 2015, 242. Landemore and Page call simple problems, in my sense, simply "problems." They call complex problems, in my sense, "predictive" ones. See Friedman 2017c for a slightly more detailed engagement with this aspect of their paper.

as intuitively obvious. To answer this objection, we need examples of counterintuitive claims that are, nonetheless, plausible. But how could a claim be both counterintuitive and plausible?

We can make some headway here by starting with two examples of technocratic claims that are both counterintuitive and *im*plausible. They are implausible because, as I will present them, they lack a mechanism that would explain how they could conceivably be true. Thus, they are akin to the claim that we should boost the number of biology/biomedicine doctorates awarded annually by increasing the number of lawyers in New Mexico. (I will refer to this as the New Mexican lawyers problem, not that there's anything wrong with lawyers from New Mexico.) Consider, then, first, that while one might assume that the availability of health insurance will positively affect people's health, it has been alleged in real-world policy debate that health insurance has no positive effect, in the aggregate, on health.[41] Second, while one might assume that education spending will positively affect educational outcomes, it has been alleged that, in the United States, a doubling of federal spending on education has had no effect on student achievement scores.[42]

If these two claims are true, it is possible that immense sums are unintentionally being wasted on health insurance and education that could better be spent elsewhere. Thus, they are claims about indirect unintended consequences. No direct harm (at least no harm of which we are aware) follows from spending unnecessarily on health insurance and education. But if, in fact, little or no good is produced by this spending, the money diverted to it could have been devoted to significant problems that might thereby have been solved, mitigated, or prevented. However, while the two correlations may be true—just as it is true, presumably, that there is a .928 correlation between the number of biology/biomedicine doctorates awarded annually and the number of lawyers in New Mexico—all three claims, as *causal* claims, are implausible, for they lack causal mechanisms. The remaining types of unintended consequence are counterintuitive yet plausible, because they do not lack (plausible) causal mechanisms.

5. One such type of counterintuitive unintended consequence would be direct. In such cases, it is alleged that technocratic initiatives "aggravate the very problems they are intended to solve," as Cass Sunstein puts it.[43] Some familiar claims of this type, which I will call "regulatory backfire," are that the Americans with Disabilities Act (ADA)—which was designed, in large part, to end employment discrimination against the disabled—actually caused greater employment discrimination against them;[44] the claim that federal student-loan programs actually made college less affordable for the poor;[45] the claim that rent control actually makes housing both scarcer and less affordable for the poor;[46] and

---

[41] Levy and Meltzer 2008.

[42] E.g., Bachelder 2014.

[43] Sunstein 1990, 32.

[44] Acemoglu and Angrist 1998.

[45] Schuck 2014, 263.

[46] Sunstein 1990, 56.

the claim that minimum-wage laws increase unemployment among low-wage workers.[47] Each of these claims, unlike the claims about health insurance and education spending, comes with a plausible causal mechanism. Thus, Sunstein contends that rent control has "discouraged new investment in housing, decreased the available housing stock, and benefited existing tenants, many of them financially well off, at the expense of others, many of them poor."[48] How might this work? Sometimes it is said that rent control encourages parents to hang onto their rent-controlled (and thus relatively cheap) apartments even when their children have grown up and moved out, leaving the parents with less need for as much space; as a result, there is less space available for the poor, as the parents are often affluent. This mechanism is counterintuitive in that it is unlikely that most people would think of it unprompted. But it is nonetheless plausible in the sense that, once one is prompted to consider it, one finds nothing logically invalid about it; and in the sense that it does not require heroic empirical assumptions to imagine that the posited mechanism *might* produce the hypothesized contraction of the housing supply for the poor. The fact that the posited mechanism is logically and empirically plausible does not establish, of course, that it has had the hypothesized counterintuitive effect in a given instance. But it does constitute a reason for doubting the self-evident desirability of rent control. Therefore, it constitutes reasonable grounds for sincere disagreement about rent control.

Similarly, some researchers believe that the ADA led employers to fear that a given disabled employee could only be fired, if need be (e.g., if she proved to be incompetent), at great risk to the employer: in response to being fired, the employee might baselessly sue the employer for discrimination under the ADA, which would impose large legal costs on the employer whether the suit succeeded or not. Rather than risk costly litigation, then, even unbiased employers may (according to these researchers) have started to avoid hiring the disabled.[49] While this is not a consequence that would spring to mind when considering whether discrimination against the disabled should be outlawed, it is not absurd to think that such a consequence is not only logically possible but may in fact have occurred, such that disagreement about whether it occurred would be reasonable.

In the case of federally guaranteed student loans, colleges may have responded to the enlarged pool of funds that the loans created by charging higher tuition than they otherwise would have, knowing that students could now borrow to pay for the higher tuition. This would have enabled colleges to spend the increased income on such items as more administrators and more student amenities. If so, students may have ended up footing the bill for these new costs by incurring debts that take decades to repay; and impoverished high-school graduates may have been priced out of attending college, scared off by the prospect of such debts.[50]

---

[47] E.g., Neumark and Wascher 2008.

[48] Sunstein 1990, 56.

[49] Winston 2006, 88.

[50] Gordon and Hedlund 2015.

Finally, it is often suggested that minimum-wage laws reduce employers' incentives to employ low-skilled workers.[51] Here the counterintuitive claim is that if the minimum wage rises above a given employee's level of productivity, the employer may look to find a cheaper substitute for the employee's labor, such as automation or new methods of production that involve a few highly skilled employees rather than many low-skilled employees.[52] In extremis, a minimum-wage hike might cause payroll to exceed revenue for employers who cannot introduce such innovations, forcing them to close down.[53] Either way, low-wage employment would (potentially) suffer.

Any or all of these counterintuitive theories may be untrue. For example, while early studies suggested that the ADA had indeed caused disemployment effects among the disabled, a 2015 study appears to have vindicated the ADA by showing that large employers, which are covered by the act, tended to respond favorably to fake employment-solicitation letters purportedly sent by disabled applicants, while small employers, which are not covered, tended to respond unfavorably.[54] This suggests that post-ADA discrimination was not primarily motivated by fear of ADA lawsuits, as the discrimination in the study occurred mainly among employers who were not affected by the ADA. However, if a naive technocratic realist were to cite this study to rebut the counterintuitive claim that the ADA backfired, she would be tacitly conceding that social problems are too epistemically difficult to yield, a priori, to our intuitions. If the veracity of intuitions is self-evident, they should not need to be backed up by empirical research. To cite empirical research about policy effects is to engage in policy debate, and policy debate would be unnecessary if the truth about policy effects were self-evident.

An adequate defense of naive technocratic realism would thus have to avoid co-optation by the existence of policy debate. That is, the naive realist would have to give us reason to think that our intuitions about modern social problems *must* tend to track reality, in principle, such that the counterintuitive claims presented in policy debate can be presumptively dismissed as absurd—or, more to the point, disingenuous. This burden of argument rests with the naive technocratic realist because it is surely conceivable, as we know from personal experience, that any action that we take *may* backfire. By the same token, any technocratic initiative may (conceivably) cause direct unintended consequences that, being counterintuitive, cannot be dismissed a priori. Whether or not a particular assertion of such consequences is justified must depend on the plausibility of the asserted mechanism and on empirical research into whether the effect has actually occurred in the past—two of the key questions at issue

---

[51] See Chapter 4.
[52] E.g., Lordan and Neumark 2017.
[53] E.g., Luca and Luca 2017.
[54] Ameri et al. 2015.

in ideal policy debate, but questions about which disagreement is always reasonable, in principle.

Bracketing the seemingly lethal effect that the possibility of direct, counterintuitive unintended policy consequences should have on naive technocratic realism, it is worth noting that such consequences are particularly important, from a theoretical perspective, because they would not only entail inadequate Type 4 knowledge (knowledge of the costs of technocratic actions), but would affirm the importance of the other three types of technocratic knowledge in a new way. *Indirect* unintended consequences, as we saw, may flow from the misallocation of scarce problem-solving resources to problems that are relatively insignificant (because we may lack adequate and reliable Type 1 knowledge), or to problems the causes of which cannot be affected by technocratic interventions (which we could know only if we have adequate, reliable Type 2 knowledge), or to interventions that are ineffective (which we could know only if we have adequate, reliable Type 3 knowledge). This is clearest in cases of public spending, where, lacking adequate, reliable technocratic knowledge, financial resources might be directed toward ineffective policies. However, regulatory policy, unlike fiscal policy, may not require the expenditure of significant problem-solving resources, at least when the administrative and compliance costs of regulation are low. Yet if a regulatory measure backfires, the aggravation of the social problem it aims to mitigate may outweigh any benefits of the regulation. Thus, if we impose regulations to address insignificant problems, or problems that cannot be solved through regulation, or if we impose poorly designed regulations, we are risking adverse unintended consequences. To minimize this risk, a regulatory technocracy would need reliable knowledge of all four types. By the same token, it is conceivable that any given spending initiative may (counterintuitively) backfire, a direct cost that would be undesirable apart from the indirect cost in wasted problem-solving resources. Thus, in light of the possibility of policy backfires, adequate technocratic knowledge of all four types would be desirable before undertaking spending initiatives as well as regulatory initiatives.

6. Unintended consequences may not only be counterintuitive ex ante but invisible ex post, and thus empirically undetectable. Yet such consequences, doubly challenging to the naive technocratic realist, would affirm the reasonableness of technocratic disagreement, and, once again, this could be true of all technocratic initiatives, in principle. Assertions of invisible consequences might, after all, be made about any action. Of course, precisely because the posited consequences are invisible, such assertions may be met with skepticism. But we cannot reject such assertions out of hand, as they may be coupled with plausible mechanisms.

For example, it has long been maintained that the FDA's regulation of new drugs to ensure their safety and efficacy may save fewer lives than it costs and cause more suffering than it relieves. Mandatory testing regimens designed to weed out ineffective and dangerous new drugs add enormously to the expense of drug development (it is argued), and this may preclude the development of drugs that could have saved more lives and reduced more suffering than the lives lost and the suffering avoided by keeping unsafe and ineffective drugs off the market.[55] However, since the putative undeveloped drugs do not exist, the lives they would have saved, and the suffering they would have alleviated, must remain invisible.[56] There cannot be letters to the editor, investigative journalism, or social-scientific studies of people who would have been saved from a fatal disease if only FDA regulations had not prevented a nonexistent drug from coming into existence. Yet there might, for all we know, be many such tragedies. Again, failures of Type 4 knowledge would be responsible. Again, too, reliable knowledge of the other three types would be more important than if only indirect unintended consequences were possible, because we should not risk invisible, direct adverse consequences for the sake of ineffective regulations or regulations that address insignificant or unsolvable problems. And again, the possibility of such consequences would make it reasonable to disagree about the wisdom of any technocratic initiative, provided that a plausible mechanism is invoked, as in this example.

7. A final type of counterintuitive, direct unintended consequence further suggests the reasonableness of disagreement about any and all technocratic initiatives. This type of consequence would occur if a technocratic policy directly created *new* social problems— regardless of whether it failed to solve the problem against which it was directed (thus wasting resources on it), regardless of whether it aggravated the problem (thus backfiring), and regardless of whether its unintended costs were invisible. However, like policy backfires and invisible policy costs, *misguided policy missiles* would result from gaps in our Type 4 knowledge, even while putting an equal premium on the other types of technocratic knowledge. Let me list 10 such claims drawn from real-world policy debate, not because misguided policy missiles are necessarily more prevalent or severe than indirect unintended consequences, policy backfires, or invisible costs—in this chapter we are interested solely in possibilities, not realities—but because claims about misguided policy missiles are particularly counterintuitive, yet can be plausible nonetheless.

(1) The prohibition of alcohol is thought to have led to the creation of vast networks of murderous criminals whose actions were worse than the problems Prohibition was intended to solve. The prohibition of narcotics is believed to have produced similar unintended consequences.[57]

(2) The high unemployment rate that plagued Western Europe even before the financial crisis, and that persisted afterward, is sometimes said to have been

---

[55] Peltzman 1973 makes the argument about efficacy testing; see also Bhidé 2017. On safety testing see, e.g., Mandel 2011, Miller 2010, and Huber 2013.

[56] Sometimes the release of new drugs in countries with less-stringent regulations enables researchers to calculate lives lost in countries with more-stringent regulations due to the failure to introduce those drugs, or due to delays in introducing them (Winston 2006, 35). But such calculations cannot estimate the cost of discoveries that are prevented from happening by regulations that impede a drug company in a given country from developing a drug that nobody else would have developed, about which we will, therefore, never know.

[57] E.g., Frydl 2013.

an unintended consequence of the social benefits and work rules attached to new jobs by law, which made hiring workers more expensive than it otherwise would have been.[58]

(3) The Affordable Care Act (ACA) may have caused employers to reduce millions of workers' hours below the 30 per week that triggered mandatory employer health-insurance payments, and may therefore have been partly responsible for the agonizingly slow US recovery from the recession following the financial crisis.[59]

(4) The ACA is also said to have exerted pressure on small businesses to stop expanding when they reached 49 employees, since the 50th employee would trigger the employer mandate.[60]

(5) "Depressed areas in cities," according to a classic paper in the unintended-consequences literature, "arise from *excess* low-income housing rather than from a commonly presumed housing shortage. The legal and tax structures have combined to give incentives for keeping old buildings in place. As industrial buildings age, employment opportunities decline. As residential buildings age, they are used by lower-income groups who are forced to use them at higher population densities. . . . A social trap is created where excess low-cost housing beckons low-income people inward"[61]—inward, that is, to areas where there are few jobs.

(6) Occupational licensing laws, it is argued, deprive as many as 2.85 million Americans of the opportunity to work in many fields, due to the (purportedly) unnecessary difficulty of obtaining a license.[62]

(7) Across the developed world, mandatory employer child-care and paid maternity-leave rules have allegedly caused employers to reduce female employment and wages, thereby avoiding the financial cost of female employees who take maternity leave and then require child care.[63]

(8) The financial crisis has been attributed, in part, to a series of regulations, designed to protect bond investors, that had the cumulative effect of conferring oligopoly status on three "ratings agencies": Moody's, Standard and Poor's, and Fitch. In turn, these so-called agencies (actually corporations) were responsible for conferring triple-A ratings on the mortgage-backed securities that threatened the solvency of major banks during the crisis.[64]

---

[58] Andrews 2002; Atkins and Steinglass 2011; Siebert 1997.

[59] Goodman 2015; Puzder 2014.

[60] Cowley 2015.

[61] Forrester 1995, 9.

[62] E.g., Alchian and Kessel 1962; Bernstein 2001; Kleiner, Krueger, and Mas 2011; White House 2015.

[63] Miller 2015.

[64] White 2009; Calomiris and Haber 2014, 266.

(9) The crisis has also been attributed, in part, to policies aimed at encouraging affordable housing for low-income borrowers, which had the side effect of introducing subprime mortgages into mortgage-backed securities.[65]

(10) Finally, the crisis has also been attributed, in part, to mark-to-market accounting regulations, which were enacted to protect investors from corporate accounting manipulations. It is said that by requiring corporations—including banks—to value their holdings of mortgage-backed securities at rapidly falling market prices during the panic phase of the crisis, these regulations transformed paper losses on the securities into bottom-line losses that jeopardized banks' solvency.[66]

These examples suggest the possibility that misguided policy missiles can land anywhere. In other words, we may be ignorant even of the areas where the unintended consequences of technocratic measures may manifest themselves, which would make them extremely difficult to anticipate. Thus, according to claim (1), a policy that was intended to curb a variety of social ills such as poverty (caused by men who were too drunk to work) ended up causing an organized-crime problem. According to claims (2), (3), and (4), policies intended (inter alia) to improve people's health negatively affected people's ability to work. According to claim (5), policies intended to reduce urban blight caused poverty. According to claim (6), policies designed to ensure consumer safety had disemployment effects. According to claim (7), regulations intended to help children purportedly ended up hurting women with children. According to claims (8), (9), and (10), policies intended to protect investors and stimulate affordable housing ended up causing an economic calamity.

How might a naive technocratic realist respond to such claims? She might assert that they are *inherently* implausible—regardless of whether the posited mechanisms are plausible—because self-evident truths cannot possibly be counterintuitive. This response might barely be reasonable with regard to counterintuitiveness within a given policy domain: if one considers, say, education to be a domain that yields to intuitive insights—after all, each of us has been in the position of being educated, and many of us have been in the position of educating—then it might be reasonable to deny that education policies could backfire, no matter what backfire mechanisms might be adduced. However, to deny that an education policy can counterintuitively cause problems *outside* the realm of education would be tantamount to a claim for omniscience about causal relationships over an entire society. Such a claim is inconsistent with human fallibility, and is therefore—I take it—unreasonable in principle.

It seems to me, then, that technocratic disagreement is always reasonable, even discounting the difficulty of obtaining the first three types of technocratic knowledge. Even

---

[65] Calomiris and Haber 2014, ch. 7; Financial Crisis Inquiry Commission 2011, 444–445.

[66] Geanakoplos 2010; Isaac 2009; International Monetary Fund 2008, 65; Isaac 2010, ch. 12; Financial Crisis Inquiry Commission 2011, 227.

if one considers knowledge of the significance of social problems, of their causes, and of the efficacy of proposed policies to be self-evident, one cannot deny the very possibility of Type 4 knowledge failures without making unreasonable claims about the reach and accuracy of human knowledge. Thus, contrary to what the naive technocratic realist believes, technocratic policies that seem self-evidently necessary might do more harm than good.

1.2.2.   Unintended Consequences, Neoclassical Economics, and Social Theory

Confirmation of the reasonableness of technocratic disagreement can be discovered by examining three rare meta-analyses of studies of technocratic policies' costs and benefits.

A 2006 meta-analysis by Clifford Winston, jointly commissioned by the Brookings Institution and the American Enterprise Institute, concluded that overall, the cost of federal regulations exceeded the benefits in every area except environmental regulation.[67] A 2012 meta-analysis by Peter H. Schuck found that, of 270 retrospective policy studies, "the vast majority were either clearly negative or showed mixed results,"[68] while only a few showed positive results. Yet a 1990 meta-analysis by Sunstein pointed to bright spots amid the (alleged) policy failures, leading him to argue that technocratic regulation is a promising venture if done correctly.[69] Disagreements of this sort are reasonable for the same reason that a technocracy needs policy studies in the first place. If technocratic knowledge were self-evident, there would be no need for research about social problems and policy remedies, let alone for meta-research about them. To the extent that such research seems to be necessary, it is because the truth about the success of the policies is not self-evident.

As Sunstein writes of retrospective policy assessments,

> In many cases it is difficult to make confident statements of causation. Scientific uncertainty is pervasive in this context. Postregulation decreases in accident and death rates may, for example, be attributable to factors other than regulatory controls. It is necessary to look at (among other things) economic, industrial, and demographic trends preceding regulatory intervention. Moreover, it is extremely hard to control for possible confounding variables.[70]

Consider the large drop in industrial air pollution that took place after the creation of the Environmental Protection Agency in 1970. We might naively view this as an obvious win for environmental-protection legislation (leaving aside whatever anticipated and

---

[67] Winston 2006.
[68] Schuck 2014, 23.
[69] Sunstein 1990.
[70] Ibid., 76.

unanticipated costs there might have been), but a different interpretation is that the decline in air pollution was caused by rising energy prices, not EPA rules.[71] Interpretive conflicts of this sort are frequent in technocratic policy debate.

However, despite acknowledging many instances in which (he believes) the costs of various regulations have exceeded their benefits, Sunstein argues that regulatory technocracy can be reformed so that it does more good than harm. This would happen, he maintains, if regulators added to the usual neoclassical microeconomic toolkit lessons drawn from behavioral economics,[72] and if they devoted greater efforts to cost-benefit analysis.[73] However, each of the components of Sunstein's reformed technocracy—neoclassical microeconomics, behavioral economics, and cost-benefit analysis—is as controversial as the policies whose epistemic shortcomings he describes. Indeed, Chapter 4 will maintain that neoclassical economics, of which behavioral economics and cost-benefit analysis are offshoots, is far too epistemologically naive to be the basis of a reliable policy science.

On the other hand, if neoclassical economics and its offshoots are suspect, then so are most of the policy studies reviewed by Sunstein, Schuck, and Winston, which use the conceptual tools of neoclassical economics. So, too, are many of the counterintuitive theories presented earlier. For example, my explanation of the mechanism through which minimum wages might cause unemployment could have been lifted from a microeconomics textbook written by a mathematically primitive neoclassical economist.If we are to transcend naive technocratic realism in pursuit of an internal evaluation of technocracy, it would seem that we will need to use different concepts than the ones that produce technocratic disagreement about the consequences of technocratic policies. Instead, we will need to construct a theory of technocracy that allows us to evaluate those very concepts.

I intend this book to present such a theory. But I would not have written it if not for qualms about unintended consequences that were inspired by countless neoclassical economic critiques of various policies and policy proposals. Such critiques, like the claims of unintended consequences listed above and the many more cited by Schuck, Sunstein, and Winston, need not be treated as accurate if they are to have a salutary effect on our thinking about technocracy. They may instead be treated as inspirations to deeper reflection than naive technocratic realism allows.

It is not self-contradictory to reject neoclassical economics while having been inspired by certain applications of it, because the source of inspiration—neoclassical economists' frequent attention to unintended consequences—is orthogonal to the tools they use in reasoning about the possibility of such consequences, and the epistemological assumptions on which those tools rely. Neoclassical economists happen to be the social scientists who have pursued the possibility of unintended consequences in a technocratic context.

---

[71] MacAvoy 1987.

[72] E.g., Sunstein 2014; Thaler and Sunstein 2008.

[73] E.g., Sunstein 1998, 2000, 2002, and 2018.

Yet neoclassical economists lack a theory that would account for the possibility that negative unintended consequences are ubiquitous or even important. Neither economists nor anyone else has, so far as I can tell, ever put forth a plausible "law of unintended consequences," although the phrase is often bandied about. The neoclassical economist's propensity to look for unintended consequences is not the same thing as a theory of what might cause them (let alone a law dictating that they will happen everywhere and always). And the crude epistemology deployed, as we will see, by neoclassical economists makes it almost inevitable that they would have failed to develop such a theory. Yet while the epistemological naiveté of neoclassical economics should warn us to treat with great caution its claims about particular unintended consequences, we would be foolish to reject the economist's desire to be on the lookout for them. We can push back against neoclassical economics with both hands, as I will, even as we recognize that neoclassical economists' claims about unintended consequences illustrate the reasonableness of technocratic disagreement—especially if we theorize that such consequences stem from the difficulty of obtaining reliable technocratic knowledge, a problem that afflicts neoclassical economists along with everyone else.

Admittedly, a Marxist might argue that the idea of unintended technocratic consequences originated with bourgeois political economists, classical as well as neoclassical, who thereby mystified issues that would otherwise be clearly susceptible to popular understanding and political action. However, unintended consequences are very nearly inescapable in the study of history, from Herodotus to the present, and as Robert K. Merton pointed out in 1936, unintended consequences were a central preoccupation of such widely varying figures as Vico, Machiavelli, Pareto, Weber—and Marx himself.[74] It would be special pleading to allow that historical actors are plagued by the unintended consequences of their actions but that technocrats are somehow free of them, unless one proposed that technocrats have escaped from the ignorance that afflicts historical actors, perhaps because they have access to esoteric knowledge that other historical actors lack (which is entirely possible, but is a proposition that must be defended, not merely assumed). Whatever it is about the world that makes unintended consequences possible—the subject of the next two chapters—one would have to have a powerful reason to cordon off technocratic policymaking as comparatively simple, epistemically, and thus exempt from a problem that seems ubiquitous in other realms.

At least for the moment, then, it seems fair to conclude that it will always be possible for reasonable people to disagree about the effects of technocratic policies, inasmuch as gaps in technocratic knowledge *might* lead to policies that produce unintended consequences; and, in particular, inasmuch as these consequences might be counterintuitive, might occur in unexpected areas, and might be invisible—yet real. The reasonableness of technocratic disagreement, in turn, suggests that the naive technocratic realist's cynical

---

[74] Merton 1936, 894.

response to the fact of technocratic disagreement—namely, to repudiate it as a smoke-screen generated by malevolent political actors—is unsustainable as a general position even though, on particular occasions, it may be warranted.

1.3. NAIVE REALISM AS A METHODOLOGICAL PROBLEM

> Each generation is disposed to regard its main assumptions as self-evident even when in fact they have merely been adopted uncritically.
> —WALTER LIPPMANN, *The Good Society*

It follows that, insofar as naive technocratic realism is widespread (as Part II will suggest is the case), empirical political epistemologists should probe the historical or psychological origins of technocrats' "intuitions" about putatively self-evident technocratic truths. For if such intuitions can be faulty, they cannot originate in sheer receptivity to the manifest truth, as the naive technocratic realist would have it. For the same reason, normative political epistemologists should critically inspect the adequacy of technocrats' policy opinions.

Political epistemologists, both normative and empirical, have pursued such questions with increasing frequency in recent decades. However, their efforts have themselves been marked by a tendency toward naive technocratic realism. This threatens to make of political epistemology in general, and in particular the political epistemology of technocracy, the illicit continuation of technocratic policy debate in the guise of political theory and social science.

Consider *The Myth of the Rational Voter* (2007), a theoretical account of public opinion written by a neoclassical free-market economist, Bryan Caplan. Caplan infers that citizens' opinions about certain economic issues tend to be inadequate—indeed, irrational—because these opinions diverge from the consensus opinions of neoclassical economists about markets (that they are generally good), foreign trade (that it is generally good), economic trends (that they are generally good), and labor-saving technology (that it is generally good). By equating irrationality with the rejection of neoclassical and basically free-market policy opinions, Caplan treats those opinions as products of unbiased reflection about self-evident economic realities, not as products of free-market doctrinal teachings shared by economics graduate students' neoclassical economics professors, or by the authors of neoclassical economics textbooks for undergraduates, or by the authors of articles in neoclassical economics journals, and so on.

As a naive technocratic realist, Caplan is compelled to conclude that citizens who subscribe to opinions with which he and his colleagues disagree must be aware of, but averse to, the manifest truth. Thus, they must be letting their "emotional and ideological" predilections take precedence over the truth.[75] Schematically, he contends that (1) the

---

[75] Caplan 2007, 128.

economic truth is self-evident, a matter of "common sense."[76] However, (2) most people reject the self-evident truth, as demonstrated by survey data showing that they disagree with the opinions shared by those with doctorates in economics. Therefore (3) most people must be irrational: they must be letting "emotions or ideology" run roughshod over common sense.[77] Caplan then produces a theory of "rational irrationality" to explain their rejection of the truth, a theory that involves three more claims: (4) most people know that their political opinions are unlikely to matter, because of the very low odds that a single vote informed by these opinions will swing an electoral outcome; (5) they therefore feel free to indulge their emotions and ideology on economic issues, as this indulgence, translated into an individual vote, will be unlikely to have undesirable consequences;[78] and (6) they gain some sort of satisfaction from this indulgence—that is, from voting for counterproductive policies, meaning those opposed by neoclassical and free-market economists such as Caplan.

No evidence is offered to support assertions (2)–(6), although each is a claim about empirical realities that could be empirically investigated.[79] In place of evidence, what drives the entire argument is assertion (1), which credits noneconomists with knowing intuitively what Caplan thinks that he and his fellow economists know: the manifest economic truth. Thus, he is simultaneously a first-person and a third-person naive realist, equating both his own opinions and those of his fellow economists with knowledge of intuitively obvious economic realities—and attributing the same knowledge to those with whom he disagrees.

However, Caplan also calls this knowledge "counterintuitive."[80] This would mean that it is *not* self-evident and would not necessarily enter the minds of noneconomists even if they were rational—contradicting assertion (1) and therefore annulling the whole argument. Criticized on this score, Caplan later responded:

> I stand by my claim that basic economic truths are obvious to any adult of normal intelligence who calmly considers them. It is obvious that trade is mutually beneficial; it is obvious that trade remains mutually beneficial even if the traders come from different countries; it is obvious that protecting unproductive jobs makes society poorer; and it is obvious that, over the long run, living standards have drastically improved. [The critics write] that when "Caplan allows that economic theory is 'counterintuitive,' we believe that he has made a slip." I agree. I misspoke. Adam Smith's observation that the market gives businesses an incentive to please

[76] Ibid., 15.

[77] Ibid.

[78] Ibid., 123.

[79] Bennett and Friedman 2008 argues that none of Caplan's assertions survive confrontation with empirical evidence; it also challenges the coherence of Caplan's notion of irrationality. On point (4), see Chapter 6.

[80] Caplan 2007, 32.

consumers is yet another truism that is obvious to any person of normal intelligence who calmly considers it. Instead of "counterintuitive," I should simply have said "unpopular."[81]

Caplan's problematic is captured in the last sentence. Given that his own and his fellow economists' economic doctrines are supposed to be so obvious that they are intuitive, how can these doctrines be so widely unpopular? (This, of course, resembles the question Lippmann and Mutz find naive citizens asking themselves about the existence of their political opponents.) Caplan's answer is that noneconomists *must be* irrationally denying the self-evident, intuitively obvious truth.

However, the only empirical evidence presented in his book—evidence of disagreement between economists and noneconomists—is compatible with noneconomists' rationality if they are as naively realistic about their economic opinions as Caplan is about his. Like Caplan, they may simply assume that their views would be self-evident to any adult of normal intelligence who calmly considered them. Therefore, we would have no need to attribute their views to unchecked emotional or ideological impulses. Even if we agreed with Caplan's free-market opinions, we could be interpretively charitable toward those who do not share them by recognizing that these opinions, being counterintuitive, are unlikely to be recognized as true by naive economic realists (even assuming, counterfactually, that large numbers of ordinary citizens had been exposed to economists' ideas to begin with).

Alternatively, we could take Caplan's interpretively uncharitable route but use the evidence he presents against him. By his own account, he used to disagree with economists' opinions, prior to his professional training in economics; and by his own account, it takes him "hours of patient instruction to show [his] students the light of [the economic theory of] comparative advantage,"[82] which is the basis for his conviction that foreign trade is beneficial. This suggests that economics is indeed counterintuitive for Caplan's students, just as it once was for him. Using Caplanesque logic, the contradiction between, on the one hand, the counterintuitiveness of economics revealed by his biographical and pedagogical experience, and, on the other, his insistence on the intuitive obviousness of economics, suggests that this insistence must be driven by Caplan's own "emotion or ideology."

Conversely, if we accept Caplan's claim that neoclassical economics is intuitive, his finding of disagreement between untutored US citizens and neoclassical economists might best be explained by saying that the opinions of the former are *likelier* than those of neoclassical economists to be right, as the former opinions are likelier to be grounded in intuition than in such mediated, fallible channels of opinion formation as undergraduate and graduate instruction.

---

[81] Caplan 2008, 385.
[82] Caplan 2007, 11, 10.

Apparently, Caplan is prevented from considering these possibilities by his treatment of his own economic opinions, and those of his epistocratic peers, as self-evidently true, such that the general public, in disagreeing with these opinions, is self-evidently irrational. Thus, Caplan's attempt at political epistemology is in fact—as a product of naive technocratic realism—anti-epistemological, as it leaves no room for ignorance, misperception, or misinterpretation.

1.3.1. Naive Realism in Thinking about the Media

Caplan's book was, in part, a rejoinder to Page and Shapiro's *The Rational Public*, an analysis of twentieth-century survey research from which I drew several findings discussed in the introduction. Page and Shapiro are, like Caplan, naive technocratic realists, but they reach the conclusion that public opinion is rational. This antithesis to Caplan's conclusion can be attributed to the fact that Page and Shapiro's own positions on questions of public policy, which they treat as manifestly warranted, happen, in most cases, to be diametrically opposed to the positions that Caplan treats as manifestly warranted. Thus, the same public opinions that are self-evidently irrational to Caplan are self-evidently rational to Page and Shapiro.

Page and Shapiro advance two primary claims: (1) that in general, journalists tend to deliver "enlightening" information and interpretations to the public;[83] and (2) that members of the public tend to be rational enough to process this information into "reasonable" or "sensible" policy preferences.[84] Thus, "rationality" denotes, for Page and Shapiro, the application of logical reasoning to enlightening information and interpretations. "Reasonable" or "sensible" policy preferences tend to result from this rational process if and only if the process involves weighing "enlightening" information and interpretations rationally; without the enlightenment provided by the information and interpretations, the public would be rational but not reasonable.

Secondarily, Page and Shapiro claim (3) that, given the general public's application of logical reasoning to enlightening information and interpretations, any individual voters' errors in information processing will tend to be random, such that they cancel each other out. This claim has come to be called "the miracle of aggregation" and is often considered Page and Shapiro's main contribution.[85] Yet the authors recognize that mainstream public opinion could be misguided *regardless* of whether deviant opinions cancel each other out in the aggregate. Only a putative flow of "enlightening" information from journalists to the public justifies the assumption that the opinions left over after deviant opinions cancel each other out are themselves reasonable. In turn, the rationality of the public is demonstrated by the fact that, in response to enlightening information, its opinions are

---

[83] Page and Shapiro 1992, 356.
[84] Ibid., 385.
[85] Philip E. Converse (1970) appears to have originated the phrase.

reasonable. Thus, the reasonability of public opinion stems not from the miracle of aggregation, but from the authors' assumption that, during the five decades they analyze (ending in 1990), journalists tended to convey to the public information and interpretations that *adequately* represented the societal factors, such as social problems, to which the public's opinions then logically responded.

However, while the authors call such journalism "enlightening," the only evidence for this enlightenment is the fact that the authors find reasonable the opinions to which it seems to have led. When the public's policy preferences were agreeable to Page and Shapiro's way of thinking over the years, the authors contend that journalism *must have* had an enlightening influence on public opinion. Conversely, on the rare occasions when the public's opinions departed from what Page and Shapiro consider to have been reasonable, they conclude that the public must have been misled by journalism rather than enlightened by it.

Consider two of Page and Shapiro's specific findings. First, as we saw in the introduction, the five decades in question saw "high and generally stable public support for government action on Social Security, education, jobs, medical care, the cities, the environment, consumer safety, and the like."[86] Public opinion here is reasonable only if one finds the listed policy initiatives reasonable, but Page and Shapiro offer no reason to think we should. In declaring public opinion on these issues reasonable, not merely rational, they are relying on nothing but their own tacit agreement with the public's conclusions. A second finding is that when public opinion shifted over time, the shifts usually "represented comprehensible and generally reasonable reactions to events and circumstances and new information."[87] For example, public support for "do[ing] more to expand employment" tended to go up in response to rising unemployment rates.[88] While such shifts in public opinion are indeed rational responses to new information or interpretations (about unemployment), they are reasonable only if one assumes that government efforts to expand employment are likely to do more good than harm. Page and Shapiro count public opinion here as reasonable for no other apparent reason than that they share this assumption. Page later wrote that if it were not the case that he personally "agree[d] with the public on most issues," he could not have reached such sanguine conclusions about the reasonableness of public opinion.[89]

Unlike Caplan, Page and Shapiro do not overtly claim that any calm, intelligent adult would agree with their opinions on these particular policy questions. But they do imply that *most* calm, intelligent adults—the overwhelming majorities to which I referred in the introduction—would agree with the authors' opinions after having received enlightening information about such matters as rising unemployment rates from journalists. In

---

[86] Page and Shapiro 1992, 169.
[87] Ibid.
[88] Ibid., 122.
[89] Page 2007, 44.

turn, given the immense influence of journalism on public opinion (about which we will need to say more), the authors contend that journalists *must have* conveyed enlightening interpretations of germane information to the public, since the net result of the journalists' efforts was a body of public opinions that the authors find reasonable.

The authors are arguing in the same circle that trapped Caplan, with the difference that Caplan equated *rationality* with agreement with him and his peers and proceeded to attribute disagreement to irrationality, while Page and Shapiro equate *reasonableness* with agreement with them and proceed to attribute it to the enlightening effects of journalism. In both cases, however, what should be an a posteriori demonstration (of public irrationality or of enlightening journalism) becomes an a priori assertion, and in both cases this is due to the authors' naive technocratic realism. In both cases, this produces a potentially significant distortion of empirical realities. Subtract Caplan's naive realism about his own and his fellow economists' opinions and we are left with no reason to think that public opinion tends to be irrational. Subtract Page and Shapiro's naive realism about their own opinions and we are left with no reason to think that public opinion tends to be reasonable—and, therefore, no reason to think that the information mediated to the public by journalists tends to be enlightening rather than misleading.

The latter point deserves further attention, as Lippmann's concern about the potentially misleading stereotypes deployed by journalists led him to develop the argument I will present in the next two chapters.

Page and Shapiro provide powerful evidence for the potential impact of journalism on public opinion. They cite an *American Political Science Review* paper that they coauthored with Glenn Dempsey, which found that from 1971 to 1986, when 80 policy issues were discussed on the evening news, "a single 'probably pro' commentary" by a reporter "was associated with more than four percentage points of opinion change" in the "pro" direction. Similarly, "after a single [broadcast] story indicating that experts favor a particular policy, public support tended to rise by about three percentage points."[90]

Given such significant media effects, one might conclude that it is important to see whether the media have reliable means of distinguishing "enlightening" from misleading information and interpretations before passing them on to the public. However, Page and Shapiro present no research about journalistic practices. Instead, they put forward a stylized depiction of the circulation of ideas in a modern society in which journalists are part of a "highly decentralized" and extensive "division of labor," where information and interpretations move from the scientific community to journalists and then to citizens.[91]

Before we get to the role of science, let us consider the idea of an epistemic division of labor. Like the authors' inattention to the cognitive processes of journalists, this idea obscures some of the basic problems we can expect an actual technocracy to face.

---

[90] Page and Shapiro 1992, 344, citing Page, Shapiro, and Dempsey 1987, 31.
[91] Page and Shapiro 1992, 364.

1.3.2. The Division of Epistemic Labor and the Conundrum of the Radically Ignorant

We can begin with an observation about all divisions of labor, not just the epistemic variety. Specialization and decentralization do not automatically tell in favor of the adequacy of whatever output is produced by a division of labor. Any given division of labor may suffer from being overspecialized, underspecialized, or specialized in the wrong ways, or from being populated with incompetent specialists. Merely dividing up labor into specializations may accomplish nothing—or it may backfire.

For example, in a division of epistemic labor, such as the one posited by Page and Shapiro, the specialists may not achieve an adequate grasp of the subjects they investigate. Mere epistemic specialization does not necessarily ensure enlightenment; it may simply ensure narrowness of focus or pedantry. Nor does decentralization ensure enlightenment, as we can now see in contemplating the massive epistemic decentralization brought about by the internet—a kaleidoscope of "fake" and "real," misleading and enlightening information and interpretation. The question, then, is whether a particular division of epistemic labor can, on the whole, *reliably* distinguish information and interpretations that are misleading from those that are enlightening. Neither specialization nor decentralization tell in favor of an affirmative answer to the question, as there is no reason to think that either specialization or decentralization per se will adequately reveal the societal realities being investigated. Thus, the division of labor metaphor may obscure more than it illuminates.

In the ideal type of an *economic* division of labor, the right degree of specialization and decentralization, the competence of the personnel, and the overall adequacy of the process are supposed to be ensured by the fact that consumers will pay only for satisfactory outputs from the process. Companies whose workers under- or overspecialize, who specialize in doing the wrong things, or who do them inadequately will (it is said) tend to produce products that consumers find unsatisfactory. As a result, these companies will, in principle, lose money and ultimately get weeded out by competitors that produce more satisfactory products. Thus, consumers putatively serve as anchors to reality and, therefore, as checks against dysfunction in the division of economic labor. The functionality of the system is ensured, however, only insofar as consumers are able to distinguish adequately between satisfactory and unsatisfactory products. In a "market" for political information and interpretation, "consumers" (voters) cannot possibly play such an anchoring role, because a consumer shopping for enlightenment finds herself facing *the conundrum of the radically ignorant* (where, again, radical ignorance means ignorance of unknown unknowns).

As W. V. O. Quine and J. S. Ullian say about human populations in general, "Widespread misbeliefs can thrive" because "ignorance of relevant truths is often accompanied by ignorance of that ignorance"[92]—that is, by radical ignorance. When one is

---

[92] Quine and Ullian 1978, 59.

radically ignorant of which information is true and which interpretations are adequate, one cannot know if one is "buying" bad information or interpretations, so one will be unable to exert a selection pressure against those who purvey the bad information and interpretations. The division of epistemic labor may produce nothing but misleading information and interpretations, and nobody will be the wiser.

The conundrum of the radically ignorant stems from the fact that radically ignorant epistemic consumers—that is, those who need "enlightenment"—are, by definition, unenlightened ex ante about whether the selection of information and interpretations delivered to them by the division of epistemic labor is enlightening rather than misleading. Indeed, insofar as someone is radically ignorant and therefore in need of enlightenment (in Page and Shapiro's sense of the term), she may not know that she needs information and interpretation at all, making her unlikely to comparison shop among the purveyors of information and interpretation (as might a consumer of, say, refrigerators in the ideal type of a market division of labor). Yet even if she does comparison shop for information and interpretation—perhaps spurred by warnings that she might otherwise be the victim of "fake news"—*efficacious* comparison shopping for nonfake news is logically impossible insofar as one is radically ignorant ex ante of which information and interpretation is reliable.

This is part of the human condition, insofar as human beings are ignorant—that is, insofar as the truth is not self-evident. Before we know the truth, we cannot know which information is true or which interpretations are adequate; if we knew this, we would not be ignorant of the truth. Prior to the consumption of enlightening information and interpretations, radically ignorant voters will not be able to distinguish misleading information and interpretations from enlightening information and interpretations, because they are, by definition, ignorant of the truths about which they are seeking enlightenment. If instead they receive misleading information and interpretations, they will not have the knowledge of the totality that would allow them to recognize the inadequacy of that information and those interpretations.

As Lippmann wrote in 1922, in politics, "where all the facts are out of sight . . . a true report and a plausible error read alike, sound alike, feel alike. Except on a few subjects where our own knowledge is great, we cannot choose between true and fake accounts. So we choose between trustworthy and untrustworthy reporters."[93] This choice too, however, is subject to the constraint of the chooser's radical ignorance. Later in the same work, Lippmann makes this point in terms of the choice among rulers, but it is the same with reporters: "Even if you assume with Plato that the true pilot knows what is best for the ship, you have to recall that he is not so easy to recognize, and that this uncertainty leaves a large part of the crew unconvinced. By definition the crew does not know what

---

[93] Lippmann [1922] 1990, 143.

he knows."[94] Unless we assume that the truth is self-evident to the consumers of news, we must conclude that they will be unequipped to comparison shop for it.

Ultimately, a "market" for enlightenment cannot work in the way that ideal-typical consumer-goods markets work because in the latter, the ultimate guarantor of efficacy is supposed to be the feedback consumers get from the products they buy: the knowledge they acquire, by using the products, about whether their purchases have been unwise. There is no such feedback with most political knowledge, including the four types of technocratic knowledge. If people have been politically misinformed, how would they know it? If they were capable of knowing it on their own, they would not need the division of epistemic labor to enlighten them.

1.3.3. The Problem of Epistocratic Identification

However, when we turn to the supply side of Page and Shapiro's stylized division of labor, we might wonder if "science" could allow information consumers to avoid the conundrum of the radically ignorant, as the authors suggest. If the only information they receive is scientific information, and therefore is "enlightened" by definition, they will not need to distinguish between the truth and "fake news," because all the news will be true.

This is a logical possibility but not a realistic one, at least if we are discussing technocratic issues. For with technocratic issues we will have to confront the fact of *epistocratic* disagreement.

If experts disagree, at least some of them must be wrong. This is to say that, on the question at issue, at least some of them must be false experts. In turn, journalists cannot reliably screen out false expertise unless they have a kind of meta-expertise that allows them to be reliable adjudicators of disagreements among experts. This, too, is unlikely, as it would entail that journalists are more expert than the experts. In reality, journalists are usually unqualified to judge the adequacy of the information and interpretations they relay to voters from experts who disagree among themselves. Moreover, even if some journalists were meta-experts, radically ignorant consumers would be unable to tell which journalists these are. The problem of choosing among expert opinions will reproduce itself when one chooses which journalists to listen to, as Lippmann suggested.

The depth of this problem can be gauged by considering that even genuine experts will experience what I will call the problem of epistocratic identification.[95] Suppose that somewhere within the division of epistemic labor of a mixed technocracy such as ours, in which there are both democratic and epistocratic elements, the Ideal Epistocrat (IE) comes up with an adequate interpretation of the cause of a significant social problem and devises a policy solution that objectively passes the cost-benefit test. How can the

---

[94] Ibid., 249.
[95] See Friedman 2017c.

other actors in the system—voters, journalists, editorialists, amateur opinion-mongers, and epistocrats other than the IE—identify who the IE is? (Indeed, how can the IE know this?) The other policy analysts will have their own analyses; the other actors in the system, not being policy analysts, will have to choose the analysis that seems most plausible to them. But unless the truth is self-evident—in which case they would not need to identify an IE to begin with—their judgments of plausibility may be unreliable if they are not themselves IEs. They might try to evaluate the putative IEs by using heuristics such as their educational pedigrees, but these clearly can be misleading.[96] So long as the truth is not self-evident, everyone in the system may be radically ignorant of the identity of the IE, such that the system as a whole may be said to experience the conundrum of the radically ignorant. "The system" will not "know" which information and interpretations to mediate to consumers—the information and interpretations that originate with the IE—as the system will be unable to distinguish the IE's views from the views of putative IEs whose information or interpretations are in fact misleading.

Page and Shapiro's discussion suggests three possible paths of escape from this quandary, but all three are variants of naive technocratic realism.

First, the authors appeal to the "daily experience" of the citizen as a check against the possibility that journalists and others in the division of intellectual labor will ply them with "outrageous nonsense."[97] If we were discussing the daily experience of product consumers with the products' performance, this might be plausible. But as we saw in Section 1.2, personal experience is an invalid basis for judging information about, and interpretations of, social problems in a modern society—except, in some cases, information about the severity of a social problem—as personal experience may be unrepresentative of the experiences of the millions of other members of the society. Moreover, it must surely be the case that, in a society that is opaque enough to require scientists to analyze its problems and prescribe cures, the intuitive insights one derives from personal experience cannot be presumed adequate: science is an effort to go beyond uninterrogated experience and is, as such, almost necessarily counterintuitive.

The second escape route would be a full embrace of "science," with no admixture of personal experience, as the arbiter of divergent interpretations. If policy debate can be considered scientific, then whatever it is about science that warrants the reliability of a scientific community's consensus in a given case—for example, what Page and Shapiro call an "elaborate process of research and discussion in which ideas are tested and filtered"[98]—may (according to some philosophers of science) be relied upon to ensure that consensual scientific judgments, if they were faithfully transmitted to the people by journalists, would justify confidence in the policy decisions that the people then reach. In this scenario, the proof that journalists are enlightening public opinion rather than

---

[96] For a defense of heuristics for expertise, see Anderson 2006; for a critique, Friedman 2017c, 298–302.

[97] Page and Shapiro 1992, 170, 381.

[98] Ibid., 364.

misleading it would not be whether Page and Shapiro (or other political epistemologists) find the public's policy opinions reasonable or sensible; it would be whether these opinions track the opinions of policy scientists. This is not something that Page and Shapiro attempt to ascertain, but it is the one empirical question that Caplan investigated, and he found that on the questions he chose to look into, public opinion did not track the opinions of policy "scientists": neoclassical economists. Page and Shapiro fail, moreover—like Caplan—to consider whether the policy "sciences" to which they allude truly deserve that appellation.

Third, Page and Shapiro perform an impressionistic calculation of the frequency of cases in which the public was misled during the decades covered by their research versus cases in which it was enlightened.[99] This is their attempt to ensure that in reality, "all works well" in the division of epistemic labor that they lay out as an ideal type.[100] They conclude that, on the whole, the public was usually enlightened. But this conclusion is, again, based on nothing but the authors' agreement with the public in most cases. It does not occur to the authors that this agreement may result from the fact that the public and the authors themselves might have gotten their information and interpretations from the same journalistic sources, which may have been misleading. After all, the authors are Americans who lived through most of the period they analyzed. The authors, then, are members of the very public whose opinions they are analyzing, and there is no reason to think that these two members of the public, Page and Shapiro, were exempt from the dramatic effects of journalism on public opinion that they illustrate in their work with Dempsey.

1.3.4. The Problem of the Technocrat-Epistemologist

The naive realism plaguing both *The Myth of the Rational Voter* and *The Rational Public* is not only objectionable in itself; it illustrates a problem that may have devastating effects on the tenability of political epistemology. At the risk of proliferating labels, let us call this the problem of the technocrat-epistemologist.

As epistemologists of public opinion, the authors of these books are asking whether citizen-technocrats' political beliefs represent real knowledge, not mere opinion. But they answer the question by tacitly equating it with the question of whether the public's beliefs match their own (the authors') beliefs. Their first-person naive technocratic realism thus leads them to beg the question they are trying to answer, since they do not confront the possibility that their own technocratic beliefs might express unreliable opinions, not real knowledge.

---

[99] Ibid., ch. 9.
[100] Ibid., 364–365.

This problem has beset not only economists, such as Caplan, and empirically oriented political scientists, such as Page and Shapiro, but a growing number of theorists who have, like Caplan, used their disagreement with various widely held policy opinions as evidence that the citizens holding these opinions are misinformed, the victims of lies, or irrational—failing to wonder if instead the theorists themselves are the ones who are misinformed.[101] In treating their own policy opinions as expressing the manifest truth, these scholars overlook the possibility that policy issues are too complex for them (or for the trained, credentialed experts from whom they sometimes derive their opinions) to master reliably. At the same time, more optimistic normative political epistemologists have used their agreement with public opinion on various issues as grounds for confidence in public opinion, neglecting to ask whether both they and the public might be wrong.[102] Then there are normative political epistemologists who deliver a mixed verdict on public opinion, depending on whether the public does or does not agree with the political epistemologists about a given topic.[103] In all of these cases, the analysts exempt their own opinions from critical scrutiny, such that their political epistemologies beg the epistemological question.

One might wonder, however, if the problem of the technocrat-epistemologist is really a problem. If one is trying to test the reliability of other citizen-technocrats' opinions, what better indicator can one use than those opinions' coincidence with one's own opinions or the opinions of experts one trusts, that is, their coincidence with what one takes to be *true*? What other indicator could there be? And even if some other gauge of epistemic reliability were available, if its readouts contradicted what one takes to be true, how could one trust these readouts without contradicting one's belief in the truth of what one takes to be true?

I think the appropriate answer to such questions, and to the problem of the technocrat-epistemologist, is to distinguish between first- and second-order technocratic opinions. The normative political epistemologist who affirms the reliability of the knowledge possessed by a given group of technocrats, such as citizen-technocrats, social scientists, or

---

[101] E.g., Brennan and Lomasky 1993; Pincione and Tesòn 2006; Oreskes and Conway 2008. Brennan 2014; Achen and Bartels 2016; and Brennan 2016. The last of these works declares, for example: "While I no doubt suffer from some degree of confirmation and self-serving bias, perhaps I justifiably believe that I—a named professor of strategy, economics, ethics, and public policy at an elite research university, with a PhD from the top-ranked political philosophy program in the English-speaking world, and a strong record of peer-reviewed publications in top journals and academic presses—have superior political judgment on a great many political matters compared to many of my fellow citizens, including to many large groups of them. If I *didn't* believe that about myself, I'd feel like a fraud every time I teach a political economy course" (Brennan 2016, 121). The begged question is whether the author perhaps *should* feel like a fraud. The fact that he fails to ask himself this question suggests that what comes across as a festival of intellectual complacency is better understood as a serious bout of radical ignorance: ignorance of the author's own fallibility, despite his abstract acknowledgement of the possibility of his "bias."

[102] E.g., Dryzek 2006.

[103] E.g., Hochschild 2013; Hochschild and Einstein 2015a; Hochschild and Einstein 2015b.

neoclassical economists, on the basis of the group's agreement with her first-order technocratic opinions—for example, her opinions about the costs and benefits of government efforts to boost employment—begs the epistemological question by assuming that the first-order technocratic opinions of at least one citizen-technocrat, herself, *are* epistemically reliable. In contrast, consider a normative political epistemologist who, for example, adduces second-order considerations about the reliability or unreliability of the *types of information* available to various political actors (such as the information produced by personal experience, journalism, neoclassical economic assumptions, statistical analysis, big data, or field experiments). Such a political epistemologist can reach inferential conclusions about the general reliability or unreliability of various types of political actors' technocratic judgments without invoking her first-order agreement or disagreement with any of them. She therefore frees her conclusions about the adequacy of technocratic knowledge from the question-begging assumption that her own technocratic knowledge is adequate. Likewise with empirical political epistemologists: if Page and Shapiro had conducted an investigation of how journalists or social scientists actually go about their business, they might have come up with noncircular second-order reasons for trusting or distrusting the reliability of journalistic or social-scientific output. Caplan, too, might have studied the processes by which economic "truth" is "discovered" by economists and propagated in doctoral programs in economics. Whatever conclusions such a study reached, they would not have inherently begged the epistemic question.

Political epistemologists are like sojourners in a desert who see what looks like a lake on the horizon. Assume that they disagree with each other about whether it is a lake or a mirage. The fact of their disagreement entails that it would beg the question for any of them to insist that since it is *obviously* a mirage, those who think it is a lake must be unenlightened, such that a division of epistemic labor that reaches the conclusion that it is a mirage is ipso facto a system that produces enlightenment. But it would not beg the question for an advocate of the mirage hypothesis to point to optical considerations that suggest that those who think it is a lake are likely mistaken.

One indicator of the value of relying only on second-order considerations is the fact that a political epistemologist who did so might thereby find her first-order opinions altered. Landemore, for example, opens *Democratic Reason: Politics, Collective Intelligence, and the Rule of the Many* (2013) by recalling her outrage at her French conationals for rejecting the EU constitution in 2005. But then she rethought her position because a second-order epistemological consideration, the Condorcet Jury Theorem, led her to question whether so many of her fellow citizens were likely to be wrong.[104] At least arguably, this is what any political theory should help us to do: distance ourselves from our relatively unreflective first-order political views so we can judge their adequacy from a wider perspective.

---

[104] Landemore 2013, xv.

Robert Shapiro, one of the authors of *The Rational Public*, provides another example. He eventually found a second-order path to skepticism about the accuracy of the public's political ideas when he noticed that various citizens' opinions about important facts often contradict each other. He inferred from such disagreements that at least some of these citizens must not be getting the adequate, accurate flow of enlightening information that he and Page had previously assumed is the norm.[105] The obvious next step for an empirical political epistemologist would be to examine the sources of the information that might lead citizens to disagree with one another about important facts.

As for normative political epistemology, consider the contrast between, on the one hand, Page and Shapiro's suggestion that "scientists" originate the ideas mooted in policy debate, which assumes that the social "sciences" produce reliable conclusions; and, on the other hand, a defense of social science based on second-order considerations. Jason Brennan proposes such a defense. First he analogizes social science to natural science.[106] Then he invokes the recent philosophical tradition of social epistemology in support of the idea that the consensus views of social scientists should be treated with deference, as social epistemologists sometimes argue that the consensus views of natural scientists should be treated.[107] Just as we should defer to natural scientists' consensus views, Brennan maintains, we should defer to those of social scientists, especially neoclassical economists.[108] The advantage of this procedure is that Brennan's version of social epistemology can be disputed at the second order, without circularity and without begging the question. For example, it is by no means clear that scientific consensus corresponds to scientific truth.[109] Every natural-science consensus is built on the ruins of a past scientific consensus; it is reasonable to infer that today's consensus in a given science may very well be superseded at a later date, calling into question the notion that it should receive our deference.[110] Similarly, Brennan's analogy between natural science and social science fails to answer well-rehearsed arguments against this very analogy.[111] And his singling out of neoclassical economics as an exemplary social science flies in the face of the sustained and nearly unanimous arguments to the contrary that have been made by philosophers who have devoted attention to the matter.[112] (*The consensus* among these experts is that neoclassical economics is, in fact, a uniquely unscientific social "science.") But these

---

[105] Shapiro and Bloch-Elkon 2008, 115.

[106] Brennan 2011, 104–105.

[107] Ibid., 104.

[108] Brennan 2014, 50, and Brennan 2016, 191 and *passim*.

[109] Solomon 2001 argues for the irrelevance of scientific consensus to both veridicality and predictive success.

[110] See Laudan 1981.

[111] For example, arguments made by Max Weber ([1904] 1949), R. G. Collingwood ([1946] 1993), Michael Scriven ([1956] 1994), Charles Taylor ([1971] 1985), Brian Fay ([1983] 1994), and Clifford Geertz ([1983] 1994). In Chapter 3, I dispute some aspects of Taylor's and Geertz's approach, but this does not imply that one should simply ignore what they say, as Brennan does.

[112] Some of the most important critical examinations of the scientific status of neoclassical economics are Mirowski 1991, Hausman 1992, Rosenberg 1992, Lawson 1997, Hodgson 2001, and Reiss 2008. See Chapter 4.

deficiencies in Brennan's argument reveal its methodological strength: since it relies on second-order claims, it can be challenged by the same type of claim, or by third-order claims—without the need to invoke anyone's question-begging first-order agreement or disagreement with this or that economics or social-scientific claim.

By bracketing their first-order political opinions, political epistemologists would not achieve objectivity or a view from nowhere. The goal, however, would not be to eradicate personal bias; the goal would be to make a genuine political epistemology possible. Political epistemologists are, as such, assessing the sources and reliability of the knowledge that is likely to be possessed by political actors. It is inconsistent with this role for them to base their assessment on their own political knowledge, or that of others whose first-order opinions they happen to trust, without adducing second-order reasons to view this knowledge (or, rather, putative knowledge) as reliable. Once second-order reasons are adduced, however, the theorists' first-order views become irrelevant.

I.4. A CRITERION OF TECHNOCRATIC LEGITIMACY AND THE THEODICY OF TECHNOCRACY

> One of the great insights of the science of society—found already in Vico and Mandeville and elaborated magisterially during the Scottish Enlightenment—is the observation that, because of imperfect foresight, human actions are apt to have unintended consequences of considerable scope. Reconnaissance and systematic description of such unintended consequences have ever since been a major assignment, if not the raison d'être, of social science.
>
> —ALBERT O. HIRSCHMAN, *The Rhetoric of Reaction*

The rest of the book will be a second-order evaluation of the reliability of technocratic knowledge. Before we begin, we should establish a preliminary criterion of technocratic legitimacy to serve as a background norm.

My account of the four types of technocratic knowledge may have seemed to imply that such a criterion should be unrealistically demanding. Complete possession of the various types of knowledge would *guarantee* against technocratic error,[113] but as a human enterprise, technocracy should not be held to standards of perfection. It fulfills its negative-utilitarian aim so long as it alleviates more discomfort than it causes. Thus, I suggest that as a working assumption, we deem a technocratic regime internally legitimate if it tends to do more good, overall, than the harm it creates in the form of costs, including unintended ones. According to this criterion, technocratic decision-makers need to know, more often than not, how to establish the existence of social problems, how to roughly prioritize them according to their significance, how to discern their causes, and

---

[113] That is, except where unpredictable exogenous factors, such as earthquakes and unusual weather, interfere with otherwise-sound solutions to social and economic problems.

how to solve them well enough to do more good than the costs these solutions generate. This standard of adequacy cuts technocrats a great deal of epistemic slack without licensing too many policy backfires, invisible costs, and misguided missiles. We can, therefore, keep it in the back of our minds as we consider the epistemic problems technocrats are likely to encounter.

However, in Chapter 7, when it comes time to make a judgment on whether, all things considered, technocracy is legitimate on internal grounds, I will introduce a final criterion of technocratic legitimacy that allows us to base our conclusions on a comparison of its likely consequences, intended and unintended, with those of an alternative system.

1.4.1. Unintended Consequences, Good and Bad

The intervening chapters will concern the likelihood of technocratic malfunctions that produce unintended consequences. But a defender of technocracy might concede in advance that technocratic actions are likely to cause unintended consequences, while pointing out that unintended consequences can be beneficial rather than adverse. If so, then perhaps we should take technocratic policy actions even if we are completely innocent of the four types of knowledge: despite our ignorance, we might end up doing more good than harm.

Albert O. Hirschman makes essentially this argument in *The Rhetoric of Reaction*, a polemic against all internal and external objections to technocracy (and other types of social reform).[114] In this work, the plaudits he assigns to "social science" for seeking out and analyzing unintended consequences, quoted in the epigraph on the previous page, are rendered ironic by his two most salient substantive claims: that while "purposive social action" (1) only "occasionally" has adverse unanticipated consequences, (2) "it is obvious that there are many unintended consequences or side effects of human actions that are *welcome* rather than the opposite."[115]

Hirschman's first claim is a generalization of naive technocratic realism. It tacitly appeals to the reader's agreement that if we tally up our first-order assessments of technocratic wins and losses, technocracy comes out ahead, begging the epistemological question by assuming the reliability of these tallies. However, his second claim can be read in a second-order manner, as arguing from, say, personal experience—everyone has taken actions that turn out better than expected—to the legitimacy of technocracy.

---

[114] Hirschman 1991.

[115] Ibid., 38–39. Strictly speaking, in this passage Hirschman is trying to rebut only claims that policies are "perverse" in accomplishing the opposite of their intention: that is, that they backfire. However, he later classifies the "perversity thesis" as a subset of a larger objection to technocratic reforms: that their costs may outweigh their benefits (ibid., 136). If the costs outweigh the benefits, it might be due not only to policy backfires but to misguided policy missiles, invisible costs, or misallocated resources caused by an error in judgment about the existence or severity of a problem.

However, such an argument would not get Hirschman to where he wants to go. To counteract worries about the adverse unintended consequences of technocracy, he would have had to contend that the unanticipated consequences of technocrats' actions will *tend* to be beneficial, not merely that they *may* be beneficial. Thus, he would have had to argue not that "there are many unintended consequences or side effects . . . that are welcome," but that, even though policymakers may be ignorant of the side effects of their actions, something or other ensures that these effects will be more welcome than unwelcome overall. This claim would not be naively realistic, as it would gesture toward a second-order factor or factors that might explain the on-balance beneficial valence of unintended consequences. However, since Hirschman does not specify what this factor or factors might be, it is hard to imagine how the claim could be supported, save through a quasi-religious providentialism.

In *On Voluntary Servitude*, Michael Rosen argues that a providentialist faith in the positive unintended consequences of human action connects Smith's invisible hand to Hegel's cunning of reason.[116] Rosen's argument prompts the thought that in responding to such a claim, it would be appropriate to deploy a secularized version of the argument from evil against the existence of the providentialist Christian God—omnipotent, omniscient, and benevolent. If God is omniscient and omnipotent, then he must not be benevolent, or he would have constructed the world in a way that avoided the evils we so often witness. Similarly, if modern society were such a benevolent environment that the unknown consequences of human actions, including technocratic actions, tend to be good ones, it would be difficult to explain how the social problems we are trying to solve could have come into existence; or why so many of them persist; or why more of them keep appearing.[117]

A defender of technocracy might reply by asserting that while there is a benevolent tendency that makes most unintended consequences positive, this tendency is not completely dominant, and that where it fails, social problems crop up. However, we would still lack a second-order explanation for such a tendency (and for the exceptions to it). All we would have is faith that it exists.

A less providentialist approach would be to claim that there are even odds that unintended policy consequences will be beneficial/positive or that they will be harmful/negative. While such a claim would be difficult to refute, it is also arbitrary and thus difficult to defend. On what grounds might we conclude that unintended consequences have precisely a .5 probability of being positive?

A more persuasive possibility is that while the tendency of unintended consequences might either be more harmful than beneficial or more beneficial than harmful, we do not know which is the case. It is difficult to say that this thesis is irrefutable, but if it can be refuted, I do not know how. If we eschew a religious faith in either the beneficence or the

---

[116] Rosen 1996, chs. 4–6.

[117] If one denies that social problems exist, one would deny the reason for technocracy.

maleficence of the social universe, I can see no way around the conclusion that we must, in fact, be ignorant of the valence of whatever unintended consequences technocracy might produce. The question, then, is whether our ignorance of the valence is more damaging to epistemological criticisms of technocracy or to defenses of it.

In favor of the former possibility is, arguably, the preliminary criterion of technocratic legitimacy itself. If the critic cannot hope to establish that the unintended consequences of technocracy are likely to be harmful, the case would seem to be closed: technocracy is legitimate, because we have no overall reason to think that its costs will outweigh its benefits.

However, that line of reasoning assumes that the burden of argument rests with the critic of technocracy, who must therefore overcome our ignorance of the valence by showing that it is in fact negative rather than positive. If, instead, the burden of argument rests with the defender of technocracy, technocratic illegitimacy follows from our ignorance of the valence— if we can establish not only that unintended consequences *may* occur, as I argued in Section 1.2, but that they are likely to occur, as I will contend in the rest of Part I.

With whom, then, does the burden of argument rest?

If we follow the lead of technocrats in the real world, the burden of argument rests with the proponent of technocracy. In actual policy debate, the proponents of a given policy have the burden of showing that its benefits will outweigh its costs (a claim that, once made, critics have the burden of rebutting). Otherwise, proponents would not argue for a policy by adducing its putative benefits, entailing the claim that they know what these benefits are. Instead, they would argue for it on the grounds that it was selected through a randomized method of some kind. For example, they could put every conceivable policy into a hat and draw from it, blindfolded.[118] It is always possible, after all, that since we do not know the overall valence of unintended consequences, such a procedure might produce policies that do more good than harm.

Randomized policy selection might be justified if one had a providentialist faith in the benevolence of the social environment that technocracy attempts to shape. Randomized policy selection is thus the logical terminus of Hirschman's second claim. But whatever one might think of it, randomized policy selection is not technocracy. The legitimacy of the governments under which almost everyone now lives is grounded not in the right of the people or an elite to gamble on doing anything it randomly chooses to do, but the right of the people or an elite to do what it has reason to think will serve the people's interests. Thus, technocratic politics implicitly demands that technocrats rationally establish that particular policies will indeed serve people's interests. This demand gives rise to the first-order knowledge claims that would be made in ideal policy debate, along with

---

[118] Of course, this would not be practicable, as there would be no criteria for paring down the infinite universe of possible actions in such a way as to yield a set of discrete "policies" to put into the hat. To avoid the New Mexican lawyers problem, policy selection in actual technocracies is limited by tacit assumptions or explicit claims about the knowable or known costs and benefits of the discrete policies debated, just as the limits of field experiments are set by the tacit or explicit judgment that the treatment mechanism could (plausibly) produce desirable results.

those that are actually made in its real-world simulacra. It also gives rise, more generally, to the inherently epistemic nature of "technocracy," as reflected in the common use of that term to denote government by an *epistemic* elite—an elite with technical *knowledge*. If randomized policy selection were adopted, decision-makers would not need to know what the results of the various policies would be, so a technocratic elite would have no conceivable function. In a technocracy, though, the decision-makers do need to know.

It appears, then, that we must proceed *as if* the overall tendency of unintended consequences—if there are any—will be negative. The opposite procedure would fly in the rationalist face of technocracy, would for it would license the adoption of policies that—like policies pulled from a hat—are justified not by knowledge, but by hope. To be sure, it would be foolish to be deterred from introducing a given policy by the mere fact that human fallibility might cause any human action to backfire. But if we have reason to think that we cannot accurately know the results of a certain action (such as a specific technocratic action), then our knowledge of the beneficial outcome of taking that type of action cannot serve as the rationale for it, as technocracy demands, since we lack such knowledge. Likewise, if the defender of technocracy concedes that it is likely to produce unintended consequences but allows, too, that she does not know what they are likely to be, then her putative knowledge of the beneficial results of technocracy (the prevention, alleviation, and solution of social problems) cannot serve as the rationale for it, for she lacks knowledge of what lies on the cost side of the ledger.

My aim in the rest of Part I will be to suggest that there are specific reasons to think that we are unlikely to know the consequences of technocratic actions, which involve manipulating the behavior of masses of anonymous others with legal carrots and sticks (as opposed, say, to manipulating the behavior of iron filings with magnets). If my argument goes through, those advocating technocratic manipulation are, in effect, advocating that we pick the specific shape that manipulation takes, in a given instance, out of a hat. In short, we can proceed as if the valence of technocratic consequences tends to be negative, even though I cannot demonstrate that it is. If we proceeded otherwise— that is, if a defender of technocracy could legitimately object to my argument because I have not demonstrated a negative valence, but without herself demonstrating a positive valence—she would fail to meet the burden of showing that technocracy will do more good than harm, for she would tacitly acknowledge that she does not know *what* it is likely to do. Accordingly, in Chapters 2 and 3, my task will be to show that unintended policy consequences, valence unspecified, are indeed probable.

However, a caveat is in order. Just as I cannot pretend to be able to show that the valence of unintended policy consequences is likely to be negative, I will not be able to show, at least not definitively, that their collective *magnitude* is likely to be so large that it outweighs the possible benefits of technocracy. Part II will get us close to that point, however, by establishing the unlikelihood that technocrats will be able to come up with strategies to tame the unintended consequences to which Chapters 2 and 3 point. Part III may then resolve the remaining second-order uncertainty.

There are few big issues in public life where cause and effect are obvious at once. They are not obvious to scholars who have devoted years, let us say, to studying business cycles, or price and wage movements, or the migration and assimilation of peoples, or the diplomatic purpose of foreign powers. Yet somehow we are all supposed to have opinions on these matters.

—WALTER LIPPMANN, *Public Opinion*

Observations of consequences are at least as subject to error and illusion as is perception of natural objects. Judgments about what to undertake so as to regulate them, and how to do it, are as fallible as other plans. Mistakes pile up and consolidate themselves into laws and methods of administration which are more harmful than the consequences which they were originally intended to control.

—JOHN DEWEY, *The Public and Its Problems*

2

Lippmann and Dewey

THE UNJOINED DEBATE

WHEN THE TECHNOCRATIC project was still young, one of its most ardent supporters stumbled on a problem: modern society is difficult for human beings to understand. In recognizing this problem, Walter Lippmann opened a new door that political theorists have not yet passed through. The difficulty he spotted was not getting people to overcome self-interest and favor the public good, or getting people who hold different conceptions of the public good to tolerate, respect, or listen to each other. Instead he worried about whether, in a complex society, well-meaning people who favor the public good, who agree on roughly what it would entail, and who are willing to listen to each other's arguments about how to achieve it, can determine which of these arguments are correct.

In principle, it was fortunate that John Dewey had been born 30 years before Lippmann, in 1859. By the 1920s, when the younger man published his epistemological worries in *Public Opinion* and *The Phantom Public*, Dewey had established himself as perhaps the leading proponent of democratic technocracy. This, as well as his eminence as a philosopher and public intellectual, made his one of the most prominent voices in

Power Without Knowledge. Jeffrey Friedman, Oxford University Press (2019). © Oxford University Press.
DOI: 10.1093/oso/9780190877170.001.0001

the Progressive movement—to which Lippmann's epistemological doubts posed a potentially fatal threat. Dewey was ideally situated to respond to this threat.

Progressives had little use for epistemological qualms, and in this respect Dewey was typical. His philosophical career had amounted to a sustained campaign against "the industry of epistemology."[1] However, he was far more sophisticated in his opposition to epistemology than other Progressives were. In 1912, Theodore Roosevelt, accepting the presidential nomination of the Progressive Party, announced that "we stand at Armageddon, and we battle for the Lord." Whether they took his words literally or not, most Progressives seem to have been just as certain as TR that they knew how to mend industrial society, and that only blackguards could oppose the social reforms they advocated. The Progressives, in short, tended toward naive technocratic realism. While Dewey shared with many Progressives an anti-epistemological cast of mind, his pragmatism was anything but simplistic.[2] Indeed, as we will see in the next chapter, he might have forcefully responded to Lippmann's epistemological doubts by simply reiterating his own quite sophisticated philosophy of science. Regrettably, that did not happen. This chapter tells the story of what did happen.

The now-famous Lippmann-Dewey debate began in 1922, with the publication of Lippmann's *Public Opinion*. This book coupled an epistemological critique of democratic technocracy with the hope that "information bureaus," staffed by statisticians, could provide reliable technocratic knowledge to elite decision-makers. Round 1 of the debate, as it were, concluded when, in the same year, Dewey reviewed *Public Opinion* in *The New Republic*. In 1925, Lippmann began round 2 when he published *The Phantom Public*, to which Dewey responded in *The New Republic* once again. However, Lippmann's new book did not acknowledge Dewey's review of his first book, so the first two rounds of the debate were self-contained. And when the debate entered its third and final round with the appearance of Dewey's own book, *The Public and Its Problems* (1927), which more elaborately responded to some aspects of Lippmann's argument, Lippmann again failed to reply. Thus, the "debate" was entirely one-sided.[3]

More important than Lippmann's failure to respond to Dewey's replies to his work is the question of whether these replies warranted a response. Dewey's performance in the debate has troubled many sympathetic scholars as intellectually complacent or, at best, vague.[4] The view I will present below is similar but has several moving parts:

---

[1] Dewey [1917] 2011, 122.

[2] As we will see, however, his application of pragmatism *to politics* did rest on naive technocratic realism.

[3] Schudson 2008 traces the recent notion that there was a "debate" at all to scholars intent on branding Lippmann "an enemy of democracy."

[4] E.g., Festenstein 1997, 98; Kloppenberg 1986, 394; MacGilvray 1999, 2010; Ryan 1995, 218; and Westbrook 1991, ch. 9. For more positive views of Dewey's performance, see Ralston 2005; Rogers 2008, ch. 5; and Bohman 2010.

1. By the time he published *The Public and Its Problems*, Dewey had come to agree, in principle, with Lippmann's chief premise, that modern society is epistemically complex. However, Dewey did not recognize that this complexity entailed the need to *interpret* society, let alone that the interpretations might be unreliable.

2. In his mind, Dewey's broad agreement with Lippmann seems to have left one important question in dispute: whether it is necessary, as Lippmann suggested, to respond to epistemic complexity by cutting the public out of the policymaking loop, leaving decisions about means to epistocrats. In the first two rounds of the debate, Dewey did not allow that esoteric social-scientific knowledge might be necessary to penetrate the complexities of modern society, as Lippmann contended in *Public Opinion*. Instead of epistocracy, then, Dewey called for a new brand of journalism that would inform the public about complex social problems. However, his case for the adequacy of such journalism failed to respond in any way to Lippmann's interpretive concerns. In the third round of the debate, Dewey conceded the need for a new social science, but his ideas about it were unresponsive to Lippmann's reasons for pessimism about the likelihood of coming up with reliable interpretations of a modern, mass society. Thus, Dewey's acknowledgment of epistemic complexity (when it comes to technocracy) remained skin deep.

3. One upshot of this superficiality was Dewey's faith that technocracy could be democratic. The promise of a new type of journalism was that it would enlighten the public about the complex causes of social problems; yet if, as Dewey proposed in *The Public and Its Problems*, journalists would accomplish this by conveying to the public the findings of social scientists, it becomes difficult to avoid the conclusion that the social scientists would actually be in charge. Moreover, Dewey's defense of the reliability of social-scientific knowledge on the grounds that it would be experimental was underargued, at best.

4. Lippmann, too, was less than consistent in recognizing the implications of epistemic complexity. In his case, the inconsistency emerged in *Public Opinion*'s untenable call for a statistical social science that would produce reliable technocratic knowledge.

5. After the debate concluded, Dewey seems to have recognized how naive his previous ideas about social science had been. Thus, in 1931, he defended the central planning of an entire society on the Soviet model, in the interest of being able to gain epistemic clarity about the results of technocratic experimentation—a need that he had not recognized during the debate. In 1939, however, he retreated from this position to an endorsement of a humbler epistocracy of civil servants operating, it would seem, in a capitalist framework.

6. A productive Lippmann-Dewey debate might have pitted Lippmann's latently antitechnocratic political epistemology against Dewey's evolutionary philosophy of science. Chapter 3 reconstructs this counterfactual debate, juxtaposing

Dewey's Darwinian defense of the reliability of scientific knowledge against the ontology of complexity implied by Lippmann's political epistemology.

Unfortunately, the actual debate accomplished little. Why, then, devote a chapter to examining it? I have two reasons.

First, nearly a century on, Lippmann's contributions to the debate and Dewey's responses still represent the state of the art in the epistemology of technocracy. Nobody since Lippmann has so deftly scrutinized the ability of political actors to understand modern society, and thus modern social problems. My analysis of technocracy, presented in the next chapter, will largely be a systematization of observations he made in the 1920s, which I will lay out more carefully than has been done before. And Dewey's responses to Lippmann—particularly his endorsement of journalistically mediated public discussion, and his "pinching shoe" analogy—are still routinely invoked by political theorists.

Second, the debate exposes an important aspect of our polity that has been insufficiently recognized by political theorists and political scientists alike: the gravitational pull exercised on democratic technocracy by epistocracy. As soon as we acknowledge the epistemic complexity of modern society, we will have to doubt citizen-technocrats' ability to master the knowledge necessary to make technocracy work well. For if intuition is inadequate to deciphering the truth—which is the case, by definition, if the reality in question is epistemically complex—then it is unclear how people relying on their intuitions alone, or even their intuitions enlightened by journalism, could reach reliably accurate conclusions about public-policy issues. Thus, if naive technocratic realism is unwarranted, a natural response—among those raised in a scientistic culture—will be to assume that there must be social scientists who, unlike the rest of us, have access to reliable technocratic knowledge. In turn, it would be logical to conclude, on technocratic grounds, that if policy-relevant truths about modern social problems, such as the truths embodied in the four types of technocratic knowledge, are not self-evident, then the public will, at best, have to be enlightened by scientific experts who somehow manage to cut through the epistemic complexity. In that case, however, any public participation in the selection of policies themselves (as opposed to the ends they are to serve) can only be harmful, as it would risk the public's misunderstanding of what the social scientists are trying to tell them. Thus, epistocracy proves itself to be the regulative ideal of technocracy—so long as we assume, as both Dewey and Lippmann did at various points in the debate, that some identifiable group of experts can reliably cut through the complexity.

That will be one of the assumptions challenged in both this chapter and the next.

2.1. LIPPMANN AND PROGRESSIVE EPISTEMOLOGY

Public opinion deals with indirect, unseen, and puzzling facts, and there is nothing obvious about them.

—WALTER LIPPMANN, *Public Opinion*

We cannot rely upon intuition, conscience, or the accidents of casual opinion if we are to deal with the world beyond our reach.

—WALTER LIPPMANN, *Public Opinion*

Before matriculating at Harvard in 1906, Lippmann had received a spectacular education in literature and art, but had shown no sign of interest in politics.[5] Soon after his arrival in Cambridge, however, he began reading Marx, the Webbs, Edward Bellamy, William Morris, George Bernard Shaw, and H. G. Wells.[6] During his sophomore year, he wrote to a woman he was courting that "the curse of great fortunes is the degradation of the poor," and that "social position is built upon the slum."[7] His ideal, he told her, was "to build a citadel of human joy upon the slum of misery" and to "give the words 'the brotherhood of man' a meaning."[8] In the spring of that year he organized a Socialist Club that took Harvard by storm.[9] His classmate John Reed, later the semiofficial chronicler of the Russian Revolution, hailed Lippmann as the "all-unchallenged Chief" of the Harvard left.[10]

However, the end of Lippmann's college years brought seeds of doubt. He would later credit Graham Wallas, a British Fabian who lectured at Harvard in the spring of 1910, for "divert[ing]" him from socialism.[11] Wallas suggested to Lippmann the vastness and invisibility of the "Great Society" of the modern world; he also argued that politics can be irrational. These considerations led Wallas to worry about how socialism would work in practice, worries that seem to have affected Lippmann deeply—but not immediately.[12] Indeed, three months after graduating, he became the apprentice to a famous muckraker, Lincoln Steffens, who was working on an exposé of Wall Street.[13] Lippmann next worked in Schenectady for the first Socialist mayor of an Eastern city, but he resigned when his employer proved unwilling to go beyond creating a few public services. Lippmann's very public condemnation of the mayor gained him even wider fame on the left than had his highly successful college activism, which had involved lecturing at various campuses for the Intercollegiate Socialist Society.[14] Yet he was now drifting from socialism toward Progressivism, and in 1914, he became a founding editor of *The New Republic*, which was immediately recognized as the leading highbrow organ of extreme Progressives. Progressivism channeled hostility toward capitalism away from revolution and toward the expansion of government's regulatory and redistributive power, but Progressives

---

[5] Steel 1980, ch. 1.

[6] Ibid., 23–24.

[7] Ibid., 14–15.

[8] Ibid., 16.

[9] Ibid., 24.

[10] Ibid., 28.

[11] Ibid.

[12] Lippmann, quoted, ibid.

[13] Ibid., 34–37.

[14] Ibid., 41–42, 24.

could be quite radical in the aims they sought to achieve through this power. Thus, in 1917 Lippmann editorialized against the "intellectually . . . timid" United States, which "trundles along without nationalized railroads or shipping, its mineral resources unsocialized, its water power exploited, its fundamental industries whipped into competition, its food distribution a muddle, its educational system starved, its labor half organized, badly organized, and unrecognized in the structure of society."[15] His Progressivism puts to shame the democratic socialism of our day.

Lippmann's writings of the 1910s offer an outlook on Progressivism that has, like the rest of his work, been unduly neglected. His contemporaneously acclaimed book of 1914, *Drift and Mastery*, declared a sweeping intellectual victory for the Progressive cause, albeit not one that had entirely been translated into public policy. Still, in dozens of states, an aroused public had enacted Progressive policies such as minimum wages, workers' compensation, inheritance taxes, compulsory education, municipal socialism, and child-labor prohibitions. These measures were accompanied by political reforms that reflected what an historian of the era calls the "great burst of democratic enthusiasm that had been the progressive movement's most tangible element":[16] populist reforms such as initiative, primary, referendum, and recall elections; the popular election of senators; women's suffrage; and bans on corporate campaign contributions.[17] The Progressives also enjoyed wide popular support in erecting a new constitutional order centered on the presidency, where—in direct contrast to the norms that had prevailed until Theodore Roosevelt's administration—it became appropriate, indeed obligatory, for the chief executive to call directly on the people to pressure Congress to enact social reforms.[18]

As *Drift and Mastery* noted, the cultural ground for this political revolution had long since been cultivated.[19] After the Civil War, public doubts about industrial capitalism began to be stoked by wildly popular works such as *An Iron Crown or: The Modern Mammon: A Graphic and Thrilling History of Great Money-Makers and How They Got Millions . . . Railway Kings, Coal Barons, Bonanza Miners and Their Victims*, written by "An Irate Chicagoan."[20] The cumulative effect of works of this sort is suggested by the success of Edward Bellamy's *Looking Backward*, which sold more than 300,000 copies between 1888 and 1890 and spawned thousands of "Bellamy Clubs."[21] (Bellamy's reach was as high as it was wide: not only did Lippmann read *Looking Backward* in college, but Dewey would later rank it as one of the greatest influences on his own political development.)[22] Bellamy's message was that the evils of capitalism were caused by monopolies, but

---

[15] Lippmann [1917] 1970, 149.

[16] Forcey 1961, 307.

[17] For figures on states' adoption of these measures, see Eisenach 1994, 242 n. 35.

[18] See Tulis 1987; on the connection to Progressivism, Friedman 2007.

[19] Lippmann [1914] 1985, 17.

[20] Cawelti 1973, 85.

[21] Shurter 1951.

[22] Ryan 1995, 43.

that monopolies are economically efficient. This notion led him to predict a surprisingly pleasant outcome of capitalist development: the emergence of one all-encompassing, superefficient monopoly that could be seized and run by the people.

The Progressive Era proper saw continued exposés of capitalist excess by muckraking journalists and the authors of such literary blockbusters as Theodore Dreiser's *Sister Carrie* (1900), David Graham Phillips's *The Great God Success* (1901), Frank Norris's *The Octopus* (1901), Steffens's *The Shame of the Cities* (1904), Ida Tarbell's *History of the Standard Oil Company* (1904), and Upton Sinclair's *The Jungle* (1906). By 1914, the barrage of anticapitalist writing had so influenced public opinion that, according to Lippmann, "no one, unafflicted with invincible ignorance, desires to preserve our economic system in its existing form." The generation preceding his, he proclaimed, "inherited a conservatism and overthrew it; we inherit freedom, and have to use it. The sanctity of private property, the patriarchal family, hereditary caste, the dogma of sin, obedience to authority—the rock of ages, in brief, has been blasted. . . . The artillery fire of the iconoclasts has shattered its prestige."[23] Some type of major reorganization of society now seemed to be endorsed by all but the most hidebound reactionaries.

In 1914 Lippmann applauded the Progressives' triumph, but he also argued that, having won the war of ideas, Progressives, including himself, faced a new adversary: "an enormously complicated world." "The modern man," he wrote, "is not yet settled in his world. It is strange to him, terrifying, alluring, and incomprehensibly big."[24] Eight years later, in *Public Opinion*, he would conclude that "the illimitable complexity of society" makes it almost (but not quite) incomprehensible, and thus "unpredictable."[25] But as of 1914, he still hopefully located the source of the "chaos" of the modern world in the intellectual revolution that had upended the old order. "There are no precedents to guide us," he wrote, "no wisdom that wasn't made for a simpler age."[26] He expected the confusion to end once people got used to the new world, for the source of the problem was transient: disorientation caused by historical change.

However, at some point between 1914 and 1920, Lippmann's politics changed again. Ronald Steel hypothesizes that, in working as a government propagandist during World War I, Lippmann "learned how easy it was to manipulate public opinion. That lesson had a powerful effect on him, leading him to question the Progressive inclination to think that the public is always right. What if the public doesn't know what it doesn't know? And what if the problem is not only faulty information, but also an unconscious channeling by the public of unfamiliar material into familiar, but deceptive, categories?"[27] Steel

---

[23] Lippmann [1914] 1985, 17.

[24] Ibid.

[25] Lippmann [1922] 1997, 228, 171.

[26] Lippmann [1914] 1985, 92.

[27] Steel 1997, xii. Steel's biography of Lippmann does not, however, specify any particular incidents during his time as a propagandist that might have given rise to these thoughts.

nicely captures the sharp break in Lippmann's perspective, although the ascription of Lippmann's epistemic worries to his role as a propagandist is speculative and somewhat at odds with the direction in which Lippmann soon went. In what seems to have been the standard Progressive perspective, the people *could* be wrong—but only if they were deliberately misled, as by propagandists.[28] After World War I, however, Lippmann began to argue that public opinion is likely to go wrong because of *inadvertent* failures to understand a complex society. This is the insight upon which the rest of Part I will elaborate.

Two years before he wrote *Public Opinion*, Lippmann thoroughly explored the *intentional* manipulation of public opinion in *Liberty and the News* (1920). Even then, however, the more disturbing realities of unintentional cognitive failure were crystallizing in his mind:

> The world about which each man is supposed to have opinions has become so complicated as to defy his powers of understanding. . . . Even the things that are near to him have become too involved for his judgment. I know of no man, even among those who devote all of their time to watching public affairs, who can even pretend to keep track, at the same time, of his city government, his state government, Congress, the departments, the industrial situation, the rest of the world. What men who make the study of politics a vocation cannot do, the man who has an hour a day for newspapers and talk cannot possibly hope to do.[29]

By 1920, then, Lippmann had begun to wonder if information overload is a problem that cannot be solved. This led almost inevitably to a break with the Progressive assumption that only deceivers can keep the people from knowing what they need to know. The people may not know what they need to know because it is in the nature of modern society to generate more information than they (meaning we) can possibly understand.

In the Progressive version of naive technocratic realism, citizen-technocrats reliably perceive the existence and nature of social problems and reliably know how to solve them, so long as they are not deliberately hoodwinked. This tacit epistemology led directly to the long list of Progressive political (as opposed to social) reforms, such as initiatives, referenda, and primaries, each designed to empower the electorate. As Roosevelt explained during the 1912 campaign, "We advocate, not as ends in themselves, but as weapons in the hands of the people, all governmental devices which will make the representatives of the people more easily and certainly responsible to the people's will."[30] Roosevelt's premise was that the people's will is adequately informed, or easily enough could be. Consider his account of how he formed his own views about public policy:

---

[28] See, for example, Page and Shapiro 1992, 374.

[29] Lippmann [1920] 2008, 22–23.

[30] Roosevelt 1912a, 120.

I usually found that my interest in any given side of a question of justice was aroused by some concrete case. . . . The need for a workmen's compensation act was driven home to me by my knowing a brakeman who had lost his legs in an accident, and whose family was thereby at once reduced from self-respecting comfort to conditions that at one time became very dreadful. Of course, after coming across various concrete instances of this kind, I would begin to read up on the subject, and then I would get in touch with social workers and others who were experts and could acquaint me with what is vital in the matter. Looking back, it seems to me that I made my greatest strides forward while I was police commissioner [of New York], and this largely through my intimacy with Jacob Riis, for he opened all kinds of windows into the matter for me.[31]

Riis, a photojournalist, had scandalized the public with his exposés of New York slums in the 1880s, culminating in *How the Other Half Lives* (1890). Photojournalists portrayed dramatic visual fragments of a vast reality as emblems of the nature and extent of a social problem, with the cause of the problem as self-evident as its existence and its cure. At one point, for example, Riis declared war against "the exploiting employers and landlords" who were so obviously "responsible for the physical, moral, and spiritual degradation of thousands of the city's men, women, and children."[32] Simply "by showing what their surroundings were doing to the young, Riis stirred hundreds of sympathetic readers who joined his attack with energy."[33] Cause, effect, and solution: all seemed to flow self-evidently from the vivid image of reality captured in a photograph.

Epistemological naiveté of this sort linked hard-bitten Progressive journalists such as Riis and more theoretical writers such as Bellamy. As an historian of the era's investigative journalism writes, "beginning with Bellamy's *Looking Backward* in 1888—a book which influenced nearly every one of the muckrakers—utopian projections flourished until the end of the Progressive period. . . . One of the leading muckrakers, David Graham Phillips, summarized the source of this impulse for his age: a 'Messiah-longing,' he wrote, 'has been the dream of the whole human race, toiling away in obscurity, exploited, fooled, despised.' "[34] Bellamy's book, though, was neither messianic nor unrealistic in any obvious sense. It proposed a solution to the effects of unrestrained capitalism that was the soul of common sense—given his assumptions about the coming capitalist mega-monopoly. Once this leviathan was nationalized, Bellamy maintained, it would be an exceedingly simple matter for the people to operate it, that is, the entire economy.[35] For they would benefit not only from the efficiencies achieved by present-day monopolies, but from

---

[31] Roosevelt 1912b, 316–317.
[32] Dilliard 1973, 3.
[33] Ibid.
[34] Martin 1973, 102.
[35] Bellamy [1888] 1951, 147, 151.

abolishing what Bellamy thought was the only source of economic complexity: the need to anticipate what one's business competitors might do. With that complication removed, running an advanced industrial economy would be easy. Similarly, muckrakers and photojournalists saw themselves as merely publicizing the plain facts they had seen with their own eyes or recorded with their own cameras. Where Bellamy considered controlling the economy a simple matter, muckrakers and photojournalists considered the identification of social problems, their causes, and their cures to be equally straightforward. It has been pointed out that the muckrakers "resembled advocacy journalists in making emotional appeals [and] in personalizing complex issues."[36] But in their defense, the muckrakers' oversimplifications conformed to their commonsensical perceptions of the causes of the problems about which they were reporting. Their assumption that the deliberate actions of evil men were responsible for the ills they publicized was of a piece with the idea that only deliberate propaganda could keep the public from recognizing the self-evident truths of modern political life.

Lippmann ended up proposing a very different political epistemology, one that began with the non-self-evidence of the truth in a modern society. This premise led him to concentrate on defects in the mental "pseudo-environment" that we build up in attempting to picture and understand nonmanifest social truths. In *Public Opinion*, he argued that "the very fact that men theorize at all is proof that their pseudo-environments, their inferior representations of the world, are a determining element in thought, feeling, and action. For if the connection between reality and human response were direct and immediate, rather than indirect and inferred, indecision and failure would be unknown."[37] The source of indecision and failure is, according to Lippmann, the difficulty of aligning the pseudo-environment with the real environment. This is an epistemic form of complexity, not one brought about by the collapse of moral traditions, as in *Drift and Mastery*. A crisis caused by epistemic complexity is not easy to resolve, nor can one assume that it will pass in time.

Thus, where *Drift and Mastery* had been optimistic if sober, *Public Opinion* strained to offer any hope of reaching reliable judgments about the problems of societies where "the pictures inside people's heads do not automatically correspond with the world outside."[38] Three years later, in *The Phantom Public*, Lippmann was even more explicit about the contrast between Progressive political moralizing and the political epistemology he had developed. "It will require more than a good conscience to govern modern society," he wrote. "In the issues engendered by the rise of the national state and the development of large scale industries are to be found the essentially new problems of the modern world."[39] These issues create "a nerve-wracking increase in the incalculable forces that bear upon"

---

[36] Harrison and Stein 1973, 14–15.

[37] Lippmann [1922] 1997, 17.

[38] Ibid., 19.

[39] Lippmann [1925] 1927, 181.

the fate of each individual. In short, the modern world is epistemically complex. Insofar as "the world is complicated" in this sense, "conscience is no guide."[40] He added:

> When I am tempted to think that men can be fitted out to deal with the modern world simply by teaching morals, manners and patriotism, I try to remember the fable of the pensive professor walking in the woods at twilight. He stumbled into a tree. . . . Being a man of breeding, he raised his hat, bowed deeply to the tree, and exclaimed with sincere regret: "Excuse me, sir, I thought you were a tree."
>
> Is it fair, I ask, as a matter of morality, to chide him for his conduct? . . . Here was a moral code in perfect working order, and the only questionable aspect of his conduct turned not on the goodness of his heart or the firmness of his principles but on a point of fact.[41]

Lippmann continued to share the Progressives' opposition to laissez-faire, to individualism, and to constitutional barriers against social legislation. But he could no longer assume that the people's good hearts would, in a complex modern society, enable them to know the policy difference between a man and a tree.

2.2. LIPPMANN'S POLITICAL EPISTEMOLOGY

> There is a bias in all opinion, even in opinion purged of desire, for the man who holds the opinion must stand at some point in space and time and can see not the whole world but only the world as seen from that point. So men learned that they saw a little through their own eyes, and much more through reports of what other men had seen. They were made to understand that all human eyes have habits of vision, which are often stereotyped, which always throw facts into a perspective; and that the whole of experience is more sophisticated than the naïve mind suspects.
>
> —WALTER LIPPMANN, *The Phantom Public*

Lippmann's works of the 1920s adduced countless examples of wartime illusions that demonstrated the gravity of our epistemic shortcomings. "Let him cast the first stone," he said in *Public Opinion*, "who did not believe in the Russian army that passed through England in August, 1914, did not accept any tale of atrocities without direct proof, and never saw a plot, a traitor, or a spy where there was none."[42] But the most remarkable aspect of Lippmann's work in these years is its emphasis on the inadvertence of false beliefs. Even if, as Steel speculates, Lippmann's experience with World War I propaganda had caused his first doubts about the wisdom of the people, his works of the 1920s transcended the

---

[40] Ibid., 18, 16.
[41] Ibid., 18–19.
[42] Lippmann [1922] 1997, 8.

crude attribution of popular misconceptions to propagandistic conspiracies against the truth. There is no need to insist that propaganda is at the root of the public's errors if the public is *inherently* prone to err in its attempts to understand the politics and policies governing a vast, unseen society. If, as Lippmann wrote in *The Phantom Public*, government actions are "altogether too numerous, too complicated, and too obscure in their effects" for the public to understand, then it is likely to err on its own, even when it is not deliberately nudged into doing so.[43] Propaganda may contribute to error in a given case, but Lippmann increasingly abandoned propaganda as a general explanation of popular misunderstandings.

In its place, he put a theory that began with the observation that "the facts of modern life do not spontaneously take a shape in which they can be known. They must be given a shape by somebody," namely the journalist.[44] Reporters and editors mold the "pseudo-environment of reports, rumors, guesses" that we, the people, tend to mistake for the real societal environment. "Where all news comes at second-hand, where all the testimony is uncertain, men cease to respond to truths, and respond simply to opinions." In this context, "the power to determine each day what shall seem important and what shall be neglected is a power unlike any that has been exercised since the Pope lost his hold on the secular mind."[45]

Lippmann concluded that the issue now known as "media bias" had to be confronted. Unlike propaganda, though, media bias is, in Lippmann's conception of it, anything but deliberate. It is rather, he thought, a reflection of the untenable situation in which all human beings find themselves when attempting to interpret modern society.

2.2.1. *Inadvertent Bias and the Determination of Ideas*

Lippmann first investigated media bias in 1920 for a special supplement to *The New Republic*, where he and Charles Merz published a long study of coverage of the Russian Revolution by the *New York Times*. They concluded that the coverage had been heavily slanted against the Revolution. The *Times* had, for example, "reported no fewer than ninety-one times that the Bolshevik regime was on the verge of collapse."[46] However, the agent of misinformation was not, as Progressives might have predicted, conservative newspaper owners spreading lies. The source of bias was the journalists' own preconceptions. "The chief censor and the chief propagandist were hope and fear in the minds of reporters and editors."[47] This conclusion represented two of the defining features of

---

[43] Lippmann [1925] 1927, 31.

[44] Lippmann [1922] 1997, 218.

[45] Lippmann [1920] 2008, 33, 32–33, 28.

[46] Lippmann and Merz 1920, 10.

[47] Ibid., 3.

Lippmann's work of the 1920s: its pessimism about journalists' ability to overcome their biases; and an epistemological rather than motivational reason for pessimism.

In turn, Lippmann became *politically* pessimistic because he considered epistemic bias, unlike deliberate bias, to be unavoidable. The significance, the implications, and indeed the truth of political information has to be imputed to it by journalists, who necessarily report on a small subset of an incomprehensibly large universe of events—a subset that they interpret as particularly significant—and on claims that they interpret as plausible. Given the vastness and invisibility of the society in which they are operating, journalists may err in their judgments of significance and plausibility. Only if the truth were noninterpretive—that is, self-evident—would these errors be presumptively attributable to an intention to deceive their readers. The erroneous coverage of the Russian Revolution was the product of inadvertent mistake, not a deliberate will to deceive.

That human perception is fallible was hardly a novel idea. But in applying this truism to politics, Lippmann's *Liberty and the News*, also published in 1920, parted decisively with the Progressives and their obsession with the influence on public opinion of sinister interests (also an obsession of Utilitarians such as Bentham). "Once you know the party and social affiliation of a newspaper," Lippmann wrote, "you can predict with considerable certainty the perspective in which the news will be displayed"—a passage that would surely gain Progressive assent. Then came the unexpected twist: "This perspective is by no means altogether deliberate." Journalists, like everyone else, "believe whatever fits most comfortably with their prepossessions." In turn, their prepossessions stem from "the prevailing *mores* of [their] social group"—and these mores, Lippmann maintained, are "of course in large measure the product of what previous newspapers have said."[48]

As of 1920, then, Lippmann was enunciating an almost completely subjectivist epistemology of politics. The public relies on journalists for virtually all the politically relevant information it receives; journalists determine which information is worthy of being reported to the public; yet the basis of this determination is the journalists' judgments of significance and plausibility, which rest on perceptions formed by their own exposure to previous journalism. In principle, journalists' perceptions, and therefore those of the public, may form a closed loop. Appearance and reality, phenomena and noumena, may bear little or no resemblance to each other, because previous appearances predispose journalists to notice similar appearances and to relay them to their readers, even if the appearances are misleading—inadvertently—in that they miss aspects of reality that journalists' prepossessions have not equipped them to notice, or have not equipped them to interpret adequately.

In *Liberty and the News*, however, this radical epistemological vision was artificially circumscribed by the assumption that journalists' biases are acquired from previous journalism, rather than from any and every ideational influence journalists might have

---

[48] Lippmann [1920], 28–29, 33, 29.

encountered, from whatever source—not only journalistic sources but books, movies, plays, documentaries, formal instruction, informal conversation, and so on. In *Public Opinion* this assumption would be abandoned, while another key innovation of *Liberty and the News* was retained. This was Lippmann's distinction between two types of mediation through which subjective ideas about objective social conditions must pass.

Ideas are usually communicated from one person (such as a journalist) to another (such as a newspaper reader). But before this interpersonal mediation can occur, an idea must seem to the first person to be congruent with her established, interconnected web of beliefs; otherwise she will not find the new idea plausible or significant enough to relay to others. Before the journalist can decide how to mediate the world to her audience, she must mediate the world to herself, and here she has little choice but to follow the most plausible interpretation generated by the ideas about the world that she has already accumulated. Her decisions about which ideas are plausible and which developments are newsworthy have to be based on her current view of how the world is and how it works. Thus, Lippmann was describing the *determination* of journalists' biases by their standing networks of perceptions, assumptions, beliefs, and theories. He was suggesting that these biases are as involuntary as journalists' sense perceptions. Thus, journalists' misperceptions about public affairs are as inadvertent as optical illusions.

Public Opinion also carried over from *Liberty and the News* the idea that our perceptions of society constitute it as a pseudo-environment, which in turn "stimulates" our actions in the real world.[49] If the pseudo-environment were *completely* disconnected from the real environment, that is, if our beliefs about the real environment formed a completely closed loop, we would be entitled to no confidence in their accuracy. However, the completely closed loop is an ideal type of my devising; it is designed to convey Lippmann's clear distinction between the political things in themselves and the appearances to which we have access. Lippmann did not deny that this gap could be bridged; he even said at one point that, in "the ideologies of politics," there is always a "foothold of realism."[50] However, he insisted that even if interpersonal and conceptual mediation achieves verisimilitude, it is our perceptions that determine our ideas; reality itself does not.

That is the point that the naive technocratic realist does not grasp. Having grasped it, Lippmann puts us on the threshold of a sophisticated political epistemology, for he suggests that what we accept as salient empirical data about society are tainted by our interpretive expectations. "The facts" may seem obvious, and our opinions may seem to express self-evident truths. Those who disagree with us may seem to be driven by emotion, ideology, or, at best, propaganda. But this is only because we do not realize how much work our preexisting webs of belief do in constructing our seemingly intuitive perceptions of facts and truth.

---

[49] Lippmann [1922] 1997, 10.
[50] Ibid., 109.

Even in the simple case of an observable political "event," for example, the facts reported by journalists are not nearly so straightforward as they seem. If a politician gives a speech, the journalist must decide if the speech is significant enough to warrant reprinting. Then, in the accompanying story, she must tell the reader what is so significant about it, or must quote opinions about its significance produced by others whom the reporter deems important enough to quote. These journalistic actions train the reader's attention on certain aspects of the speech, de-emphasizing the rest of it. The reporter will also have to judge whether to report other political figures' disagreements about the significance, the meaning, or the implications of the speech. Too, the reporters' and others' interpretations must be put into a sequence in the news story, but any sequence will tend to color the reader's impressions. To overcome a negative impression conveyed in the opening statement of a story's facts, a stronger positive impression must later be conveyed than would be necessary otherwise. A quoted claim will tend to be less believable if it contradicts assertions made by the reporter, who functions as an omniscient narrator. An editor must put a headline over the story, select and caption a photo, and choose how prominently to place the whole package. At every step, journalistic judgment is exercised. This judgment cannot possibly be determined by the sheer facts being reported, for if the facts could speak for themselves, judgments about them would not be necessary. The judgments, and thus the selection and presentation of facts, are products of journalists' webs of explicit and tacit beliefs. A similar process occurs when someone reads the story, skims it, skips it, or stops in the middle. On both the sender's and the recipient's side, messages are screened and shaped by interpretations that fit the messages into an extant web of beliefs—or by interpretations that reject the messages that do not fit.

The role of interpretation is even greater when journalists mediate not "news" as such but large-scale or long-term processes that, unlike a speech, cannot be directly observed. The mediation of such processes is necessary in a democratic technocracy, assuming that social problems have a large scale and develop over a long time. In such cases, gaps between reality and pseudo-reality will be invisible and possibly undetectable. While long-term and large-scale phenomena are as real as are observable news events, the facts about these unobservable phenomena are inferences that can be established only through interpretation. That they can be established—or corrected—by sheer sense impressions is an illusion.

Thus, the photojournalism that Roosevelt found so illuminating was, to Lippmann, dangerously misleading. "Photographs," he wrote, "have the kind of authority over imagination to-day, which the printed word had yesterday, and the spoken word before that. They seem utterly real. They come, we imagine, directly to us without human meddling, and they are the most effortless food for the mind imaginable." Likewise movies and documentaries:

On the screen the whole process of observing, describing, reporting, and then imagining has been accomplished for you. Without more trouble than is needed to stay awake the result which your imagination is always aiming at is reeled off on the screen. The shadowy idea becomes vivid; your hazy notion, let us say, of the Ku Klux Klan, thanks to Mr. Griffith, takes vivid shape when you see the Birth of a Nation. Historically it may be the wrong shape, morally it may be a pernicious shape, but it is a shape, and I doubt whether anyone who has seen the film and does not know more about the Ku Klux Klan than Mr. Griffith, will ever hear the name again without seeing those white horsemen.[51]

However much the media may convey the impression of direct access to reality, according to Lippmann, this impression is inaccurate, for even if there is a kernel of truth on the page or the screen or in the photo, it cannot possibly be the whole truth: that is entailed by the overabundance of information. Yet in trying to convey a representative sample of the truth, what choice does the journalist have but to rely on her partial perceptions of the way things are "out there"? All reports about large-scale or long-term social processes, even dry and formal scholarly studies, paint pictures of reality that are judged holistically, according to their conformity with one's web of beliefs. Yet the beliefs in anyone's web are themselves fallible perceptions of reality, so when we combine them into a holistic assessment, we may inadvertently misrepresent the real whole in the shape that we expect it to have. While there may be some overlap between reality and our webs of belief, we cannot know where the overlap does or does not lie. All of our beliefs *seem* worthy of belief, but if we have rejected naive realism, we must recognize that some or all of them may actually be unworthy of belief. The problem is that we are radically ignorant of which beliefs are, in fact, unworthy. That is an unknown unknown.

Thus, Lippmann contends that when we "establish schools, build navies, proclaim 'policies' and 'destiny,' raise economic barriers, make property or unmake it, bring one people under the rule of another, or favor one class as against another . . . some view of the facts is taken to be conclusive, some view of the circumstances is accepted as the basis of inference and as the stimulus for feeling"—but we can do little to verify our view of the facts. "What each man does is based not on direct and certain knowledge, but on pictures made by himself or given to him."[52] Therefore, "under certain conditions men respond as powerfully to fictions as they do to realities, and . . . in many cases they help to create the very fictions to which they respond."[53] Clearly the fictions to which Lippmann refers are not perceived as such, or else we would not respond to them as we would to (self-evident) realities. Nor need these fictions be lies.[54] They may be inadvertently incorrect extrapolations from perceptions that we take to be accurate.

---

[51] Lippmann [1920] 2008, 61.
[52] Lippmann [1922] 1997, 16.
[53] Ibid., 14, 10.
[54] Ibid., 10.

Lippmann called these fictions "stereotypes." Stereotypes are never deliberately used if one knows they are false, but they are constantly used because we don't know which ones are false—and because we have no choice but to use some stereotype or another. "The alternative" to stereotyping, he wrote, "is direct exposure to the ebb and flow of sensation. But that is not a real alternative," for "the real environment is altogether too big, too complex, and too fleeting for direct acquaintance. We are not equipped to deal with so much subtlety, so much variety, so many permutations and combinations. And although we have to act in that environment, we have to reconstruct it on a simpler model before we can manage with it."[55] With simplified reconstruction comes the possibility of error.

2.2.2. The Primacy of Interpretation

The main theoretical advance of *Public Opinion* over *Liberty and the News* is in its analysis of the second of the two forms of mediation—not the mediation of readers' perceptions by those who report "the facts" to them, but the mediation of both readers' perceptions of these reports, and journalists' perceptions of what to report, by stereotypes about cause and effect in the relevant aspects of the unseen society.

Such stereotypes, Lippmann contends, are generalizations that would be "shifting and haphazard" if not for the efforts of "a comparatively few men in each generation": those who are "constantly engaged in arranging, standardizing, and improving" our stereotypes into "logical systems, known as the Laws of Political Economy, the Principles of Politics, and the like."[56] Stereotypes, then, are not mere prejudices, as we might be inclined to think by the contemporary usage of the term. They are elements of the conceptual schemas that allow us to make sense of the world. They form patterns of interpretation. As such, they may be provincial or they may be sophisticated. In combination, they may enable us to think we understand a narrow issue or one so broad that they amount to an ideology or a social theory that can, in turn, organize a great deal of information.

The starting point of Lippmann's analysis of stereotypes is his argument for the primacy of interpretation. Without interpretive mediation, he contends, the overabundance of information about politics would strike adults in the same way that, according to William James, with whom Lippmann studied at Harvard, a newborn sees everything: as "one great, blooming, buzzing confusion."[57] To familiarize ourselves with what would otherwise be an incomprehensible chaos, we rely on stereotyped interpretations of what is going on. Stereotypes make some of the features of the buzzing confusion legible; we focus our attention on them, which we are thus able to perceive. We ignore the rest,

---

[55] Ibid., 10–11.

[56] Ibid., 69.

[57] Ibid., 54, quoting James [1890] 1918, 488. Lippmann then quotes Dewey on the application to adults of James's claim about infants. On James and Lippmann at Harvard, see Steel 1980, 17–18.

which remains illegible. "For the most part we do not first see, and then define, we define first and then see."[58]

A stereotype makes part of society legible by mentally predisposing us to see aspects of the otherwise formless chaos as objects connected by causal relationships. A stereotype also highlights whichever pseudo-features of society seem to confirm the accuracy of the stereotype. These are merely pseudo-features because they extrapolate from a small set of mediated "facts" to a possibly erroneous representation of the state of things in society at large. "In putting together our public opinions, not only do we have to picture more space than we can see with our eyes, and more time than we can feel, but we have to describe and judge more people, more actions, more things than we can ever count, or vividly imagine. We have to summarize and generalize. We have to pick out samples, and treat them as typical."[59] If interpretation were not anterior to perception, we could perceive nothing distinct. Thus, "the perfect stereotype precedes the use of reason; is a form of perception, imposes a certain character on the data of our senses before the data reach the intelligence. . . . It stamps itself upon the evidence in the very act of securing the evidence."[60]

Our need to attend only selectively to the otherwise overwhelmingly vast reality is thus an *unavoidable* source of epistemic partiality. Our only defense against overabundant information is to use stereotypes as interpretive lenses that screen out most of the chaos while focusing on interpretation-congruent information, which we take to represent larger realities. The appearance and reappearance of such information seems to confirm the accuracy of the initial interpretation. "If what we are looking at corresponds successfully with what we anticipated, the stereotype is reinforced for the future."[61] The result is a growing but skewed data sample that increases our confidence in its adequacy as it expands, or so Lippmann suggests. I will take up this suggestion in Chapter 5.

2.2.3. *Too Much Information*

The political problem described by Lippmann is readily misunderstood, and this misunderstanding has plagued the many public-opinion scholars who have taken their cue from him. Generally—universally, to my knowledge—they have held that the problem to which he pointed is that the public is grossly *under*informed—rather than that the public is vulnerable to *erroneous* perceptions of facts, and misleading generalizations from them, because it must use questionable interpretations of overabundant information. Lippmann's view has therefore been thought to dovetail with the main direction of contemporary opinion scholarship since the 1940s, in which Lippmann's problematic

---

[58] Lippmann [1922] 1997, 54–55.
[59] Ibid., 95.
[60] Ibid., 65.
[61] Lippmann [1925] 1927, 33.

was cashed out as the mass public's ignorance of a sufficient *quantity* of political "information" or "knowledge."[62] The researchers' tacit (and often explicit) assumption has been that if people would just get more political knowledge into their heads, they would make reliably good political decisions.[63] I will call this the additive view of knowledge. In the additive view, more knowledge is better than less, and "full information" is not an impossible dream. In the additive view, the problem is a deficit of information that needs to be supplemented, not a surfeit of information that needs to be selectively attended to if it is to be understood.

Nothing is easier than to show that Lippmann did not accept the additive view. Thus, as we have just seen, he deplored the confirmation of stereotypes when confirmatory information is *added* to the small stocks of information that a stereotype initially highlights. Confirmatory information, Lippmann thought, can easily lead away from the truth—even though it leaves us with more information than before. Yet a careless reading of *Public Opinion* might easily produce the opposite impression. The book begins by emphasizing that people have limited time for and interest in learning about politics and government. Its first five chapters (out of 28) enumerate, in vivid detail, a variety of additional factors that restrict people's "access to the facts."[64] If one stops reading the book too soon, one can logically conclude that the problem with public opinion is that it suffers from an information deficit, not an information surfeit. That has been the default reading of political scientists for nearly a century, but it omits the problem Lippmann raises in Chapter 6, the first of five chapters on stereotypes. This is the problem of interpretation, which stems from information overload, which in turn entails information selection, which leads to confirmation bias and thus the possibility of a closed loop. The whole process begins with the need to make sense of too much information, not too little.

The very concept of interpretation has been absent from the mainstream of opinion research since the 1940s. Yet the "blooming, buzzing confusion" that was Lippmann's conceptual starting point indicates that we *must* interpret because we need to screen out the noise if we are to hear a signal. Only after sifting the oversupply of information down to a manageable sample can we understand it, and what we understand we interpret as representative of conditions at large. *The problem of interpretation* is reducible to the fact that what we know (or what we think we know) may not accurately represent what we do not know. This means that we may lack the *right* knowledge, regardless of how much information we have. The potential problem is a biased sample, not a small one. The facts we know about might be consistent with a given interpretation, and thus may buttress our acceptance of it; but other facts might overturn this interpretation if we knew about them, if we knew how to interpret them properly, or if we were not encouraged, by our extant interpretation, from discounting them. In accepting an interpretation as accurate,

---

[62] See Friedman 2013b.
[63] See Chapter 6.
[64] Lippmann [1922] 1997, 18.

we are necessarily and radically ignorant of whatever unknown information might falsify the interpretation or render it inapplicable to the situation being interpreted.

Chapter 4 of *Public Opinion* complains that (according to an unscientific survey) 14 percent of educated Chicagoans "read but one paper" per day, while 46 percent read two, 21 percent three, 10 percent four, 3 percent five, 2 percent six, and 3 percent all eight of the newspapers then available. Here Lippmann might be construed as saying that everything would be fine if only more Chicagoans read eight papers a day—as someone who holds the additive view might believe.[65] But two years prior to *Public Opinion*, Lippmann had already contended that "the man who has an hour a day for newspapers and talk cannot possibly hope to do" what is expected of him as a political decision-maker—and that neither can "men who make the study of politics a vocation,"[66] men such as Lippmann himself, who read about as much political news as any human being could. Consider, too, what he wrote in Chapter 24 about the muckraker Upton Sinclair, who assumed "that news and truth are two words for the same thing." In reply, Lippmann maintained that "if newspapers are to be charged with the duty of translating the whole public life of mankind, so that every adult can arrive at an opinion on every moot topic, they fail, they are bound to fail, in any future one can conceive they will continue to fail."[67] They must fail because newspapers do not report the truth; they report, at best, a sample of the truth, and samples are necessarily biased. (A sample may in fact be representative of the larger reality being interpreted, but the sample itself cannot possibly be based on knowledge of that larger reality; it is necessarily "biased" not in the sense of being wrong, but in the sense of being a partial and thus *potentially* incorrect interpretation.) Sinclair's equation of news with truth ignored "the illimitable complexity of society"[68]—something that scholars of public opinion also ignore when they question the public's political competence because so few voters read one (or more) good newspapers, or the electronic equivalent.

Perhaps it was a mistake for *Public Opinion* to have discussed the "quantity" of information at all. In so doing, it conveyed the opposite of Lippmann's most important message. But in his quest for an encyclopedic political epistemology, he also discussed such factors as readers' lack of sufficient background for understanding news reports; reporters' factual errors; the manipulation of symbols by politicians; the deliberate "manufacture of consent," that is, propaganda; the need to sensationalize in order to capture readers' attention; and emotional distractions from a clear perception of the truth. Thus, *Public Opinion* exemplifies the central problem it describes: there is so much in it that readers can find virtually anything they are prepared to discover. Among all the factors to which Lippmann ascribes the public's propensity to make bad political decisions, one is

---

[65] Ibid., 38.

[66] Lippmann [1920] 2008, 22–23.

[67] Lippmann [1922] 1997, 226, 228.

[68] Ibid., 228.

sheer lack of information. But he always comes back to the problem of interpretation, a problem that would persist even if we could read a dozen papers a day, even if were thoroughly schooled in politics and policy, and even if nobody were trying to manipulate us.

The Phantom Public should put to rest any misunderstanding about whether Lippmann believed that "more" knowledge would solve the problem. Here Lippmann wrote that "it used to be thought"—presumably by Progressives such as himself, his many acquaintances in politics and journalism, and his colleagues at *The New Republic*—that if only the voter "could be taught more facts, if only he would take more interest, if only he would read more and better newspapers, if only he would listen to more lectures and read more reports, he would gradually be trained to direct public affairs." But "the whole assumption is false."[69]

2.2.4. The False Promise of Statistics

As an alternative to the vain hope that journalists could bring the requisite selection of knowledge to the general public, Lippmann suggested at the end of *Public Opinion* that "bureaus of governmental research" could be attached to each cabinet department, and that the statisticians employed in these bureaus could convey the pertinent knowledge directly to government decision-makers, as well as enlightening the public at large. Such bureaus would "reverse the process by which interesting public opinions are built up. Instead of presenting a casual fact, a large screen of stereotypes, and a dramatic identification, they break down the drama, break through the stereotypes, and offer men a picture of facts, which is unfamiliar and to them impersonal."[70]

It might seem, then, that in its concluding pages, Lippmann forgot what the book had said about the ineluctability of stereotypical interpretation in dealing with too much information. However, he took literally the notion that the problem with overabundant information lay in sampling bias. If, "in putting together our public opinions . . . we have to pick out samples, and treat them as typical,"[71] a solution seemed to present itself: scientific sampling. "The science of statistics"[72] would enable information bureaus to surmount the interpretive problems to which Lippmann had pointed. However, Lippmann confessed that his understanding of statistics was poor, and one can only agree.[73] He failed to notice at least three problems with the science of statistics, all of which indicate that one cannot rely on statisticians to achieve the goal he had in mind for them: the goal of transcending interpretation.[74]

---

[69] Lippmann [1925] 1927, 36.
[70] Lippmann [1922] 1997, 233.
[71] Ibid., 95.
[72] Ibid.
[73] Ibid.
[74] Ibid.

First, statisticians must treat the measured phenomena as equivalent to one another in order to count them. But this may homogenize phenomena that are heterogeneous: for example, the many different types of unemployment, or unemployment of the same type but caused by many different factors. It is not impossible to sort out these issues, but doing so requires interpreting statistics, not imagining that they can speak for themselves. Interpretation is, according to Lippmann, the problem; statistics, then, can hardly be the solution. It may be possible for a given statistician to come up with measures that adequately deal with this problem. Yet since this solution will require an adequate interpretation of the very phenomena the statistics are intended to represent, it cannot rely on statistics alone.

Second, *causality* among statistical variables is always a matter of interpretation, not measurement; this is why correlation is not causation. A statistic is an inert readout from an illegible universe until a fallible interpreter relates it to a causal theory. A statistic about illiteracy among high-school graduates may seem to dictate a certain action to solve a normatively important educational problem—but only if we interpret the statistic (however tacitly) through the lens of a causal theory or several of them: say, a theory about the sources of illiteracy in the past, a theory about the effects of past efforts to increase literacy, and a theory about the continuity of current sources of illiteracy with past sources, culminating in a theory about how to increase literacy in the future. Each theory meshes with the theorist's web of beliefs. Such webs, however, may differ from theorist to theorist, such that a plausible theory, in the eyes of one interpreter, will appear implausible to another. The gathering of additional statistics may sometimes be helpful in resolving such disagreements, but it may also multiply the points about which there is reasonable disagreement. Moreover, even a unanimous consensus among statisticians may betoken nothing but their common exposure to a hegemonic interpretation. So again, it is not logical to expect that "exact record and quantitative analysis" will solve the problem of interpretation.[75]

Third and most fundamentally, in using a statistical sample one assumes that it represents the larger whole. But if the whole is heterogeneous in a manner that cannot be predicted, the assumption will be false. The use of statistics presupposes the assumption of "uniformity" in "the operations of nature,"[76] as Hume put it, an assumption without which natural science would be impossible. To use statistics to understand or predict human behavior, it would have to be uniform in the same way nature is—not identical on the surface, but identical underneath, in the causes that create diverse appearances. An implication of Lippmann's own argument in *Public Opinion*, however, is that human nature cannot be assumed to be uniform in this sense. Developing this point will require reconstructing the ontology implicit in Lippmann's political epistemology. Ontology,

---

[75] Ibid., 222.
[76] Hume [1772] 1999, 159.

unfortunately, was left undiscussed in the course of the debate with Dewey, so I will post-pone the matter until the next chapter.

It may be worth noting that Lippmann was not the first to fall victim to the siren song of statistics. By the time *Public Opinion* appeared, a statistically based science of social reform had already been attempted by the Progressives' scholarly progenitors, and it had already been judged a failure by many of them. This may have escaped Lippmann's no-tice because the first wave of statistical social science had crested by the time he entered college.[77]

The surge of interest in statistics had originated in the late nineteenth century with the "younger" school of German Historical economists, led by Gustav von Schmoller and Adolph Wagner. Schmoller, Wagner, and like-minded colleagues were the main draws for the hundreds of American and other foreign graduate students who flocked to Germany and returned to their home countries to found the modern social sciences.[78] The younger German Historical economists condemned the egoism inherent in the uni-versal laws taught by classical and neoclassical economics. The solution, in their view, was to stop making universalistic social-scientific claims until the empirical basis for new social-scientific laws could be accumulated. Their students, equating "empirical" with "statistical," produced innumerable statistical studies of the particular, historically con-tingent social problems plaguing their countries. However, the result of their efforts was a huge pile of research that could not guide action, as it lacked theoretical interpreta-tion. A historian of the era comments that "by the 1890s, sensing [that] the historical school was becoming swamped in ever-expanding, formless empirical results, the bright-est American students were already seeking out Schmoller's rival marginalists in Vienna instead":[79] neoclassical economists.

By 1925, however, Lippmann seems to have recognized that he had been barking up the wrong tree. In *The Phantom Public*, the idea of statistical "fact-finding agencies" is duti-fully mentioned on an early page,[80] but the rest of the book argues that the true experts are not statisticians but "those who are responsibly concerned as agents" in a public dis-pute, such as labor leaders and businessmen. "They alone," Lippmann maintained, "know what the trouble really is."[81] Lippmann's new position was a distant anticipation of mid-century political-science theories such as Robert Dahl's "polyarchy," which reversed the Progressive attack on special interests by welcoming the participation of multiple inter-ested parties in the making of public policy.[82] For Lippmann, however, the point was not to represent multiple interests but to bring the interested parties' direct knowledge

---

[77] See Goodwin 2014, 9–10; Fourcade 2009, 81.

[78] Rodgers 1998, 83, 89–90; Hodgson 2001, 138. Rodgers (1998, 89–90) points out in contrast that not a single American student sat in on Max Weber's lectures.

[79] Rodgers 1998, 92.

[80] Lippmann [1925] 1927, 32.

[81] Ibid., 63.

[82] E.g., Dahl 1961.

to bear. This would be unnecessary if a statistician could duplicate or improve on such knowledge.

By 1937, Lippmann would move even farther from advocating an epistocracy of statisticians. In *The Good Society*, he jettisoned all thoughts of scientific social expertise. By then the Great Depression had produced a vogue for comprehensive central planning, in imitation of the Soviet Union (a vogue in which Dewey participated, as we will see). *The Good Society* mocked this fad. "In science there was knowledge," Lippmann wrote. "In government there was power. By their union an indispensable providence was to be created and the future of human society contrived and directed."[83] The faith in scientific central planning, however, overlooked "the essential limitation" of "all policy, of all government": to wit, that "the human mind must take a partial and simplified view of existence." "To the data of social experience the mind is like a lantern which casts dim circles of light spasmodically upon somewhat familiar patches of ground in an unexplored wilderness."[84]

> The ruler in any society is a private man doomed to take partial views. He may be looked upon as standing at the small end of a funnel which at its large end is as wide as the world in the past, the present, and the future. . . . And to understand even that small part he must turn to theories, summaries, analyses, principles, and dogmas which reduce the raw enormous actuality of things to a condition where it is intelligible.[85]

Rulers armed with statistics would confront exactly the same problem.

2.3. DEWEY'S DEFENSES OF DEMOCRATIC TECHNOCRACY

> The confusion resulting from the size and ramifications of social activities has rendered men skeptical of the efficiency of political action. Who is sufficient unto these things? Men feel that they are caught in the sweep of forces too vast to understand or master.
> —JOHN DEWEY, *The Public and Its Problems*

> The indirect and unthought-of consequences are usually more important than the direct.
> —JOHN DEWEY, *The Public and Its Problems*

One of the curiosities of the Lippmann-Dewey debate is how effusively Dewey lauded Lippmann's contributions to it, hailing the disillusioned Progressive's "brilliancy" and calling *Public Opinion* "perhaps the most effective indictment of democracy as currently

---

[83] Lippmann [1937] 2005, 23–24.

[84] Ibid., 30–31.

[85] Ibid., 29.

conceived ever penned."[86] Lippmann's dichotomy between "the world outside and the pictures in our heads" was, according to Dewey, "a more significant statement of the genuine 'problem of knowledge' than professional epistemological philosophers have managed to give."[87]

That the praise was not mere rhetoric is suggested by the paucity of criticisms that Dewey advanced. But the praise was greater than it should have been, from Dewey's perspective. In James T. Kloppenberg's unimpeachable formulation, the main argument of *Public Opinion* is that "because citizens do not see public problems in their full complexity but only through the distorting but indispensable lenses of stereotypes, they are incapable of making the intelligent choices democracy demands."[88] Dewey failed to notice that Lippmann saw stereotypes as *indispensable*, and not just for ordinary citizens but for journalists, too. This oversight led Dewey to assume more common ground with Lippmann than there actually was.

Thus, Dewey's review of *Public Opinion* portrayed Lippmann as condemning public opinion for being "shaped chiefly by tradition, by stereotyped pictures, and by emotions, by personal interests unintelligently perceived."[89] Dewey was defining "stereotypes" as we might understand them today—not as unavoidable responses to information overload, but as dispensable prejudices: "traditions and habits of mind," as Dewey said, "that form the standing 'categories' through which facts are received, illusions that have to do with *defence, prestige, morality*." If stereotypes are a function of emotion, then they are not a function of interpretation. While Dewey's reference to "categories" might be thought to hint, à la Kant, at the unavoidability of stereotypes when interpreting overabundant "facts," any such hint was lost on Dewey himself, who maintained, as would the later scholars of public opinion, that the problem facing the public is not too many facts but too few: "The data for good judgments are lacking; and no innate faculty of mind can make up for the absence of facts."[90]

A dearth of facts, not inevitably stereotyped selections from among too many facts: this is the difficulty Dewey thought Lippmann had so brilliantly identified. He seemed to think that Lippmann would agree that, given enough facts and appropriately flexible, rational attitudes, the public would be able to do away with its stereotypes and make intelligent policy decisions. For example, Dewey adduced a case where he agreed with Lippmann that the public had erred—Prohibition—to suggest that *Public Opinion* untenably portrayed the public's historically contingent "stupidity, intolerance, bullheadedness and bad education"[91] as if it were indefeasible. In reality, according to Dewey,

---

[86] Dewey 1922, 286.
[87] Ibid.
[88] Kloppenberg 1986, 392.
[89] Dewey 1922, 286.
[90] Ibid., 209.
[91] Dewey 1925b, 54.

such cases demonstrate that "the fundamental difficulty of democracy" is to deliver to the public a "thoroughgoing education" that will dislodge its bad mental habits—its stereotypes, as he understood the concept.[92] The "genuine problem of knowledge" to which Lippmann had pointed, Dewey thought, was getting the right facts into people's heads. For Dewey, this meant circumventing the public's stereotypes—which would hardly be possible if stereotypes are indispensable means of interpretation.

By the same token, Dewey suggested that journalists could upend the public's stereotypical thinking, as if Lippmann had not devoted strenuous efforts to exposing the necessity of journalists' own stereotypical thinking. Thus, Dewey's reviews of *Public Opinion* and *The Phantom Public* were largely devoted to proposals for media reforms that would enable journalists to carry out their stereotype-busting assignment. Prohibition was a mistake, yes, but while its proximate cause was the public's "stupidity" (a misconstrual of Lippmann's concern with *mistake*), its ultimate cause was, for Dewey, nothing more permanent than the failure of "the press" to educate the public properly.[93] He couched his proposals for media reform as attempts to remedy the ills Lippmann had diagnosed, when a true understanding of the diagnosis would have revealed Dewey's prescriptions to be the product of a fundamentally different construal of the malady.

Dewey's starting point was the domination of journalism by "advertising, propaganda, invasion of private life, the 'featuring' of passing incidents in a way which violates all the moving logic of continuity."[94] These deformities stemmed, in Dewey's view, from the fact that the newspaper owners had not yet been reckoned with. It is they "who have ability to manipulate social relations for their own advantage."[95] Until their influence was reversed, public opinion would be "casually formed and formed under the direction of those who have something at stake in having a lie believed."[96] But with the power of newspaper owners removed, public opinion could be set aright. Dewey agreed with Lippmann that journalism had failed to educate the public, but this did not mean that it would always fail. What was needed was a new form of journalism.

Reforming journalism had long been a favorite project of Dewey's. While teaching at the University of Michigan in the early 1890s, he had enthusiastically lent his support to a stillborn Ann Arbor newspaper, *Thought News*, which aimed to bring to its readers arguments for democratic socialism not by means of theoretical discussion, but by reporting "the truth about the actual conduct of [Ann Arbor's] business."[97] *Thought News* was advertised as the "one journal which shall not go beyond the fact; . . . which instead of dwelling at length upon the merely individual processes that accompany the

---

[92] Dewey 1922, 288.
[93] Dewey 1925b, 54.
[94] Dewey [1927] 1954, 169.
[95] Ibid., 168.
[96] Ibid., 177.
[97] Dewey quoted in Westbrook 1991, 54.

facts, shall set forth the facts themselves."[98] Three decades later, in his review of *Public Opinion*, Dewey maintained that a properly reformed journalism would simply report "the news as the truth," conveying "events [that are] signalized to be sure, but signals of hidden facts, of facts set in relation to one another." Once informed of these facts, "Men can act intelligently."[99] The distance between Dewey and Lippmann could not have been greater. Recall Lippmann's gibe against Sinclair, contained in the very book Dewey was reviewing. Sinclair's folly, according to Lippmann, was to overlook the illimitable complexity of society—enabling him to believe "that news and truth are two words for the same thing."[100]

The main difference between Dewey's ideas about *Thought News* and the views about journalism he expressed in the 1920s was that the latter included a dose of instrumentalist aestheticism. For example, in his review of *The Phantom Public*, he argued that journalists not only should "discover, record, and interpret all conduct having a public bearing" (a literally impossible task, according to Lippmann), but that in doing so, they should use "methods which make presentation of the results of inquiry arresting and weighty."[101] Such methods are needed, Dewey maintained, because the most serious enemies of political knowledge are the "emotional habituations and intellectual habitudes on the part of the mass of men," of which "the exploiters of sentiment and opinion only take advantage."[102] Fortunately, he wrote, "The function of art has always been to break through the crust of conventionalized and routine consciousness."[103] A new breed of journalists could purvey the facts artistically. This would get around the emotions and intellectual sloth of the stereotype-besotted public (as Dewey understood stereotypes: lazy mental habits). Artistic journalism would knock people out of their intellectual ruts. Once they were awakened, they would see the significance of the hidden facts that the new breed of journalists reported. The problem of political knowledge would be solved.

The key to this aestheticized journalism would be its separation from the profit motive. "The assembling and reporting of news would be a very different thing," according to *The Public and Its Problems*, "if the genuine interests of reporters were permitted to work freely," liberated from the class interests of their employers. With journalists' artistic and truth-seeking interests set loose, "the results of accurate investigation" could be presented in a fashion that had "direct popular appeal."[104] An aesthetically arresting

---

[98] Announcement of *Thought News* quoted in ibid., 55.

[99] Dewey 1922, 288.

[100] Lippmann [1922] 1997, 226, 228. Dewey overlooked Lippmann's condemnation of the notion that "a more or less conscious conspiracy of the rich owners of newspapers" was responsible for the sorry state of journalism (ibid., 212). If this were true, Lippmann argued, the socialist press, vigorous at the time, would be a paragon of unbiased reporting, but anyone familiar with it, he thought, would recognize that this was hardly the case (ibid.).

[101] Dewey 1925b, 54.

[102] Dewey [1927] 1954, 169.

[103] Ibid., 183.

[104] Ibid., 182–83.

journalism "would be more sensational" than even the sensationalist journalism of the day, Dewey maintained in his review of *Public Opinion*. "To see underlying forces moving in and through events seemingly casual and disjointed will give a thrill which no report confined to the superficial and detached incident can give."[105]

Dewey may well have been right about that, but it was wholly unresponsive to Lippmann's argument. Dewey was presupposing that there is no question about *which* "facts" are relevant, in which case there is no room for sincere interpretive disagreement. Thus, if the public is misinformed, the "deceptions and propaganda"[106] of capitalist newspaper owners must be at fault. By contrast, *Public Opinion* held that newspaper publishers "honestly see the world through the lenses of their associates and friends," such that published untruths or distortions are usually inadvertent.[107] Dewey completely missed Lippmann's emphasis on the inadvertence of media bias, and, more important, on the need for biased interpretation if we are to make sense of too much information. Making journalists' biases more aesthetically appealing would only make matters worse.

A subtler problem was Dewey's failure to grapple with Lippmann's reflections on economic determinism. Capitalists' material self-interest, Lippmann argued, like everything else in politics, must be interpretively constructed. Therefore, capitalists' perceptions of their interests are fallible and will vary according to the ideas of a given capitalist. "There is no fixed set of opinions on any question that go with being the owner of a factory, no views on labor, on property, on management, let alone views on less immediate matters," according to *Public Opinion*. "There is no magic in ownership which enables a business man to know what laws will make him prosper."[108] Dewey's response to this argument was to call it "the best criticism I have ever read of the doctrine of the economic determination of interest."[109] But if capitalist newspaper owners' interests are not self-evident to them, why should we think it is any different for the public's interests, as perceived by journalists? This question escaped Dewey, caught up in the Progressive commonplace that the core problem with the media was that "the privileged few," motivated by self-interest, foisted self-serving lies on the public. If this problem could be solved, journalists could artistically convey "the facts" about its interests to the public.[110]

Public Opinion as a whole might be cited as a rebuttal to Dewey's view of journalism, but the heart of this rebuttal would have to be the primacy of interpretation. "The story of why John Smith failed," Lippmann wrote, "his human frailties, the analysis of the economic conditions on which he was shipwrecked, all of this can be told in a hundred different ways. There is no discipline . . . which has authority to direct the journalist's mind

---

[105] Dewey 1922, 288.
[106] Dewey 1925b, 53.
[107] Lippmann [1922] 1997, 206.
[108] Ibid., 118.
[109] Dewey 1922, 286.
[110] Ibid., 287.

when he passes from the news to the vague realm of truth. There are no canons to direct his mind, and no canons that coerce the reader's judgment or the publisher's."[111] Dewey's failure to grasp this point, or even to recognize that Lippmann was making it, explains his insistence that institutional reforms could remedy the epistemic problem that Lippmann had identified. Lippmann was skeptical of journalism for the same reason that he was skeptical of public opinion: he could not see how either the journalist or the ordinary citizen could find a reliable interpretive basis for decoding the blooming, buzzing confusion of modern society. Responding to this type of skepticism by calling for a more gripping form of journalism, freed from the self-interested imperatives of newspaper owners, entirely missed the point.

2.4. THE FUNDAMENTAL DILEMMA OF DEMOCRATIC TECHNOCRACY

When distant and unfamiliar and complex things are communicated to great masses of people, the truth suffers a considerable and often a radical distortion. The complex is made over into the simple, the hypothetical into the dogmatic, and the relative into an absolute. Even when there is no deliberate distortion by censorship and propaganda . . . the public opinion of masses cannot be counted upon to apprehend regularly and promptly the reality of things.
—WALTER LIPPMANN, *The Public Philosophy*

Questions of science, agriculture, industry and finance, are highly technical. How many voters are competent to measure all the factors involved in arriving at a decision? And if they were competent after studying it, how many have the time to devote to it? . . . How many citizens have the data or the ability to secure and estimate the facts involved in its settlement?
—JOHN DEWEY, *The Public and Its Problems*

In the third round of the debate, however, Dewey did begin to address the epistemological issues Lippmann had raised. Indeed, at several junctures in *The Public and Its Problems*, Dewey expressed the problem of epistemic complexity with greater eloquence than even Lippmann had mustered. "The local face-to-face community," he wrote, "has been invaded by forces so vast, so remote in initiation, so far-reaching in scope and so complexly indirect in operation that they are, from the standpoint of the members of local social units, unknown. . . . They act at a great distance in ways invisible to" them.[112] As a result, he acknowledged, the policy actions endorsed by ordinary citizens may cause adverse unintended consequences. "Observations of consequences are at least as subject to error and illusion as is perception of natural objects," he said, and the resulting

---

[111] Lippmann [1922] 1997, 228.
[112] Dewey [1927] 1954, 131.

mistakes are "more harmful than the consequences which they were originally intended to control."[113]

This position was far more pessimistic than Dewey had been in his reviews of Lippmann's books. Accordingly, Dewey now added, to his calls for a new type of journalism, a plea for a new type of social science. Investigation adequate to the complexity of modern society, according to *The Public and Its Problems*, "devolves upon . . . technical experts in the sense that scientific investigators and artists manifest *expertise*."[114] "The social sciences" would have to develop the relevant expertise, and Dewey complained that they had not yet begun to do so.[115]

It is easy to underestimate the significance of this epistocratic element in Dewey's argument, impressed as we must be by his deep commitment to democracy. Yet if social-scientific experts cannot meet the high expectations he placed on them in *The Public and Its Problems*, a technocracy that does more good than harm may be impossible—so long as one allows, as he now did, that modern society is epistemically complex. Moreover, if epistemic complexity means that the truth about policy effects is counterintuitive, as suggested by his remark about unintended consequences, then it would seem that an instrumentally rational technocracy *must* be an epistocracy. For if technocratic truths are inaccessible to intuitive inspection, then the chance that an untutored voter will recognize these truths drops below .5, and the Condorcet Jury Theorem produces the conclusion that the electorate is bound to get things wrong unless it is "enlightened" by an elite that can point the way past the public's superficial impressions.

Dewey had unwittingly laid the groundwork for this conclusion (sans Condorcet) long before 1927. To insist that the people need to be enlightened by a new type of journalist, after all—as Dewey had been doing since the 1890s—is, pro tanto, to deny, at least tacitly, that the truth is self-evident to the people. However, Dewey had also been assuming that the truth would be self-evident to journalists freed of capitalist bosses. Inasmuch as he had not explained how journalists would be any better equipped than ordinary citizens to set aside their stereotypes and recognize the truth, his long-standing endorsement of a democratic technocracy led by journalists had been epistemologically incomplete: it contained within it an unacknowledged epistocratic element, but without any rationale for it.

The Public and Its Problems came to grips with this problem, at least in principle. According to Dewey as of 1927, the elites to whom the people must turn for enlightenment are not journalists, but experts distinguished by their use of a method—the scientific method—that renders their perceptions superior to those that would occur, unbidden, to the rest of us. The role of journalists, accordingly, is to convey these findings to the masses in arresting fashion. Thus, an epistemologist of technocracy must consider

---

[113] Ibid., 29–30.
[114] Dewey [1927] 1954, 208–209.
[115] Ibid., 203.

whether Dewey's vision of social science was coherent. Bracketing this issue for a few moments, however, let us pursue the threat to democracy posed by Dewey's newfound emphasis on social science.

The very purpose of science is to advance beyond what is (or seems) intuitively obvious. Scientific knowledge is, in this sense, inherently esoteric. Thus, if a reliable social science is necessary, and if it is possible, why should the nonscientists play any policymaking role at all? At best, the involvement of the people in making policy would merely ratify the conclusions of the social scientists. But at worst, the people might misunderstand scientific findings and make the wrong policy decision.

I will call this *the fundamental dilemma of democratic technocracy*. It suggests that the regulative ideal of a technocracy that recognizes epistemic complexity is to assign policymaking powers to a social-scientific elite—if such an elite can be found. One might still argue, as Dewey (and Habermas) did, that there remains an important role for the public: to specify the ends toward which technocracy should aim. But there would seem to be a strong reason to exclude the people from the process of formulating policy means to those ends: insofar as esoteric social-scientific knowledge is necessary, it is as a corrective to untutored intuitions that would, if translated into policy, do more harm than good. Therefore, to allow any space at all to the enactment of popular measures that conflict with esoteric social science would contradict the purpose of a technocracy: doing more good than harm by solving, mitigating, or preventing social problems. Restricting ourselves to the internal reasoning of a technocracy, then, the people's participation in the specification of ends should, ceteris paribus, be coupled with a social-scientific epistocracy to choose the means.

The Public and Its Problems proposed three different resolutions of this dilemma. Two of them were epistemological; none of them succeeded.

The non-epistemological resolution depended on an argument concerning motives, not knowledge. Here Dewey warned that "a class of experts is inevitably so removed from common interests as to become a class with private interests and private knowledge, which in social matters is not knowledge at all." Therefore, he contended, social scientists need to be subordinated to the people, such that they serve "the needs which they are supposed to serve."[116] Apparently, the problem with the experts' "private knowledge" is not that it is epistemically deficient, but that it would enable them to pursue their own interests at the expense of the public interest.

To subordinate the experts' interests to those of the people, Dewey offered a version of a proposal Lippmann had made in *Public Opinion*: barring the experts from offering policy advice *per se*. Lippmann had suggested that the experts' role be restricted to recording statistics about policy effects and conveying the records to policymakers.[117] Dewey likewise argued that "expertness is not shown in framing and executing policies,

---

[116] Ibid., 207, 206.
[117] Lippmann [1922] 1997, 242.

but in discovering and making known the facts upon which the former depend."[118] If experts could be restricted to the latter role, their interests could be kept from subverting their scientific function. This solution, however, was as unrealistic in Dewey's hands as it had been in Lippmann's. Surely the experts could use their superior knowledge to game the facts presented to policymakers (be they cabinet officials, as Lippmann proposed, or journalists and thus members of the general public, as Dewey proposed), manipulating their audience into enacting whatever measures they favored, including those that served their own interests. Those to whom the experts conveyed their findings could avoid being gulled only if they could see through social scientists' distortions of the facts. But if they could do this, it would entail that they had a superior command of the facts, so why would they need social scientists to begin with? According to Dewey in *The Public and Its Problems*, like Lippmann in *Public Opinion*, we need social scientists to unravel the complexity of modern society. We would not need them to do it for us if we could do it for ourselves. If we do need them, it must be because we do not know what we would need to know if we were to police them effectively. We find ourselves in the conundrum of the radically ignorant.

As if to preempt this objection, Dewey produced a question-begging defense of democratic wisdom, maintaining that "it is not necessary that the many should have the knowledge and skill to carry on the needed investigations; what is required is that they have the ability to judge of the bearing of the knowledge supplied by others upon common concerns."[119] But he did not explain why the many are likely to have this ability, let alone the ability to tell whether the experts have been corrupted by self-interest—except through a bald assertion that constituted his first epistemological argument for democratic participation in technocratic policymaking.

Dewey asserted that "it is easy to exaggerate the amount of intelligence and ability demanded to render" technocratic policy judgments. He continued: "Until secrecy, prejudice, bias, misrepresentation, and propaganda as well as sheer ignorance are replaced by inquiry and publicity, we have no way of telling how apt for judgment of social policies the existing intelligence of the masses may be."[120] The second sentence makes the first sentence sound reasonable. But it does so only by effectively negating Dewey's eloquent acknowledgments, elsewhere in the book, of epistemic complexity. Secrecy, prejudice, bias (of the lazy, avoidable variety recognized by Dewey), misrepresentation, and propaganda might, in principle, be overcome through an adjustment in motives—for example, by removing the profit motive from the newspaper industry. But the invisible action of indirect causes in a modern society—the operation of "forces so vast, so remote in initiation, so far-reaching in scope and so complexly indirect in operation that they are, from

---

[118] Dewey [1927] 1954, 208.

[119] Ibid., 209.

[120] Ibid.

the standpoint of the members of local social units, unknown"[121]—poses an epistemic problem, not a motivational one. If social scientists are needed to reveal the complex social forces that would otherwise remain hidden, it can only be because citizens' intuitive understanding of these forces is inadequate. By calling in social scientists to solve this problem, Dewey is suggesting that we, the people, cannot make sufficient sense of modern society on our own. Does this suggestion itself exaggerate "the amount of intelligence and ability" necessary to make accurate technocratic policy judgments? If so, then social science may not be necessary after all. But if not, then an unchecked epistocracy, when it comes to the determination of policy means, is the regulative ideal.

Dewey's second epistemological argument also elides the problem of epistemic complexity. "The man who wears the shoe," he points out, "knows best that it pinches and where it pinches, even if the expert shoemaker is the best judge of how the trouble is to be remedied."[122] This famous argument is as empty, upon closer examination, as it is beguiling.

Dewey is saying that ordinary people can identify the social and economic problems that beset them, but that experts will have to figure out the solutions. Note that this is the opposite of the scenario we have just examined, in which the experts deliver the facts and the public crafts, or at least judges, the "social policies" to be pursued, lest the experts be allowed to enact self-interested policies. I will return to this contradiction in Section 2.5. For now, let us examine the seemingly commonsensical shoe analogy itself.

As we saw in Chapter 1, personal experience is insufficient to establish that a social problem is significant enough to warrant public action. It would seem that the same goes for interpersonal discussion, to which Dewey turns at the end of the book.[123] When people bring contrasting personal experiences to the discussion of their metaphorical shoes, how will their disagreements be reconciled without an appeal to statistics, and other esoteric knowledge as well? Whether the metaphorical shoe is unemployment, unaffordable housing, bad education, or costly health insurance, one needs more than personal experience with the problem if one is to conclude, legitimately, that government should try to solve it. Such a conclusion entails the claim that the problem is widespread and that it is more pressing than other problems that compete for problem-solving resources. It also entails the claim that the problem is susceptible to a collective solution that would be more beneficial than it is costly. Citizen-technocrats who somehow knew all these things could dispense with the services of epistocrats. Insofar as the people need social-scientific advice—because reliable knowledge of the significance and the cause of their painful shoes, and of the efficacy and the costs of policies to relieve or prevent the

---

[121] Ibid., 131.

[122] Ibid., 207.

[123] I do not interpret his call for discussion as being intended to solve an epistemic problem, but discussion, albeit not necessarily face-to-face discussion, has taken on that role in some contemporary forms of deliberative democratic theory. See Landemore 2017.

pain, cannot be gleaned from personal observation or interpersonal discussion alone—then the people will have to be told by the experts which of its pains should be treated, not just which treatments should be attempted. If pinching shoes are not widespread, in the experts' judgment, or if they are widespread but cannot be relieved through techno-cratic action in a cost-beneficial manner, then complaints about them should be ignored, from a strictly technocratic point of view.

Suppose, conversely, that the public does *not* complain about a problem that *is* suscep-tible to technocratic correction, because the public fails to recognize an indirect, invis-ible, but remediable cause of the problem. Suppose, too, that social scientists have reliable technocratic knowledge, and that this knowledge leads them to conclude that the public *should* complain about this problem because it is widespread and relatively significant, and because its causes can be corrected, mitigated, or prevented at a lower cost than the benefits of corrective action. In such a case, it would seem necessary that the social scien-tists have the power to implement what they know to be the solution to the problem—in defiance of public indifference to it. Withholding this power from the social scientists would run counter to the purpose of technocracy.

Whether or not people complain about their pinching shoes, then, is largely irrelevant to the question of whether the painful shoes should be the object of technocratic action. Given the epistemic complexity of modern society, but assuming (as Dewey did) that this complexity is not too great for an identifiable group of experts to decipher, the logical ter-minus of technocracy is not only that this group should craft the policy means to collec-tively decided ends, but that it should specify which social problems should be addressed by collective action. This is not to say that the experts should specify the general values (such as the relief of discomfort) to be pursued, or that the people's opinions about which problems ought to be solved should be entirely disregarded. But such opinions should not be considered binding on the epistocrats, whose (putative) expertise would have to settle the question of whether a given painful shoe can be fixed without doing more harm than good. This conclusion would seem inevitable unless we abandon technocratic con-sequentialism and attribute to democracy an intrinsic value that cannot be overridden—even at the expense of unsolved social problems and of solutions that, as Dewey put it, "pile up and consolidate themselves into laws and methods of administration which are more harmful than the consequences which they were originally intended to control."[124]

Three commitments tug against each other in *The Public and Its Problems*: a commit-ment to an unstated but clearly negative-utilitarian consequentialism, in the form of a desire to solve social problems, which pulls us toward technocracy of some kind (dem-ocratic or epistocratic); a recognition of epistemic complexity, which pulls us toward the epistocratic option if one assumes, as Dewey did, that an epistemically reliable tech-nocratic social science is feasible; and a commitment to democracy, which pulls toward

---

[124] Dewey [1927] 1954, 29–30.

democratic technocracy.[125] As we will see in the next section, Dewey later came up with a form of technocracy that, at least in principle, would acknowledge the need for a social science that made visible what is too epistemically complex to be self-evident, while retaining popular control of policy. But this form of technocracy had not yet taken shape in *The Public and Its Problems*. Thus, the book's acknowledgment of epistemic complexity was more verbal than real.

2.5. DEWEY'S DEFENSES OF POLICY SCIENCE

> Even the specialist finds it difficult to trace the chain of "cause and effect," and even he
> operates only after the event, looking backward, while meantime social activities have moved
> on to effect a new state of affairs.
> —JOHN DEWEY, *The Public and Its Problems*

Let us return now from the fundamental dilemma of democratic technocracy to the question of whether even social science can solve the epistemic problems to which *The Public and Its Problems* was attuned.

On the very first page of the book, Dewey appears to back away from the uncritical empiricism that had characterized his promotion of journalistic reform in the first two rounds of the debate. Dewey now denies "that facts carry their meaning along with themselves on their face." It is not true, he writes of facts, that "their interpretation stares out at you" if you "accumulate enough of them." Thus, "no one is ever forced by just the collection of facts to accept a particular theory of their meaning, so long as one retains intact some other doctrine by which he can marshal them."[126] These remarks are consonant with the main thrust of Lippmann's political epistemology and therefore are, at least at first glance, in tension with Dewey's hopes for democratic technocracy. If the facts are consistent with many interpretations, how are citizen-technocrats to decide which interpretations are relatively accurate and which are off the mark?

A similar question might also impugn the reliability of epistocratic knowledge if social scientists, too, must grapple with competing interpretations of facts. However, Dewey denies that this is necessary. The passage about the facts not speaking for themselves opens a discussion of *natural* science in which Dewey argues that adequate scientific interpretations are not self-evident. In natural science, "the human imagination might run wild in its theories of interpretation even if we suppose the brute facts to remain the same"—but in natural science, interpretative proliferation is suppressed by "laboratory apparatus" and "mathematical technique."[127] One might therefore expect Dewey either

---

[125] At the end of *The Public and Its Problems*, he went "beyond the field of intellectual method" to defend democracy as "face-to-face intercourse." The basis of this defense was that "happiness" may be found "only in enduring ties with others" (ibid., 211, 214).
[126] Ibid., 3.
[127] Ibid.

to bemoan the absence of such devices in the social sciences or to suggest some substitute device. But it turns out that he sees no need for such devices, for he views social science as much *easier*, interpretively, than natural science.

Thus, he continues, if students of "the facts of politics" would "confine themselves to observed phenomena," it would not be difficult to obtain "a reasonable consensus"[128]—despite the absence, in politics, of laboratories and mathematics. For "the main facts of political action, while the phenomena vary immensely with diversity of time and place, *are not hidden even when they are complex*. They are facts of human behavior accessible to human observation."[129] Thus, while allowing that an interpretation-free registration of "facts" is impossible in natural science, Dewey maintains that it is possible, indeed essential, in social science.

However, several pages later comes the passage quoted earlier: "Observations of consequences are at least as subject to error and illusion as is perception of natural objects," such that "mistakes pile up and consolidate themselves into laws and methods of administration which are more harmful than the consequences which they were originally intended to control."[130] Here Dewey seems to be saying that interpreting modern social forces—or at least observing their consequences—is *more* difficult than interpreting physical forces. Yet he swings back in the other direction after a few more pages, in a passage that reveals why we should not think that the occurrence of political errors, illusions, and unintended consequences might preclude an effective technocracy:

> The formation of states must be an experimental process. The trial process may go on with diverse degrees of blindness and accident, and at the cost of unregulated procedures of cut and try, of fumbling and groping, without insight into what men are after or clear knowledge of a good state even when it is achieved. Or it may proceed more intelligently, because guided by knowledge of the conditions which must be fulfilled. But it is still experimental. . . . Political philosophy and science . . . may . . . aid in creation of methods such that experimentation may go on less blindly, less at the mercy of accident, more intelligently, so that men may learn from their errors and profit by their successes.[131]

An experimental approach to public policy, then, will not stop us from blundering, but it should allow our blunders to be corrected over time. Just as natural science replaces "cut and try" with "intelligent" laboratory experimentation, social science can replace random improvisation with genuine learning from policy experimentation. If so, then natural science and technocracy should be equally effective, on the whole.

---

[128] Ibid., 4, my emphasis.
[129] Ibid., 19, my emphasis.
[130] Ibid., 29–30.
[131] Ibid., 33–34.

The idea that natural and social science are both reliable because both are experimental is consistent, as we will see in the next chapter, with Dewey's evolutionary epistemology. And if *The Public and Its Problems* were to have contained an argument from evolutionary epistemology justifying the reliability of experimental social science, this argument would have provided a prima facie valid case for the adequacy of epistocracy. But *The Public and Its Problems* contains no such argument. When, at the end of the book, Dewey finally returns to the question of experimental policy science, he does not mention an evolutionary warrant for the reliability of experimentation in natural and social science alike. Instead he once again contrasts natural and social science, repeating the book's initial claim that intelligent political experimentation is fundamentally easier than what goes on in "the mathematical and physical sciences."[132] "When we say that thinking and beliefs should be experimental" in policy science, he explains,

> we have then in mind a certain logic of method, not, primarily, the carrying on of experimentation like that of laboratories. Such a logic involves the following factors: First, that those concepts, general principles, theories and dialectical developments which are indispensable to any systematic knowledge be shaped and tested as tools of inquiry. Secondly, that policies and proposals for social action be treated as working hypotheses, not as programs to be rigidly adhered to and executed. They will be experimental in the sense that they will be entertained subject to constant and well-equipped observation of the consequences they entail when acted upon, and subject to ready and flexible revision in the light of observed consequences.[133]

As of 1927, these four sentences constituted Dewey's entire solution to what he called "the problem of method"—that is, the problem of the method of a reliable social (policy) science. The brevity of the passage suggests how insignificant Dewey found the problem to be. The content of the passage explains why: Dewey's treatment of social science, unlike his treatment of natural science, ignored the problem of interpretation.

Given the significance of this problem in Lippmann's argument, Dewey's four sentences merit close inspection. The precise nature of the methodological "factors" listed in the sentences is fuzzy, but the passage as a whole suggests that Dewey had in mind two general guidelines to direct policy scientists: open-mindedness and careful observation. Let us consider them in turn.

The directive to be open-minded tracks Dewey's view of stereotypes as lazy stupidities—not inescapable means of interpretation. Lippmann argued that stereotypes grow from the need to screen out most of the overabundant information available to us, and that the dogmatism to which stereotypes can lead is inadvertent: we become increasingly convinced that the world is a certain way because the stereotypes screen in

---

[132] Ibid., 7.
[133] Ibid., 202–203.

information congruent with that picture while screening out incongruent information. If so, it is pointless moralizing to demand that we try to force ourselves to be open-minded, that is, to screen in information that conflicts with our stereotypes. We haven't done so already not because we didn't want to, but because we can't. Stereotypes render the universe of overabundant information intelligible by identifying a fraction of the universe as indicative of the totality, even while they make other information incomprehensible or implausible. Thus, the very thing that makes stereotypes indispensable—their interpretive function—makes it impossible to *will* ourselves to accept the plausibility of stereotype-incongruent information. If we could somehow force ourselves to see all information as equally intelligible and equally plausible, we would have no need for stereotypes in the first place.

Dewey's second methodological principle is equally unrealistic. We must, he counsels, constantly and carefully "observe" the consequences of policy experiments. This principle contradicts his contention, at the beginning of the book, that in politics "observations of consequences are at least as subject to error and illusion as is perception of natural objects."[134] A scientific method of policy analysis must include a means of correcting such errors. Otherwise, the injunction to observe the consequences of policy experiments will amount to another empty exhortation. The question is how to observe these consequences *reliably* if error and illusion are indeed common. Had Dewey factored into his account of social science the epistemic complexity that he articulated regarding natural science, he might have recognized that social-scientific observations may be ambiguous, subject to a variety of interpretations, or biased. If so, however, an appeal to careful observation is as pointless as an appeal to open-mindedness.

Of course, one might want to reply, with Dewey, that social science is indeed easier than natural science, because the facts of politics can be "observed." By this, he seems to have meant that human beings, unlike atoms or cosmic rays, can be seen with the naked eye, as can their bodily actions. But the sheer observability of people taking actions is irrelevant if, as he also maintained, "the local face-to-face community has been invaded by forces so vast, so remote in initiation, so far-reaching in scope and so complexly indirect in operation that they are, from the standpoint of the members of local social units, unknown," as "they act at a great distance in ways invisible to him."[135] Such passages suggest agreement with Lippmann's view that modern society is "an invisible and most stupendously difficult environment."[136] But if so, then it is unclear how the open-minded observation of what is visible to the naked eye—people, as visible bodies—will produce a reliable social science.

Given this gap in Dewey's reasoning, it is not surprising that the problem of overabundant information (leading to wild interpretive fancy), which he thought is controlled

---

[134] Ibid., 29–30.
[135] Ibid., 131.
[136] Lippmann [1922] 1997, 236.

in natural science by means of mathematics and laboratories, does not even crop up in his portrayal of social science. Thus, he makes no room for legitimate ex post interpretive disagreement about the consequences of public-policy experiments. Instead, he takes a naively realistic approach to the observability and conclusiveness of "the facts" from which technocratic citizens are to make inferences about which policies to enact ex ante. He does allow for legitimate disagreement, but it is not disagreement about the empirical consequences of past policy experiments; it is solely disagreement about what to do if "the facts" show, ex post, that a policy experiment failed to achieve the desired results. In that event, a new experiment will have to be tried, and

> differences of opinion in the sense of differences of judgment as to the course which it is best to follow, the policy which it is best to try out, will still exist. But opinion in the sense of beliefs formed and held in the absence of evidence will be reduced in quantity and importance. No longer will views generated in view of special situations be frozen into absolute standards and masquerade as eternal truths.[137]

Here Dewey might be thought to be answering Lippmann—if Lippmann had said that people form political beliefs in the absence of empirical evidence, or that their beliefs universalize historically contingent truths. But Lippmann's main point was, on the contrary, that people's convictions about the truth are not even reliable in their own time and place because they stem from the use of stereotypes to interpret empirical evidence. We need stereotypes, according to Lippmann, to bring order to the blooming, buzzing confusion *of facts*. Lippmann, then, was questioning our ability to "observe the consequences" of our political actions without the assistance of interpretive stereotypes; and he was questioning the adequacy of our interpretive stereotypes, which may misrepresent the realities at issue, and which may be circularly confirmed when they screen in confirmatory evidence while screening out incongruent evidence. Only by overlooking these issues when it comes to public policy, as opposed to natural science, was Dewey able to envision a technocratic social science that experimentally generates manifest truths—the inarguable "results" of policy experiments already conducted—and then advise the social scientist to be sure to allow that things may change in the future, calling forth an endless need for fresh experiments.

2.5.1. The Problem of Counterfactuals

Dewey's uncritical empiricism besets both sides of the contradiction, noted earlier, between the scenario in which experts come up with the facts while the public devises the policy solutions, and the scenario in which experts devise policy solutions to the fact,

---

[137] Dewey [1927] 1954, 29–30.

pointed out by citizens, of their ill-fitting shoes. In both scenarios, technocracy works reliably well only if experimentation delivers to policymakers—citizen-technocrats in the first case; epistocrats in the second—facts that speak for themselves. If the facts do not speak for themselves, then either the public or the social scientists will face the problem with which Dewey began his book, in reference to natural science: a wild profusion of interpretations of the facts.

Policy experiments *always* require interpretation because something very important is always hidden: the counterfactual. What would have happened in the absence of the experiment? If the experiment is a macroeconomic stimulus, one might "observe" that unemployment continues to rise after its implementation. But this observation is worse than useless without a theory that suggests whether unemployment would have risen even more without the stimulus. Technocrats, then, face the practical problem of deciding which changes in extant statistics are effects of a given policy experiment. The mere temporal coincidence of a statistical change with an antecedent experiment does not establish causation any more than the failure of an experiment to reverse a statistical trend shows that the experiment failed; other variables may explain the spurious appearance of success, and countervailing factors may have intervened to create the spurious appearance of failure. Conversely, all too much is observable in the absence of an ordering theory. An endless variety of observations can be made after a policy experiment occurs. Consider the vast range of economic statistics that are now collected. Only resource constraints keep this range from extending to infinity.

If a technocracy cannot determine why or even whether a given policy experiment failed, its next experiment *will* be a matter of "cut and try," not intelligent learning. The determination of what would have happened without the experiment, and the determination of which observations are relevant, do not follow from the facts themselves, but from social scientists' interpretations of the facts. Normative theorists of technocracy must therefore ask whether these interpretations will tend reliably to track reality; and whether, given a profusion of interpretations, a polity can reliably decide which one to accept.

The Public and Its Problems offered no answers to these questions. The notion that social scientists can gaze out at all the things happening in a modern society and "observe" those that stem from a specific policy experiment entails that, somehow or other, they can do what natural scientists sometimes do—but that social scientists can do it without the help of laboratories, mathematics, *or* interpretations. In 1927, Dewey breezed past this problem with his assurance, so like his old confidence regarding *Thought News*, that "the facts" relevant to public policy can easily be identified. On this unsatisfactory note, the debate with Lippmann closed.[138]

---

[138] I have discussed only the parts of the debate that are relevant to the normative epistemology of technocracy. Therefore, I have ignored the bulk of *The Public and Its Problems*, which takes up the question of how "publics" of those affected by the indirect consequences of private or public action might become cognizant of

2.5.2. Controlled Policy Experimentation

Four years later, however, Dewey sharply broke from the simplistic positions he had taken during the debate. "Social Science and Social Control" (1931), an essay in *The New Republic*, directly repudiated the view of social science he had expressed in *The Public and Its Problems* (although he did not announce this fact).

In this essay, Dewey acknowledged that a "morass of speculative opinion" would follow from attempts to interpret the effects of uncontrolled policy experiments, the very thing he had (in effect) denied in *The Public and Its Problems*. Once again, he adduced the example of Prohibition. In his review of *The Phantom Public*, he had used Prohibition to suggest that Lippmann confused the temporary "stupidity" of the public with a permanent defect in its epistemic capacities. In "Social Science and Social Control," however, Dewey presented a more pessimistic view, according to which—even ex post—conflicting interpretations of the success or failure of Prohibition are reasonable. This interpretive ambivalence, according to Dewey, stems from the fact that Prohibition was

> not an experiment in any intelligent scientific sense of the term. For it was undertaken without the effort to obtain the conditions of control which are essential to any experimental determination of fact. The Five Year Plan of Russia, on the other hand, whether noble or the reverse, has many of the traits of a social experiment, for it is an attempt to obtain certain specified social results by the use of specified, definite measures, exercised under conditions of considerable, if not complete, control.[139]

Apparently, then, Dewey no longer believed that open-mindedness and the observation of experimental policy effects would suffice. Just as in natural science, *controlled* experimentation would be necessary in policy science.

Thus, while he declined to say directly whether the Soviet Union's version of central planning was "noble or the reverse," Dewey made it clear that he would welcome central planning in the United States.[140] After coyly suggesting that he was "not arguing for the desirability of social planning and control"—its desirability, he maintained, "is another question"—he immediately went on to say, clearly referring to the Great Depression, that

---

their own existence as such. This is relevant to the evaluation of technocracy only if such publics would then have a reliable means of deciding how to prevent, mitigate, or undo unwanted indirect consequences.

[139] Dewey 1931, 276.

[140] I use "central planning" as the term is used by economists, which is congruent with what Dewey meant by "social planning." A central plan imposes one elaborate blueprint of activity on an entire economy, just as a scientist imposes elaborate controls in a laboratory. Such plans are "central" in the sense that the plan is imposed from a metaphorical center, but the plan could be arrived at by a dictator, a deliberative council, ordinary political debate, a mass plebiscite, or decentralized debate followed by one of these decision methods. Thus, the totalistic scope and detail of a centralized social plan do not preclude democracy.

"those who are satisfied with present conditions and who are hopeful of turning them to account for personal profit and power will answer the question [of central planning] in the negative." Wealthy capitalists, in other words, would oppose central planning, leaving little doubt where Dewey stood. He concluded the essay even less ambiguously:

> If we want something to which the name "social science" may be given, there is only one way to go about it, namely, by entering upon the path of social planning and control. Observing, collecting, recording and filing tomes of social phenomena without deliberately trying to do something to bring a desired state of society into existence only encourages a conflict of opinion and dogma in their interpretation.[141]

Dewey recognized, then, that policy experimentation requires interpretation, and that social scientists will not necessarily tend to converge on an accurate consensual interpretation. That outcome could be ensured only by making society into an experimental laboratory.

Thus, it seems that Dewey had in mind vesting the state with the absolute power over society that the Soviet Union claimed to enjoy, but for epistemic reasons. Such a state could, in principle, so arrange things that only one independent variable, the experimental policy, would be altered during a five-year period. That way, all changes that occurred after a policy experiment was instituted could plausibly be attributed to the policy alone. One might add that the same method could also (in principle) solve the problem of detecting unintended consequences. The intention of a government's central plan might be to see whether a certain measure, M, would or would not cause result X. Regardless of whether X happened, however, if unexpected phenomenon Y occurred, there would be little doubt that Y had been caused by M—so long as one had controlled every other aspect of the society that might have caused Y.

Dewey's endorsement of central planning was a needed corrective to *The Public and Its Problems*. There he had naively asserted that retrospective policy science is easier than natural science because it does not pose interpretive problems. Having now recognized that retrospective policy science would actually confront very serious interpretive problems—as in the case of retrospective analyses of Prohibition—he called upon controlled experimentation to work the wonders it seemed to work for natural scientists.

However, while controlled policy experimentation might be thought to resolve interpretive disputes in the abstract, it would confront two rather serious drawbacks in practice.

---

[141] Dewey 1931, 277. Six years later, Dewey ([1937] 1987, 489) castigated Lippmann for objecting to social planning in *The Good Society* ([1937] 2005), a book Dewey flayed for giving "encouragement and practical support to reactionaries." This is remarkable given Dewey's abandonment of central planning in 1939—which suggests that the left and central planning have no necessary connection, a suggestion I take up in Chapter 7 and the Afterword.

First, the number of social problems—and plausible solutions—that could be solved would be very small, since each successive five-year plan could rigorously test but a single solution to a single problem. (Otherwise, confounding interactions might be introduced.) If there were, say, 15 social problems and four plausible solutions to each of them, it could take 300 years to test them experimentally through five-year plans. Perhaps one might defend this result as acceptable, since after (at most) three centuries our descendants would live in a society improved in 15 different ways. But during those 300 years, all other changes within the societal laboratory would have to cease. Otherwise the experimenter could not even hope to settle interpretive disputes, since other variables might account for changes she would like to attribute to the experiment. To preclude a "morass of speculative opinion," subnational experiments to solve all other problems would have to be forbidden during the course of a given policy experiment. Yet Dewey believed, not unreasonably, that all of life involves experimental problem-solving. In that case, all of life would have to be frozen during each five-year plan so that any observed changes could be linked to the single policy experiment underway. In exchange for the possible solution of one problem in five, ten, 15, or 20 years, the billions of problems that would otherwise be solved daily by experiments performed *by individuals* would have to wait.

Second, of course, we would have to give even more power to the state than was actually bestowed on virtually any Stalinist regime, all of which—save China during the Great Leap Forward, and perhaps North Korea during the twentieth century—tolerated black markets and other deviant (uncontrolled) behaviors that would ruin the experimental control Dewey sought.[142] In exchange for solving social problems, we would trade away the blessing of living our lives without being constantly surveilled and supervised, disciplined and punished. For without draconian behavioral controls, we might act in ways that would spoil the precondition of the experimental method: laboratory control. Life in such a society would be a totalitarian nightmare worse than any actually witnessed in the twentieth century. The social policing necessary to ensure experimental control would be oppressively intrusive, and the constraints on individual problem solving intolerable.[143]

It is a testament to Dewey's intellectual honesty that he was willing to contemplate such a scenario rather than fuzzing over the requirements of a truly scientific technocracy. But if we do not want to sacrifice human life on the altar of science, we would seem to be stuck with uncontrolled technocratic experimentation.[144] This would also appear

---

[142] See, for example, Scott 1998, 350–351.

[143] Mentioning the totalitarian implications of central planning of this sort does not transcend the internal, negative-utilitarian perspective of technocracy. To live in a society in which every single action was decided from the center, lest it upset the experimental control (even if this were possible), would be quite an unhappy experience, violating the negative-utilitarian imperative of technocracy—for people such as ourselves. One might ask, however, following Marx, whether a true species being would not enjoy conforming to the social plan, and indeed whether, for such a being, conformity would not be constraining.

[144] I discuss another option, randomized field tests, in Chapter 4.

to mean that we are stuck with the conflicting interpretations that Dewey blamed on the lack of scientific control. Without controlled experimentation, we cannot expect social science to deliver conclusive observations. Instead, we can expect it to generate long and possibly endless debate among social scientists using different theoretical paradigms to interpret less-than-conclusive evidence.

Dewey seems to have reached this very conclusion by 1939. With the Depression grinding on, despite the many policy experiments in which the US government had engaged, he gave up on policy science—yet he now declared allegiance to a new version of epistocracy. "The faculty of reason or of common sense with which the optimistic rationalism of the eighteenth century supposed men to be equipped," according to his *Freedom and Culture*, "would not go far in judging causes and effects of political and legal action at the present time."[145] For relief from this difficulty, he turned not to journalists, nor to open-minded scientific observers of policy experiments, nor to central planning, but to "an intelligent and capable civil service."[146] For "the economic situation is so complex, so intricate in the interdependence of delicately balanced factors, that planned policies initiated by public authority are sure to have consequences totally unforeseeable—often the contrary of what was intended."[147] Moreover, "social events are sufficiently complex ... that the development of effective methods of observation, yielding generalization about the correlation of events, is difficult."[148] Borrowing a metaphor from Lippmann, Dewey pointed out that "attention and interest are not freely ranging searchlights that can be directed at all parts of the natural universe with equal ease."[149]

Thus, 12 years after the conclusion of the debate, Dewey had come to see the real difficulty as too much information and too many plausible interpretations of it—just as Lippmann had seen it. Yet he did not explain how civil servants could solve this problem any better than could ordinary citizens, journalists, or social scientists lacking experimental control. How can civil servants be expected so to direct their attention as not to produce a biased picture of a given problem?[150]

Perhaps Dewey failed to ask this question because he continued to attribute biased interpretations to intellectual conservatism, not to the deeper problem he had finally

---

[145] Dewey [1939] 1989, 55.

[146] Ibid., 56.

[147] Ibid., 53.

[148] Ibid., 91.

[149] Ibid., 105. Cf. Lippmann [1922] 1997, 229.

[150] Dewey may have been thinking of what Charles Lindblom and David Cohen (1979, 12) would later call bureaucrats' "usable knowledge," i.e., their experiential seat-of-the-pants knowledge: their "common sense, casual empiricism, or thoughtful speculation and analysis"—their *phronēsis*, as opposed to their *epistēmē*. But important as *phronēsis* undoubtedly is, it is no substitute for *epistēmē*. *Phronēsis* may well teach bureaucrats how to "get things done" politically or institutionally. But I am assuming that technocrats (whether citizen-technocrats or epistocrats) know how to get things done in that sense. If they do not, this is an additional problem for technocracy. But even if they do, they would still face the problem of deciding what *should* get done, i.e., which policy means to given ends should be adopted.

acknowledged. The searchlights of attention and interest, he wrote, "operate within certain channels, and the general state of culture determines what and where the channels are."[151] Once again, it seems, he was blaming transitory cultural narrowness for what Lippmann had argued were inherent epistemic limitations. I think we must conclude that, despite the striking evolution of Dewey's thinking about technocracy in the 1930s, he failed to come up with a formula that would solve the epistemological problems that Lippmann had identified.

In the first two rounds of the debate, Dewey had tried to turn the epistemological problem over to journalists, but this was naively realistic. In the third round, in which he attempted to acknowledge epistemic complexity, he invoked a new social science as the answer, but the public would be in no position to argue with social scientists; epistocracy would triumph over democracy except in the sense that the public could establish the general ends that epistocrats should pursue, and could voice suggestions about which problems should be solved. More important for our purposes, an epistocracy guided only by the injunction to observe open-mindedly would not solve the problem of interpretation that Lippmann had identified.

Ironically, though, the central planning that Dewey endorsed in 1931, while entailing a hideous form of state power, veered away from the road to epistocracy he had been following. At least arguably, the results of totalitarian experiments could be reliably interpreted by ordinary citizens, given that only one variable at a time would be in play. Central planning thus offered a logical and democratic solution to the problem of interpretation, albeit an unfeasible and undesirable one. However, Dewey's subsequent retreat to civil-service epistocracy left him essentially where Lippmann had been in 1922: endorsing a form of epistocracy that, like Lippmann's information bureaus, could not meet the challenge posed by epistemic complexity.

---

[151] Dewey [1939] 1989, 105, my emphasis.

Politics is more difficult than physics.

—ALBERT EINSTEIN

3

Technocracy and Interpretation

STRANGELY, DEWEY FAILED to recognize that Lippmann had created a new, political branch of the "industry of epistemology"[1] that had long been the main target of Dewey's own philosophy. Had he been aware of this fact, he might have reacted more cogently and carefully to the epistemological problem that Lippmann had underscored. All Dewey would have needed to do is draw on what I will call his evolutionary epistemology.[2]

As no attention has been paid to this puzzle in the scholarly literature, I will venture a hypothesis about it. By the time *Public Opinion* was published in 1922, it had been more than two decades since Dewey's evolutionary epistemology had taken shape. Toward the end of the nineteenth century, he had concluded that natural selection bequeathed to us an all-purpose problem-solving capacity, "intelligence," that not only ensured our ancestors' survival but eventually gave rise to experimental natural science.[3] In addition, as we have seen, he thought that social problems are easier to unravel than are the problems tackled by natural science. It would seem to follow that if our evolved intelligence can create a reliable natural science, it can create an even more reliable policy science (or "social science," in Dewey's terminology). However, Lippmann too had, at least initially, thought that a reliable policy science (grounded in statistics) is feasible. In the face of Lippmann's scientism, Dewey might logically have seen no reason to defend his own

---

[1] Dewey [1917] 2011, 122.
[2] I borrow the term "evolutionary epistemology" from Munz 1985; Radnitzky and Bartley 1987; and Jarvie 1988. These writers, however, had something more specific in mind than the vague Darwinism deployed by Dewey.
[3] See Dewey [1898] 1975.

Power Without Knowledge. Jeffrey Friedman, Oxford University Press (2019). © Oxford University Press. DOI: 10.1093/oso/9780190877170.001.0001

analogy between natural and social science, let alone to insist that the analogy is plausible because of the evolution of our intelligence.

Still, it was unfortunate that Dewey missed the chance to confront Lippmann's skepticism with his own, Darwinian alternative. Natural selection presupposes environmental pressures on species, to which their traits may be more or less adaptive. Thus, if Dewey had argued for the reliability of social science on the basis of our evolved intelligence, he would have drawn attention to the environment to which this trait is supposed to be adapted: modern society. The debate might then have confronted the question of precisely what it is about modern society that (according to Lippmann) makes it epistemically complex, and whether this ontological something might make it too epistemically complex for even intelligent, evolved human beings to understand and predict.

Lippmann and Dewey both accepted that epistemic complexity is real, but neither was compelled to explore the reasons for this complexity in any depth. That is what I will do in this chapter. The conclusion I will reach is that modern society may be too opaque to be successfully manipulated by a technocracy, for the modern environment is primarily constituted by human action. Human actions are driven by human ideas, and human ideas are, as a practical matter, unpredictable—to some degree. The question for Part II, then, will be whether technocrats are likely to be able to deal with this degree of unpredictability.

The road to Part II will follow some twists and a lengthy detour. Section 3.1 will construct a rebuttal to Lippmann of the type Dewey might have mooted if he had recognized that Lippmann was turning Dewey's lifelong nemesis, epistemological doubt, against technocracy. Section 3.2 will explore how Lippmann might have responded to this rebuttal, drawing on *Public Opinion* and, to a lesser extent, *The Phantom Public* to derive several theses about the *ideational determination* of human actions. In defending these theses, I will sketch a picture of the ontological complexity of modern minds, and thus the pragmatic unpredictability of the society created by those minds. Here I will invoke certain features of human history that explain the heterogeneity of the *interpretations* produced by people in the modern world, and thus the unpredictability of the actions that follow from these interpretations.

Section 3.3 is an excursus on the methodological implications of the previous section. It contrasts Charles Taylor's methodologically collectivist form of interpretivism against the methodology I derive from Lippmann, which I call "epistemological individualism." Section 3.4 proposes that intellectual history, broadly defined, is the model of an epistemologically individualistic social "science," in that it is attuned to people's heterogeneous ideas; but that this fact militates against the reliability of social science as traditionally practiced, which bears almost no resemblance to intellectual history (a theme to be taken up in Part II). Moreover, while intellectual history, broadly defined, is a good model, even it cannot achieve the reliable knowledge, let alone the reliable predictive knowledge, that a technocracy requires. However, Section 3.5 points out that people's ideas are sometimes homogeneous, and that their actions are sometimes more homogeneous than their ideas might suggest. These facts might enable a judicious, empirically oriented technocracy to make limited, reliable behavioral predictions. Part II will explore the likelihood of such a technocracy.

3.1. DEWEY'S EVOLUTIONARY EPISTEMOLOGY

Reflection is an indirect response to the environment, and the element of indirection can itself become great and very complicated. But it has its origin in biological adaptive behavior and the ultimate function of its cognitive aspect is a prospective control of the conditions of the environment.

—JOHN DEWEY, "The Development of American Pragmatism"

By the time Lippmann published *Public Opinion*, Dewey had spent decades trying to counter epistemological doubt. In a typical passage from 1906, he deplored modern philosophers' transformation of "the Greek conception of two orders . . . *within* existence," one "the domain of knowledge," the other "the territory of opinion, confusion, and error," into two separate and mutually unapproachable realms of existence. Modern philosophers had fixed "the region of the 'unreal,' the source of opinion and error," in the realm of " 'subjective states,' 'sensations' and 'ideas' " that could not be guaranteed to correspond to the objective world. In making the subject-object dichotomy unbridgeable, Dewey continued, modern philosophers had retained "the Greek conception of two orders of existence," but "instead of the two orders characterizing the 'universe' itself, one *was* the universe, the other was the individual mind trying to know that universe." He concluded that "this scheme would obviously account for error and hallucination; but how could *knowledge,* truth, ever come about on such a basis? The Greek problem of the possibility of error became the modern problem of the possibility of knowledge."[4] Where modern epistemologists assume that knowledge claims are suspect until proven innocent, Dewey sided with the Greeks (as he interpreted them) in holding that knowledge claims should be assumed reliable until proven false.

This argument reflected a key commonality between the two main periods of Dewey's career: the Hegelian period, which ended during the mid-1890s, and the Darwinian period, which began then and lasted until his death in 1952. In both periods, Dewey held that knowledgeability rather than ignorance is the default human condition. First the dialectic, then the theory of natural selection showed, in Dewey's estimation, that humanity possesses a tendency toward knowledgeability. Therefore, skeptics must do more than ask how we can know. They must show why we cannot.

In 1882, when Dewey had recently begun graduate studies in philosophy, he wrote to his college mentor that for empiricism, in contrast to Hegelianism, "nothing exists for the

---

[4] Dewey [1906] 1977, 188.

subject except . . . sensation or impression." Consequently, "nothing can be known of real being, and the result is skepticism, or subj. idealism, or agnosticism." Unlike the empiricists, however, Hegel "takes *the facts* & endeavors to explain them—that is to show what is necessarily involved in knowledge." Thus, Hegel reaches "the conclusion that subject and object are in organic relation, neither having reality apart from the other." This approach, it seemed to Dewey, is "science as opposed to nescience," as it replaces doubt with knowledge.[5] In effect, Hegel had reversed the modern transformation of the "Greek" acknowledgment of the possibility of error into the suspicion that error may be ubiquitous. By integrating subject and object, Hegel made what we (moderns) think of as "subjective" perception tend, if only diachronically, to reflect objective reality—"the facts" from which Hegel began. This presumption of human knowledgeability was preserved when Dewey exchanged Hegel for Darwin and Idealism for natural science.

Dewey's defense of natural science against epistemological doubt was, in part, historical. Across the very centuries during which empiricist philosophers tried unsuccessfully to overcome their worries about our knowledge of anything but the cogito, natural science had delivered astonishing knowledge of the external world. According to modern epistemologists, however, this knowledge is of questionable validity because it originates outside the self-knowing subject, who is epistemically severed from the external objects that scientists claim to know. Dewey argued, in contrast, that scientific knowledge is real enough; only a default epistemological skepticism had kept modern philosophers from embracing it.

Strictly speaking, Dewey was begging the question against the modern philosophers: according to them, after all, we cannot be sure that scientific knowledge is real knowledge. However, Dewey supplemented his historical argument with perhaps the best available defense of (or explanation of) the reliability of natural science, even now. This defense is premised on two ideas: that we are creatures of nature, dependent on interaction with the natural environment; and that we are evolved creatures whose interaction with the environment selects for adaptive abilities and reliable knowledge. The union of these two ideas is what I call Dewey's evolutionary epistemology.

To survive in a given environment, Dewey assumed, a creature's interactions with it must, on the whole, be successful.[6] Thus, we should expect this creature's descendants, over time, to accumulate adaptations that enable increasingly successful engagements with the environment. "Settled and regular action" by naturally selected beings "must contain an adjustment of environing conditions; it must incorporate them in itself."[7] Such adjustment builds on reliably accurate, evolved knowledge of the environment, whether encoded in instinct and habit or consciously registered in thought. Dewey

---

[5] Dewey to H. A. P. Torrey, October 5, 1882, quoted in Westbrook 1991, 19; my emphasis.

[6] Dewey, however, did not distinguish between day-to-day success in mundane activities, success in passing on one's genes to reproductively successful descendants, and the success of a species in surviving.

[7] Dewey 1921, 84.

extrapolated this evolutionary approach to natural science. "The adaptations made by inferior organisms, for example their effective and coordinated responses to stimuli, become teleological in man and therefore give occasion to thought," which "has its origin in biological adaptive behavior."[8] Scientific knowledge is the result of thoughtfully using the experimental method that is natural to evolved humanity.

The evolved origins of human thought also underwrote Dewey's confidence in political knowledge, including knowledge of how to solve social problems. In an essay published three years before the debate with Lippmann began, Dewey wrote that, "in order to get an intellectual warrant for our [political] endeavors"—that is, "a reasonable persuasion that our undertaking is not contradicted by what science authorizes us to say about the structure of the world"—we must ask the following questions:

> How shall we read what we call reality (that is to say the world of existence accessible to verifiable inquiry) so that we may essay our deepest political and social problems with a conviction that they are to a reasonable extent sanctioned and sustained by the nature of things? Is the world as an object of knowledge at odds with our purposes and efforts? Is it merely neutral and indifferent? Does it lend itself equally to all our social goals, which means that it gives itself to none, but stays aloof, ridiculing as it were the ardor and earnestness with which we take our trivial and transitory hopes and plans? Or is its nature such that it is at least willing to cooperate, that it not only does not say us nay, but gives us an encouraging nod?[9]

In this essay, Dewey indicated his agreement with the last possibility—nature's encouraging nod—only indirectly, by stating his commitment to democracy and thus, by implication, his optimism about the people's ability to solve their social problems. This epistemological optimism would not have served as an argument against Lippmann, as it would have begged the question of whether democracy, or rather democratic technocracy, is in fact adequate to its problem-solving task. But Dewey also argued in the other direction, from evolution to human competence in dealing with the environment. For example, he maintained that a natural organism equipped by evolution with "intelligence" is able to infer from "what is surely known to something else accepted on its warrant."[10] "The plain man," by implication, can reliably predict the "objective consequences" of his actions—"their bearing upon future experiences."[11] For he can "use given and finished facts as signs of things to come," and can "take given things as evidences of absent things." He can thus "form reasonable expectations."[12] Inasmuch as he "can read

---

[8] Dewey 1925a, 10. Here "teleological" clearly means "aimed at ends," such that the resulting actions are efficiently caused and preveniently informed, albeit teleologically inspired.

[9] Dewey [1919] 1998, 75.

[10] Dewey 1910, 26.

[11] Dewey [1917] 2011, 116–117.

[12] Ibid., 118.

future results in present on-goings," his "bias grows reasonable."[13] This could have been the basis of a rebuttal to Lippmann.

Dewey was not saying that the plain man's biases grow infallible. He noted, in a passage that might in fact have influenced Lippmann, that the human condition is punctuated by "ignorance which is fatal; disappointment; the need of adjusting means and ends to the course of nature." These failures are Dewey's grounds for recognizing as "indubitable" the "existence of an external world": our disappointments establish the persistence of a gap between our knowledge and the environment that frustrates our intentions.[14] Lippmann too, as we saw, viewed our disappointments as signs of a gap between the real environment and the pseudo-environments built up in our minds.[15] However, Dewey maintained that despite the ignorance suggested by our disappointments, "matter of fact positivistic knowledge . . . gradually grows up,"[16] because the environment enforces "a certain minimum of correctness under penalty of extinction."[17] Our knowledge becomes reliable over evolutionary time to the extent that it reflects unchanging environmental uniformities. And when the environment changes, experimentation, or "the method of intelligence," can be brought to bear. "That which was unconscious adaptation and survival in the animal, taking place by the 'cut and try' method until it worked itself out, is with man conscious deliberation and experimentation."[18] In response to a change in the otherwise-regular environment, human beings envision various behavioral responses and then try them out. Dewey saw such experimentation as the prerequisite of both an intelligent politics and an intelligent science. In both, we use our evolved capacity to understand and control the environment with which we interact. In contrast to both empiricists and rationalists, who see intelligence as a matter of "copying the objects of the environment," for Dewey the function of intelligence is "a prospective control of the conditions of the environment."[19] While he admits that "the realness of error, ambiguity, doubt and guess pose a problem," he proposes that "it is a problem which has perplexed philosophy so long and has led to so many speculative adventures, that it would seem worthwhile, were it only for the sake of variety, to listen to the pragmatic solution." This solution is to recognize that "the appropriate subject-matter of awareness is not reality at large, a metaphysical heaven to be mimeographed at many removes upon a badly constructed mental carbon paper which yields at best only fragmentary, blurred, and

---

[13] Ibid.

[14] Ibid., 119.

[15] See Lippmann [1922] 1997, 17: "If the connection between reality and human response were direct and immediate, rather than indirect and inferred, indecision and failure would be unknown."

[16] Dewey [1920] 1948, 10.

[17] Ibid.

[18] Dewey [1898] 1975, 53.

[19] Dewey 1925a, 10. In *The Public and Its Problems*, Dewey ([1927] 1954, 12) shrank the definition of "intelligence" down to "the observation of consequences as consequences, that is, in connection with the acts from which they proceed."

erroneous copies. Its proper and legitimate object is that relationship of organism and environment in which functioning is most amply and effectively attained; or by which, in case of obstruction and consequent needed experimentation, its later eventual free course is most facilitated."[20] Here, as in the passage on the difference between Greek and modern epistemology, Dewey shifts the burden of argument vis-à-vis the epistemological skeptic. While he acknowledges that an obstruction may occur in our otherwise functional, learned relationship with our environment, he portrays such an event as exceptional. In response to it, we experiment intelligently and interpret the results in a manner that frees us from the obstruction—returning us, eventually, to a sort of epistemic equilibrium, however temporary it might be. Only on the basis of this equilibrium as the default can we assume that our knowledge tends to be reliable until proven otherwise—or until the environment changes. At that point, we can draw on our knowledge of other environmental regularities to envision an experimental solution to the obstruction and then test it. Obstructions to our predictive knowledge stem from relatively small changes in the environment, not from anything that our intelligence might be unequipped to handle through experimentation.

If Dewey had recognized the skeptical thrust of Lippmann's argument, he could easily have mobilized this version of pragmatism against it. He could have said that just as we are able to deal with the physical environment successfully because we evolved in interaction with it, the same should be true of the societal environment. Just as, in our interactions with nature, we "can use given and finished facts as signs of things to come" and "can take given things as evidences of absent things, and can, in that degree, forecast the future,"[21] we should be able to forecast the effects of policies enacted to solve problems caused by societal change. This ability to forecast reliably would reduce the many conceivable policy options to a manageable few with which we could experiment. The proliferation of possible interpretations of the evidence would be dramatically narrowed by the application of our evolved intelligence, which would detect environmental regularities that would rule out most interpretations.

Thus, Dewey's evolutionary epistemology would have constituted a plausible defense of technocracy against Lippmann's doubts—albeit not, in the end, an adequate one.

3.1.1. Evolutionary Epistemology and Evolutionary Psychology

Before getting to the inadequacy, it is important to avoid a misunderstanding. We need to distinguish Dewey's evolutionary epistemology from the evolutionary *psychology* that has flourished since the 1980s.

---

[20] Dewey [1908] 1998, 129.

[21] Dewey [1917] 2011, 118.

Unlike evolutionary psychologists, Dewey did not posit anything like modules of cognition that have been passed down genetically from our "environment of evolutionary adaptation" (EEA), which is usually identified as the Pleistocene.[22] This is fortunate for Dewey's position. Had he propounded a version of evolutionary psychology, it could have been rebutted by pointing out that recent human activities have caused the modern environment to change so rapidly that our genes are unlikely to have caught up—a popular notion called the adaptive-lag hypothesis. Had Dewey relied on evolution having selected for modules specifically adapted to the Pleistocene (or to pre-Pleistocene EEAs), then the possibility would arise that these modules are not in sync with the novel circumstances of modernity and are therefore maladapted to the epistemic demands of a technocracy.

The adaptive-lag hypothesis has recently been brought into question, for it turns out that genetic adaptation has continued at a rapid pace during the Holocene, which dates from the introduction of horticulture and agriculture about 12,000 years ago.[23] However, the continuation of human evolution during the Holocene does not imply that recent evolution could have fostered the spread of new mental modules that would help solve peculiarly modern social problems. Someone who understood how to solve these problems—or who understood modern society itself—better than everyone else (a superlative economist or sociologist, for example) would not thereby gain a significant reproductive advantage: one's reproductive success in a modern society is in no significant manner affected by one's ability to understand that society or its problems at a global level. Therefore, whatever modules might make possible this person's superior understanding would not come to dominate the gene pool of technocratic decision-makers.

Evolutionary psychology is inherently a dysfunctionalist paradigm when applied to modern conditions insofar as they differ from those that characterized our EEAs; this is reflected in the adaptive-lag hypothesis. Were evolutionary psychology to be applied to technocracy, its dysfunctionalist implications would show up in the irrelevance of an understanding of modern social problems to one's reproductive success. Dewey's evolutionary *epistemology*, however, is inherently functionalist; this is why it might serve as grounds for trusting in the reliability of our knowledge of modern society, rather than grounds for doubting it. In this sense, Dewey was well served by his inattention to whether specific cognitive traits may have been adapted to particular environmental conditions encountered in past eras.

In place of special-purpose mental modules tailored to specific environmental conditions, Dewey posited intelligence as a general characteristic that enables our species to tackle whatever environmental changes frustrate our purposes. "Intelligence" in his usage—the ability to draw appropriate predictive inferences from "observed

---

[22] E.g., Barkow et al. 1992; Pinker 2002. I refer to our EEAs in the plural because adaptations from the environments that preceded the Pleistocene should also, ceteris paribus, have been carried forward into our genome.

[23] Holden and Mace 1997.

facts"—could explain our ability to make spectacular advances in understanding and controlling the natural environment. Similarly, it might, when applied to the social environment, enable us to construct a reliable policy science.

3.1.2. Is Evolutionary Epistemology Utopian?

In Dewey's evolutionary epistemology, our intelligence brings us knowledge of such facts as "that certain things are foods, that they are to be found in certain places, that water drowns, fire burns, that sharp points penetrate and cut, that heavy things fall unless supported, that there is a certain regularity in the changes of day and night and the alternation of hot and cold, wet and dry."[24] Advanced scientific knowledge is merely a refinement of mundane knowledge of this sort, using ever-more-careful versions of the experimental method.

The question, however, is whether such knowledge is of the type that technocrats need. It is a long way from knowing that sharp points penetrate and cut to knowing how to prevent a financial crisis. Precisely because Dewey did not suggest that intelligence is narrowly tailored to solving specific problems in our EEAs, there is the risk that in applying his evolutionary epistemology to the technocratic control of behavior in a modern society, we would be conflating an intelligence adapted to solving problems in the domain of rocks and sticks with an intelligence so wide as to be indistinguishable, for practical purposes, from omniscience. Nothing would have been of greater reproductive advantage to our ancestors than an intelligence that would enable them to learn precisely what they needed to know about any problem they faced. Yet one cannot infer, from the advantageousness of such epistemic powers, that our forebears possessed them and passed them down to us. Dewey's evolutionary epistemology may therefore prove too much. Surely there might be limits to what we can reliably know, despite the fact that our ability to know is a product of natural selection. Yet it is hard to discern exactly where the limits of our evolved capacity for knowledge might lie.

One way forward might follow the long tradition of drawing philosophical distinctions between the natural and social sciences. One might thus argue that evolutionary epistemology explains the success of natural science but could not underwrite a comparably successful social science. Yet when dealing with technocratic variants of social science, it is difficult to make such distinctions without begging the question. For example, one cannot very well maintain, following the pattern set by Dilthey, that while natural science pursues explanation or prediction, social science pursues understanding—and is therefore incompatible with technocratic prediction. A technocratic social science would indeed seek to discover causal explanations and to make predictions, but we cannot rule

---

[24] Dewey [1920] 1948, 10.

out these ambitions as unfeasible simply because we have chosen to *define* social science as hermeneutical rather than explanatory or predictive.

I will follow a different path. I will not deny that the ultimate epistemic goal of technocracy, reliable behavioral prediction, is obtainable in principle. But I will contend that in practice, reliable behavioral predictions may be out of reach because of the determination of conscious human behavior by human ideas. Ideas themselves might be predictable, not just hermeneutically comprehensible, if we had reliable knowledge of their causal antecedents. But in modern societies, such knowledge may, as a practical matter, be beyond our grasp.

3.2. HETEROGENEOUS IDEAS AND ENVIRONMENTAL UNPREDICTABILITY

> As rational beings it is worse than shallow to generalize at all about comparative behavior
> until there is a measurable similarity between the environments to which behavior is a
> response.
> —WALTER LIPPMANN, *Public Opinion*

While evolutionary epistemology may explain the proto-scientific ability of our intelligence to respond adaptively to environmental change, the environment must be largely stable for this to work. Otherwise, we would be unable to focus on one or a few elements that capture our attention by departing from our learned expectations and posing obstacles to our plans. In addition, after the environment changes, the basis upon which we imagine experimental responses must be inferences from "what is surely known" about the stable, pre-change environment.[25] Otherwise, experimental actions to deal with change would be no better than random "cut and try" (or random policy selection).

Thus, Dewey's evolutionary epistemology depends on the uniformity of nature as much as does the natural science that grows, in his view, out of intelligent lay experimentation. A controlled natural-science experiment is uninstructive beyond its time and place unless we assume that physical conditions elsewhere are homologous to conditions in the laboratory. Similarly, a defense of technocracy by means of evolutionary epistemology presupposes a social environment that, when tested through experimentation, can form the basis for accurate predictions of the effects of future technocratic actions. The social environment must therefore not only be stable, for the most part; it must be held together by underlying causal forces that justify inferences from one locality to another.

However, the environment that technocracy attempts to understand, and explain, and predict—in the service of attempting to control it—is the product of, and largely consists in, human behavior. Even an intelligence equipped by evolution to understand and

---

[25] Dewey 1910, 26.

anticipate human behavior would find itself unable to produce reliable scientific generalizations about the societal environment if human behavior, instead of being *knowably* uniform, varies in its uniformity according to determinants—such as ideas—that are, as a practical matter, unpredictable. Therefore, if, in response to Lippmann, Dewey had put forward his evolutionary epistemology, Lippmann would have had a counterargument ready to hand. He could have denied the knowable uniformity, and thus the predictability, of human ideas.

Lippmann raised the question of a heterogeneous environment at the beginning of *Public Opinion*. His answer is essential to his understanding of the epistemic complexity of modern society. Thus, after his first mention of the fictive or "pseudo" nature of the stereotypes on which our minds rely, he was immediately moved to ask whether we might not circumvent "the use of fictions" by means of "direct exposure to the ebb and flow of sensation." Recall that his answer was that unmediated observation

> is not a real alternative . . . for the real environment is altogether too big, too complex, and too fleeting for direct acquaintance. We are not equipped to deal with so much subtlety, so much variety, so many permutations and combinations.[26]

In other words, direct exposure to the environment—unmediated by interpretations (stereotypes)—is unfeasible, because the environment is—as far as we can tell—heterogeneous.

Exactly why would such heterogeneity block unmediated comprehension? The extracted passage provides a two-part answer.

First, the environment addressed by politics is literally too large to be understood by anyone in its totality: there is too much society, hence too much information, to comprehend. "In any society that is not completely self-contained in its interests and so small that everyone can know all about everything that happens," Lippmann had argued two pages prior, "ideas deal with events that are out of sight and hard to grasp."[27] To understand such events, these ideas must abstract away from the blooming, buzzing confusion of the totality.

It might appear that this claim could be granted by a Deweyan defender of policy science. After all, the physical universe, too, is vast and mostly out of sight—yet scientists have managed to abstract away from heterogeneity to predict many aspects of the behavior of the totality. However, the indispensable assumption behind such predictions, based as they are on empirical evidence, is that whatever empirical observations we make in one part of the universe (such as a laboratory) are applicable elsewhere, in the parts whose behavior we seek to predict. This assumption cannot survive Lippmann's second claim, if it is true: that the modern social environment varies unpredictably, which is to

---

[26] Lippmann [1922] 1997, 10.
[27] Ibid., 8.

say that its heterogeneity is of a type that blocks us from being able to extrapolate *reliably* to the unobserved parts of the whole on the basis of the parts we can observe. The size of a modern society will prove fatal to our understanding of it, let alone our explanations and predictions of it, if the parts we see—the human actions that we witness—turn out to be discontinuous with those we do not. Understanding, explanation, and prediction will all, in a vast society, be unreliable if the behavior we observe is unrepresentative of the behavior we cannot observe.

"In putting together our public opinions," Lippmann wrote, in a passage I have quoted before,

> not only do we have to picture more space than we can see with our eyes, and more time than we can feel, but we have to describe and judge more people, more actions, more things than we can ever count, or vividly imagine. We have to summarize and generalize. We have to pick out samples, and treat them as typical.[28]

If we did not treat our samples as typical, "the bewildering variety of our impressions" would render us helpless.[29] But while people's data samples might (conceivably) be typical, and thus reliable, when dealing with "the customs and more obvious character of the place where they lived and worked," it is different when "dealing with an invisible environment" about which the truth "is not self-evident" and must be inferred.[30] In such cases, the assumption of knowable uniformity may be unwarranted. In Lippmann's view, as participants in modern society, we are "gambling with the behavior of unseen men."[31] Yet we usually fail to recognize this, for we impute predictability to them by projecting onto them our theories about the behavior we see (or think that we see) when observing others. Captivated by "vivid aspects of a whole which [we] can rarely imagine," our "prevailing vice is to mistake a local prejudice for a universal truth."[32]

This homogenizing impulse is, in effect, an attempt to make the environment seem "legible" enough, in James C. Scott's terminology, to be amenable to technocratic manipulation.[33] When we give in to the homogenizing impulse, we confuse locally valid (or at least compelling) stereotypes with universally valid ones. Locale, here, is an epistemological concept, not an ontological one. An epistemically local stereotype is an interpretation imposed on a wider whole by anyone, anywhere, based on whatever partial sample of information the interpreter has encountered in the past, interpreted so as to shape it into a coherent stereotypical basis for reaching conclusions about the whole. On the

---

[28] Ibid., 95.

[29] Ibid.

[30] Ibid., 164, 202.

[31] Lippmann [1925] 1927, 165.

[32] Ibid., 171.

[33] Scott 1998.

other hand, if this procedure is inadequate, the problem must be ontological. Insofar as our local stereotypes are epistemically unreliable, it must be due to something real that causes the behavior of "unseen men" to be different from—unexpectedly heterogeneous, in comparison to—the behavior we are led to expect by our interpretation of an epistemically local sample of information. Such an ontological source of epistemic complexity would ensure that our predictions of human behavior in the unseen parts of society illicitly assume that the whole is more knowable than it really is.

The potential problem with the homogenizing impulse is not that it must overlook heterogeneity as such, but that it must overlook *unpredictable* heterogeneity. Natural scientists are able to make reliable predictions about the interaction of large numbers of heterogeneous factors by first discovering the patterns of their behavior and interaction locally, and then assuming that these patterns reflect universal regularities. Factors as heterogeneous as temperature, humidity, and barometric pressure each affect the weather, but they do so in predictable fashion inasmuch as the patterns of interaction discovered locally apply universally. The heterogeneity at which Lippmann was pointing is of a different order. Even if we stipulate, as I will now do, that all the heterogeneous processes affecting human behavior are nomological, and even if we stipulate, as I will now do, that we might someday know the laws according to which these processes operate and interact, we will remain unable to make reliable behavioral predictions if the laws describe operations on inputs that are not only heterogeneous but too inaccessible for us to know in any detail. While knowledge of the nomology plus knowledge of heterogeneous inputs would—stipulatively—produce reliable predictions, knowledge of the nomology without knowledge of heterogeneous inputs will—predictably—produce unreliable predictions.

Had Lippmann made this point, Dewey would surely have demanded to know what these mysterious inputs are. Yes, people are more complicated than rocks and sticks, but what aspect of human behavior is *so* complicated—or, rather, so epistemically complex (opaque)—that our evolved intelligence cannot figure it out? Such a question would have required Lippmann to elaborate his implicit ontology of social heterogeneity.

Part of what he might have said is again suggested early in *Public Opinion*, where he considered the possibility that human behavior is driven by knowable but diverse psychological proclivities—that is, by *predictable* heterogeneity. At the time, Freudianism was making rapid strides among American intellectuals. (Looking back on his triumphant 1909 visit to the United States, Freud would write that "my short visit to the New World encouraged my self-respect in every way. In Europe I felt as though I were despised but in America I found myself received by the foremost of men as an equal. . . . This was the first official recognition of our endeavors.")[34] Lippmann did not challenge the validity of Freudian theory, but he denied that it, or any other theory of human behavior, could deal

---

[34] Freud 1935, 102–103.

with the unknown heterogeneity of *ideational* inputs.[35] Thus, he suggested that "before we involve ourselves in the jungle of obscurities about the innate differences of men, we shall do well to fix our attention upon the extraordinary differences in what men know about the world."[36] If somebody's

> atlas tells him that the world is flat he will not sail near what he believes to be the edge of our planet for fear of falling off. If his maps include a fountain of eternal youth, a Ponce de Leon will go in quest of it. If someone digs up yellow dirt that looks like gold, he will for a time act exactly as if he had found gold. The way in which the world is imagined determines at any particular moment what men will do. It does not determine what they will achieve. It determines their effort, their feelings, their hopes, not their accomplishments and results. . . .
>
> Try to explain social life as the pursuit of pleasure and the avoidance of pain. You will soon be saying that the hedonist begs the question, for even supposing that man does pursue these ends, the crucial problem of why he thinks one course rather than another likely to produce pleasure is untouched. . . . The theory of economic self-interest? But how do men come to conceive their interest in one way rather than another? The desire for security, or prestige, or domination, or what is vaguely called self-realization? How do men conceive their security, what do they consider prestige, how do they figure out the means of domination, or what is the notion of self which they wish to realize? Pleasure, pain, conscience, acquisition, protection, enhancement, mastery, are undoubtedly names for some of the ways people act. There may be instinctive dispositions which work toward such ends. But no statement of the end, or any description of the tendencies to seek it, can explain the behavior which results.[37]

Lippmann put his finger here on an aspect of the human condition that has received all too little attention. If we do not know someone's specific ideas in a given situation, we cannot know how she will behave, even if psychology tells us precisely how her thoughts and feelings will develop, nomologically—because thoughts and feelings do not arise *de novo*. Thoughts are cognitive responses to ideational inputs; feelings are somatic responses to the inputs or to the resulting thoughts. Without first *believing* that she has struck gold, the prospector would not be jumping for joy, but the science of psychology cannot tell us whether a given person in a particular time and place will have this belief or not. Moreover, psychology cannot tell us that this belief will produce a joyful somatic response, because such a response depends on the thought's interaction with a whole skein

---

[35] Lippmann [1922] 1997, 17.
[36] Ibid., 15.
[37] Ibid., 16–17.

of other thoughts—a web of beliefs—that are, in turn, contingent on countless messages heard, understood, agreed with, remembered, and combined with one another into an interpretation of the value of a certain mineral. Whatever the psychological laws that turn the resulting interpretation, added to the perception of gold, into a feeling of joy, these laws will predict entirely different interpretations, different feelings, and different actions if the ideational inputs are different. All the psychological knowledge we might ever hope to gain, therefore, will not enable reliable behavioral predictions if we lack knowledge of people's ideas. Accordingly, insofar as people's ideas are heterogeneous, we cannot simply assume that a given person will react to a given objective situation (even if we know the details of this situation) just as those people we have observed have responded to it, nor as we ourselves have responded to it. If we do not know the actor's subjective perceptions and interpretations (which I group under the rubric of "ideas"), we cannot predict the resulting actions.

In truth, I think we have to admit that we do not even know our own ideas well enough to predict many of our future actions (under specified conditions) completely. But the modern social environment is constituted by the actions of strangers—Lippmann's "unseen men."[38] If these anonymous others' ideas tend to be unpredictably heterogeneous, then so, ceteris paribus, will be their actions. Ideational heterogeneity, then, in conjunction with ideational determinism—that is, the determination of actions by ideas, and of ideas by the reception and interaction of other ideas—is the basis for a critique of the notion that the environment created by human actions can be predicted. For if the environment is determined by others' actions, if their actions are determined by their ideas, and if their ideas are unpredictably heterogeneous, then so, too, will be the environment. Of course, if ideas were accessible to observation, as temperature and humidity are, their heterogeneity would not be a problem. And if ideas were heterogeneous but randomly distributed, we could use the laws of probability to know the environment ideas will eventually produce, by means of action. But the gold prospector's ideas are not random, nor are those of anyone else. If ideas are heterogeneous, non-random, and unobservable, the prediction of the environment created by human behavior will be problematic.

I should note that Lippmann's argument for ideational determinism was intended to target only our *political* ideas. He was arguing that these ideas are responses to a pseudo-environment, not to the real environment. The pseudo-environment consists of interpretations built up from doubly mediated ideas, in the potentially closed loop described in Chapter 2. But the point applies not only to political actors, such as journalists, citizen-technocrats, and epistocrats, but to the objects of their actions: the people whose actions must be reliably predicted by a legitimate technocracy, one that does more good than harm. The objects of technocratic action are, as much as the

---

[38] Lippmann [1925] 1927, 165.

subjects—the technocrats—in the same position as the gold prospector, the sailor, the conquistador, the hedonist, the self-interested agent, and the seeker after security, prestige, domination, or self-realization. Technocratic subjects and objects alike are ideational creatures trying to make sense of their surroundings. Insofar as their surroundings are constituted by people's actions, and people's actions are determined by people's ideas, and people's ideas are unpredictably heterogeneous, they all face a difficult task. It is reasonable, then, to apply, to the nonpolitical behavior that technocracy must control, and thus predict, Lippmann's point about the unpredictable heterogeneity of political behavior.

3.2.1. *Theses on Lippmann*

Let me thus apply the point by setting out three Lippmannesque theses about the ontology of the modern societal environment. While the theses seem to be implicit in *Public Opinion*, I am not claiming that they amount to what Lippmann "really meant." I do think, however, that he easily could have signed on to them.

For expository purposes, my statement of the theses will continue to use the term *ideas* to subsume "perceptions," "beliefs," and "interpretations," along with hypotheses, theories, strokes of inspiration, and assumptions, implicit and explicit. Little of importance will rest upon the terminology, as the basic assumption is that *any* of the ideas in an agent's web of "beliefs" (or ideas) may contribute to the agent's interpretation of her circumstances and, therefore, her reaction to them. For her understanding of, say, a hypothesis, as well as her attribution of plausibility to it, will depend on other ideas in her web—assumptions, perceptions, beliefs, and interpretations alike—that seem to her to bear on this hypothesis; while, in turn, each of these other ideas will be interpreted and treated as plausible in the light of still other ideas. Thus, the interpretive determinants of any given idea may ramify outward to her entire web of beliefs. In a nutshell, the problem for technocracy is that these ideas, and thus the resulting interpretations, are likely to vary unpredictably from person to person, or so I will suggest. Thus, there should be unpredictable interpretive heterogeneity among the agents whose actions technocrats are trying to predict, and, even more crucially, between these agents and the technocrats themselves—all of whom are human and thus subject to heterogeneous ideational inputs. Insofar as the agents' heterogeneous ideas are inaccessible to the technocrats, and insofar as the agents' ideas determine the interpretations that motivate their actions, unpredictable ideational heterogeneity creates a potentially lethal epistemic problem for technocratic prediction.

I will begin by discussing the first two theses together.

Thesis 1 (interpretive determinism). At least insofar as an agent is acting deliberately, her interpretation of which action is advisable under her perceived circumstances will determine which action she takes.

Thesis 2 (ideational determinism). An agent's interpretation of which action is advisable under her perceived circumstances will be determined by the web of those of her ideas that seem (to her) relevant to (a) the circumstances themselves, (b) the purpose of actions that (for her) count as normatively advisable in those circumstances, and (c) the effects[39] that seem (to her) likely be produced by such actions in those circumstances. Also playing a part will be the implicit assumptions and other tacit ideas that stand behind ideas about (a), (b), and (c).

From the first thesis it follows that, to the extent that technocrats attempt to predict agents' deliberate actions, they must predict the agents' interpretations of their circumstances. This makes the technocrat's task much *more* difficult than that of the natural scientist, contra Dewey. Inanimate physical entities do not act on the basis of interpretations of how best to respond to their objective circumstances; they act on the basis of the objective circumstances themselves. Unlike natural scientists, then, technocrats need to anticipate not the objective circumstances to which behavior will respond, but agents' subjective interpretations of how they should deal with whichever objective circumstances they find relevant to their actions (which itself is a matter of interpretation). The ultimate question for technocracy, as a practical matter, is whether technocrats can reliably predict such interpretations—lacking access to the agents' webs of belief, and thus the ideas that determine the agents' interpretations, according to the second thesis. Put differently, the question is how to make the pseudo-environment constituted by the technocrats' webs of belief correspond to the pseudo-environments constituted by the agents' webs of belief— even though, as I will contend, these webs will may well be heterogeneous, such that any given technocrat may interpret things differently than any given agent, ceteris paribus.

I will suggest in Chapter 4 that epistocracy has the internal appearance of legitimacy only because epistocrats ignore that question. In practice, this means that instead of interpretive and ideational determinism, epistocrats default to psychological determinism (Freudianism is but one example), or, more often, economic determinism. These objectivist forms of determinism, with which we can also group various kinds of sociological structuralism and functionalism, have the effect of treating the agents whose behavior is being predicted as if they were mindless machines—suitable objects of control by Berlin's robotic technocrats, who "automatically" know what to do. It is assumed that the actions of the robotic objects controlled by robotic technocrats can be predicted with reference to such determinants as the robotic objects' internal drives, economic or psychological, or with reference to external social forces, factors,

---

[39] Of course, not all actions are instrumental to some end; some actions are ends in themselves. In such cases it may seem that the actions' anticipated effects are irrelevant. But effects need not be empirical. Any duty or normative tradition that identifies certain types of action as obligatory still requires that those who wish to obey the duty or tradition identify when and whether circumstances are such as to enjoin the obligatory action, so that the effect of acting in a certain way will be to fulfill the duty or follow tradition.

structures, or systems that govern them, as physical laws govern iron filings; or, in undertheorized, positivist iterations, with reference to whatever "objective" (statistically constructed) variables the technocrat can think to correlate with the machines' behavior. Epistocracy relies, then, for its appearance of legitimacy, on ideationally dehumanizing those it attempts to control. In Chapter 6 I will suggest that in a more complicated way, the same is often true of democratic technocracy.

Thus, an epistemological critique of technocracy can be said to entail a form of humanism. But this form of humanism need not rely on moral considerations external to technocratic reason, nor on such traditional humanistic ideas as the notion of free will. Indeed, the notion of free will is directly antithetical to the critique of technocracy I will be developing, for an agent whose action stemmed from her free (underdetermined) will would lack sufficient reasons for action: that is to say, ideational determinants.[40] Human minds, however, are saturated with reasons for action, and we know that these are sufficient to determine their actions because otherwise (lacking sufficient reasons for an action) a human being would be unable to act. Like Buridan's Ass, she would be unable to "choose." However, the determination of actions by reasons will not allow us to predict the agents' actions if we do not know what their reasons are. This is what *may* make them unpredictable, even in the absence of free will—if these reasons are interpersonally heterogeneous and inaccessible.

By contrast, a free will *must* be unpredictable because of its spontaneity, that is, its underdetermination. Thus, if one were to insist that the will is free, or that human beings are creative in a sense that is *not* reducible to the opaque yet fully determined interplay of the ideas in their webs of belief, there would be no need for an investigation of internal technocratic legitimacy. True spontaneity would pose an insurmountable barrier to technocratic efforts at behavioral prediction, case closed. However, to believe in such spontaneity is to believe in uncaused causes: determinants of action that come from nowhere to close the putative gap between reasons and actions. A premise of all modern science, including the project of behavioral prediction, is that there are no uncaused causes. A critique of technocracy based on free will or genuine spontaneity, then, would be external to technocracy. An internal critique must treat free will as a myth, in that all human actions have efficient causes that therefore *could* be predicted, in principle; while recognizing the evidence that those causes are, in significant part, ideational, which may raise serious problems for technocracy, in practice.

This evidence is of the following sort. When I believe it advisable to make a bodily motion of which I am physically capable, I do it. This is the causal sequence, from belief to physical action, that governs much of our conscious lives. A recognition of the ubiquity

---

of this causal sequence is the minimal element of humanity we must acknowledge if we are to notice that technocratic reason may regularly misfire.

The fundamental fault of technocratic reason, then, at least according to the internal critic, is not a moral one—the immorality, as some might argue, of thinking of people as machines. After all, people might *be* machines, in the relevant sense, and it would be unscientific to insist that we not think of them as such because it is somehow immoral to do so, or unseemly. Rather, the fundamental problem with technocratic reason, at least from an internal vantage point, is that it cannot deal with the peculiarly ideational nature of the human "machine."

Thesis 3 (ideational heterogeneity). The ideas, and thus the interpretations, that determine agents' deliberate actions, as well as the ideas of the technocrats attempting to predict and control agents' actions, vary from person to person to some extent, making each person's actions somewhat unpredictable to the others.

Let us consider this thesis conditionally. *If* there is ideational heterogeneity, it would tend to produce some degree of behavioral unpredictability, given the other two theses. Ideational heterogeneity between my web of beliefs and yours would keep me from knowing how you will interpret your situation, and thus how you will act in response to it. Even if I know what your situation is, then—itself a difficult matter, if you are anonymous to me, as are most agents to the technocrats attempting to predict their behavior—I cannot know how you will subjectively interpret it, and thus how you will act in response to it, if you and I are ideationally heterogeneous. Moreover, even if I could somehow know the full contents of your web of beliefs right now, I would have to have learned these ideas in the same interpretive sequence as you did if I were to have any hope of predicting their implications for your future thought and action. Therefore, heterogeneity in the sequence of ideational exposures would block predictability just as effectively as heterogeneity in the contents of different webs of belief produced by these exposures.

Consider a 14-year-old whose first exposure to a compelling picture of society (at T_1) came from *The Communist Manifesto*, leading her to explore longer works by other critical theorists—all interpreted through a web of beliefs initially shaped in large part by Marx; but who then, at age 18 (T_2), happened to read *Atlas Shrugged*, followed by other libertarian writers (say, as an assignment in a college course). The interpretations of society produced by her web of beliefs at T_3, when she is 22, are likely to be very different from those produced at T_3 by the web of beliefs of someone who, as a 14-year-old, read Ayn Rand first, leading her to explore other libertarian writers during the next four years, only getting to Marx and other critical theorists at age 18—even if, by the time she was 22, she had read exactly the same list of works as had her counterpart at T_3. For the sequence in which these works were encountered would ensure that at each point along the way, the interpretive context in which a given item on the list was read would be cumulatively and radically different between the two people. As Lippmann put it, "In human conduct the smallest initial variation often works out into the most elaborate differences."[41] Assuming the truth of this claim, technocrats would need access to the entire prior history of an agent's encounters with various relevant ideas at $\{T_1 \ldots T_n\}$ in order truly to understand her relevant web of beliefs in the present, let alone predict her future beliefs and thus her actions. *If* we commanded the complete history of someone's relevant ideational exposures, then, given the determination of her current and future ideas by the nomological interaction of these exposures in her web of beliefs, we would achieve perfect understanding of her current ideas and Laplacean knowledge of her future ones (assuming we could also know all of the intervening exposures), and thus perfect knowledge of her future behavior. But as a practical matter, that would be even more difficult than mind reading. In practice, we cannot know what a current agent's past ideational exposures were, nor the interpretive sequence in which they occurred. Therefore, we face an immense practical difficulty in attempting to predict her future ideas or the behavior they will produce.

The heterogeneity of people's ideas should not be written off as random noise that can be dealt with through probability theory. Ideational heterogeneity does not have random causes that would produce a normal distribution. *Idiosyncratic* ideas, which is what we are discussing, are not random ideas. They are ideas that have an interpretive, path-dependent logic of their own; behavior caused by this logic is not random (although it may seem to be random because we cannot easily understand it, lacking access to the webs of belief that cause it). Nor are we entitled to assume that ideational heterogeneity will merely produce *negligible* perturbations from a central tendency—even if we do not claim to be able to predict the scope of these perturbations statistically—as we cannot know if there is such a tendency, or what it might be, lacking a full sequential knowledge of agents' relevant ideational exposures. It is doubtful that it even makes sense to speak of "randomness" when it comes to fully determined systems such as the human mind (absent freedom of the will). For this reason, the generalizations produced by modern social science always work well until they suddenly stop working well, or at all. People, unlike physical particles, can change their minds.

3.2.2. *Predictable Sources of Unpredictable Ideational Heterogeneity*

This critique presupposes, however, that ideational heterogeneity is in fact a significant aspect of the modern mind. The following considerations help to sustain the conclusion that it is:

1. Toward the beginning of the Holocene, the spread of agriculture allowed social stratification to occur. The production of an agricultural surplus made it possible to maintain cultural (ideational) elites who, like military and bureaucratic

---

[41] Lippmann [1922] 1997, 260.

elites, were not wholly preoccupied with food production. Cultural elites must have generated ideas of far greater complexity than had been possible before. (Specialization will do that—even though it will not necessarily produce *better* ideas.)

2. In the Paleolithic, culture had been a congeries of ideas invented by small bands of people who, being illiterate, could pass down only those ideas that could be remembered or encoded in oral tradition, ritual, or art. Ideational complexity must therefore have experienced another leap forward, even beyond that produced by the activities of cultural elites, once writing was invented approximately five millennia ago.[42] When they could be written down, the ideas produced by cultural elites could accumulate over time and build up limitlessly, unconstrained by the bounds of memory.

3. Once *mass* literacy came about, the number of *diverse* ideas that might reach a member of a given society would have risen exponentially. Similarly, the translation into a given vernacular of works produced by cultural elites writing in other languages expanded the universe of written work far beyond the point where anyone could master a significant portion of it. Consequently, each literate person would have been increasingly likely to be exposed to a somewhat different stream of ideas than any other literate person would experience.

A recent estimate has it that electronic devices now enable people to read about 100,000 words daily.[43] No two people, however, are reading precisely the same words. To the extent that the ideas expressed in these words enter their webs of belief, the effect is bound to be somewhat heterogeneous.

4. Before the advent of city-states, people lived in hunter-gatherer bands small enough that everyone with whom one was acquainted would have been extremely well known to her.[44] Close observation and discussion must have rendered people fairly predictable to one other, just as we now are able to predict, with tolerable reliability, the behavior of our intimates—despite the opacities caused, for us, by the first three factors. City-states, however, were too large to allow everyone to be personally acquainted; and city-states saw a diversification in the experiences interpreted by their various inhabitants that were inaccessible to other inhabitants. Thus, city dwellers would have—to some considerable degree—lost the ability to make reliable behavioral predictions about most of those with whom they came into contact. The same holds for us: while the

---

[42] Scott 2017, 140.

[43] Howard 2018.

[44] Turner and Maryanski 2008, 57; Mameli 2007, 26. On the transition from hunting and gathering to the city-state, see Scott 2017.

ideas of even the closest lovers are not completely pellucid to each other, as one moves outward to friends, acquaintances, and occupational associates, toward anonymous participants in the same culture, and finally toward anonymous participants in other cultures, transparency of belief and predictability of behavior should decline radically, ceteris paribus. As a practical matter, lacking personal knowledge of the overwhelming majority of people in a modern society, we cannot know anywhere near all the ideational influences on them. Therefore, their webs of belief should tend to be not only heterogeneous but opaque—to us, as observers of them.

These factors are not supposed to constitute a complete list. Their additive effect, however, should be apparent. They amount to an ontological explanation of unpredictable ideational heterogeneity in the modern world, or what Brian Fay calls the "pragmatic epistemic unpredictability of human thought."[45] Taken together, the factors suggest that, insofar as human actions are determined by human thought, technocrats are, as a practical matter, poorly equipped to predict them. Yet such predictions are required of technocrats. They must predict the behavioral effects of technocratic policies if they are to weigh their benefits against their costs. If technocrats are poorly situated to make such predictions reliably, technocratic policies are likely to generate unanticipated costs, in the form of unintended behavioral consequences.

3.2.3. The Question of Frequency

Thus, a recognition of ideational heterogeneity grounds an internal critique of technocracy—assuming, however, that ideational heterogeneity is not only significant, but so significant, i.e., so *frequent*, that it can be expected to produce (presumptively adverse) unintended consequences that are of sufficient *magnitude* as to outweigh the benefits of technocratic action. Yet a critic of technocracy on the basis of ideational heterogeneity might seem to be unable to make reliable claims about its frequency or about the magnitude of the resulting consequences. Such claims would constitute predictions of the very type whose reliability the critic is calling into question. Insofar as others' ideas are inaccessible to me, I cannot establish with any precision how frequently they will be different from my own, nor, therefore, how great will be the magnitude of unintended consequences of the actions caused by those ideas. I can no more establish these things than I can establish that the valence of unintended consequences is likelier to be negative than positive, as discussed at the end of Chapter 1. These are known unknowns.

---

[45] Fay [1983] 1994, 102. As Fay writes, "The possible influences on the minds of people are practically innumerable, and the amount and intensity of interaction between such collections [of individuals] so great, that the idea that a human group might be isolated enough so that a scientific prediction about its conceptual developments might be forthcoming sounds like a mad millenarian dream" (ibid.).

Borrowing a page from that discussion, though, it would seem that expecting the critic of technocracy to assume the burden of argument here would be asking too much. Technocrats claim to know that the policies they advocate will do more good than harm. When a critic points to a factor, such as ideational heterogeneity, that might plausibly be expected to confound this knowledge *when it obtains*, it would seem that defenders of technocracy should assume the burden of showing either that this factor will rarely obtain or that, while it may be ubiquitous, it will generally be rendered harmless by some other factor.

In Section 3.5, I will consider a defense of the latter type: the suggestion that factors such as homogenizing norms might render behavior manageably predictable, despite frequent ideational heterogeneity. Part II will then explore whether either epistocrats or citizen-technocrats can be expected to detect such norms, or other neutralizing factors, without downplaying ideational heterogeneity or ignoring it altogether. If they can, then the magnitude of predictably unpredictable behavioral effects could be reduced, and it is not inconceivable that it would shrink to the point where it would be outweighed by the benefits of technocracy.

Let me turn here, then, from the magnitude of unintended consequences to the frequency of the ideational heterogeneity that might cause such consequences. It seems to me that factors such as the four enumerated previously (there are undoubtedly others) suffice to establish *a presumption of ideational heterogeneity*, for the following reason. Insofar as our ideas are not innate, they have human origins. Only if there were some unitary human idea generator, however, would the resulting ideas be uniform. If the messages we receive are heterogeneous, and assuming that the psychological processing of these messages is nomological, the outputs (the messages that we understand and allow, as it were, into our webs of belief, as well as the ideas that emerge once we think about these messages) should be heterogeneous as well. The four factors, then, can stand in for any human source of diversity in the ideas that enter our minds. Given diverse ideational inputs, we have no reason to posit uniformity as the default assumption about the outputs, leaving us with the default assumption that they will tend to be heterogeneous.

We can run a check on the presumption of ideational heterogeneity by reflecting on our interpersonal experiences, in which two or more minds encounter one another. It seems to me that the lesson of these experiences is, overwhelmingly, that no two minds are uniform. One indication of this is the frequency with which we disagree with those we encounter, which (I suspect I will not encounter many readers who disagree with me about this) is high. If I may generalize from my experience, one *always* disagrees about at least one thing with any other person with whom one is acquainted, and usually about many things—often, nearly everything. Conversation with a given other rarely discloses only ideas *that one had already thought of.*

The emphasized words, however, suggest a second indicator of ideational heterogeneity. Conversation does not always express (or imply) disagreement, but even when we do not disagree with one another, we are frequently surprised by one another's ideas. One does not have to be *startled* by another's ideas to be surprised by them in the weak sense I have in mind, but discovering startling ideas in another's web of belief is not all that unusual, either. In less startling cases, one finds that one had never thought of something before in precisely the way the interlocutor does, or that one is learning something from her that one did not previously know. There would be little point in conversing—the exchange of pleasantries aside—if not for the fact that conversation is (to varying degrees, of course) interesting; what makes it interesting is that it offers a constant stream of weak (and occasionally strong) surprises.

A third indicator of the ubiquity of ideational heterogeneity is of particular relevance to technocracy. If I may again invoke personal experience, even people whom I have known all my life continually express weakly surprising (and sometimes shocking) ideas to me, sustaining endless conversation about matters small and large. As I move outward on the gradient of familiarity, the ideas of people I have known for a mere decade or two are both more weakly and more strongly surprising than those of very close friends; the ideas of professional acquaintances whom I have known for a few years, students for whom I serve as a mentor, and so on tend to be even more surprising; still more so the ideas of those who were anonymous to me until very recently, such as students in the classroom or airplane seatmates. Conversely, as someone emerges from anonymity into familiarity, she becomes nongeneric. Her particularity, which may be defined as her ideational strangeness, becomes apparent to me. She is strange in the sense of being interesting, and interesting in the sense of being surprising: otherwise, I would completely know her already. Yet technocrats are usually trying to predict and control the behavior of people they have never even met. This is bound to lead to surprises.

Before considering behavioral homogeneities that may offset the presumption of ideational heterogeneity, let us now step back and survey the methodology implicit in the Lippmannite theses, so that, in Section 3.4, we can use this methodology to think more specifically about the difficulties technocrats will have in trying to predict the behavior of diverse, surprising others.

3.3. EPISTEMOLOGICAL INDIVIDUALISM

> Until we know what others think they know, we cannot truly understand their acts.
> —WALTER LIPPMANN, *Public Opinion*

If we follow the Lippmannite theses, we are led toward a methodological orientation I will call epistemological individualism. Section 3.4 will show that this orientation is embodied, as an ideal type, in the practice of intellectual history—a fact that crystallizes the improbability of reliable technocratic prediction. For (I will argue) the problem of ideational heterogeneity makes even the findings of intellectual history unreliable on the whole, despite the value of particular contributions to intellectual history. Yet intellectual historians have important epistemic advantages over technocrats, rendering the predictions of the latter even less reliable than the findings of the former.

To set the stage for that argument, let me flesh out epistemological individualism by contrasting it against methodological collectivism as defended, paradoxically, by a leading intellectual historian, Charles Taylor. This methodological detour will prove worthwhile in the end, as Part II will not only make frequent use of collective concepts such as "the public," "the economy," "modern society," and, of course, "social" problems, but will depict "technocracy" as a "system" that exerts pathological epistemic "pressures" on technocrats. A critique of Taylor's methodological collectivism will establish bearings for using such collective metaphors in a manner compatible with the individualistic ontology of ideas that I have drawn from Lippmann.

3.3.1. Epistemological Individualism and Cultural Collectivism

Epistemological individualism unites four elements: methodological individualism, the fallibility and potential ignorance of individuals, communication among individuals, and the possibility that their ideas will be heterogeneous.

The epistemological individualist seeks to explain human behavior in terms of *individuals'* ideas simply because, pragmatically speaking, supra-individual analysis, while often heuristically valuable (as when using collective metaphors), may distract us from the individual actors who are the creators and the loci of ideas. This is important, of course, when the supra-individual analysis is explicitly concerned with ideas, but it can also be a problem when we treat "states" and other "institutions" as if they had minds of their own in more than a metaphorical sense. This occurs when they are treated as unitary actors infallibly following the logic of their situations, as if the situations did not have to be interpreted by someone. Only individuals can produce such interpretations (or any other interpretations), according to the epistemological individualist, because individuals are the biological loci of the webs of belief that give rise to interpretation. But individuals produce heterogeneous interpretations, and these are fallible not only because individuals may make logical mistakes, but because they are (by definition) ignorant of whatever their webs of belief heterogeneously omit.

The epistemological individualist is not, then, a methodological individualist of the type familiar from neoclassical economics and rational-choice theory. Such methodological individualists tend to assume that agents have knowledge that is adequate to their situations. As Chapter 4 will show, this assumption is critical to neoclassical economists' attempts to render the behavior of individual agents predictable. In contrast, for the epistemological individualist, one of the key defects of methodological *collectivism* is that it inclines us to overlook the heterogeneity and fallibility of the individuals who compose the collectivity. That is, methodological collectivism can obscure the inadequacy of people's knowledge just as much as neoclassical economics can. The converse of methodological collectivism, in this respect, is a form of methodological individualism that, unlike neoclassical economics, is not committed to unrealistic knowledge claims.

That methodological collectivism may obscure the fallibility of individuals' ideas is exemplified in Taylor's influential essay "Interpretation and the Sciences of Man" (1971). By critically inspecting this essay, we can bring out the connection between methodological individualism, the fallibility and possible heterogeneity of individuals' ideas, and the role of the communication of ideas among individuals.

Taylor begins by objecting to the notion that a "subjective realm" underlies objective social and political realities—exactly the notion that animates Lippmann's project.[46] The problem with appeals to a subjective realm, according to Taylor, is that they are too individualistic: they lack "the notion of meaning as not simply for an individual subject; of a subject who can be a 'we' as well as an 'I.'"[47] Taylor maintains, then, that ontologically (not just metaphorically), there is a linguistic-cultural community apart from its individual members that acts in some sense as a subject: an intersubjective subject. The task of a hermeneutical social science, in his view, is to understand the intersubjective meanings that stand behind (or above) the actions of the members of such a community.

Culture, then, according to Taylor, is not an ensemble of individuals' interpersonally communicated but, nonetheless, subjectively held ideas. Rather, it is a constellation of linguistically given, emotionally laden "common meanings" that the members of a linguistic community all share because they speak the same language.[48] "The range of human desires, feelings, and hence meanings," he writes, "is bound up with the level and type of culture, which in turn is inseparable from the distinctions and categories marked by the language people speak."[49] (We will need to consider the effect of putting feelings rather than ideas under the rubric of "meanings.") Interpretation is, for Taylor, the act of trying to understand the intersubjective meanings expressed in, or rather determined by, this shared language—*in contradistinction to* trying to understand the subjective interpretations determined by the webs of belief of individual subjects. These webs will undoubtedly overlap to some degree, because their content will in many cases have entered the webs by being communicated from others to a mass audience; yet the resulting interpretations may vary intersubjectively, because *all* of the ideas in any two individuals' webs are (presumptively) unlikely to be the same. The communication of ideas

---

[46] Taylor [1971] 1985, 31, quoting Almond and Powell 1966, 23.

[47] Taylor [1971] 1985, 40. Although Taylor's criticism of Almond and Powell is couched as an attack on their subjectivist individualism, theirs is a poorly chosen exemplar of subjectivism, for as Taylor points out (ibid., 42), their analysis of politics is functionalist. In functionalist analyses, the determinants of the subjective realm are, in the end, objective systemic needs, not subjective, fallible beliefs. Taylor's own analysis of politics, at least in this article, is also functionalist, as we shall see: bereft of interpreting individuals, it depicts culture as a noninterpretive (unmediated) response to objective conditions. By contrast, Lippmann's methodology blocks functionalism because it does not attribute ideas, or behavior, to extra-interpretive sources such as objective needs.

[48] Ibid., 24.

[49] Ibid., 25.

among individuals is intersubjective in itself, and it can create intersubjective ideational overlap in some instances, but if individuals are not exposed by communication to the same messages in the same sequence over the course of their lives, it can be expected to create diversity as well. The latter possibility is obscured by positing a supra-individual ontology that makes intersubjective "meanings," bound up as they are in language, more than just "ideas in [the] heads" of "the people in our society";[50] such meanings, Taylor insists, cannot be "the property of a single person, or many, or [even] all."[51] In that case, they can *only* overlap, not diversify.

Taylor justifies this ontological claim by appealing to the constitutive role played by intersubjective meanings in social practices. Intersubjective meanings "are not just in the minds of the actors," he contends, "but are out there in the practices themselves, practices which cannot be conceived as a set of individual actions, but which are essentially modes of social relation, of mutual action."[52] In fact, however, they can indeed be conceived as individual actions. Mutual action is always and everywhere mutually undertaken by individuals and by them alone. Social practices, likewise, are engaged in, without exception, by individuals. It is true, however, that insofar as individuals are able to participate jointly in a certain practice, they will almost certainly share similar (if not necessarily identical) subjective ideas, often tacit ones, about the meanings intrinsic to it. The question, then, is whether the constitutive role, in practices, of intersubjectively shared ideas is better explained by epistemological individualism, which "locates" the shared ideas in several individual minds—having gotten there, often, by means of interpersonal communication—or by methodological collectivism, which, in Taylor's variant, connects "meanings" through a uniform (shared) language, allowing him to locate them in a supra-individual ontological realm.

The question cannot be answered by claiming that all ideas are, by virtue of their rendition in language, *inherently* intersubjective, in contradistinction to being subjective, merely because they are shared. Even if most linguistic meanings within a given, stipulatively defined cultural whole are linguistically shared, some linguistic meanings are individual, if for no other reason than that an individual may draw on her web of shared yet somewhat heterogeneous ideas to innovate in a way that would not be possible for another individual—because the overlap between any two individuals' webs of belief is likely to be incomplete. Whenever an individual has to invent a neologism or use an old word in a new way, it is because she has an idea that was not, to her knowledge, previously expressible in the shared language of her culture, just as it is the case that whenever an individual has a new idea of any kind, it must stem from treating old and often shared ideas in a novel way—a treatment that must be due to some deviation of her web of beliefs from others' webs. Moreover, some ideas may not be expressible in language at all.

---

[50] Ibid., 36.
[51] Ibid., 37.
[52] Ibid., 36.

Everyone has had the experience of trying, without success, to find words for an idea that is "there" ("in one's head") even though one lacks words to express it. Finally, all shared meanings (and other shared ideas) are nonetheless the meanings (and ideas) of the individuals who share them.

Taylor may mean to acknowledge the latter point by saying that meanings "are not *just* in the minds" of individual actors.[53] But once we acknowledge the subjectivity of meanings, such that a given individual's meanings may or may not overlap with those of other subjects, what do we gain by contending that meanings also exist elsewhere than in the subjects' individual minds—that is, that they are intersubjective in contradistinction to being subjectively shared? Similarly, what do we gain by denying that the practices in which individuals engage can be conceived of entirely as individuals' actions, based on individuals' ideas—sometimes shared, sometimes not? The example Taylor adduces, the practice of negotiation, inadvertently shows that nothing is gained and much is lost.

Taylor asserts that negotiation "in our society . . . requires a picture of the parties as in some sense autonomous, and as entering into willed relations."[54] Such a picture, he adds, "must be the common property of the society before there can be any question of anyone entering into negotiation or not. Hence they are not subjective meanings, the property of one or some individuals, but rather inter-subjective meanings which are constitutive of the social matrix in which individuals find themselves and act."[55] These assertions are either false or tautological.

They are false in the sense that someone in our society who is forced to enter into a relationship unwillingly may try to deal with the situation by offering to the dominator something different from what she is trying to get from her victim. Thus, even the slave can sometimes negotiate with the master. Such negotiations, grounded in power asymmetries, directly violate the autonomy precept that Taylor takes to be a universal presupposition of negotiation in our society. If, however, one were to defend Taylor's position by saying that negotiations under duress or oppression are not "true" negotiations as sanctioned by "our society's" collective meanings, one would be right about the collective nature of such meanings, but only tautologically. One would have erased the possibility of heterogeneity in the meanings held by individual members of our society, but only by defining it away.

On the other hand, any *given* meaning of negotiation (defined tautologically as "the" meaning of negotiation), of the sort that might be explicitly invoked by someone engaged in the social practice of negotiation—who might say to her interlocutor, "*That's not what 'negotiation' means!*"—will almost always have originated outside of her mind. Otherwise she would have no grounds for assuming that her interlocutor will understand the concept as she invokes it. But this does not justify the claim that the origin

---

[53] Ibid., my emphasis.
[54] Ibid., 35.
[55] Ibid., 36.

is supra-individual. Rather, it will surely have originated in the individual minds of the negotiator's cultural predecessors, who communicated the concept to her and (she assumes, or hopes) to her interlocutor by means of such prosaically "cultural" processes as news reports, treatises, dramatizations in popular culture—and, of course, the process of learning "the" meaning of the word "negotiation" when she is learning the English language. In such prosaic processes, there are no agents except individuals and no mechanisms but individuals' subjective ideas and actions, including the actions by means of which they communicate their ideas amongst one another. If we had perfect historical hindsight, and thus could investigate the sources of a given speaker's understanding of what "negotiation" means, we would invariably discover messages about the meaning of negotiation that originated with and were mediated prosaically from other individuals, not from an empyrean intersubjective realm that is not reducible to individuals, their ideas, and the messages by means of which these are communicated.

This is not to suggest that a practice or other nonverbal activity may not *implicitly* communicate messages. Taylor's fellow communitarian, Alasdair MacIntyre, provides hockey as an example of an intersubjective practice that may fit this description (although he would not necessarily acknowledge it). According to him, a hockey player who, "in the closing seconds of a crucial game[,] has an opportunity to pass to another member of his or her team better placed to score a needed goal," knows exactly what to do—because playing hockey is a "well-defined social rol[e]," well defined by collective expectations to which the individual conforms.[56] True enough, but invoking "collective expectations" does not explain where they originated. If we could investigate with perfect hindsight the history of hockey, we would surely find that the game was originated by individuals, either deliberately or through the evolution of forms of play over time brought about by individual innovations, deliberate or accidental. The mutual expectations that thus arose might, in turn, have been communicated to other individuals either deliberately or implicitly. One can deliberately learn such expectations by reading a rulebook or studying hockey games; one can learn them unintentionally by watching games for pleasure or playing them and learning as one goes along. There is no mystery here that requires a supra-individual ontology for its resolution. Indirect communication is a prosaic but crucial epistemologically individualistic cultural mechanism by which the meanings of (or, better, ideas about) social practices are transmitted from some individuals to others.

Thus, to speak of "culture" in the prosaic, epistemologically individualistic sense captures an important source of individuals' ideas: the ideational influences exerted by one individual on another by means of direct or indirect communication. Such influences are effaced if we treat culture as intersubjective *in contradistinction to* being communicated from one individual subject to another.

---

[56] MacIntyre 1988, 140–141.

3.3.2. Language and Heterogeneity

Taylor insists that "inter-subjective meaning is not a matter of [individuals'] converging beliefs or values," because "apart from the question of how much people's beliefs converge is the question of how much they have a common language of social and political reality in which these beliefs are expressed."[57] It is important that Taylor at least recognizes, here, that there is a distinction between "beliefs and values"—both of which are types of idea—and a third type of idea: the "meanings" expressed in language. Too often his discussion treats the meanings of words as the only ideas there are, and thus the interpretation of meanings as the only type of interpretation there is. Most of our interpretations, however—especially those relevant to "the sciences of man"—amount to attempts to understand not what people mean by a particular word or concept, but what they intend or intended to do by taking a particular action. If I want to understand your behavior, it usually requires interpreting not so much how you define words or concepts as interpreting *which* concepts you use to build your theories about your environment, including your social environment—and how you put these concepts together. Puzzlement over the behavior of another may, but usually does not, concern what she means by a word or a concept. Words and concepts are mere building blocks: they are essential (at least arguably) to thought, but they can be used to create all sorts of ideational structures of very different shapes. Precisely because your concepts will likely be similar to mine due to our induction into a common language, the difficulty in interpreting your behavior and your ideas will probably lie elsewhere than in the meanings of the concepts you use. For example, it may lie in the inaccessibility, to me, of the *content* of your theories about your environment (i.e., the content of your interpretations of other people's behavior)— theories that guide your actions. Thus, it is critically important that, despite having distinguished between meanings and other ideas at this point in his discussion, Taylor fails to recognize that interpretive puzzles among the speakers of a completely uniform, intersubjectively shared language may be caused by diversity in the speakers' beliefs, values, and other ideas—not just in the meanings they attach to their concepts. Even while denying that a shared language causes interpretive puzzles, Taylor treats language as if it were the only potential source of puzzlement, and this is a serious mistake.

It is true that if people are to communicate their beliefs or values or other ideas— at least if they are to do so explicitly—they must have a language that makes this possible. Arguably, too, they may need to put their ideas into words in order to think about them—although introspection suggests, if I am not mistaken, that thinking is frequently done less explicitly than that. However, none of this entitles us to think that even the meanings of the words people use are dictates of intersubjective language (in contradistinction to subjectively communicated but nevertheless subjective language), as shown by continued changes to language, such as neologisms. These changes always originate

---

[57] Taylor [1971] 1985, 37.

with individuals, who communicate them to other individuals. With rare exceptions such as Esperanto, languages are the cumulative product of countless individual contributions over time, and they enable countless divergent uses, in accordance with innovations (such as neologisms) made by the divergent thoughts of individual language users. Languages, then, are no more intersubjective—in a nonprosaic sense that demands a special ontology—than are houses, which are produced by the cumulative efforts of countless individuals and are then the site of divergent activities by other individuals (or the same ones). Languages enable individuals within a stipulatively given "culture" to express an infinite array of heterogeneous and often contradictory ideas—the ideational content produced by various arrangements of concepts that, themselves, can often (although not always) be treated as if they were linguistically fixed. This content, not the meaning of the concepts themselves or the words that express them, is what is usually so hard to understand (and predict). The possibility of intralinguistic content heterogeneity, however, as much as the possibility of heterogeneity in people's words and concepts, will be disregarded if we view culture as a collective whole that impresses itself on individuals through their common language, causing them to think and act solely in ways that are consistent with the intersubjectively approved meanings of their words. Such a view reverses the order of causality. Culture does not cause individual action through language. Rather, language enables culture by allowing individuals to communicate their variable, often contradictory ideas to one another, thus contributing to the individual webs of belief that produce individuals' interpretations and thus actions.

This does not eliminate the possibility that language may homogenize thought, in some cases, by standardizing people's words or the meanings they attach to them. But the people whose meanings are thus homogenized remain individuals with potentially idiosyncratic usages. As Mark Bevir points out, speakers of the same language sometimes misunderstand each other, so "we cannot assume that hermeneutic meanings will always overlap with linguistic ones."[58] Linguistic misunderstandings are possible, it seems to me, because languages are taught and learned by fallible individuals. Each fallible teacher and each fallible student of a language will occasionally attach to a word a slightly different meaning than do other speakers of "the same" language—or even a grossly different meaning. Often, this diversity is revealed in the dialogical recognition that two language speakers, whether children or adults, mean different things by the same word. Up until that moment, each speaker may have been unaware of the fact that the meaning she had learned could be mistaken, in the sense that other meanings were possible. In such cases, each speaker was a naive linguistic realist about her understanding of the word. We should not reproduce their naiveté in our theorizing about language and culture. Language is intersubjective, but that does not in any way efface the fact that it is subjective. The intersubjectivity is a product of communication among individual minds, that is, among

---

[58] Bevir 1999, 48.

fallible and thus somewhat diverse webs of belief, despite the communication of usually homogeneous conceptual meanings through the teaching of a common language.

Despite its flaws, Taylor's perspective is widely shared among interpretivists. Clifford Geertz, for example, insists that culture "is public" and that, "though ideational, it does not exist in someone's head."[59] While it is indeed public in the sense that it is communicated, it is communicated from one head to others. Bevir notes that "pupils learn what they do from individual teachers, not a social tradition; they listen to lectures by individuals, not society; they discuss affairs with individuals, not society; they read books written by individuals, not society; they watch television programmes made by individuals, not society; and they reflect on beliefs held by individuals, not society."[60] The waters are only muddied if we conceptualize this inter-individual process of culture production as supra-individual, as when we pit intersubjectivity against subjectivity by omitting a factor that makes both ideational homogeneity and ideational heterogeneity possible: communication among individual human subjects.

3.3.3. Cultural Change and Fallible Ideas

None of this is to say that individuals are more ontologically real than societies or cultures. The ontology to which Lippmann points us is that of heterogeneous *ideas* that may make individuals' actions unpredictable. But "the individual" is a methodological construct that we routinely surpass when we break the individual down into parts or subsystems, such as the lymphatic system, the brain, or "someone's" various ideas, plural. "The individual," then, has no ontological reality greater than the ontological reality of any other metaphor. However, the utility of continuing to speak of "individuals" who stand above their separate (individual) ideas is threefold. First, there is a holistic interaction among the different ideas in any "individual's" "web of beliefs," presumably made possible by the physical wiring of the single "brain" (yet another metaphor) that is contained in any "individual's" head. Second, these webs of belief plausibly determine the actions taken by the "individual's" body, of which all social action consists. Third, in contrast to ideational interactions within an individual's head, ideational interactions *between* individual heads can take place only if mediated by some technology other than a biologically shared nervous system, since there is no such system. This nonbiological mediation is what we call communication, but to understand it, we must see it as mediating between the "webs of belief" of biological "individuals." So long as we understand communication individualistically in this sense, however, we are entitled to construct metaphorical entities at the supra-"individual" level that capture the effects of communication—entities such as "public opinion," "cultures," and "institutions"—just

---

[59] Geertz [1983] 1994, 218.
[60] Bevir 1999, 204.

as we construct metaphorical entities at the subindividual level that capture the effects of, say, lymph nodes.

To recognize the metaphorical nature of these constructs is, of course, to avoid their reification. Reifications are objectionable not so much because they are metaphysically incorrect as because theydistract us from important realities, such as the fact that "individuals" can introduce neologisms and (more importantly) other types of ideational innovation. Taylor's reification of "culture" likewise distracts us from the ontological reality of ideational heterogeneity. In contrast, epistemological individualism reduces all metaphorically collective cultural phenomena to the "ideas" and "actions" of metaphorical individuals, who may differ from one another and may communicate these differences among themselves. In this way, it not only allows for ideational heterogeneity but helps to explain it.

Communication among individuals introduces a potentially wide array of heterogeneous ideas into the individuals' webs of belief. In turn, individuals can synthesize these ideas into heterogeneous interpretations and thus actions that are unpredictable, to the extent that the interpretations are not shared by those who are trying to predict the resulting actions. (Synthesis is a product of individuals' creativity, but if they can synthesize new ideas only according to fixed psychological laws, as I am assuming, the new ideas are fully determined by the conjunction of the laws and heterogeneous ideational inputs; the creativity, then, is not truly spontaneous.)

Thus, the epistemological individualist explains cultural change as proceeding, schematically, in three steps. First, what we can figure, metaphorically, as an individual's web of beliefs will sometimes produce an idiosyncratic interpretation by synthesizing ideas that are, to some extent, different from the ideas in other individuals' webs. Second, the resulting innovation may be communicated to (some) other individuals by means of the individuals' bodily actions, such as writing and reading a book. Finally, some of the webs of the individuals on the receiving end of a communicated, innovative idea may interpret the innovation as being plausible enough to count as true or probably true, such that it is admitted into those webs, adding a new element to them that may enable further innovations to be synthesized by them.

To quote Bevir once more, "Change occurs because people deliberately or inadvertently make innovations, so we cannot explain change unless we allow for innovations, and we cannot allow for innovations if we try to fix the meanings of utterances by reference to abstract social meanings."[61] In turn, people's ability to innovate is (in my view, not necessarily Bevir's) explained by the idiosyncrasies in their webs of belief. Even bracketing linguistic error, people who speak the same language, engage in the same practices, and partake of the same culture (in the prosaic, epistemologically individualistic sense) may nonetheless be exposed within that culture to teachers, lectures, conversations, books,

---

[61] Ibid., 49.

television programs, blog posts, social media debates, and so forth, that express subtly or even diametrically opposed points of view. This may cause some of the agents exposed to these diverse ideas to create idiosyncratic syntheses of them that may, in turn, change their interpretations of their or others' situations. In effacing the idiosyncrasy of individual webs of belief, methodologically collectivist understandings of culture dampen our ability to explain cultural change.[62] They thereby impede our recognition of the *fallibility* of interpretation.

Both limitations are exemplified in Taylor's closing discussion of "the strains in contemporary society, the rise of deep alienation" in the 1960s. Taylor, writing just after the close of that decade, enlists his collectivist hermeneutics to explain why "the structures of [modern] civilization, interdependent work, bargaining, mutual adjustment of individual ends, are beginning to change their meaning for many, and are beginning to be felt not as normal and best suited to man, but as hateful or empty. And yet," Taylor contends, "we are all caught up in these inter-subjective meanings in so far as we live in this society."[63] This is a paradox that ought to have troubled Taylor. How can people who are constituted by a univalent, collective linguistic culture suddenly find its meanings hateful or empty? How, that is, can masses of people renounce the meanings that are supposed to be constitutively theirs unless at least some of them individually synthesize *objections* to these meanings—communicated, in turn, to masses of others—in ways that are, from the standpoint of the culture "as a whole" (i.e., the webs of belief of most of those who hear these objections), not only idiosyncratic but wrong?

Since Taylor ignores the possibility of ideational heterogeneity, let alone the possibility that this will enable individuals to synthesize new ideas, criticize old ones, and spread these novel and critical ideas by means of interpersonal communication, he is barred from noticing individual bearers of revolutionary cultural messages in the 1960s (and the 1950s)—whose objections to prevalent "meanings" (here Taylor conflates meanings, beliefs, and values), once communicated to other individuals, might themselves have *fostered* alienation and thus cultural change. Yet since Taylor does not invoke the *Weltgeist*,

---

[62] Collectivist understandings of culture do not, however, entirely erase the ability to explain cultural change. A Hegelian would explain cultural change as a developmental working-out of the logic of ideas that are already "there" in a culture, as potentialities or implications, at the start of the developmental process of *Geist*. But the same type of process can be envisioned by the epistemological individualist: individuals, over time (and in communication with each other), work out some of the logical implications presupposed by their individual webs of belief. Thus, for example, Kant worked out what he took to be some of the implications presupposed by the aspects of Rousseau's thought that Kant interpreted as particularly significant; Hegel worked out some of the implications of Kant's and Rousseau's thought in like manner, and Marx worked out some of the implications of Hegel's, Kant's, and Rousseau's thought. This understanding of ideational development is preferable to Hegel's not because it is ontologically individualistic per se, but because it builds in the possibility that the presuppositions of the individuals' thought are mistaken; while Hegel's view, by ascribing agency to a collective *Geist*, builds the omniscience associated with a monotheistic God into the developmental process of fallible human beings.

[63] Taylor [1971] 1985, 49, my emphasis.

at least not explicitly, he cannot attribute the cultural changes of the era to a literal collective being's change of mind, or to its dialectical development. Therefore, he is left with little choice but to explain the *subjective* "feelings" of alienation besetting his unspecified "us" by pointing to the *objective* failure of the social "structures" from which "we" "felt" alienated during the 1960s. That is, he suggests that—without the mediation of rebellious cultural thinking on the part of specific individuals communicating with one other (including individuals from the past whose ideas were communicated in writing)—"we" subjectively *but accurately* perceived the objective failure of these "structures." In turn, Taylor's language of emotion, rather than ideation, suggests an act of untheorized and uncommunicated perception: "we" (subjectively) *intuited* that the structures of modern civilization were hateful or empty—because *they really were*, objectively.

Taylor's naive cultural realism is consistent with his monolithic view of culture. It stands to reason that, if culture is monolithic, dissidents from the cultural mainstream can be inspired to dissent from it only by an extracultural, noninterpretive, direct apprehension of the truth—for culture, interpretation, and mediation are swallowed up in a univalent linguistic whole, leaving no space for dissenting ideas: where would they originate, since they dissent from the shared meanings that are treated as the only sources of culture? A picture emerges, then, of people's feelings as infallible reflections of objective reality. Thus, Taylor maintains that before the 1960s, "the free, productive, bargaining culture [had] claimed to be sufficient for man," but that then "the children," in particular, came to see the truth: that "it was not."[64] The free, productive, bargaining culture was objectively insufficient, and the children happened to be the ones who saw (or felt) this self-evident truth, as there is no other way that they might have come to *disagree* with the beliefs and values (not just the concepts) constitutive of bourgeois culture. "The notion of a horizon to be attained by future greater production (as against social transformation) verges on the absurd in contemporary America," Taylor asserts, and the obvious fact of this absurdity was recognized with special acuity by the young. "Placed in a private haven of security" by the affluent society, the young found themselves "unable to reach and recover touch with the great realities: their parents have only a negated past, lives which have been oriented wholly to the future; the social world is distant and without shape; rather one can only insert oneself into it by taking one's place in the future-oriented productive juggernaut. But this now seems without any sense."[65] The evocativeness of the language and the plausibility of the thought should not obscure the fact that Taylor is describing idiosyncratic ideas that particular individuals might have come up with by some means other than their unmediated recognition of Reality.

In contrast, if one were to investigate what happened in the 1960s from an epistemologically individualistic perspective, one might notice that many people in the

---

[64] Ibid., my emphasis.

[65] Ibid., 50. (Notice that the claim that such a horizon is absurd is a claim about its unlikelihood or, in this case, its valuelessness—not about the correct meaning of "horizon.")

affluent West, even young ones, disagreed with the critique of bourgeois life that Taylor takes to be self-evidently warranted. Yet how could they have failed to apprehend the truth if it was indeed self-evident? One might also notice that 1960s youth rebellions took place in such places as Mexico City, Prague, and the inner cities of the United States, places where the affluence Taylor identifies as an objective precondition of alienation had not been achieved.[66] To understand these anomalies, an epistemological individualist might read contemporaneous accounts, such as memoirs and books, in search of the communicated ideas and the heterogeneous webs of belief that led different "children" of the era in various contradictory directions. By contrast, methodological collectivism lures the theorist into massively undifferentiated claims and sweeping conclusions. It also pulls the theorist toward understanding both her own interpretations of reality and those of others as unmediated reflections of it. In this respect, methodological collectivism is insidiously anti-epistemological and self-confirmatory.

The avowed purpose of Taylor's methodological position is to displace a social science focused on subjective beliefs, but in practice this can easily mean that the observer ascribes to those she is observing an intuitive grasp of objective realities that happen to match the observer's own subjective beliefs about those realities. The epistemologically individualistic alternative treats subjectivity as capable, in the limit case, of complete autonomy from objectivity, such that "culture" may be a closed loop with no truth value at all.

3.4. INTELLECTUAL HISTORY AND THE PRACTICAL PROBLEMS OF TECHNOCRACY

> The uniqueness of historical sequences and the meaningfulness of human behavior mean that there is a latitude of interpretation always confronting the social scientist which the natural scientist is luckily spared.
> —W. G. RUNCIMAN, *Social Science and Political Theory*

> Philosophy is perfectly right in saying that life must be understood backward. But then one forgets the other clause—that it must be lived forward.
> —KIERKEGAARD, *Journals*

In sharp contrast to Taylor, Quentin Skinner has pointed out that "the concept of truth is irrelevant to the enterprise of explaining beliefs."[67] That is, whether or not the observer

---

[66] Taylor acknowledges that "alienation is most severe among groups which have been but marginal in affluent bargaining societies," such as "blacks in the USA" (ibid., 51), but this means that his thesis explains too much: those who have been bathed in affluence and those who have been deprived of it are equally alienated by it.

[67] Skinner 2002, 2. Cf. Bloor 1991, 8.

finds a belief to be accurate is irrelevant to explaining why the observed believes it to be accurate. Skinner's insight points the way toward the ideal-typical embodiment of epistemological individualism: intellectual history.

If people's ideas presumptively mirrored reality, as Taylor suggests, we would have no reason to try to understand their ideas rather than trying to understand the realities they mirror. At most, we would explicate people's ideas glancingly, as Taylor did in gesturing toward the "feelings" of "the children"; but there would be no need to interpret these ideas from the agents' own perspective, as there would be no mystery about them: they simply reflect the truth. Nor would we have any reason to try *explain* them (causally), as we would assume that we already know the explanation: they are caused by the unforced force of self-evident reality.

On the other hand, if ideas—others' or our own—do not mirror reality (or, rather, if they do not *necessarily* mirror it), we will have many reasons to try to understand and explain them. For one thing, taking a genealogical approach, we may discover among others' ideas mistakes that have been communicated to us, or to contemporaries with whom we disagree, in the form of inherited but unjustifiable assumptions or conclusions. (Intellectual history can therefore serve both a critical function and a self-critical one.) For another thing, we may want to escape the solipsism of the present by encountering the historical other on her own terms, precisely because, on our terms, it is difficult to understand the other. (This would not be the case if the observer and the observed are reflecting upon self-evident truths.) In pursuit of such goals, Skinner lays down a "golden rule" for intellectual historians: "however bizarre the beliefs we are studying may seem to be, we must begin by trying to make the agents who accepted them appear as rational as possible."[68] Finally, there is this: insofar as people's ideas determine their deliberate actions; insofar as these actions, in turn, shape the social environment; and insofar as this environment is sometimes hostile to human well-being; intellectual history—in the broad sense of any attempt to understand the ideas of real people, even if they are not "intellectuals"—may be essential to furthering the cause of human well-being. For, by means of intellectual history in this broad sense, we might be able to understand environmental problems in Dewey's sense of "environmental": social problems.

Thus, there is a degree of overlap between the goals of the intellectual historian and those of the technocrat, constituting a motive for the technocrat to want to be an intellectual historian in the broad sense, or at least an epistemological individualist. However, while intellectual history exemplifies epistemological individualism, we will now see that intellectual history itself is not reliable, on the whole. Technocracy is even less so, because it must deviate from intellectual history in several crucial respects.

---

[68] Skinner 2002, 40.

3.4.1. The Interpretive Problem and Intellectual History

The aspiration to critical or self-critical genealogy, the revulsion against solipsism, and the attempt to understand and explain challenges to human well-being all presuppose a gap between the web of beliefs of the intellectual historian, as subject, and that of the subject who is the object of her understanding and explanation—in contrast to the unity between subject and object suggested by Taylor's treatment of the ideas of "the children." In his depiction of the historical children-objects as recognizing the same truth that is self-evident to the historian-subject (Taylor himself), the "text-analogue" constituted by the behavior of the children presents no aspect that seems, to Taylor, "confused, incomplete, cloudy, seemingly contradictory—in one way or another unclear,"[69] that is, no aspect that requires interpretation. The historical other's ideas are not opaque, in this view, nor is there opacity in the "structures" of modern "civilization"[70] that, in the case of the cultural revolutionaries of the 1960s, were the objects of the other's ideas: these objective structures are clearly seen by object and subject alike.

The intellectual historian, by contrast, is necessarily immersed in the opacity of the other's ideas, because the objects of her investigation are plural, diverse—they tend to disagree among one another—rendering their ideas (not just the meanings of the concepts they used) puzzling enough to require interpretation: Why, after all, do they differ with each other, and often with us, the observers? The intellectual historian is at the rock face of individuals' ideational mystery and heterogeneity. To ignore either the mystery or the diversity would be to withdraw from the practice of intellectual history.

Taylor himself did not withdraw. In 1975, four years after the publication of "Interpretation and the Sciences of Man," his monumental *Hegel* devoted more than five hundred pages to the interpretation—not the mere exegesis—of Hegel's work. Along the way, Taylor investigated disagreements between Hegel and Rousseau, Hegel and Kant, Hegel and Fries—Hegel and each of the dozens of figures analyzed in the book. Hegel's web of belief was different from theirs, and theirs were different from one another's—despite the fact that in most cases they wrote in the same language, German. Taylor makes no attempt to sweep the differences aside.[71] Yet disagreement entails fallibility: disagreeing parties cannot all be equally right. The realities about which they disagreed, then, could not very well have been self-evident, and Taylor does not treat them as if they were.[72] *Hegel* is a standing rebuke to the methodology suggested by "Interpretation and

---

[69] Taylor [1971] 1985, 16.

[70] Ibid., 49, my emphasis.

[71] Taylor 1975, *passim*.

[72] Taylor does, however, treat many of Hegel's beliefs as if they stemmed from his simply seeing farther and deeper than did his interlocutors, and this is a common vice among intellectual historians. A thoroughgoing intellectual historian in the Skinner mold would not explain any belief by referring to its insightfulness, that is, its truth value, rather than to antecedent ideational factors. (Thus, for example, my treatment of Lippmann, which does refer to his insightfulness, cannot be considered an exercise in intellectual history.) Still, Taylor does not treat Hegel's opponents as stupid or irrational. Therefore, their disagreements with Hegel cannot have stemmed, in

the Sciences of Man," for *Hegel*, like any competent work of intellectual history, is episte-mologically individualistic.

The intellectual historian is, in effect, a specialist in the problems we all encounter in trying to understand the behavior of other people—predecessors or contemporaries, historically prominent figures, anonymous strangers, or intimate acquaintances. The dif-ficulty is that no two human beings, at least in the modern world, have been subjected to exactly the same set of ideational determinants in exactly the same sequence. However, this is a problem that even specialists are hard-pressed to solve, because they themselves are modern individuals whose webs of belief are different from those whose webs they seek to understand. Otherwise there would be nothing to seek: the other would be as transparent to them as Taylor thought "the children" of the 1960s were to him.

Skinner aptly describes the problem:

> The models and preconceptions in terms of which we unavoidably organize and adjust our perceptions and thoughts will themselves tend to act as determinants of what we think and perceive. We must classify in order to understand, and we can only classify the unfamiliar in terms of the familiar. The perpetual danger, in our attempts to enlarge our historical understanding, is thus that our expectations about what someone must be saying or doing will themselves determine that we understand the agent to be doing something which they would not—or even could not—have accepted as an account of what they *were* doing.[73]

An imperfect indicator of the severity of the problem is the profusion of conflicting interpretations of even exhaustively studied historical figures. Interpretive profusion can be attributed to the fact that each historian's interpretation is determined, tacitly, by what seems (to her) to be the relevant portion of the panoply of ideational influences to which she has been exposed in her own life up to the moment of interpretation, which combine to determine her interpretation of the historical object. The historical object, however, was exposed to a different panoply of ideational influences, creating a different web of beliefs—the contents of which are mostly inaccessible to the historian. The mismatches between the webs of belief of various historians of a given figure and the figure's own web of beliefs may incite heterogeneous interpretations, as reflected in scholarly disputes among the interpreters—manifestations of disagreement and surprise.

This is not to deny that logic and evidence can give us reasons to prefer one inter-pretation over others, regardless of our initial webs of belief; nor that intellectual his-torians will sometimes converge on a single interpretation. But the application of logic and evidence, and the achievement of consensus, are constrained not by the objective

---

Taylor's view, from their blunt failure to recognize the self-evident truths seen by Hegel. Hegel would not have needed to see farther and deeper than others if the truths he discovered were self-evident.

[73] Skinner 2002, 58–59.

truth-value of the interpretations of the objects of interpretation, but by the interpreters' subjective webs of belief about how to interpret the evidence regarding the objects that they find relevant. Variation in the interpreters' webs of belief will dispose some interpreters, but not others, to reject as implausible certain logically valid inferences from the evidence they find relevant, and it will also cause interpersonal variation in the evidence they find relevant. Therefore, interpretive error is a real possibility, such that we are best advised to treat even the most widespread and heartfelt historiographical consensus as Weber advised that all scientific opinion should be treated: as a provisional stopping point, probably to be superseded. Admittedly, we need not go so far as to agree with him that "each of us knows that what he has accomplished will be antiquated in ten, twenty, fifty years."[74] It is always possible that in any given case the truth has been discovered, that it has been recognized as the truth, and that this recognition will never fade. But the truth may also never be discovered, or it may already have been discovered but left behind because historians' webs of belief (about the truth) changed, such that they mistakenly came to believe that what they used to think of as true is false. Or an interpretation may be false but so compelling that the consensus in favor of it will never die. Thus, if we apply to intellectual historians themselves Skinner's dictum about the irrelevance of truth to understanding the ideas of the historian's object of scrutiny, all we will be able to say about an historiographical consensus, even a lasting one, is that it bespeaks agreement among historian-subjects—not that it is likely to be true.

The tenuous nature of historical interpretation does not undermine the integrity of historical research as an activity. The motive for science as a vocation is the chance of discovering the truth, even if the chance is small. We have no reason to deny that any given participant in the activity may discover the truth, but the problem of interpretation renders any given interpretation untrustworthy, ceteris paribus, along with any given historiographical consensus. We have reason to doubt the reliability of the findings of intellectual historians as a group, but inasmuch as any of them as individuals may succeed in their attempts to reach the truth, they themselves, as individuals, have every reason to attempt it.

The problem of interpretation is a general one, transcending historiography. Whenever we need to engage in interpretation in order to understand or explain others' actions, the truth about the ideas behind these actions cannot be self-evident. We seek, as Collingwood put it, to "re-thin[k] the same thought which created the situation we are investigating."[75] But in the end, we have only our own thoughts about the situation and our own thoughts about the thinkers who created it, because what we consider to be the relevant evidence can be interpreted only through the lenses provided by our own webs of belief.

---

[74] Weber [1918] 1946, 138.
[75] Collingwood [1946] 1993, 218. See van der Dussen 2013 on Collingwood's ideational determinism.

3.4.2. *The Problem of Anonymous Others*

The general problem of interpretation confronts technocracy in four particular respects that render technocratic reasoning even more unreliable, on the whole, than intellectual history. The first of these problems is itself historical.

If we are weighing the costs and benefits of a technocratic initiative, we need to compare the magnitudes on both sides of the ledger. Therefore, we need not only reliably accurate behavioral predictions but fairly exact ones, and they must be quantitative to facilitate weighing. However, neither magnitudes nor other quantities can be derived a priori. Charles Manski calls this lacuna "the silence of theory."[76] Technocrats must fill the lacuna with the only data there are: historical data.

Therefore, technocrats must be historians. Yet their task is even more difficult than the task facing intellectual historians, because technocrats must predict future behavior by drawing inferences from the statistically aggregated behavior of anonymous others in the past. This behavior, like all human behavior, requires interpretation. But statisticians cannot, as such, engage in the intensive biographical interpretation undertaken by intellectual historians. Their interpretation of past behavior is, therefore, even less likely to be accurate than is intellectual history. Where intellectual historians are particularistic, probing the idiosyncrasy of each individual's ideas, technocrats in the real world, driven by quantitative data, must be sweepingly general. Data-driven technocracy does not posit supra-individual cultural entities, as Taylor did. But the effect of attempting to interpret the behavior of anonymous others is similar. In both cases, what is missing is access to individuals' webs of belief.

In daily life, we gain imperfect access to people's webs of belief as they emerge from anonymity and become known to us personally. In like manner, intellectual historians may sometimes be able to create intellectual intimacy with their subjects by immersing themselves in the available evidence about their webs of belief, drawing their own webs closer to those they are investigating. But with populations consisting of more than a few members, there is little reason to think that the analysts' webs of relevant belief will, on the whole, adequately overlap with those of the objects of their investigation—assuming the ubiquity of ideational heterogeneity. When there are thousands, millions, or billions of anonymous agents, a great deal of analytical mismatch is inevitable, as a practical matter. Such mismatches are obscured by the homogeneity attributed to past actions by turning them into statistics.

3.4.3. *The Problem of Novel Circumstances*

When the technocrat turns from retrodiction to prediction, she encounters a second interpretive problem. She is interested in how agents will respond to a technocratic

---

[76] Manski 2013, 88.

initiative designed to alter their behavior by changing their circumstances. For example, she may want to know how businesspeople will respond to a regulation aimed at encouraging higher pay by mandating a higher minimum wage. The regulation is intended to change their incentives by imposing legal penalties for hiring below the new minimum. This adds another layer of speculation to the interpretive task that would face them if they were *merely* historians of anonymous others' behavior—others with webs of belief presumptively different from their own. Technocrats must not only understand why agents did what they did under given circumstances in the past; they must predict how agents will act under the new circumstances produced by a technocratic policy. How will businesspeople respond to a higher minimum wage: by raising wages or by cutting employment? To answer such questions, technocrats must forecast how agents will interpret novel circumstances.

That presentation of the problem underplays its difficulty, however, because the circumstances that will be interpreted by the agents whose behavior the technocrat needs to predict will not solely be shaped by the technocrat. (This is the problem Dewey sought to address by endorsing central planning, which would control for all changes not initiated by the central planners.) Therefore, the technocrat must predict agents' behavior in response to unpredictable circumstances, not merely in response to the predictable change of circumstance introduced by the technocrat's own regulatory intervention.

For example, US regulatory policy prior to the financial crisis encouraged banks to invest in mortgage-backed securities, each of which consisted of claim rights on the mortgage payments flowing from thousands of individual or "whole" mortgages. This policy was enacted because, while there had never been a nationwide housing bubble, there had been regional bubbles that threatened the solvency of local banks holding whole mortgages. A federal banking regulator told the Financial Crisis Inquiry Commission that "if you had a regional . . . real estate downturn[,] it took down the banks in that region along with it, which exacerbated the downturn." So, he continued, "we said to ourselves, 'How on earth do we get around this problem?' And the answer was, 'Let's have a national securities market so we don't have regional concentration.' "[77] Mortgage-backed securities would facilitate a national market, so banking regulators encouraged mortgage-backed securities.[78] They predicted that the result of this policy would be to disperse the historically regional concentration of mortgage risks in banks' portfolios.

However, the new market in mortgage-backed securities would be vulnerable to a nationwide housing bubble, as opposed to a regional one. Why, then, did a nationwide housing bubble form? One explanation—which is itself a matter of interpretive speculation—is that a great many house buyers in the early 2000s thought that with house prices going up for what they believed were "secular" reasons (America's rising

---

[77] Financial Crisis Inquiry Commission 2011, 43.

[78] See, for example, Acharya and Richardson 2009 and Financial Crisis Inquiry Commission 2011, 99–100, 119, 196.

population and Americans' rising incomes),[79] they could buy houses that would otherwise be unaffordable, confident that if they became unable to make mortgage payments, they could sell their houses for more than the purchase price. Thus, their interpretation of what was actually an unsafe real-estate "bubble" as a safe real-estate "boom" may have prompted them to buy more houses than otherwise, in the aggregate, inflating the bubble by driving up housing prices—thereby endangering the viability of the mortgage-backed securities into which whole mortgages were bundled, and thus the solvency of the banks that held these securities, if the house buyers' interpretation was incorrect, as it turned out to be.

The novel circumstances that, in retrospect, it seems that banking regulators "should" have recognized in this scenario—the interpretive dynamics of what turned out to be the first nationwide housing bubble—were not themselves created by technocratic policies, but they may have contributed to the failure of the policy described by the banking regulator.[80] These dynamics exemplify the type of vast, invisible "forces" to which Dewey attributed the epistemic complexity of modern society. Epistemological individualism allows us to see that such invisible forces may actually be people's interpretations of their circumstances, interpretations that may seem clear in retrospect—along with the mistakes embedded in them—while being difficult to predict in advance. Unless technocrats have totalitarian control over society, though, they will have to predict the behavior of people who are interpreting new circumstances over which the technocrats often do not have control, and that they may not, therefore, have anticipated.

3.4.4. The Problem of Heterogeneous Agents

The most obvious problem in moving from retrodiction to prediction is that the agents whose behavior is being predicted are likely to be different people than those whose aggregated historical behavior was the basis of the prediction. This suggests that technocrats may need to forgo anything akin to intellectual history altogether, even in their retrodictive activities. Intellectual history is the most reliable way to understand and explain the anonymous other, as it deanonymizes her. It particularizes what would otherwise be an abstraction. Yet it is only in an abstract sense that "the behavior" of past individuals can be considered a guide to that of entirely different individuals in the future. Evidence that technocrats derive from past behavior has relevance to future individuals' behavior

---

[79] See, for example, the widely quoted 2005 denial, by the head of the President's Council of Economic Advisers, that there was a nationwide housing bubble, as opposed to a housing boom justified by secular factors (Bernanke 2005).

[80] A further complication, however, is that changes in regulatory policy to encourage a nationwide market in privately issued mortgage-backed securities, or collateralized debt obligations (CDOs), may themselves have helped to pump up the housing bubble by increasing banks' demand for whole mortgages to be packaged into CDOs, pushing house prices higher and, as well, leading banks to reduce underwriting standards for whole mortgages. See Friedman and Kraus 2011, ch. 2.

only to the extent that all individuals are ideationally alike. This is where Hume's assumption of "uniformity" in "the operations of nature" makes itself most clearly evident in the workings of technocratic reason, and where its inappropriateness is perhaps most glaring.

3.4.5. The Problem of Time's Arrow

Fourth and finally, the objects of technocratic prediction and control have yet to act. Thus, even if they were the same people as those whose behavior the technocrat has retrodicted, even if these people's webs of belief were accessible to the technocrat, and even if the situations in which they will act were *not* novel, there would be an interim period that intervenes between their past actions and the future actions being predicted. During this period, the webs of belief that governed their past actions may change, even if objective circumstances do not. Thus, agents' future actions, even in identical circumstances, may differ from their actions in the past. Not only may the webs of belief of the technocratic subject and the object of her control differ—in parallel with the interpretive problem facing intellectual historians; not only may the objective context of the objects' interpretations change; and not only may the objects themselves be different agents than those about whom the technocrat has gathered evidence; in addition, the ideational basis of the agents' interpretations may change.

Popper pointed out that, to be able to predict future inventions and scientific discoveries, we would already have to know what future inventors and scientists will know—meaning, effectively, that we would be able to invent their inventions and make their discoveries.[81] Predicting future actions of any kind requires that we know what future actors will believe. However, lacking Laplacean knowledge of all the ideational influences on the actors up to the moment of their actions, and thus of the evolving intricacies of their webs of belief, the reliability of such knowledge is highly improbable, even if we could start from data about the actions produced by the same actors' webs of belief in the recent past concerning the same circumstances, and even if the agents, past and future, were not anonymous.

In light of these problems of interpretation, one must attribute to sheer thoughtlessness Berlin's claim that "experts or machines" can settle questions of means in politics. He must not have paused to consider whether these questions might not be far *more* difficult to answer than those he spent his life tackling—questions of intellectual history. The technocrat must ask, "What might unknown agents [about whose thoughts we have no evidence] do in a dimly specified future?" The intellectual historian merely asks, "Why did a specific agent [about whose thoughts there is often extensive evidence] take action X?" (an action such as writing a certain passage in a book). Yet no competent intellectual

---

[81] Popper 1957.

historian would claim that this question is an easy one to answer, let alone one that could be answered automatically, by a machine.

3.5. HOMOGENIZING FACTORS

If agents differ in unspecifiable ways, then . . . very little [*sic*], if any, predictive inferences can be made.
—KENNETH J. ARROW, "Rationality of Self and Others in an Economic System"

The living impressions of a large number of people are to an immeasurable degree personal in each of them, and unmanageably complex in the mass.
—WALTER LIPPMANN, *Public Opinion*

Fortunately for the technocrat, however, ideational heterogeneity is not the whole story, for there may be slippage—or, more accurately, apparent slippage—between ideas and action, and thus between unpredictable ideational heterogeneity and somewhat predictable behavior. This would reduce the frequency of heterogeneous behavior and, therefore, the magnitude of unintended consequences. Put in different terms, there may be homogenizing behavioral counterforces to the heterogeneity of people's ideas.

The presence of at least one type of homogenizing counterforce is suggested by personal experience. Anonymous people often behave in fairly predictable ways. Seatmates on an airplane do not often perform cartwheels in the aisle. Customer-service personnel do not often venture beyond the rote and frequently unhelpful behavior with which we have all become familiar. This might conceivably be due to homogeneity across the webs of belief of millions of different customer-service personnel, but a different explanation is that they share not homogeneous beliefs in general, but specific normative tenets (norms) that they view as obligatory in their situations, as they interpret them—despite the fact that, apart from this shared interpretation of their situations, their webs of belief may be wildly heterogeneous. Shared norms can act as a counterweight to the heterogeneous behavior that would otherwise be expected to issue from such webs of belief. The intercession of shared norms, then, may create a gap between the (presumptively great) frequency of anonymous others' unpredictable ideas and the frequency of their unpredictable behavior.

Lippmann quotes G. K. Chesterton about the contrast between ideational heterogeneity and behavioral regularity in a passage well worth excerpting:

"Modern society," says Mr. Chesterton, "is intrinsically insecure because it is based on the notion that all men will do the same thing for different reasons. . . . As within the head of any convict may be the hell of a quite solitary crime, so in the house or under the hat of any suburban clerk may be the limbo of a quite separate philosophy. The first man may be a complete Materialist and feel his own body as a horrible machine manufacturing his own mind. . . . The man next door may be a Christian Scientist and regard his own body as somehow rather less substantial than his own shadow. . . . The third man in the street may not be a Christian Scientist but, on the contrary, a Christian. . . . The fourth man may be a theosophist, and only too probably a vegetarian; and I do not see why I should not gratify myself with the fancy that the fifth man is a devil worshiper. . . . Now whether this sort of variety is valuable, this sort of unity is shaky. To expect that all men for all time will go on thinking different things, and yet doing the same things, is a doubtful speculation. . . . Four men may meet under the same lamp post; one to paint it pea green as part of a great municipal reform; one to read his breviary in the light of it; one to embrace it with accidental ardour in a fit of alcoholic enthusiasm; and the last merely because the pea green post is a conspicuous point of rendezvous for his young lady. But to expect this to happen night after night is unwise."[82]

It is true, as Chesterton suggests, that any behavioral homogeneity would be unstable if it required the convergence of *completely* heterogeneous webs of belief on the same actions. But it seems more likely that such regularity, to the extent that it exists, stems from such factors as the stabilizing behavioral effect of shared norms that are superordinate within webs of belief that may otherwise be heterogeneous. Thus, customer-service personnel are required by their employers to behave in a certain manner, and even if some employees find this behavior odious, they may decide to perform it for the sake of their continued employment. A norm is thus imposed on the employees; more precisely, the employees adhere to the norm as if it were their own, because (to some extent) they share among themselves a homogeneous commitment to getting the wages paid by the employer. The behavioral heterogeneity that would otherwise follow from their heterogeneous ideas is thereby suppressed—not, as in Chesterton's account, by coincidence, but because superordinate ideas shared by heterogeneous agents limit the behavior to which their otherwise-diverse webs of belief would lead. Airline passengers have been socialized in a culture (in the prosaic sense) where disobedience to authoritative rules is considered inappropriate, so (to some extent) they tend to sit in their seats as instructed, even if they have diverse reasons to disobey. Patterns of behavior such as these can be so stable as to tempt social scientists to reify the "institutions" it allows them to construct, metaphorically, out of the patterns—as if the institutions have minds of their own.

For defenders of technocracy, however, the question is not so much how stable the ideas causing the "existence" of "institutions" such as "states" are likely to be, but how regularized are the ideas that cause the behavior of the human objects of technocratic regulation. How often is it likely that the normalization of behavior, or the creation

---

[82] Lippmann [1922] 1997, 14.

of some counterweight to ideational heterogeneity other than widely shared norms—such as the mass inculcation of homogeneous ideas across a population through the mass media—will occur; to what extent; and in which specific areas of life? In the face of potential conflicts between the heterogenizing force of ideas and homogenizing counterweights, what technocrats must do is determine, fairly precisely, when specific counterweights can reliably be expected to constrain the unpredictable effect of presumptively frequent heterogeneous ideas. If technocrats are unable to do this, then the degree of predictability produced by norms would itself be unpredictable, leaving technocrats in an unpredictably heterogeneous social environment, such that their interventions produce a profusion of unintended consequences. Whether it turns out that, in general, islands of unpredictable behavior are surrounded by an ocean of predictable behavior, or vice versa, this would not affect the presumptive illegitimacy of technocracy. What matters is whether, in particular cases, technocrats are likely to know where the areas of predictability are located, how wide they are against a backdrop of presumptively unpredictable ideas, and the behavior they are likely to cause. For if technocrats assume predictable behavior in cases where it is absent, or if they overestimate its extent where it is present—or if they misinterpret its interpretive implications for the agents whose actions they are trying to control—their policies will tend to produce unintended consequences.

This state of uncertainty offers a measure of hope for technocratic legitimacy. If theorists of technocracy could demonstrate on second-order grounds that, for example, technocrats should be reliably able to determine the effects of various superordinate norms (or other homogeneous or behavior-homogenizing ideas), as well as being reliably able to discern the limits of their knowledge of the predictability conferred by such homogenizing factors, then we could expect that technocrats might be reliably able to predict people's behavior in those cases, despite the presumptive heterogeneity of human ideas. This might reduce the magnitude of the unintended consequences caused by ideational heterogeneity, rescuing technocratic legitimacy. Otherwise, we would have established, I think, that technocrats cannot justifiably claim to know that the benefits of their actions will outweigh the costs.

3.5.1. *The Possibility of a Judicious Technocracy*

I cannot preclude the possibility that a defense of technocracy on the basis of homogenizing ideas would suffice, because I cannot presume to know either the magnitude of the unintended consequences caused by ideational heterogeneity or the magnitude of the reduction in unintended consequences caused by technocrats' discovery of homogenizing ideas. This is a thorny issue that I will take up in Part III. For the purposes of Part II, however, we can stipulate that even if the magnitude of the problem caused by frequent and unpredictable ideational heterogeneity is very high, the discovery of homogenizing ideas can reduce it to a manageable level, rescuing technocratic legitimacy according to the preliminary standard of doing more good than harm. But a defense of technocratic legitimacy along these lines would have to keep several things in mind.

One is that norms are often obeyed as a matter of habit, while technocracy is inherently disruptive of habit. Technocrats produce "interventions" designed to change behavior: the behavior to which they attribute social problems. It may be illogical, then, at least in some cases, to expect that technocracy can latch onto norms as the necessary source of behavioral predictability; in the act of latching onto them, technocrats may disrupt them.

There may nonetheless be cases where the change in habits caused by a technocratic intervention will not jeopardize stabilizing norms or other counterforces, such as homogenizing mass culture. Yet a defender of technocracy would have to show that technocrats are likely to be able to identify such cases reliably. As with the need to identify areas in which particular norms impose homogeneous behavior despite the heterogeneous ideas bubbling under the surface, technocrats would need to be judicious enough to distinguish cases in which behavioral homogeneity would be likely to persist, even after an intervention, from cases in which it would not.

Another consideration is that even nonhabitual norms are customary in many cases: that is, the behavior they govern is deliberate rather than habitual, but the agents regularly settle on traditional behavior. Yet in the modern era, custom itself has increasingly been subject to critical scrutiny and dissolution. Thus, traditional norms may no longer exert the stabilizing behavioral effects that they once did. The decline of traditional behavioral patterns is too obvious to require elaboration, but there is an interesting implication: conservatism, in the sense of a dedication to traditional behavior, is a natural ally of technocracy.

A final consideration corresponds to two methodological requirements that would seem incumbent on a technocracy capable of identifying the limits of its predictive knowledge.

In general, such a technocracy would have to be a careful, discerning, and empiricist enterprise—again, a judicious one. The identification of areas of predictability that could withstand technocratic disruption would probably have to occur case by case, based on deep familiarity with the ideas, including the norms, of those whose actions need to be predicted. Such an enterprise would presumably require open-mindedness and meticulous observation—the very qualities that Dewey required of his hoped-for social science. This is a tall order, for as we saw, injunctions to be open-minded amount to pointless moralizing if there are plausible grounds for conflicting interpretations of the evidence; and injunctions to observe carefully are vacuous if what is being observed is the effect of invisible society-wide forces, such as behavior that might be caused by unobservable ideas, or the behavior of masses of anonymous others.

Still, technocrats might be able to get around these problems if, for example, they confine their observations to the visible behavior of relatively small groups of people whom they come to know intimately enough to tease out their webs of belief. In this respect, the piecemeal nature of technocracy might be helpful, as it sometimes allows relatively small subsets of the general populace to be targeted for behavior modification. Such groups—bankers, for example—are more ethnographically observable, at least in principle, than is the general population at large, or "society" as a totality. Perhaps other epistemologically individualistic methods of technocratic governance might be devised, too.

On the other hand, if a technocracy experiences pressures against judicious empirical observation and open-mindedness, its legitimacy may not survive the internal critique presented in this chapter. This is the possibility I will pursue in Part II, where I will call such pressures "pathological." This is not to suggest psychological pathologies but "systemic" ones. If dogmatic or aprioristic technocrats are systematically selected for in a technocracy, the technocracy, as a system, is unlikely to be reliably able to separate predictable from unpredictable zones of behavior, and is likely therefore to do more harm than good—regardless of whether the dogmatism or apriorism is a psychological trait of the individual technocrats or has some other cause. The same is true if empiricist technocrats are systemically selected who are averse to investigating the ideational basis of people's actions.

Asking whether we can expect pathological systemic pressures in a technocracy would seem to be a more tractable approach than attempting to anticipate theoretical defenses of the ability of technocrats to judiciously identify the scope and limits of their knowledge of behavioral homogeneities. Pathological pressures may be identifiable a priori; and their effects may be detectable, a posteriori, in really existing technocracies. Of course, after identifying such pressures, I will have to specify how they might be produced by processes that are consistent with epistemological individualism. The "pathological pressures of a technocratic system" are collective metaphors—but they may help us envision realities that can then be reduced to the metaphorically individual, biologically ideational level.

3.5.2. *Technocracy and Social Theory*

Specifically, we will have a priori reason for skepticism about the prevalence of open-minded epistocrats if the very process of acquiring expertise inherently tends to imbue individual experts with dogmatic inclinations; or if, alternatively, regardless of such a process, we can reasonably expect dogmatic epistocrats to win out in the struggle for influence over public policy. Chapter 5 will argue that both reasons for skepticism are warranted, and will provide a posteriori evidence that these pathological pressures are, at present, realities. This gives citizen-technocrats an unexpected advantage over epistocrats: the relative open-mindedness of the former. Chapter 6 will then consider whether systemic pressures in democratic forms of technocracy can be expected to counteract or override this advantage.

First, however, Chapter 4 will discuss the prospects for judicious empiricism among epistocrats, setting aside the issue of dogmatism. This chapter will pay special attention to the dominant policy science of our age, economics. Among economists, I will contend, there is a pathological aversion to acknowledging the causal force of ideas. The question motivating the chapter is whether this pathology is somehow selected for by the "system" of technocracy. Let me set the table for my answer by suggesting a parallel between technocratically pathological social science and social theory in the grand tradition.

Grand social theorists—whether their theories are closest to the modern disciplines of economics (e.g., Smith, Marx, Hayek), psychology (e.g., Montesquieu, Rousseau, Freud), or sociology (e.g., Tocqueville, Durkheim, Foucault)—are vulnerable to pathologies very much like those I will discuss in Chapter 4. This is because grand social theorists make claims about human behavior across entire societies or historical epochs, or across all societies in all epochs, a practice that almost necessarily ignores heterogeneity in the ideas of the agents whose actions shaped those societies.

Thus, a better term than grand social theory might be oracular social theory. Grand theorists seize on this or that feature of the blooming, buzzing confusion—whichever features happen to catch their eye, which is to say features that happen to be highlighted by their webs of belief—so as to transform the epistemic chaos of thousands, millions, or billions of webs of belief into a legible pattern. In elaborating upon economic, psychological, or sociological "factors," "forces," "structures," "variables," or (yes) "pressures" and "systems" that might impose a clear pattern—factors such as rational self-interest, class struggle, spontaneous order, passions specific to certain times and climes, amour propre, unconscious drives, moeurs, collective consciousness, anomie, discourses, power—grand theorists impose legibility on the total social whole, ascribing orderliness and comprehensibility to it. As Georg Simmel pointed out, however, "The very image of the *whole*, which seems to imply the fullest and purest objectivity, reflects the peculiarity of its possessor much more than the objective image of any particular thing usually reflects it."[83] In turn, the peculiar organizing principle imposed by any given grand social theorist will overshadow the heterogeneity, the unpredictability, the causal importance, and sometimes even the existence of individuals' ideas. By contrast, when an epistemological individualist makes claims about, say, "modern society"—for example, by pointing out consequences to be expected from historical developments in the Holocene—the effect (I hope) is to highlight heterogeneity and thus complicate our understanding of what we think of as modern society, bringing us closer to the chaos, not sweeping it aside. Thus, one of the challenges I will face in Part II is to square my invocation of "systemic pressures" in favor of *homogeneously* dogmatic technocrats and technocrats who are homogeneously inattentive to ideas, on the one hand, with epistemological individualism on the other, so as to avoid the charge that I myself am engaging in grand theorizing.

---

[83] Simmel [1910] 1950, 294, as translated in Weingartner 1962, 166. Simmel, however, was referring to peculiarities caused by different personalities, not different webs of belief.

Grand theory can be seen as manifesting what Lippmann called the "impulse to seek stability in an incalculable environment by standardizing for one's own apparent convenience all those who form the context of one's activity."[84] However, if we are to be more charitable than Lippmann was about this impulse, we might attribute it not to a desire for convenience, but to the fact that any intelligent person may readily believe that the global truth is represented by whatever patterns are rendered visible by her epistemically local interpretive stereotypes. Hence the fact that many highly intelligent people embrace conspiracy theories. Clearly they do not *think* these theories oversimplify reality, for the sake of convenience or anything else; if they did, they would not believe in them. However much others might find the theories simplistic, the conspiracist thinks that the theory she accepts captures reality in all its important details (which conspiracy theorists often think are quite numerous and complicated)—because of congruence between the claims and assumptions connected with each other by the theory and the claims and assumptions that were already in her web of beliefs before encountering (or inventing) the theory. The grand social theorist is an extremely intelligent person, albeit (unlike most conspiracists) an extremely learned one, who is naively realistic about her own web of beliefs and the contribution it makes to the social regularities she thinks that she sees. However, regardless of the subjective origins of grand theories, it seems clear that objectively, their effect is as Lippmann suggested: they oversimplify human reality, creating the impression that the theorist has achieved a profound understanding of a complex social totality—indeed, that the totality is real, not merely a construct—precisely to the extent that the theorist overlooks the opaque reality of human ideas. Heterogeneous and perhaps incomprehensible sources of behavior are thus replaced by much simpler, homogeneous social factors, structures, forces, and so on.

The homogenizing effect is essential, no matter how numerous a theorist may think the factors or how complicated their interactions. In this respect, grand theory is similar not only to conspiracy but to technocracy. Where the grand theorist usually imputes homogeneity so as to make sweeping retrodictions about the behavior of anonymous others, the technocrat does so to make sweeping predictions of their behavior. The imputation of homogeneity, however, is antithetical to the intellectual historian's concern with idiosyncrasy. Even when grand theory is strictly retrospective, then, it is not genuinely historical, as it does not treat human behavior as if it were caused by *human* beings. The contrast between "theory" and "history" in this sense parallels the contrast between the social sciences, which are congruent with technocracy, and the humanities, as an ideal type—although one way of stating the lesson of this chapter is that the only truly scientific social science would be one that is akin to intellectual history, and is therefore humanistic.

---

[84] Lippmann [1925] 1927, 169.

None of this is to say that the generalizations produced by grand theorists are uniformly false. It is possible that some or all of them may be true, just as any given intellectual-historical or social-scientific claim or any conspiracy theory may be true, especially if we define "true" as "an accurate but partial description of a complex whole." However, an *epistemically* complex whole, one that is opaque to some significant extent, as opposed to a complicated whole—which has many moving parts and interactions, all of which combine to yield reliable totalistic generalizations—is unlikely to be so easily mastered as the grand theorist assumes.

This is to say that the validity of grand theory, as a genre, is unreliable—assuming that the societies or epochs being analyzed are indeed epistemically complex, as they must be if they are populated by ideationally determined, unpredictably heterogeneous people. So, too, with technocratic predictions, as a genre—at least if they do not judiciously take account of the possible effects of ideational heterogeneity.

By contrast, a judicious grand social theory, if that is not a contradiction in terms—a grand theory of ideationally determined epistemic complexity—and a judicious technocracy alike would specifically have to confront the question of whether agents' presumptively diverse webs of belief might disrupt any behavioral regularities ascribed to the whole by the theorist or the technocrat. Both the judicious theorist and the judicious technocrat would have to begin, then, with something like the following proposition, from Baron d'Holbach: "Beings essentially different by their natural organization, by the modifications they experience, by the habits they contract, by the opinions they acquire, must of necessity think differently" from one another.[85] If so, then the burden of proof falls on grand theorists and technocrats, who must show that the homogeneities they think they see can survive contact with the reality of individuals' presumptively heterogeneous ideas. As we will see in the next chapter, then, a cardinal rule, both for a judicious technocracy and for a nonoracular social theory of ideationally determined epistemic complexity, would be Skinner's dictum for intellectual historians, the dictum of interpretive charity. Simply put, the judicious technocrat or social theorist would have to try to put herself in the shoes of those whose actions she wants to explain or predict.

It is not surprising, in this light, that Holbach's discussion of heterogeneity was part of an argument for toleration—political charitability. "For one man to exact from another that he shall think like himself," he maintained, would be "to insist that he shall be organized precisely in the same manner—that he shall have been modified exactly the same in every moment of his existence: that he shall have received the same temperament, the same nourishment, the same education: in a word, that he shall require that other to be himself."[86] Thus, if

---

[85] Holbach 1770, 114. He goes on to say that from "the multiplicity of imperceptible differences, which is to be found in their modes of seeing and thinking," can be derived the conclusion that each has "a language which is peculiar to himself alone, and this language is incommunicable to others" (ibid.), which is introspectively obvious but was lost on the Herder- and Wittgenstein-influenced philosophers of the last century.

[86] Ibid.

prejudice had been laid aside ... the most trifling reflection would have shewn him the necessity of this diversity in his notions, of this contrariety in his imagination, which depends upon his Natural conformation diversely modified: which necessarily has an influence over his thoughts, over his will, and over his actions. In short, if he had consulted morals, if he had fallen back upon reason, every thing would have conspired to prove to him, that beings who call themselves rational, were made to think variously.[87]

It is ironic that Holbach is usually classified as a materialist. For he pointed toward a type of social science that would be deterministic, as all science must be, but, given its ideational focus, would *not* be materialistic (at least not single-mindedly so) or otherwise reductionist; thus, it would be intellectually charitable. Moreover, its empiricism, alert to at least the possibility of unpredictable ideational diversity among human beings, would be open to recognizing discrepancies between the ideas of the researcher and the ideas of those she studies.

Social scientists and theorists who followed Holbach's lead would be careful, discerning, open-minded practitioners of interpretive understanding. My question in Part II will be, in effect, whether they could therefore be technocrats—or whether interpretively charitable, empirically scrupulous, open-minded technocracy is impracticable in the real world.

---

[87] Ibid., 116. Shterna Friedman brought this passage to my attention, and pointed out the nonmaterialistic nature of Holbach's "materialism."

PART II

Toward an Empirical Epistemology of Technocracy

Few economists can remember that their reasoning is built upon an unreal picture of man and industry. By the time the details are worked out, economists have the greatest difficulty in recalling the fact that they have been talking about an imaginary world, a world which pleases their fancy because it yields to their logic.

—WALTER LIPPMANN, *Drift and Mastery*

The fantastic claim has occasionally been made for economic theories—e.g., the abstract theories of price, interest, rent, etc.—that they can, by ostensibly following the analogy of physical science propositions, be validly applied to the derivation of quantitatively stated conclusions from given real premises, since given the ends, economic behavior with respect to the means is unambiguously "determined." This claim fails to observe that in order to be able to reach this result even in the simplest case, the totality of the existing historical reality including every one of its causal relationships must be assumed as "given" and presupposed as known. But if *this* type of knowledge were accessible to the finite mind of man, abstract theory would have no cognitive value whatsoever.

—MAX WEBER, " 'Objectivity' in Social Science and Social Policy"

4

The Pathological Pressure to Predict

ONE COULD HARDLY imagine a body of theory more foreign to Holbach's approach than neoclassical economics. Neoclassical economists relentlessly disregard the very possibility of ideational heterogeneity—a habit that perfectly suits the practice of behavioral prediction, although not reliable prediction. And so, as if by an invisible hand, neoclassical economics has become the premier technocratic policy science, but an epistemically pathological one. A policy science that, like neoclassical economics, ignores ideational heterogeneity may be able to issue a steady stream of behavioral predictions, but these predictions cannot be judicious in the requisite sense.

My goals in this chapter are to explain why a discipline so averse to considering the role of idiosyncratic ideas in human behavior has become the hegemonic policy science, and to ask whether a policy science might arise that, unlike economics, judiciously balances homogenizing tendencies such as behavioral norms against the presumptive

Power Without Knowledge. Jeffrey Friedman, Oxford University Press (2019). © Oxford University Press.
DOI: 10.1093/oso/9780190877170.001.0001

heterogeneity of people's webs of belief. Sections 4.1 and 4.2 will follow Herbert Simon in suggesting that economists feel themselves able to predict behavior because they impute to agents adequate knowledge of their circumstances. This imputation bypasses the need to consider agents' fallible ideas and interpretations at all, let alone to consider whether their ideas and interpretations might be unpredictably idiosyncratic. Section 4.3 suggests that the branch of cognitive psychology that has come to be known as behavioral economics may suffer from a similar pathology. Section 4.4 discusses the historical, empirical side of economics—econometrics—and the fact that, toward the end of the twentieth century, many econometricians came to believe that something was interfering with the retrospective analyses on which their quantitative behavioral predictions relied. The resulting methodological revolution, in which empiricist economists have downplayed theory in favor of natural and controlled experimentation, has led to the discovery of heterogeneity where neoclassical theory would predict uniformity.

Could this discovery portend a reformed, judicious policy science? Section 4.5 tries to answer this question by looking at a nontechnocratic branch of social science, social psychology (specifically, the part of that subfield dedicated to studying the authoritarian personality), which has always been empiricist and, at best, theoretically ad hoc, yet is nearly as insensitive to the possibility of ideational heterogeneity as are neoclassical economics and behavioral economics. If even nonepistocratic social sciences share pathological traits with policy sciences such as economics, it suggests that these traits have origins that are external to technocracy as a "system": cultural factors, understood from an epistemologically individualistic perspective. In this light, Section 4.6 assesses the prospect of a judicious epistocracy.

This chapter will be pointing toward homogeneities in epistocrats' and social scientists' ideas. Chapter 6, similarly, will suggest homogeneities in the ideas of citizen-technocrats, and Chapter 5 will suggest homogeneities in epistocrats' *manner* of thinking. All of this may seem to contradict Chapter 3's emphasis on ideational heterogeneity. Moreover, Chapters 5 and 6 will try to establish technocratic homogeneities by using empirical evidence gathered by positivist social scientists, evidence of the same sort that I critically scrutinize at the end of this chapter. I need to distinguish at the outset, then, among (*a*) the injudicious use of social-scientific evidence for predictive purposes, where behavioral homogeneity (regularity) is assumed as the default—based on the unexamined assumption of uniformity in the operations of human nature; (*b*) the judicious use of social-scientific evidence for predictive purposes, where unpredictability is taken to be the default—based on the presumptive heterogeneity of human ideas; and (*c*) the use of social-scientific evidence for an entirely different purpose, the purpose of the three chapters comprising Part II: the construction of a plausible theory about the preconditions of a political "system" such as technocracy.

The premise of Part II is that a judicious technocracy might come into existence if epistocrats, citizen-technocrats, or both find a way to balance the presumptively heterogeneous effects of ideas against any behavioral homogeneities they discover. Thus,

I will be assuming that synchronic behavioral regularities (such as those produced by behavioral norms) may exist and may, in principle, be unearthed by social scientists. My critique of social science will concern its injudicious inattention to the possibility that the predictable behavior produced by such homogeneities is limited by ideational heterogeneity. The posited injudiciousness, then, has to do with social scientists' tendency, in practice, to assume that their data bespeak predictable behavioral regularities without considering the causal importance of idiosyncratic ideas. I will not be questioning the validity of social scientists' data themselves, nor the use of such data to establish behavioral regularities—so long as social scientists think through the ideational mechanisms of these homogeneities, and so long as they pay due attention to the counteracting force of presumptively heterogeneous ideas. I will therefore feel free to use such data for my own quasi-retrodictive, merely suggestive purposes: to highlight what may be significant ideational patterns in one really existing technocracy, that of the United States; to speculate about how such patterns might have originated; and to speculate, further, about the types of ideational change that could make for a judicious technocracy.

In turn, I will use empirical evidence regarding real-world American technocrats' behavior to suggest patterns of an injudiciousness that might plausibly be viewed as a precondition of real-world technocracy, with the intention not of predicting whether these patterns will persist, but of thinking about whether a technocracy would be unable to function in the absence of patterns such as these. In other words, I will be asking whether pathologies that seem to exist in the here and now are somehow necessary to the existence and reproduction of technocracy—as suggested, figuratively, by the notion that technocracy as a "system" is exerting metaphorical "pressures" for epistemic pathologies among individual technocrats—or, instead, whether these pathologies can somehow be overcome.

4.1. ECONOMICS AND THE ASSUMPTION OF EFFECTIVE OMNISCIENCE

> By attributing perfect knowledge to individuals, one makes their beliefs match whatever the
> facts are and thereby avoids the problem that action depends on subjective belief.
> —DANIEL HAUSMAN, *The Inexact and Separate Science of Economics*

In 1971, Wassily Leontief, later a recipient of the Nobel Prize in Economics, wrote, of his discipline, that "uncritical enthusiasm for mathematical formulation tends often to conceal the ephemeral substantive content of the argument behind the formidable front of algebraic signs."[1] In 1985, future Nobel laureate Robert Solow complained, of his fellow economists, that "there is enough for us to do without pretending to a degree of completeness and precision which we cannot deliver."[2] In 1991, Nobel laureate

---

[1] Leontief 1971, 1.
[2] Solow 1985, 329.

Gérard Debreu's presidential address to the American Economic Association defensively cataloged what he viewed as the achievements of formalization, but even he allowed that "in the past two decades, economic theory has been carried away further by a seemingly irresistible current that can be explained only partly by the intellectual successes of its mathematization."[3]

Critical commentary by respected economists was not the only form taken by late-twentieth-century doubts about the field. During the 1980s and 1990s, scholarly analysts of economics tended simply to take it for granted that "the profession" was in a state of crisis; as the analysts saw it, their job was not to document the crisis but to explain it. Characteristically, one of their studies began by observing, without the felt need for substantiation, that "contemporary academic economics is not in a healthy state.... While economic forecasters do not forecast sufficiently accurately, 'theorists' fail to provide non-arbitrary explanations of any real economic phenomenon of interest."[4] Another work concluded that while "the edifice of contemporary microeconomics is elegant, even gorgeous," its "empirical difficulties are legion" and perhaps insurmountable, and that "current work lacks any clear explanatory or predictive purposes."[5] A third author argued that "much of the mystery surrounding the actual development of economic theory— its shifts in formalism, its insulation from empirical assessment, its interest in proving purely formal, abstract possibilities, its unchanged character over a period of centuries, the controversies about its cognitive status—can be comprehended and properly appreciated if we give up on the notion that economics any longer has the aims or makes the claims of an empirical science of human behavior. Rather, we should view it as a branch of mathematics."[6] Perhaps most famously, Philip Mirowski claimed that ever since the nineteenth century, economists had suffered from such a strong degree of "physics envy" that economic theory should be seen as literally nothing but the elaboration of physical metaphors: "physics is the dog and economics is the tail."[7]

Yet, in a classic case of cultural evolution caused by ideational innovation, economics soon changed. Laboratory experimentation, quasi-random natural experiments, randomized field experiments, and randomized controlled trials began to come into vogue among economists in the 1990s, revolutionizing the methodological side of economics. This shift toward empirical methods hardly seems consistent with a discipline that has either mathematical formalism or physics envy in its DNA. The new empiricism has even been characterized as rendering the "neoclassical" label obsolete—along with criticisms of neoclassical apriorism.[8]

---

[3] Debreu 1991, 5.

[4] Lawson 1997, 3, 4–5.

[5] Hausman 1992, 280, 55.

[6] Rosenberg 1992, 247.

[7] Mirowski 1991, 396.

[8] Colander 2007, 15.

A different type of critique would focus on continuities in the substance of neoclassical economics, not its methods. Such a critique might target an idea that seems to have been in the back of the mind, if not on the tip of the tongue, of virtually every economist since Adam Smith. This is the notion—neither the conclusion of a mathematical proof nor an empirical finding, but what David Colander revealingly calls the "intuition"—that "incentives matter."[9] I will suggest that the more one's thinking is shaped by this intuition, the more one's economics will seem suited to the predictive task of epistocracy; but the less suited it will be to judiciously determining the limits of epistocratic knowledge. This is because incentives alone cannot actually produce behavioral predictions or, therefore, policy advice. Therefore, the incentives-matter intuition has to be supplemented by a sub rosa epistemology that is so naive that it lacks conceptual space for any acknowledgment of agents' fallibility, let alone their heterogeneity.

Consider the predicament in which an epistemologically sophisticated economist would find herself if she critically inspected her reliance on the intuition that incentives matter. First, she would notice that an incentive is powerless to affect behavior if it is not first perceived as an incentive by the agents whose behavior it is supposed to affect. Second, knowing that the perceived incentive will affect these agents' behavior is useless—for predictive purposes—if the economist does not also know exactly *how* it will affect it. But this requires knowing exactly how agents will interpret their situations in light of the perceived incentive. Only if they interpret their situations the way the economist does will the incentive "matter" *in a way the economist will be able to predict*.

Yet the economist cannot read minds. How, then, can she know how anonymous agents who may not even have appeared on the scene will perceive and interpret their situations? The only way she can know this, or believe that she knows it, is by tacitly assuming that the truth about the agents' situations will be self-evident to them, requiring neither fallible perception nor fallible interpretation. In that case, the agents' fallible ideas—whether homogeneous or heterogeneous—will not come into play, and the economist can infer the agents' behavior from the economist's own (putatively accurate) perception of agents' objective circumstances alone.

Borrowing from a manifesto issued by David Tuckett and twelve other social scientists challenging economists' epistemic blinders, I will call this tacit assumption the sub rosa epistemology of "effective omniscience."[10] Effective omniscience is not knowledge of everything; it is knowledge of everything an agent needs to know if she is to make the optimal decision in a given situation. By assuming agents' effective omniscience, economists turn the incentives-matter intuition into the basis for a technocratic policy science that can, they believe, reliably predict the behavior of agents about whom the science knows nothing—except the incentives the agents will objectively face if a given policy is enacted.

---

[9] Ibid., 44.

[10] Tuckett et al. 2015, 214; see the epigraph to this subsection.

4.1.1. The Economist as Naive Realist

The theoretician who did the most to explore the epistemic role of the incentives-matter intuition was another Nobel laureate in economics, Herbert A. Simon (although he received his doctorate in political science). Simon called the agent imagined by economists "the nearly omniscient *Homo economicus* of rational choice theory."[11] *Homo economicus* is not merely, in Simon's estimation, a self-interested agent, nor an agent who is instrumentally rational. After all, a selfish, instrumentally rational member of the species *Homo sapiens* is nonetheless ignorant and fallible—not effectively omniscient. The crucial point about the species *Homo economicus* is that economists ascribe to its members accurate knowledge of their objective circumstances, including accurate perceptions of the incentives they face and accurate forecasts of the effects of their possible actions on the goals they would like to achieve. This imputation of effective omniscience is, according to Simon, the original sin of economics, as it effaces human fallibility and one of its consequences: that fallible people may (in effect) disagree among themselves about the best course of action, making it difficult to predict the actions they will decide to take.

Simon's term for effective omniscience is *objective rationality* (or, alternatively, *substantive rationality*).[12] He explains that "the term 'rational' denotes behavior that is appropriate to specified goals in the context of a given situation." He continues: "If the characteristics of the choosing organism are ignored and we consider only those constraints that arise from the external situation, then we may speak of substantive or objective rationality, that is, behavior that can be adjudged objectively to be optimally adapted to the situation."[13] By contrast, Simon dubs the instrumental rationality of fallible, heterogeneously ignorant agents "procedural" rationality, by which he means that fallible, heterogeneously ignorant agents attempt to determine the most efficient means for achieving their ends—but that these attempts may fail while remaining rational.[14]

Simon maintains that economists rest their conviction that "every actor . . . always chooses the alternative with the highest utility"[15] on the assumption that actors are objectively rational, and thus that their attempts succeed. By tacitly equating instrumental rationality with objective rationality, rather than with procedural rationality, they impute effective omniscience to agents who are actually fallible and ignorant. That is, economists are naive third-person realists about economic agents. Just as the naive first-person realist treats her own perceptions as unmediated by interpretation, the economist analyzes economic agents as if their situations require no interpretation. Insofar as situations do require interpretation, however, and insofar as the interpreters are fallible and ignorant, they might fail to know about some important aspect of their situations. They might also

---

[11] Simon 1985, 303.

[12] Ibid., 294.

[13] Ibid.

[14] The distinction between procedural and objective rationality first appears in Simon 1976.

[15] Simon 1985, 296.

fail to know the best interpretive context for making sense of the aspects of which they are aware. Any such gaps in their knowledge would make their reactions to their situations unpredictable, assuming that these gaps are idiosyncratically heterogeneous, which the argument of the last chapter allows us to assume as the default.

Without the assumption of objective rationality or effective omniscience, incentives would not matter in a predictable fashion. And so—as if "technocracy" were exerting a pressure on economists to produce the unending stream of behavioral predictions for which they have become notorious—they have accepted this assumption unquestioningly, despite the violence it does to the fallible and heterogeneous nature of people's ideas. Thus, I will refer to this epistemically pathological behavior as, metaphorically, the economist's response to a systemic "pressure to predict," although I will aim to render the metaphor in epistemologically individualistic form by disaggregating the "system" into the prosaic operations of culture, and by locating the "pressure" in a mechanism that operates at the individual level.

4.1.2. The Red Herring of Irrationality

Critics of economic theory typically contend that economists err in treating agents as instrumentally rational and self-interested, overlooking real people's "irrational" other-directness and emotionality. But such criticisms, unlike Simon's, do not cut very deep. The assumption of self-interestedness can certainly cause distortions when noneconomic (e.g., political) behavior is being analyzed, as I suggested in my comments about public-choice theory in the introduction.[16] As grand theories go, however, the assumption of self-interestedness seems plausible when it comes to modern economic behavior, as is the assumption of instrumental rationality. Whether because of capitalism itself, the Protestant Ethic, or other cultural factors—and whether one deplores it or not—contemporary Westerners, at least, do seem, for the most part, to be rather homogeneously self-interested in their economic affairs. Nor is it reasonable to think that they are too emotional to behave with *procedural* rationality—driven, it is often said, by "animal spirits" rather than dispassionate calculation.[17] Emotions do not simply materialize for no reason. To take an example of great importance to economists, people become bullish (optimistic) or bearish (pessimistic) because they receive information that they interpret as either promising or worrisome. If their response to this information is suboptimal, the fault lies with the inadequacy of the information or its interpretation, not with the emotion that stems from the interpretation.

Thus, in ascribing self-interest and instrumental rationality to *Homo economicus*, economists merely do part of the job of judicious epistocrats: they identify behavioral

---

[16] See also Friedman 1996.

[17] Akerlof and Shiller's *Animal Spirits* (2009) is a book-length development of Keynes's idea (Keynes 1936, 161). For an epistemological critique, see Friedman and Kraus 2011, 53–55.

norms and other homogeneous or homogenizing ideas. Although economists do not think about it this way, the culturally transmitted homogenizing norm of self-interest might, in principle, counteract the presumptive heterogeneity of agents' actions—if we ignore the fact that agents must fallibly interpret their situations prior to acting. Once we take this fact into account, though, we find that even in principle, the norms of procedural self-interest significantly underdetermine an agent's actions. Neither procedural rationality nor self-interestedness does away with agents' need to perceive and interpret their circumstances, the fallibility of the resulting interpretations, or the unpredictable heterogeneity of the resulting actions. Instrumental rationality is merely a propensity to weigh the costs and benefits of one's actions—a propensity that, if anything, increases agents' unpredictability by incorporating their estimates of consequences into their behavior. Consequences are always uncertain, especially in the modern world. As for self-interestedness, it concerns ends, not means, and means are just as epistemically fraught as ends, if not more so. Just as citizen-technocrats may be divided over how best to achieve consensual ends, individual agents may not know which means will achieve their ends—regardless of whether these are selfish. Indeed, the actions of an agent whose every action was determined not by self-interest but by ethical or traditional precepts would be far *more* predictable than those of an agent acting in accordance with an uncertain calculus of gain.

Economists elide these uncertainties by assuming, as Simon puts it, "that the actor will choose the alternative for which the expected utility is the highest." He elaborates: "By expected utility of an alternative is meant the average of the utilities of the different possible outcomes, each weighted by the probability that the outcome will ensue if the alternative in question is chosen."[18] Yet economic theory "does not postulate anything about the way in which the actor makes probability estimates of uncertain events."[19] Thus, "the mere assumption of [instrumental] rationality provides little basis for the prediction of behavior. To be of much use, that assumption must be supplemented by considerable empirical knowledge about the decision maker."[20] Without such knowledge, an economist cannot know how an ideationally determined and fallible but idiosyncratic actor will make probability estimates. Even harder to fathom is how the economist can reliably predict the estimates of anonymous *future* actors whose ideas are idiosyncratically fallible. But the imputation of objective rationality to economic agents makes the *economist's* need for knowledge of the agents seem to disappear.

In targeting objective rationality, then, Simon took aim at the Achilles heel of economics as an epistocratic science: that is, a discipline that purports to be able to predict the behavior of real people in the real world. Real people may be selfish, and they may be instrumentally rational, but they are not omniscient about how to behave in given

---

[18] Simon 1985, 296.
[19] Ibid.
[20] Ibid., 295.

circumstances; nor are economists omniscient about how agents should behave in given circumstances, let alone, crucially, how they will *think* they should behave.

4.2. ECONOMICS AS A POLICY SCIENCE

The economic analyst has opted for Reason. His guide is a single principle. He assumes that men pursue their interest by applying reason to their circumstances. And he does not ask *how they know* what those circumstances are.

—G. L. S. SHACKLE, *Epistemics and Economics*

Without economics we lose even the illusion that we understand the probable, or potential, long-term or merely possible consequences of choices that policy makers are forced to make.

—ALEXANDER ROSENBERG, "If Economics Isn't Science, What Is It?"

If we seek to "deduce the substantively, or objectively, rational choice in a given situation," Simon noted, "we need to know only the choosing organism's goals and the objective characteristics of the situation. We need to know absolutely nothing else about the organism."[21] Thus, by assuming away her own need for agent-specific knowledge, the economist is able to sidestep all the difficulties of interpersonal understanding that are exemplified, in more manageable form, by the challenges of intellectual history.

The resulting practices are perfectly suited to the prediction of technocratic policy effects. In treating as unproblematic the actors' (subjective) knowledge of the optimal action dictated by a technocratic initiative, the economist can derive a prediction of the actors' rational behavior from the economist's own (subjective) perception of the optimal action. An unparalleled measure of *Verstehen* is achieved—because the actor is nothing but an imagined replica of the economist.

Suppose the economist envisions a policy that will create incentive I, which would, the economist believes, make action A_1 optimal for agents (about whose idiosyncratic ideas she knows nothing) who find themselves in situation S_1. By enacting the policy, the economist predicts, the higher incidence of A_1 will solve, prevent, or mitigate an economic problem. But if some of the agents in S_1 were to interpret A_2 or A_3 or A_4 as the optimal action, and if no homogenizing norm counteracted this conclusion by dictating A_1 (in the agents' judgment), the economist's prediction about these agents' behavior would be rendered inaccurate. This is possible insofar as the agents are ignorant or fallible. Ignorant or fallible agents might misconstrue the objective situation: they might think that S_1 is actually S_2 or S_3 or S_4. Or they might misinterpret which action is optimal when S_1 is conjoined with I. Furthermore, if agents interpret their situation *correctly* but the economist does not, or if agents are *right* to deem A_2 or some other action optimal

---

[21] Ibid., 296.

when the economist does not, the economist's behavioral predictions will once again be inaccurate.

What a technocrat needs if she is to make reliably accurate behavioral predictions is not the ability to infer optimal actions from future agents' objective circumstances, but the ability to predict future agents' subjective interpretations of how to behave under future circumstances as the agents themselves will perceive and interpret them. The objective optimality of A_1 is no more relevant to any particular agent's behavior than the truth value of the beliefs of an historical actor is relevant to our understanding or explanation of those beliefs. Indeed, if both the economist and the agent *wrongly* believe that A_1 is optimal, their convergent error will ensure that the economist's behavioral prediction is accurate. It is when the beliefs of the technocrat differ from those of the agent that unanticipated behavioral consequences may follow—regardless of whether the beliefs of either party, or both of them, track objective reality. Thus, the effect of the economist's imputation of objective rationality to economic agents is not just empirically objectionable because it credits them with superhuman powers of perception and interpretation. It is epistemically pathological—even while being functional for technocracy—because it seems to establish a homogeneity of ideas as between the economist-technocrat and the agents, and among the agents too, enabling the economist-technocrat to think she can predict their behavior. If, in reality, agents and the economist-technocrat have heterogeneous ideas about which action is objectively best for the agents to take, then a misalignment between predicted action and actual action may occur, and the policy based on the bad prediction will unintentionally encourage behaviors not predicted by the economist-epistocrat.

Consider, for example, a somewhat dated but tractable example of how an economist of the sort criticized by Simon might, prior to the empiricist methodological revolution to be discussed in Section 4.4, analyze a proposal to establish a minimum wage. The economist might begin by noticing that (1) if it is to have any positive effect, the new law will have to raise wages above their current level, increasing employers' costs. This would be an objective change in conditions—a tax on labor, in effect—that, the economist might argue, (2) creates an objective disincentive for employers to employ labor, ceteris paribus. Simon's argument does not fault these two steps in the economist's reasoning. However, to predict what employers will do in response to the theorized disincentive, the economist must further assume (3) that employers will notice the tax on labor (that is, perceive it accurately), (4) that employers will infer that the optimal response to the tax is to economize on labor, and thus (5) that they will reduce employment beneath the level it otherwise would have reached. Unless this reduction in employment is outweighed, normatively, by higher wages paid to the workers who keep their jobs, then a technocratic policy recommendation—do not establish a minimum wage—appears to follow straightforwardly from the behavioral prediction. But the behavioral prediction itself follows only from the assumption that employers will see their new situation just as the economist does in the third and fourth steps. If employers fail to perceive and interpret their situation as the economist does, the economist's prediction will fail—regardless of whether the economist is right about the optimality of the employers' predicted response.

The accuracy of this type of reasoning was called into question by the first major salvo of the new economic empiricism: a natural experiment investigated by David Card and Alan Krueger, who compared employment in New Jersey after the statewide minimum wage was raised in 1992 to employment in eastern Pennsylvania, where the statewide minimum stayed the same. Card and Krueger concluded that raising the minimum wage had *reduced* unemployment.[22] In response, however, Nobel laureate James M. Buchanan contended that any minimum wage that increases the wages of the covered workers *must* increase unemployment, a priori, due to "the inverse relationship between quantity demanded and price," that is, "the law of demand." This law, according to Buchanan, is "the core proposition in economic science," as it "embodies the presupposition that human choice behavior is sufficiently rational to allow predictions to be made." (Buchanan was referring, of course, to objective rationality, or effective omniscience—not fallible, subjective, procedural rationality.) Thus, "just as no physicist would claim that 'water runs uphill,' no self-respecting economist would claim that increases in the minimum wage increase employment. Such a claim, if seriously advanced, becomes equivalent to a denial that there is even minimal scientific content in economics."[23]

In Buchanan's view, then, the scientific status of economics is contingent on its ability to predict behavior. But if the incentives-matter intuition is to ground this ability, as Buchanan is assuming, it can only be by linking otherwise-powerless objective incentives (2) to agents' predicted actions (5) by means of the assumption that agents will accurately perceive and interpret the objective dictates of the incentives in the same way that economists do (3–4). Thus, in the case at hand, Buchanan has to assume that future employers will believe certain things that Buchanan believes, even though he knows nothing about these employers except the incentives they will objectively face if the minimum wage is raised.

Thus, in the interest of "science" as understood by an epistocrat, Buchanan ascribes to unknown, anonymous agents the subjective propensity to take actions that *would* follow from their accurate knowledge of objective circumstances—but without explaining where this knowledge will originate. This is more like magical thinking than science.

4.2.1. *A "Systemic Pressure" for Naive Economic Realism*

In a lecture to the American Political Science Association, Simon urged his audience to avoid the epistemological fiction of objective rationality that is foundational to neoclassical economics. Thus, he recommended that political scientists commit themselves to

---

[22] Card and Krueger 1994.
[23] Buchanan 1996.

a research program strikingly similar to that of the intellectual historian—broadly conceived as the student of past actors' ideas, whether the actors are one or many, "elites" or "masses." Political scientists should, he said, "carry on painstaking empirical research at both macro and micro levels" with the aim of discovering the subjective reasons for political actors' actions, and also the reasons for those reasons—that is, to discover "where political ideas come from."[24] He argued that these discoveries are sometimes within reach, because people "do appear to behave in a [procedurally] rational manner—they have reasons for what they do, and a clever researcher can usually obtain data that give good clues as to what those reasons are."[25]

Whatever data this might require must perforce be drawn from the past. Political science, then, must be retrospective if it is to be empirical and thus truly scientific, in sharp contrast to Buchanan's assumptions about scientificity. "The key premises in any theory that purports to explain the real phenomena of politics," Simon argued, "are the empirical assumptions about goals and, even more important, about the ways in which people characterize the choice situations that face them. These goals and characterizations do not rest on immutable first principles, but are functions of time and place that can only be ascertained through empirical inquiry. In this sense, political science is necessarily a historical science."[26]

Simon went on to point out that acknowledging people's instrumental rationality "is very different from claiming," as economists do, "that we can predict the behavior of these rational actors by application of the objective rationality principle to the situations in which they find themselves." "Such prediction" is, he maintained, "impossible," for in the real world, behavior depends not only on "the structure of the actors' utility functions" (i.e., what they desire) but on "their representation of the world in which they live, what they attend to in that world, and what beliefs they have about its nature"[27] (i.e., how they perceive and interpret their situations). Clearly, however, "there is no way, without empirical study, to predict which of innumerable reasonable specifications" of their situations "the actors will adopt."[28] Thus, Simon said at a conference in 1985, economists "fail to distinguish between the real world and the decision maker's perception of it"; they insist that those whose actions they are trying to predict see "the world as it really is."[29] Because they do not notice that fallible agents must *interpret* the world, economists think they can "predict the choices that will be made by a rational decision maker" by drawing solely on economists' own

---

[24] Simon 1985, 303.
[25] Ibid., 300.
[26] Ibid., 303.
[27] Ibid.
[28] Ibid.
[29] Simon 1987, 27.

"knowledge of the real world and without knowledge of the decision maker's perceptions or modes of calculation."[30]

However, if economists *were* to recognize that people's choices can be predicted only if one knows their interpretations of the world, and further that this knowledge is, as a practical matter, unavailable when it comes to the interpretations of anonymous agents, especially future anonymous agents, then economists' qualifications to be epistocrats would be called into question—not just objectively but subjectively, that is, in their own minds. I am not suggesting, however, that, in an effort to retain their roles as epistocrats, economists deliberately set out to ignore behavioral unpredictability. It seems far likelier that their training in the incentives-matter tradition obscures from them the very possibility of deviations from objective rationality due to agents' ideational differences from economist-observers and from each other, that is, their ideational heterogeneity. In the incentives-matter tradition, theorizing about the effects of incentives on unknown agents is equated with theorizing about the agents' behavior, because the intervening role of agents' fallible, heterogeneous ideas is entirely overlooked. Economists trained to theorize this way will be able to produce behavioral predictions with no knowledge of agents' webs of belief—and no awareness that they need this knowledge. That is, they will be radically ignorant of their epistemic blind spot. By contrast, economists who transcended their training in the incentives-matter tradition or never received it—and who followed Simon in concluding that, to be truly scientific, they should consign themselves, in effect, to being intellectual historians—would thereby select themselves out of the pool of epistocrats, for the sine qua non of technocracy is to make predictions about unknown agents' future behavior.

Thus, self-selection is an epistemologically individualistic mechanism that could account for what otherwise looks like a systemic "pressure" to predict. *If* there is a regime in the real world that qualifies as technocratic in my sense, it must, by definition, have decision-makers who make ex ante predictions of human behavior. If the regime is an epistocracy, in whole or in part, these decision-makers, or those who advise them, must, by definition, claim access to esoteric knowledge (such as the "knowledge" produced by rational-choice theory) that, they believe, enables reliable behavioral predictions. Social scientists who were unable to generate such predictions, such as economists who internalized Simon's critique, could no longer be epistocrats, by definition, unless they managed to come up with a judicious way to turn intellectual history toward predictive purposes. Assuming for now that this is a practical impossibility, these social scientists would have selected themselves out of the epistocracy, replaced by people who had selected themselves into it by ignoring ideational heterogeneity and fallibility—people such as Buchanan.

Figuratively speaking, the "response" of such people to the "pressure" exerted by "technocracy" is to make aprioristic behavioral predictions premised on naive economic realism.

---

[30] Ibid.

4.2.2. *Taming Radical Ignorance*

> To search for a solution to a problem is an absurdity. For either you know what you are
> looking for, and then there is no problem; or you do not know what you are looking for, and
> then you are not looking for anything.
> —MICHAEL POLANYI, *Science, Faith, and Society*

The preceding analysis of economic theory may seem to be contradicted by mid-twentieth-century attempts to take account of economic agents' ignorance. But a brief look at some highlights of these attempts, which go under the heading of "the economics of information," will suggest that the opposite is the case.

This literature was inaugurated by future Nobel laureate George Stigler's 1961 paper, "The Economics of Information." Stigler treated information as neoclassical economists treat any other scarce good: it will be purchased only to the extent that agents have an incentive to consume it after weighing its utility against its cost. "If the cost of search is equated to its expected marginal return," according to Stigler, "the optimum amount of search will occur, and thus the optimal information will be learned."[31]

For Stigler, learning presupposes a search for information, a search whose costs and benefits are known in advance by the searching agent. Stigler equated the marginal return that an agent expects to receive from an information search with the *optimal* return by simply imputing to her accurate knowledge of the value of the information she does not yet know (not yet having conducted the search). Only in this way could Stigler predict the optimality of the search ex ante. Thus, his model of search is contingent on the assumption of objective rationality, that is, effective omniscience, even though he was purportedly analyzing agents who, lacking information, are ignorant.

As Shaun P. Hargreaves Heap and Yannis Varoufakis point out, Stigler's model "begs the question of how the agent knows how to evaluate the potential utility gains from a bit more information *prior to gaining that information*."[32] One cannot know the benefits of unknown information (and thus whether it would be objectively rational to "learn" it) without already knowing the information. In Stigler's view, agents fail to learn only what they have *accurately* calculated would not be worth learning. Thus, they are radically ignorant of nothing; there are, for them, no unknown unknowns. Were Stigler to have allowed that agents are radically ignorant, he could not have predicted the optimality of their information searches: they might end their searches before it was optimal to do so or extend them after it was optimal to do so. Or the information they need might not have been discovered yet, making their searches pointless. Or their interpretations of their situations might wrongly persuade them that they have all the information they

---

[31] Stigler 1961, 216. (This section draws on Evans and Friedman 2011.)

[32] Hargreaves Heap and Varoufakis 1995, 21.

need, such that they keep themselves in the dark because they are not even aware that that is where they are.

The main refinement of Stigler's model came in 1970, when future Nobel laureate George A. Akerlof introduced the concept of asymmetrical information in a paper called "The Market for 'Lemons.'"[33] Akerlof's idea was that people can lack relevant information that cannot be searched for. To use his example, the most feasible way for a used-car buyer to discover if a given car is a lemon may be to buy it and then find out; usually, it is hard to detect a lemon in advance. The prospective buyer's ex ante ignorance here is suboptimal, while in Stigler's view all ignorance is optimal.

However, Akerlof did not allow that prospective buyers may be radically ignorant— unaware of the existence, relevance, content, or interpretive significance of the information they lack. He assumed that prospective buyers know that they are ignorant about whether a given car is a lemon. Moreover, he assumed that this ex ante ignorance is not inadvertent but is the product of lemon sellers' incentive to withhold from buyers information that is known to the sellers; accordingly, the economist can know about the ignorance of the buyers, ex ante, by deriving it from the incentives the sellers face. Thus, the economist can predict both parties' behavior. These assumptions may be plausible in the context of buying a used car, but they are unlikely to be applicable in many other situations. By focusing on the unusual situation of used-car sales, Akerlof avoided the intractabilities of radical and thus unpredictable ignorance. The missing information about whether a given car is a lemon is, to Akerlof's buyer, a known unknown, and to Akerlof's seller, a known known. There are no unknown unknowns for either party, nor for the economist making predictions about them.

The locus classicus in the literature on "signaling" in labor markets suffers from the same defect. In the model developed by future Nobel laureate Michael Spence, employers are ignorant of the productivity of job applicants; this "makes the decision one under uncertainty."[34] However, employers know that they are ignorant in this way, while potential employees are assumed to know about their employers' ignorance. In response, employees signal their productivity to employers by means of heuristics such as educational degrees. Indeed, a "wage schedule" (an objective statistical distribution) tells prospective employees the precise value of such signaling, enabling them rationally to decide if they should, say, graduate from high school or attend college. A prospective employee "will invest in education" as a signal "if there is sufficient return" for sending this signal, "as defined by the offered wage schedule."[35]

---

[33] Akerlof 1970. Not coincidentally, Akerlof coauthored *Animal Spirits* (Akerlof and Shiller 2009), which attempted to introduce realism into economic theory not by abandoning the assumption of objective rationality, but by focusing on predictable emotional barriers to objectively rational behavior.

[34] Spence 1973, 356.

[35] Ibid., 358.

As with the market for lemons, the problem here is not a complete lack of verisimil-itude, as it was in Stigler's original version of the economics of information. While the notion of a knowable wage schedule is ridiculous in many cases, and while many people "invest" in education for reasons other than their employment prospects, the idea that employees and employers may be wary of each other is no more absurd than the idea of wary used-car buyers. The problem is that the only type of ignorance allowed for by Spence is ignorance that is known about by employers and prospective employees—and thus by economists. Such ignorance is a *predictable* response to incentives, just as in Stigler's model.

Thus—as if it were perversely devised by technocracy as a "system"—the eco-nomics of information acknowledges but carefully hems in agents' ignorance. If, as the theorists assume, agents' effective omniscience is the default, and if departures from this default are due to objective incentives knowable to agents and econo-mists alike, then the resulting behavior can be unproblematically predicted both by other agents and by economist-epistocrats. But if economic agents could be radi-cally ignorant—simply, straightforwardly, accidentally ignorant, in the sense that each of us rediscovers about ourselves whenever we are surprised by a mistake we have unwittingly made—then their actions could not be reliably predicted, either by other agents or by economists. And in that case, economists could not be epistocrats. Economists who recognized this type of unpredictability would thereby select them-selves out of the pool of potential epistocrats—unless they found a judicious way to discern the existence, and extent, of homogenizing factors that might cause slippage between ideas and actions.

4.3. THE ERASURE OF IGNORANCE BY BEHAVIORAL ECONOMISTS

In the limit, each individual's psyche and patterns of cognition are unique.... Psychologists who strive to reduce this complexity to more general laws, such as Freud or Skinner, raise the same questions as do neoclassical economists who do the same thing. Logically, how do you take aggregate measures on incommensurable individual attributes?
—LAWRENCE E. LYNN JR., "The Behavioral Foundations of Public Policy Making"

"Behavioral" economics offers an interesting comparison to economics proper, because despite its name and its clear epistocratic implications, it is a branch of cognitive psy-chology. A brief examination of some work in behavioral economics will suggest that the pathological epistemic tendencies self-selected for by neoclassical economists, including economists of information, can have other sources than the incentives-matter tradition. For behavioral economists share the same epistemic tendencies as economists such as Buchanan, Stigler, Akerlof, and Spence, even though incentives play no essential role in their paradigm.

4.3.1. Economics and Psychology

The founders of behavioral economics, Daniel Kahneman and Amos Tversky, were trained psychologists who never taught in an economics department. This makes the rapid assimilation of their approach by economists all the more striking. Nobel Prizes in economics were awarded in 2002 to Kahneman, after Tversky had died; in 2013 to Robert Shiller, who revived Keynes's "animal spirits," but as a predictable psychological regularity (in the spirit of behavioral economics); and in 2017 to Richard Thaler, a behavioral economist who had joined with Cass Sunstein to create guidelines for technocratic "nudging."[36] Assuming that the prize committees accurately represented sentiment in "the profession," these awards suggest that, contrary to the criticisms made by so many observers during the late twentieth century, neoclassical economics is only as formalistic, and only as inattentive to empirical data, as seems necessary to produce sweeping behavioral predictions. If empiricists can make such predictions, economists are not only willing to listen, but eager to learn, even if the empiricists hail from another discipline. And if these empiricists portray *Homo economicus* as *procedurally* irrational, that is acceptable too. Even more strikingly, the research agenda of behavioral economists is to enumerate *deviations* from the objective rationality that Simon identified as the cornerstone of neoclassical economics. However, these deviations, as canonized in the ever-growing list of irrational "heuristics and biases," are supposed to be shared by everyone, at least in the aggregate—such that they can ground ex ante behavioral predictions. Where an orthodox neoclassical economist such as Buchanan attributes predictability to agents by assuming a priori that they tend not to make mistakes, behavioral economists attribute predictability to them by assuming that their mistakes, established a posteriori through laboratory experimentation, reflect homogeneous cognitive defects rather than unpredictably idiosyncratic ignorance, or the unpredictably fallible interpretations of either the agents or the psychologists studying them. Again, then, as with the economics of information, while behavioral economics offers the superficial promise of epistemic realism, the actuality so constrains the realism as not to disturb technocratic faith in the predictability of human behavior. Behavioral economics complicates the simple model of predictable behavior used by economists such as Buchanan, but it does not complexify it in the epistemic sense. The default remains agents' objective rationality, which enables the ex ante behavioral prediction of agents' behavior, and empirically established deviations from the default are equally predictable.

I will examine just two of these deviations in detail, in the hope of showing that behavioral economics may be just as epistemically pathological as economics—such that the epistemic pathologies exhibited in the latter field need not necessarily stem from the incentives-matter tradition. This may allow us to get a better handle on why that tradition itself was selected for.

---

[36] Thaler and Sunstein 2008.

4.3.2. Problems of Interpretation in Behavioral Economics

In perhaps their most celebrated experiment, Tversky and Kahneman described to experimental subjects a former philosophy major, "Linda," who, while a college student, had been "deeply concerned with issues of discrimination and social justice, and also participated in anti-nuclear demonstrations."[37] The subjects were then asked if it is more "probable" that Linda would become a feminist bank teller than that she would become a bank teller simpliciter; they tended to say yes.

Tversky and Kahneman maintain that in making this judgment, the subjects failed to notice that a part must be smaller than the whole. Feminist bank tellers are a subset of all bank tellers and must therefore be less numerous than the latter, so it was illogical for the subjects to impute feminism to Linda. According to Tversky and Kahneman, then, the subjects had manifested a psychological bias, the "conjunction fallacy," that is procedurally irrational, but that is used with enough regularity that it will predictably crop up outside the psych lab.

However, a replication of the experiment largely eliminated the apparently illogical responses by asking the question about Linda in terms of frequencies, not probabilities.[38] As Zeljka Buturovic and Slavisa Tasic explain, "If we do not assume that the subjects understand *probable* to mean what Bayesian statisticians mean by the term, we may recognize that instead [the subjects] may ask themselves, 'How *frequently* would one find a philosopher/left-wing political activist/bank teller who is not a feminist as compared to one who is?' "[39] Tversky and Kahneman, however, seem to have tacitly assumed that their subjects were using the Bayesian definition of "probable" that Tversky and Kahneman themselves were using. The authors' hidden premise was that the "true" definition of the term *probable* is self-evident, such that the Bayesian definition is not a matter about which the subjects might rationally (albeit tacitly) differ from the experimenters, or about which they might rationally but unpredictably disagree among themselves, or which they might simply fail to know about or understand. Only this naively realistic premise justifies the inference that the subjects' responses were fallacious and, in turn, that they must have stemmed from psychological miswiring (rather than ignorance, misunderstanding, or disagreement), manifesting a discrete "bias" that can be generalized to the human race as a whole (insofar as we all share the same wiring).

Naive realism is even more clearly at work in behavioral-economics research purporting to show predictable heuristics and biases in the use of particular statistics, rather than biases in statistical reasoning in general. Consider another landmark study that, like the Linda paper, gets its own chapter in Kahneman's popularization of behavioral economics, *Thinking: Fast and Slow* (2011). In this 1973 experiment, Kahneman and Tversky

[37] Tversky and Kahneman 1983, 297.
[38] Fiedler 1988.
[39] Buturovic and Tasic 2015, 136–137, emphases added.

presented subjects with a character sketch of "Tom W." The psychologists told the subjects that Tom is

> of high intelligence, although lacking in true creativity. He has a need for order and clarity, and for neat and tidy systems in which every detail finds its appropriate place. His writing is rather dull and mechanical, occasionally enlivened by somewhat corny puns and flashes of imagination of the sci-fi type. He has a strong drive for competence. He seems to have little feel and little sympathy for other people and does not enjoy interacting with others. Self-centered, he nonetheless has a deep moral sense.[40]

The subjects were then asked to rank various fields of graduate specialization "in order of the likelihood that Tom is now a graduate student in each of these fields."[41] Ninety-five percent of the subjects believed that Tom is likelier to be a graduate student in computer science than in "the humanities or education" (which Kahneman and Tversky treated as a single field). This belief is irrational, according to Kahneman and Tversky, because the subjects "*were surely aware* that there are many more graduate students in the latter field,"[42] such that the odds are greater that Tom is in the humanities or education.

Kahneman and Tversky thus assume that the subjects were effectively omniscient about a topic to which most of them had probably never given a moment's thought before entering the laboratory: the statistical distribution of graduate students across academic disciplines in the United States circa 1973. Surely such statistics are not self-evident. Yet if the subjects were simply ignorant of them, there is no reason to assume that they irrationally preferred to use the stereotype of a computer geek *instead of* using the statistics.[43] In the Linda experiment, Kahneman and Tversky were naive realists about the meaning of "probable." In the Tom experiment, they were naive realists about the statistical distribution of graduate students in the United States circa 1973.

Kahneman and Tversky called such statistics "base rates." "Base-rate neglect" is one of the most important errors predictably committed by the human mind, in their view. However, if experimental subjects do not happen to know the relevant base rates, they will have little alternative but to use the information they do possess, which in the case of the Tom experiment seems to have been the stereotype of the computer geek conveniently handed to them by Kahneman and Tversky. Subjects who considered the option of guessing at the base rates might have decided that mere guesses were not good enough.

---

[40] Kahneman and Tversky 1973, 238.

[41] Ibid., 238–239.

[42] Ibid., 239, my emphasis.

[43] In *Thinking: Fast and Slow*, Kahneman retrospectively confirmed that he and Tversky had attributed effective omniscience to the subjects, asserting that "the members of the prediction group knew the relevant statistics" (Kahneman 2011, 149). The 1973 paper contains no evidence that the subjects knew the relevant statistics.

Or they might have inferred that they were being tested for their ability to deduce that Tom fit the stereotype handed to them by the experimenters, a deduction they proceeded to make.

Thus, Kahneman and Tversky failed to consider that experimental subjects, like everyone else, must interpret their situations before acting. In answering psychologists' questions, they may interpret what they are being asked differently than the psychologists do. They may also factor into their answers their interpretations of the intentions of the psychologists, and these interpretations can be mistaken. Kahneman and Tversky intended the Tom question as a test of the subjects' willingness to ignore putatively known base rates in favor of a stereotype, and they intended the Linda question as a test of the subjects' ability to recognize the logical relationship between a whole and its parts, but the subjects may have interpreted the Tom question as a test of their ability to infer his computer geekiness from the stereotype provided by the experimenters, and the Linda question as a test of their ability to infer her feminism from her undergraduate major and political ideas. Why else, they might have reasoned, would the psychologists have given them information about these things?

The Linda and Tom experiments are but two of many; the literature produced by behavioral economists is enormous. My selective reading of the literature suggests that these examples are typical expressions of a gigantic epistemic blind spot, but in this space I can only refer readers to other critics who have noticed similar problems.[44] However, I am not suggesting that we should disregard the claims of behavioral economists any more than that we should disregard the claims of economists. I am merely suggesting that it is possible to be a naively realistic epistocrat even without a grounding in the incentives-matter tradition; and that naive realism is pathological, from a technocratic point of view, even if it is not aprioristic. Therefore, we cannot simply hope that if it *were* to disregard the claims of aprioristic economists in favor of the claims of more empirically grounded social scientists, our technocracy could escape the epistemic pathologies exemplified by Buchanan's reaction to the Card and Kreuger study. A technocratic deformity wider than orthodox neoclassical economics seems to be at work. Indeed, if we examine in more detail the shift of economists themselves away from aprioristic orthodoxy, we will find that the orthodox repudiation of the subjective is not the only barrier to a judicious recognition of ideational heterogeneity. The positivist alternative is equally unfriendly to ideational heterogeneity, because it is committed to the assumption that empirical correlations necessarily indicate homogeneous regularities.

---

[44] See, e.g., Levi 1985, Funder 1987, Fiedler 1988, Gigerenzer 1991, Koehler 1993, Fletcher 1994, Madrian and Shea 2001, Hintikka 2004, Gigerenzer 2005, Plott and Zeiler 2007, and Buturovic and Tasic 2015.

4.4. POSITIVISM AND THE CONFRONTATION WITH HETEROGENEITY

We stand accused, not without reason, of ignoring history, psychology, and other behavioral
sciences, of arrogance and condescension toward "literary" practitioners of these subjects,
and now of inflating the contributions our quantitative methods can make to them.
—MARTIN BRONFENBRENNER, "Economics as Dentistry"

As I have noted before, a policy science needs to provide estimates of the costs and benefits of proposed or enacted policies. Thus, even an epistocracy run by orthodox neoclassical economists would require empirical research to attach weights, preferably precise
quantitative weights, to the behaviors that a priori theory predicts.

This is what econometric research provided during the middle decades of the twentieth century: the perceived ability to generate reliable quantitative behavioral predictions based on historical data. Thereafter, econometrics was displaced, to some extent,
by new methods that might seem to suggest the transformation of economics into a judiciously empiricist discipline. As of this writing, however, what seems actually to have
happened is that the pathology criticized by Simon—aprioristic naive third-person (and,
to an extent, first-person) realism—has been increasingly displaced by a quite different,
naively empiricist pathology that, once again, does not disturb the economist's perceived
ability to produce reliable behavioral predictions. The imputation of effective omniscience to agents by mere assumption has been displaced, to some extent, by a positivism
that effaces agents' beliefs and interpretations by dispensing with any economic anthropology at all, including the implausible one expressed by the notion of *Homo economicus*.

In criticizing positivism, I do not mean to invoke the elaborate theoretical and historical structure developed by Comte, or the ambitious philosophical agenda of the Vienna
Circle. Instead, I simply have in mind the widespread assumption that by probing behavioral "data" we can discover reliable behavioral homogeneities—without reference to,
and even in defiance of, agents' ideas.

4.4.1. Taking the Con Out of Econometrics

Econometricians assume that statistical findings about the past represent regularities that
can be extrapolated into the future. As we might expect, then, they tend to overlook the
problem of historical interpretation and the problem of time's arrow. They do try to deal
with the problem of novel circumstances, though, a problem that, after all, has to do with
objective realities, not with what positivists might view as subjective pseudo-realities.
Econometricians cope with novel circumstances in two ways: by attempting to predict
future agents' reactions to the changed objective incentives that would be created by a
given policy initiative; and by attempting to predict agents' reactions to whatever other
objective changes seem plausible and relevant to a given researcher, such as those suggested to her by forecasts about changing demographic or macroeconomic variables.

These efforts entail the manipulation of statistics. Straight-line extrapolations from historical statistics (the only kind there are) could not anticipate behavior in reaction to new circumstances, whether objective or subjective. As a result, econometrics is shot through with arbitrariness—or so economists began to think in the 1980s, giving rise to the methodological shift toward experimentalism that is still underway.

Edward Leamer's 1983 paper, "Let's Take the Con Out of Econometrics," was an early statement of the problem. "The econometric art as it is practiced at the computer terminal," Leamer pointed out, "involves fitting many, perhaps thousands, of statistical models. One or several that the researcher finds pleasing are selected for reporting purposes," and she tweaks the results to fit her preconceptions about the plausibility of this or that assumption.[45] Thus, as Tony Lawson later said, "Econometricians often appear to know *prior* to any formal analysis when certain sets of projections or estimates are at least plausible."[46] Deirdre McCloskey put the point more forcefully:

> People say, "We do econometrics, and that tests our hypotheses." Baloney. We do theory. I was just rereading last night Paul Krugman's famous article where he tries to introduce geographical considerations into economics, and it is a very skillfully done article. It's rhetorically very skillful. I can show you how it works rhetorically, but it is complete nonsense scientifically, not because it is wrong but because it is arbitrary.
>
> There are a zillion other ways of formalizing geography in economics that would come to opposite conclusions to those he comes to, and yet he's kind of airily saying that this is a contribution. Then there are a thousand other articles modifying that. It doesn't get anywhere: they modify it and get completely different conclusions. If you change your assumptions, you get different theorems.[47]

In time, sentiments like these came to be widely shared among economists, as suggested by a 2003 survey of students enrolled in the top seven US doctoral programs in economics. A Columbia student complained that "much of the econometrics work by applied economists . . . is simply manipulation of the data to say what they want to say."[48] A University of Chicago student put a more defensible gloss on the situation, however: "You have an idea about how the world works and you make a model to fit your idea."[49] Even if such practices were acceptable, however—given the need to generate quantitative behavioral predictions—the result of engaging in them was, as Leamer wrote, that "hardly anyone [took] anyone else's data analyses seriously."[50] A related issue was that, as McCloskey put

---

[45] Leamer 1983, 37. Cf., for example, Cooley and LeRoy 1981 and Manski 2013, 21.

[46] Lawson 1997, 37.

[47] McCloskey interviewed in Colander et al. 2004, 32.

[48] Colander 2007, 222.

[49] Ibid., 201.

[50] Leamer 1983, 37.

it, "most economists feel that conclusions from data sets are fragile. . . . Somebody claims to have found something, and then six months later a new equation is estimated, and the same finding seems to be reversed."[51] Lawson concluded that "the observed practices of econometricians indicate that the models actually derived are not sufficiently stable to allow the successful forecasting of events occurring outside the period for which the models were initially constructed."[52]

Unsurprisingly, however, economists did not produce any deep epistemological analysis of what was going wrong. Indeed, they appear to have seen the problem as a matter of unscrupulous data analysis. In order to take the con out of econometrics, therefore, they did not give up the attempt to extrapolate behavioral data into the future; if they had, they would have selected themselves out of the pool of potential epistocrats. Instead they turned to natural (quasi-controlled) and controlled (laboratory and field) experimentation to predict future behavior less arbitrarily, or so they seem to have thought.[53]

4.4.2. Interpretive Conundrums of Natural Experiments

> It does not even make sense to ask . . . what a minimum wage does in the absence of
> everything else.
> —JULIAN REISS[54]

The new empiricism was launched by Card and Krueger's finding that employment rose in New Jersey fast-food restaurants, compared to those in eastern Pennsylvania, even though the former had to pay a higher minimum wage. Card and Krueger attempted to render this finding plausible, in the eyes of orthodox neoclassical theorists, by invoking the theory of monopsony, but the force of their argument was a posteriori, not a priori.[55] More than a hundred empirical studies of minimum wages were conducted around the world during the next 15 years, most based on natural experiments like the one in New Jersey and Pennsylvania; the findings were then collected and analyzed by David Neumark and William L. Wascher.[56] This immense literature exemplifies the epistemic problems inherent in the use of empirical data for predictive purposes.

Consider first the problem of historical interpretation. Neumark and Wascher uncovered an ambiguity in the survey question Card and Krueger had used to elicit employment information from restaurant managers. Therefore, Neumark and Wascher substituted payroll data for managers' survey responses, and they concluded that Card and Krueger's findings were erroneous. According to the payroll data, the rise in New

---

[51] In Hendry et al. 1990, 187.
[52] Lawson 1997, 71. Cf. Heckman 2000, 49 and 90.
[53] Angrist and Pischke 2010.
[54] Reiss 2008, 176.
[55] Card and Krueger 1994.
[56] Neumark and Wascher 2007 and 2008.

Jersey's minimum wage encountered an employment elasticity of −0.2, meaning that a 10 percent increase in the minimum wage would have caused a 2 percent decline in employment—consistent with the orthodox view expressed aprioristically by Buchanan in reaction to Card and Krueger.[57] However, Card and Krueger responded to Neumark and Wascher by pointing out, inter alia, that payroll data varied significantly depending on whether restaurants reported their payrolls weekly, biweekly, or monthly. Card and Krueger attributed this discrepancy to the fact that the different types of restaurants "were differentially affected by seasonal factors, including the Thanksgiving holiday and a major winter storm in December 1992," which might have affected their short-term hiring.[58] Still, after controlling for these objective heterogeneities and making other adjustments, Card and Krueger concluded that "the increase in New Jersey's minimum wage probably had no effect on total employment in New Jersey's fast-food industry, and possibly had a small positive effect."[59] In short, their original findings and conclusions were probably wrong, but might have been a little bit right.

On the other hand, these findings are so sensitive to the interpretation of historical particularities that conclusions could shift again if, say, an eastern Pennsylvania restaurant manager from those days were to write a memoir. (Card and Krueger point out that the lower unemployment detected by Neumark and Wascher in the control area of Pennsylvania was "driven by data for restaurants from a single Burger King franchisee who provided all the Pennsylvania data.")[60] The appalling certitude displayed by both sides in the subsequent minimum-wage debate may be a function, in part, of the neat homogeneity of quantitative data, which hides the many ambiguities of the individual actions the data aggregate. These ambiguities, in the end, may be plausibly attributed to the variety of individual ideas that may lead to the same action: the Chesterton problem.

Neither side in the debate allowed that the conflicting findings produced by the many studies might have demonstrated heterogeneous *subjective*, interpretive responses to the incentives created by a rise in the minimum wage. Rather than uniformly firing employees, one restaurant manager might have reasoned that the best way to respond to the higher minimum was by reducing nonlabor costs, e.g., by eliminating menu items whose components were particularly expensive. But to avoid losing too many customers due to the smaller menu, this manager might have hired more workers to reduce waiting times or to increase the cleanliness of the bathrooms. The savings on food, she might have reasoned, might help to offset the wages of the larger staff, and the activities of the larger staff might help to offset the customers lost because they could not order the dropped menu items. If employment *had* risen in response to the higher minimum wage, but for ideational reasons such as these, we would be unable to conclude that higher employment

[57] Neumark and Wascher 2008, 73.

[58] Card and Krueger 2000, 1398.

[59] Ibid., 1419.

[60] Ibid., 1398.

would also occur in other times and places with other managers facing other objective circumstances and interpreting them idiosyncratically. Yet such a response to a higher minimum wage is no more idiosyncratic, in the sense of being *unlikely*, than any other response would be—including the orthodox response insisted upon by Buchanan.

Idiosyncratic managerial ideas might also explain the wide range in the magnitudes, as opposed to the directions, of various employment responses to higher wage minima. The employment elasticities of the studies listed by Neumark and Wascher ranged from 2.65 to −2.23, such that a 10 percent increase in the minimum wage would cause effects ranging from a 26.5-percent increase in a given population's employment to a 22.3-percent reduction.[61] This enormous variation in behavioral magnitudes might have been explained by different employers' heterogeneous ideas about how to respond to higher wage costs. If so, it would only go to show that natural experiments did not and could not solve, nor even address, the fundamental interpretive problems entailed by any attempt to extrapolate the past behavior of anonymous others into the future.

4.4.3. Controlled Experimentation and the Burden of Proof

However, natural experiments were soon replaced on the cutting edge of economic empiricism by randomized field trials and randomized controlled trials. Because these technologies assign treatment and control groups randomly, they came to be considered the methodological "gold standard." But the widely recognized problem with these methods is their external validity, or lack of it, which is essentially the same problem that plagues both natural experiments and old-fashioned econometrics.

How can one know that the behavior of agents in a field experiment or laboratory will be reproduced by agents elsewhere? The answer is the same as the answer to such questions as, How can one know that the statistical aggregates used by econometricians do not mask ideational variations that portend unpredictability? How can one know that a given statistical model of past behavior represents what will happen in the future, under different circumstances? How can one know whether New Jersey and eastern Pennsylvania fast-food restaurants were truly (homogeneously) comparable? The only way to "know" such things while knowing nothing about the agents' subjective ideas is to impute homogeneity to human behavior by *ignoring* the role of subjective ideas.

In this respect, the new empiricism is not so revolutionary after all, for it perpetuates the epistemic blindness of a priori economic theory. However, it is not identical to a priori theory, as it does not impute objective rationality to agents. Instead, it treats them as if they act homogeneously in response to whatever objective variables the economist deems worthy of investigating experimentally. *Homo economicus* as a creature of self-interest and omniscience is displaced by a cipher that uniformly reacts, for undertheorized reasons, to

---

[61] Neumark and Wascher 2007, Tables 5.1 and 5.2.

various objective factors, but the result is the same: its behavior can be predicted. Again, it is as if a technocratic pressure to predict perversely constrained the new empiricists' attempts to introduce realism into economics.

Could their positivist mindset nonetheless portend a judicious technocratic approach? By way of analogy, consider the increasingly recognized fact that psychological experiments often fail to replicate outside the "WEIRD" (Western, Educated, Industrialized, Rich, and Democratic) populations on which they have traditionally been conducted.[62] The positivist response to this fact would be to rein in the *universalist* assumptions of psychology, of which we will get a taste in the next section, by assuming henceforth that findings produced among Westerners are generalizable only to other Westerners. Is this not what we would want a technocratic discipline to do: judiciously limit its knowledge claims about homogeneities when heterogeneities are discovered?

That would be a step in the right direction, but it would not suffice. If heterogeneous behavior stems from people's heterogeneous ideas, we have reason to think that behavioral heterogeneity is the rule, not the exception. But in that case, the proper procedure would not be to assume behavioral homogeneity as the default until we identify a heterogeneity (such as non-WEIRD-ness) that makes us pull in our horns. Instead, heterogeneity should be the assumed default, and the burden of argument should rest with those who claim knowledge of homogeneities, not those who challenge these claims. Those who make homogeneity claims should have to explain why we should generalize from their local data to universalistic conclusions, even if the universe is "the West" rather than "everyone," or "unemployment in America" rather than "everywhere," or "unemployment among teenagers working at fast-food restaurants" rather than "among teenagers at large"—or rather than "unemployment among teenagers at this restaurant on this particular day," or rather than "the unemployment of this particular teenager." Julian Reiss points out that participants in randomized tests of the ultimatum game "made more generous offers in two experiments in Kansas City than in an identical experiment in Vermont," and that "students in a Kansas City community college offered more than workers in a nearby warehouse."[63] Once behavioral heterogeneity is unveiled by randomized experiments, as it was also unveiled in natural minimum-wage experiments, Lippmann's point about epistemic parochialism becomes very concrete: generalizations from one epistemic locale to another may express nothing more than the limited imaginations, or knowledge, of those making the generalizations.

It may also illustrate Lippmann's point about the "impulse to seek stability in an incalculable environment by standardizing for one's own apparent convenience all those who form the context of one's activity."[64] Consider the aspirations of Abhijit Banerjee and Esther Duflo, the leading proponents of randomized experimentation in economics.

---

[62] Henrich et al. 2010.

[63] Reiss 2008, 95, citing Carpenter et al. 2005.

[64] Lippmann [1925] 1927, 169.

Experimental work, they write, aims at answering such questions as "does better access to inputs (textbooks, flipcharts in classes, lower student-teacher ratios) matter for school outcomes (attendance, test scores), and if so, by how much?"[65] If we recognize that external validity problems may be rooted in the variability of people's ideas, we will wonder why we should think there is one answer to such questions across any two textbooks, flipcharts, students, teachers, schools, or other "variables," let alone across all of them everywhere. Surely the ideational content of *particular* textbooks and flipcharts, and the idiosyncratic webs of belief of the particular students and teachers who read this content, may have important effects on educational outcomes. But these "variables" are inherently heterogeneous, and thus cannot legitimately be tested with experiments any more than with multivariate regression analysis.

4.4.4. *General Heterogeneity and the Ideational Variety*

The wide variations in experimental findings lead Reiss to conclude that "human behavior appears to be extremely sensitive to the precise setting in which it occurs," and that "there seem to be few factors that are genuinely stable."[66] However, the mere possibility of unpredicted behavior caused by unidentified factors should not be enough to call behavioral extrapolations into doubt, for if we recognize this possibility (as we should), it amounts to saying nothing more than that social scientists are fallible, leaving us where we were at the end of Chapter 1: with the logical possibility of predictive error, and thus unintended technocratic consequences, but no reason to think that predictive error is likely. To go farther than that, we need to specify particular factors that might undermine the basis for reliable generalizations from a given experiment. Otherwise, positivist social scientists will say, with justice, that we simply need to test empirical variables that might cause the apparent heterogeneities—homogeneously, across all situations in which the heterogeneities might crop up.

Unlike aprioristic responses to the figurative pressure to predict, positivist responses do not rely on an overarching causal theory, such as one grounded in the intuition that incentives matter, that might allow the theorist to do without empirical data altogether (if not for the need to attach quantitative weights to theoretical predictions). Indeed, for the positivist, data are *all* one needs; causal theory is an afterthought or is dropped entirely. Thus, for example, Donald P. Green, Shang E. Ha, and John G. Bullock, leaders of the experimentalist movement in political science, argue that "one can learn a great deal of theoretical and practical value simply by manipulating variables and gauging their effects on outcomes, regardless of the causal pathways by which these effects are transmitted."[67] In technocratic terms, randomized experiments allow us to eschew the search for

---

[65] Banerjee and Duflo 2014, 80.

[66] Reiss 2008, 145.

[67] Green et al. 2010, 207.

causal knowledge (Type 2, in the schema I used in Chapter 1) in favor of efficacy knowledge (Type 3). Yet it is injudicious to assume that the efficacy knowledge gathered from an experiment can be considered relevant beyond the observed treatment population unless we have identified a homogenizing factor that could override ideational heterogeneity. Otherwise, assuming external validity entails the assumption of the uniformity of human behavior, an assumption that I hope to have called into question.

In the neoclassical orthodoxy, the assumption of behavioral uniformity is vouchsafed by the incentives-matter intuition. By renouncing causal theory, positivists formally repudiate this intuition, but this leaves them reliant on an ungrounded belief in behavioral uniformity, and thus in the external validity of this or that experimental (or observational) study. What we might call a "true" positivist, one who goes on nothing except this ungrounded belief, would have to accept any conceivable experimental result as externally valid, running into the New Mexican lawyer's problem. Recall that changes in the number of US. biology/biomedicine doctorates awarded annually strongly correlate (.928) with changes in the number of lawyers in New Mexico.[68] A true positivist would proffer such correlations among variables as the basis of policy advice, despite her ignorance of the causal pathways that might have produced the correlations and, therefore, her lack of a theory that would warrant the assertion of external validity in a given case. Only a *false* positivist would disregard such a correlation on the grounds that it seems implausible, inasmuch as the judgment of implausibility would stem from an a priori refusal, not driven by "the data," to take seriously correlations that have no apparent causal explanation.

True positivism is injudicious. The true positivist, letting the data "speak for themselves," might, if she wanted more biology PhDs, lobby for a new law school in Albuquerque. But false positivism is injudicious, too, because claims of implausibility need to be brought into the open and assessed: it is not enough merely to have a sneaking suspicion that a given correlation cannot be indicative of a behavioral regularity; one must provide a reason for suspicion—such as the absence of an epistemologically individualistic mechanism. Otherwise, claims of implausibility are little better than "intuitions" that are treated as self-evident, pre-empting any need for empirical research and returning us to an apriorism like Buchanan's—but without the explicit theorizing.

Thus, traditional neoclassical economists have criticized experimental positivism on the grounds of its theoretical ungroundedness. Nobel laureate James Heckman, for example, contends that natural experiments "often run the risk of producing estimates of causal parameters that are difficult to interpret [in that they are] . . . difficult to relate to the body of evidence about the basic behavioral elasticities of economics. The lack of a theoretical framework makes it difficult to cumulate findings across studies, or to compare the findings of one study with another."[69] Heckman is assuming, as so many

---

[68] As mentioned in Chapter 1; see http://www.tylervigen.com/.
[69] Heckman 2000, 85.

social scientists do, that the purpose of theory and empirics alike is to identify behavioral regularities or even universalities, not particularities—which, as such, may not be technocratically actionable. Reiss points out that for such critics of experimental positivism, "theories—by virtue of being general—ensure the external validity of the experimental hypotheses. Suppose that a certain hypothesis is internally valid for some experimental population. But since this hypothesis is derived from the theory (the theory of rational choice, say), it confirms the theory, and since the theory is general it applies (in principle) everywhere."[70] Invoking a theorized homogeneity in response to heterogeneous findings, then, begs the question raised by heterogeneity—the question of external validity. Yet this response is understandable if there is no ontological explanation for the heterogeneity. Without such an explanation, such as the possibility that agents' ideas are heterogeneous, what alternative do economists have to doubling down on theory—assuming that they must, figuratively, to respond to the pressure to predict?

Reiss proposes that economists "bite the bullet and accept that in economics there may be truths that are entirely local and not at all exportable."[71] If economists were to take his advice, they would be going in the same direction Simon recommended to political scientists: all the way from prediction and technocracy toward retrodiction and intellectual history, broadly speaking. From a technocratic perspective, however, a more judicious proposal would be to go only part of the way, with the extent determined by empirical findings about behavioral norms or other epistemologically individualistic factors—factors that are consistent with ideational determinism—that might counteract ideational heterogeneity. But this would presuppose that economists replace the default assumption of the uniformity of human nature with the default assumption of ideational and thus—until proven otherwise—behavioral unpredictability.

Given that both of the vulnerable parts of neoclassical economics—its positivist empirical tradition and its naively realistic theoretical tradition—are antithetical to a recognition of the causal role of ideas, it seems likelier that some discipline other than economics might become the site of judicious social science and, thus, policy science. Therefore, it may be helpful to consider epistemic pathologies in an almost completely nontechnocratic branch of social science, social psychology, as opposed to the cognitive psychology that gave birth to behavioral economics (which has clear technocratic implications, e.g., those fleshed out in work on nudging). It turns out that social-psychology research on the authoritarian personality offers striking parallels to the situation I have described in economics. The "pressure to predict," then, seems to extend even to social scientists who have no reason to want to predict—indeed, even to social scientists who are adamantly antitechnocratic, such as Theodor Adorno.

---

[70] Reiss 2008, 91.
[71] Ibid., 182.

4.5. NONTECHNOCRATIC SOCIAL SCIENTISTS WHO THINK
LIKE TECHNOCRATS

Statistical research is for the historian a good servant but a bad master. It profits him nothing
to make statistical generalizations, unless he can thereby detect the thought behind the facts
about which he is generalizing.
—R. G. COLLINGWOOD, *The Idea of History*

The Authoritarian Personality (1950), coauthored by Adorno and the social psychologists Else Frenkel-Brunswik, Daniel Levinson, and Nevitt Sanford, has exerted tremendous and ongoing influence on the field. In just the first six years after it appeared, the
book inspired at least 230 studies, of which at least 193 were authored by psychologists
or were published in psychology journals[72]—exceeding even the initial impact on economics of Card and Krueger's minimum-wage study. Although the intense interest in
The Authoritarian Personality tapered off over time, by 1989 there were, by one count,
1,200 studies of "the authoritarian personality," and by October 2018, *The Authoritarian
Personality* had been cited 17,138 times.[73] Much of the contemporary psychological literature in other areas, such as ethnocentrism, acknowledges its profound debt to Adorno
and his colleagues.[74]

In at least one respect, this is odd. *The Authoritarian Personality* is as close as a work
of modern social science can be to an exercise in grand, oracular theorizing—which has
never been the dominant mode in social psychology. Thus, even in the 1950s, the great
majority of publications sparked by the book were positivistic attempts to replicate, falsify,
or apply its narrow empirical claims, particularly those having to do with the infamous
F-scale, by means of which the authors measured fascist psychological tendencies. For the
most part, social psychologists were uninterested in either confirming or challenging the
book's Freudian theoretical superstructure: that is, the hypothesis that "future authoritarians were . . . raised by threatening, forbidding, status-conscious parents who punished
unconventional impulses harshly and arbitrarily. The child repressed hostility toward
these distant parents and covered his or her tracks with reaction formations of abject
submission and overglorification. The repressed aggression was displaced and projected
onto various outgroups. Hence authoritarianism and ethnocentrism were two sides of
the same coin."[75] It seems to have been as true in the middle of the twentieth century as
at the beginning of the twenty-first that social psychologists were far less concerned with
such theoretical claims than with positive data and the measurement thereof. Thus, it
may seem paradoxical that their attention was so consumed, for years after its publication, by a thousand-page book so thoroughly drenched in theory—and grand theory, at

---

[72] See the bibliography to Christie and Cook 1958.
[73] Van Ijzendoorn 1989, 37; citation count from Google Scholar.
[74] E.g., Jost et al. 2003, *passim*; Altemeyer 1996, 45.
[75] Altemeyer 1988, 52.

that. But whatever the book's theoretical "excesses," it was, from a positivist perspective, a cornucopia of testable hypotheses about behavioral regularities. Appropriately, then, *The Authoritarian Personality* not only ignored the causal role of ideas, and the unpredictable heterogeneity that goes with it; it explicitly repudiated such a role.

In the book's introduction, Adorno et al. note that "in modern society, despite enormous communality in basic culture, it is rare for a person to be subjected to only one pattern of ideas, after he is old enough for ideas to mean something to him"[76]—a nice summary of the third Lippmannite thesis. Immediately after the quoted sentence, however, the authors reach the conclusion that in the face of an individual's exposure to heterogeneous ideas, "some selection is usually made, according, it may be supposed, to the needs of his personality."[77] At a stroke, this disposes of both the ideational determination of people's ideas and their heterogeneity. If the authors' supposition is warranted, then people's ideas can justifiably be considered epiphenomena of their psyches, not their webs of belief. And if, as Freud taught the authors, the psyche follows known tendencies, the psychologist can produce justifiably sweeping explanations or even predictions of the ideas held by vast numbers of anonymous others. Yet the authors' supposition would be warranted only if the individual's selection of some "patterns of ideas" over others could not occur inadvertently and nonfunctionalistically—the result, for example, of path dependence in her web of beliefs—rather than being deliberately chosen for her, as it were, by a homunculus concerned with satisfying the needs of her personality.

If the foundation laid by earlier ideas forms the interpretive environment in which candidate ideas are evaluated, we do not need to posit a homunculus (Freudian or otherwise) to make the "choice" of the individual's ideas: it will be determined by her prior ideational exposures, woven together in an interpretive web. Because the authors seem to have been radically ignorant of this possibility, they were able to justify the reduction of people's ideas to psychological epiphenomena on the grounds that human "opinions . . . depend upon human needs," meaning the needs of the psyche.[78] This functionalism is hegemonic in social psychology even now, although the needs of the psyche are no longer viewed through a Freudian lens, or any other coherent theoretical lens.

4.5.1. Psychological Reductionism and Interpretive Charity

Psychological functionalism leads to the conclusion that if one knows people's psychological needs, one can predict their beliefs. This conclusion, of course, violates Skinner's "golden rule" of interpretive charity.[79] Social psychologists do not attribute *their own* beliefs (for example, their beliefs about the psychological functionality of beliefs) to a

---

[76] Adorno et al. 1950, 9.
[77] Ibid.
[78] Ibid., 5.
[79] Skinner 2002, 40.

psychological "need" to believe this or that; like all of us, social psychologists attribute their beliefs to their efforts to understand the truth. Only when trying to explain *others'* beliefs, and only when these beliefs are too odious or mysterious to be easily understood, does one resort to psychologizing. By psychologizing the other, one drives a wedge between understanding the meaning of the other's beliefs phenomenologically—in the heterogeneous ways they themselves might understand them—and explaining them scientifically.

Doing violence to others' beliefs is the result, as can be seen most clearly, but not exclusively, in the chapters of *The Authoritarian Personality* in which Adorno analyzed interviews with particularly authoritarian and ethnocentric subjects. Herbert Hyman and Paul Sheatsley's famous methodological critique of *The Authoritarian Personality* devotes some 20 pages to Adorno's painful leaps of interpretive logic,[80] but nothing conveys the magnitude of the problem like reading his chapters in their entirety. It would be worthwhile for any student of technocracy to explore these chapters because they show that qualitative social science and, indeed, qualitative social science drenched in grand theory can be just as positivistic, and thus as insensitive to ideational heterogeneity, as is quantitative social science. It will have to suffice, here, to offer two examples of Adorno's lack of interpretive charity, selected because they allow for detailed but relatively brief analyses.

First, Adorno discusses a woman who related to her interviewer that she once dated a lawyer who "was very well-educated and knew languages." The man proposed to her after three weeks during which "she had dates with him and saw quite a lot of him." However, simultaneously with his proposal he revealed that he was Jewish (he asked, "Would you object to marrying a Jew?"). At this, according to the interviewer, the woman "said that it was as if she had been struck a great blow. He did not look Jewish, his name was not Jewish, and he even sang in the choir of her church, so that she never suspected that he was Jewish." She rejected his offer. "The thing that is most impossible to her in the idea of marrying a Jew," the interviewer continues, "is the thought of bearing *Jewish children*." Upon seeing her suitor 10 years later, the woman "felt that he did look more Jewish, but added that that was perhaps because she now knew that he was Jewish."[81]

An intellectually charitable interpreter would say that while the woman was evidently anti-Semitic, we are not in a position either to understand her anti-Semitism or to explain it causally, as the interviewer did not ask the woman what she thought is so terrible about Jews.[82] An intellectually charitable understanding and explanation of belief X requires, at the very least, that we know what X is, in at least some particularity. (This is the basis of the problem of historical interpretation, and it is, *in nuce*, the difficulty

---

[80] Hyman and Sheatsley 1954, 89–109.

[81] Adorno et al. 1950, 642.

[82] Hyman and Sheatsley (1954, 97) point out that the interviews fail to "solicit the *reasons* for particular ideologies" or to inquire "into the way in which Negroes, Jews and other minority groups are *perceived*."

confronting technocracy.) All we can infer about this woman's beliefs is that they were, in some fashion that we cannot specify, anti-Semitic.

Adorno, however, thought he knew much more than that. "It is hardly going too far to assume," he asserted, that her anti-Semitism was based on a stereotype of Jewish "aggressiveness," and that this stereotype, in turn, "re-enacted old childhood taboos against sexuality and that it was only afterwards that these were turned against the Jew as an individual. Primary attraction is the basis for subsequent repulsion."[83] Yet the woman said nothing about either the man's aggressiveness or Jewish aggressiveness. Perhaps Adorno imputed to her this particular stereotype of Jews because of how quickly the man proposed marriage, but if the woman thought this behavior was overly aggressive she failed to say so. All we know is that she found *something* extremely objectionable about the fact that he was Jewish.

There is also no basis in "the interview data" for Adorno's suggestion that, upon running into the man 10 years later, the woman found him repulsive; she merely said that he now looked more Jewish than he had. But I will say nothing more about the extravagant Freudianism of Adorno's interpretation of her. That shiny object would distract us from the real problem: his utter lack of interpretive charity. It is inconceivable that the woman could, in principle, understand her anti-Semitism as Adorno does. To be sure, interpretive charity is not obligatory in all cases. But—from the perspective of the intellectual historian, broadly speaking—it is inexcusable to jump to reductionist conclusions about some belief without even pausing to understand what it is. Adorno completely omits the woman's beliefs, except as epiphenomena to be explained nonideationally.

The interpretive malpractice here is not a lapse. It is just one volley in a relentless barrage of tortured hermeneutics covering 140 pages of the book. Adorno's lack of interpretive charity is so unselfconscious, so matter-of-fact, that psychologists might be tempted to explain it as manifesting some deep-rooted "need" not to understand the other as the other might understand herself. Yet we need not psychologize Adorno to explain his interpretive procedures if we begin by understanding them *as if* they were selected for by a technocratic pressure for prediction. This approach suggests the following possibility: his lack of interpretive charity has the effect of homogenizing the subjects' anti-Semitism, ethnocentrism, and authoritarianism, which enables sweeping generalizations about the *real* causes of their behavior. In the case at hand, Adorno treats the woman as indistinguishable from other American anti-Semites of the era, many of whom did indeed believe in the "aggressiveness" stereotype (as shown by some of the other interviews analyzed in this chapter of the book). Ironically, then, Adorno may have stereotyped the woman as having stereotyped the man as aggressive. Lippmann teaches that stereotyping is not a psychological syndrome but a cognitive necessity—if one is attempting to make

---

[83] Ibid.

sweeping generalizations, for example, across the population of all anti-Semites (or, for that matter, all Jews). That is what technocrats do.

Yet Adorno would have been the last person on earth to harbor technocratic ambitions. To his mind, technocracy partakes of the instrumental rationality on which he ultimately blamed all the horrors of the modern era.[84] Besides, there was no collective agent with technocratic goals who might have smuggled pathological ideas into Adorno's web of beliefs against his every inclination. The similarity of his approach to that which would be taken by an ideal-typical technocrat, then, is puzzling if we take literally the figure of a pathological systemic pressure to predict. An epistemological individualist will therefore have to seek ideational causes for Adorno's lack of interpretive charity. What specific ideas might have led him to think that his stereotyping of this woman and other interview subjects could be justified by such scant evidence? A second example of his interpretive procedures provides a valuable clue.

4.5.2. Psychology and Naive Realism

Thirteen pages before his analysis of the woman, Adorno discusses a college "girl" who told her interviewer:

> Jews are aggressive, bad-mannered, clannish, intellectual, clean, overcrowd neighborhoods, noisy, and oversexed. I will admit that my opinion is not based on much contact, however; I hear these things all the time. There are very few Jewish students in my school, and I have already referred to my good contact with the one girl.[85]

Adorno claims that the contradiction between the student's "judgment and experience is so striking that the existence of prejudice can be accounted for only by strong psychological urges."[86] Strictly speaking, Adorno is quite wrong: the student herself offers a nonpsychological account, whatever one might think of it, namely that her prejudices reflected what she had heard repeatedly about Jews. To reject this account as inherently incredible, such that only psychopathology can explain her acceptance of what she had heard about Jews (in defiance of her personal experience with one Jewish student), entails that any psychologically healthy person would necessarily privilege personal experience over culturally communicated messages. However, no personal experience can reliably testify to the accuracy or inaccuracy of a sweeping stereotype concerning unknown others. To assume that it can and should, as Adorno does, is to assume that personal experience reveals truths both self-evident and universal. For him, the student's privileging

---

[84] Horkheimer and Adorno [1944] 2002.

[85] Adorno et al. 1950, 629.

[86] Ibid.

of what she heard over what she experienced means, apparently, that she was rejecting the self-evident truth, which would indeed suggest that a psychological explanation is called for.

The previously discussed woman's anti-Semitism, too, does not seem to have been the result of her personal experience with her rejected suitor, in that she was shocked when, despite that experience, he turned out to be Jewish. Ipso facto, Adorno may have reasoned, her anti-Semitism must have had a psychological source, regardless of what she might have heard about Jews (about which the interviewer did not trouble to ask). If personal experience reveals the manifest truth, then to believe stereotypes that contradict personal experience must be evidence of a deep-rooted disorder.

Naive realism of this sort is the theoretical heart of *The Authoritarian Personality*, including its statistical chapters. Adorno and his colleagues routinely dichotomize people's ideas into those that self-evidently track objective truth and those that, having "no basis in reality," demand psychological explanation.[87] Self-evidently false beliefs must, as such, be attributed to the "deep-lying needs of the personality," and that is the attribution the authors proceed to make, over and over again. After all, they argue, in the deep-lying needs of the personality, "Psychology has already found the sources of dreams, fantasies, and misinterpretations of the world."[88] Misinterpretations of the world, then, cannot simply be mistakes traceable to erroneous ideas that people have picked up along the way. Being manifestly "irreconcilable with reality,"[89] misinterpretations *must* have their source in some nonideational factor, such as people's need "to conform and to belong and to believe."[90]

Just like neoclassical economists, then, and economists of information, and behavioral economists, Adorno et al. assume that the default human condition is knowledge. Thus, they maintain that

> the fact that people make general statements about "the Jew," when the Jews are *actually* so heterogeneous . . . is vivid evidence of . . . irrationality. . . . When the belief that Jews possess financial power out of all proportion to their numbers persists *in the face of overwhelming evidence to the contrary*, one is led to suspect not only that the individual holding this belief has an unusual preoccupation with power but also that he might himself wish to assume the kind of power which he supposes Jews to have. It is clear that research into the emotional sources of ideology is required for the understanding of such phenomena as these.[91]

---

[87] Ibid., 618.
[88] Ibid., 9.
[89] Ibid.
[90] Ibid.
[91] Ibid., 57, my emphases.

The authors' conclusion is "clear," of course, only if anti-Semites somehow know that Jews are heterogeneous, and only if they somehow know that there is overwhelming evidence against the Jews' financial power. But how would they know these things? As Hyman and Sheatsley point out, Adorno et al. tend to "substitute their own knowledge, that of the scientific observer, for the less accurate knowledge of the ordinary subject they interview."[92] The alternative is to allow that people are credulous and can easily be led to believe whatever they hear about matters of which they are largely ignorant.

In the book's introductory discussion of fascism, by which the authors actually mean Nazism, they assert that

> since *by its very nature* it favors the few at the expense of the many, *it cannot possibly demonstrate* that it will so improve the situation of most people that their real interests will be served. It must therefore make its major appeal, not to rational self-interest, but to emotional needs—often to the most primitive and irrational wishes and fears. If it be argued that fascist propaganda fools people into believing that their lot will be improved, then the question arises: Why are they so easily fooled? Because, it may be supposed, of their personality structure; because of long-established patterns of hopes and aspirations, fears and anxieties that dispose them to certain beliefs and make them resistant to others.[93]

Such passages indicate the merely secondary importance of Freudianism to the authors' project. Freudian theory gives the authors a psychological explanation for why people might endorse a system that is *self-evidently* against their interests. But no psychological explanation would be needed absent that naively realistic premise. The premise excludes the possibility that supporters of Hitler were ignorant ex ante of the negative effect of Nazism on their own real interests (which seems to be what the authors have in mind—as opposed to the real interests of Jews), which is to say that, for example, they did not realize that Hitler would actually go to war against virtually the entire world, and lose.

We are entitled to say, I think, that the authors do not merely fail the test of interpretive charity by omitting any attempt to make rational sense of beliefs they find bizarre; but that they violate Skinner's proscription against letting the truth or untruth of a given belief enter into one's explanation of it. Since the truth is, in the authors' eyes, self-evident, they have little alternative but to explain untrue beliefs nonideationally. Conversely, they assert, with equal naiveté, that the actual (rather than the perceived) truth of a belief will (somehow) contribute to its acceptance by "an objective and thoughtful man."[94] If they had instead allowed that truth may be opaque, they might have recognized that ideational sources of belief such as folk wisdom, propaganda, journalism, or high culture

---

[92] Hyman and Sheatsley 1954, 109.
[93] Adorno et al. 1950, 10, my emphases.
[94] Ibid., 11.

can easily persuade even objective and thoughtful men of notions that the authors find incredible. This would have compelled them to consider such standard historiographical questions as whether anti-Semitism was particularly widespread or deep-rooted in Germany and, if so, what prosaic cultural factors might have explained it. By turning instead to homogenizing social-scientific explanations for stereotyped beliefs, the authors produced a seemingly profound but actually quite superficial theory of Nazism—one that was long on assertion but short on concreteness, and one that failed to reckon with one of the most sobering aspects of the human condition: that people can believe awful things—and do monstrous things—*without* being crazy.

Even when Adorno explicitly turns, late in the book, to the subject of ignorance, he struggles to deal with the possibility that, as he puts it, "the ultimate reason" for ignorance "might well be the opaqueness of the social, economic, and political situation to all those who are not in full command of all the resources of stored knowledge and theoretical thinking." By implication, it seems, these epistemic resources would reveal the truth in all its fullness if one commanded them; but this would imply that anti-Semites, lacking these resources, may be victims of opacity, not psychopathology. However, immediately after articulating the possibility that ignorance stems from opacity, Adorno begins backpedaling, asserting that "our social system tends objectively and automatically to produce 'curtains' which make it impossible for the naive person really to see what it is all about," which implies that if the curtains came down, the naive person—despite lacking the resources of stored knowledge and theoretical thinking—would see the self-evident truth. Along the same lines he then adds that "these objective conditions are enhanced by powerful economic and social forces which, purposely or automatically, keep the people ignorant," suggesting again that in the absence of such forces, the truth would be manifest to the people. But in the next sentence he goes back to allowing that the truth is *inherently* opaque, requiring illumination by means of special insight: "Capitalism . . . has to maintain itself somewhat precariously and to block critical insights which were regarded as 'progressive' one hundred years ago but are viewed as potentially dangerous today."[95] If seeing the truth requires insight, the truth is not self-evident. Yet Adorno's brand of social-systemic analysis soon pulls him in the other direction once again. Instead of viewing the theory that social and economic "forces" block progressive insights as merely a metaphor for such prosaically cultural factors as the barrage of journalism launched against the Bolshevik revolution (as analyzed, for example, in Lippmann and Merz's 1920 study of the *New York Times*)[96]—in which case Adorno would have had to allow that people might simply have been confused about the veracity of progressive insights by the ideational inputs to their webs of belief—he treats capitalism as a real agent that somehow or other, "purposely or automatically," inserts insight-blocking ideas into

---

[95] Ibid., 661–662.
[96] Lippmann and Merz 1920.

people's heads. This only deepens the epistemic mystery: If not for this nebulous, system-ically self-protective mechanism, would the people know the truth or would they not?

In the end, Adorno resolves his epistemological quandary by siding firmly with naive psychological realism. He concludes that those who, "for reasons of vested interests or psychological conditions, identify themselves with the existing setup," must be ignorant of the obvious problems with this setup not because it is opaque, not because they are be-reft of stored knowledge and theoretical thinking, and not because social and economic forces manage to keep progressive insights out of their heads, but because "they uncon-sciously do not *want* to know too much and are ready to accept superficial or distorted information as long as it confirms the world in which they want to go on living."[97] Thus, it seems, if not for their unconscious desire to be ignorant, they would know which infor-mation is superficial or distorted and presumably would, by screening out this informa-tion, know the deep and undistorted truth.

An intellectually charitable biographer might begin trying to understand these con-flicting epistemological sentiments by remembering that Adorno was strongly influ-enced by Marxism, which is similarly conflicted (at least arguably). Marx claimed to have knowledge of the true nature of the social whole, knowledge that proletarians would someday win by virtue of the oppression self-evident to those in their position. Yet Marx was not himself a proletarian. How, then, did he come to see the truth about the totality? If he merely saw what is self-evident, then everyone else should see it, regardless of their class position, such that those who do not see it must be the victims of economic, social, or (as Freud would later to suggest to the Frankfurt school) psychological forces that hide the truth from them. But in that case proletarians, too, might forever be kept in the dark by these forces. Alternatively, Marx might have seen the truth because of his "stored knowledge and theoretical thinking," or simply because of his genius. But in that case, too, (most) proletarians, lacking access to these epistemic resources, might never discover the truth. A third possibility is that if the truth is not self-evident and must be revealed by theorists such as Marx, it might in the end be out of everyone's reach, in-cluding Marx's, as even theorists of genius are fallible.

If we were to pursue the hypothesis that this (putative) Marxian conundrum influ-enced Adorno, we would not only have to work through his relationship with Marxism, but we would have to confirm that the conundrum was really there in Marxian texts that Adorno knew well. To confirm that the conundrum was there might, in turn, require an investigation of what happened, epistemologically, when Marx inverted Hegel. This, in turn, might require an investigation of Hegel's epistemology, which might, in turn, re-quire a rethinking of Kant, and so on. To explain Adorno's idiosyncratic web of beliefs, we would be drawn ever further into the somewhat knowable but somewhat opaque and unreliable history of social theory. The social scientist, in contrast, like the technocrat,

---

[97] Adorno et al. 1950, 661.

in order to explain the putatively homogeneous—the predictable—is drawn toward the present and even the future, which she believes she can reliably know.

Yet Adorno was no more a social scientist, by training, than he was a technocrat by aspiration. One advantage of a hypothesis such as the one about Marxism is that it could explain Adorno's sweeping psychological (and economic) reductionism by dialectically overcoming the initial figure of technocratic pressures. The Marxism hypothesis allows us to reconceive of these pressures as efficient ideational pushes (such as the influence of Marx on Adorno) toward homogenizing, naively realistic ideas, not as teleological pullings toward homogenizing, naively realistic ideas exerted on him (somehow or other, "purposely or automatically") by a reified political system, "technocracy." By the same token, in constructing intellectual histories of those naive realists who are *not* merely moonlighting as social scientists, and of those who *are* epistocrats, we could arrive at (conjectural) efficient causes for the epistemic pathologies displayed by those, such as Buchanan, Kahneman, and Tversky, who presumably were not influenced by Marxism: for example, by inquiring into their disciplinary training—leading, in turn, to historical questions about the origins of this training, and so on. This would be part of the project of an empirical political epistemology of technocracy. For example, Teppo Felin argues that "Kahneman's focus on obviousness comes directly from his background and scientific training in an area called psychophysics. Psychophysics focuses largely on how environmental stimuli map on to the mind, specifically based on the *actual* characteristics of stimuli, rather than the characteristics or nature of the mind. From the perspective of psychophysics, 'obviousness'—or as it is called in the literature, 'salience'—derives from the inherent nature or characteristics of the environmental stimuli themselves," sans interpretation.[98]

Paradoxically, then, such intellectual-historical hypotheses are complementary with the metaphorical figure of a technocratic selection pressure for prediction, as they could explain, ideationally, why epistocratic social scientists *and* nontechnocratic social scientists *and* a seminal opponent of technocracy were averse to ideational explanations—thereby making sense, with intellectual charity, of their lack of intellectual charity. Social scientists (and philosophers) whose practices can be explained in this fashion would be expected, ceteris paribus, to select themselves into enterprises that eschew intellectual charity. For a normative rather than empirical political epistemologist, however, the key point is that when we find social scientists and philosophers in the grip of epistemic pathologies such as naive realism even when they are *not* engaged in technocratic enterprises, we have evidence that the causes of the pathologies are cultural, not "systemic," raising the question of whether they can be culturally reversed in the interest of producing a judicious technocracy.

---

[98] Felin 2018.

4.5.3. *Psychological Reductionism and Positivism*

However, this discussion of the lack of interpretive charity among social scientists and epistocrats is as yet far too simple, as we have not said anything about noneconomist, nontechnocratic, positivist social scientists who are *not* naive realists.

In neoclassical economics, as we have seen, policy scientists have moved from merely fleshing out predictive expectations with empirical findings (econometrics), to treating economic theory as an afterthought (Card and Krueger), to abandoning it altogether (Banerjee and Duflo). As this process has unfolded, the role of naive realism à la Buchanan has shrunk. It would be a gross exaggeration to say that it has been sidelined, because economic theory itself has not been sidelined by most economists. But inasmuch as economic theory is built on the "intuition" that incentives matter, inasmuch as this intuition is operationalized by imputing effective omniscience to economic agents, and inasmuch as that imputation entails naive realism, naive realism is essentially irrelevant to the new empiricism within the larger discipline, as the new empiricists do not attribute effective omniscience or any other trait to agents a priori. Yet the new empiricists have as much faith that they can predict agents' behavior as do traditional neoclassical theorists. The new empiricists' faith is rooted not in naive realism, but in the positivist assumption that gold-standard empiricist technologies will turn up reliable behavioral regularities. It appears, then, that ideational factors other than the epistemically naive teachings of neoclassical economics—such as, perhaps, the ethos of social science, or the preoccupation with methods in graduate training programs—can produce pathological positivist responses to the technocratic "pressure to predict."

The situation in social psychology looks to be similar, or so I will argue, yet social psychology is not a technocratic field. Just as the correlations among statistical variables captured by the F-scale received much more attention in the literature than did the Freudian theory that inspired it—let alone the naive realism by means of which Adorno et al. justified their psychological reductionism—what continues to matter to social psychologists are "the data." This renders naive realism peripheral to their thinking, and it pushes their explicit theorizing toward ad hocery, not oracular pronouncement. Rather than assuming that the truth is so obvious to the people they study that only psychological blinders can stop them from seeing it, social psychologists seek primarily to correlate behavioral variables with each other, including ideas treated as dependent variables—but excluding, except haphazardly, ideas treated as independent variables. This is to say that social psychologists are, not surprisingly, psychological reductionists, and that psychological reductionism can be as interpretively uncharitable as naive realism.

This can be illustrated by considering an influential recent theory of authoritarianism that is even more sweeping than the one produced by Adorno et al., yet lacks any explicit ideational superstructure such as Freudianism. Even more paradoxically, it is couched as a reaction against other positivists' theoretical eclecticism, yet it is equally undertheorized.

In *The Authoritarian Dynamic* (2005), Karen Stenner asserts that there is a primal psychological force, "authoritarianism," that "is the primary determinant of intolerance of difference across domains, cultures, and time." That is, "intolerance of racial diversity, [of] political dissent, and [of] moral deviance are all primarily driven" by this authoritarian disposition, now and forever.[99] Not for Stenner the proliferation of ad hoc theories of intolerance "packed with proper nouns." She contends, indeed, that social and political psychologists' "attention to [the] names, dates, and places" of actual intolerance, such as when they explore the racism of twentieth-century Americans, "risks obscuring important regularities in human behavior" that her approach will reveal.[100] Even Adorno and his colleagues claimed only to be discovering regularities produced by tyrannical child-rearing, which is not a necessary aspect of the human condition forevermore. Stenner's claims apply, by contrast, to some large and fixed proportion of *Homo sapiens*, everywhere and always. Yet despite its self-consciously grand sweep, her theory, unlike that of *The Authoritarian Personality*, is almost wholly positivistic. The data indicating Stenner's homogeneities are supposed to speak for themselves, brute facts that explain but need not themselves be explained. Thus, Stenner's rebuke to ad hocery ends up being itself ad hoc, although it studiously avoids proper nouns.

Stenner's main claim is that each of the following intercorrelated variables is a product of a persona that is "concerned with minimizing difference in all its manifestations":[101] "obedience to authority, moral absolutism and conformity, intolerance and punitiveness toward dissidents and deviants, animosity and aggression against racial and ethnic outgroups."[102] Her implicit theory, then, is that the homunculus in the authoritarian breast, or genome, is afraid of difference per se. Upon inspection, this theory makes as little sense as any nugget of folk psychology, such as the notion that partisan conflict is ultimately "tribal," or that lockstep agreement among ideologues is due to a "herd mentality," or that protests against social injustice are mere "virtue signaling" or express the psychological fragility of "millennial snowflakes." That is, such notions are plausible—if one does not think about them very hard—to everyone but those whose ideas (about the merits of their party and the faults of the other party, about the nature of the social and political realities described by their ideology, or about the gravity and subtlety of social injustice) are thereby explained away. *Folk psychology*, as I will use the term, is the psychologizing engaged in by those—laypeople or professionals—for whom the need for interpretive charity is alien, and who thus dismiss ideas or ways of thinking they do not understand.

---

[99] Stenner 2005, 3.

[100] Ibid., 7. I equate social and political psychologists—Stenner herself is a member of the latter group—because they use the same methods and rely on pretty much the same literature. Political psychology is social psychology applied to political phenomena.

[101] Ibid., 269.

[102] Ibid., 3.

One should suspect that an explanation of ideas or behavior is of the folk-psychological type when one cannot use the explanation to achieve *Verstehen*. Thus, one might ask whether, if one were to put oneself in the shoes of the psychologized other, it is plausible that one could fear "difference" per se. It might seem so if one does not think about it carefully, but when one does, a problem arises: Every person is different from every other person along any number of dimensions. Is it plausible that large numbers of us could find *all* of these differences equally fearful, such that every single person they meet would be equally frightening? If not, then perhaps we will need to investigate the specific types of differences that some individuals fear and others do not. This, however, would require an interpretively charitable inquiry into people's beliefs about one another's differences, and this cannot be provided if one is convinced that such beliefs are mere reflexes of their "fear of difference."

The global "fear of difference" stems, according to Stenner, not from specific beliefs about particularly threatening differences, but from an acute psychological "need" for "oneness and sameness."[103] The existence of such a need, however, has no theoretical or empirical basis other than the correlations among survey variables that she construes as indicators of predispositions toward (1) obedience to authority, (2) moral absolutism and conformity, (3) intolerance and punitiveness toward dissidents and deviants, and (4) animosity and aggression against racial and ethnic out-groups. Even if we bracket the questionable appropriateness of construing such measures as indicating fear of difference, the correlations are consistent with an alternative, interpretively charitable possibility that Stenner never considers: that authoritarians are intolerant not of "difference" per se, but of particular "differences" that violate their normative standards. That is, they might be intolerant only of what they believe are *harmful* types of "difference," such as the single-parent households that they believe (according to Stenner's data) are linked to poverty, crime, and other "societal ills,"[104] rather than opposing single-parent households on the generic and logically incoherent grounds that they are different from dual-parent households (which are, of course, just as different from single-parent households as the latter are different from the former). Conversely, they might *oppose* certain types of sameness when they (believe that they) have specific reasons to think the samenesses are undesirable, as in the case of the sameness that (they believe is) the goal of "political correctness."[105] But investigating such possibilities might require introducing proper names, and it would certainly entail the possibility that authoritarians, as much as anyone else, have beliefs, not mere psychological reflexes. Once we investigate these beliefs, we may discover that fear of "difference" is an empty and misleading construct, because what is actually at work is fear of (or objections to) specific types of people or behavior. We would

---

[103] Ibid., 150.
[104] Ibid., 264.
[105] Ibid., 243.

then want to know where these fears originate, which would lead us toward intellectual/ cultural history.

Similar points can be made about the four "predispositions" that, according to Stenner, "authoritarianism" brings together. Stenner's data correlations do not suggest that authoritarians advocate obedience to *progressive* "authority," or "absolutist" adherence to *progressive* morality, or "conformity" to *progressive* ideas, or animosity and hostility against racial and ethnic out-groups that have not acquired, or have lost, a specific, ideationally negative charge, such as (in the United States) the descendants of Irish immigrants. Her data, then, are consistent with the possibility that authoritarians favor obedience only to (what they believe are) legitimate authorities, absolutist adherence only to (what they believe are) legitimate moral precepts, conformity only to (what they believe are) legitimate expectations, and hostility only to groups that they view as posing specific threats. Pursuing this hypothesis, however, would require that we descend from abstractions about difference and sameness that may seem intuitively plausible to a social psychologist folk-psychologizing about anonymous others, but that probably would not make sense to the others themselves.[106] And if we want to *explain* the others' beliefs, we would search for their ideational roots, drawing us even farther away from the abstract and generic and—at least potentially—toward heterogeneous cultural influences.

Stenner's lack of interpretive charity, like that of Adorno, is best illustrated by her long chapters on interview data. The interviews were conducted on her behalf in Durham, North Carolina, while she was teaching at Duke University. The most important finding from the interviews, in her judgment, is that "authoritarian" interviewees repeatedly displayed clear signs of agitation when the interviewers were black. According to her theory, these interviewees must have been "frightened and unhinged by difference"[107]— not frightened and unhinged by the fact that black people were sitting in their living rooms. (Stenner does not wonder if male interviewees would have been unhinged by female interviewers, or vice versa, despite the high salience of gender "differences" to most people.) The unmentioned possibility that the interviewees were racists, as opposed to being authoritarians, is interpretively charitable so long as it is nonreductionist, such that the subjects' anxiety is attributed to their at least minimally coherent (if false) ideas about blacks in particular, not to racial difference in the abstract. (Interpretive charity demands a recognition of the existence of subjects' ideas and an attempt to understand how they cohere in the subjects' minds, not an acceptance of their truth value.) If no plausible account along these lines could be produced, then, and only then, would a judicious social scientist resort to psychologizing.

Stenner's lack of interpretive charity is also evident in her statistical measures. Her only data on the posited authoritarian disposition itself, as opposed to the correlations

---

[106] Stenner's interviews do quote *anti*authoritarians praising "diversity," but it is clear from the context that they mean not diversity per se but racial diversity.

[107] Stenner 2005, 217 and chapters 7 and 8.

among dependent variables that it is supposed to explain, consist of responses to a survey question asking which traits are more important to encourage in children: (1) independence or respect for their elders; (2) curiosity or good manners; (3) self-reliance or obedience; (4) being considerate or being well-behaved.[108] Astoundingly, social psychologists consider respondents who choose the second option in each pair to have authoritarian personalities. Yet virtually anyone raised in the United States (and perhaps any other Western country) prior to the publication of Benjamin Spock's *Baby and Child Care* in 1946 might very well have chosen the second, "authoritarian" option in each pair. Dr. Spock's book, unmentioned by Stenner and apparently unknown among social psychologists, sold 50 million copies, was translated into 42 languages, and was widely credited with sparking a "permissiveness" revolution in child-rearing that had profound behavioral repercussions. Assuming that this putative cultural revolution could have radically changed people's answers to Stenner's questions, then such answers should not be considered valid measures of their deep-seated personality traits. Instead, we might speculate that ideas about how children should behave may originate in norms that are taught to children by parents and that persist into adulthood, where they can be measured in opinion surveys such as those used by authoritarian-personality researchers. A given parent's norms may, in turn, originate in her own parents' instructions, advice, and examples to her—or in other cultural sources (in the prosaic sense), such as the teachings of Dr. Spock, that may have influenced her or her parents. Thus, what Stenner is measuring may be ideas all the way down; innate personality traits may play no role in generating the authoritarianism variables. In particular, a plausible alternative interpretation of the variables is that they reflect not a dedication to "sameness," or even authoritarianism, but to traditional norms of child rearing. (Just such norms might be of interest to a judicious technocrat, as they might supervene, for example, on parents' desire to indulge their children in various ways.)

Stenner would surely reply by pointing to correlations between the "authoritarianism" variables and the four intercorrelated variables suggesting intolerance of "difference." But these correlations, too, might be explained ideationally if one charitably considers the type of parents who might teach or model traditional norms of child behavior to their children *after* the putative permissiveness revolution had spread far and wide. For example, one might suspect that parents whom the revolution passed by would tend to be relatively sequestered from the type of popular culture in which books such as Dr. Spock's become sensations—a fairly literate, up-to-date type of popular culture in which credentialed experts are deferred to and traditional norms readily abandoned. Sequestration from this type of culture could be brought about by rural isolation, by regional cultural norms, by an aversion to newfangled ideas or book learning, or even by an intelligence deficit. (Stenner convincingly depicts the "authoritarian" interview subjects as almost

---

[108] See Feldman and Stenner 1997.

uniformly inarticulate, poorly educated, and stupid).[109] Conversely, the cultural sequestration that might account for the persistence of traditional child-rearing norms might
also account for the traditionalists' persistent racism, obdurate nationalism ("Love it or
leave it"), unthinking opposition to communism, impatience with avant-garde sexual
mores, and so forth—as reflected in Stenner's "intolerance" variables. The culturally sequestered might also be less likely than others to have received a progressive primary, secondary, or postsecondary education that would have taught them to question authority,
cherish self-expression, and celebrate racial and sexual diversity. Thus, sequestration from
progressive ideas might be all the explanation we need for why the sequestered are intolerant *and* why they do not view children through the "permissive" lens Stenner equates
with libertarianism (her term for antiauthoritarianism). Putatively authoritarian attitudes toward children and intolerance alike, then—and thus their correlation—might be
explained by the parents' insulation from the cultural transmission of progressive ideas.
Thus, ideas may be the true explanatory variable for *all* of Stenner's correlations.

It turns out, in fact, that Stenner's quantitative data confirm that intelligence and
higher education strongly and inversely correlate with both the "authoritarian predispo-
sition" and intolerant political attitudes, and not just in Durham, North Carolina. This
suggests that tolerance is taught, such that intolerance may thrive among those who do
not attend college. Injudiciously, however, she dismisses the fundamental challenge this
finding poses to her theory with an ad hoc auxiliary hypothesis that explains it away. In
"modern liberal democracies," she writes,

> it is largely the case that academic, educated, and higher-status environments
> tend to promote libertarian values more than [do] lower-status and less-educated
> circles. . . . [However,] one would be hard-pressed to maintain, for example, that
> higher-status environments are pervaded by libertarian norms in Azerbaijan, or
> that education in China tends to promote libertarian values.[110]

Thus, since higher education in China is inversely correlated with authoritarianism,
as it is in the West, the correlation cannot be due to antiauthoritarian norms taught to
highly educated Chinese, since we all know, apparently, that Chinese higher education
actually teaches authoritarian norms. Stenner therefore proposes as more "plausible" the
theory that "the beneficial effects of knowledge and cognitive skills on one's ability to
deal easily and comfortably with complexity and difference" explain the negative correlations between intelligence and higher education on the one hand and "authoritarianism"

---

[109] To notice that someone is unintelligent may be characterologically uncharitable, but it is not interpretively
uncharitable, as one can still put oneself in her shoes and understand how her actions and beliefs "make sense"
from her standpoint.

[110] Stenner 2005, 160.

and intolerance on the other, since we all know that higher education, including that in China, teaches (generic) knowledge and cognitive skills.[111]

It is worth noting that even if Stenner were right to imply that Chinese higher education toward the end of the twentieth century promoted authoritarian values (she offers no evidence, apparently relying on an unexamined stereotype), higher education might still have an antiauthoritarian ideational effect in other countries, depending on a vast array of other, heterogeneous cultural influences. But I am informed that Chinese higher education during that period taught—as one might expect, a priori—not generic "authoritarianism" and "intolerance," but the need to obey *the Communist Party* and intolerance toward threats to its hegemony. Moreover (I am informed), especially in the wake of the Tiananmen Square massacre, these teachings came to be widely considered a joke by many students, such that attitudes of toleration toward or support of dissent (from the Communist authorities) were the unintended effect of the authorities' teachings. In sum, tolerance may, like intolerance, be ideational, not psychological, even in China.

It is also important to note that Stenner's higher-education variables—attendance at and graduation from college—are easy to quantify but poorly represent exposure to antiauthoritarian teachings, which, one may hypothesize, are less likely to be propagated in vocational, scientific, and religious colleges than in liberal-arts colleges, to take just one gross dichotomy. If we were to investigate such hypotheses, however, we would again be drawn away from sweeping generalizations and toward particularity, because (for example) the antiauthoritarian effect of liberal-arts psychology courses might differ dramatically from those of liberal-arts economics courses, and because a nearly infinite array of other ideational heterogeneities might arise, such as differences in what is taught in similar courses at different schools, in what is taught by different professors at the same schools, in how what is taught is interpreted by heterogeneous students, and so on—just the sort of issue that Banerjee and Duflo, too, ignore. Thus, while the impact of the tolerationist, antiauthoritarian ideas that might be taught to some college students would be well worth exploring, an adequate exploration would have to set aside the assumption of homogeneity that here, as in positivist economics, grounds the propensity to predict behavior.

A brief final example can bring this part of the discussion to a close. One of Stenner's main targets is Bob Altemeyer's research on authoritarianism. In the 1980s, Altemeyer devised a Right-Wing Authoritarianism (RWA) scale that revivified the field after it had become bogged down in disputes over the validity of the F-scale.[112] His approach was even more positivistic than Stenner's, in the sense of being more data-driven and, therefore, more ad hoc and less insistently universalistic, and these are her grounds for objecting to it.[113] But his approach, if not the particular measures he used, is just as conducive as

---

[111] Ibid., 161.

[112] Altemeyer 1981, 1988, and 1996.

[113] Stenner 2005, 4–5.

hers to sweeping generalization and prediction, because it is just as lacking in interpretive charity. To take one of many examples, Altemeyer ascribes to people with high RWA scores an "acceptance of government injustices." Thus, his survey data show that they tend to favor "blocking peaceful protests against government policies."[114] This particular measure of "authoritarianism," being less abstract than measures of opposition to "difference," is slightly less universalizable than they are, as it would clearly be inapplicable in parts of the globe, or historical eras, in which peaceful protests against government policies were unheard of. Nevertheless, it is as interpretively uncharitable as any of Stenner's measures. If one favors blocking peaceful protests, one must surely think that blocking them is *justified*, not that it is an "injustice." But in that case this attitude, or rather this belief, is in need, not of a psychological explanation, but an ideational one: an exploration of the subjects' ideas about justice and protest in particular contexts, an investigation that would, again, draw us ever farther toward the particular.

Unlike Stenner, Altemeyer does not avow that he has cracked the authoritarian code for all time. But the two social psychologists share common ground in failing to think about their subjects' ideas as they themselves might understand them, and this allows both of them to make sweeping retrodictions and predictions, even if Altemeyer's fall short of universalism—as do the retrodictions and predictions of social psychologists who positivistically restrict themselves to making claims about WEIRD populations. Lack of interpretive charity, then, may flow as easily from positivism as from naive realism. It may also flow as easily from positivism that is theoretically ad hoc (Altemeyer) as from positivism that is universalistic (Stenner) or, on the other hand, from positivism that is altogether bereft of explicit theorizing (Banerjee and Duflo, or Kahneman and Tversky). However, in an interesting counterpoint to the other psychologists we have examined, and to all of the economists as well (except Simon, if he can be considered an economist), Altemeyer explains his findings through the lens of "social learning theory,"[115] which, in principle, allows for learning *from culture*. According to social learning theory, behavior stems from the cognitive mediation of environmental inputs, and Altemeyer recognizes, in principle, that these inputs could include ideational influences such as "direct teaching."[116] Yet when push comes to shove, Altemeyer, like Stenner in discussing Chinese higher education, injudiciously dismisses such influences. Thus, when he finds himself wrestling with the discovery that RWA scores dropped precipitously among (a sample of) "liberal arts students" as their time in college progressed, he never seriously investigates the hypothesis that this is because the students were taught antiauthoritarian ideas in the classroom—even though he does acknowledge that possibility briefly.[117]

---

[114] Altemeyer 1988, 9.

[115] Bandura 1977.

[116] Altemeyer 1988, 54.

[117] Altemeyer 1996, 85. Altemeyer jokes that RWA scores among liberal-arts students do not merely decline "because their marvelous professors expose them to a wide range of ideas" (ibid.), but he never undertakes to investigate the possibility systematically.

Instead, he insists that their declining RWA scores must primarily be due to their *experiences* in college, as duly measured by another of his inventions, the Experiences Scale (which fails to measure the experience of reading antiauthoritarian assignments or hearing antiauthoritarian lectures and discussions).[118] And so—again, as if by an invisible hand—the generalizations he derives from his correlations are preserved against the great confounder: ideas.

4.6. THE PRESSURE TO PREDICT IN LIGHT OF ITS IDEATIONAL SOURCES

We are now in a position to say much more than that social scientists who thoroughly, hence particularistically, explored the causal role of ideational influences would thereby select themselves out of the pool of candidate epistocrats, unless they found a way to combine this exploration with a probing of behavioral regularities. While such self-selection can be styled, metaphorically, as resulting from a technocratic pressure for epistemic pathology, the actual sources of the pathologies of those who select themselves *into* the pool of candidate epistocrats may be a diverse array of ideational influences on them. Among these are not only naive realism but a positivist form of intellectual uncharitability—one that may also inhere in the aims, the scope, the ethos, and the methods of social psychology and, one might easily imagine, in the other empirical social sciences too (except ethnographic anthropology), even when they are not technocratic. All social sciences are primarily dedicated to the identification and retrodiction of behavioral homogeneities, with the unintended consequence of ignoring or dismissing heterogenizing, particularizing, and potentially unpredictable "forces" such as ideas. Even when positivist social scientists have no predictive ambitions, and even when they treat ideas as dependent variables, they seem disinclined to treat them as robust causal forces that might scatter behavior idiosyncratically rather than regularizing it conveniently. When Stenner and Altemeyer notice this possibility, they swat it down as quickly as they can, leaving themselves no interpretive options but uncharitable ones. But then, so did Adorno et al., on the basis of a theoretical defense of naive realism.

Thus, both naive realism and positivism appear to pose formidable barriers to a judicious technocracy. But this situation is not set in stone. In the cases we have examined, important homogeneities, such as anti-Semitism, racism, and child-rearing norms, seem to have been misconstrued as non-ideational due to what can be figured as a pathological "pressure" to predict. But ideationally sensitive treatments of these themes are certainly possible. If social scientists' own positivistic ideas are the actual cause of the pathological "pressure," it might be relieved if there were to be a massive ideational shift among those who become social scientists. We might find it difficult to imagine a day when social scientists have internalized the possibility that "variables" may be at work that are too

---

[118] Altemeyer 1988, 76.

idiosyncratic to be generalizable, too richly dependent on inaccessible combinations of inputs—such as ideas—to be predictable, or fully predictable; and who accept that, in consequence, behavioral homogeneities need to be established as exceptions to the heterogeneous rule, and their limits intensively explored. But it is not *impossible* to imagine.

Thus, there is no reason, in principle, that intellectual history, broadly speaking, could not be the foundation of a different kind of social science, a kind closer to Holbach than to Adorno, Akerlof, Altemeyer, Banerjee and Duflo, Buchanan, Card and Krueger, Kahneman and Tversky, Spence, Stenner, and Stigler. The methods of such a social science might be primarily hermeneutical or phenomenological (to investigate ideational heterogeneity) and ethnographic (to investigate the existence, nature, and extent of homogenizing factors such as behavioral norms), rendering the vast technical and intellectual superstructure of modern social science largely redundant. But it could happen, and a new superstructure, the intellectual scaffolding of a reliable policy science and a legitimate epistocracy, might conceivably be built.

On the other hand, there is no sign that such a social science—or such an epistocracy—is in the offing.

The field of economics offers a lens through which to view the world. For those who buy into it and pursue it as a career, it provides a foundation of a personal and political philosophy. It forever sets you apart—for better or worse—from mere muggles.

—N. GREGORY MANKIW, "Politics Aside, a Common Bond"

5

Epistocracy and the Spiral of Conviction

SEVENTY-EIGHT PERCENT OF the empirical studies that appeared in the 13 years after the publication of Card and Krueger's paper affirmed the orthodox view that minimum wages cause unemployment.[1] Yet opposition to raising the minimum wage dropped from 90 percent among surveyed economists in 1978 to 46 percent in 2000, and by 2005— five years after Card and Krueger acknowledged, in the pages of the *American Economic Review*, that they could no longer sustain their original claims—some 52 percent of surveyed economists favored *raising* the US minimum wage or keeping it the same.[2] Indeed, a number of economists took to declaring adamantly, on empirical grounds, that "the record is clear"—minimum wages do *not* cause unemployment—mimicking the certitude of economists such as Buchanan, who had previously reached the opposite conclusion on theoretical grounds.[3]

In a book published three years before the original Card and Krueger paper appeared, David Colander may have laid the groundwork for understanding economists' apparent

---

[1] By my count, Neumark and Wascher 2007, Tables 5.1, 5.2, 6.1, and 6.2 describe 69 studies of minimum-wage increases that showed increases in unemployment or statistically insignificant effects, and 15 showing statistically significant declines in unemployment. (Statistically insignificant results are consistent with the orthodox view, as they could stem from minimum-wage increases that were insufficient to create an incentive to reduce employment appreciably.) Some of Neumark and Wascher's descriptions of the results produced by individual studies are ambiguous; these are excluded from my count.

[2] Kearl et al. 1979; Fuller and Geide-Stevenson 2003; Whaples 2006, Table 3. Forty-seven percent favored abolishing it.

[3] Reich and Jacobs 2014. Cf. Saltsman 2013.

Power Without Knowledge. Jeffrey Friedman, Oxford University Press (2019). © Oxford University Press.
DOI: 10.1093/oso/9780190877170.001.0001

overreaction to it. According to Colander, liberal economists such as himself, who constituted a clear majority in the discipline, had, in general, been "extremely hesitant to apply economic analysis to real-world situations because it often comes to results that don't fit their moral view of how things should be."[4] If Colander was right, then when the Card and Krueger study opened the door to doubts about the minimum-wage orthodoxy, liberal political predispositions may have pushed those doubts farther than the evidence would appear to have justified. In other words, ideological doctrine may have displaced the old theoretical doctrine.[5]

Consider a counterfactual. Had economists concluded that heterogeneous empirical findings showed that employers may react to a higher minimum wage unpredictably, sometimes raising employment and sometimes contracting it, they would have been unable to motivate opinions about the policy question: Should the minimum be raised in the here and now? Instead of a decline in the proportion of economists who opposed raising the minimum wage, there would have been a decline in the proportion who had any opinion one way or the other. That is, economists would have become truly uncertain and would thereby have selected themselves out of the pool of potential epistocrats on this issue. What happened instead was a polarization of certainties.

The polarized economists must have believed that those of their colleagues with whom they disagreed were simply bad at making behavioral predictions, at least in this case, or were using the wrong predictive technology (flawed natural experiments, for example), or were using the right technology badly. In short, polarization may have been due to the polarized economists' dim view of the quality of the evidence used by "the other side," not merely their high estimation of the quality of the evidence used by their own side. But why did *both* sides (apparently) take such a dim view of the other side's evidence? Indeed, why did economists, as fair-minded social scientists, polarize into "sides" to begin with?

This looks for all the world like a classic case of dogmatism. Dogmatism could explain not only the apparent partiality of at least one, and possibly both, of the two groups of economists, but both groups' ability to advocate (or oppose) their favored policies even though the evidence in its totality seemed to violate *both* of the two sides' behavioral predictions about the employment effects of the minimum wage—or, to put the point in slightly different terms, when the evidence was ambivalent or ambiguous enough to raise doubts about whether the truth was yet known. Thus, it seems that dogmatic economists may have been selected into the epistocratic pool—economists whose dogmas enabled them to take technocratic policy positions even when, for those who cared about empirical evidence, the evidence was ambivalent or ambiguous. As if by an invisible hand, then, dogmatism could serve the perverse function of perpetuating firm epistocratic opinions

---

[4] Colander 1991, 6.

[5] Of course, several orthodoxies may have been at work both before and after the Card and Krueger study changed the landscape, and on both sides of the debate. Buchanan, for example, was not only an orthodox neoclassical economist but a libertarian.

in the face of ambivalent or ambiguous evidence thrown forth by heterogeneous, unpredictable behavior.

The dogmas at work could be political, theoretical, or of any other kind, so long as they give human behavior the appearance of predictability. In so doing, they would serve the systemic "function" of bolstering confidence in a given response to the pressure to predict by obscuring evidentiary ambiguity or ambivalence, or even by obscuring the falsification of one's own response by the evidence. Where the pressure to predict might itself (figuratively) produce an injudicious neglect of the causal role of people's ideas, then (as we saw in the last chapter), a pressure for dogmatism could produce a separate epistemic pathology: the injudicious dismissal of ambiguous, ambivalent, or incongruous evidence— or of disagreement about what counts as good evidence or how best to interpret it.

Put in terms of the stylized division of epistemic labor mooted by Page and Shapiro, discussed in Chapter 1, such dogmas can persuade someone that she is the Ideal Epistocrat, that is, the one who has gotten hold of the truth about the matter at hand, even when large numbers of other epistocrats disagree with her. Thus, dogmas can be essential to solving (or, rather, appearing to solve) the problem of epistocratic identification. The systemic need for a solution to this problem should therefore exert a figurative selection pressure of its own, in the sense that undogmatic social scientists would tend to be less interested than dogmatic ones in arguing for a particular policy when evidence against its ability to pass the cost-benefit test arises, or when the evidence is (in the undogmatic epistocrats' view) unclear. Open-minded social scientists would in this manner tend to select themselves out of the pool of potential epistocrats on the particular issue being debated.

Like the figurative pressure to predict, the figurative pressure for dogmatism would undermine the ability of a technocracy to discover the limits of the homogeneities that a given group of epistocrats claims to have discovered. This entitles us to call the pressure pathological. How can such a pressure arise? In Section 5.1, I begin working toward an answer by considering how experts become experts, a process that I call the spiral of conviction—an ideational alternative to the leading psychological theory of dogmatism, the theory of motivated reasoning. In the second section, I apply the spiral-of-conviction model to Philip E. Tetlock's findings about the dogmatism of experts. In the third section, I illustrate the applicability of the spiral-of-conviction model to the real world of technocracy by examining the answers given by several prominent epistocrats to the question of what caused the financial crisis of 2007–8. A final section transforms the spiral model into an epistemologically individualistic "systemic" theory.

5.1. THE SPIRAL OF CONVICTION

The people best informed on the issue are the ones least likely to change their minds. Much of this represents attitudinal stability; some of it may represent rigidity.
—BERNARD BERELSON, "Democratic Theory and Public Opinion"

Speaking, as I just did, about the "usefulness" of a dogma to an epistocrat should not be taken to suggest that epistocrats (or others) have the power to choose whether to adopt a dogma, or to believe in this or that doctrine dogmatically. I am assuming that one's web of beliefs, not her "free will," determines not only her interpretations of techno-cratic issues, but the degree to which she adheres to these interpretations dogmatically, such that dogmatism is inadvertent. We will see that in effect, the theory of motivated reasoning revives the notion of free will but projects it into the unconscious, where some non-doxastic motive such as ego defense allows the self, or a homunculus acting in its stead, to "choose" beliefs dogmatically, even while the self knows, at one or another level, that in doing so it is choosing to believe in what is false. If not by means of a deliberate decision of this kind, conscious or unconscious, how could epistocratic dogmatism be generated inadvertently?

An alternative mechanism, the spiral of conviction, is suggested by Lippmann's theory of belief formation. According to Lippmann, a stereotype (an interpretation) allows one to make sense of part of the world's blooming, buzzing overabundance of information. But in the process, it tends to screen in a biased and self-confirming sample of infor-mation: information that is consistent with the stereotype. Other information will tend to be screened out as unintelligible, irrelevant, suspect, absurd, or, at best, anomalous. Ceteris paribus, then, the process of interpretation-based learning—the only type of learning there can be in a technocracy, other than rote memorization (which itself would have to begin with someone's interpretation of what is important enough to be memo-rized)—should initiate a self-reinforcing pattern of interpretive confirmation: a progres-sive strengthening of one's belief that one's interpretation of the evidence is correct, due to a progressive expansion of one's knowledge of confirmatory evidence.

I avoid the term *confirmation bias* to describe this process because it is often taken to mean a deliberate attempt to seek out confirmatory information. My suggestion, on the contrary, is that spirals of conviction are inadvertent and involuntary, just as are the perceptions, beliefs, interpretations, and biases that may be reinforced by a given spiral.

5.1.1. *Predictions about Cognition versus Predictions about Cognitions*

What is the scientific status, if any, of the spiral-of-conviction model, as I have just pre-sented it? And would arguing for it contradict my strictures against making sweeping generalizations about human behavior?

No doubt, the model is sweeping. But I have argued against only sweeping general-izations about human behavior that ignore or discount the causal role, in people's be-havior, of their presumptively heterogeneous webs of belief. The spiral-of-conviction model not only does not ignore or discount this role; it accepts it and contributes to an understanding of how such webs are formed and strengthened. Its predictions and ret-rodictions concern how people organize, make sense of, and add to their webs of belief, but without purporting to predict or retrodict the content of the webs, which remains opaque, at least in the absence of intellectual-historical investigation of particular individuals' webs. To the extent that the spiral-of-conviction model is accurate, it is part of the nomology of human belief, but it does not determine *what* people believe. The victim of the spiral of conviction could be dogmatically committed to racism, fascism, liberalism, Progressivism, Marxism, libertarianism, idiosyncratic isms, isms as yet uninvented—or to social-scientific positivism, or the dogma that "incentives matter," or naive economic, psychological, political, or technocratic realism.

As for the scientific status of the spiral-of-conviction model, it is supported by an interpretively charitable, introspectively plausible understanding of positivist social-scientific evidence. (Chapter 4's criticism of positivist social science applies only to social scientists' uncharitable interpretation of evidence, not to the evidence itself.) I follow Weber in making *Verstehen*, or interpretive charity, the prime criterion of theoretical rigor in the social sciences. To be sure, the presumption of ideational heterogeneity should stand in the way of confident retrodictions or predictions of people's ideas or behavior based on empirical data, regardless of how charitable one's interpretations of the data. But this does not rule out using patterns in such data, identified theoretically and interpreted charitably, to hypothesize about the nomology of our mental processes.

Still, the most prudent stance to take toward social-scientific evidence is to treat it as merely suggestive of real possibilities. This is how I will treat the empirical evidence I adduce in this chapter and the next.

5.1.2. *Evidence for the Spiral of Conviction*

The idea of a spiral of conviction was inspired by Philip E. Converse's "The Nature of Belief Systems in Mass Publics" (1964), which remains the most important contribution to the study of ideology in American political science. Converse hypothesized that political ideologies get their apparent coherence—the coherence that is experienced by the ideologue—from their grounding in "some superordinate value or posture toward man and society, involving premises about the nature of social justice, social change, 'natural law,' and the like." Thus, he contended, "a few crowning postures—like premises about survival of the fittest in the spirit of social Darwinism—serve as a sort of glue to bind together many more specific attitudes and beliefs" into a belief *system*.[6] The specific attitudes and beliefs that are consistent with the crowning postures seem, to the ideologue, to fit together for "abstract and quasi-logical reasons developed from a coherent world view."[7]

---

[6] Converse 1964, 210–211.
[7] Ibid., 211.

Converse's argument suggests that "belief systems" or ideologies are webs of belief, which is consistent with introspection. Our own political beliefs are not random collections of propositions but constellations of ideas that are well-enough organized to yield interpretations of the political world that are, to some extent, coherent. If one treats as an "ideology" any subset of one's own ideas that seem to "go together"—such as the beliefs held by liberals, conservatives, anarchists, communists, libertarians, neoclassical economists, positivists, naive realists, ideational determinists, and so on—one can see, I think, that they are interconnected in a manner that allows one to interpret the relevant part of the world (accurately or not). And if one introspects deeply enough, one will find that some of these beliefs serve as crowning postures around which the others are organized.

The organization of a belief system might begin with someone's reception of a crowning posture communicated from someone else, which then allows the recipient to interpret some aspect of politics or society. That is, the interpretive role played by the crowning posture may allow the nascent ideologue to make sense of, and therefore to become knowledgeable about, a growing quantity of seemingly relevant reasoning, claims, and information about this aspect. Using Converse's example, the crowning posture of social Darwinism can be stated as the belief that success is caused by fitness and failure by unfitness. Someone who reads or hears this interpretation of success and failure, without having first been shielded against it by what she interprets as a conflicting interpretation (such as that success and failure are functions of luck), may unproblematically accept the crowning posture into her web of beliefs, which would then make her receptive to congruent claims, such as that those who are financially successful are fit, while those who receive public assistance are unfit. Notice that, at this early stage, where one's belief system is still germinal, it can take very little in the way of persuasive argumentation to convince someone of a crowning posture or of subsidiary claims. Mere assertion might even be persuasive, which would explain the reproduction of religion: very young people, especially, are credulous because of their relatively underdeveloped webs of belief, and religions are most effectively inculcated among the very young. So, too, are political ideologies.

Once someone accepts the crowning posture of, say, social Darwinism into her web of beliefs, it would allow her to learn information, claims, and arguments about, say, policy issues concerning welfare and income redistribution—but primarily information, claims, and arguments that are congruent with the crowning posture. Incongruent information, claims, and arguments would tend, ceteris paribus, to strike her as irrelevant or implausible—or even, in the limit case, unintelligible. Anyone, I think, can confirm introspectively that the information, claims, and arguments of those who are one's political adversaries often seem irrelevant, implausible or even incomprehensible. This, indeed, would appear to be the source of a great deal of the mutual vitriol that is a given in politics: the fact that those on the other side seem to have such plainly wrong or unfathomable ideas, prompting the thought that they are irrational or evil. This thought may stem from one's inability to understand ideas that have been screened out of one's own web of beliefs because they are incompatible with the interpretations of the world produced by the web. Recall Lippmann's dictum that "the perfect stereotype precedes the use of reason; is a form of perception, imposes a certain character on the data of our senses before the data reach the intelligence. . . . It stamps itself upon the evidence in the very act of securing the evidence."[8] In this view, a web of beliefs both produces and confirms perceptions consistent with it. As the confirmations multiply, those who have different webs of belief than one's own become increasingly difficult to understand with interpretive charity, because one's own web has rendered incongruent beliefs implausible or incredible.

It seems likely, however, that even the most sophisticated and heavily reinforced interpretive screens are imperfect: through confusion, inattention, or the presence of contradictory crowning postures in one's web, one might end up accidentally screening in ideas that are incongruent with any given crowning posture and with the web that has developed around it. This would explain how dogmatic ideologues can nonetheless be intellectually creative (one thinks of Adorno and Buchanan): their webs of belief are idiosyncratically permeable and thus heterogeneous in comparison to others who hold the same dogmas. Still, it would seem that the ideas screened in by one's web of beliefs should be *largely* consistent with a given posture and should therefore have the effect, over time, of strengthening one's confidence in its validity as the web grows in size. Thus, Quine and Ullian contend that "what we come to believe derives much of its support from the sheer bulk of past cases."[9]

The growing amount of congruent information screened in by the interpretation made possible by a crowning posture would tend to reinforce the budding ideologue's impression that the interpretation is sound. At this point we can expect that the budding ideologue will have become recognizably "ideological," that is, doctrinaire about the crowning posture, because her growing web of relevant beliefs tends overwhelmingly to confirm its validity.[10] At the same time, if she discovers that certain sources of ideas (such as a given news outlet, given authors, or the leaders of a given political party) are trustworthy, in the sense that they share her positions on the crowning posture or the subsidiary issues, it is logical that she would start screening in information from these sources, further deepening her information (or misinformation) base and thereby inadvertently strengthening her faith in the crowning posture—which seems to her to prove itself reliable, with ever-greater frequency, because of the confirmatory ideas she receives from trusted sources.

The ideologue's goal in screening ideas and sources for congruence with her extant web would *not* be to confirm, say, social Darwinism. It would be to learn the truth without wasting time and effort on unintelligible, "obviously" wrong, or annoyingly obtuse

---

[8] Lippmann [1922] 1997, 65.

[9] Quine and Ullian 1978, 84.

[10] Moreover, interpretive schemas may allow one to *remember* schema-congruent information better than would otherwise be the case (Lodge and Hamill 1986).

arguments for truth-claims that are inconsistent with her growing and increasingly persuasive web of beliefs. Thus, while she would be aiming at the truth, as interpreted by her web of beliefs, she would unintentionally be achieving dogmatism (and perhaps naive realism about her dogmas). Even assuming that she could understand the true intellectual challenge posed by ideologically incongruent ideas, it would be increasingly rational for her to discount such ideas as anomalous or untrustworthy the larger her stock of confirmatory ideas grew, because this growing stock of congruent ideas would render incongruent ideas increasingly implausible.

The rationality of this process—even though it leads to dogmatism about inaccurate beliefs as well as accurate ones—is crucial, as it indicates that the spiral-of-conviction model is interpretively charitable. As one gains confidence in one's beliefs from the accumulating mass of evidence in favor of them, one *should* tend to become doctrinaire about one's conclusions, not because one is deliberately closing one's mind, but because one's conclusions are based on a growing sample of information that seems reliable—but that, one may fail to recognize, is biased. It is rational to trust one's sense of reliability because there is an overabundance of information out there and one needs a way to focus one's attention on only the most telling bits, disregarding the rest. There is no other way to do this than to judge as "telling" the information that seems plausible because it is congruent with one's standing web of beliefs. That, I think, is what introspection tells us that we all do, unavoidably. Bias is unavoidable in a world of overabundant information, because there has to be an interpretive screening mechanism to allow one to understand such a world, assuming that one does try to understand it, or assuming that one inadvertently thinks that one understands it. Only the entirely ignorant can avoid bias entirely—which, as we will see in the next chapter, offers a measure of hope for democratic technocracy.

Dogmatism produced by the spiral of conviction would close the minds of the dogmatic, but not in the uncharitable sense of dogmatism. The dogmatic mind produced by a spiral of conviction rationally draws conclusions from a wide and often impressive web of relevant beliefs. The crowning postures of this mind's belief system are backed up by large amounts of evidence and large numbers of logically connected claims and arguments, which are screened in along with the confirmatory evidence and may also be developed as one reflects on what one thinks one knows. It is rational to require evidence, claims, and arguments that challenge such a belief system to meet the standards of verification set by the belief system itself, as there is no other feasible standard to use. Bayesian updating is not an option in the real world, because it would require that the "data" of the world stream in unimpeded to correct the interpretive priors that make any data comprehensible. But data cannot stream in unimpeded by interpretive priors when there are far too many data for anyone to understand, sans interpretation.

Interpretations are the screening devices that make understanding possible, but only by focusing attention on a small and biased sample of "the" data. Like all rational but radically ignorant human beings, the ideologue must continually distinguish between ideas that seem to be worth considering and ideas that seem so outlandish that their consideration would likely be a waste of time. Faced with overabundant information, the only reasonable way to draw the line is by inferring, from her interpretation of what she (thinks that she) already knows, which new "data" are likelier to be true than false, or likelier to be more revealing than misleading about the big picture. Thus, it is rational for her to demand that if she is to take new data seriously, they must be consistent with her standing interpretations of old data (and old arguments, claims, and other ideas). Ceteris paribus, the deeper one's prior knowledge base, the stronger one's priors will be.

5.1.3. The Causal Relationship Between Knowledgeability and Dogmatism

The workings of the spiral of conviction would explain Converse's well-known findings about attitudinal "constraint" over time.[11] Converse found, as of 1956, "a very sharp dichotomy within the population" between, on the one hand, a relatively small "hard core" of citizens who, over time, had fixed issue positions that he called "constrained"; and everyone else, whose opinions about political issues fluctuated almost randomly from one survey to the next. He interpreted the fluctuating opinions as "non-attitudes,"[12] but this was a misnomer. He was not referring to people who answered "Don't Know," or who gave no opinion, but people who gave inconsistent opinions at different interviews separated by nearly a year. A better label for their "non-attitudes" would have been "shallow attitudes." The attitudes of the hard core, by contrast, which were constrained enough to persist over time, must have been anchored by something lacked by those whose attitudes were relatively shallow. The anchor seems to have been a greater quantity of political information. "Extreme instability" of attitudes was "associated with absence of information," according to Converse, while those with more information were relatively ideological.[13]

The spiral-of-conviction model easily explains these correlations. Those whose belief systems gave them an interpretive screen were able to assimilate more information than those who lacked a belief system; in turn, the greater information base accumulated by the former produced more dogmatic convictions that, therefore, persisted over time, regardless of counterevidence, counterargument, or counterclaims the respondents

---

[11] Decades later, Converse (2006, 310) denied my interpretation of his findings (Friedman 2006) by disputing whether the respondents whom he had labeled "ideologues" were "extremists." The spiral of conviction, however, concerns not the development of extreme beliefs but the development of dogmatic ones. A "moderate" can be just as dogmatic as can an extremist, given an interpretive framework that favors information that is congruent with a moderate outlook.

[12] Converse 1964, 242, 245; Converse 1970.

[13] Converse 1964, 245. In saying "absence" of information, Converse lent himself to another misconstrual. Even the citizens in his survey (the 1956 survey also used in *The American Voter*) who were judged to be the least informed politically were usually not *completely* uninformed: they tended to know the names of the two major parties, the names of the two major candidates for president, and so on. To formulate a political opinion, one does need some information, even if it is scant or false information (and even though no amount of information will, alone, *suffice* to create an opinion absent an interpretation of the information).

might encounter from month to month. The nonideological citizens may have been un-informed, in part, *because* they lacked an interpretive screen, so whatever information did make it into their webs of belief between surveys would have had a greater ability to change their minds.[14]

Converse's finding that ignorance correlated with attitude instability (lack of tem-poral constraint) also meshes with later work on the fluctuation of poorly informed vot-ers' opinions in response to survey question-order and framing effects.[15] Changing the wording or order of survey questions tends to have strong effects on the responses of the poorly informed; weak effects on the responses of the well informed. This can be attributed to the fact that a poorly informed respondent may be prompted by a question's framing to think of the issue in a way that is, to her, entirely novel, whereas such changes of frame are less likely to be either novel or persuasive among respondents who already have an issue frame in mind—a frame buttressed by the ideas that were rendered legible, and plausible, by the frame itself, or by a belief system that lent itself to that framing of the issue.

5.1.4. The Far Reaches of One's Web of Beliefs

The association between political information, political ideology, and attitudinal con-straint has been repeatedly confirmed since 1964 but has not been intensively studied or analyzed. What analysis there is tends to take it for granted, strangely enough, that to be dogmatic is *desirable*—because it is associated with greater political information.[16] This misunderstanding has obscured the silver lining in Converse's findings about the general public's ignorance: that it is associated with open-mindedness. This is a point I will develop in the next chapter. The dark cloud, on the other hand, is that those who are relatively knowledgeable—such as epistocrats, by definition—are likely to be rela-tively doctrinaire. Thus, the spiral-of-conviction model suggests that the prospects for a judicious epistocracy are slim, ceteris paribus.

I will restrict myself, here, to the dark cloud. Consider, first, that epistocrats might well have become interested in public policy to begin with because of strong political or polit-ically relevant ideas. If these ideas act as interpretive screens, they would enable a young citizen-technocrat to amass a large amount of policy-relevant information, making her a

---

[14] See also Stimson 1975, Neuman 1981, and Jennings 1992.

[15] E.g., Zaller 1992, ch. 4.

[16] Thus, the article on the study of ideology in the centennial edition of the *American Political Science Review* says that "Converse's contribution" was to remove "the negative implications of bias or false consciousness" from the concept of ideology, which is untrue of Converse's contribution but does seem to be true of how he was interpreted by later scholars. "Ideology became a beneficial characteristic and a mark of sophistication," the article continues. "An 'ideologue' would have a reasonably well-organized set of attitudes and preferences that were stable across time and informed by knowledge of what the government was doing" (Knight 2006, 623). See also, e.g., Kinder 1983, Carmines and D'Amico 2014, and Achen and Bartels 2016, 13.

good candidate epistocrat, ceteris paribus. Thus, in line with Colander's suggestion, the ideologies about which epistocrats are dogmatic may be political.

One might think that epistocratic training could overcome the effects of political ideology, even if one allows that the training might replace political ideology with a theoretical or methodological ideology, such as that "incentives matter." But evidence about people's "online processing" of information suggests that ideologies (of any kind) that are acquired early in life may be particularly hard to shake as, over time, the evidence and arguments for the conclusions of the ideology may be forgotten, with only the conclusions remembered.[17] "Source memory"—the recollection of how and why one came to believe something—develops slowly in children and then deteriorates quickly as adults age.[18] Adults may therefore be vulnerable to the ongoing influence of messages they heard in childhood or adolescence that left them convinced of certain political conclusions; for they may not remember the sources of the messages and may therefore be unable to check their trustworthiness. Even if, as an adult epistocrat or one in graduate training, one encounters a challenge to a given legacy conclusion, one might be unable to test the challenge adequately against the feeling one retains from some point in the past (one knows not when) that the challenge *must* be wrong somehow. This would make it very difficult to root out ideological convictions, and might help to account for the depressing fact that a great many epistocrats consistently uphold one ideological position across their entire careers. Thus, for example, there are reliably Republican and reliably Democratic economists, reliably liberal, conservative, and radical economists, reliably Austrian, Chicago school, Keynesian, and institutionalist economists, reliable proponents and reliable opponents of raising the minimum wage.

Yet it is not irrational to trust one's vague feelings from the past. If one were to ignore a conclusion for which one has no source memory, one would be trusting in the argument or evidence that now challenges the conclusion while ignoring the challenge to *it* represented by the original, now-forgotten evidence or argument. This would be unwise, for when one heard the now-forgotten message, one must have thought it provided a good reason to accept the conclusion that now persists, and good reasons are exactly what *should* undergird one's conclusions. In resisting counterarguments and counterevidence to a conclusion, then, one may merely be defending a truth whose demonstration lies just beyond the remembered fringes of one's web of beliefs. On the other hand, as Quine and Ullian put it, "The cause of a belief may have been some unqualified person's irresponsible remark. It may even have been a misunderstanding on our part of someone's words, or a subconscious association of ideas. . . . The cause may have gone unnoticed, or have been forgotten; but the belief is there, and by chance it may even be true."[19]

---

[17] E.g., Lodge et al. 1989; Lodge et al. 1995; Butler et al. 2009; Umanath et al. 2012.
[18] Johnson 1998; Gopnik 2010.
[19] Quine and Ullian 1978, 15.

5.1.5. The Spiral of Conviction and Radical Ignorance

The spiral-of-conviction interpretation of dogmatism is different from standard accounts in that it does not suggest that the dogmatist engages in improper forms of reasoning or that she lets emotions—such as an irrational attachment to her current beliefs, wishful thinking, ego defense, or an equation of her beliefs with the integrity of her intellectual or political "tribe"—drive her responses to new information. This is important, because such folk psychologizing might lead us to think that epistocrats could avoid ideological bias if they were selected for emotional detachment or a fierce devotion to reason and evidence. Such a selection strategy would be ineffective against spirals of conviction because they are rational (not emotional), and, indeed, normatively unobjectionable, as there is no practical alternative to the interpretation-based, selective learning of large amounts of information.

The reason for the difference between the spiral model and other accounts of dogmatism is that the spiral model postulates the ideologue's radical ignorance of her dogmatism—in effect, her ignorance of the fact that imbibing the tenets of a different belief system might have led her to endorse with certainty conclusions directly opposed to those that she is now certain are singularly sustained by fact and logic. By contrast, an account of dogmatism that interprets it as stemming from irrationality might depict it as akin to akrasia. According to such an account, if one's devotion to reason is strong enough, one can, at least in principle, resist a dogma's emotional pull and courageously confront unpleasant truths, just as the akratic might be able to overcome her weak will and force herself to do the unpleasant thing that she knows she should do. The comparison between dogmatism and akrasia, however, presupposes that the ideologue recognizes that she is not *already* confronting the whole truth (or the most relevant aspects of it), just as the akratic *knows* that she should do what she has trouble doing. Thus, the akrasia model forecloses the possibility that the ideologue is radically ignorant, and in so doing it overlooks the basis of the spiral of conviction: the reasonableness (because there is no real alternative) of interpreting the world consistently with the way it is depicted by one's web of beliefs. The akrasia model, one might say, is moralistic where what is needed is not condemnation of the dogmatist but understanding. Moralizing and epistemology do not mix well, because moral condemnation presupposes that the one who is being condemned *knows* that she should not believe what she believes rather than being radically ignorant of the fact that the belief is untrue.

Bryan Caplan's argument in *The Myth of the Rational Voter* uses something like the akratic model.[20] As we saw in Chapter 1, he starts from the premise that voters know that in large electorates, no single vote is likely to tip an election. I will dispute this premise in Chapter 6, but let us accept it here for the sake of argument. Because they know that their votes and thus their opinions almost certainly do not matter, according to Caplan, voters

---

[20] See Bennett and Friedman 2008, 215–219 and 232–238.

feel free to "indulge" their "demand for political delusion" by believing in ideologies that, he asserts—in a striking act of uncharitable interpretation—*they know* are untrue, but that they find emotionally gratifying.[21] In contrast, the spiral-of-conviction model interprets the ideologue as assuming that she is, so far as she knows, pragmatically adjusting her beliefs to the incoming flow of "information," let the chips fall where they may (*as if* she were a discipline of Reverend Bayes). The resulting opinions are those the ideologue thinks are justified by "the" evidence, claims, and argumentation, meaning the evidence, claims, and argumentation that she finds persuasive. There is no thirst for delusion, nor must the resulting beliefs be emotionally comforting. Indeed, a signal advantage of the spiral model is that it allows us to recognize that ideologues frequently believe things that are emotionally quite disturbing to them. In the real world, political ideologies may as easily convince people that their society is inevitably corrupt or on the brink of destruction as that its best days lie ahead, just as religious ideologies may persuade people that they are destined for hell or destined for heaven. The notion that ideologues are carefree because they have deliberately chosen self-satisfying beliefs is a classic example of folk psychologizing that bespeaks little familiarity with living, breathing ideologues.

The victim of a spiral of conviction has her opinions shaped by whatever "truths" are at her disposal, whether they are upsetting, gratifying, or emotionally neutral. The difference between an ideologue and a nonideologue is not a greater or lesser indulgence of emotion or a greater or lesser commitment to truth. It is the greater plausibility of conclusions that seem to have been confirmed by a great deal of credible evidence and argumentation, as compared to the lesser plausibility of conclusions that seem to be based on scant evidence or tentative argumentation. The normative fly in the ideological ointment is not some morally culpable decision or deplorable character flaw, but the fact that evidence and argumentation of which the ideologue is radically ignorant may reveal that her ideology is wrong—something that the ideologue may never learn because this news is screened out by her ideology. This is tragedy, not grounds for condemnation.

Another advantage of the spiral model over the akrasia model is that, on logical grounds alone, the latter view is so intellectually uncharitable as to be incoherent. Whatever suspicions self-aware people may have about the biases that *might* drive their own conclusions, they cannot possibly believe that their own ideas are so "ideological" (in the sense of being both dogmatic and biased toward an untruth) that they are unjustified or likely to be unjustified; yet that is the belief attributed to the ideologue by the akrasia model. Just as the akratic putatively knows that she really should do something that she nonetheless fails to do, the ideological akratic would have to believe that, say, social Darwinism *is false* (or is likely to be false), and thus should *not* be believed, even though she believes it nonetheless. Needless to say, however, one cannot believe in what one believes is false; "belief"

---

[21] Caplan 2007, 3, 18, 2. Bennett and Friedman 2008, 244–248, shows that the "rational" component of the theory of "rational irrationality" entails the incoherent claim that voters believe that their beliefs are false.

that *p* means belief that *p* is true.[22] More technically, a belief in *p* that is unjustified by one's perception of the truth of *p* would violate what Ward E. Jones has dubbed the first-person constraint on doxastic explanation, that is, the fact that one cannot recognize one's own beliefs as being caused by epistemically inadequate reasons lest one abandon those beliefs due to their recognized inadequacy.[23] If, as Caplan holds, ideologues know that their beliefs are false, this knowledge would immediately deprive their beliefs of any plausibility in their own eyes, extinguishing their "belief" in their beliefs. This is the very opposite of what happens with ideologues.

5.1.6. Spirals of Conviction or Motivated Reasoning?

A more coherent alternative to the spiral-of-conviction model is the motivated-reasoning model that political scientists have borrowed from psychology to explain political dogmatism. According to this model, people have two conflicting motives for belief, which are generally termed "accuracy" and "directional" motives. Directional motives are supposed to push people toward believing in conclusions that they "want" to believe in, regardless of the evidence against the accuracy of these conclusions.[24]

It would seem that here again, undertheorized and interpretively uncharitable folk psychology has been picked up by positivist psychologists. Motivated reasoning is "wishful thinking" decked out in positivist language; like the folk version, the positivist version holds that people stubbornly cling to beliefs that *at some level they know* are false. Yet unlike the akrasia theory, the theory of motivated reasoning is—at least arguably—logically coherent, because it assigns the putative directional motive to an unconscious "level." It divides the self into a phenomenological realm, where one consciously believes that one's beliefs are accurate, and an unconscious realm, where it is as if someone else is in charge: a homunculus dedicated not to accuracy but a directional goal, such as ego defense. The figurative homunculus achieves this goal by getting the conscious self to dogmatically reaffirm its extant beliefs, regardless of the cost in accuracy; but, contrary to the akrasia model, this is a cost of which only the homunculus is aware. Thus, neither the homunculus nor the conscious self is in violation of the first-person constraint on doxastic explanation. The metaphorical homunculus is a rational agent manipulating a nonmetaphorical rational agent, but without believing the untruths the latter is manipulated into believing. Consequently, the conscious agent is unaware of the falseness of the beliefs she takes to be true. Motivated-reasoning theorists themselves, being positivists, do not, of course, attach the directional motive to anything so metaphysical as a homunculus, but it is helpful to envision their splitting of the self in this way because it shows up not only the potential strength of the theory (its logical coherence) but its weaknesses, as we will see.

---

[22] By implication, the notion of akrasia entails an incoherent understanding of human psychology.

[23] See Jones 2002.

[24] See Abelson 1986 and Abelson and Prentice 1989 for the ego-defense view; for a critique, Friedman 2012b.

In political science, the motivated-reasoning study that exerted the most influence was probably Charles Taber and Milton Lodge's 2006 paper, "Motivated Skepticism in the Evaluation of Political Beliefs" (cited more than 2,000 times as of late 2018).[25] Taber and Lodge gave undergraduates in their laboratory the opportunity to read arguments identified in advance as congruent or incongruent with the students' initial beliefs about affirmative action and gun control. The authors found, first of all, that students tended to read the congruent arguments, not those that would challenge their priors. However, students required to read both congruent and incongruent arguments spent more time reading incongruent arguments than congruent ones. Afterward, these students tended to rate the congruent arguments as stronger than the incongruent ones. Indeed, most of these students became more persuaded of the veracity of their prior beliefs than they had been before the experiment. That is, exposure to contradictory arguments strengthened belief in what was being contradicted.

Crucially, these effects were predominantly found among subjects who were likely to be relatively well informed about affirmative action and gun control ahead of time, as indicated by their greater stores of general political information; and among those who had stronger initial beliefs about affirmative action and gun control. "By contrast with the most knowledgeable and most 'crystallized' thirds of our sample," according to Taber and Lodge, "the least sophisticated [i.e., most poorly informed] respondents and those with the weakest prior attitudes on these issues show little or no prior belief effect."[26] They conclude that "rather than moderating or simply maintaining their original attitudes, citizens—especially those who feel strongly about the issue and are the most sophisticated—strengthen their attitudes in ways not warranted by the evidence."[27]

All of these findings, however, are consistent with the spiral-of-conviction model. No imputation of a directional motive is necessary.

According to the spiral model, the relatively well-informed students, seeing little point in reading arguments that they already (thought that they) knew were wrongheaded, would have logically chosen to read arguments they had reason to think would be accurate. And when instructed to read arguments that challenged their prior beliefs, they would have logically tended not to be persuaded by them. The spiral model is also consistent with the finding that the students instructed to read incongruent arguments spent more time on them than on congruent arguments. Insofar as incongruent arguments were unfamiliar to the students, they may have needed more time to understand them than they needed with congruent, familiar arguments. Another not-incompatible possibility is that they needed time to search their memories for counterarguments when confronting arguments that, being incongruent with their priors, seemed implausible. "Because memory searches are time consuming," write Kari Edwards and Edward Smith,

---

[25] See the symposium on this paper in *Critical Review* 24(2) (2012).

[26] Taber and Lodge 2006, 760.

[27] Ibid., 756. See also Gaines et al. 2007.

"participants would take longer to evaluate arguments that are incompatible with their prior beliefs."[28] Note that searching for counterarguments is *good* scientific practice for those whose only motive is to determine the truth.

As for the finding that exposure to incongruent arguments strengthened the subjects' prior beliefs, Lee Ross suggests that Taber and Lodge's subjects may have said to themselves, in effect, " 'If that's the best [the other side] can do to support their argument, I'm even more certain [than before] that they are wrong.' "[29] Ross's conjecture is supported by a similar experiment conducted in 2012 by James Druckman, Jordan Fein, and Thomas Leeper, who found that subjects' views about health care reform grew more certain after they read more about the subject, *regardless* of whether the readings were congruent with their initial opinions.[30] The subjects' initial interpretation seems only to have been susceptible to being strengthened, not weakened, by exposure to more information—pro or con—as, arguably, the initial interpretation allowed them to understand the new information and classify it as plausible or implausible, such that more information would serve as confirmation of the interpretation, even if it seemed incongruent with the interpretation. If the new information was congruent with the interpretation, it would seem plausible, redoubling confidence in the interpretation. If the information was incongruent, it would ipso facto be classified as implausible—thus confirming that the interpretation is consistent with all plausible evidence, again redoubling confidence in it.

Like Taber and Lodge, Druckman, Fein, and Leeper assume that their experiment vindicates the motivated-reasoning paradigm, but in fact their experiment, like Taber and Lodge's experiment, is compatible with the view that people can rationally but unwittingly behave dogmatically because their initial beliefs serve as a plausibility screen against new evidence and arguments. Thus, the motivated-reasoning interpretation of the experiments does not explain any evidence that the spiral-of-conviction interpretation cannot explain just as well. However, the spiral-of-conviction model better explains the greater propensity to dogmatism of the relatively well informed. For if anything, one would expect an unconscious directional motive to produce higher levels of dogmatism among relatively *uninformed* people, because they would unconsciously recognize that opinions based on a relatively narrow foundation of evidence will require stronger buttressing by unreasoned dogmatism than those based on a wider foundation. If directional motives exist, they should make someone with little evidence for her beliefs all the more determined, at the unconscious level, to reject any shred of counterevidence, as, ceteris paribus, each shred of it should pose a greater threat to her beliefs than it would pose to someone whose beliefs were based on a greater amount of evidence.

Let us make this more concrete by appealing to the construct of a homunculus rather than the construct of an unconscious level. The homunculus should recognize that the

---

[28] Edwards and Smith 1996, 6.

[29] Ross 2012, 236. Cf. Shah et al. 2002.

[30] Druckman et al. 2012, 439.

conscious self, if it is to achieve the directional goal, will need to be more dogmatic in rejecting counterevidence to its weakly supported beliefs than in rejecting counterevidence to its more strongly supported beliefs. In reality, though, it seems that those subjects whose beliefs were supported by a greater evidentiary base were the ones who more strongly resisted counterevidence. The interpretively charitable view is that this behavior was not determined by an incompetent homunculus but by the subjects' sense that their beliefs were rationally worthy of reaffirmation in the face of what the subjects interpreted as *implausible* counterevidence and counterargument—presumably because the beliefs in question had been confirmed, as far as the subjects were concerned, by a relatively large amount of prior evidence and argument.

Taber and Lodge explain the propensity to dogmatism among the relatively well informed as a matter of using their greater stores of information as "ammunition" to fend off incongruent information.[31] This ad hoc martial metaphor, however, suggests a homunculus inexplicably dedicated to scientific rigor in the war it is fighting against the accuracy motive—itself the embodiment of scientific rigor. If the homunculus is trying to get the ego to defend its beliefs regardless of their truth value, why should it require that this defense use evidence as ammunition? Why would the homunculus tie its own hands in the battle for dogmatism by compromising in this manner with the forces of accuracy? Again, then, the homunculus seems not to know what it is doing. Conversely, if the motivated-reasoning model were modified to afford the homunculus absolute competence and absolute power—unconstrained by empiricist values and, therefore, unconstrained by the need for evidentiary ammunition to achieve its directional objectives—it is unclear why our conscious selves would ever be able to change their minds about anything. Yet in reality we are quite capable of changing our minds, under the right circumstances: that is, when faced with evidence that *we interpret* as showing that we are wrong. (Thus, we have no trouble changing our minds about whether it will be raining in a few minutes if it has just begun to rain, even if, before it began to rain, we had been convinced that it would not.) Moreover, Converse's study, like the motivated-reasoning data themselves, suggests that poorly informed people change their minds much more readily than do those with wider, deeper webs of belief—such as epistocrats.

The key to understanding this is to recognize that one rarely evaluates a new candidate belief, or new evidence or arguments relevant to an existing belief, de novo and atomically—that is, free of interpretive context. Rather, one evaluates inbound information as plausible or implausible by virtue of its congruence or incongruence with the totality of the "salient" evidence and reasoning of which one is aware, and the interpretations to which the evidence and reasoning give rise. That was Quine's point in "Two Dogmas of Empiricism."[32] As he and Ullian later put it, "It is in the light of the full body

---

[31] Taber and Lodge 2006, 757.
[32] Quine 1951.

of our beliefs" that candidate beliefs "gain acceptance or rejection; any independent merits of a candidate tend to be less decisive."[33]

5.2. THE SPIRAL OF CONVICTION AMONG EXPERTS

> If we did not rely on our preconceptions to organize the past, we would be hopelessly
> confused. . . . And if we relied solely on our preconceptions, we would be hopelessly
> closed-minded.
> —PHILIP E. TETLOCK, *Expert Political Judgment*

The best-known study of the predictive abilities of social-scientific experts is undoubtedly Philip E. Tetlock's *Expert Political Judgment* (2005). Tetlock showed that 284 experts in various social-scientific fields were unable to make event predictions, relevant to the areas of their expertise, that would improve upon simple extrapolations from the status quo. This is to say, in effect, that the experts either failed to interpret recent history correctly or that, in trying to extrapolate their interpretations into the future, time's arrow, heterogeneous agents, or novel circumstances produced changes that they failed to anticipate, or that they failed to anticipate with sufficient precision.[34]

More directly relevant here, however, is Tetlock's finding that the worst predictions were made by the most dogmatic experts. "Political belief systems," he writes, "are at continual risk of evolving into self-perpetuating worldviews,"[35] and it is mainly "hedgehog" experts, who think in terms of a single paradigm, who actualize this risk. He contrasts them against "foxes" among his experts, who brought a variety of paradigms to bear and who tended to make more accurate predictions than hedgehogs did.

The hedgehog/fox contrast may suggest, to motivated-reasoning theorists (such as Tetlock himself), that a technocracy could place its trust in nondogmatic experts, who somehow manage to escape the clutches of unconscious directional motives. Yet while Tetlock's "foxes" were *relatively* undogmatic, spirals of conviction seem to have been at

---

[33] Quine and Ullian 1978, 16. I am not suggesting assent to all aspects of Quine and Ullian's account, such as their claim that a web of beliefs is ultimately grounded in observation statements.

[34] The predictions the experts failed to make were much simpler than policy predictions would have to be. Tetlock did not ask the experts to do counterfactual thinking about the behavioral changes that would be wrought by a proposed policy. They were asked to predict what would happen to Argentina's GDP in the next two to five years, or whether there would be a nuclear war in the Indian subcontinent in the next five to 10 years—not what would happen if a new Argentine economic policy were adopted, or if peace talks between India and Pakistan were undertaken (Tetlock 2005, 45 and 247). As Tetlock (2010, 475) later said, his failure to ask his experts for counterfactual predictions makes his findings even grimmer for epistocracy than they appear to be at first glance. After all, if the experts cannot make reliable extrapolations from recent trends, they can hardly be expected to make reliable predictions about the complications introduced by policy changes (see also Buturovic 2010). Thus, his findings could form the basis of an a fortiori argument against epistocratic knowledge: If experts cannot get the easy questions right, how likely are they to get the hard ones right?

[35] Tetlock 2005, 4.

work among them, too. "Hedgehogs and foxes alike," he found, "impose more stringent standards of proof on dissonant discoveries (that undercut pet theories) than they do on consonant ones (that reinforce pet theories)."[36] Hedgehogs and foxes alike challenged ideologically incongruent data while rarely challenging congruent data.[37] In short, both hedgehogs and foxes (rationally, in my view, although not in Tetlock's) doubted the veracity of data that were inconsistent with their interpretations of the way things are. Hedgehogs and foxes alike were, after all, experts, with large knowledge bases to justify their priors. Therefore, if the spiral model is correct, Tetlock was measuring differences of degree among dogmatists, not differences of kind.

Advocates of nonideological expertise might suggest on the contrary that foxes learn simply by "opening their minds" to a wealth of empirical information. But even were this possible, whatever facts they thereby learned would then require interpretation if they were to make predictions, and this interpretive process should, over time, have the effect of screening in congruent evidence while screening out incongruent evidence. The only alternative to interpretively selective attention and retention would be indiscriminately memorizing whatever information happens to cross one's path, leading not to expertise but the accumulation of trivia. Thus, we need a different explanation for the existence of foxes than their sheer absorption in "the data."

One possibility is that foxes were relatively open-minded because they were less attentive or rigorous than hedgehogs, and therefore inadvertently allowed more contradictory information into their webs of belief. Alternatively, it is possible that, relatively early on, they were persuaded of the merits of more than one nonexclusive crowning posture, and that the various interpretations then screened in competing webs of evidence, assertion, and argumentation. Another possibility is that they were persuaded of interpretive frameworks that are less comprehensive than, say, classic political ideologies or the ideology of rational-choice theory. Someone exposed early on to one or several less-comprehensive interpretations of a given subject should be relatively well placed to recognize her own radical ignorance, for she may notice potential conflicts among different interpretations of the same evidence, ambiguity in the evidence when it is viewed from various theoretical perspectives, or heterogeneity in the evidence picked out as significant by various interpretive frameworks.

However, while such epistemological sophistication should be conducive to judicious policymaking, it should also reduce a given expert's confidence in her ability to make accurate predictions. There should thus be a trade-off between foxiness and suitability as an epistocrat (or epistocratic policy adviser). The less dogmatic the epistocrat, the less she should be able, in principle, to advocate one or another interpretation of evidence with confidence, at least when the evidence is ambivalent or ambiguous. Policies, however, have to be advocated with confidence if they are to be adopted. Decision-makers

---

[36] Ibid., 145.
[37] Ibid., 158–160.

need definitively supported policy choices, ceteris paribus; hence the perennial wish, first voiced by Harry S Truman, for "one-handed economists"—those who do not say, "on the one hand X, on the other hand not-X." The more tentative the advocates of a given policy, then, the less likely its adoption, ceteris paribus, compared to policies strongly supported by hedgehoggier epistocrats.

In a policy debate between a hedgehog and a fox, other technocratic actors, including other epistocrats, will face a problem of epistocratic identification. Faced with a candidate epistocrat who backs her claims with a great mass of evidence and a candidate epistocrat who instead acknowledges the weakness, ambivalence, or ambiguity of the evidence on her side, it is only logical to identify the first epistocrat as likelier to be right than the second—not because of the character of the first epistocrat, which might seem dogmatic (if, as the stereotype holds, dogmatic people "seem" dogmatic, which I doubt), but because of the apparent conclusiveness of the evidence she brings to bear. Admittedly, the other actors, if they recognized that they might inadvertently select for dogmatism, could instead defer to the least-confident epistocrats, but this would amount to choosing the policy that appears to be least supported by the evidence. It seems logical, then, that the relatively dogmatic epistocrats will tend to win, even when they should not, because the evidence they present will make it appear that they should.

It is in this sense that I began the chapter by suggesting that dogmas may prove "useful" to epistocrats. In the limit case, pure foxes, who are so perceptive that they notice the uncertainties—or are so unrigorous or inattentive that their webs of belief leave them hopelessly conflicted—would remain undecided on a given issue, selecting themselves out of the pool of those offering what technocracy demands: policy recommendations. Even short of the limit case, however, systemic selection for persuasive epistocrats should amount to systemic selection for dogmatic ones, other things equal.

5.3. THE FINANCIAL CRISIS IN RETROSPECT: THE ECONOMIST AS IDEOLOGUE

> The disaster that grew from these flawed incentives can be, to us economists, somewhat
> comforting: our models predicted that there would be excessive risk-taking and short-
> sighted behavior, and what has happened has confirmed these predictions.
> —JOSEPH E. STIGLITZ, *Freefall*

In this section I will present a case study that may be taken to illustrate the pathological effect of the technocratic "pressure for dogmatism." I will suggest that an assumption that seems to be all-but-universally shared among epistocrats—that the financial crisis of 2007–2008 was caused by bankers who were incentivized to take excessive risks—has found no evidentiary confirmation and a great deal of disconfirmation; but that, when disconfirming evidence has been confronted by prominent epistocrats, it has been dismissed by means of reasoning that strongly suggests dogmatism in action.

My selection of the case study stems from intensive research about the crisis that I undertook in 2010, resulting in a coauthored monograph on the subject.[38] In the course of this research I was persuaded of the dogmatism of economists, leading to the analysis in this chapter. Thus, this case study is a severely biased sample (although there is no such thing as an unbiased sample, according to my argument in Chapter 2). I hope this will be excused on the grounds that the evidence I present is merely suggestive. This brief case study is not intended to establish the breadth or depth of dogmatism among American economists, let alone epistocrats in general, but rather to suggest that it *may* be broad and deep. It will also suggest that the particular economists who are chosen to be epistocrats are not somehow immune to the pathological thinking we would expect of those who are profoundly gripped by webs of belief that they find (of course) extremely convincing.

5.3.1. The Orthodox View of the Crisis

The orthodox epistocratic understanding of the causes of the financial crisis consists of two compatible theories, both of which blame the crisis on bankers' incentives to take excessive risks. First, it is argued that because many bankers' compensation packages paid them bonuses for profits but did not penalize them for losses, they had everything to gain and nothing to lose from taking excessive risks that might produce high profits; therefore, they deliberately bet on mortgage-backed securities that they knew were excessively risky.[39] Second, it is argued that the executives of too-big-to-fail (TBTF) banks knew, or strongly suspected, that they would be bailed out if their banks got into trouble, again giving them an incentive to take excessive risks without fear of loss.[40]

While both of these arguments are very widely accepted as beyond dispute, it is remarkable that there is (to my knowledge) no evidence in favor of either except repeated assertions that they *must* be true—seemingly because, as Nobel laureate Joseph Stiglitz says in the section epigraph, both arguments comport with what economic theory (i.e., the intuition that incentives matter in a predictable fashion) would predict. Even more remarkably, there is abundant evidence against both theories. Most of this evidence is

---

[38] Friedman and Kraus 2011. My narrow argument here, about how economists have treated evidence about the crisis, does not depend on the conclusions of this book—a contribution to policy debate in which I have lost confidence for second-order reasons that should be obvious by this point.

[39] See, e.g., Acharya and Richardson 2009, 206–207; Admati and Hellwig 2013, 162; Barth et al. 2012, 66–69; Blinder 2013, 82; Dewatripont et al. 2010, 46–47; Johnson and Kwak 2010, 179; Roubini and Mihm 2010, 68–69; Posner 2009, 93–100; Stiglitz 2009, 331; Stiglitz 2010, 13–14, 151–153. The claim that this is how most bankers' pay was structured, as opposed to the claim that the result was excessive risk taking, is itself asserted rather than proved by these authors; see Murphy 2012 for evidence that the assertion is false.

[40] E.g., Acharya and Richardson 2009, 209; Admati and Hellwig 2013, 142ff; Calomiris and Haber 2014, 259; Hart and Zingales 2010, 20; Johnson and Kwak 2010, ch. 6; Stiglitz 2009, 333; Stiglitz 2010, 15, 164.

widely known by economists, as I will show, yet it has almost never been confronted by them (at least in print). When it has, dogmatic thinking appears to have kept them from questioning the orthodox understanding of the crisis.

The dogma in question is the assumption of effective omniscience. Both theories of the crisis trade on the assumption that bankers "knew" (that is, subjectively believed) ex ante that by investing in mortgage-backed securities, they were taking excessive risks. Otherwise—if the bankers did not believe that these securities were excessively risky— nothing would be explained by the objective incentives to take excessive risks postulated by the two hypotheses (the one that targets banks' compensation structures and the one that targets banks' putative status as TBTF). Rather than attempting to prove a negative by giving chapter and verse on the many publications in which economists assert the va- lidity of the two theories but fail to provide any supporting evidence,[41] I will concentrate on how economists have treated evidence against the theories; or rather, evidence against the underlying assumption that bankers knew that they were taking excessive risks prior to the crisis.

5.3.2. The Paradox of the Banks' Holdings of Triple-A Mortgage Bonds

The first piece of evidence requires a bit of background.

The behavior that is supposed to have been motivated by the bankers' putative know- ledge that they were taking excessive risks was their purchase of triple-A-rated residential mortgage-backed securities (RMBS). However, such securities are contractually struc- tured so as to make those of them that command triple-A ratings *less risky* than those rated AA, A, BBB, BB, or B. Because of this structuring (called "tranching"), AAA-rated RMBS paid much lower interest rates to their investors than did lower-rated RMBS tranches, which were riskier. The investors in the triple-A tranches were trading lower in- terest payments for greater safety, while investors in the lower-rated tranches were being compensated with higher interest payments for the greater risk they were taking. Yet bankers almost always bought the triple-A RMBS, as we will see. Economists do seem to recognize this fact, but they fail to see that it directly contradicts their theory that bankers were seeking excessive risk because of their incentives to do so. Such incentives should have spurred bankers to invest in low-rated, relatively lucrative RMBS tranches, not high-rated, relatively unlucrative ones.

An RMBS is a collection of bonds—promises to pay revenue in installments—issued against a pool of thousands of mortgages. Under the terms of an RMBS, the owners of bonds issued against the AAA tranche of the RMBS have a priority claim on all mortgage payments made by any of the mortgagors in the asset pool. Only after all AAA investors are paid what they are contractually owed in a given period does the remaining revenue

---

[41] See the sources cited in the previous two footnotes.

from the mortgage pool flow, like water in a multitiered waterfall, to investors in the AA tranche. In turn, only after all obligations to these bondholders are met does revenue flow to investors in the A tranche, who get paid before the BBB investors are paid, followed by the BB investors. As a matter of contractual obligation, then, the higher-rated tranches are safer than the lower-rated ones. Any banker who invested in AAA tranches was buying the safest available type of RMBS—not the riskiest.

The relative safety of the AAA tranches went with relatively low returns. It is a truism about bonds, including RMBS, that higher ratings produce lower revenue for bond investors, because high ratings connote high safety, while lower ratings, connoting greater risk, produce higher returns: investors in riskier bonds require an inducement to assume the greater risk. In the case of mortgage bonds, this requirement is reinforced by the contractual structure of tranching. With corporate or government bonds, ratings are merely opinions about risk formulated by staff members of the "ratings agencies" (Moody's, Standard and Poor's, and Fitch). However, with RMBS and other asset-backed securities (ABS), such as securities issued against pools of student loans or auto loans, the rating agencies' opinions are translated into the contractual obligation to receive payments at a specific level of the waterfall. As a result, the rates of return on the higher-rated tranches tended to be much lower than the rates of return on the lower-rated tranches. In late 2006, just before doubts about the subprime mortgage market began to spread, a newly issued Goldman Sachs RMBS paid investors in the AAA tranche 30 basis points (0.30 percent) over LIBOR (the London Interbank Offered Rate, the rate banks charged each other on three-month loans). But the same RMBS offered a BBB tranche that paid 150 basis points over LIBOR (1.5 percent), along with a BB tranche that paid 375 basis points over LIBOR (3.75 percent)—more than 10 times the "spread" paid to investors in the AAA tranche.[42] Thus, investors, including bankers, who were greedy for higher yields and heedless of risk should have bought the lower-rated, highly lucrative, but relatively risky BB or BBB bonds, ceteris paribus. But according to the only published study of US commercial banks' aggregate holdings of ABS (including RMBS), banks' investments in lower-rated tranches were "economically trivial."[43] In direct contradiction to the two leading theories of the crisis, this study, coauthored by Isil Erel, Taylor Nadauld, and René M. Stulz and published in 2014, suggests that bankers were in fact highly risk averse.

Calculations by Wladimir Kraus have used the method pioneered by Erel et al. to paint a picture of the risk aversion of just the four largest US commercial banks on the eve of the crisis.[44] Kraus used the Big Four's regulatory filings to determine their holdings of ABS (including RMBS) that were rated A, AA, or AAA at the end of 2006. He shows that the Big Four made relatively small investments in A-rated tranches, collectively

---

[42] Ashcraft and Schuermann 2008, 30, Table 17 (AAA, 30 basis points over LIBOR; AA, 47 bps; A, 56 bps; BBB, 150 bps; BB, 375 bps).

[43] Erel et al. 2014, 435.

[44] See Friedman 2011 for details.

totaling $13 billion, as compared to their investments in AA- and AAA-rated tranches, totaling $60 billion—more than a 4:1 ratio of safer and less lucrative tranches to less-safe, more-lucrative tranches. (Unfortunately, the regulatory filings group AAA and AA holdings together, and they do not record holdings of BBB or lower-rated tranches.) Using the Goldman Sachs RMBS as an example, investors in the A tranche would have received 56 basis points over LIBOR, or nearly twice what the AAA tranche paid and 63 percent more than the AA tranche.[45] Bankers who were greedy for profit and heedless of risk should have been piling into the A tranches rather than the AA and AAA tranches, yet the Big Four banks did the opposite.

A similar piece of evidence requires a word about the entities that issued mortgage-backed securities. Tranched, rated RMBS were issued by investment banks, such as Goldman Sachs, and the investment-bank arms of commercial bank holding companies.[46] However, another, much larger category of mortgage-backed securities, "agency MBS," were unrated, as they were issued by two government-sponsored agencies: Fannie Mae (the Federal National Mortgage Association) and Freddie Mac (the Federal Home Loan Mortgage Corporation). These two agencies (unrelated to the "ratings agencies" that assigned letter grades to the tranches of RMBS issued by investment banks) were created by Congress in 1938 and 1970, respectively, to buy mortgages from commercial banks and package them into unrated mortgage-backed securities, with the (technocratic) goal of encouraging banks to issue more mortgages. Because their congressional charters and their technocratic role virtually guaranteed that they would be bailed out if necessary (as they were, in September 2008), investments in agency MBS were considered safer than even the waterfall-protected AAA tranches of privately issued RMBS, and so they were even less lucrative for investors. Nonetheless, agency MBS were, by far, the preferred mortgage bonds among the Big Four, garnering investments of $329 billion—nearly six times these banks' $60 billion investment in higher-yielding triple- and double-A ABS tranches of all kinds, and 25 times their investment in even higher-yielding single-A tranches.[47] Erel, Nadauld, and Stulz show that this pattern was even more pronounced among smaller banks.[48]

For our purposes, the most important point is not the precise extent to which this evidence shows that bankers did the opposite of what the leading theories of the crisis would predict that they did. After all, Kraus's calculations, and those of Erel, Nadauld, and Stulz, were unknown to economists when they began to pronounce on the crisis, and they probably remain unknown to most of them even now. Yet, judging from their writings about the crisis, most economists did know (or thought they knew) that the triple-A

---

[45] Ashcraft and Schuermann 2008, 30, Table 17.

[46] Investment banks do not accept federally insured deposits and do not lend to businesses, mortgagors, and so on; commercial banks do.

[47] Friedman 2011.

[48] Erel et al. 2014, Table 4.

tranches of privately issued RMBS got the banks into trouble. One would be hard pressed to find an economist's account of the crisis that fails to mention the unwarrantedly wide triple-A tranches in which banks invested (a scandal that economists tend to attribute to the rating agencies' misaligned incentives).[49] Economists who mention this scandal thereby confirm their belief that it was banks' investments in triple-A RMBS tranches that nearly brought down the banking system. Moreover, it is probably safe to say that every living economist knows the truism that triple-A bonds produce lower yields than do lower-rated bonds. That is as basic as it gets in economics.

The conjunction of these two known knowns—that bankers invested in triple-A tranches, and that greater revenue would have flowed to bankers who invested in lower-rated tranches—should suggest, on purely logical grounds, that it is wrong to assume that bankers greedy for profit and insensitive to risk must have caused the crisis. Yet economists have consistently presented this assumption as an unquestionable truth. The alternative conclusion would be that bankers got into trouble because they did not know how risky these highly rated investments actually were. (Recall, from Chapter 3, that there had never been a nationwide US housing bubble.)

5.3.3. *Further Evidence of Bankers' Radical Ignorance*

The economists' assumption that bankers understood the risks they were taking is also belied by the fact that executives of the banks that turned out (in retrospect) to be exposed to the greatest risks lost billions of dollars in personal wealth that they could have held onto by selling their own banks' stock before the deflation of the housing bubble reached its crisis phase in September 2008, with the implosion of Lehman Brothers. Bank executives who knew that their firms had invested in excessively risky mortgage bonds, as posited by the orthodox view of the crisis, could have locked in huge gains in the value of their bank stock had they sold their shares earlier, when the housing bubble began to deflate. The first signs of trouble came when Ownit Mortgage Solutions filed for bankruptcy in December 2006, followed by New Century Financial Corporation in April 2007. In June, Moody's and S&P downgraded or placed warnings on $12 billion worth of subprime mortgage bonds, leading Bear Stearns, the fourth-largest investment bank (after Goldman Sachs, Lehman Brothers, and Morgan Stanley), to close down its two subprime mortgage hedge funds. Even then, there was plenty of time for bankers to sell off their banks' stock. Bear Stearns was still nine months away from crashing; its bailout, in March 2008, would wipe out its shareholders, paying them $2 per share for stock that had commanded $172 per share in January 2007 and $98 per share as late as February 2008. Lehman Brothers did not become insolvent until September 2008. Because of their

---

[49] See, for example, the discussions of the rating agencies in Acharya and Richardson 2009, Barth 2010, Blinder 2013, Dewatripont et al. 2010, Gjerstad and Smith 2009, Hull and White 2012, Jarrow 2012, Johnson and Kwak 2010, Roubini and Mihm 2010, Shiller 2008, Stiglitz 2009, and Stiglitz 2010.

failure to sell their own stock before their banks went under, Bear and Lehman CEOs James Cayne and Richard Fuld personally lost about $1 billion each, and the chairman of Citigroup, the most highly exposed commercial bank, lost approximately $500 million.[50]

The most obvious hypothesis by means of which we can explain the bankers' failure to sell their bank stock is that, contrary to the orthodox view, they were radically ignorant that triple-A mortgage bonds were excessively risky and that their banks' holdings of these bonds were dangerous. We will later consider an alternative, folk-psychological view (that they "did not want to know" about the risks they were taking).

Before turning to economists' defenses of the orthodox view, I should note that nothing I have said definitively establishes that bankers were ignorant of the risks they were taking. I am not, in short, attempting to make a first-order claim about what caused or did not cause the financial crisis. I am simply pointing out that the case in favor of the economists' orthodox first-order claim is not prima facie valid. It flies in the face of evidence that is known by economists. Thus, we face a potentially pathological lapse in epistocratic thinking.

5.3.4. Economists Analyze the Crisis

To my knowledge, not a single economist has published an attempt to defend the orthodox view against the fact that banks were heavily invested in the least-lucrative forms of RMBS. This silence speaks volumes. As we have seen, there is every reason to think that economists know, or think they know, that the banks invested in triple-A RMBS tranches, *and* that these tranches were less lucrative than lower-rated tranches. The conjunction of these two facts, or putative facts, appears to directly contradict the claim that, in the aggregate, bankers deliberately took excessive risks in search of higher yields. Yet economists make this claim repeatedly, fervently, and, so far as I can determine, almost universally. I attribute this contradiction to the cognitive force exerted by the factor identified in Stiglitz's epigraph above: the consistency of this claim with the dogma that incentives matter in a predictable way.

However, regarding the bankers who lost huge amounts of money by failing to sell their stock, I have identified four economists—Stiglitz himself, James Barth, Gerard Caprio Jr., and Ross Levine—who have tried to address the threat it poses to the orthodox theory of the crisis. Before getting to Stiglitz's efforts, let us examine the lengthier treatment developed by Barth, Caprio, and Levine—three justifiably respected finance specialists with many years of epistocratic service—in their 2012 book, *Guardians of Finance*, published by MIT Press. Barth, a professor of business at Auburn University, has worked at both the Office of Thrift Supervision and the Federal Home Loan Bank Board. Caprio, a professor of economics at Williams College, has worked at the World Bank. Levine, a

---

[50] Cohan 2009.

professor of business at the University of California, Berkeley, has worked at the Fed, the IMF, and the World Bank.[51]

So far as I know, *Guardians of Finance* contains the only full-scale scholarly attempt to refute the hypothesis that the cause of the crisis was the fact that, as the authors put it, "experienced professionals were incredibly myopic":[52] in other words, that bankers were radically ignorant. Against this hypothesis, Barth, Caprio, and Levine marshal three arguments.

First, they contend that "a first-semester business school student might venture that if highly rated mortgage instruments were paying a greater return than comparably rated corporate securities, as was the case, then the former must be riskier."[53] However, such a student's venture would be wrong: different types of securities may be subject to different risks, regardless of whether they share the same rating. More important, objective risk is irrelevant unless it is perceived. What the authors need to show is that "experienced professionals" *considered* highly rated RMBS tranches riskier than corporate bonds with the same rating, but they would have no reason to have done so. When comparing highly rated tranches with lower-rated tranches, investors, such as bankers, who understand how tranching works will ipso facto know that the lower-rated tranches are objectively riskier than the higher-rated tranches (because of their contractual structure). As the authors themselves say, "The first tranche, or slice of the deal, comprised the safest and highest rated (AAA) portion of the new securities,"[54] but they proceed to ignore this fact, preferring to compare apples and oranges. When someone buys a highly rated mortgage bond that pays a premium over a highly rated corporate bond, she may simply think she is getting a bargain made possible by different investors' heterogeneous interpretations of the risks of heterogeneous bonds (or by the fallibility of the rating agencies' judgments). However, the very possibility of ideational heterogeneity and thus disagreement would be invisible to an economist committed to the naive realism of the incentives-matter school, according to which the truth about risk, like all other relevant truths, is self-evident (at least to experienced professionals).

Second, the authors provide what they deem "harder evidence" against the radical-ignorance hypothesis: research showing that those in the financial sector were making an "excess wage" compared to comparably skilled people in other sectors. The authors claim that this demonstrates "the undeniable role of compensation in the crisis,"[55] but it

---

[51] The authors' argument that bankers knew they were taking excessive risks has been picked up by other respected epistocrats, such as Charles W. Calomiris and Stephen H. Haber (2014, 268). Calomiris, a Columbia Business School professor, previously served on the Advisory Scientific Committee of the European Systemic Risk Board, the International Financial Institution Advisory Commission of the US Congress, and the Federal Reserve System's Centennial Advisory Committee. Haber, a Stanford professor of political science and (by courtesy) economics, was a consultant to the IMF and the World Bank.

[52] Barth et al. 2012, 57–58.

[53] Ibid., 69.

[54] Ibid., 72.

[55] Ibid., 73–74.

does not. The question of whether bankers were overpaid has no bearing on the question of whether they were ignorant of the risks they were taking. Perhaps the authors are suggesting that because they were so well paid, bankers looked the other way when taking self-evident risks. But this suggestion would, at best, provide only a self-interested *motive* (greed) for neglecting the risk—not evidence that those motivated to ignore the risk did, in fact, know of and understand the magnitude of the risk. Thus, the authors' suggestion would beg the question.

It may seem that the dogma the authors are defending is that of *Homo economicus* as self-interested. But they contradict this possibility when they turn to the failure of bank executives to sell their banks' stock once the crisis began to unfold in early 2007. To the authors, this failure demonstrates that the bank executives were *not* greedy, and in fact that they did not even care about protecting themselves against stupefying financial loss. By 2007, according to the authors, bank executives had made so much money that "the eventual collapse of their firms just didn't matter much."[56] Thus, the fact that the executives "suffered great personal financial losses" in the crisis "is moot" because these losses were offset by the gains made through their stock sales in previous years, which had apparently satiated these financial professionals' interest in money.[57]

The most striking aspect of this argument is not that it attributes, to the very same people whom the authors accuse of seeking financial gain without regard to the risks incurred (prior to 2007), a subsequent indifference to financial losses of astonishing magnitude; nor that it implicitly locates this dramatic change in bankers' preferences at just the right moment to explain away their failure to sell their stock; nor even that it jettisons the assumption of self-interestedness, which is usually seen as a linchpin of economic theory. It is, rather, the epistemological nature of the doctrine sustained by these intellectual gymnastics: namely that, notwithstanding all appearances to the contrary, the bankers *knew* that their banks were taking excessive risks. The dogma being defended is not *Homo economicus* as selfish, but *Homo economicus* as effectively omniscient. When selfishness and omniscience collide, these economist-epistocrats choose the less-plausible assumption (omniscience) over the more-plausible one (selfishness among American bankers).

If we were to treat the posited systemic "pressure" for behavioral prediction literal-mindedly, we might think that the economists' behavior manifested a desire to remain epistocrats in good standing. But if we treat the pressure as a metaphor for the causal force of ideas, the story is more complicated. I speculate that the assumption that "incentives matter" has, in the authors' minds, not only enabled them to make behavioral predictions over the courses of their careers, but to do so with great confidence, because it has seemed to be so frequently affirmed long after it was inculcated (presumably) in their academic training—biasing them, thereafter, against the plausibility of interpretations

---

[56] Ibid., 69.
[57] Ibid., 74.

of evidence that contradict it. If so, then dogmatism—in the inadvertent, spiral-of-conviction sense—has triumphed over a judicious weighing of the evidence. Thus, the metaphorical pressure at work is a pressure for dogmatism more than a pressure to predict. But in this case, the dogma happens to be the ability to predict agents' behavior without acknowledging the possibility of agents' ignorance—a dogma the content of which is, figuratively, a response to the separate pressure to predict.

5.3.5. History Without Agents

Guardians of Finance is noteworthy not only because of the authors' far-fetched rebuttal to the radical-ignorance hypothesis, but because of their ahistorical approach to history. They are attempting to explain the well-documented actions of specific bankers in a particular time and place, yet they do not name a single bank executive who suddenly decided in 2007 that holding onto his or her wealth didn't matter. Accordingly, they provide no evidence of such a decision. Instead, their putatively historical argument is deductive and circular. Rather than showing, as advertised, that "experienced professionals" knew what they were doing, it tells a story about a convenient reversal in preferences that could explain the professionals' failure to sell their bank stock only *given* their ex ante knowledge that their banks were taking excessive risks. (They knew they might well be on the verge of losing their fortunes, but they suddenly didn't care.) But whether they had this ex ante knowledge is exactly what is in question.

By dealing with "experienced professionals" in the abstract, the authors obscure this circularity. The general triumphs over the particular, homogeneity over heterogeneity, and epistemological dogma over interpretive charity, because proper names are avoided, such that no investigation of what actual bankers were actually thinking need be undertaken. Such investigation has been done by others, though, and it turns out that Lehman Brothers' Fuld was proud of his resurrection of the investment bank after its ill-fated merger with Shearson, another brokerage firm, had been unwound in 1994. Fuld saw Lehman's success after the Shearson debacle as a "personal validation," according to former Federal Reserve chair Ben Bernanke.[58] This information was not publicly available until after *Guardians of Finance* was published, but that is not the case with similar information about Bear Stearns's Cayne, who was discussed at length in *House of Cards* (2009), a book on Bear's collapse by financial reporter William D. Cohan. In the years preceding the crisis, Cayne was obsessed with building a new headquarters skyscraper for Bear that would testify to the permanence of its leap in stature under his stewardship. Having once been a "Jewish" investment bank that had been disrespected by the WASP banking establishment, Bear had, under Cayne, risen into the upper echelon of investment banking, and he was determined to memorialize this achievement.[59] It is implausible to think that

---

[58] Bernanke 2015, 249.
[59] Cohan 2009.

he or Fuld would have knowingly allowed their banks to take potentially fatal risks that could lead to the destruction of what they viewed as their life's work.[60]

5.3.6. The Economist as Folk Psychologist

Similar weaknesses are evident in Stiglitz's postcrisis writings. Stiglitz is the most prominent living economist of information, a recipient not just of the Nobel Prize but the John Bates Clark Medal and more than 40 honorary degrees. He is, as well, the consummate epistocrat, having served as head of the President's Council of Economic Advisers, chief economist of the World Bank, chair of the international Commission on the Measurement of Economic Performance and Social Progress, cochair of the High Level Expert Group on the Measurement of Economic Performance and Social Progress, and chairman of the UN Commission on Reforms of the International Monetary and Financial System.

In both a 2009 journal article and a 2010 book, Stiglitz made much of the fact that the rating agencies conferred triple-A ratings on the "toxic" RMBS.[61] Thus, he was aware of the ratings of these tranches, and (being an economist) he must have been aware that this means that bankers passed up higher rates of return by failing to invest in low-rated tranches. But in neither the article nor the book did he wonder why the avaricious, risk-seeking behavior on which he blames the crisis would have produced investments in low-yield AAA tranches rather than higher-yield BB, BBB, A, or AA tranches. Turning from evidence to theory, the journal article maintains that "the banks adopted incentive structures that were designed to induce short-sighted and excessively risky behavior,"[62] and that the objective incentive created by these structures explained bankers' shortsighted and risky behavior. But the article also acknowledges that "the bankers seemingly didn't understand the risks that were being created by securitization."[63] If the second statement is true, then the incentives cited in the first statement are irrelevant. If the bankers did not understand that they were taking excessive risks, their objective incentives to take these risks could not possibly have affected their behavior.

Stiglitz's book on the crisis, *Freefall*, fails to escape the same contradiction. On page 12, Stiglitz suggests "a simple explanation [for the crisis]: flawed incentives." On page 13 he articulates the executive-compensation version of this explanation: "With its pay dependent not on long-term returns but on stock-market prices, management naturally does what it can to drive up stock market prices." Note the present, theoretical tense when speaking of past actions by specific bank executives, who are never named. Page 15 gives a theoretical account of "agency problems and externalities" at the beginning of

---

[60] This paragraph is based upon Friedman and Kraus 2011, 160.
[61] Stiglitz 2009, 331–332; Stiglitz 2010, 92–94.
[62] Stiglitz 2009, 331.
[63] Ibid.

a paragraph that concludes by enunciating the TBTF variant of the flawed-incentives theory: "Knowing that they were too big to fail provided incentives for excessive risk-taking." Again, Stiglitz names no names and provides no evidence for any bankers' "knowledge" that their institutions were TBTF. Nor does it occur to him that bankers might not have wanted to risk legal jeopardy, public obloquy, and their billions of dollars in bank stock by gambling on the chance that their banks would be bailed out (Lehman Brothers, of course, was not; Bear Stearns was, but only nominally, as we saw).

On page 154, however, Stiglitz recognizes that the bankers' failure to sell their stock in 2007 or the first half of 2008 poses a problem for both variants of the skewed-incentives theory. His initial response is similar to the one later proposed by Barth, Caprio, and Levine. Even though some bankers "may have been foolish enough to keep much of their wealth in bank shares," he writes, "many are now wealthy, in some cases very wealthy."[64] The fact that bankers are wealthy may reflect the fact that their institutions took excessive risks, but it is irrelevant to whether they *knew* that they were taking excessive risks. The question raised by Stiglitz himself is why, if they knew about those risks, they held onto their bank stock rather than selling it, passing up the chance to preserve much of the wealth they had accumulated.

Yet in calling them "foolish" for failing to sell, Stiglitz may again have been admitting (as in his article), however backhandedly, that the bankers did not know what he claims they did know. Elsewhere in the book, he similarly gropes for a muddy middle ground: "They didn't *want to know*."[65] Folk psychologizing of this sort again begs the question. The question is whether bankers knew about excessive mortgage risks, as the orthodoxy holds—not whether they "wanted" to know about them. Just as wanting to be informed, in a general sense, does not make it possible to know that of which one is radically ignorant, not wanting to be informed does not abolish one's knowledge, or what one thinks of as one's knowledge. Regardless of whether bankers wanted to know that they were taking excessive risks, their behavior suggests that they did not know that they were taking them.

By treating the various possibilities (ignorance, knowledge, and wishful thinking) as if they were equivalent, Stiglitz renders his claim that the bankers "knew" impervious to falsification. As such, the claim invites ad hoc auxiliary hypotheses to explain away the bankers' apparently ignorant behavior, no matter how bizarre or self-contradictory the hypotheses might seem to someone not wedded to the dogma of effective omniscience. Stiglitz, like Barth and his colleagues, is treating the bankers' knowledge as an unquestionable assumption, rather than as a possibility to be investigated with an open mind. That is what the doctrinaire do: they treat as self-evidently true what is called into question by alternative interpretations of evidence.

---

[64] Ibid., 331–332.
[65] Stiglitz 2010, 14.

In the hands of an epistocrat, dogmas displace the uncertainty that would erase the ability to predict and, thus, to prescribe. According to the spiral-of-conviction model, dogma is both a product of learning and a smotherer of doubt. In both respects, it facilitates epistocratic confidence. Thus, we should expect that even epistocrats who are not in the grip of the incentives-matter dogma will tend to be in the grip of some other dogma—whether disciplinary, methodological, or ideological—that provides them with the confidence required by epistocratic debate.

We may therefore be entitled to conclude that when epistocrats discover (or seize upon) a homogenizing force, such as incentives, that might tame behavioral unpredictability, this discovery is not likely to reflect an accurate understanding of the true balance of homogenizing and heterogenizing forces. Instead, it is likely to reiterate an inadvertently biased understanding of the world that seems, to the epistocrats, to have been amply confirmed by the facts, time and again. Confronted with disastrous behavior by bankers, economists misconstrued it as resulting from a homogenizing omniscience that their training and experience may have led them to expect but that, in reality, does not exist. Thus, they failed to investigate whatever real (ideational) factors might have led different bankers to make similar mistakes—a failure that is bound to lead to injudicious policy prescriptions, such as attempts to change bankers' incentives rather than attempts to guard against their fallibility.

5.4. FOUR PATHOLOGIES OF EPISTOCRACY

In this chapter and the last one, I have suggested that two metaphorical pressures are likely to call forth pathological responses in any real-world epistocracy: a pressure to make behavioral predictions and a pressure for confidence in those predictions.

Candidate epistocrats may (figuratively) respond to the first pressure in at least two ways: by self-selecting either for naive realism or for positivism, both of which will tend to downplay, elide, or ignore the causal role of fallible ideas, and thus of heterogeneous interpretations, in the determination of human behavior. In epistemologically individualistic terms, this is to say that, truistically, social scientists whose beliefs or assumptions happen to be naively realistic or positivistic will tend to think themselves capable of making behavioral predictions, thereby selecting themselves into the pool of candidate epistocrats, while those who do not hold such ideas (or similar ones) will tend to select themselves out, perhaps becoming intellectual historians, critics of epistocracy, or other harmless scholars. However, inasmuch as epistemically pathological responses to the first pressure are contingent upon social scientists' ideas, they could be stilled, at some future date, by an ideational shift against naive realism, social-scientific positivism, and similar intellectual orientations.

There are also at least two pathological responses to the second pressure, both of which would seem to be more robust against ideational change than the two responses to the pressure to predict. First, if the spiral model is roughly accurate, then epistocrats will (in effect) self-select for dogmatism, because a spiral of conviction should ensue from learning a great deal of information about public policy. In epistemologically individualistic terms, the process of learning will reduce awareness of the provisional, interpretive, and possibly incorrect nature of what is learned, and thus the need to be sensitive to incongruous, ambiguous, or ambivalent evidence. Second, political decision-makers, in attempting to identify which epistocrats can be trusted, can be expected to select those who are more dogmatic than most, even from among a group that is dogmatic on the whole—because those who are less dogmatic than most will tend to be less persuasive in advocating their points of view, even as those who are the least dogmatic of all, and thus the most likely to be judicious, will not even participate in the competition.

However: there is injudiciousness and injudiciousness. If epistocrats respond (as it were) to the "pressure" to predict by ignoring the causal role of ideas entirely, then even if they are open minded, their policy making will necessarily be injudicious (according to my definition of injudiciousness). But if an ideational shift sensitized epistocrats to ideational heterogeneity, even as their dogmatic tendencies went unabated, the resulting policy making would surely be less judicious than might be ideal, but it is at least conceivable that it would be judicious enough to do more good than harm.

Thus, if economists had been dogmatic, not about the effective omniscience of bankers, but about the opposite hypothesis—that bankers were ignorant of the fact that the housing boom was actually a housing bubble—their policy recommendations, whatever they might have been, could at least have had a chance of being on target. Dogmatism in defense of such recommendations might therefore have had the effect of enacting on-balance beneficial policies. For a technocracy, open-mindedness is not an end in itself. Ignoring ambiguity or ambivalence is a good thing, from a technocratic perspective, if the result is public policy that does more good than harm. But if dogmatism is coupled with an anti-ideational belief system, such as naive realism or positivism, the results would seem almost predestined to be unfortunate. The behavioral effects of heterogeneous and thus fallible ideas cannot be taken into account if one does not acknowledge that ideas have any behavioral effect at all. If one then encounters a case in which fallibility is apparent but one resists this appearance dogmatically, technocratic lessons will not be learned. The case of the financial crisis suggests that the results may be catastrophic.

This leaves us essentially where we were at the end of the last chapter: looking for an alternative to epistemically pathological variants of epistocracy, pending a cultural shift that shows no signs of arriving. However, the analysis in this chapter suggests that there may be such an alternative: democratic technocracy. For according to the spiral-of-conviction theory, ordinary citizen-technocrats should be the least dogmatic technocrats there are.

Lack of information may be a bar to the holding of an opinion in the minds of the theorists but it does not seem to be among the electorate (where, of course, it is not experienced as lack of information at all).

—BERNARD BERELSON, "Democratic Theory and Public Opinion"

The ignorance of relevant truths is often accompanied by ignorance of that ignorance.
—W. V. O. QUINE AND J. S. ULLIAN, *The Web of Belief*

6

Public Ignorance and Democratic Technocracy

BEING RELATIVELY UNINFORMED, citizen-technocrats should, according to the spiral-of-conviction model, be relatively open-minded. The question, then, is whether they can overcome their relative ignorance in a way that enables them to make judicious predictions about the effects of technocratic policies—without, in the process, becoming dogmatic.

I will answer the question indirectly, first asking whether we can make sense of the well-documented political ignorance of the mass public by thinking of its members as citizen-technocrats. From this vantage point, we will get a fairly comprehensive picture of how relatively uninformed citizens, bereft of the guidance that a dogmatically held ideology might otherwise provide, might manage to participate in politics in the real world of democratic technocracy. This will, in turn, help us think about whether the public's ignorance is likely to create pathologies that outweigh the theoretical advantage of democratic technocracy over epistocracy: the relative open-mindedness of the citizen-technocrat, in comparison to the epistocrat.

In Section 6.1, I will contend that mainstream research on public ignorance provides an initial basis for skepticism about the epistemic capacities of citizen-technocrats, but that this research makes use of an untenable understanding of the importance of political "knowledge," according to which more of this homogeneous stuff necessarily tends to be better than less. Section 6.2 will examine the revisionist literature on "heuristics" (a term that, in political science, has a positive connotation, diametrically opposed to behavioral

Power Without Knowledge. Jeffrey Friedman, Oxford University Press (2019). © Oxford University Press.
DOI: 10.1093/oso/9780190877170.001.0001

economists' use of it).[1] Unlike mainstream opinion researchers, the revisionists recognize that knowledge is of variable importance, such that a single good heuristic is better than a mountain of irrelevant or misleading information. But they have not established that good heuristics are what the public tends to use. Section 6.3 targets the rational-choice explanation of public ignorance, to which the revisionist scholars appeal in explaining the public's use of heuristics. I will argue that radical-ignorance theory provides a better explanation of both public ignorance and the public's use of heuristics than does rational-ignorance theory. Section 6.4 examines evidence for the public's radical ignorance of societal complexity and, thus, of the very possibility of unintended policy consequences. Section 6.5 argues that two apparently widespread and epistemically pathological heuristics dovetail with radical ignorance of societal complexity. These two heuristics can be used by citizens with very little political information to generate opinions about almost any technocratic policy or political actor. In Section 6.6, I examine whether the use of these pathological heuristics is likely to block the public from engaging in the judicious policymaking that, as we have seen, may also elude epistocrats.

6.1. PUBLIC IGNORANCE AND THE A FORTIORI ARGUMENT FOR EPISTOCRACY

> The political ignorance of the American voter is one of the best-documented features of contemporary politics.
> —LARRY M. BARTELS, "Uninformed Votes"

> The widespread ignorance of the general public about all but the most highly salient political events and actors is one of the best-documented facts in all of the social sciences.
> —RICHARD R. LAU AND DAVID P. REDLAWSK, "Advantages and Disadvantages of Cognitive Heuristics in Political Decision Making"

> Let us be honest. The average voter is called on to make decisions on questions about which he knows nothing. In other words, he is incompetent.
> —GIOVANNI SARTORI, Democratic Theory

In 1964, at the height of the Cold War, only 38 percent of the American public knew that Russia was not a member of NATO.[2] In 1979, only 24 percent knew the gist of the First Amendment.[3] In 1989, only 57 percent knew what a recession is.[4] In 2002, 35 percent said that "From each according to his ability, to each according to his needs" is part of the US

---

[1] Kuklinski and Quirk 2001, 295.
[2] Page and Shapiro 1992, 10.
[3] Ibid.
[4] Ibid.

Constitution, and another 34 percent were unsure.[5] In the light of such findings, it is not surprising that the public's political ignorance has been a central theme in public-opinion research since the 1940s.

The resulting literature suggests the presence of a behavioral regularity that can be expressed as follows: most members of the American mass public, at least, have, since the 1940s, paid scant attention to public affairs, and this is reflected in their very poor command of public-affairs information.[6] The implications for empirical political episte-mology are profound and wide ranging. For example, journalists, pundits, and scholars are probably wrong to think of "national conversations" as dialogues or even monologues with the public, for most members of the public are (usually) too inattentive to be able to know about, let alone follow, what is said in such conversations. And if, as this literature has repeatedly demonstrated, significant majorities do not know what major legislation has been recently enacted,[7] or which candidate favors which policies,[8] or the meaning of common terms for political ideologies (such as "liberalism" and "conservatism"),[9] then we are probably ill advised to speak about electoral mandates as anything but myths.

However, for normative theorists of technocracy, the most important implication of the literature is that the public may make what John Zaller, a pre-eminent contributor to this literature, calls "technically stupid" political decisions.[10] Fear of such decisions was a red thread in research on public ignorance in the twentieth century, and interest in the topic has only grown in the twenty-first.[11]

The research began with the Columbia school of sociologists in the 1940s and 1950s, led by Bernard Berelson and Paul Lazarsfeld, and continued with the Michigan school of political scientists in the 1960s, who set the main direction of research on public opinion ever since.[12] Philip E. Converse, whose work was discussed in the last chapter, was, along with Angus Campbell, Warren E. Miller, and Donald E. Stokes, one of the University of Michigan scholars who coauthored the school's seminal text, *The American Voter* (1960). This book remains the foundational document in the literature, and I will have much to say about it in Sections 6.3 and 6.5. Michigan-school research reached its apogee with Zaller's *Nature and Origins of Mass Opinion* (1992), which he ended with a parable about "Purple Land," an idealization of the status quo that offered a quasi-Platonic solution to the problem of public ignorance. In Purple Land, the electorate's ignorance is short-circuited by politicians who manipulate public opinion but who are,

---

[5] Somin 2013, 19.

[6] See, e.g., Delli Carpini and Keeter 1996, appendix 3; Page and Shapiro 1992, 10–11; and Somin 2013, ch. 1. For evidence that the phenomenon extends beyond the United States, see Lewis-Beck 1988.

[7] Somin 2013, 1–2.

[8] Ibid., Table 1.2.

[9] Converse 1964.

[10] Ibid., 331.

[11] See, for example, Achen and Bartels 2016 and the symposium on it in *Critical Review* 30(1–2) (2018).

[12] See Friedman 2013b for an overview of the literature.

in turn, manipulated by wise epistocrats. In this way, Zaller supposed, public opinion might be steered away from making technically stupid decisions (and morally dubious ones, too).[13] He has since withdrawn the idea as utopian,[14] but the very fact that he contemplated it, in a last-ditch attempt to save what he thought of as democratic legitimacy from the problem of public ignorance, suggests how serious public-opinion researchers tend to think this problem is.

6.1.1. *The A Fortiori Argument from Public Ignorance*

It also suggests that these scholars recognize the technocratic dimension of modern democracy (even though they consistently confuse the legitimacy of democratic technocracy with the legitimacy of democracy simpliciter). Zaller's reference to technically stupid decisions recalls the distinction among opinion researchers, mentioned in the introduction, between "easy" political issues—which are either purely symbolic or else deal with choices among ends—and "hard" ones, which deal with means and are difficult precisely because they are "technical."[15] In making this distinction, the researchers have observed that a great many political issues in modern "democracies" are of the hard variety, the resolution of which requires technical knowledge that they seem to think is difficult to obtain and understand. Their research provides ample grounds for pessimism about whether citizens are, at present, apt to acquire this knowledge, although this would not suggest the illegitimacy of democracy, as opposed to the illegitimacy of democratic technocracy.

Critics of this research have contended that it merely shows that ordinary citizens tend to be ignorant of civics trivia, such as constitutional provisions and the names of public figures—not truly important information.[16] The critics certainly have a point, as the public-ignorance findings typically concern respondents' failure to possess substantively insignificant "neutral, factual public-affairs knowledge,"[17] as Zaller puts it. However, by testing for such neutral knowledge, survey researchers prescind from their own views about the specific things the public must know if it is to make good policy choices. Were the researchers to test for knowledge that they think is important for making such choices, they could be accused of bias in concluding that the public is ignorant, as this conclusion would be equivalent to saying that the public does not know the things that the researchers, as tacit proponents of a particular policy choice, think it should know. In other words, the researchers could be accused of letting their first-order opinions color

---

[13] Zaller 1992, epilogue.

[14] Zaller 2012.

[15] Carmines and Stimson 1980, 80.

[16] E.g., Page and Shapiro 1992, 12; Lupia and McCubbins 2000, 77; Lupia 2006; Landemore 2013, 200; Landemore 2014, 23.

[17] Zaller 1992, 43.

their second-order conclusions, thereby failing to transcend the question-begging role of technocrat-epistemologist.

Because of its punctiliousness in avoiding this accusation, Michigan-school research can be said to establish the basis for an a fortiori second-order argument against public participation in technocratic policy decisions: namely, that if voters do not pay enough attention to politics and government to pick up neutral, factual public-affairs knowledge—however trivial it might be—it is all the more unlikely that they will pick up the four types of technocratic knowledge (assuming that this knowledge exists).[18] While it is true that the neutral, factual public-affairs knowledge tested by survey researchers is often unimportant in its own right, it is also true that if citizens lack this knowledge, it is probably because they are so inattentive to politics, government, and current events that they will lack technocratically necessary knowledge, too.

The a fortiori argument, however, is tenuous for several reasons, one of which is that there is no reason to think that most or all citizens could not be much better informed than they have recently been. Findings of political ignorance may have pointed to a behavioral regularity in mass publics of the twentieth century, but this regularity would seem to be contingent on low levels of attention to politics; at any time, large numbers of people might begin to find politics interesting, ending the regularity. On the other hand, even if this occurred, the newly attentive members of the public might not make judicious use of the technocratic knowledge, or putative technocratic knowledge, that they would then (hypothetically) acquire. (Indeed, as I will suggest later on, they might not think that such knowledge is important to acquire.) After all, we now have reason to believe that epistocrats in our day, who are, by definition, highly informed relative to ordinary citizen-technocrats, tend to be confused about what constitutes true knowledge of human behavior and that they tend to use what knowledge they do acquire injudiciously. If members of the mass public became more technocratically informed, moving into the epistocratic class, they might merely end up re-enacting the pathological behaviors identified in the last two chapters, especially dogmatism. Thus, there is no justification for treating the public-ignorance findings as premises that lead to epistocratic conclusions, as at least one writer has recently done, even when these premises are inserted into an a fortiori argument.[19] The fact that ordinary citizens pay little attention to public affairs does not imply that those who pay more attention, and are therefore *relatively* well informed, will know what they need to know if they are to make sound political decisions, nor that they will use their technocratic knowledge wisely, to the extent that they have it.

---

[18] To be sure, even the most skeptical researchers have tended to bend over backward to "deny" or "extenuate" public ignorance, as Robert Luskin (2002) memorably put it. But this is because they themselves have a simplistic view of the types and "amounts" of knowledge that citizen-technocrats need.

[19] See Brennan 2016, which suggests making high scores on tests of political trivia a qualification for voting. For a critique, see Gunn 2019.

6.1.2. The Additive View of Knowledge Redux

Arguments for epistocracy premised on the empirical literature appear to be unthinking products of the additive view of knowledge implicitly adopted in that literature. In the additive view, as we saw in Chapter 2, what matters in making political decisions, including technocratic decisions, is the quantity of knowledge possessed by the decision-maker, such that more knowledge necessarily tends to produce better decisions. Zaller, for example, infers the mass public's propensity to make technical mistakes from its dearth of neutral, factual public-affairs knowledge. Once we amend his inference so that the dearth of such knowledge implies, a fortiori, a paucity of technocratically necessary knowledge, a further implication is that if ordinary citizens had more of this type of knowledge, they would make fewer technical mistakes. The logical conclusion seems to be that those who have the most knowledge of this sort—epistocrats—should rule. Thus, Zaller put epistocrats in charge of Purple Land.

Many of his colleagues, however, have been hindered from seeing the epistocratic implications of the additive view of knowledge, for they combine this view with the assumption that it does not take all that much knowledge to make reliably accurate technocratic decisions. More knowledge is better than less, then, but the public does not need that much more than it already has, and the extra amount that it needs is readily obtained—say, by reading a good newspaper. This view of political knowledge suggests the scholars' ideational determination by precepts of democratic technocracy such as those that were common in the Progressive Era, according to which citizens who keep up with the news are capable of making wise policy decisions. Thus, the mainstream literature, despite regular obeisances to Lippmann, has failed to absorb his most elementary teaching: that even full-time students of politics and government, such as Lippmann himself, could not possibly attain the requisite knowledge, no matter how many good newspapers they read.

The reason for the mainstream disconnect with Lippmann is that the additive view of knowledge, which he rejected, takes no account of whether a given quantity of knowledge contributes to an adequate interpretation of the reality one is attempting to understand. Information that is accurate and therefore "factual," strictly speaking, can be useless if it fails to point toward an approximately accurate interpretation of the relevant realities, and worse than useless if it misleadingly points toward an inaccurate interpretation. Information can be accurate but misleading if it is correct in itself but contributes to a skewed picture of the totality. Contrary to the additive view, then, more knowledge is not necessarily better than less, and there may in fact be no scalar relationship between knowledge and truth.

Heterogeneity in the importance of knowledge is different from heterogeneity of ideas across individuals. My point here is not, as in Chapters 3–4, that each individual is likely to have an idiosyncratic web of beliefs that will render her behavior somewhat unpredictable because it diverges from the webs of others, including those trying to predict her behavior. Instead, I am suggesting that the knowledge that might inform a given agent will vary *in value* according to whether it helps the agent reach an accurate interpretation of the issue at hand. This suggestion offers another reason for thinking that a democratic technocracy might be internally legitimate, at least in comparison to an epistocracy, as the probative value of a small amount of knowledge may outweigh that of a great heap of it. Therefore, we should not assume that those who are more knowledgeable than their peers are likely to make better technocratic decisions.

Consider a disagreement about a Type 4 technocratic issue, such as what the effect of raising the minimum wage is likely to be, among highly informed participants in policy debate—for example, those who possess doctorates or even Nobel Prizes in seemingly relevant fields, such as economics, and are therefore superlatively well informed, according to the additive view. Assuming for the sake of exposition that there are just two sides in the debate, and that the epistocrats are evenly split on the merits of the policy; and assuming that one side in the debate is more correct than the other; then citizen-technocrats who use meager scraps of information, or even the flip of a coin, to reach the same conclusions as the 50 percent of the epistocrats who are right are, therefore, more entitled (by technocratic standards) to decision-making power than the 50 percent of the epistocrats who, despite their possession of far greater quantities of information than these citizen-technocrats possess, are defending a mistaken position. More knowledge, in short, may be *worse* than less. By the same token, *all* of the epistocrats could be misled into endorsing a mistaken interpretation by an unrepresentative sample of knowledge, or by graduate training in a faulty interpretive paradigm; while poorly informed citizen-technocrats—even *negatively* informed citizen-technocrats (those whose only information is incorrect)—may nevertheless end up endorsing a policy that has greater benefits or fewer costs than the one endorsed by the epistocrats. One can, after all, reach a good conclusion for a bad reason.

In Chapter 2, I contended that, insofar as modern social problems are epistemically complex, democratic technocracy faces a logical slide toward epistocracy—if we assume, as Lippmann did in 1922, and as Dewey did in 1927, that social science can enable policy scientists to produce reliably accurate predictions of human behavior. In that case, however, epistocracy would be desirable on technocratic grounds by virtue of the accuracy of the epistocrats' reliably accurate interpretations of human behavior, not by virtue of their sheer accumulation of large quantities of knowledge about it. The additive view of knowledge, by contrast, implies epistocracy as the regulative principle of democratic technocracy *regardless* of the adequacy of epistocrats' interpretations, merely because epistocrats know "more" than citizen-technocrats. This implication exposes the logical deficiency of the additive view—and it raises the question of whether a citizen-technocracy could be as efficacious in solving problems as an epistocracy, or more so.

6.2. THE UNFULFILLED PROMISE OF HEURISTICS RESEARCH

The focus on voters' lack of textbook information ... is a red herring. It focuses on what voters don't know instead of on what they do know.

—SAMUEL L. POPKIN, *The Reasoning Voter*

As early as 1988, dissenters from the Michigan mainstream began to defend citizens' use of "low-information rationality"[20] and "heuristics," or knowledge proxies, as substitutes for the neutral, factual public-affairs knowledge the public seemed to lack.[21] These revisionist scholars recognized that less knowledge can, in principle, be as good as more of it. This enabled them to gesture toward a more realistic view of public opinion than was possible by merely measuring the public's "knowledge deficits."

However, the revisionists' main goal was to advance a normative claim that was unjustified by their empirical findings: the claim that citizens are likely to arrive at heuristics that are *adequate* substitutes for large quantities of relevant political information.[22] While the revisionist scholars were right to point out that a good heuristic may be as valuable as a great deal of relevant knowledge, they failed to recognize that, by the same token, a bad heuristic can be worse than no knowledge at all. Thus, they wrongly supposed that by showing that ordinary citizens do in fact use heuristics, they could prove that ordinary citizens are as qualified to make political decisions as those with "more" knowledge.

The heuristics literature's combination of gesturally rich empiricism and underargued normative optimism was exemplified in Samuel L. Popkin's pioneering revisionist work, *The Reasoning Voter* (1991). Popkin recognized the importance of "the interpretations offered by elite opinion leaders on television," as well as the fact that the media will necessarily be selective in the information they report; and he distinguished between the ideational experiences that citizens have in "daily life" (such as noticing that gasoline prices are going up) and their interpretations of these experiences as politically relevant—interpretations that require ideas about the representativeness of these conditions in society at large. Such ideas, he suggested, are relayed to citizens by the media.[23] Had Popkin succeeded in fixing political scientists' attention on the interpretive role of the media, he would have done a tremendous service to the field, rectifying what Larry Bartels once called "one of the most notable embarrassments of modern social science": the paucity of media-content and media-effects research.[24]

---

[20] Popkin 1991, 7 and *passim*; Sniderman et al. 1991.

[21] See Graber 1988, Stimson 1990, Popkin 1991, Lupia 1994, Lupia and McCubbins 1998, Erikson et al. 2002.

[22] Lupia 2006.

[23] Popkin 1991, 25–28.

[24] Bartels 1993, 267. Since then, a great deal of laboratory experimentation has demonstrated the persuasive capacities of the news media (see Chong and Druckman 2011 for a brief survey). However, this literature underplays media effects, as the three main categories of experimentally demonstrated effects—agenda setting, priming, and framing—each presuppose fixed voter predispositions, uninfluenced by the media. Agenda setting makes one issue rather than others appear to be important at a given moment; priming emphasizes one issue rather

However, the importance of the media in shaping public opinion suggests, as Lippmann emphasized, that citizens might well be misguided in their political judgments—depending on whether the interpretations, and the selections of information, that are mediated to citizens by journalists are misleading. This suggestion directly cuts against Popkin's normative project: rescuing the public from the charge of incompetence. Thus, he asserted that heuristics such as gasoline prices are *sufficient* substitutes for the knowledge of objective social realities that most citizens seem (a fortiori) to lack. The weakness of this position is exemplified by his infamous discussion of the tamale heuristic: during the 1976 campaign, Mexican American voters, by his account, turned against President Ford for failing to shuck a tamale before trying to eat it. Where Lippmann would have worried that the tamale heuristic reflected a stereotype with little or no probative value, Popkin extolled it on the grounds that "a president who understands and is familiar with an ethnic group is more likely to help ease that group's way into the American mainstream."[25] At best, this is true only if it would be self-evident to such a president how to do so.

By assuming that heuristics are sufficient substitutes for adequate knowledge, revisionist political scientists replaced the dark outlook of earlier public-opinion research with a sunny optimism that normative theorists, too, have found appealing. In 2006, for example, Habermas, having been worried by the "rather sobering portrait of the average citizen as a largely uninformed and disinterested [*sic*] person" that had been painted in the pages of *Critical Review* (drawing on Michigan-school research), announced that "this picture has been changed by recent studies on the cognitive role of heuristics and information shortcuts in the development and consolidation of political orientations." These studies, Habermas contended, suggest "that in the long term, readers, listeners, and viewers can definitely form reasonable attitudes toward public affairs."[26] Habermas's contention was unjustified. To be sure, the revisionist scholars *claimed* that the heuristics used by citizens are reasonable, in the sense of being reasonably accurate and sufficient

---

than another in the retrospective evaluation of a politician's performance; and framing emphasizes one or another dimension of an issue. All three types of media effect alter "the weight component of an attitude through changes in [the] availability, accessibility and/or applicability" of media consumers' preexisting beliefs about the issues in question (ibid., 310). None of the three addresses the possibility that these beliefs themselves are shaped by the media (including non-news media, such as cinema and formal education). Thus, they may considerably understate the impact of the media. Zaller 1992 makes a promising start in rectifying this problem, but by the end of the book the author's agenda changes, perhaps for methodological reasons, and the issue of the mediated origins of voters' predispositions, with which he opens the book, is never joined (see Friedman 2012a). Political scientists' reluctance to study media effects outside the laboratory contradicts their recognition that "well informed" citizens have different policy opinions than do those who are less well informed (e.g., Althaus 2003); the information that seems to change the opinions of the relatively well informed, after all, has to come from somewhere. For evidence of media effects, see Page, Shapiro, and Dempsey 1987, Preiss et al. 2007, and Bryant and Oliver 2008.

[25] Popkin 1991, 3.

[26] Habermas 2006, 420, citing Somin 1998, Friedman 2003, and Weinshall 2003.

substitutes for "perfect information," but their research did not support this claim. To establish the reasonableness and sufficiency of heuristics, it is not enough to show, as the revisionists did, that citizens use heuristics; one must appeal to second-order considerations that would suggest that the specific heuristics used by citizens tend to be epistemically adequate. This, the revisionists failed to do.

That is not surprising, as the revisionists found their theoretical inspiration in economics, where it is simply assumed, as we have seen, that agents respond optimally to objective incentives. Popkin's book was directly influenced by rational-choice theory, as was the later, even more influential work of Arthur Lupia and Matthew D. McCubbins. Building on what they called "the premise that 'incentives matter,'" they depicted citizens' use of heuristics as a functional response to the "incentive to learn."[27]

Lupia and McCubbins repudiated the additive view even more forcefully than Popkin had. "You can know a long list of facts and fail to put them together in a way that allows you to make accurate predictions," they noted, such that "you can have information but not knowledge." They wisely advised, then, that "information is valuable only if it prevents costly mistakes." But they immediately added, with no justification but the premise that incentives matter, that citizens *agree* with this wisdom: "*This is why* people reject so many opportunities to acquire political information."[28] By implication, people not only know that acquiring too much information would be a waste of time and effort—which is itself, as we will see, a claim that is never demonstrated—but they know how much information, and which information, is enough to serve as a sufficient substitute for more. According to Lupia and McCubbins, citizens' search for the smallest possible quantity of probative knowledge turns up heuristics that allow them to avoid costly mistakes, because citizens "have an incentive to attend to stimuli that promise high returns."[29] Apparently, then, the incentive to know which stimuli are probative somehow creates knowledge of which stimuli are, in fact, probative, just as, for neoclassical economists, the incentive to know if mortgage-backed securities were excessively risky magically put this knowledge into bankers' heads. As in a Stiglerian information search, heuristics users know when they have found just what they need, the nugget of heuristic information that obviates further knowledge, and they know where to look for it. How they could know this without also knowing the very information the heuristic allows them to avoid knowing is as much a mystery in the heuristics literature as in the economics of information.

Lupia's most famous finding concerned several 1988 ballot propositions regarding auto-insurance regulation in California. He discovered that a sample of Los Angeles voters who knew only the insurance industry's position on the propositions—without knowing what the propositions required—tended to vote the same way as did a sample

---

[27] Lupia and McCubbins 1998, 43, 23.
[28] Ibid., 24–25, 25, 28, my emphasis.
[29] Ibid., 30.

who knew some of the actual provisions of the propositions.[30] Thus, for example, voters who used the insurance industry's opposition to Proposition 100 as a reason to vote *for* it mimicked the behavior (in effect) of those who knew some of the proposition's provisions. As James Kuklinski and Paul Quirk note, however, the use of the insurance industry's position as a negative heuristic is adequate only if we assume that "those who knew the provisions relatively well were indeed adequately informed."[31] Lupia did not even attempt to demonstrate that the relatively well-informed voters, who knew about some of the provisions of Prop 100, were adequately informed about its *effects* when they, like their less knowledgeable counterparts, voted yes.

However, if we drop the normative agenda of the heuristics literature, and the rational-choice framework that facilitates it, we are left with findings of great potential significance. "Knowing that the insurance industry was against Proposition 100," according to Lupia, "increased by 48 percentage points the probability that a respondent who could provide no correct answers to proposition knowledge questions voted for Proposition 100."[32] A 48-point increase in favorability to one of the insurance propositions is telling, but if we do not assume that it bespeaks heuristics users' effective omniscience, what exactly does it tell us? This is a question I will try to answer in Section 6.5. In the meantime, we can agree with the revisionists that heuristics use is, *in principle*, a valid approach to decision-making, since more knowledge cannot be assumed to be better than less, while we acknowledge that any given quantity of knowledge, large or small, may be misleading, such that neither "more" knowledge nor "less" should be assumed, in principle, to be adequate. The adequacy of heuristic knowledge—or putative knowledge—will vary from case to case. The mere fact that citizen-technocrats use heuristics, then, is of no normative significance in itself.

Arguments for the other main types of heuristics use that have been identified by revisionist political scientists—the use of party labels as heuristics, and the retrospective evaluation of candidates or parties—are also strong empirically but normatively irrelevant.[33] Taking party labels first, the normative question is whether an ignorant citizen-technocrat is likely to know whether a party's general orientation and goals will lead to beneficial policy results. A voter who knew that, in regard to technocratic issues, would first have to possess all four types of technocratic knowledge regarding most of the technocratic issues likely to be confronted by a party's office holders. Thus, it begs the question to assume that merely because voters use party labels as heuristics, they have gotten hold of sufficient substitutes for the requisite knowledge.

A similar circularity besets the idea that retrospective voters need not worry about the details of proposed policies; instead, they can "simply sit back and see what works"—or

---

[30] Lupia 1994.
[31] Kuklinski and Quirk 2000, 158.
[32] Lupia 1994, 70.
[33] See, e.g., Fiorina 1981, Ferejohn 1986, Kiewiet and Rivers 2005, and, on party labels, Rahn 1993.

rather, what worked or failed to work under the current government.[34] If economic conditions are good, the retrospective economic voter uses this information as a heuristic for the incumbent's technocratic competence or that of the incumbent party, so she votes to re-elect. If the economy is doing poorly, she votes for the out-party. This procedure is supposed to relieve voters of the need to be knowledgeable about politics and policy, in the sense that "watching 'Meet the Press' and reading the *New York Times*"[35] makes one knowledgeable—since watching *Meet the Press* and reading the *New York Times* are activities that most voters, at least in our day and age, seem unwilling to undertake. In fact, however, epistemically *reliable* retrospective voting would require voters who are much "more" knowledgeable than the most careful reporter or pundit and, indeed, more knowledgeable than policy specialists—who often disagree with one other about the cause of a recent recession, the effects of a president's economic stimulus program, the feasibility of a challenger's proposals, and so on.

The retrospective voter would need, first of all, reliably accurate perceptions of whether things are going badly or well society-wide. Retrospective-voting theorists tend to assume that voters can use "changes in their own welfare" to gauge whether things are going well society-wide,[36] but as we saw in Chapter 1, this assumption does not hold water: one would have to back up one's knowledge of personal welfare with statistics, at the very least, if one were to draw legitimate sociotropic conclusions from it, but adequate statistical knowledge is one thing we would expect ignorant voters to lack, a fortiori. Moreover, voters who tried to get the statistical and other knowledge necessary for adequate retrospective voting would be at the mercy of messages conveyed by fallible, stereotype-driven mediators such as journalists, who have been known to misreport even such matters as whether the economy is in recession.[37] That is not all. Even if mediators (not just journalists but friends, relatives, internet trolls, and so forth) manage to relay an accurate retrospective assessment of recent conditions to citizen-technocrats, such information cannot, in itself, tell them whether the incumbent's policies made things better or worse than they otherwise would have been, or indeed whether the incumbent's policies had any effect at all. Finally, a vote against the incumbent based on past performance presupposes that in the future, under different circumstances than those that affected the past, the challenger would probably do better than the incumbent would have done; but this relies on the assumption that there is such a trait as "competence" in the management of a vast economy, such that if the incumbent lacks it, it would be worth gambling that the challenger may have it. It is as if those who have this putative trait are oracular beings who just *know* how to

---

[34] Fiorina 1981, 8.

[35] Ibid., 10.

[36] Ibid., 5.

[37] Hetherington 1996 argues that the media misreported this issue during the 1992 presidential campaign.

"steward" the economy—a notion suggesting a primitive form of naive third-person technocratic realism.

The normative failings of the heuristics program in political science, however, should not obscure three conceptual advances pioneered by the movement.

First, the revisionists underscored the variable importance of knowledge, which is embodied in the fact that a good heuristic is better than any amount of irrelevant or misleading information. Absent the normative agenda, this might have inspired reflection on the fact that a bad heuristic can be even worse than any given quantity of information, prompting scholars to explore (rather than assuming) the adequacy of the heuristics voters actually use.

Second, there are hints in the heuristics literature of the problem of too much information—an alternative to the epistemically utopian rational-choice understanding of why real people might use heuristics, which assumes their effective omniscience. "Relative to our ability to comprehend it," Lupia and McCubbins write, "our environment is very complex," so heuristics are needed to navigate it.[38] It follows that *everyone* uses heuristics, not because they accurately calculate the costs and benefits of doing so, and not because they somehow know which heuristics are adequate, but because they have no alternative. Nobody can have "perfect knowledge," so we must each take the information we think we understand and try to interpret its larger significance. (What are heuristics if not condensed interpretations?) One normative consequence is that epistocracy is not necessarily desirable in comparison to democratic technocracy, as we have seen. Another is that neither epistocracy nor democratic technocracy may be justifiable according to internal normative criteria, because both epistocrats and citizen-technocrats may be unlikely to arrive at adequate interpretations of an entire society or its problems.

Finally, the heuristics literature pointed to specific heuristics, such as party labels, the perceived intentions of the insurance industry in California, and the perceived retrospective performance of the economy, that might explain a great deal of actual political behavior. By viewing heuristics as interpretations, we will be able to reach a more refined understanding of what people using such heuristics might be doing, allowing us to answer the normative question of whether citizen-technocrats are likely to perform their task adequately well.

6.3. PUBLIC IGNORANCE: RADICAL, NOT RATIONAL

It is, heaven knows, often difficult in a world as complex as ours to know enough to judge accurately where your interests lie. But it's infinitely more daunting to acquire an adequate understanding of the good of other people in your society. The problem is even more

---

[38] Lupia and McCubbins 1998, 22.

acute in modern democratic countries because our fellow countrymen are so numerous that none of us can possibly know more than a small fraction of them. Consequently we have to make judgments about the good of people we don't know personally and can know about only indirectly. In social science-ese, the information costs in trying to acquire an understanding of the interests of all our fellow citizens are far too high for most of us to bear.

—ROBERT A. DAHL, *Democracy and Its Critics*

Nobody knew health care could be so complicated.

—DONALD J. TRUMP, February 27, 2017

There are two kinds of uninstructed voter. There is the man who does not know and knows that he does not know. He is generally an enlightened person. He is the man who waives his right to vote. But there is also the man who is uninstructed and does not know that he is, or care.

—WALTER LIPPMANN, *Public Opinion*

Even as the revisionists were using the theory of rational choice to vindicate voters' use of heuristics, mainstream public-opinion scholars were gravitating toward the same theory to explain voters' allegedly indomitable ignorance.[39] In what soon became the consensus view shared by both types of scholar, the ignorant voter *knows* that her lone vote is highly unlikely to tip the outcome in an election with many voters. In turn, this putative knowledge reveals to the voter that she has an objective incentive to be politically ignorant, because there is no reason to spend time and effort learning about public affairs if the well-informed vote one thereby casts does not matter. In addition, heuristics scholars held that knowledge of the low odds that one's vote will matter leads to the decision to use heuristics as low-cost information substitutes. Thus, *rational-ignorance theory* assumes that ignorant citizens are ignorant, and that they may therefore use heuristics, because they happen to know the most important thing they need to know about politics: the minuscule odds that their votes will be decisive.

However, if we give up the economistic assumption that the public's ignorance is a deliberate choice, responsive to incentives, we can arrive at an epistemologically plausible account of public-opinion findings that roots both ignorance and heuristics use in an environment of overabundant information that needs to be interpreted. Such an account will enable us to think systematically about the types of heuristic that are likely to be used in a democratic technocracy.

---

[39] E.g., Zaller 1992, 16; Gilens 2001, 379; Althaus 2003, 63, 250; Converse 2006; Fishkin 2009, ch. 2; Goren 2012, 505. See also Page and Shapiro 1992, 13.

6.3.1. Empirical Evidence against Rational Ignorance

The theory of rational ignorance was first enunciated in 1957 by Anthony Downs in *An Economic Theory of Democracy*.[40] Downs's theory joins the low odds that one vote in a large electorate will be decisive with three claims about voters' motives and knowledge:

1. Voters are acting instrumentally: they seek to influence public policy by casting what might be the decisive vote in favor of the candidate or party of their choice.

This is not equivalent to saying that they are acting selfishly. The goal to which one's vote is an instrument may be sociotropic. I will assume that this is indeed the goal, as demanded by a democratic technocracy, even though anecdotal evidence suggests that many voters do not vote instrumentally, but rather as a duty; and even though, in reality, other voters may vote instrumentally but selfishly. The literature on sociotropic voting[41] suggests that selfish voting is less common than is commonly assumed, but selfish voting certainly occurs, and in any given election it might occur predominantly or exclusively. Such an election would pro tanto be outside the bounds of democratic technocracy.

2. Voters know, at least vaguely, the very steep odds against any one vote in a large electorate being decisive.

This claim, as we shall see, is not supported by the available evidence.

3. Therefore, voters deliberately choose not to become politically well informed, as it would be a waste of their time and other resources to do so.

This claim, as we shall see, is illogical.

The second claim would appear to be false on its face given that billions of people do vote, despite being members of large electorates. This is known as the paradox of voting—as a leading revisionist famously put it, "the paradox that ate rational choice theory."[42] The paradox is this: If voters are instrumentally rational, and if it is not instrumentally rational to vote, why do they vote?

Aaron Edlin, Andrew Gelman, and Noah Kaplan provide the following answer, designed to rescue rational-*voting* theory, as opposed to rational-*ignorance* theory, from the paradox.[43] If the costs of voting are low enough, and if a sociotropic citizen multiplies the small chance of casting a decisive ballot by a high enough estimate of

---

[40] Downs 1957, ch. 13.
[41] E.g., Kinder and Kiewiet 1979; Sears et al. 1980; Kinder and Kiewiet 1981; Kiewiet 1983; Citrin and Green 1990; Sears and Funk 1990; Blinder and Krueger 2004; Lau and Heldman 2009; Kiewiet and Lewis-Beck 2011.
[42] Fiorina 1990, 334.
[43] Edlin et al. 2007.

the benefits to society of a victory for her candidate or party, it *will* be instrumentally rational for her to vote. The reasoning seems inarguable. On its basis, Ilya Somin has tried to rescue the theory of rational *ignorance*. He points out that if the conditions stipulated by Edlin et al. hold; and if, in addition, the cost of becoming politically well informed is substantially greater than the cost of voting, as seems plausible; then people with a high estimate of the sociotropic benefits of seeing their candidate elected might find it worthwhile to vote, but not worthwhile to become well informed.[44] The relatively high cost of becoming well informed would outweigh the sociotropic benefit of doing so, while the relatively low cost of voting might be outweighed by the socio-tropic benefit of doing so. Thus, Somin's argument could explain why so many citizens bother to vote but not to inform themselves adequately (using an additive notion of epistemic adequacy).

Within the terms set by rational-choice theory, Edlin et al. successfully defend claim 2 from the paradox of voting, and Somin successfully defends claim 3. But that is not the same thing as showing that either claim is warranted, because the terms set by the theory are arbitrary. To show that the claims are warranted, someone would have to demonstrate that voters actually do know the high odds against their votes making a difference (claim 2, which is presupposed by claim 3). Neither Edlin, Gelman, and Kaplan nor Somin nor anyone else seems to have even attempted to do so.

One way of attempting it would be to ask voters to estimate the odds that a single vote will be decisive. Although this does not appear to have been tried, there is indirect evidence that most American voters in recent years have not known the odds, even approximately. For example, 78 percent of a national sample of 1,000 likely US voters in 2016 agreed that "one person's vote really matter[s]."[45] And 89 percent of recent voters said in 1990 that influencing government policy was an "important" reason for having voted.[46] This would hardly make sense if they believed that their individual votes were unlikely to be, or to have been, decisive, for in that case their individual votes could not influence government policy.

A less direct way to find out if voters know the odds against their vote mattering is to ask nonvoters why they do not vote. I have been unable to find a survey containing both that question and the relevant response prompt: that the odds against one's vote counting are too high to justify voting. But in 2004, the Census Bureau asked US citizens who did not *register* to vote if it was because "my vote would not make a difference."[47] Only 3.7 percent of the respondents said yes.

---

[44] Somin 2013, ch. 3.

[45] Rasmussen 2016.

[46] Campbell 2006, 52.

[47] Census Bureau 2006, Table E. The Census Bureau regularly asks why people do not register to vote, but it does not allow them to answer that the odds against their vote counting are too high, nor even to answer, more vaguely, that their vote would not make a difference.

It would seem, then, that at least in the United States in the late twentieth and early twenty-first centuries, the available evidence is inconsistent with claim 2, upon which claim 3 relies. Neither voters nor nonvoters seem to have realized, by and large, that the odds against their votes being decisive are astronomically high. Therefore, they cannot very well have decided to underinform themselves because of those odds.

If claim 2 is indeed false, it would not be surprising. The theory of rational ignorance was not even propounded until mass democracies had been functioning for nearly two centuries.[48] Before Downs noticed it, the arithmetic premise of the theory had escaped the attention of several generations of democratic theorists (and even economists).[49] How, then, would ordinary voters know about it?

Somin suggests that such knowledge is "intuitive."[50] Otherwise he would be committed to the implausible claim that, since the advent of mass suffrage, billions of citizen-technocrats have been *explicitly* making calculations of the following sort to determine, respectively, whether they should vote and whether they should acquire political information—

$$D^*(300 \text{ million} / 1000) / (100 \text{ million}) - C_V = U_V$$
$$D^*(300 \text{ million} / 1000) / (100 \text{ million}) - C_{pi} = U_{pi}$$

—even though these formulae did not appear in print until 2013 (in Somin's *Democracy and Political Ignorance*).[51] However, there is no reason to think that what escaped so many democratic theorists prior to Downs is intuitive. We did not evolve in societies consisting of hundreds of millions of anonymous others, so there is no reason to think that we would we have acquired the ability to intuit complicated formulae for calculating the costs and benefits of acting as members of such large groups.

Let us therefore chalk up the rational-choice theory of voting, and thus its offshoot, rational-ignorance theory, to the fantastic assumption, stemming from economic theory,

[48] Richard Tuck (2008, 31) finds predecessors to Downs among utilitarian philosophers of the early 1950s.

[49] Tuck (2008, 10) points out that prior to the middle of the twentieth century, both democratic political theorists and economists who thought long and hard about collective action not only failed to see voluntary participation in large groups as instrumentally irrational; they decidedly thought otherwise. Even now, moreover, there is substantial disagreement among scholars in the Downsian tradition about how to calculate "the odds" of a vote being decisive (compare Brennan 2011, ch. 1 to Edlin et al. 2007, and to Somin 2013, ch. 1). Both facts tell against the notion that these odds are intuitively obvious.

[50] Somin 2013, 71. Similarly, Jason Brennan (2016, 31) asserts, without providing any evidence at all, that while "few citizens know how to calculate the exact probability that their votes will be decisive," they "do know intuitively that their votes are unlikely to make a difference."

[51] Somin 2013, 67, 69. D is the expected difference in welfare per person if the voter's preferred candidate defeats her opponent; C_V is the cost of voting; U_V is the utility of voting; C_{pi} is the cost of acquiring political information; U_{pi} is the utility of acquiring it. Somin is assuming an electorate of 300,000,000, a 1/100,000,000 chance of casting a decisive vote, and voters who value the welfare of their fellow citizens an average of a thousand times less than their own.

that human beings are effectively omniscient. A more realistic approach would recognize that knowledge of something as arcane as the odds of a vote turning the outcome in a large election is probably transmitted culturally—if at all—rather than being intuitive. One might therefore undertake a cultural investigation, looking at (for example) discussions in the mass media and popular culture of the efficacy of voting. Pending such research, I will hazard that the odds of a vote being decisive are rarely mentioned in movies, on television, or anywhere else in mass culture—except in the form of repeated, inaccurate assertions that every vote *does* "count." Thus, we have no reason to think that the depressing mathematics of voting has entered many people's minds. Yet if people have not thought about the odds that their votes are likely to tip the outcome, then they cannot possibly have decided that because the odds are low, they should not bother to inform themselves about public affairs.

The chance that one will cast a decisive vote is thus a good example of a fact about which most people can probably be assumed to be radically ignorant. For most people, whether or not their vote will affect the outcome is probably an unknown unknown: not a question about which they have declined to learn the answer because they have calculated that it would not be worthwhile to know it, nor a question they have wondered about but cannot answer, but a question they have not even thought to ask. This hypothesis may be confirmed by the following consideration. Whenever we are surprised to learn something, we must have been radically ignorant of it before the surprise occurred. Discussions with ordinary citizens (in classrooms, in taxicabs, in grocery store checkout lines) reveal that when they are made aware of the high odds against one vote mattering, they are so surprised that they immediately begin trying out implausible arguments for why the odds must in fact be low, or for why the odds do not matter.[52] That is where their "intuitions" lead them: toward astonished *resistance* to the rational-choice theory of voting (and, by implication, rational-ignorance theory).

6.3.2. The Logical Incoherence of Rational-Ignorance Theory

Not only does rational-ignorance theory fail to tally with the available empirical evidence. It is logically incompatible with the casting of *nonrandom* votes—that is, votes determined by one's beliefs about which option is better, rather than by a coin toss.

Edlin et al., and Somin, overcome the paradox of voting by assuming that voters calculate that the cost of voting is not so high as to overcome the *perceived* sociotropic benefit of casting the decisive vote, multiplied by a more or less accurate estimate of the odds of that happening. Bracketing the (unsubstantiated and implausible) notion that voters do, empirically, have a more or less accurate estimate of the odds, the idea that voters base

---

[52] Hardin 2009, 70.

their decision not to inform themselves on their perception of sociotropic benefits poses an apparently insuperable logical difficulty for the theory of rational ignorance.

The perceived sociotropic benefit of casting the decisive vote depends on what is designated as D in Somin's formulae: the expected sociotropic difference that would be made by the election of one candidate or party over the others. However, a voter who had, according to claim 3, *deliberately* decided to underinform herself about public affairs (due to a more or less accurate estimate that her vote, and thus her opinion, are unlikely to matter) would thereby have mandated her own ignorance of D when it came time to choose among the options on the ballot. At the moment of attempted choice, she would surely remember that her estimate of the high odds against her vote mattering had led her deliberately to underinform herself about D, by her own standards of epistemic adequacy (whatever those standards might be). Believing herself, therefore, to be underinformed about D, she could not enter a plausible estimate of it into her calculations. Thus, she would have no basis for choosing one candidate or party over another: that is, no basis for voting except, perhaps, the flip of a coin. This applies to using heuristics such as party labels or voting retrospectively, too, as she would know that she had deliberately underinformed herself about what party labels indicate and about the state of the economy or the society.

None of this is to say that rationally ignorant voters would need, but lack, *reliable* knowledge of D. That may be, but we are now considering the empirical question of how it is that ignorant voters are able to motivate their votes, not the normative question of whether their ignorance renders them epistemically unqualified to vote (in their capacity as citizen-technocrats). They may turn out to lack reliable technocratic knowledge, but in determining whether rational-ignorance theory can explain this possibility, what matters is whether they meet their own standards of epistemic reliability, not whether we judge those standards to be deficient. *Whatever* their epistemic standards are, and however inadequate we might judge them to be, they themselves must believe that they have met these standards before they can decide which candidate or party to vote for. Only citizen-technocrats who consider themselves—rightly or wrongly—to be adequately informed about the net sociotropic benefits of a specific candidate's or party's victory could be motivated to vote for that candidate or party, as opposed either to not voting or to choosing randomly among the candidates or parties on the ballot.

Voters who do not consider themselves adequately informed, then, because they have deliberately chosen not to inform themselves adequately by their own standards of adequacy, would be unable to cast nonrandom ballots. Such voters—according to rational-ignorance theory, *all* instrumentalist voters (except those who decided to underinform themselves but then accidentally encountered what seemed to them adequate information about whom they should vote for)[53]—would think that they are too ignorant to

---

[53] I owe this qualification to David Schraub.

know whom they should vote for, since they would have deliberately made the choice to be precisely that ignorant. It would seem, then, that (with the exception noted in parentheses in the last sentence) rational-ignorance theory cannot account for nonrandom instrumentalist votes.

Of course, there sometimes *is* random voting, e.g., for obscure offices when a voter thinks this necessary to prevent a spoiled ballot. But if a voter felt inadequately informed about the electoral contests that she considers important (because, as per the theory of rational ignorance, she had deliberately chosen to inform herself inadequately about these contests, according to her own standards of adequacy), she would have no way of knowing, by her own lights, which candidate or party to favor. Thus, not only would she have to vote randomly if she found herself inside a voting booth; for the same reason, she would not take the trouble to get herself there.

In sum, the theory of rational ignorance cannot explain why people would vote nonrandomly or, indeed, at all, as the theory holds that they would have chosen to be too ignorant (according to their own epistemic standards) to know for whom or for what they should vote. Voting nonrandomly after having made the choice to be ignorant would be blatantly illogical. Thus, we must reject the theory of rational ignorance.

However, a theory of *radical* ignorance can readily explain the nonrandom voting of voters who are inadequately informed, according to epistemic standards that are *not* their own—for example, the standards of political scientists concerned about the voters' ignorance of neutral, factual public-affairs knowledge, or the standards of normative epistemologists of technocracy. This is the real issue lurking behind rational-ignorance theory. Its actual starting point is an observer's judgment that voters are ignorant according to the standards of the observer: for example, the rational-ignorance theorist. In an attempt to explain this, the theorist illicitly ascribes to the voters themselves the judgment that they are underinformed, which is no more justified than is ascribing to them the knowledge that their votes do not matter. Without these two ascriptions, however, a solution to the puzzle of ignorant voters reveals itself: they do not know, or even think, either that their votes do not matter or that their opinions are too uninformed to produce sociotropic ballots. Lacking knowledge of their ignorance, according to the theorist's standards—or rejecting these standards—and lacking knowledge that their votes almost certainly do not matter, it is entirely rational for them to vote without becoming "well informed" according to the observer's standards. We do not need Edlin et al.'s solution to the paradox of voting, and we do not need Somin's solution to the paradox of ignorant voting, because these are paradoxes only if we impute knowledge to voters that we have every reason to think that they lack.

Thus, a voter who does not pay much attention to politics and government may be able to estimate D—to her satisfaction—because she is radically ignorant of the fact that she is underinformed about D according to the epistemic standards of rational-ignorance theorists (or scholars of public opinion, or normative theorists of technocracy); or, on the off chance that she has heard of these standards, because she does not agree that they are appropriate. According to *her* standards, she knows enough to estimate D, and that is the only knowledge she needs if she is to make nonrandom electoral choices.

Any voter necessarily believes that whatever knowledge enables her to cast a non-random vote is adequate knowledge, no matter how inadequate others may find it. If, in fact, a given voter is mistaken about the adequacy of her knowledge, she must be ignorant of this fact, that is, ignorant of her ignorance of the knowledge she lacks or of its (puta-tive) normative importance. If one wants to understand such a person's political behavior charitably, then, one would not ask why she votes, as the answer is clear: she votes be-cause she assumes that she knows enough to cast a ballot that will achieve a worthwhile objective; to the extent that she is a citizen-technocrat, this would mean a ballot that achieves a sociotropic objective. One would ask instead: What are the standards of epi-stemic adequacy that make her think she can achieve a worthwhile objective by casting a nonrandom ballot, given her low level of neutral, factual public-affairs knowledge and, a fortiori, her low level of technocratically necessary knowledge?

6.3.3. Radical Public Ignorance and the Naive Technocratic Worldview

The initial basis of the Michigan school's bleak outlook on mass democracy was open-ended interviews with randomly selected citizens during the presidential campaign of 1956. A sample of the interviews was excerpted in the chapter of *The American Voter* ti-tled "The Formation of Issue Concepts and Partisan Change."[54] These excerpts strongly suggest that at least in 1956, American voters simply failed to recognize (or, rather, to agree with observers) that they were inadequately informed. There is certainly no sign that the interviewees had deliberately underinformed themselves, nor any evidence that they recognized that their votes, hence their opinions, were unlikely to matter. And if they lacked knowledge that could have or should have changed their votes—technocratic knowledge or knowledge of any other kind—this ignorance appears to have been radical (in the sense of unintentional), not rational (in the economistic sense of being deliberate and effectively omniscient). However, it bears emphasizing that radically ignorant voters and other radically ignorant agents *are* "procedurally" rational.

Here are snippets from each of the published interview extracts with voters in the three highest "levels of conceptualization" into which Campbell, Converse, Miller, and Stokes divided their sample. The authors randomly selected these extracts to illustrate the beliefs shared among respondents in each level. Respondents who used ideologically relevant concepts (relevant, primarily, to liberalism or conservatism, as interpreted by the authors) were grouped in Level A. Those who instead drew on perceptions of which social groups, such as business or labor, were favored by the parties or candidates in the 1956 presidential campaign fell into Level B. Those who were primarily concerned with

---

[54] Campbell et al. 1960, ch. 10.

the "nature of the times"—whether things were or were not going well economically, in foreign policy, and so on (in revisionist argot, retrospective voters) were put into Level C. Everyone else—whose comments had "no issue content"—was sorted into a fourth level, D, not excerpted here for reasons of space and to avoid tedium.[55] In parentheses, I provide the proportion of eligible voters in each level and the proportion of actual voters (eligible voters minus nonvoters). The respondents in Level D made up 22.5 percent of eligible voters but just 17.5 percent of actual voters.

Level A (11.5 percent of eligible voters; 15.5 percent of actual voters):

1. Well, the Democratic Party tends to favor socialized medicine—and I'm being influenced in [opposing] that because I came from a doctor's family.[56]

2. I think of the Republicans as being more conservative and interested in big business.[57]

3. I like [the Democrats'] platform. . . . They're more inclined to help the working class of people, and that is the majority in our country. . . . [Republicans] play up to individual rights, which is good. That's good—it makes a person feel more independent.[58]

4. [The Democrats] certainly have passed beneficial legislation like social security and unemployment insurance, which the average man needs today.[59]

5. I think the Democrats are more concerned with all the people. . . . They put out more liberal legislation for all the people. . . . [Republicans are] for a moneyed group.[60]

6. The Democratic Party is more for higher social security. They're more for old age pensions and better working conditions for the working man. They want a higher standard of living for all people, not just a few. The promises that are made by the Democrats are kept if at all possible. The facts are told to the American people. . . . I was growing up at the time of the Hoover Administration. What a time I had, too. There was barely enough to eat. I don't think the Republicans wanted that, but they did nothing to stop it. Not until Roosevelt came along and made things start to happen. Now the Republican Party still stands for big business, at the expense of the farmer and the working man. Promises made are not kept—ask the poor farmer, if no one else.[61]

---

[55] See Campbell et al. 1960, 249, for a tabular presentation of the statistical breakdown by level of conceptualization.
[56] Ibid., 228.
[57] Ibid., 229.
[58] Ibid., 230.
[59] Ibid., 231.
[60] Ibid., 232.
[61] Ibid., 233.

Level B (42 percent of eligible voters; 45 percent of actual voters):

7. [Republicans] are more for big business. . . . The little man gets crowded out. They cater to the big men.[62]

8. [Democrats] have always helped the farmers. . . . We have always had good times under their Administration. They are more for the working class of people. . . [Republicans] promise so much but they don't do anything. . . . I think the Republicans favor the richer folks.[63]

9. I've just always before been a Democrat. My daddy before me always was. . . . I just don't believe [Republicans] are for the common people.[64]

10. [The Democrats] are more interested in small businessmen and farms. . . . I've always heard this.[65]

11. I know nothing about politics but I like the Democratic Party because I know they are more for the poorer people. . . . [Republicans] are out to help the rich people.[66]

12. I don't know anything about the Democratic Party. [Respondent was thinking awfully hard and getting nowhere at all.] Well, for one thing, they were hard on the farmers.[67]

Level C (24 percent of eligible voters; 23 percent of actual voters):

13. Promises were made that weren't kept. . . . It confuses the public and it confuses me. A person don't know who to vote for. All the same, both parties are guilty in some instances of breaking campaign promises. . . . More should be done for human beings, for the good of the people. . . . [Eisenhower] is a former Army man and saw the horrors of war and therefore would want to keep the peace.[68]

14. They's a lot of nice Democrats. They's not too much difference in the parties. . . . Politics is something I don't study on much. . . . I don't know whether I'll even vote or not.[69]

15. Stevenson will see to it that they stop testing the bomb and I'm in favor of that. I don't want them to explode any more of those bombs. . . . I don't know much about the parties. . . . I don't know much about the whole thing. . . . [Under Eisenhower,] my husband's job is better. . . . His investments in stocks are up. They go up when the Republicans are in. . . . [But] as I mentioned before,

---

[62] Ibid., 236.
[63] Ibid.
[64] Ibid., 237–238.
[65] Ibid., 238.
[66] Ibid.
[67] Ibid., 239.
[68] Ibid., 242.
[69] Ibid., 243.

[Stevenson]'s saying stop testing the bomb because it can do so much damage. My husband says that's such a minor point, but I don't think so.[70]

16. Well, I really don't know enough about politics to speak. I never did have no dealings with it. . . . [As for the Democrats,] I like the good wages my husband makes. [*It is the Republicans who are in now.*] I know, and it's sort of begun to tighten up since the Republicans got in. . . . Truthfully, the Republican Party just doesn't interest me at all. . . . I haven't read enough about either one of the candidates to know anything about them at all.[71]

Notice, first, that if we follow Campbell and his colleagues in linking the levels of conceptualization to levels of neutral, factual public-affairs knowledge, as seems defensible from the extracts, then as knowledge declined, so did the propensity to vote. Relatively knowledgeable citizens (in Levels A and B) overvoted in comparison to their share of the population, while relatively uninformed citizens (in Levels C and D) undervoted. Accordingly, one of the Level C respondents (number 14) was on the borderline between thinking that she knew enough to be able to vote nonrandomly and thinking that she did not. Yet rational-ignorance theory predicts that *all* voters[72] believe that they have crossed this border into the realm of the inadequately informed—as a result of their deliberate decision not to invest in adequate knowledge. The declining propensity to vote as knowledge of neutral, factual public-affairs information declined suggests that in reality, as logic demands, those who voted did not believe themselves to be inadequately informed, and that when citizens did believe they were inadequately informed, they selected themselves out of the pool of citizen-technocrats, as respondent 14 was on the verge of doing.[73] Similarly, subsequent research has found that poorly informed respondents to survey questions are more likely to answer "Don't Know" (DK) or to give no opinion (NO) than better-informed respondents.[74] According to rational-ignorance theory, however, *all* voters should think of themselves as poorly informed, such that all voters in opinion surveys should give DK/NO responses.

A few of the respondents in Level D, not excerpted above, did indicate an awareness of nearly disabling levels of ignorance. For instance, a Missouri woman said she did not

---

[70] Ibid.

[71] Ibid., 244.

[72] With the exception, noted earlier, of voters who decide to underinform themselves but then accidentally encounter information that they consider adequate to inform a nonrandom choice. A more fanciful exception would be voters who find "entertainment value" in following politics, as if it were a hobby or a spectator sport, despite knowing (allegedly) that their political opinions do not matter (Somin 2013, 78–82). "Politics fans," however, give every sign of feeling that their rooting interests are grounded in fact and logic. Sports fans, by contrast, tend to recognize that their emotional investment in a given team is arbitrary. This is part of what makes it fun.

[73] Unless they decide to vote randomly.

[74] Althaus 2003, 278 and passim; Bullock and Luskin 2011, 553.

"know about either one of the men [running for president] enough to give an opinion." Such respondents constituted 5 percent of Level D and 3 percent of actual voters.[75] But most Level D respondents, while offering no specifics about either the candidates or their parties, were nonetheless able to motivate opinions: "I'm a Democrat, that's all I know"; "I just like Eisenhower better"; "I have no use for Stevenson whatsoever."[76] This type of response can easily be characterized as irrational if we are interpretively uncharitable. But we should not confuse our own lack of insight into someone's reasons, or her unwillingness or inability to articulate her reasons, with an absence of reasons. Inasmuch as they voted nonrandomly, we can be assured that even the most uninformed of these voters (by their standards or ours) had reasons of some sort, even if they could not put their finger on them. Whatever these reasons were, the voters themselves could not have perceived them to be inadequate; that is, they could not have believed that they were *too* uninformed to distinguish good candidates or parties from bad ones. Thus, if they were ignorant of normatively important information about the candidates or parties—for our purposes, technocratically important information that would have changed their votes or moved them into the undecided category—they must have been ignorant of this ignorance.

Three more observations about the quoted respondents strike a theorist of radical ignorance.

First, most of the respondents appear not to have known which policies were favored by the competing candidates or their parties; nor did most respondents express specific policy preferences of their own. Only respondents 1, 4, 6, and 15 mentioned specific policies. However, *everyone* in Levels A, B, and C seemed to perceive "obvious" sociotropic differences between the parties or candidates—differences that were sufficient to motivate nonrandom votes in every excerpted case except, possibly, that of respondent 14. This suggests that it is not inaccurate to characterize them as citizen-technocrats. Moreover, the confidence with which political opinions were expressed, even in the apparent absence of policy preferences, and even by most of the respondents who recognized their political ignorance in the abstract (respondents 11–13 and 15–16), suggests that if respondents were ignorant of important sociotropic effects of the policies favored by their candidate or party, they were unaware of this ignorance.

Second, even the respondents who did mention specific policies seemed unaware of the possibility that other citizens might disagree with their assessments of these policies' merits. Respondent 15, for example, who opposed atomic testing, seems to have been saying that her husband believed this to be an unimportant election issue. But regardless of its importance, she did not betray awareness that there might be arguments against her position on the issue. Only respondent 1 seemed to recognize that there might be arguments against her position (that is, her opposition to socialized medicine). The other

---

[75] Campbell et al. 1960, 249.
[76] Ibid., 247, 247, 248.

respondents who mentioned specific policies (respondents 4, 6, and 15) appeared unaware of the possibility of reasonable debate about the policies they favored or opposed. It is not that they seemed to know about the existence of cogent arguments against their policy opinions but were unwilling to pay the price of learning what these arguments were. Rather, it did not seem to occur to them that such arguments might exist.

Third, the respondents' general unawareness of the contestability of their opinions suggests as well that they were unaware of the fallible conceptual and interpersonal sources of their own political beliefs, and thus of the potential gap between their beliefs about reality and reality itself (with the instructively glaring exception of the first respondent). That is, the respondents tended to be naive political realists in general and naive technocratic realists in particular. Several respondents did acknowledge their own fallibility, in principle. But such acknowledgments are empty if one does not see that a *particular* opinion is not a direct deliverance of objective reality, but originates in ideas communicated from fallible human beings. None of the respondents except the first one seemed to recognize this about their particular opinions.

Summing up: the respondents seemed not only to be ignorant of their preferred parties' and candidates' policy positions, but radically ignorant of the possibility that their own votes, hence their opinions, hence their informedness or uninformedness, did not matter, contrary to rational-ignorance theory. As well, the respondents seemed, by and large, to be radically ignorant that there could be alternatives to their political opinions, or that these opinions might not be informed by the knowledge necessary to lead to sociotropically adequate votes.

6.4. A BIAS FOR TECHNOCRATIC ACTION

Everything that is broken in our country can be fixed. Every problem can be solved.
—DONALD J. TRUMP, Address to Joint Session of Congress, February 28, 2017

Where there is a wish, there is not necessarily a way. Devotion to an end does not ensure
discovery of the means.
—WALTER LIPPMANN, *The Good Society*

Does citizen-technocrats' radical political ignorance include ignorance of unintended policy consequences?

It seems likely. Policy debate is the arena in which claims about unintended consequences are usually made; but the *American Voter* interviews, and the public-ignorance literature more broadly, suggest widespread disengagement from policy debate, a fortiori. At the very least, it is hard to imagine where people who are disengaged from policy debate might get the idea that a given policy might run afoul of unintended *counterintuitive* consequences. Moreover, without regular exposure to such claims about many different policies, there would be little reason for them to think about whether unintended counterintuitive consequences might pose a general problem for citizen-technocrats, such as themselves.

6.4.1. The Naive Technocratic Worldview

In the absence of such thoughts, it would be logical for citizen-technocrats to default in favor of problem-solving action. In *Congress as Public Enemy* (1995) and *Stealth Democracy* (2002), John R. Hibbing and Elizabeth Theiss-Morse provide grounds for suggesting that this is what does happen in the real world, at least in the United States in recent decades.

The authors write, about the participants in focus groups they conducted in 1992, that there was "overwhelming sentiment . . . that the government should 'do something' about key problems."[77] Even the most casual student of politics will have noticed the same thing, and not just in 1992. I reviewed some of the evidence for this conclusion in the introduction, in the form of Americans' overwhelming proclivity to favor policies that are aimed at solving social problems. More abstractly, Christopher Ellis and James A. Stimson point out that, in every year between 1953 and 2008, Americans tended to prefer government action to inaction.[78] Conversely, as Hibbing and Theiss-Morse show with focus-group and survey evidence, disillusionment and anger can follow from the perception that government is failing to act. The authors' angry, disillusioned respondents did not allow that inaction might be caused by arguments about which actions will succeed or what their effects might be, let alone that such arguments might be justified. On the contrary: they seemed to agree that, as one put it, all it would take to solve the extant problems is for the two parties' leaders to get together and say to each other, "There's a problem. We won't leave this room until it's fixed." Another participant warmed to the theme: "They need to be put in small spaces in the summertime that is [*sic*] not air conditioned, and say, 'Get on the ball and do something!' and they'd do it."[79] Thus, Hibbing and Theiss-Morse suggest, American citizens tend to see policy disagreements as nothing but pointless partisan bickering.[80] This, too, will ring true to any student of daily politics in the United States and perhaps elsewhere.

Hibbing and Theiss-Morse's evidence seems to me to indicate, like the *American Voter* interviews, that citizen-technocrats in the United States (at least in recent decades) have tended to have in mind a naively realistic worldview: not a dogmatically held ideology, but a series of logically connected but tacit ideas that make sense of the evidence we have before us, as well as other evidence about public opinion and voter behavior to be discussed in a moment. If we were to make this worldview explicit by asking one of its

---

[77] Hibbing and Theiss-Morse 1995, 55.
[78] Ellis and Stimson 2012, 45.
[79] Hibbing and Theiss-Morse 1995, 97.
[80] Ibid., 65; Hibbing and Theiss-Morse 2002, 137.

adherents why she thinks politicians in the hot room would know how to solve the social problems, I suspect she would say, in effect, that the truth about such matters would be self-evident to them. This form of naive technocratic realism is the link between all the tendencies I will portray as components of the naive technocratic worldview.

The first of these tendencies is what I will call a "bias" for technocratic action. Like the heuristics uncovered by revisionist scholars of public opinion, this bias—whether or not it is justified—would be entirely *rational* given the assumption of self-evidence. We *should* take technocratic action to solve any and every problem that arises if the appropriate solution would be self-evident to decision-makers who sat down in a hot room and thought about it. To make this assumption, however, one must also assume (tacitly) that there will not be complicating factors such as counterintuitive unintended consequences that, as such, are *not* self-evident. Thus, the naive technocratic worldview may flow not only from radical ignorance of the mediated nature of our perceptions and interpretations of the world, as in naive realism simpliciter, but from radical ignorance of the possibility of unintended consequences. When we see citizen-technocrats demanding unspecified technocratic action, as if the correct action will be self-evident, we must conclude that they are radically ignorant of the possibility of such complications as unintended consequences, particularly those that are counterintuitive.

6.4.2. From Truman to Trump

A bias for technocratic action would explain Americans' apparently unending frustration with political "gridlock" and the popular chord struck by presidents who run against a "do-nothing" Congress. Harry S Truman hit upon the latter trope in his 1948 re-election campaign, and presidents have been trading on his success ever since. Nonincumbents too, such as Donald Trump in 2016, are able to harp on a similar theme by dismissing their opponents as "all talk, no action." Hillary Clinton tried to play a similar card in portraying herself as a "fighter" who "gets things done." But Trump's disinclination ever to back down in any controversy may have demonstrated to some voters, in deed—far more effectively than Clinton could demonstrate about herself, in words—that he would not let anyone get in the way of his determination to *act*. His continuous attack mode may likewise have signaled a propensity for action; so, too, his disparagement of Clinton for lacking "stamina," of Mitt Romney for having "disappeared" from the battle for the presidency at the end of the 2012 campaign, and of Jeb Bush for his "low energy."

To critical observers of Trump, his comical ignorance of public policy (and so much else) was a clear disqualification for the presidency. But citizen-technocrats who tacitly adhere to a naive technocratic worldview would have no reason to recognize that an ignorant politician might lack knowledge not only of civics trivia but of policy effects—inasmuch as they assume that such effects are self-evident to those who sit down and think about them. Hibbing and Theiss-Morse's respondents, who made that assumption, logically concluded that the reason social problems persist is that elected officials have "the ability but not the will to take care of the nation's problems."[81] The ability was, for them, the easy part, or so it seems; the hard part was the will. For such citizen-technocrats, Trump's bullheaded willfulness alone may have signaled his qualification for the office of citizen-technocrat in chief.

In "Causal Stories and the Formation of Policy Agendas," an analysis of real-world policy discourse, Deborah A. Stone maintains that the inhabitants of modern societies "have two primary frameworks for interpreting the world—the natural and the social." In the natural world, she points out, "there is no willful intention" behind whatever happens. But in the social world, "we understand events to be the result of *will*. . . . We usually think we have an understanding of causation when we can identify the purposes or motives of a person or group and link those purposes to their actions."[82] Let us call "technocratic voluntarism" the assumption that a strong will is crucial to the achievement of sociotropic ends. This is the second element of the naive technocratic worldview. Trump portrayed himself as the ideal recipient of support from technocratic voluntarists. Citizens who are technocratic voluntarists should respond well to purely aspirational appeals by politicians who identify no policy mechanisms, or only vague ones, to accomplish their objectives: crush terrorism, revive industry, end poverty, and solve every other social problem. Viewed in this light, voluntarism complements the action bias as an offshoot of the naive technocratic worldview. If technocratic action is self-evidently needed, it follows almost (but not quite) necessarily that we should prefer strong-willed politicians to those who offer detailed policy agendas. The will to get things done should suffice if what needs to be done is self-evident.

6.5. SIMPLE HEURISTICS FOR A COMPLEX WORLD

> People for the most part . . . organize the world into neat evaluative gestalts that couple
> good causes to good effects and bad to bad. Unfortunately, the world can be a morally messy
> place in which policies that one is predisposed to detest sometimes have positive effects and
> policies that one embraces sometimes have noxious ones.
> —PHILIP E. TETLOCK, *Expert Political Judgment*

The technocratic action bias and technocratic voluntarism imply a third element of the naive technocratic worldview: the tacit assumption that society has an ontology that is so simple that it is epistemically transparent. In such a society, causal forces are straightforward enough to be understood without the assistance of social-scientific technology. In such a society, the solutions to social problems should follow directly from political actors' will to solve them.

---

[81] Hibbing and Theiss-Morse 1995, 97; Hibbing and Theiss-Morse 2002, 13.

[82] Stone 1989, 283, author's emphasis.

A simple-society ontology, in turn, would logically undergird the deployment of the two final elements of the worldview: two heuristics that treat the disposition of political agents' wills as if they are reliable proxies for the effects to be achieved by the agents' actions, that is, two heuristics that treat the intentions governing agents' wills as equivalent to the results to be expected from agents' actions. First, a simple-society ontology implies that political actors of goodwill, who genuinely intend to solve social problems, will be able to do so without counterproductive consequences (which are not contemplated), such that good technocratic outcomes will follow from good intentions. Second, if social problems nonetheless persist, an explanation suggests itself: namely, political actors with bad intentions, that is, people who do not want the problems solved; political actors who are selfish, not sociotropic. Why would it be important to pick a strong-willed leader if not because people of goodwill must have the "strength" and doggedness to prevail over people of bad will?

In this analysis, technocratic voluntarism and the bad-intentions heuristic might best be understood as add-ons to the good-intentions heuristic, brought into play by frustration at the seeming inability of the well-intentioned to solve social problems. Given a simple society, the persistence, and perhaps even the existence, of social problems is most easily explained by the resistance to change of political actors with bad intentions, who must be overcome by uniting good intentions with a strong will.

Stone argues that "complex causal explanations are not very useful in politics, precisely because they do not offer a single locus of control, a plausible candidate to take responsibility for a problem, or a point of leverage to fix a problem."[83] The epitome of a complex but politically useless causal explanation, she writes, is the claim that "it is impossible to anticipate all possible events and effects; so failure or accident is inevitable"—the claim, in other words, that political actors' ignorance leads them to make serious *mistakes*. Such claims, she suggests, are far less persuasive than are narratives of blame, of which conspiracy theories are only the most obvious example. According to her research, "books and studies that catalyze public issues have a common structure to their argument. They claim that a condition formerly interpreted as accident is actually the result of human will."[84] Hibbing and Theiss-Morse present survey data on Americans' understandings of their elected officials that may be relevant to this thesis. As of 1998, those surveyed judged elected officials to be far better informed and much more intelligent than the American people as a whole, but far more selfish, too.[85] The respondents' chronic dissatisfaction with elected officials was due, it would seem, to the conviction that the officials had bad

---

[83] Stone 1988, 289.

[84] Ibid., 289. Thus, neoclassical economists' naively realistic insistence on the bad-intentions narrative of the financial crisis and, in general, on incentives, and thus intentions, as predictive of human behavior may stem, at least in part, from their internalization of the citizen-technocratic culture in which they were raised, and not merely from their professional training. The former might also make the latter seem plausible when an economics student raised in a democratic technocracy goes into an economics classroom.

[85] Hibbing and Theiss-Morse 2002, Fig. 5.1.

intentions, not inadequate knowledge, such that they deliberately, willfully declined to solve problems they knew how to solve. Indeed, politicians' bad intentions seemed, to most respondents, to be the central threat to the common good.

The *American Voter* excerpts sustain the further hypothesis that the intentions of politicians and parties provide a central organizing heuristic for citizen-technocrats who (a fortiori) tend to lack the four types of technocratic knowledge. The primary basis for most respondents' endorsement of a candidate or party was the perception that the candidate or party intended to benefit people who deserved to be helped: a good intention. And the primary basis for most respondents' antipathy to the other candidate or party was the perception that that party or candidate intended to benefit those who did not deserve to be helped: a bad intention. Fully 75 percent of the respondents whose comments were excerpted (by Campbell et al.) in Levels A, B, and C aligned themselves politically on the basis of the results that they thought a politician or a party "want[ed]" to accomplish for people who needed help (respondents 6 and 13); or on the more general grounds that a party or politician was "interested in" or "concerned with" helping, or was "inclined to" help, people who needed to be helped (or did not) (2, 5, and 3); or on the grounds that a party or politician "cater[ed] to" (7), "favor[ed]" (8), or simply was "for" (8, 9, and 11) people who needed (or did not need) to be helped. By contrast, respondents 4, 6, 8, 12, 14, 15, and 16 referred to retrospective perceptions of actual policy effects. Of these, however, only respondents 4, 12, 14, and 16 failed to discuss political actors' intentions in addition to retrospectively perceived results.[86]

The use of intentions as heuristics should not be confused with what Campbell and his colleagues termed voting on the basis of "group benefits." In their schema, respondents who cared primarily about group benefits comprised only Level B (represented by respondents 7–12), but those who appear to have used the intentions heuristics dominated both Level B and Level A (together representing 60.5 percent of the 1956 electorate). The intentions heuristics' penetration into Level C as well (judging from the comments of respondents 14–16) suggests that these heuristics were much more prevalent than was group-benefits voting. Notably, "group-benefits" voting may suggest voting in favor of benefits for *one's own* group, but when citizen-technocrats prefer one party over another because of its intention to help "the common people" or a group such as "the working class," it does not necessarily mean that they want to help that group on selfish grounds. They may just want the majority of Americans, or those who deserve help, to be helped. As respondent 3 said, "The working class of people . . . is the majority in our country."[87]

To update these findings, I asked a research assistant to generate a random sample of 500 of the 4,272 responses to the open-ended American National Election Survey of

---

[86] Only one of the *American Voter* respondents, number 6, allowed that there may be a gap between intentions and results: he acknowledged that the Republicans did not want the Great Depression to occur.

[87] Campbell et al. 1960, 230.

2016. (*The American Voter* was based on the 1956 version of the same survey.) He classified 139 of the 500 responses as having "no issue content" (Level D), leaving 361 responses to be further analyzed. Of these, 235, or 65 percent, attributed to Hillary Clinton, Donald Trump, the Democratic Party, or the Republican Party the intention to help or hurt people who did or did not warrant this treatment; or, alternatively, the intention to help themselves (that is, the politicians or the party's own members alone), or to help special interests. Thus, 65 percent of the respondents appear to have been using good intentions as heuristics for desirable results or bad intentions as heuristics for undesirable results. An additional 34 respondents referred to one or the other candidate's bigotry. Arguably, this, too, constitutes a use of the bad-intentions heuristic, with a candidate's hostility to minorities serving as a proxy for the intention to work against their interests. If we count the bigotry responses this way, then a grand total of 269 respondents, or 75 percent of the 361 being analyzed, used good or bad intentions as heuristics, exactly as in 1956.[88]

Similarly, survey research undertaken by Sean Freeder in 2015–2017 finds that "a rough majority of citizens attributes negative motives to political outgroups, broadly construed (e.g., people who differ in terms of vote choice, partisan affiliation, or policy preference)," and that, "while ingroup motive judgments are almost universally positive, assumed outgroup ill-intent is commonplace."[89] These results were based on asking a group of survey respondents to provide the reasons people might have for disagreeing with them about various political issues, or for identifying with the other political party. (A separate group was provided a fixed list of such reasons, including both intentions- and non-intentions-based reasons; the results were the same.) Additionally, Freeder showed experimentally that "the impact of motive attribution on outgroup affect appears to be equal to or larger than that of position distance," meaning that people seem to care more about the other party's members' putative motives in favoring a given policy than they care about the policy itself.[90] This may seem irrational on its face, an example of psychological "identification" with the in-group and hostility to the out-group, but not if people lack strong opinions about specific policies, as we saw was the case in 1956. If people see society as simple in that they are unaware of the hard, technical issues that are raised in policy debate—for example, issues relating to unintended consequences—it would stand to reason that the most important thing about political actors is their intentions,

---

[88] In contrast to 1956, however, only seven respondents, or 2 percent, made retrospective references to the actual results that had been achieved by either party or candidate. (In 2016, unlike 1956, neither candidate was an incumbent.) An additional 20 respondents in 2016, or 5.5 percent, were classified as "ideological or near-ideological," corresponding to Level A, on the basis of using abstract, ideologically relevant terms such as "socialism." The remaining 70 respondents (19 percent) gave only unclassified responses, often regarding candidates' qualifications for office or endorsements of the policies a candidate supported, but not including references to ideology, intentions, or results. I thank Eli Davey for doing this research, and Matt Grossmann for getting me the raw 2016 ANES data.

[89] Freeder 2018, 6.

[90] Ibid., 26.

not the particular policies they advocate, as good intentions should lead to good policies in the end. By the same token, one's own political views can be policy-free because they are grounded in good intentions. Besides, if bad intentions are responsible for unsolved social problems, one would expect those with these intentions to be deceptive. They might *say* they are for beneficial policies even while they end up breaking their campaign promises—itself a trope that is consistent with the simple-society ontology.

Laboratory experimentation on "the illusion of explanatory depth" likewise suggests the presence, in the subjects who participated, of the good-intentions heuristic, and its possible connection to both a bias for technocratic action and a simple-society ontology. Philip M. Fernbach, Todd Rogers, Craig R. Fox, and Steven A. Sloman significantly reduced subjects' stated support for various public policies merely by asking them to explain the mechanisms by which they would achieve their intended results. By contrast, subjects did not lose confidence in their policy opinions when they were asked to state their *reasons* for them—i.e., the ends the policies were intended to achieve.[91] Fernbach et al. explain this contrast by speculating that when subjects were asked about mechanisms, they recognized the (ontic) complexity involved and wisely lost (epistemic) confidence in their policy opinions.[92] (The fact that they did not lose confidence when asked about their reasons suggests that they did not suspect that "the right answer" was to report lower confidence upon merely being challenged in any way by the researchers.) Thus, it seems that before being asked about it, the subjects were radically ignorant of how their favored policies might work, as we would expect of citizen-technocrats who tacitly accept a simple-society ontology. Contemplating such a society, one would default in favor of action because—so long as a proposed policy is well intended—there would be no reason to worry about whether its mechanisms will produce bad consequences. The subjects' undiminished confidence after they were asked about the intended goals of a policy rather than the means by which they would be achieved suggests, therefore, that they unwittingly treated a policy's perceived intention as a proxy for its results.

6.5.1. The Bad-Intentions Heuristic in Action

Hibbing and Theiss-Morse write that, as their respondents see it, "interest groups are invariably evil, and Congress's members are evil for being in any way associated with them."[93] "A popular myth," they note, is "that if members of Congress listened to the people rather than to the special interests, most disagreements would magically disappear."[94] As one of

---

[91] The policies were unilateral sanctions on Iran for its nuclear program, raising the Social Security retirement age, a single-payer health care system, a cap-and-trade system for carbon emissions, and merit-based pay for teachers (Fernbach et al. 2013, 941).

[92] Ibid., 940.

[93] Hibbing and Theiss-Morse 1995, 147.

[94] Ibid., 19.

their respondents put it, congressional representatives "may have good intentions, but when they get in there it's like a corrupt system. They have to start going alone against the whole works, you know."[95]

Special interests exemplify bad intentions by definition, as they work for their own good, not that of the public. Fully 86 percent of the respondents to a 1992 survey conducted by Hibbing and Theiss-Morse agreed that "Congress is too heavily influenced by interest groups when making decisions."[96] In a 2001 poll, 65 percent of the respondents said that "officials choose to follow what special interests want."[97] A 2010 survey showed that 78 percent "believed the government to be run by a few big interests, not for the benefit of the people."[98] Such results stand to reason if the public is using the bad-intentions heuristic. This possibility puts Lupia's finding about Proposition 100 in a new light. The 48 percent shift in public opinion can be accounted for by attributing to respondents the use of the insurance industry's presumed bad intentions as a heuristic for sociotropically undesirable results.

The importance and scope of the bad-intentions heuristic are suggested by Trump's 2016 campaign, in which he claimed that he was "self-funded" and thus immune to the corrupting power of special interests, as well as the campaign of his apparently polar opposite, Bernie Sanders, who accepted only small campaign contributions for the same reason. But this is not a recent development. As late as five months before the 1992 presidential election, the polls showed independent candidate Ross Perot substantially ahead of both President George H. W. Bush and his Democratic challenger, Arkansas Governor Bill Clinton. Perot's campaign later self-destructed, but for a long stretch he proved to be a far more credible and successful candidate than Trump was at comparable points in his campaign.[99] Perot was charismatic and funny, he was willful and "strong," and unlike Trump, he could not plausibly be accused of racism, sexism, ignorance, or stupidity. But he was explicit about his epistemically naive model of social problem solving, where Trump was merely suggestive. Perot, he told his audiences, would simply go to Washington, "look under the hood," and "fix" whatever was broken. Perhaps equally important, he was, like Trump, a billionaire. In a 1992 Harris poll, 55 percent of all respondents agreed that Perot would not "be influenced by the special interests who make big campaign contributions."[100]

---

[95] Ibid., 100.

[96] Ibid., 64. We need not assess whether these suspicions are warranted. Very few citizens have any direct contact with what goes on in Washington, so they cannot know whether their suspicions are warranted. The question, then, is what accounts for their suspicions, not whether or not they are accurate.

[97] Roper 2001, 18.

[98] Galston 2010.

[99] *Time* 1992.

[100] Hibbing and Theiss-Morse 2002, 143.

6.5.2. *Irrationality or Intentions Heuristics?*

People's use of good and bad intentions as heuristics would explain certain anomalies in the public-opinion literature that have increasingly tempted political scientists to attribute irrationality to vast numbers of their fellow citizens. One of these anomalies is the "inverted" relationship between many voters' surveyed policy positions and those of the candidates and parties they support. When informed that their party or candidate supports a policy with which they disagree, such voters alter their position to conform to that of the party or candidate, rather than using independently arrived-at policy positions as criteria for judging a candidate or party.[101] Inverted issue positions are often taken to show that voters "rationalize" their issue positions to match those of politicians—to whom, it is therefore assumed, the voters must be groundlessly, irrationally loyal.

An interpretively charitable take on inverted policy stances would start from the fact that many voters seem to be indifferent about the policy instruments through which politicians "get things done," but not at all indifferent about *what* they get done. (This would be consistent with the unimportance of issue positions to the vast majority of *American Voter* respondents.) As Hibbing and Theiss-Morse put it, "people tend to believe that all policy solutions driven by a concern for the general welfare (rather than special interests) are more or less acceptable, or at least not worth arguing about."[102] "They want to see certain ends [achieved]—such as a healthy economy, low crime rates, good schools—but they have little interest in the particular policies that lead to those ends."[103] They care about solving problems, in other words, more than they care about *how* to solve problems—because, once again, they assume that how to solve them will be self-evident (at least until someone such as Fernbach asks them how the problem would be solved).

If citizen-technocrats tacitly assume that, insofar as politicians intend to solve social problems, it will be easy for them to come up with effective ways of doing so, it would follow that if a politician is well intentioned, she can be delegated the task of sitting down and figuring out which solutions should be adopted. After all, there would be no need for elected representatives, or so the thinking seems to go, if the people themselves had the time to sit down and think about public policy. Hibbing and Theiss-Morse's *Stealth Democracy* assembles an impressive array of evidence suggesting that this thinking is widespread. The voter's main function, in this view, is to suss out the politicians' intentions, especially by judging whether they are tools of special interests—not to do the politicians' policymaking job for them. In this light, it is rational for such voters to adjust whatever policy views they express, when questioned by survey researchers, in accordance with the views of politicians whom they trust: that is, politicians who seem to have good intentions.

---

[101] See Lenz 2012 and Achen and Bartels 2016, ch. 2.
[102] Hibbing and Theiss-Morse 2002, 9, my emphasis.
[103] Ibid., 13.

Use of the intentions heuristics may also shed light on seemingly irrational framing effects. In an influential paper, Bartels noted that in various surveys, "the proportion saying that too little was being spent on 'solving problems of big cities' exceeded the corresponding proportion [saying that too little was being spent on] 'assistance to big cities'" by 25–31 points in surveys conducted in 1985, 1986, and 1987; that "63 to 65 percent said that too little was being spent on 'assistance to the poor,'" while only "20 to 25 percent of the respondents in each year said that too little was being spent on 'welfare'"; and that "the proportion of the public saying too little was being spent on 'dealing with drug addiction'" exceeded "the corresponding percentage proportion [saying that too little was being spent on] 'drug rehabilitation'" by an average of nine percentage points.[104] While Bartels conceded that respondents might rationally perceive a difference between drug rehabilitation and dealing with drug addiction, he could not persuade himself that the apparently large framing effects observed in the other cases were rational, since "assistance to big cities" and "solving problems of big cities" seemed to him equivalent, as did "welfare" and "assistance to the poor"—which, he emphasized, refer to "the *same* set of programs and policies."[105] The paradox is resolved, however, if we notice that in each case, the framing that mentioned the general problem-solving intention of a policy got much more support than the framing that mentioned the specific policy by means of which the general intention was to be achieved—an example, perhaps, of the phenomenon explored by Fernbach and his colleagues.

6.5.3. *What It Means for Radically Ignorant Citizens to "Use" a "Heuristic"*

As these examples should remind us, it is important to avoid the mistake of attributing our own opinions or (putative) knowledge to those whose opinions we are analyzing, a phenomenon we might dub "reverse *Verstehen*." Reverse *Verstehen* is the master error of rational-ignorance theorists (who attribute to the public the theorists' own knowledge of the low odds that a single vote will matter), neoclassical economists, behavioral economists, and naively realistic social psychologists. To ensure that I have not made a similar mistake in analyzing the opinions of radically ignorant voters, it may be worth clarifying what it means to say that they are "using" intentions as "heuristics" for results.

In rational-ignorance analysis, the use of heuristics is a deliberate decision made by citizens attempting to economize on knowledge. To be sure, this may sometimes happen. Some voters using the intentions of California insurance companies as a negative heuristic for the results produced by Proposition 100 probably said to themselves, "I'll bet those damned insurance companies intend to rip us consumers off, so I don't need to find out what Prop 100 would do; I can just vote the way the insurance companies don't want

[104] Bartels 2003, 58–59.
[105] Ibid., 59.

me to vote." But a *radical*-ignorance analyst would not insist on such deliberateness in the use of heuristics. We need not imagine, therefore, that the 75 percent of *American Voter* respondents who discussed the good or bad intentions of parties and candidates said to themselves, "I don't need to pay attention to the unintended consequences discussed in policy debate; I can simply try to discern the intentions of political actors and use them as proxies for policy consequences." While citizen-technocrats can use the good- and bad-intentions heuristics in that way, they can also use them even if they are unaware of the existence of policy debate (and are therefore ignorant of their ignorance of its content); and, more generally, even if they are unaware that they lack necessary technocratic knowledge (including knowledge of unintended consequences). If they are unaware that they lack it (or need it), it stands to reason that they will also be unaware that they are using the knowledge that they do have (or think that they have) about political actors' intentions as, *in effect,* a proxy for the knowledge they lack. The good- and bad-intentions heuristics can thus be used inadvertently, without knowing that one is "using" heuristics at all.

The same applies to the simple-society ontology. I infer the tacit presence of such an ontology from people's apparent propensity for technocratic action even when they seem to lack knowledge of policy mechanisms, from their apparent use of intentions as heuristics, and from their apparent technocratic voluntarism. Although, in conversation with someone who partakes of the naive technocratic worldview, one might be able to elicit explicit declarations of belief that are consistent with the ontology, and with the other elements of the worldview, none of these elements would normally operate at the explicit or conscious level. Unlike interpretively uncharitable understandings of the unconscious level, however, this understanding of it is predicated on the assumption that those who partake of the worldview unconsciously *could*, if prompted, explicitly acknowledge the tacit elements of the worldview, as there is nothing irrational or even illogical about them. Thus, lacking an understanding of how societal complexity might confound reliable technocratic knowledge—which is to say an understanding of how a complex societal ontology might produce epistemic problems, such as those that might obscure the consequences of a technocratic policy—people would have little reason to treat those consequences as difficult to discern; and therefore little reason to imagine a disconnect between technocratic will and technocratic results, that is, between the intended results of technocratic action based on goodwill, or ill will, and the actual effects of the action.

Thus, for them to think and behave *as if* they were naive technocratic realists, *as if* they had a technocratic action bias, *as if* they were technocratic voluntarists, and *as if* they were using intentions as proxies for technocratic results would be entirely reasonable, even though they may not, and probably do not in most cases, understand themselves to be doing this. They are not, after all, thinking about "technocracy" and the complications that might be posed for it in an epistemically complex society, nor about the unpredictable ideational heterogeneity that causes the complexity, any more than, in deciding whom they should vote for, they are thinking about the odds that their vote will be decisive. Thus, if one tacitly accepts a naive technocratic worldview predicated, logically but only implicitly, on a simple-society ontology, one can "use" heuristics such as those I have discussed even if one is unaware that one is doing so or, indeed, that one is subscribing to such a worldview in the first place.

6.5.4. Resolving Some Riddles of Public Ignorance

One puzzle that might be solved by people's acceptance of a naive technocratic worldview is that "nonattitudinal citizens," in political science jargon—citizens whose political attitudes seem to fluctuate almost randomly over time—are nonetheless able to vote nonrandomly; and are able, when asked, to express nonrandom political opinions. They might simply be indifferent to most of the policy issues about which surveys ask them, because they treat the answers to policy questions as easy for politicians to answer but beyond their own purview. Thus, they might not care very much about the surveyed questions and thus, in answering them, are buffeted about by whatever bits of information they happen to have recently heard about the policies.[106] Another, not-incompatible, explanation is that even when they do care, they are so open-minded that they are able to motivate "genuine" opinions on the basis of these slight gusts of information, but that these opinions are so shallowly rooted—as they are not grounded in a self-reinforcing base of ideologically selective information—that they can change if the next gust of information is blowing the other way.

"Nonattitudinal" citizens, then, may simply be those who have a lower information base than more dogmatic citizens; accordingly, their minds (about intentions and any other seemingly relevant factor) would more easily be changed from moment to moment. Thus, we might understand Donald Trump as a classic nonattitudinal citizen (on most, but not all issues; immigration and trade would be exceptions). Although he naively equated his every opinion with indisputable truth, these opinions were so frequently based on slender evidence, or none at all, that he was able to abandon them more easily than has any politician in living memory, reversing course at the drop of a hat again and again due to something he had learned from (or had heard asserted by) the last person to wander into the Oval Office, or an item he had read in the most recent issue of the *National Enquirer*, or a sound bite from that morning's episode of *Fox & Friends*.

The bigger puzzle, to which both rational-ignorance theory and radical-ignorance theory attempt to provide a solution, is why such citizens think they need so little knowledge to motivate their political opinions—"little" and "important" from the perspective of rational-choice theorists, scholars of public opinion, or normative theorists of democratic technocracy. Unlike rational-ignorance theory, radical-ignorance theory answers

---

[106] See Zaller 1992, ch. 4. The idea of nonattitudinal citizens stemmed from Converse's finding that non-ideological citizens tended not to hold consistent issue positions over time (Converse 1964).

the question without projecting onto politically ignorant voters the knowledge that their votes do not matter, and, therefore, without projecting onto them the logically incoherent decision to underinform themselves before nonrandomly voting. Instead, the theory suggests that their epistemic standards are very low (from the perspective of others) because they assume that social problems are simple enough to be easily understood and fixed. Being radically ignorant of the question of whether technocratic policies will yield the intended results, they believe that, to vote sociotropically, all they must know is, for example, what those intended results are—knowledge that, they might assume, can be inferred from (putative) knowledge of politicians' intentions, or those of partisans, or of interest groups, or even the intentions inscribed in the titles of technocratic measures, such as the No Child Left Behind Act.

Ignorant citizen-technocrats who are in this sense radically ignorant (ignorant of their need for, and ignorant of their lack of, the four types of technocratic knowledge) would see most of the vast universe of information about public affairs as irrelevant to the task of voting. Therefore, instead of trying to arbitrate the difficult, contested technical claims made in policy debate—about which, a fortiori, they are probably unaware—such citizen-technocrats would be expected to think, and to think almost exclusively, about whether a given politician seems to be concerned about herself, her comfort, her salary, her perks, and the demands of special interests; or, instead, whether she seems to care about the public interest, or such proxies for it, or components of it, as the interests of "people like me," or the interests of the middle class, the working class, the common man, or even the disadvantaged. That is all they would think they need to know.

This is not to say, however, that only the intentions heuristics, or intentions-related heuristics such as party labels, can solve the puzzle of the ignorant citizen-technocrat. Retrospective voting is another rational heuristic for a voter deemed ignorant by political epistemologists of technocracy, but who has a simplistic understanding of modern society. There may well be others, such as the nationalist us/them binary, that enable people to take technocratically oriented political action and hold technocratically oriented political opinions while being innocent of technocratic knowledge.

6.5.5. *Technocratic Debate, Moral Conflict, and the Transformation of Means into Ends*

An additional empirical puzzle that might be solved, in part, by radical-ignorance theory is political enmity. If technocratic issues can be settled by simply determining which side favors sociotropic ends, then technocratic politics takes on the appearance of a moral battle over ends, not a debate over difficult-to-parse means. Indeed, those who insist that it is the latter may appear to be not just obtuse, but to be actuated by the evil intention to disrupt the problem-solving process by derailing it into technical discussions—or by the intention to remove power from the hands of the people, who obviously know what to do (since the solution to social problems is self-evident), only to place it in the hands of "elites." Such people do not merely disagree about an opaque reality; indeed, since reality is not opaque enough to foster disagreement, they do not actually disagree. They deliberately favor what they know is wrong. Such people *deserve* enmity or even hatred.

Consider President Trump's speculation that the "caravan" of Central American migrants that "threatened America" before the 2018 midterm elections may itself have been paid for by liberal financier (and cosmopolitan elite) George Soros.[107] Assuming for the sake of argument that Trump supporters' opposition to open borders was, as they claimed, based not on xenophobia but on concerns about the effect of illegal immigrants on such social problems as drug trafficking and unemployment, blaming the caravan on Soros would have transformed what in their eyes had been a technocratic issue into a battle of good Americans such as themselves against uncaring elitists such as Soros, who (for some reason) did not want these problems to be solved. Similarly, opponents of minimum-wage increases frequently portray the proponents as mouthpieces for labor unions' relatively well-paid members, rather than as activists who actually care about low-wage workers.[108] The opponents' contention is that minimum wages keep low-wage workers from getting jobs that would put competitive downward pressure on the wages of better-paid, unionized workers, such that the self-interest of the latter is the only conceivable reason that anyone would want higher minimum wages. In cases such as these, technocratic debates over policy effects are transformed into controversies over the intentions of those on "the other side." A similar transformation is brought about when minimum-wage proponents insist, as did the Senate majority leader in 2014, that "it's about whether or not it is right that people who are working 40 hours a week get a fair shot at being able to provide for their families."[109] This moralized framing of the issue enables citizen-technocrats to make decisions about the question without considering, or even being aware of, such data as those contained in the scores of dueling studies of the effects of the policy discussed earlier. A side effect is to cast those who disagree with them as unjust or simply evil. Yet, from a purely technocratic perspective, the moralized framing is indefensible. The desirability of a specific policy instrument designed to solve, mitigate, or prevent a social or economic problem depends on the instrument's actual effects. While it is indeed unjust for people to have to work for low wages, this does not make into a matter of right the adoption of any specific policy intended to rectify the injustice. If raising the minimum wage in a specific time and place had the effect, on balance, of hurting the low-paid workers who were supposed to be helped, no sociotropic citizen-technocrat should support the measure, regardless of whether the ability to work at a living wage is a right.

However, it seems to be easier to mobilize people by contending that a policy is just or unjust in itself than by making complicated, technical claims about its empirical effects

---

[107] Samuels 2018.

[108] E.g., Gómez 2018.

[109] Peters 2014.

for good or ill. Thus, politicians who trade in complicated, technical claims about public policy are less likely to be successful, ceteris paribus, than politicians whose rhetoric transforms such claims into nonnegotiable moral demands; the same goes for politicians who depict their opponents as having base motives rather than as disagreeing with them on technocratic grounds. In the charged environment created by such politicians, even the most dispassionate observers may understandably tend to feel that they are getting to the real essence of what is (in reality) technocratic politics if they see it as a clash of good and evil rather than as a rhetorically disguised wrangle over technical details. This feeling may even persuade them that technocratic politics, and technocratic polities, are not technocratic at all.

This is not, of course, to say that all politics *is* technocratic, even in a fundamentally technocratic polity. Politics is not technocratic when minority rights are at stake, for example, or when other nonnegotiable demands are at stake—that is, when the consequences of meeting these demands do not matter.

6.6. SYSTEMIC PRESSURES IN A DEMOCRATIC TECHNOCRACY

> In a modern society ... citizens' total experiences are disparate enough for their judgments to diverge, at least to some degree, on many if not most cases of any significant complexity.
> —JOHN RAWLS, *Political Liberalism*

My analysis of citizen-democrats' heuristics and biases may seem to contradict Chapter 3's argument about the heterogeneity of human ideas. If citizen-technocrats' heuristics and biases are (presumptively) heterogeneous, how can we draw reliable conclusions—and sweeping conclusions, at that—from interviews with a few thousand people conducted in 1956 and 2016, or from opinions expressed in focus groups in 1992 and 1998? Similarly, the evidence I have presented comes solely from the United States. Surely things may be different elsewhere. And if the conclusions I drew are to be incorporated into a normative political epistemology of technocracy, would they not be functioning as predictions about the ideas of future citizen-technocrats about whose ideas we know next to nothing?

While such qualms are always appropriate when one purports to describe the opinions of millions of anonymous others—even when one is not trying to predict their future behavior—cultural homogenization through mass education and media messaging may in some cases justify sweeping conclusions such as the ones I have drawn, with due allowance for the fact that any two citizen-technocrats are as unlikely to have identical webs of belief as are any two economic actors. So long as we are not attempting to forecast behavior, the heterogeneity of the beliefs of those being analyzed is less important than otherwise, as the putative soundness of the analysis remains even if the number of people to whom it applies cannot be specified, nor the resulting actions (such as whom they might vote for) predicted. Thus, the enterprise of mass opinion analysis may be as worthwhile as (if far less precise than) the enterprise of intellectual history. While the results of the enterprise as a whole are untrustworthy, a given analyst may hit upon the truth occasionally, so it is no more senseless to set oneself the goal of trying to understand in outline form the "mentalities" that govern public opinion in a given time and place than to set oneself the goal of trying to understand what, say, Rousseau meant when he wrote that one can be forced to be free—even though any particular answer is likely to be wrong. (It is the same with policy debate: any given policy analyst can try to set herself the goal of discovering the true effects of a policy, even when this requires predicting behavior. Although the additional epistemic burdens entailed by novel circumstances, heterogeneous agents, and time's arrow further reduce the chances of reaching the truth, this merely diminishes the legitimacy of the "system" of technocracy, which depends upon discovering *which* policy analyst's prediction is correct; it does not necessarily debunk any particular prediction.)

However, for the normative theorist of technocracy, as opposed to the empirical political epistemologist, there is another reason to engage in an analysis of heuristics, biases, and ontological assumptions such as the one I have set out thus far: namely, that widespread acceptance of these heuristics, biases, and assumptions would seem to be preconditions for the production and reproduction of a democratic technocracy, *given* an electorate that (on the whole) lacks the four types of technocratic knowledge. Nothing is to say that such a democratic technocracy will exist in a given time and place. But to the extent that it does exist, its citizen-technocrats *must* rely on assumptions or heuristics that so simplify the world of public affairs that they feel equipped to carry out their perceived function in that world despite their dearth of technocratic knowledge. The simple-society ontology, the action bias, technocratic voluntarism, the intentions heuristics, and naive technocratic realism itself are ideal for doing just that. Moreover, to the extent that they are in play, they would constitute efficient ideational causes of pathological responses to the (figurative) pressure to predict policy effects; such responses would tend to ensure that judicious policy making is not engaged in. If we do not acknowledge the epistemic complexity of modern society, we cannot possibly recognize its (putative) ontological source in unpredictable ideational heterogeneity, and thus we cannot attempt to take this heterogeneity into account.

One task of empirical evidence in a normative theory of technocracy, then, is to suggest the concrete form that abstract possibilities such as these may take in the real world. The more questionable task, that of the empirical political epistemologist, is to discern if they *do* take such forms in a given time and place; yet it is a task that may produce real insight, despite the unreliability of the enterprise as a whole. On January 20, 2017, it does seem (to this observer) as if a randomly selected voter of the sort long feared by empirical scholars of American public opinion—a voter with virtually no knowledge of public affairs and no awareness that he needed it—had been parachuted into the Oval Office. If we set ourselves the goal of understanding why this happened, it may be useful to hypothesize that for at least some voters, the reason was Trump's loudly proclaimed intention to fight stubbornly for "the American people" against the creatures of the Washington "swamp"—lobbyists, criminals, and globalist elites, that is, enemies of the self-evident interests of the American people.[110] Voters may rationally gravitate to portrayals of the world in such simplistic, Manichaean terms if they assume that a good (and strong) will is all that matters in making wise public policy, because there are no inherent barriers to accomplishing whatever such a will might choose to accomplish; and if they assume that bad wills must be responsible for social problems or for their persistence because, the truth about social problems being self-evident, only such wills could be blocking the problems' solution.

6.6.1. An Optimistic Scenario

Citizen-technocrats who use intentions as heuristics for results are not taking very seriously the possibility of unintended consequences, if they are considering this possibility at all. And if they do not think they need to know much beyond political actors' intentions, the other types of technocratic knowledge are likely to go missing too, even if they are made available for citizen-technocrats to "consume." Real-world citizen-technocrats' heuristics and assumptions, then, as much as real-world epistocrats' methods and assumptions, seem for all the world as if they were deliberately designed to perpetuate a dysfunctional "system." But, of course, they were not. Epistemic pathologies are the products of human ideas, not of metaphorical systems. So, as with a judicious epistocracy, one hope for a judicious democratic technocracy lies in the fact that ideas may change.

However, bracketing ideational change for a moment, it is possible to piece together an optimistic picture of future possibilities predicated on the radical-ignorance interpretation of really existing democratic technocracy.

For one thing, even if they are not sufficient, good intentions will probably be an important component of a judicious technocracy in most cases. Intentionally aiming at a sociotropic target is a good start on judicious technocratic policy making. Of course, one also needs to know where the target is and how to hit it, but in this regard it is not unimportant that citizen-technocrats are, by virtue of their stipulated ignorance relative to epistocrats, less likely to be dogmatic, at least according to the spiral-of-conviction model. The Fernbach experiment suggests the salutary effect that can be expected from an open mind when it comes to technocratic issues. Even though, prior to the experiment, the subjects seem to have used the good-intentions heuristic to choose which policies to support, their confidence in these policies was deflated by asking them to explain how they would work, and such deflation would be a prerequisite to judiciously exploring whether a proposed policy mechanism would be likely to have the intended effects. In addition,

---

[110] Of course, this speculation not only ignores the possible role of racism and sexism in Trump's victory, but the role of his opposition to "political correctness." This is to say that technocratic politics is only one of the threads of democratic politics in the real world, and that in any given case it may not be the most important thread. That depends on the heterogeneous ideas of the electors interpreting the choice before them.

it is conceivable that citizen-technocrats' molding by mass culture might provide them with reliable insights into the expected behavior of the targets of technocratic regulation, at least in some cases. Alerted (somehow) to the need to examine policy mechanisms, citizen-technocrats might simply ask themselves how they themselves would respond to a given policy, X. Their own self-knowledge might provide reliable predictions of how the targets of X would respond, assuming that the targets share with citizen-technocrats behavioral homogeneities, such as those that might be effected by shared norms communicated through mass culture. By drawing on their own exposure to mass-mediated norms and other mass-mediated ideas, citizen-technocrats might be better able to identify ideational homogeneities than epistocrats are, inasmuch as the latter may be distanciated from these cultural currents by their specialized training. Citizen-technocrats might also be better placed to gauge the strength or weakness of such norms and ideas, not merely their prevalence. There may, then, be a role for the "common sense" of the "common man" in the making of technocratic policy.

Yet there are some obvious problems with this scenario.

First, even accepting the premise that citizen-technocrats have privileged insight into certain behavioral regularities, this may not matter in a great many cases, such as when bankers or airline pilots are being regulated, as opposed to when "ordinary" people similar to citizen-technocrats are being regulated. Moreover, determining the boundaries around those objects of technocratic regulation who do and do not match the ideas of "ordinary" people would itself be a difficult, perhaps insurmountable task, equivalent to reading the minds of agents whom the citizen-technocrats have not met and who may not even exist yet.

Second, the premise itself is questionable, because the source of the insight is supposed to be citizen-technocrats' participation in mass culture. Culture is multifarious and subject to idiosyncratic interpretation; even if it is the source of homogeneous behavioral norms to which citizen-technocrats have privileged access, they may nonetheless disagree among themselves about the existence and content of these norms (not merely their reach), and disagreement entails that some or all of the resulting technocratic ideas would have to be wrong.

Disagreement, in turn, would create a third problem: deciding among the divergent views. This is a democratic analogue to what I have been calling the problem of epistocratic identification: when epistocrats disagree, how can they decide who in their number to trust? The same type of problem would occur once citizen-technocrats disagreed with one another about behavioral norms or, indeed, about any other aspect, or perceived aspect, of technocratic policymaking.

Fourth, even if citizen-technocrats sometimes have privileged access to knowledge of relevant behavioral regularities, this knowledge would bear only on whether a given policy would be efficacious (Type 3 knowledge) and, perhaps, on whether it would produce unintended consequences (Type 4 knowledge). Even if they could derive such knowledge from their own experience of mass-mediated behavioral norms or other ideas, they would continue to lack knowledge of whether a social problem is widespread and serious (Type 1) and knowledge of what has caused it (Type 2). Such knowledge can, even in the best-case scenario, reach citizen-technocrats only after having been mediated by fallible, stereotype-driven human beings such as journalists.

Being inexpert themselves, moreover, journalists would have to relay this information from putative experts who, being heterogeneously fallible interpreters of a complex reality, are likely to disagree among themselves. Journalists as such are unqualified to adjudicate disputes among experts; and if journalists differ about which information to relay to the public, the citizen-technocrat will be unqualified to adjudicate which journalists are relaying reliable information. These variants of the problem of epistocratic identification—which were suppressed, to some extent, in the mid-twentieth-century days of media oligopolies—have broken out across the world with the multiplication of competing media outlets and sources that all claim to offer the unvarnished truth, despite offering contradictory information and contradictory interpretations of it.

In this context, it will not do for us to advise citizen-technocrats simply to pick real experts and legitimate media sources over fabulists, propagandists, and trolls, since the truth of a given expert's expertise and the legitimacy of a given media source are the very points at issue. If these things were self-evident, fabulists, propagandists, and trolls would have no audience. Media consumers are caught in the conundrum of the radically ignorant. Indeed, inasmuch as all experts and all mediators are biased in one way or another, owing to the need to winnow down overabundant information by interpreting it, it is part of the human condition to be caught in the conundrum of the radically ignorant. This is to say that, lacking effective omniscience, we cannot know whom to trust. We may rightly assume that some experts are more expert than others, some sources more trustworthy, but as a practical matter, the only way to judge which is which is to look for congruence of one kind or another with our own webs of belief. This is true even if we turn to heuristics such as academic pedigree, which resonate or fail to resonate based on one's ideas about the probative value of such heuristics and the legitimacy of the academic disciplines, such as economics, that confer them. These ideas are likely to have been shaped by the very types of expert or source that they then pick out as trustworthy, creating the real possibility of a closed loop that confirms a pseudo-reality that we confuse with the unvarnished truth.

Fifth and finally, naive technocratic realism may easily lead to polarization among citizen-technocrats. If we see the technocratic other as someone who is denying the *self-evident* truth, then this other—whether a politician, an expert, a journalist, or a next-door neighbor—"presents himself," as Lippmann wrote, "as the man who says, evil be thou my good. . . . Rarely in politics or industrial disputes is a place made for him by the simple admission that he has looked upon the same reality and seen another aspect of it. . . . Thus . . . out of the opposition we make villains and conspiracies."[111]

---

[111] Lippmann [1922] 1997, 83.

6.6.2. *Naive Technocratic Ideology*

Polarization, like dogmatism, is not inherently pathological, from a technocratic perspective—where all that counts is whether the enacted policies do more harm than good. On its face, it is neither here nor there if the process of enactment leads citizen-technocrats to hate each other, unless this eventuates in outright civil war (which would be a serious social problem indeed).

Bracketing the possibility of civil war, however, polarization can have knock-on effects that are technocratically problematic. For one thing, polarization can cause political grid-lock, as is so often feared, and this could hinder the enactment of the judicious tech-nocratic solutions that, in the optimistic scenario, citizen-technocrats might be able to endorse. In addition, polarization can, in conjunction with the bad-intentions heuristic, inspire citizen-technocrats to become knowledgeable enough to be victimized by spi-rals of conviction. A nonattitudinal, open-minded citizen-technocrat who is radically ignorant of societal complexity, but who becomes aware of conflict among technocratic experts, or journalists, or other citizen-technocrats, might simply be mystified and alien-ated by the spectacle. How, she may wonder, can people disagree about what should be self-evident, namely, how to solve her fellow citizens' problems? The same citizen, how-ever, once armed with the bad-intentions heuristic, might be moved to want to know which of the contending parties has self-interested motives that would explain a con-flict that by all rights should not exist. This appears to be recognized by politicians who transform technocratic disputes over means into battles of good against evil. They find it easier to motivate political action by getting people angry at those with whom they disa-gree than by getting them to think about complicated policy mechanisms and uncertain policy effects. In turn, a side effect of citizen-technocrats' anger may be a burning interest in learning more about the evildoers.

As they gain such knowledge, or putative knowledge, initially open-minded citizen-technocrats might become members of a particularly pathological subspecies of "epis-tocrat" by virtue of a spiral of conviction—if they are able to find some interpretive framework for assimilating this knowledge. The bad-intentions heuristic itself might give them such a framework, serving as the crowning posture of what we might call a naive technocratic ideology (as opposed to worldview). In such a belief system, disagree-ment would be explained by the ability of bad actors to cloud people's recognition of self-evident solutions to the people's problems. This ideology could enable its adepts to acquire esoteric knowledge, but it would primarily be knowledge, or putative know-ledge, about politics rather than policy—yet knowledge that, in appearing to shed light on bad motives, would seem adequate (if one is a naive technocratic realist) to determine positions on policy questions. Consider the California voters who thought that their knowledge of the insurance industry's opposition proved that Prop 100 warranted their support. They seem to have inferred their policy position solely from political know-ledge (or pseudo-knowledge) of the industry's motives, with no knowledge of what the proposition would have done, let alone knowledge of the costs and benefits of doing it. Knowledge of the motives of the technocratic other can be expected to give previously disengaged citizen-technocrats the sense that now, they finally understand what is really going on in the opaque world of politics. But in the process, it can be expected to generate spirals of conviction that deprive the affected citizens of their former, pre-epistocratic open-mindedness, even as it also leaves them without the technocratic knowledge they actually need.

Another route from polarization to dogmatization might run, not through the greater political knowledgeability attendant upon interest in learning about evildoers, but the self-righteousness attendant on viewing oneself as fighting them. In such a battle, one may well feel entitled to reject whatever one's opponents say, on the grounds that it is obviously false—given the self-evident truth of one's own position. This attitude would have the effect of inflating a citizen-technocrat's confidence in what she perceives to be true, even if these perceptions are poorly grounded in either technocratic *or* political "knowledge."

6.6.3. Journalists and the History of Their Ideas

Since these dark scenarios are predicated on citizen-technocrats' use of the bad-intentions heuristic, it might be thought that they could be forestalled if the journalists who mediate knowledge of disagreement made sure always to depict it as stemming from each side's perception of what Lippmann called "a different set of facts." Even though this policy would have the effect of portraying some dishonest cases of policy debate as if they were honest, the noble lie might be worth telling, from a technocratic perspective, if it prevented polarization and thus dogmatism.

If this were to work, however, it would require that journalists themselves refrain from using the bad-intentions heuristic. There are at least two reasons to think that this is probably unrealistic. First, journalists are drawn from the general population. Whatever beliefs or assumptions might lead ordinary citizens to use various heuristics should lead journalists to do so as well, ceteris paribus. Second, there is reason to think that journalists will be particularly prone to using the bad-intentions heuristic, because there is reason to think that they will self-select for naive realism.

A presupposition of nonopinion, nonpartisan news journalism is that it is possible to perceive and convey to the reader the truth, untainted by bias. Journalism is, effectively, an ongoing process of fact transmission and fact checking, with all the epistemological naiveté one would expect of an enterprise in which discrete and unambiguous "facts" are the coin of the realm. Such journalism must downplay the journalist's interpretive role in selecting which facts to present (or to check) and the journalist's interpretive role in establishing criteria of these facts' importance (or truth).[112] Journalists, then, are likely to be naive technocratic realists of both the first- and third-person varieties. They should,

---

[112] See Uscinski and Butler 2013.

ceteris paribus, tend to self-select for the belief that they can discern "the facts"; and when the facts do not seem self-evident to them, they should tend to assume that they are self-evident to someone else: the expert, whom journalists treat as having a direct line to the truth.

This speculation is borne out historically. The ideal of objective news journalism seems to have originated in the naive technocratic realism of the Progressive Era. As Michael Schudson's history of American journalism puts it, "Reporters in the 1890s saw themselves, in part, as scientists uncovering the economic and political facts of industrial life more boldly, more clearly, and more 'realistically' than anyone had done before. This was part of the broader Progressive drive to found political reform on 'facts.'"[113] When Dewey advocated "the news as truth," he was pushing on a wide-open door; journalists were already doing their best to achieve this ideal, as illustrated by the muckrakers and photojournalists whose works were so influential in the Progressive Era.

The naively technocratic historical origins of modern journalism do not entail that journalists must have remained naively technocratic down to the present day, but there is little reason to suspect any significant break with the past. Nonopinion journalists in the United States give every indication of viewing themselves as neutral mediators of the facts, even when reporting on complex policy questions. Thus, in reaction to Trump's aspersions on their motives, veracity, and biases, and in response to the explosive growth of alternative sources of "news," mainstream journalists rarely contended that they had superior *methods* for unearthing the truth (such as patient investigative journalism); instead, they tended to portray themselves as worthy of trust simply because of their dedication to reporting "the truth" (that is, their *intention* of reporting it), such that Trump and the alternative sources were cast as being opposed to reporting the truth (rather than being ignorant of what it was). Mainstream American journalists during the twentieth century, too, seem to have found themselves puzzled by the very accusation of bias. No such first-order accusation can be adjudicated by a political epistemologist, but political epistemologists are entitled to say, for second-order reasons, that bias is baked into the human interpretive condition. Thus, while in a given case we cannot know a priori what the bias is (or what the biases are), or whether it produces an interpretation that distorts reality—a bias might coincide with the truth—we *can* know that there must be bias of some kind; otherwise, a journalist would be unable to decide which news is newsworthy and how to report it. Yet in response to the accusation of bias, American journalists typically say that their professional standards require them to check their biases, if any, at the office door. These standards, which also originated in the Progressive Era, presuppose that bias is voluntary and can be shed like a raincoat. The standards themselves, then, are naively realistic.

---

[113] Schudson 1978, 71.

It is a short step from naive journalistic realism to the bad-intentions heuristic. If the facts are self-evident, political conflict over factual questions—which are, by definition, always the questions at issue in technocratic policy debate—must stem from "willful ignorance" (the "akratic" version of motivated reasoning) on one or both sides of a given conflict, or else from a confrontation between those with good intentions and those with bad ones—who must be *lying* about the facts. Both possibilities impute bad motives to one or the other side, even if only the bad motive of ego defense.

Journalists drawn from the culture of a democratic technocracy, who have also self-selected for naive realism, are thus unlikely candidates to defuse the bad-intentions heuristic. Admittedly, one might recruit journalists who were not intelligent enough to notice a conflict between, on the one hand, the tolerant message that all parties to disagreement are seeing different sets of facts, and, on the other hand, the ethos and practices of their trade, which presuppose a society so simple that it presents itself to journalists (and the experts they quote) as a self-evident collection of checkable facts. But these unintelligent journalists' tolerant message to their audience would be undercut by the same presupposition on the reader's side: that following the news will convey the "factual" knowledge needed to understand a simple society. If that is the case, identifiable journalists or experts can understand it and pass this understanding on to us. But this would make it mysterious, to us, why anyone could disagree with the facts thus transmitted to us—sending "us" down the road toward hating "them." If, on the other hand, one is persuaded that the facts are selected by fallible interpretations and are, therefore, contestable, then there would be little reason to follow the news, as one would recognize that the news will inevitably deliver biased information, and that one would have no way to determine if the bias is accurate in a given case.

A related consideration should be mentioned. In the optimistic scenario, I assumed that citizen-technocrats could be pulled back from their overreliance on the *good*-intentions heuristic if they were simply asked to think about policy mechanisms, à la Fernbach et al. However, someone would have to ask them to do that. Given the epistemic naiveté that would seem inherent in nonopinion, nonpartisan journalism, it seems likely that the task would fall either to opinion or partisan journalists or to politicians, parties, interest groups, or experts who oppose a particular technocratic measure that seems destined to prevail (unless they intervene) because it taps into voters' good intentions. Consider, for example, Trump's proposal to "build a wall," which, at least arguably, played on its supporters' sociotropic intention to protect "America" from drugs, crime, and unemployment. Opinion journalists and Democratic politicians rushed to point out the needlessness, unfeasibility, and high cost of this proposal, making classic technocratic knowledge claims. Yet their intervention, rather than deflating Trump supporters' support for the wall, sparked a backlash of accusations against these "elites'" partisan (or "globalist") motives in attempting the deflation. Had Fernbach and his colleagues asked people to think about the mechanisms of the policies they favor even as protestors in the hallway shouted that the psychologists were bad actors bent on reducing the subjects' enthusiasm for measures that would obviously advance the public good, the outcome of the experiment might not have been so encouraging.

6.6.4. No Exit

There might be another path to the deflation of the bad-intentions heuristic. This would be to criticize the naive technocratic worldview (as opposed to the naive technocratic ideology) of which both of the intentions heuristics may be seen as components.

An ideology enables the ideologue to accumulate a knowledge base that confirms its crowning postures, producing dogmatism about them as a side effect. In contrast, a *worldview*, as I have been using the term, is a bundle of logically related positions, some or all of them tacit, that *can* have a dogmatizing effect if it becomes the interpretive basis of information gathering (that is, if it becomes an ideology), but can otherwise merely have the effect of creating latent predispositions toward certain conclusions that, in the limit case, are not supported by any information at all. Insofar as the intentions heuristics, the action bias, and technocratic voluntarism presuppose a simple-society ontology, one can "use" the resulting worldview as the basis of a naive technocratic ideology. But one can also use it to motivate technocratic opinions in the absence of almost any technocratic *or* political knowledge, as so many uninformed voters seem to do.

Consider the *American Voter* interviewees one last time. Not only were most of them innocent of left- or right-wing ideology, but they also did not seem to be using idiosyncratic ideologies of their own devising. Converse established this by showing that they were nonattitudinal and thus lacked the intertemporal issue constraint that we would expect any ideology to impose. Since their issue positions fluctuated almost randomly over time, it would appear that there was no ideology to "constrain" them. Moreover, inasmuch as these citizens were, on the whole, politically ignorant, no ideology seems to have enabled them to accumulate much political knowledge. Yet they were able to vote and hold definite political opinions, primarily (it appears) by using the intentions heuristics; and as we have seen, they also seemed unaware of the possibility of either unintended policy consequences or justified political disagreement. Thus, the voters appear to have assumed that society is so simple that intentions track results, and so simple, too, that technocratic disagreement is anomalous. Their radical ignorance of the possibility of disagreement may have been reinforced by their apparent unawareness of the mediation to them of their own opinions—naive realism in the classic sense discussed in Chapter 1. Thus, they seem to have been both classic naive realists and adherents of the naive technocratic worldview—but not adherents of a naive technocratic ideology, because they were, by and large, adherents of no ideology.

For the most part, dogmatism should make it hopeless to argue with adherents of an ideology. In a longitudinal study of 1,528 gifted students over the course of 37 years, only two respondents (0.01 percent) "changed from being a strong ideologue on one side to being a strong ideologue on the other" (although 13 percent moved from strong left or right positions to the center).[114] Given the dogmatizing functions of ideology, it would be unreasonable to expect otherwise. How, after all, can anyone persuasively criticize an entire web of beliefs and all the supporting evidence it has screened in? Even if one were to criticize its crowning postures effectively, the subsidiary beliefs and data screened in by them would persist, as would the conclusions whose sources have been forgotten. In contrast, the adherents of the naive technocratic worldview may change their minds frequently, as Converse showed. Given their open-mindedness, it might be possible to demonstrate to them that modern society is complex enough that results do not necessarily track intentions. By deflating the intentions heuristics, this demonstration might prevent them from becoming polarized and hence dogmatic.

However, those who engineered this demonstration would have to be motivated by the conviction that the naive technocratic worldview is a danger in the real world of democratic technocracy, and this conviction would entail putative second-order knowledge of that world. Thus, the naive technocratic worldview would have to be criticized by those whose own, putatively sophisticated alternative worldview would itself probably be an ideology that had enabled them to gather the necessary critical information, and in sufficient abundance that they would want to engage in political debate about the inadequacies of the naive worldview.[115] Just as deplorably, it seems likely that in response, naive technocratic ideologues would arise to attack the motives of the critics, leading the critical ideologues to counterattack.

The two sides in this political war would not be evenly matched. Naive technocratic realism has been abroad for more than a century, and the intentions heuristics seem to be much older. Western culture has, for thousands of years—since the spread of Christianity, if not Roman Stoicism—lavished praise on good intentions while condemning bad ones. A measure of the profound effect these traditions have had on us is that the previous sentence has a certain absurd ring to it—as if praise of good intentions and condemnation of bad ones must be rooted in historical tradition rather than in common sense or the nature of morality. Yet reflection on Greek philosophy and non-Christian cultures reveals, I think, the falseness of our reflexive idea that worrying about people's intentions— let alone fixating on them, as we so often do—is natural.[116]

While, as a matter of logic, the assumption of a simple society may undergird both naive technocratic realism and the intentions heuristics (as well as technocratic voluntarism and a bias for technocratic action), as a matter of history, it is unlikely that

---

[114] Sears and Funk 1999, 14.

[115] Perhaps I have fallen victim to such an ideology; or perhaps I have managed to escape a spiral of conviction through a lack of rigor in policing my web of beliefs. But any ideologue would think that he has escaped the spiral somehow. Another possibility is that I have not escaped the spiral, but that the beliefs reinforced by this particular spiral are true.

[116] This is not to suggest that Greek *politics*, as opposed to Greek philosophy, was free of a strong concern with motives.

very many people have been taught the simple-society ontology, which almost nobody explicitly avows. A great many do, however, explicitly avow the bad intentions of their political opponents, and the Fernbach experiment suggests the pivotal role that their own good intentions may play in their technocratic thinking. When the intentions heuristics were exported from the West's moralistic, Christian culture into technocratic politics, they may have given rise to the tacit inference that the society whose problems needed to be solved is a simple one, one in which the problems will succumb to goodwill—unless impeded by bad will. If this historical speculation is roughly accurate, anyone attempting to deflate the naive technocratic worldview would find herself facing down an imbricated, intertwined, interrelated complex of pervasive cultural influences that would seem to be difficult or even impossible to uproot. But if it *could* be uprooted, it would require a cultural revolution—not mere tinkering with, say, the messages sent by journalists.

6.6.5. *The Hobson's Choice of Technocracy*

Having now put on the table both causes for hope and causes for concern, we may be able to sort out the prospects for a judicious technocracy, either democratic or epistocratic, given all the factors discussed in Part II.

First let us consider the role of naive realism. I hope to have established, in Part I, the default expectation that human behavior will be unpredictable, which might constitute a prima facie case for the illegitimacy of technocracy—if not for the possibility that heterogenizing factors such as superordinate norms or mass acculturation might make people reasonably predictable. Technocrats who attempted to seize upon such factors, however, would need to treat unpredictability as the default and show that, case by case, they had identified exceptions to the rule. This is a tall order, perhaps one that cannot be achieved in many or most cases. But what we seem to find in really existing technocracies is widespread ignorance that any such achievement is necessary. Consequently, both epistocrats and citizen-technocrats are prone to one or another pathological means of oversimplifying a complex reality, and in the United States, at least, this often means that they are naive realists. However, the object of naive realism seems to differ as between contemporary US epistocrats and citizen-technocrats.

Among citizen-technocrats, it often seems to be naively but tacitly assumed that technocratic policies will achieve the intended results (and only those results). This assumption, in turn, implies a tacit ontology of societal simplicity (and the attendant worldview). Without such an ontology, or one equally incompatible with epistemic complexity, the radically ignorant citizen-technocrat would not be able to form opinions about either particular technocratic policies or the parties and politicians entrusted with choosing them. She would then select herself out of the pool of citizen-technocrats by refusing to vote and by answering DK/NO in opinion surveys.

Thus, it is not surprising that in at least one real-world democratic technocracy, there seems to be abundant evidence that, among those who do feel able to motivate non-random technocratic votes and opinions, there is indeed (a fortiori) radical ignorance of technocratic knowledge, coupled with apparently widespread naive technocratic realism. Citizen-technocrats often seem to think that all they need is simple heuristic information, such as information about whether politicians have wills good (and strong) enough to aim public policy in a sociotropic direction. This thought, like any ideational phenomenon, might be undermined by an ideational shift. But the dimensions of such a shift, involving, as it would, a repudiation of intentions heuristics that seem tightly and extensively woven into our moralistic culture, would be so great as to offer even less hope than there might be for a shift away from naive realism of the sort displayed by neoclassical economists and behavioral economists.

The latter type of naive realism, however, is not naive *technocratic* realism, at least in the United States. Among US economists, epistemic naiveté concerns not the policies to be recommended but the situation facing the agent whose actions the policymaker needs to predict. This form of naive realism, which we can call naive *epistocratic* realism, injudiciously effaces the complications introduced by agents' idiosyncratic, heterogeneous ideas. A judicious epistocrat would have to address those complications directly and locate a source of homogenizing control over agents' actions, such as superordinate behavioral norms. But an ideational shift away from naive epistocratic realism might enable epistocrats to arise who can do this because they are adequately sensitive to agents' unpredictable ideas and potentially unpredictable actions. Another such shift might overturn positivism, which also effaces agents' unpredictably heterogeneous ideas. These ideational shifts would not be as far-reaching as a shift away from our moralistic culture, so a judicious epistocratic culture might be more readily attainable than a judicious democratic technocracy.

However, such a culture would have to be cordoned off from the general culture that fosters the naive technocratic worldview and, in particular, from the intentions heuristics. If the good-intentions heuristic shaped epistocrats' webs of belief, they would find themselves unable to take seriously the very idea of unintended adverse consequences. If the bad-intentions heuristic shaped them, they would tend to produce morality tales in place of sound technocratic analyses. This—not just training in the incentives-matter tradition—may have been part of what was happening when neoclassical economists leapt to the conclusion that greedy bankers *deliberately* took the risks that caused the financial crisis. Of course, even if epistocrats could, à la Plato, be sequestered from birth against the wider culture they would attempt to manipulate, this would weaken their ability to understand those they were attempting to manipulate.

Even if epistocrats were to be cordoned off from, or were to experience ideational shifts away from, naive epistocratic realism, positivism, and the elements of the naive technocratic worldview that they might have absorbed from the wider culture, epistocratic judiciousness would face the hurdle of dogmatism, a pathological response to the "systemic pressure" for confidence in one's policy judgments. In epistemologically individualistic terms, the self-selection of overconfident epistocrats would tend to be ensured (although it would not be guaranteed) by their success in competition with other epistocrats in policy debate. The mechanism creating such epistocrats' dogmatism, as I have suggested, might be the spiral of conviction rather than motivated reasoning. Dogmatism would arise as citizen-technocrats gained expertise, removing them from the ranks of the ignorant but also the ranks of the open-minded. Epistocrats might also be plagued by spirals of conviction arising from ideologies they imbibe or concoct separately from their epistocratic training, such as political ideologies. Dogmatism would seem to be a robust problem for epistocracy that might never be overcome systemically, even if it can be overcome, to varying degrees, by individual epistocrats. The systemic problem would be how to identify the latter without overcompensating by selecting for those who are relatively open-minded merely because they are too ignorant or unintelligent to be dogmatic. On the other side of the ledger, citizen-technocrats, as distinct from epistocrats (by definition), will tend to be open-minded only insofar as they are ignorant, and thus unaffected by spirals of conviction. The only systemic way to fill their knowledge gaps—without expecting them to become epistocrats while somehow *avoiding* spirals of conviction— would seem to be through a bootstrapping operation such as journalism, which we have reason to think will not be reliable.

And so we seem to face a dilemma: Would we rather be ruled by epistocrats who are relatively well informed but doctrinaire, or by citizen-technocrats who are relatively open-minded but ignorant? While *democratic* theorists have, in effect, proposed a variety of external reasons to choose the second horn of the dilemma, if we consider the matter using exclusively technocratic normative criteria, it is a choice that, at best, must leave us searching for an alternative.

PART III

Exitocracy

ASSUMING THAT THE arguments of Parts I and II hold, they leave us with (at least) three quandaries.

The first is that it may be impossible to determine whether a technocracy transformed by the hoped-for, ideationally sensitive approach to public policy could reasonably be expected to pass the test of doing more good than harm (regardless of whether the technocrats tended to be dogmatic). Even were they judiciously attentive to ideational heterogeneity, would technocrats, on the whole, be able to overcome the problems identified in Part I sufficiently to reduce the magnitude of their errors to an acceptable level? No matter how persuasive one finds the critique of injudicious technocracy offered in Part II, it does not establish the magnitude of the relief that would be afforded by a judicious alternative.

Nor, second, does either Part I or Part II establish the magnitude of the unintended consequences we can expect from an *in*judicious technocracy. This is, in part, because of my self-denying ordinance against making first-order technocratic claims. If there is a *second*-order method of determining the frequency and the severity of injudicious technocratic errors (as distinct from the frequency of unpredictable ideational heterogeneity), I cannot imagine what it is. For example, we cannot appeal to disasters unintentionally caused by really existing technocracy (e.g., the financial crisis, according to some of the claims about counterintuitive unintended consequences listed in Chapter 1) without begging the question of the reliability of our knowledge of the technocratic origin of these disasters. It is one thing to recognize that technocracy—whether judicious or not—*could* cause disastrous unintended consequences, or merely negative consequences that incrementally add up to more harm than good. It is another thing to point to specific undesirable conditions and blame them on technocracy, which would seem necessary if we are to judge the magnitudes on either side of the ledger. That would entail making question-begging first-order judgments. Nor can we, conversely, argue that the "clear" benefits of really existing (injudicious) technocracy outweigh its unintended costs without again begging the epistemological question.

Moreover, even if we were to relax the constraint against first-order arguments, there is little reason to think that lessons we might derive from the past are applicable to the future. Suppose that, both in perception and in reality, the benefits of really existing technocracy have outweighed the costs thus far. A string of enormous technocratic failures (or putative failures) might then cause us to become overly pessimistic, conflating several one-off catastrophes with a systemic tendency. Only after even more time had passed might we be able to determine, retrospectively, whether this newfound pessimism had been justified, in that an interim run of technocratic success (or good luck) might now seem to call for optimism. But that, too, might prove illusory; ad infinitum. Retrospection cannot answer the magnitude question, then, even if it could tell us whether technocracy in the past did pass the cost-benefit test.

Thus, the magnitudes on both sides of the ledger—the magnitude of the costs and benefits of judicious technocracy and the magnitude of the costs and benefits of injudicious technocracy—appear to be imponderables.

The third quandary is that even if we were to conclude that either injudicious technocratic action or technocratic action of all kinds is illegitimate on internal grounds, technocratic *inaction* is not necessarily a logical alternative. "Inaction" is as much a choice as action is. "Doing nothing," that is, leaving the status quo as it is, holds no inherent epistemic advantages over "doing something" unless the status quo has some inherently beneficial epistemic property in comparison to technocratic action. If it has no such property, then doing nothing cannot reasonably be expected to minimize adverse consequences, which may stem from inaction as easily as from action.

Suppose that US foreign policymakers, aware of the difficulty of predicting the outcome of any war, had chosen to do nothing after Pearl Harbor. Nazi Germany and Imperial Japan might have won World War II. Every technocratic "intervention" has a rationale akin to the one for entering World War II. In every case, technocratic actors believe that there is a social problem against which "state" action is likely to be effective, and the costs of which are likely to be outweighed by the benefits. Although such action may cause adverse side effects, as we have seen, an adverse side effect of inaction—among others—is that the social problem may fester. If there were a reliable means of determining that the costs of letting identified social problems fester are lower than the unintended costs of intervening, we could decide in favor of inaction or, in the context of "the state," in favor of "laissez-faire" as a general policy position. But I know of no such means.

As a way around these quandaries, Chapter 7 will attempt to think through an alternative to really existing technocracy that I will call exitocracy. An exitocracy would facilitate forms of action that are based on the exit mechanism—which, I will argue, *does* possess inherently beneficial epistemic properties. Thus, the ideal type of an exitocracy can resolve the third quandary by providing an alternative to both technocratic action and technocratic "inaction": exitocratic action. The comparative nature of this use of exitocracy, as an ideal type, will also resolve the first two quandaries by allowing us to judge both judicious and injudicious technocracy comparatively rather than absolutely. That way, we do not have to try to divine the magnitude of the costs and benefits of either type of technocracy. We have obvious reason to prefer judicious technocracy *relative to* injudicious technocracy, even though we cannot know the magnitude of relief from error offered by judicious technocrats. Thus, the epistemic case for exitocracy can establish a hierarchy of legitimacy: exitocracy is preferable to judicious technocracy, but judicious technocracy is preferable to injudicious technocracy. However, this does not entirely dissolve the problem of magnitudes, to which I will suggest that the solution may ultimately be to reconceive the nature of the critique of technocracy I have offered.

In the ordinary run of often repeated decisions the individual is subject to the salutary and rationalizing influence of favorable and unfavorable experience. . . . And so it is with most of the decisions of daily life that lie within the little field which the individual citizen's mind encompasses with a full sense of its reality. Roughly, it consists of . . . the things under his personal observation, the things which are familiar to him independently of what his newspaper tells him.

—JOSEPH A. SCHUMPETER, *Capitalism, Socialism and Democracy*

Choice in the political arena generally involves decisions among alternatives whose consequences tend to be quite remote, both in time and in space. When you buy a pair of shoes, you quickly discover through wearing the shoes and later comparative window-shopping whether your decision was an optimal one. The feedback is direct and immediate.

—SHAWN ROSENBERG, "Against Neoclassical Political Economy"

7

Capitalism, Socialism, and Technocracy

IN THIS CHAPTER, I will use Albert O. Hirschman's distinction between exit and voice to argue that exit-based action, along with other individual actions in the "private sphere," while imperfect at best, may better solve social problems than would voice-based technocratic action in the "public sphere," even if such action were undertaken judiciously. My analysis will aim to show that the ability to exit from a given situation is desirable—from a technocratic point of view—because it allows the exiting individual to improve on a personally unsatisfactory state of affairs without understanding the society-wide significance or cause of the problem, without knowing the efficacy of a society-wide solution, and without weighing the costs and benefits of such a solution. The individual, I will maintain, is likely to have a *relatively* reliable, and corrigible, understanding of the effects of a solution on her own well-being. This makes exit-based actions less epistemically demanding than technocratic actions, by and large (with exceptions to be discussed). It comes down to the difference between judging, and improving upon, one's own pinching shoes and judging, and improving upon, the shoes of an entire population of anonymous others.

Power Without Knowledge. Jeffrey Friedman, Oxford University Press (2019). © Oxford University Press.
DOI: 10.1093/oso/9780190877170.001.0001

Exit, however, is not a substitute for attempts to address social problems. It is a way to address them more effectively than through what Charles Lindblom and David Cohen once called "deliberatively cooperative problem solving through thought or analysis"[1]— that is, public, collective, or "political" problem solving by means of the voice mechanism.[2]

Section 7.1 compares "exitocracy" and technocracy conceptually. Section 7.2 provides an epistemological critique of Hirschman's development of the exit/voice dichotomy. This critique allows us to see that epistemically, the public and private spheres are asymmetrical, with the public sphere hobbled by its reliance on voice-based macro-solutions that necessarily block exit-based micro-solutions. Section 7.3 considers a second advantage of the private sphere, contingent not on its use of the exit mechanism but on its epistemically superior use of voice. Section 7.4 examines some of the epistemic limits of the exit mechanism. Section 7.5 discusses the need for wealth redistribution in the interest of maximizing exit opportunities across a given population. Section 7.6 asks whether even an exitocracy would be prone to worsening the human condition rather than bettering it.

7.1. A REVISED STANDARD OF TECHNOCRATIC LEGITIMACY

An exitocratic government would unquestionably be a state. But it would differ from a technocratic state—judicious or injudicious—in that, instead of attempting, case by case, to produce solutions to any and all social problems that might arise, its cardinal goal would be to provide a framework within which individuals could attempt to solve— or, better, escape—the problems that afflict them as individuals, whatever their origin (society-wide or not). Where this is possible, such a state would allow exit to trump technocratic voice. What would remain of technocracy would be the attempt to provide public goods, including those that are foundational to a private sphere in which individuals using exit can flourish.

We might say, then, that exitocracy is an unusual or "extraordinary" version of technocracy, one that attempts to forego, wherever possible, the frontal analytic assault on social problems, society-wide, that typifies "ordinary" technocracy, whether judicious or injudicious. Instead, exitocracy favors indirect maneuvering in the private sphere, primarily but not solely by means of the exit mechanism.

To make this type of maneuvering possible, an exitocracy would need to undertake the traditional liberal project of enacting coercively enforced rules that create a capacious private sphere. An exitocracy would also need to undertake wealth redistribution far more ambitious than a universal basic income—redistribution along the lines of Rawls's Difference Principle—to make the exit mechanism accessible to all. Both of these liberal projects would be justified by the role that the exit mechanism can play in people's

---

[1] Lindblom and Cohen 1979, 24.
[2] Ibid., 30.

attempt to alleviate the problems that affect them personally or those whom they know intimately well.

Because of its ambitious redistributive agenda, an exitocracy can be considered a form of socialism. However, inasmuch as people would be able to profit by providing goods and services that may (in effect) help other people to solve their own problems through the exit mechanism, an exitocracy would also have a capitalist dimension. Both the socialist and the capitalist aspects are captured by H. L. A. Hart's distinction between "power conferring" and "duty imposing" laws.[3] An exitocracy is a regime in which the policies of government are, wherever possible, power conferring—or, more conventionally put, where the policies are conducive to roughly equal positive freedom, with exceptions covered by something like the Difference Principle; but where the rationale for these policies is not a liberal goal, such as the maximization of freedom or equality as an end in itself, but the technocratic goal of minimizing human distress. By conferring equal power on people to solve their problems in the private sphere, an exitocracy would live up to the egalitarian premise of all forms of utilitarianism and of socialism, too. But the use of the exit mechanism would depend on the availability of more than one option, and multiple options might be provided by heterogeneous capitalists, as we will see.

Because both its capitalist and socialist elements would be in the service of people's ability to solve their problems, exitocracy provides a point of comparison against which the legitimacy of both injudicious and judicious ordinary technocracy can be internally assessed. Rather than trying to judge whether technocracy does more harm than good according to negative-utilitarian standards, we can ask whether ordinary technocratic actions, judicious or injudicious, are likely to do more good according to those standards, or less harm, than the individual actions facilitated by a power-conferring exitocracy. More simply, we can ask if actions in the private sphere would tend to be epistemically superior in achieving the negative-utilitarian goal of technocracy in comparison to the voice-based public-sphere problem solving on which ordinary technocracies rely. If the answer is yes, then we can judge ordinary technocracy, judicious and injudicious alike, as illegitimate according to its own standards, even as we keep in mind that judicious technocracy is preferable to the injudicious kind. We can reach these conclusions without having to know the magnitude of the adverse unintended consequences of judicious or injudicious technocratic actions, or, on the other hand, the degree to which these actions achieve their intended objectives. Thus, we may be able to say that, in light of the interpretive difficulties that would face even judicious technocrats, ordinary technocracy is, comparatively speaking, illegitimate.

In anticipation of these results, we can now revise the preliminary internal criterion of technocratic legitimacy that I set out in Chapter 1. Rather than holding technocracy to the standard of doing more good than harm—which would require that we calculate

---

[3] Hart 1961, 94 and *passim*.

unknowable magnitudes—we should ask instead whether technocracy can be expected
to do more good, or less harm, than exitocracy.

7.2. EXIT AND VOICE

In the decades that have passed since the appearance of Hirschman's *Exit, Voice, and
Loyalty* (1970), commentators have been so taken with its counterintuitive defense of
voice, and thus of democratic politics, that the logic of this defense seems to have escaped
critical scrutiny. So, too, has the narrowness of Hirschman's perspective on exit, according
to which it should be evaluated as a means of improving the performance of institutions.
If, instead, we care about improving the well-being of the people served by institutions,
we will need to consider the epistemological advantages of exit over voice—advantages
to which Hirschman was altogether insensible.

However, before considering the exit side of the comparison, we need to notice that
Hirschman offers a number of quite different characterizations of voice. These can be
arrayed from thick to thin, revealing that only the thinnest plays a non-rhetorical role in
Hirschman's attempt to make the comparison.

The thickest version of voice is what Hirschman calls "political action par excellence."[4]
The thinnest is the communication of the bare fact that the voice user is unhappy about
something, as when a customer complains about an unsatisfactory product or service.
In the latter case, voice is merely "a signal that something has gone awry."[5] This is the
only type of voice that Hirschman's argument actually defends. Hirschman's loyalty to
anything thicker, including the type of voice that is ideally exercised in a democratic technocracy, is merely gestural. Indeed, the minimalism of his argument is in line with the
view that democratic technocracy asks too much, epistemically, of citizen-technocrats.
The agents who actually do all the epistemic work for Hirschman are the equivalent of
epistocrats. Crucially, however, their knowledge is stipulated, not demonstrated.

Hirschman's argument for thin voice is that the inconsequential signal sent by a lone
customer voicing a grievance would be amplified significantly if all the other unhappy
customers were blocked from using the exit mechanism. For example, if the company
with which they were unhappy was a state-sanctioned monopoly from which exit were
effectively forbidden, collective voice might outperform exit—judged by the standard of
improving institutional performance—by prompting such a loud chorus of protest that
the monopoly would have to change its ways. Democratic voice, then, is effective when
it is thin but loud.

Nevertheless, Hirschman insistently mentions thicker variants, as in several references
to "the art of voice."[6] This art, he says, is integral to democracy, for it allows the citizen to

---

[4] Hirschman 1970, 16.
[5] Ibid., 26.
[6] Ibid., 43.

"express his point of view," not merely to telegraph his unhappiness with goods or serv-ices.[7] Indeed, in opening the book, Hirschman equates voice with "the articulation of one's critical opinions" (and thus with "political action par excellence").[8] Yet he refrains from introducing thick voice into his formal argument. The value of thick voice, from a technocratic point of view—Hirschman's point of view—depends on whether those whose opinions are voiced know what they are talking about. If the voiced opinions were to go beyond statements of unhappiness, if they were to articulate theories about the scope of the problems, their causes, or how to solve them, the agents using voice would, whether they know it or not, be talking about things that Hirschman gives us no reason to think they can reliably know. Thus, beyond the sheer noise of their complaints, it would be advisable, technocratically, to disregard their voices—if there is a relatively re-liable alternative source of knowledge, which Hirschman assumes that there is: experts.

7.2.1. Voice, Incentives, and the Imputation of Knowledge

Mark Warren points out that Hirschman saw exit as, at best, "incentiviz[ing the] respon-siveness of [institutional] decision makers to those they claim to serve or represent."[9] Economists more orthodox than Hirschman had long taken a similar tack. They had argued, as Hirschman put it, that the threat of consumer exit will "keep a firm 'on its toes'"; and that, if the threat of exit fails to incentivize a firm to be responsive to con-sumer demand, an exodus of consumers will lead the firm's managers "to make a major effort to bring performance back up to where it should be."[10]

In making such arguments, Hirschman's predecessors had ignored the question of how a firm's managers would know how to bring performance back up to where it should be. That is, they had assumed the managers' effective omniscience. In arguing for the su-periority of voice over exit, however, Hirschman makes the very same assumption. His voice-friendly conclusion is at odds with those reached by his more orthodox colleagues, but he reaches it for the orthodox reason that voice produces a more effective *incentive* for managerial performance than does exit. This is an entirely non-epistemological ar-gument, or anti-epistemological argument, in that it treats the necessary knowledge as given and imputes it, as if by magic, to the managers—who need only be roused, by a loud chorus of complaint, to exert their wills to implement this knowledge.

Hirschman was a development economist before he turned to social theory and intel-lectual history. Accordingly, he fleshes out his argument by contending that state-owned enterprises, such as those in the Global South, could (paradoxically) enhance their re-sponsiveness to consumer needs by legally blocking their customers' exit from their

---

[7] Ibid., 32.

[8] Ibid., 16.

[9] Warren 2011, 692.

[10] Hirschman 1970, 3.

products. For example, he recounts his surprise at the failure of the Nigerian national rail-road to improve its miserable service despite successful competition from private buses and trucks. "The presence of a ready alternative to rail transport," he concludes,

> makes it less, rather than more, likely that the weaknesses of the railroads will be fought rather than indulged. With truck and bus transportation available, a de-terioration in rail service is not nearly so serious a matter as if the railways held a monopoly for long-distance transport—it can be lived with for a long time without arousing strong public pressure for the basic and politically difficult or even explo-sive reforms in administration and management that would be required. This may be the reason public enterprise, not only in Nigeria but in many other countries, has strangely been at its weakest in sectors such as transportation and education where it is subject to competition: instead of stimulating improved or top performance, the presence of a ready and satisfactory substitute for the services public enterprise offers merely deprives it of a precious feedback mechanism that operates at its best when the customers are securely locked in.[11]

The missing feedback mechanism is voice. Customers who exit from the subpar railroad do not bother to voice complaints about its service. But if the customers have no alter-native to using the rails because the exit option (the use of buses and trucks) is blocked, they will "raise hell" in protesting poor rail service, incentivizing the railroad's managers to deliver "improved or top performance."[12]

Because Hirschman does not specify the nature of the messages voiced by the angry customers, this scenario may suggest the operation of a thicker variant of voice than a mere signal of dissatisfaction—an epistemically richer variant that might inform manage-ment of the source of the problem or even how to solve it. And when initially describing the effects of exit and voice, he says that in response either to exiting customers or to those who stay and raise hell, management may "*search for* the causes and possible cures,"[13] implying that, as yet, management does not know what the causes and cures are, and also implying, perhaps, that the opinions of the customers may help managers to learn what needs to be done. However, contradicting this rhetorical recognition of managers' need to learn something, Hirschman's formal exposition of the comparative logic of exit and voice starts from the assumption that in performing badly, managers are *not* ignorant of anything they need to know, which implies that in trying to improve institutional per-formance, they will not need to learn anything from their customers' opinions or from any other sources. Thus, he stipulates, without explanation, that "the performance of a firm or an organization is assumed to be subject to deterioration for unspecified, random

---

[11] Ibid., 44.

[12] Ibid., 45, 44.

[13] Ibid., 4, my emphasis.

causes which are neither so compelling nor so durable as to prevent a return to previous performance levels, provided managers direct their attention and energy to that task."[14]

Indeed, the book's raison d'être is to grapple with the putative fact that initially satisfactory "organizations in general are subject to *lapses from* efficient, rational, law-abiding, virtuous, or otherwise functional behavior." Hirschman's task, he tells us, will be to explain how society can "marshal from within itself forces which will make as many of the faltering actors as possible *revert to* the behavior required for its [society's] proper functioning."[15] Therefore, his starting point is (1) an unexplained functional level of managerial performance. Then comes (2) an equally mysterious fall into anomalously poor performance. Once the decline has set in, the tendency of management is (again mysteriously) (3) "toward flaccidity and mediocrity" until (4) hell-raising customers jolt it to do what it already knew how to do in stage (1).[16]

Stage (3) is more important than it might seem, because it guarantees that subpar performance will not be mysteriously resolved by a random, positive performance fluctuation to match the negative one that inexplicably reduced the organization's performance. In stage (3), dysfunction continues, potentially forever, because of managers' (unexplained) laziness.[17] Laziness is a favorite neoclassical explanation for nonoptimality because laziness means, by definition, that there must be inadequate incentives. To target laziness is to assume that "incentives matter"—all the more so when, thanks to Hirschman's initial stipulation, all other factors are effaced, such that nothing else can be said to matter in a predictable fashion. What is left over—the effect of incentives—*does* matter, and in a predictable fashion, if one ascribes continued suboptimality to laziness, for one then presupposes the lazy actor's effective omniscience, and thus the predictable optimality of her behavior once she stops being lazy. The problem, then, is how to end the laziness by increasing incentives for optimal performance. Once she is adequately incentivized, she will do what the economist thinks she should have been doing—and what she knew she should have been doing—all along. The sole function of voice, in Hirschman's formal analysis, is to provide the needed incentive.

For Hirschman, then, the efficacy of voice is parasitic on the assumption that the truth is manifest to institutional managers. Angry customers change the incentives facing lazy managers (as opposed to ignorant ones), reviving the "energy and attention" that once animated them, such that, without having learned anything except that their customers are angry, they return their institution to "previous performance levels."[18] In a moment, we will consider a different possibility: that angry customers will have no effect on performance, because suboptimality indicates the managers' ignorance of what to do.

---

[14] Ibid.

[15] Ibid., 1.

[16] Ibid., 59.

[17] Ibid., ch. 5.

[18] Ibid., 4.

7.2.2. Why Exit Can Work Better Than Voice

Hirschman's scenario, so constructed as to make incentives the only analyzable variable, obscures the possibility that in the real world, exit can produce salutary benefits by allowing people to escape from social problems—regardless of whether this has any effect on institutional incentives and regardless of whether it improves institutional performance.

Consider the competition that Hirschman deplores for diminishing consumers' incentive to protest against poor managerial performance. He ignores the fact that in the reality of Nigeria as he presents it, competition solved or mitigated the social problem caused by poor managerial performance—regardless of whether the poor performance was caused by laziness or by ignorance. The exit mechanism allowed former railroad customers to use their knowledge of the fact that they were experiencing problems with the railroad to take advantage of competing modes of transport. In turn, their knowledge of the superiority of the competitors was also experiential. This knowledge allowed them to improve their situations, even though it did not improve the performance of the railroad.

For our purposes, this is important because the former customers' experiential knowledge of the personal significance of the problems they had been experiencing, and of the effects of the solutions they discovered by using the exit mechanism, was reliable relative to the interpretively fraught Type 1 and Type 3 knowledge they would have had to use if they had been put in charge of the railroad, which would have required them to gauge the significance of the problems, and the efficacy of solutions, for thousands or millions of anonymous others. Moreover, to come up with these solutions, they would have needed to know the cause of the problems, and to evaluate them, they would have needed to know the unintended costs of the solutions for those anonymous others and for still other people who were not railroad users but were affected by the solutions. All four types of technocratic knowledge, then, would have been required of them. By using exit, in contrast, the former railroad customers put to good use accessible and relatively reliable knowledge, solving or mitigating their own problems even if they had little idea what had caused them, what their global solution might be—or (an important qualification to which we will return) what the effect on anonymous others of their own use of exit to solve them might be. Thus, if we drop Hirschman's arbitrary attribution of knowledge to the managers, the former customers may be said to have commanded more reliable problem-solving (or -mitigating) knowledge than is likely to be possessed by any given group of technocrats, including managerial specialists.

It may seem, however, that I am withholding effective omniscience from the railroad's managers only to smuggle it into the heads of whichever competitors offer better service. How do the competitors know how to solve the railroad's problems (in effect)?

There is in fact no reason to think that they know this in general, such that we could say, of any given competitor ex ante, that she is more likely to solve the problem than the railroad's managers are. The epistemic advantage of economic competition is not that any identifiable capitalist is less fallible than any other, or that capitalists, as a group, are less fallible than technocrats, as a group, but that capitalism allows more than one fallible solution to be tried concurrently, with those affected by the problem using personal experience to judge which of the competing solutions is relatively acceptable. The former railroad customers are the arbiters of the success of the competitors, which they judge using their relatively reliable knowledge of whether their discomfort has been relieved by Bus Line A or Truck Line B. The fallibility and ignorance of any given competitor does not matter, from a negative-utilitarian perspective, so long as their customers can use the exit mechanism to go from goods and services they dislike to those they like. The essential requirement, then, is that there be diversity in the options available to consumers, based on diversity in various competitors' fallible ideas about what consumers need and will be willing to pay for. The same applies to diversity in the options available to workers, based on diversity in various fallible employers' ideas about what workers need and the work conditions they will be willing to tolerate.

This qualitatively changes the situation that leads to the problem of epistocratic identification. In an exitocracy, competitors offer solutions to the people's problems, and the people evaluate the solutions—not, however, by trying to adjudicate among the competitors' theories about, or interpretations of evidence about, the society-wide efficacy of various solutions; nor by trying to outguess or out-research the competitors so as to come up with solutions of their own; nor by relying on heuristics such as the competitors' educational pedigrees; nor by trusting in the competitors' dedication to the common good or their strength of will. Instead, they directly try out the competing solutions that the competitors create. In the ideal type, consumers or workers need know nothing about the attitudes, the character, or even the identity of those who sell them things or those who pay their wages. They need only know whether the results for them personally are better than the alternatives they have tried.

In this analysis, the very thing that renders the problem-solving activities of an ordinary technocracy relatively unreliable—ideational heterogeneity—enables relatively reliable (although by no means perfect) problem-solving in an exitocracy, ceteris paribus, because in an exitocracy ideational heterogeneity among producers and employers allows them to offer competing solutions. This should prove to be more effective than technocracy in solving people's problems, on the whole, assuming that the problems affect consumers or workers in a manner they are capable of reliably noticing; assuming that they have exit opportunities, and corresponding entry opportunities, by means of which they can experiment, individually, with heterogeneous solution possibilities, meaning more than one; and assuming that they are then able to notice whether a given experiment has worked. (These conditions give rise to various preconditions of and limitations on the efficacy of voice, to be considered later on.)

By contrast, if people are unhappy and their ability to exit is blocked, then they themselves or some expert or experts, identifiable ex ante, must determine what is wrong and how to fix it. Assume, contrary to Hirschman, that the experts are fully motivated to serve the public as best they can—that is, that they are sociotropic and not lazy. If their best efforts to serve the public turn out to be inadequate, causing a social problem; and if, as Hirschman proposes, exit to alternative possibilities is blocked; then it is indeed possible that angry voices will be raised in protest. Yet if the experts were able to respond to these protests by making use of prevenient knowledge of how to solve the problem, why (other than for "random" reasons) would they have implemented the policies that caused dissatisfaction to begin with? To predict that they will respond adequately to voiced complaints, Hirschman must impute to them the very knowledge whose absence is the only nonrandom, nonmysterious explanation for their initial failure. In short, Hirschman establishes the epistemic ability of experts to respond adequately to voice in a manner very similar to that by which Berlin and the young Habermas established the epistemic competence of epistocracy. He assumes what he needs to demonstrate: the adequacy of the knowledge of an identifiable group of experts. For Berlin and the young Habermas, these are experts in government or "scientific" advisers to government. For Hirschman, they are managers protected by a government-enforced monopoly. For all three thinkers, however, the knowledge is inexplicably, preveniently "there."

7.2.3. The Epistemic Asymmetry Between Exit and Voice

In addition to the ability to experiment among competing alternatives, the different scope of judgment required of the final decision-maker in the two systems creates an epistemic asymmetry between exitocracy and technocracy. To use exit reliably well, in comparison to the use of voice, the decision-maker (such as the consumer or the worker in an exitocracy) considers only the effects of the various options that she is able to experience. In using voice, however, the technocratic decision-maker must reach far beyond experiential knowledge so as to judge the significance of social problems for anonymous others, to speculate about their causes, and to speculate about the efficacy of various solutions and the side effects they may cause.

That is true even of judicious technocrats. The advantage of judicious technocrats over injudicious ones is that the former, attuned to the presumption of ideational heterogeneity; aware, therefore, of the need to understand agents' actions with interpretive charity; and of course (preferably) sensitive to ambiguities in the empirical evidence bearing on homogenizing counterforces, are likelier than the latter to do more good than harm. The exitocratic alternative is to actualize heterogeneous behavioral predictions in the form of competing goods, services, and job opportunities from which there is exit. That way, the relatively reliable knowledge of customers and workers can be put to use, but without expecting them or any other identifiable agents to have reliable society-wide knowledge. Inasmuch as it is inherently difficult for anyone to have such knowledge—even those who are judiciously attentive to ideational heterogeneity—the exitocratic alternative would appear to be the better one.

The fundamental asymmetry between the relatively reliable knowledge of exit users and the relatively unreliable knowledge of voice users entails a parallel asymmetry between the reliability of consumers' and workers' knowledge and the unreliability of capitalists' knowledge. Capitalists are in the business, from a systemic perspective, of predicting the behavior of (usually) anonymous consumers or workers when offered goods, services, or jobs. Capitalists are as fallible in making such predictions as technocrats, which is why capitalists so often lose money or go out of business. However, when capitalists err, the resulting problems for consumers or workers need not be solved either by trusting that capitalists secretly know what went wrong, as Hirschman does, or by trusting consumers or workers to figure it out (or to know it intuitively), as they would need to do in their capacity as citizen-technocrats. When the ideas of *plural* capitalists compete with one another, dissatisfied consumers or workers can exit from the problems without trying to understand them. A division of epistemic labor is enacted, but it is anchored in the relatively reliable knowledge of consumers and workers, not the relatively unreliable knowledge of experts at the summit of an intellectual pyramid or voters at its base. What makes the system work is not the accurate identification of experts (ex ante or ex post), or the spread of "enlightenment" to voters, but the testing of putative expertise against the relatively genuine (albeit very imperfect) expertise that we each have regarding our own lives.

7.3. THE PUBLIC/PRIVATE ASYMMETRY IN VOICE

A second public-private asymmetry has an epistemic basis similar to that of the first: a narrowly restricted area of knowledge. In this case, however, the knowledge is of others whom we know personally, as compared to the knowledge of anonymous others required of technocrats (and capitalists). Personal familiarity can generate knowledge that enables us to help each other in private, and knowledge that spares us the need to exit from a personal relationship that encounters problems. We can instead use voice to try to solve the problems, with greater hope of success than would be reasonable in the public sphere.

A friend or relative is better known than a stranger, so one is more likely to come up with an adequate interpretation of the patterns and reasons for a friend's or relative's behavior than one is to interpret the behavior of strangers adequately. One may also be able to offer reliable problem-solving advice customized to the other's idiosyncrasies. This asymmetry is a good reason to prefer parental governance of children over governance by the state; intimate over professional "social work"; and, in some cases, communal or governmental problem-solving at the very local, face-to-face level over larger units of government.

As well, personal familiarity with people with whom one is not necessarily friendly, such as the residents of one's neighborhood or one's coworkers or employer, can sometimes help to improve interactions and correct perceived problems without exiting from them, by using voice. In other cases, however, exit will be invaluable in such situations.

Hell may not be other people, but being locked into a relationship that has broken down and resists voiced solutions can be more hellish than most other social problems.

The fact that this second asymmetry relies on voice suggests a significant tension with the first asymmetry. The second asymmetry may well constitute an epistemic argument for withdrawing from modern society, and especially from its capitalist and technocratic sectors, the better to confine one's relationships to those with whom one is personally familiar and with whom (and about whom) one can therefore theorize reliably. In a very small-scale group, like those in which hunters and gatherers lived, everyone is known to one another intimately and should therefore be much better able, in principle, to accommodate one another deliberately and deliberatively (for instance, in anticipating one another's needs) than in mass, anonymous society. The upshot is that on epistemic grounds, life in intimate groups is preferable to life in mass society, other things equal.

Of course, one need not completely withdraw from mass society if one is to enjoy the epistemic advantages of intimacy, not to mention the emotional advantages. Almost everyone who participates in the impersonal orders of capitalism and technocracy uses the fruits of these orders to help create, sustain, and enrich intimate personal relationships. Yet it seems undeniable that the use of exit in anonymous settings, such as commodity purchase and production, is at odds with the epistemic advantages that may be conferred, in face-to-face settings, by the use of voice. Moreover, the unhappiness that seems widespread in modernity may be attributable, in part, to the contradiction between these two dimensions of the private sphere: the anonymous and the personal. Modernity adds to our personal relationships a tremendous number of abstract relationships with anonymous others, relationships with which our forebears would have had no experience and to which the emotional equipment we inherited from them is unlikely to have adjusted since the end of the Paleolithic. This would be another mark against modernity, from a negative-utilitarian perspective.

7.4. SOME EPISTEMIC LIMITS OF EXIT

The ideal type of exit differs from the reality in many cases. Restricting ourselves first to social problems to which there may be competitive solutions, and assuming the capitalistic provision of these solutions, the *resource cost* of exit can limit its efficacy. If an ineptly managed railroad offers subsidized fares while bus and truck services do not, the poor may be effectively blocked from exiting from the railroad even if they have the formal, legal ability to exit. In addition, *iterative* experimentation can be impracticable in the private sphere, as with the choice of such singular "commodities" as a college education. A similar limitation is *temporal*. Experimental decisions about what type of education to receive, what type of work to pursue, where to live, and whether to make the arduous, lasting commitments necessary for raising children cannot be exited from as easily as the decision to take a bus instead of a train. Separately, the feedback one personally receives from a given experience will sometimes be *irrelevant* to the solution of a problem, limiting the efficacy of exit.

In this section I will briefly examine the iterative, temporal, and relevance limits on exit, and the question of exitocratic paternalism when these limits are severe. Section 7.5 will examine the resource limit and a solution to it: wealth redistribution.

7.4.1. *The Temporal Limit to the Utility of Exit*

The temporal constraint on the utility of exit might suggest that the significance of exit for human happiness is negligible, as exit might seem to be restricted to transient experiments such as taking a train or a bus. But such decisions can be quite important, all told. Human life consists, for the most part, of a long series of short-term situations. It is not unimportant, then, from a negative-utilitarian standpoint, that problems with these situations be mitigated.

Moreover, the exit mechanism can be invaluable even in fairly long-term situations. People armed with the power of exit can make lasting and calamitous mistakes, wasting long stretches of their lives in poisonous personal relationships, in dispiriting careers, in bad jobs, or in pursuit of unattainable or unsatisfying goals. But this makes it all the more important for them to be able to reverse course if alternatives become apparent, so they may try to make the best of the time that remains to them. Moreover, voice in the private sphere can be a valuable epistemic tool in avoiding long-term mistakes, and a valuable supplement to exit in finding ways to correct them. One's intimate knowledge of a friend may shed light on her long-term interests in a way that theoretical or statistical knowledge of masses of anonymous others cannot.

Exit is a corrective to error, but it does not prevent error and it does not remotely approach being a total remedy for it. In general, however, exit, especially in conjunction with private-sphere voice, should improve our lot in comparison with exit blocking— the method by which voice-based decisions are imposed by an ordinary technocracy.

7.4.2. *The Iterative Limit to the Utility of Exit*

Some medical choices present extreme examples of the limited repeatability of certain types of experimentation. If one experiments with a lethal drug, one may never get a chance to exit from the experiment. Thus, if an established body of natural-scientific knowledge justifies the conclusion that some substances are likely to be lethal to the human organism, an exitocracy might have to ban them: when they are ingested, exit is not an option. Where exit cannot possibly correct error, the epistemological argument for it disappears.

The goal of this chapter is not to lay out a blueprint for an exitocracy, even in rough outline. However, by noticing limits to the epistemic utility of exit, we can avoid painting with too broad a brush. When exit is unfeasible, certain forms of technocratic paternalism are legitimate from an internal point of view.

7.4.3. *The Relevance Limit to the Utility of Exit*

In some cases, personal experience will be as unilluminating when one is making decisions in the private sphere as it tends to be in the public sphere. Even in the private sphere, after all, one frequently deals with anonymous others, at least insofar as the private sphere is capitalistic. Others' heterogeneous behavior may negate the usefulness of the behavioral generalizations one has drawn from past personal experience (based on one's interactions with an epistemically local subset of the human race). And private voice may be unavailing in such situations, as one's interlocutors, too, will have to draw on a very limited range of experience.

Still, exit can be a most effective remedy even when it is hard to learn lessons from one's experimental mistakes. One might mistakenly think, after a certain amount of dating, that one has learned what one's "type" is—until one meets an anonymous other who breaks the mold but turns out to be the love of one's life. One's predictions about the type of person one was likely to fall in love with are thus shown to be wrong, because they drew on what turned out to be misleading personal experiences. Yet it is in just such cases that one's ability to experiment may have the greatest value. An acknowledgment of the relevance limit, like an acknowledgment of the iterative and temporal limits, does not reverse the overall epistemic advantage of exit.

7.5. AN EXITOCRATIC DIFFERENCE PRINCIPLE

Exit opportunities will often require economic resources. These can allow one to enter into alternatives to the situation from which one would like to exit. Thus, if the experimentation promised by the exit option is to be possible for more than the rich, economic redistribution is called for.

The rationale for exitocratic redistribution, however, is not the achievement of social justice. While it is true that, as Rawls notes, people's talents and other resources are bound to be distributed arbitrarily from a moral point of view, an exitocracy would need to redistribute pecuniary resources not to remedy this arbitrariness, but to meet the technocratic mandate of solving social problems—but indirectly, by conferring powers rather than imposing duties. Such redistribution would be necessary even if the original distribution of talents and resources were *not* morally arbitrary.

Nevertheless, an exitocracy would not treat equality of resources as an end in itself any more than Rawls did. Rawls provided for an indeterminate amount of deviation from an egalitarian baseline through the Difference Principle, since the goal of his system of justice was to raise up the least advantaged, not to level down the most advantaged.

Therefore, the Difference Principle allows inequalities that would indirectly work to the benefit of the least advantaged, such as those that provide incentives for wealth creation that will benefit the poor. An exitocracy would need something like the Difference Principle to ensure that redistribution did not become an obstacle to the creation of entry opportunities rather than a means of making them available to all.

An adaptation of the Difference Principle to the purposes of technocracy would replace "primary goods" with "entry goods" as the resources to be redistributed. The aim of this principle would be to maximize, for as many people as possible, the opportunity to use exit to solve problems affecting them personally. It would achieve this aim by affording people the means, having exited from problematic situations, to enter into as many alternatives as possible, consistent not only with others' roughly equal opportunity to do the same, but with the expansion of such opportunities for all.[19] This goal would justify more redistribution than the allocation of some minimum level of income to everyone. And the recipients would be the poor, not everyone. In these respects, exitocratic redistribution is a form of egalitarian socialism. As an ideal type, socialist redistribution makes exit opportunities meaningful by joining them with entry goods available to all. Under Marxian socialism, by contrast, the means of production are collectively owned, making it impossible to create alternatives to what is decided upon collectively, through voice. Therefore, whatever problems people experience would have to be solved through political processes. This would put everyone in the position of railroad customers trying to determine the causes of the railroad's problems and the effects to be expected from various solutions, but lacking any reliable knowledge but the fact that they are experiencing the problems.

The difficulty here is not, or not solely, that there would be no price system to aggregate knowledge, a view popularized by F. A. Hayek in the middle of the twentieth century.[20] Hayek's argument was the upshot of the socialist calculation debate, which began in the 1920s.[21] In the most careful and detailed account of the debate, Don Lavoie points out that Hayek's opponents overlooked the fact that capitalism depends, epistemically, on "the competition of separate private owners who *disagree* about which [production] techniques are better."[22] Lavoie does not note, however, that capitalists' disagreement is at odds with the epistemic case for the price system made by Hayek. The prices of production goods (the means of production)—the prices that were at issue in the debate—are, in the ideal type of capitalism, set by the rivalrous bidding of disagreeing capitalists. Insofar as one or both parties to any disagreement must be wrong, such prices *cannot* be correct, as the capitalists who are on the wrong side of the disagreements play as much of a role in setting prices as those who are right. For example, when the Ford Motor Company

---

[19] Warren (2011) calls redistribution of this sort "enhanced exit."
[20] Hayek [1945] 1948.
[21] See Hayek [1935] 1975 and Lange 1936, 1937, and 1938.
[22] Lavoie 1985, 123, my emphasis.

introduced the Edsel in 1958, the car's production bid up the prices of all its component parts and, in turn, the prices of the capital goods, labor, and raw materials required to make those components—before low sales forced Ford to discontinue the model. In the interim, production of the Edsel made all of those prices inaccurate to some degree, along with all the prices that were affected by the prices pushed up by Ford's demand for the Edsel's components. This surely caused inaccurate prices to spread throughout the entire world economy.

Competing capitalists disagree because their fallible webs of belief produce heterogeneous, often-inaccurate interpretations of what consumers are willing to buy and how most efficiently to produce it. The inaccuracy of interpretation A is revealed when consumers, using the exit option to choose goods produced in line with interpretation B, fail to buy goods produced in line with interpretation A. It is misleading, then, to view the price system as aggregating *knowledge*, as Hayek did. Instead, it aggregates *opinions*— always including incorrect opinions. Moreover, capitalists faced with the same array of prices at a given moment will often interpret their implications differently, leading them to reach divergent conclusions about how to proceed. Thus, even if, à la Hayek, prices could be said to aggregate knowledge rather than opinion, this would not solve the epistemic problem besetting capitalists, which is a problem of interpretation, not aggregation. Capitalists' problem is to decide what they should do in the face of a blooming, buzzing confusion of information, including price information. If the information itself could explain what should be done, there would be no disagreement among capitalists about what to do, and thus no need for competition among them. This puts capitalists in the same untenable epistemic position in which technocrats find themselves (whether or not capitalists are any more aware of it than technocrats are). No given capitalist is better positioned than any given technocrat to cut through the epistemic chaos with an accurate interpretation of what needs to be done, regardless of the presence of a price system.

The epistemic advantage of capitalism, then, does not stem from the wisdom of capitalists as a group, as reflected in the market prices for production goods that result from the rivalrous bidding emphasized by Lavoie. Rather, it stems from the fact that capitalists' interpretations of what should be produced, and how to produce it, are subjected to testing by consumers and workers wielding relatively reliable knowledge of their experiences with the resulting products and the jobs required to produce them, but possessing the power to exit from them. This advantage is foregone by a planned economy. On the other hand, however, the advocates of a planned economy tend to claim that all or most social problems are caused by capitalism itself, a utopian socialist claim with which Marx agreed. This grand-theoretic claim could be the basis of an argument for forsaking the epistemic advantage of capitalism: if there are no problems to be solved, or few of them, because we have abolished capitalism, then we do not need to empower consumers and workers, as individuals, to solve them through the use of exit.

This grand-theoretic claim is made at the first order, and so cannot be addressed directly except to say that the knowledge needed to assess its accuracy would be even more speculative and unreliable than the knowledge needed to assess smaller-bore technocratic policy claims. The proponent of the claim must somehow engage on all fronts against competing (technocratic) analyses of the causes of each and every social problem, but without begging the epistemological question by simply asserting the obvious validity of her own analysis—even as she must provide a reason to think that the planners will be able so to arrange things as to avoid the inadvertent creation of new problems, again without begging the epistemic question. For present purposes, however, we need only recognize that if social problems can be ended by abolishing capitalism, then technocracy can be abolished along with it. The chief justification for technocracy has historically been to cure the ills caused by capitalism, and if social problems go away, so does the need for technocracy—a point that any Marxist aware of Marx's opposition to bureaucracy might happily endorse. Thus, even if (arguendo) one could show that a planned economy would be epistemically superior to capitalism, this would not constitute an argument for technocracy.

7.5.1. A Social Problem and Two Exitocratic Solutions

Bracketing the type of socialism that is embodied in a planned economy, one might be tempted to say that the type of socialism that is embodied in exitocratic redistribution would serve to make capitalism work for everyone (from a negative-utilitarian perspective) by giving everyone, as much as possible, the means by which to benefit from the exit options offered by capitalists. But this would leave out one of the most important uses of exitocratic redistribution, which is to allow people to *exit* from the exit options offered by capitalists. Let me illustrate this point by considering redistribution to the poor in the Global South as a means of allowing them to escape from sweated labor. This example will illustrate that redistribution is superior to exit, even as exit is superior to ordinary technocracy.

After many years spent in Southeast Asia, *New York Times* reporter Nicholas Kristof made it a personal mission to bring to light the paradoxical benefits of poorly paid work in conditions so undesirable that most of his readers could hardly imagine the upside of it, and were therefore inclined to endorse classic technocratic responses: the prohibition of sweatshops or their regulation—responses that precisely duplicate the Victorian responses to the original sweatshops, the factories of the Industrial Revolution.

Thus, in a 2009 article, Kristof described the plight of Pim Srey Rath, a Phnom Penh resident who yearned for a job in a sweatshop. Such a job would have allowed her to exit from her current place of employment, a garbage dump described by Kristof as "a mountain of festering refuse, a half-hour hike across, emitting clouds of smoke from subterranean fires."[23] In previous reporting he had noted that "in the slums of Indonesia and in

---

[23] Kristof 2009.

Thailand," as in Cambodia, "many workers even speak of sweatshop jobs as their greatest aspiration."[24] Neou Chanthou, another scavenger at the Phnom Penh dump, explained how this could be so: "It's dirty, hot and smelly here," he said. "A factory is better."[25]

Extreme poverty is the prototypical serious social problem, and in such cases as Srey Rath's and Chanthou's, the epistemic merits of exit in mitigating this problem could hardly be clearer. Srey Rath and Chanthou had direct experience working as garbage scavengers and they hated it. In comparison, entry into sweatshop labor promised a tremendous gain in their well-being and that of their families (in technocratic terms, a tremendous reduction in their distress). Naturally, this promise was not a guarantee. Their desire for sweatshop work may have been based on what Srey Rath and Chanthou had heard from others who had secured such work already; but these informants may have reacted to their jobs in given sweatshops more positively than Srey Rath or Chanthou would have reacted to jobs at those or other sweatshops. Still, the testimony of people who had actually performed the experiment of working in sweatshops might have been probative, especially if these people were well known to those whom they informed. And if this testimony had turned out to be false or inapplicable to Srey Rath or Chanthou, they almost certainly could have returned from sweated labor to scavenging, taking advantage of the exit mechanism to mitigate the mistake of having tried working in a sweatshop.

Yet from Tory outrage at dark satanic mills to the progressive antisweatshop movement of the late twentieth century, the dominant technocratic tendency has been to prohibit sweated labor or to regulate its conditions. The unreliability of the knowledge on which such actions are based is suggested by a 1998 report written by a sweatshop monitor who visited a Chinese garment factory:

We find almost every violation in the book. The workers are pulling 90-hour weeks. The place has no fire extinguishers or fire exits, and is so jammed full of material that a small fire could explode into an inferno in a minute. There are no safety guards on the sewing machines, and the first-aid box holds only packages of instant noodles.

With the bosses out of earshot, I fully expect the workers to pour out their sorrows to me, to beg me to tell the consumers of America to help them out of their misery. I'm surprised at what I hear.

"I'm happy to have this job," is the essence of what several workers tell me. "At home, I'm a drain on my family's resources. But now, I can send them money every month."

I point out that they make only $100 a month; they remind me that this is about five times what they can make in their home province. I ask if they feel like they're

---

[24] Kristof 1998.
[25] Kristof 2009.

being exploited, having to work 90 hours a week. They laugh. "We all work piece rate here. More work, more money."

The worst part of the day for them, it seemed, was seeing me arrive. "I don't want to tell you anything because you'll close my factory and ruin any chances I have at having a better life one day," one tells me.[26]

It does not seem to have previously occurred to this quasi-technocrat (not vested with official authority, but using her position as an inspector to police the regulation of sweatshops) that sweated laborers might have taken such unappealing work for what they considered to be good reasons. In other words, she was ignorant of their webs of belief and, apparently, ignorant of the possibility that their actions were motivated by beliefs at all. Had she understood their reasoning, it might not have seemed self-evident to her that sweated labor *is* a social problem—rather than being a suboptimal solution, but a solution nonetheless, to the problem of poverty.

However, given adequate levels of wealth redistribution, choices as suboptimal as those facing sweatshop workers would not be necessary. Redistribution would allow people to exit not only from barely tolerable options, such as scavenging garbage, but also from the somewhat better options, such as sweated labor, offered by competing capitalists. On the other hand, redistribution may not be politically realistic, at least in situations like this, where redistribution would have to cross national borders if it were to be of significant help. So long as nationalist ideas remain potent, exitocracies, like ordinary technocracies, will have to be nation-states, in which case the ability of workers to exit from one suboptimal job to another may be their only chance to mitigate some of the most important problems they face.

It might appear, however, that the foregoing analysis overlooks the *social* dimension of "social problems." Even if we accept that garbage scavengers can improve their lot by taking jobs in sweatshops, might that not have the effect, elsewhere in a global economy, of harming workers whose wages are pulled down, or whose jobs are eliminated, by competition from sweated labor?

More generally, does the epistemic case for exitocracy overlook the fact that everyone's fate is interconnected, such that anyone's exit decisions may have unseen and possibly undesirable effects on others? The customers who exited from the Nigerian railroad may, after all, have caused more unhappiness to railroad workers who thus had to be laid off than was gained by bus and truck employees (and by reducing the former railroad customers' discomfort). One reason that exit is less epistemically demanding than voice is, as we saw, that those who use the exit mechanism need not consider the unintended consequences of their actions *for others*.

---

[26] Esbenshade 2004, 212–213.

It seems undeniable that the welfare improvements made possible by some people's use of the exit option may come at the expense of others, for any human action may have the unintended consequence of harming others. Yet I know of no reason to expect that the unintended harms to others of actions in the private sphere will tend to outweigh the gains to those who take these actions—at least if those harmed are, in turn, able to use exit opportunities to improve their position after being harmed. This is what I meant earlier when I referred to "maneuvering" in the private sphere: not merely game-theoretic strategizing, but any individual efforts to adjust to new problems as they arise.

Let us suppose, however, that in a given case, or in general, the use of exit does turn out to be a negative-sum "game." This would constitute an argument for technocracy only if technocrats could reliably know which regulations would, by blocking some people's exit opportunities, undo or prevent the damage without causing worse damage. We now have reason to think that on the whole, even judicious technocrats will tend to lack reliable knowledge of just this sort, relative to the reliability of the knowledge possessed by those who would otherwise (if they were not blocked by technocratic action, even judicious technocratic action) be able to use the exit mechanism to cope, imperfectly, with the losses incurred in the negative-sum game. Thus, even if exit does more harm than good overall, it is difficult to see how technocracy cannot be expected to make matters worse.

7.6. EPISTEMIC DILEMMAS AND CULTURAL CRITIQUE

The administration of an exitocratic Difference Principle would require the administrators to make behavioral predictions that nobody—no matter how judiciously attentive to ideational heterogeneity—is well positioned to make. The goal of the principle would be to provide the least advantaged with greater entry opportunities than they would otherwise have, by enabling them to leave undesirable jobs or to buy more of the goods and services offered by capitalist entrepreneurs. This creates a new dilemma. If, in a given time and place, and for significant numbers of capitalists, entrepreneurship is motivated by self-interest, it would seem incumbent on judicious exitocrats, cognizant of this superordinate behavioral norm, to protect capitalists against excessively high taxes to pay for redistribution. Yet as we saw in Chapter 4, the norm of self-interest underdetermines the behavior that it homogenizes, as self-interested agents must still interpret their situations, and these interpretations may be heterogeneous. A judicious technocrat attempting to decide which level of taxation is "excessively" high, then, would have to answer the empirical question of how the ideationally heterogeneous capitalists of her time and place will respond to various possible rates of taxation. This question is no less difficult to answer than the question of how they might respond to various levels of a minimum wage or to other "ordinary" technocratic initiatives. Thus, the epistemological critique of technocracy presented in Part I would apply to redistribution in the service of enhancing people's entry opportunities. The same critique would apply, as well, to the provision of other public goods, including the good of legally establishing and defending the private sphere. All of these exitocratic activities would entail highly fallible, speculative behavioral predictions about anonymous, presumptively heterogeneous others. Thus, if the epistemological critique of technocracy gives us reason to substitute exit for voice, does it not also give us reason to reject the state functions that make exit possible? If we accept the epistemological critique of technocracy, it seems that we must accept, as well, that the unintended costs of providing public goods, including those created by these essential exitocratic activities, may exceed their benefits, because technocratic reasoning will have to be deployed in the course of these activities.

This quandary is similar to those that I presented at the beginning of Part III, and therefore may be susceptible, at least in part, to resolution by recourse to the same tactic I used there: that is, by shifting from the absolute perspective embodied in the preliminary criterion of legitimacy toward the comparative perspective embodied in the revised criterion. While technocratic reasoning will have to be deployed in providing exitocratic public goods—this is what makes exitocracy a form of technocracy, even if an "extraordinary" one—the inevitable errors that result will be offset, to some (putatively significant) extent, by the fact that these public goods will enable people to solve social problems in the private sphere. It is true that we cannot know, in an absolute sense, whether the cost of exitocrats' errors in creating and defending the private sphere will outweigh the benefits of the exit opportunities created thereby. Still, we are entitled to say that the mix of benefits and costs should be more favorable in an exitocracy than in an ordinary technocracy, despite the errors that will undoubtedly plague both exitocrats and ordinary technocrats. But this comparison between exitocracy and ordinary technocracy justifies only the provision of those public goods, such as redistribution and a legal system, that enable exit. Let us call these "primary" public goods, not in the sense that they are the most important types of public goods (they are not), but in the sense that their provision is the distinctive trait of an exitocracy. The comparison to ordinary technocracy justifies the provision of such goods by an exitocracy, but it does not justify the provision of other public goods, such as environmental protection or military defense, that are essential and, indeed, may be more important (normatively) than the creation of a private sphere, but are unconnected to its creation or its maintenance. We can call these "secondary" or "tertiary" public goods—secondary or tertiary not in their significance, but in their exitocratic justification.

Secondary public goods are those nonprimary public goods that are justified on exitocratic grounds by virtue of exitocrats' ability to build exit-like devices into the provision of the goods. No exit is available from the provision of any public good, but the exit mechanism can be mimicked in some cases. Thus, an exitocracy might address global warming through something like a carbon tax rather than through something like the Green New Deal, as a carbon tax would not require technocratic knowledge of how best to get people to reduce their carbon emissions: the discovery of how to do so would be left to individual agents seeking to reduce the tax they pay, indirectly maneuvering

based on relatively reliable feedback instead of trying to discern a (literally) global solution to the problem of climate change. This would not be a pure case of exit, as the
tax itself would be duty- rather than power-conferring. Nor would it amount to an exit
from ordinary technocracy: the size of the carbon tax, and many other details, would
have to be set through ordinary technocratic deliberation about the human behavioral
consequences to be expected from different policy designs. But similar things could be
said of exitocracy as a whole. What we may have come to view as "natural" arenas of exit,
such as the consumer goods and labor markets, presuppose artificial (human) interpretive technocratic judgments about, for example, how best to define "property" and how
to structure people's "rights" to it. Decisions about how high to set a carbon tax and how
to collect it (as well as what to do with the proceeds) are inescapably technocratic and
thus, like all technocratic decisions, are prone to error—given the presumptive ideational
heterogeneity of the people who would be paying the tax. Yet, like the construction and
enforcement of property rights, the construction and implementation of a carbon tax is
likely to reduce the scope for technocratic error in comparison to technocratic initiatives,
such as the Green New Deal, that lack exit-like devices.

There will, however, be many nonprimary public goods that are not susceptible to
exit-like fixes. For these tertiary public goods, such as territorial military defense, foreign policy, and many, many others, the normative comparison would not pit exitocracy
against ordinary technocracy, or ordinary technocratic policies with exit-like features
against ordinary technocratic policies that lack them, but judicious against injudicious
technocratic policymaking. If tertiary public goods are provided judiciously, there is
reason to think that the cost-benefit ratio will be better than if they are provided injudiciously, as judicious technocrats would, by definition, at least attempt to address the
fundamental problem identified in Part I—unpredictable ideational heterogeneity—
however imperfectly they might end up doing so. (If perfection were our standard, there
would be no point in thinking about the legitimacy of any human endeavor.) Thus, for
what it is worth, we once again have reason to desire a cultural revolution in favor of technocratic judiciousness: a revolution against the ideational insensitivity, naive realism, and
interpretive uncharitability that are embodied (for example) in neoclassical economics
and social-scientific positivism. It should be noted that the seeming unlikeliness of such
a revolution does not make it a pipe dream. In domestic policy there seems to be little
evidence that policymakers are, at present, aware of the causal role of ideas in human
behavior, but this is not the case in the area of foreign intelligence (which is, of course,
a crucial part of military defense). In *Why Intelligence Fails*, Robert Jervis draws on intelligence documents to argue that prior to the invasion of Iraq, most US and European
analysts of Iraq, being ignorant of Saddam Hussein's actual thinking, made a good-faith
effort to understand it as best they could. As Jervis sees it, the analysts' assumptions about
Saddam Hussein's beliefs were plausible enough, given the analysts' own beliefs—but
their webs of belief turned out not to overlap sufficiently with his. Yet they were, at least,
attempting to understand his beliefs with interpretive charity, so they avoided the use

of such injudicious technologies as neoclassical economics, behavioral economics, and social-scientific positivism.[27] This example emphasizes the fallibility of even a judicious technocracy, but it also suggests that it is feasible, as in some areas of policymaking it already exists.

The foregoing establishes, I think, that there is a normative hierarchy of technocratic legitimacy, allowing us to avoid the magnitude question when comparing ordinary technocracy against exitocracy as well as when comparing injudicious technocracy against the judicious variety. Yet the magnitude question cannot so easily be brushed aside. It remains possible that the problem of frequent ideational heterogeneity is so great that it renders *any* technocratic efforts illegitimate, even judicious exitocratic efforts, according to the *preliminary* standard. We shift to the comparative standard because we cannot purport to know such things without begging the question raised by the epistemological critique, leaving us with the possibility that the magnitude of the unintended consequences caused by the problem is so large that it might cause *all* forms of technocratic action to do more harm than good; or, on the other hand, whether it might be so unimportant that it should not worry us even when providing tertiary public goods injudiciously. We can bracket the preliminary standard in trying to decide *how* to proceed technocratically in a given case (preferring exit or exit-like mechanisms to voice, or judicious to judicious technocratic analysis), but there is also the question of whether we should proceed technocratically at all when such a choice is before us. Are the risks of even judicious tertiary technocratic action too high, as might be suggested by the Iraq example? While we have reason to prefer exitocracy to ordinary technocracy and judicious to injudicious technocracy, it is not clear, at least to me, that the epistemological critique tells us anything about whether to provide tertiary public goods, or any particular tertiary public good, let alone how to do so.

However, political theory need not necessarily answer such questions. It can simply be a spur to critical reflection on present realities. Thus, the epistemological critique of technocracy might be seen as a form of Adornoesque critical theory that cannot necessarily guide political action; or as a form of cultural action, not political action.

If one expects political theory to motivate political practice, this conclusion will be deeply unsatisfying. I confess that it is disappointing to conclude a critique of technocracy with the acknowledgment that it may have no political upshot. But the expectation that political theory must motivate political practice may itself be a product of the assumptions that foster technocracy, at least in democratic societies—where, as Lippmann observed, we are expected to have opinions about every political issue, no matter how unlikely it is that our opinions will be adequately grounded. As he pointed out, the reasonable course, when one is aware of one's ignorance, is to refrain from holding an opinion. Our ignorance of the magnitude of the problem underscored by the critique

---

[27] Jervis 2010, ch. 3.

presented in Part I suggests that we should refrain from seeing the critique as capable of motivating opinions about the desirability of political action, or inaction, *except* when the choice we face is between the exit mechanism and the voice mechanism, or between using the latter judiciously or not. Indeed, refraining from holding such opinions is the only *possible* course if we fully recognize the significance of the magnitude issue. People are incapable of "choosing" to hold opinions that they know are unjustified, as shown by the logical incoherence of the akrasia theory of motivated reasoning (Chapter 5). Thus, if one fully recognizes one's ignorance in a given case, one literally has no choice but to select oneself out of the pool of opinion holders in that case. Having become fully aware of one's ignorance of the magnitudes of the unintended consequences caused by technocracy, one would ipso facto be unable to motivate technocratic opinions. In the intellectual space thus created, the space of agnosticism rather than agonism, one can pursue critical cultural work.

Such work might help us to understand the forms of false consciousness that seem to go with technocracy—such as the demand that we have opinions about things we cannot reasonably be expected to understand. A conceptually related form of false consciousness is the inclination to *express* our opinions, culminating in the notion that political discussion or contestation, or political action, is constitutive of the human. This version of humanism bears a striking affinity with technocracy, both democratic and epistocratic, as if it had been shaped by the invisible hand of technocracy. And it is as if we, too, have been shaped by its invisible hand, habituated as we are to advocacy, to debate, to arguing and otherwise attempting to persuade—despite the fact that arguing is, in most cases, no more efficacious than voting; despite the fact that the ungroundedness of our opinions, at least in the technocratic realm, suggests that they are probably wrong, on the whole, such that the arguments advancing these opinions would be counterproductive if they succeeded in changing others' minds; and despite the fact that, in *any* realm, such success is rare (although not nonexistent). If one's interlocutors are worth arguing with, in principle—because they disagree with one's opinions—it probably means that their webs of belief cannot be changed by one's arguments; while one's arguments will only reinforce the prejudices of those ready to accept them into their webs. There is also the strange impulse to praise political figures, parties, or movements for doing whatever we think they should have done, or to condemn them for doing what we think they should not have done—as if the agents involved did not have reasons for doing whatever they did or did not do. People do what their webs of belief demand. Praising or blaming them for what they do presupposes a match between their webs of belief and ours, as if, when they do what our web of beliefs leads us to believe they should do, they are led to do this by some conatus of (what we consider to be) goodness rather than because their ideas *compel* them to do it; and such that when they do what our web of beliefs leads us to think they should not, they perversely refuse to do what they *know* they should not. As Holbach suggested, this presupposition effaces the distinction between them and us—and makes us intolerant of them when they refuse to act as we would.

In Chapter 6, I speculated about the Christian origins of the moralizing embodied in the intentions heuristics, but the syndrome of praising and blaming is a slightly different type of moralizing and, in any case, speculation is just that. We do not know where this or any other form of technocratic false consciousness originated, and it would be valuable to find out, insofar as we can.

Thus, having been thrown by chance of birth into technocratic culture—the culture of moralizing, and opinionating, and arguing; the culture of the inhuman humanism that effaces our ideational nature—we might explore its historical roots. As there is not really an invisible hand of technocracy that might explain them, what are the actual sources of this culture, the origins of the ideas that have made it, and us, the way we are? Investigating such questions might rescue a meaningful existence for those who are alienated by technocratic culture, even if it does not lead to political action or political opinion. Fortunately, intellectual history is still possible in the private sphere.

7.7. EXIT AND HUMAN HAPPINESS

Of course, the private sphere itself is frequently accused of fostering dehumanization. A fully developed cultural critique of technocracy would thus have to grapple with the possibility that exitocratic cultural and, thus, emotional pathologies are worse than those that seem to go with technocracy.

A preliminary comparison might pit the hot hatreds that seem to go with technocracy against the cold rationality that seems to go with exitocracy. The mental habits fostered by regular use of the exit mechanism may help us to solve problems even as it deprives us of happiness—not only because we use instrumental reason when dealing with other human beings,[28] but as an unintended consequence of the aggregation of individuals' exit decisions over long stretches of time.

Exit-oriented decision-making has been the rule for most of human existence. We have been brought to where we are—that is, to modernity, with all its problems (social and otherwise)—by uncountable exit-based decisions, few of which were designed to lead in this direction. Modernity is the greatest unintended consequence in human history, and it is far from clear that it is a beneficial one, on balance. Similar things can be said about capitalism. Capitalism may be a "spontaneous order," as Hayek maintained, but it would not follow that it is desirable. (Marx, too, thought of capitalism as a spontaneous order.) The unintended consequences of this unintended order are immense, and we are in no position to declare that the net valence of those consequences is positive.

---

[28] It has to be questioned, however, whether the use of instrumental rationality has indeed been significantly magnified by modern society or by "civilization" as a whole, as suggested by Horkheimer and Adorno's *Dialectic of Enlightenment* ([1944] 2002). The constant adaptation of hunters and gatherers to environmental changes indicates, on the contrary, a highly refined instrumental orientation, of which James Scott's *Against the Grain* (2017) gives a good sense; also see the final note to this chapter.

Viewers of the old television series on cultural anthropology, *Faces of Culture*, may remember what happened when Brazilian miners set up camp near the outskirts of an indigenous village in the Amazon. Overcoming their initial fears, the villagers chose to visit the camp and accept the miners' gifts of tools and consumer goods. The next thing they knew (at least as I recall the story), their apparently satisfying "primitive" existence had been ruined. They had been drawn into modernity unwittingly, by small but fateful choices that made them dependent on a civilization they had not intended to join, the implications of which they did not understand. They did not know where they were headed and may well have chosen differently if they had. Conversely, it is reported that while thousands of settlers on the North American frontier ran off to join Native American tribes during the seventeenth, eighteenth, and nineteenth centuries, few of these runaways voluntarily returned; and few Native Americans volunteered to join European-American civilization.[29] One interpretation of these divergent paths of exit, the first leading toward modernity and the second away from it, is that in the South American case the choices along the path were incremental and the destination unknown, while in the North American case, the choice was between two options that had been intimately experienced by those who made it: full-on modernity and an apparently happy alternative destination. In the early Holocene, by contrast, when the choice was between hunting and gathering and a small step away from it, and then another, the choosers chose out of blindness to their (our) ultimate destination.

An alternative scenario, however, emerges from a recent synthesis of archaeological evidence produced by James C. Scott. In his view, the pivotal departure from hunting and gathering—the decision to live in small city-states—was not a product of innumerable exit choices. Instead, it was a "choice" initially forced upon the slaves who made urban existence possible.[30] After this decision was made for them, it may have taken on a life of its own, sustained in part by further decisions made by their descendants under the influence of legitimating ideologies of various kinds, such as religious and eventually political and economic belief systems. In this view, modernity is a grand mistake, but it is not the outcome of exit decisions so much as of hierarchically made, coercively imposed voice decisions, where the voices were those of the militarily and then the culturally powerful. Still, the net effect of everyone else's subsequent exit decisions has been the creation of a society that nobody envisioned and that might be worse than a dead end.[31]

---

[29] See the first chapter of Junger 2016.

[30] Scott 2017.

[31] However, Jared Diamond (2012, 456) reaches happier conclusions by relying on the testimony of indigenous people who lived through the transition from traditional ways of life to modernity, such as many residents of New Guinea. The benefits of the transition, as they see it, include not only the material objects made available by an advanced economy—"salt, pepper, palm oil, pots and pans, machetes, beds, lanterns; good clothes and shoes" (one senses an extremely well-developed sense of instrumental rationality among these "primitives"); but "a healthier life; the opportunity to send one's children to school; that it is easier to obtain plant food from fields than to gather it in the forest; and that it is easier and safer and faster to hunt animals with a gun than to make nets and extract kicking, biting, and slashing animals trapped in nets"; along with the ability "to keep

Such a conclusion, however, would be a judgment on modernity, or on aspects of it—not a judgment on the choice between technocracy and exitocracy. If one finds oneself regretting modernity, and if one blames modernity on uncountable exit decisions, it would be appropriate to find a better mode of decision-making, if there is one; or to exit from modernity in favor of a more human alternative—if one could be found. It would not be appropriate to defend the use of an epistemically inferior decision-making mechanism, voice, over an epistemically superior one, exit, in the administration of modern life. Ordinary technocracy, whether democratic or epistocratic, is as modern as it gets. It can hardly be expected to save us from the ills of modernity.

Contemplating the mistakes to which exit may lead, then, or those to which it may already have led, we might explore the feasibility of other modes of life. It is conceivable that some alternative to modernity would be superior to it even if the alternative contained no private sphere and, thus, allowed no exit, although this seems unlikely given human imperfection. However, the question concerning technocracy is not equivalent to that concerning modernity. If we fail to exit from modernity, then, it would seem that the obvious course is instead to exit from technocracy, to the extent that we can.

---

themselves and their children well fed and healthy; to live longer; and to have many children survive to become adults." There is also the much greater security of body, and the freedom from fear, that Diamond attributes to the monopoly on legitimate violence enforced by the state (the very entity on which Scott implicitly blames the woes of modernity). The chance of being killed or seriously injured in interpersonal violence or organized warfare (and, too, in accidents) was, in Diamond's estimation, much higher for hunter-gatherers, by orders of magnitude, than it is for us. Thus, men of the New Guinea Highlands judged life to be "better since the government had come because a man could now eat without looking over his shoulder and could leave his house in the morning to urinate without fear of being shot" by an arrow (ibid., 148). Similarly, the decision of frontier Americans to flee "civilization" may have reflected the choice between hunting and gathering and the back-breaking requirements of pre-industrial agriculture, as opposed to choosing between hunting and gathering and the relative ease of post-industrial civilization. For a critique of Diamond's book, see Scott 2013.

Afterword

TECHNOCRACY AND THE LEFT

EVEN A CRITIQUE of technocracy predicated on a socialist alternative is likely to be understood as conservative. This is because much of the left has allowed itself to drift into the arms of technocracy.

To gain some perspective on this development, it may be helpful to take a brief look at a precursor to technocracy in early modern Germany. This will broaden the provincial historical lens I have used—focused solely on the Progressive Era in the United States—as well as illustrating the distorted allegiances entailed by the left's embrace of technocracy.

Foucault traced a recognizably technocratic type of state to the rise of the "art of government" in sixteenth-century Europe. The premise of this art was that the state should see to "the welfare of the population, the improvement of its condition, the increase of its wealth, longevity, health, etc."[1] In pursuit of this end, governments would regulate their subjects' "economic activity, their production, the price [at which] they sell goods and the price at which they buy them, and so on."[2] Although Foucault's list of regulatory initiatives was short, it suggested the expansiveness of the technocratic agenda inaugurated by the art of government. These possibilities were abundantly illustrated by Cameralism, which came to flourish in seventeenth- and eighteenth-century Germany; and which, under the pressure of its academic proponents' attempts to achieve scholarly

---

[1] Foucault 1991, 100.

[2] Foucault 2008, 7.

Power Without Knowledge. Jeffrey Friedman, Oxford University Press (2019). © Oxford University Press.
DOI: 10.1093/oso/9780190877170.001.0001

rigor, transformed the art of government (*Staatskunst*) into a "science of government" (*Staatswissenschaft*)—arguably the first attempt at a technocratic policy science.[3]

Cameralism originated in efforts to augment the power of principalities in the Holy Roman Empire by increasing their revenues from taxes and from Crown properties, such as forests and mines. (*Kammer* refers to the fiscal chamber of the Crown.) However, this restricted focus came to widen considerably, for, as the Cameralist academic Wolfgang von Schröder would argue in 1752, "The welfare and the well-being of subjects is the foundation upon which all happiness of a ruler over such subjects must be based."[4] In the academic Cameralist view, as Keith Tribe puts it, "The good of the ruler is indistinguishable from the good of the populace; the administrative apparatus is devoted to the increase of the ruler's wealth through the optimization of the happiness of his subjects."[5] Therefore, the administrative apparatus should regulate social activity—potentially *all* social activity—in the interest of the subjects' well-being.

Many German princes took Cameralist advice, creating what Tribe calls "an ever-expanding work of regulation—from rules of dress, through order and cleanliness in the streets, to rules on the export and import of goods."[6] "The range of matters that eventually became the object of regulation," he writes, "is quite bewildering in its variety," in that anything and everything, including not just the processes of industry and agriculture but the conduct of what we would call personal life, might bear on the people's well-being and therefore be a fit object of *gute Polizei*. (*Polizei*—usually translated as "police," sometimes as "policy"—was derived from *polis*.)[7] Thus, the scope of the regulations embodied in the Cameralist *Polizeiordnung* was "infinite," in Tribe's view[8]—"almost infinite," in Foucault's.[9]

The expositors of Cameralism were acutely aware of the fact that their project required a great deal of knowledge; epistemics, therefore, became their central concern. Johann von Justi, the greatest Cameralist academic, conceptually divided the realm not into state and society, or the public and the private, but the knowledgeable and the ignorant—the regulators and the regulated.[10] However, while the knowledge needed by the regulators

---

[3] Tribe 1988, 8. The periodization of Cameralism is determined, of course, by the activities and people one counts as "Cameralist." Keith Tribe's *Governing Economy: The Reformation of German Economic Discourse, 1750–1840* (1988) focuses on academic Cameralism, and thus on the eighteenth century; Andre Wakefield's *The Disordered Police State: German Cameralism as Science and Practice* (2009) focuses on Cameralist practice, and thus includes the seventeenth century; Marc Raeff's *The Well-Ordered Police State* (1983) traces the "steady stream of *Landesordnungen* and *Polizeiordnungen*" that flowed from "the chanceries of the host of German territorial sovereignties both great and small," beginning in the sixteenth century (Raeff 1983, 43).

[4] As translated in Tribe 1988, 120.

[5] Ibid., 34.

[6] Ibid., 31.

[7] Ibid., 75.

[8] Ibid., 32.

[9] Foucault 2008, 7.

[10] Wakefield 2009, 34.

for the good of the regulated was as limitless as were the activities to be regulated, this knowledge was readily obtained, the academic Cameralists assumed, and they duly began to churn out encyclopedic textbooks for epistocrats covering everything from silver mining, viticulture, fruit growing, vegetable gardening, and animal husbandry to medicinal herbs, flowers, "brewing, bleaching, advice on how to get spots off clothes, how to get rid of headaches."[11] An anonymous critic protested:

> It is true that the greatest and the smallest things—potato growing, and the oak tree, the art of preparing manure and the analysis of the infinite, pig breeding and pedagogy—have generally more or less relationship with the art of governing. But does it follow that one must know all of them intimately? And how could that possibly happen?[12]

The Cameralists had much in common, epistemologically, with the "younger" German Historical economists, such as Gustav von Schmoller and Adolph Wagner, whose late nineteenth-century lectures fostered an explosion, not of encyclopedic textbooks, but encyclopedic statistical studies of social problems. ("Statistics" originated in the German *Statistik*, another Cameralist term; it meant "knowledge of the state.")[13] Students of the German Historical school spread the Progressive gospel to the United States and elsewhere in the West.[14] But while the epistemological naiveté displayed by so many Progressives was anticipated by Cameralism, and may well have been fostered by it—both Wagner and Schmoller studied the Cameralists' writings in depth, Schmoller even receiving a degree in the subject[15]—the Progressives were naive realists about *the people's* perceptions of social problems (so long as propagandists did not interfere with the people's perceptions of the self-evident truth). Despite their reputation for elitism, they divided the realm not into the learned and the ignorant, but the people and the special interests—both of which, they thought, knew the cause of social problems and their remedies, as these were self-evident. Progressivism departed from Cameralism, accordingly, over the question of popular sovereignty. Nor did Cameralists contemplate any fundamental challenge to the hierarchy of German estates; Cameralism was inegalitarian by default as well as elitist by doctrine. In these respects, Cameralist statism was far from being a left-wing project *avant la lettre*. Yet an essentially Cameralist statism has

---

[11] The quotation and the list are drawn from Tribe 1988, 25–26, with the exception of mining, which Wakefield emphasizes.

[12] Wakefield 2009, 49.

[13] Tribe 1988, 33.

[14] Rodgers 1998, 98.

[15] On Wagner, see Tribe 1988, 183; on Schmoller, Caldwell 2004, 48. Marx was urged by his father to study the *Staatswissenschaften* (Stedman Jones 2016, 41), but he passed up the opportunity (Marx [1837] 1975, 20).

been the default position of the contemporary left—in large part, it appears, due to the Progressive Era assumption that the people can control technocracy and ensure its responsiveness to their interests. The electorate has replaced the Crown, but the goals are the same—as is the epistemic naiveté.

Like the Progressives and the contemporary left, moreover, Cameralists were hostile to unrestrained capitalism, although, lacking a conception of capitalism as a social or economic "system," this hostility was not particularly pronounced. Uncontrolled production and commerce were merely signal features of the German landscape that, along with so many other features, demanded state regulation in the interest of the people's welfare. For the Progressives, by contrast, capitalism was to be the main target of state action, a target invested with all the animus we would expect to be directed against a system—once it became known as such—to which the squalor, disharmony, and alienation of modernity were attributed. The goal of the Progressives, however, was again the same as that of the Cameralists: to use the state to solve whatever social and economic problems arose.

Marxism too, of course, gave rise to a variant of anticapitalist statism, but by the middle of the twentieth century, the left had begun to repudiate this variant (more accurately, the Stalinist variant): left totalitarianism. In contrast, there has been no reckoning with the Progressive variant: democratic technocracy. Thus, what is now known as democratic "socialism," at least in the United States, is a beefed-up technocracy wrapped in emancipatory anticapitalist rhetoric. Arguably, moreover, the anticapitalist legacy of both of the main streams of left-wing thought (Marxist-emancipatory on one side, technocratic on the other) stands in the way of such a reckoning, as many of the orthodox in both traditions fear a capitalism run wild if, failing its abolition, it is not tightly controlled.

One has to wonder, however, if this fear, and the assumption that technocracy is an appropriate response to it, has simply not been thought through. If capitalism is, in fact, an epistemically advantageous means of advancing people's welfare, why should the left resist it—short of attempting to abolish it? It is one thing to believe (for example) that capitalism, or commodity production, is inherently at odds with human self-determination and therefore must be completely done away with, regardless of the consequences or, alternatively, because the consequence will be to abolish all social problems. It is entirely different to accept capitalism, even grudgingly or merely until the revolution, and, in the interim, to use technocracy to inhibit the redeeming feature of capitalism—the exit mechanism—in order to alleviate those problems.

Consistent with this analysis, it may be that the technocratic state has been tacitly accepted on the left not because anyone since von Justi has offered a cogent theoretical defense of the ability of technocrats to know how best to block people's exit opportunities, but because the attention devoted to social problems themselves has crowded out attention to the efficacy of solving these problems technocratically. Suppose, however, that we follow Marx in attributing all social problems—including, in our day, the festering garbage dumps of Phnom Penh—to capitalism. It does not follow that people's exit from the garbage dumps should be blocked by technocratic regulation. Whatever the cause of social problems, people should be able to exit from them.

Yet our humanist culture may leave us with such a powerful revulsion against bad intentions that the case against technocracy will never have the appeal of the case against capitalism—fueled as capitalism is by greed. Technocracy may therefore continue to get a free ride intellectually, as suggested by the near-universal infatuation with it among today's self-styled socialists. The Cameralists, at least, recognized that technocracy is inseparable from high epistemic ambitions, and they sought to fulfill these ambitions—no matter how risible their efforts seem in hindsight. On today's left, even that degree of epistemological awareness is lacking. This leads by default to embracing a technocratic system that cannot reasonably be expected to fulfill humanitarian ambitions, at least until technocrats become epistemically judicious.

The same cultural revolution that might bring about such a technocracy—a revolution against the illusion of self-evident truth, and against the attendant epistemic pathologies—might also produce a left that, for the first time, did not compensate for its moral rigor with epistemological neglect. Such an ideational shift is as little in prospect on the left as it is among social scientists or non-left citizen-technocrats. However: it is not inconceivable that it, too, might occur.

REFERENCES

Abelson, Robert P. 1986. "Beliefs Are Like Possessions." *Journal for the Theory of Social Behavior* 16: 223–250.

Abelson, Robert P., and Deborah A. Prentice. 1989. "Beliefs as Possessions: A Functional Perspective." In *Attitude Structure and Function*, ed. Anthony R. Pratkanis, Steven James Brecker, and Anthony G. Greenwald. Hillsdale, NJ: Erlbaum.

Acemoglu, Daron, and Joshua Angrist. 1998. "Consequences of Employment Protection? The Case of the Americans with Disabilities Act." Cambridge, MA: National Bureau of Economic Research Working Paper No. 6670.

Acharya, Viral V., and Matthew Richardson. 2009. "Causes of the Financial Crisis." *Critical Review* 21(2–3): 195–210.

Achen, Christopher H. 1975. "Mass Political Attitudes and the Survey Response." *American Political Science Review* 69(4): 1218–1231.

Achen, Christopher H., and Larry M. Bartels. 2016. *Democracy for Realists: Why Elections Do Not Produce Responsive Government.* Princeton, NJ: Princeton University Press.

Admati, Anat, and Martin Hellwig. 2013. *The Bankers' New Clothes.* Princeton, NJ: Princeton University Press.

Adorno, T. W., Else Frenkel-Brunswik, Daniel J. Levinson, and R. Nevitt Sanford. 1950. *The Authoritarian Personality.* New York: Harper & Row.

Akerlof, George A. 1970. "The Market for Lemons: Quality Uncertainty and the Market Mechanism." *Quarterly Journal of Economics* 84: 488–500.

Akerlof, George A., and Robert J. Shiller. 2009. *Animal Spirits.* Princeton, NJ: Princeton University Press.

Alchian, Armen A., and Reuben A. Kessel. 1962. "Competition, Monopoly, and the Pursuit of Pecuniary Gain." In *Aspects of Labor Economics*, ed. H. Gregg Lewis. Princeton, NJ: Princeton University Press.

Almond, Gabriel A., and G. Bingham Powell. 1966. *Comparative Politics: A Developmental Approach*. Boston: Little, Brown.

Altemeyer, Bob. 1981. *Right-Wing Authoritarianism*. Winnipeg: University of Manitoba Press.

Altemeyer, Bob. 1988. *Enemies of Freedom*. San Francisco: Jossey-Bass.

Altemeyer, Bob. 1996. *The Authoritarian Specter*. Cambridge, MA: Harvard University Press.

Althaus, Scott L. 2003. *Collective Preferences in Democratic Politics*. New York: Cambridge University Press.

Althaus, Scott L., Mark Bevir, Jeffrey Friedman, Hélène Landemore, Rogers M. Smith, and Susan Stokes. 2014. "Roundtable on Political Epistemology." *Critical Review* 26(1–2): 1–32.

Ameri, Mason, Lisa Schur, Meera Adya, Scott Bentley, Patrick McKay, and Douglas Kruse. 2015. "The Disability Employment Puzzle: A Field Experiment on Employer Hiring Behavior." Cambridge, MA: National Bureau of Economic Research Working Paper No. 21560.

Anderson, Elizabeth. 2006. "Democracy, Public Policy, and Lay Assessments of Scientific Testimony." *Episteme* 3: 8–22.

Andrews, Edmund L. 2002. "With Germany Formally in Recession, Many Are Wondering Why." *New York Times*, February 28.

Angrist, Joshua D., and Jörn-Steffen Pischke. 2010. "The Credibility Revolution in Empirical Economics: How Better Research Design Is Taking the Con Out of Economics." *Journal of Economic Perspectives* 24(2): 3–30.

Arrow, Kenneth J. 1987. "Rationality of Self and Others in an Economic System." In *Rational Choice: The Contrast Between Economics and Psychology*, ed. Robin M. Hogarth and Melvin W. Reder. Chicago: University of Chicago Press.

Ashcraft, Adam B., and Til Schuermann. 2008. "Understanding the Securitization of Subprime Mortgage Credit." Federal Reserve Bank of New York, Staff Report 318, March.

Atkins, Ralph, and Matt Steinglass. 2011. "A Fix That Functions." *Financial Times*, August 4.

Bachelder, Kate. 2014. "The Top 10 Liberal Superstitions." *Wall Street Journal*, October 31.

Bandura, Albert. 1977. *Social Learning Theory*. Englewood Cliffs, NJ: Prentice-Hall.

Banerjee, Abhijit, and Esther Duflo. 2014. "The Experimental Approach to Development Economics." In *Field Experiments and Their Critics: Essays on the Uses and Abuses of Experimentation in the Social Sciences*, ed. Dawn Langan Teele. New Haven: Yale University Press.

Barkow, Jerome H., Leda Cosmides, and John Tooby, eds. 1992. *The Adapted Mind: Evolutionary Psychology and the Generation of Culture*. New York: Oxford University Press.

Bartels, Larry M. 1993. "Messages Received: The Political Impact of Media Exposure." *American Political Science Review* 87(2): 267–285.

Bartels, Larry M. 1996. "Uninformed Votes: Information Effects in Presidential Elections." *American Journal of Political Science* 40: 194–230.

Bartels, Larry M. 2003. "Democracy with Attitudes." In *Electoral Democracy*, ed. Michael B. MacKuen and George Rabinowitz. Ann Arbor: University of Michigan Press.

Barth, James R. 2011. *The Rise and Fall of the U.S. Mortgage and Credit Markets*. New York: Wiley.

Barth, James R., Gerard Caprio Jr., and Ross Levine. 2012. *Guardians of Finance: Making Regulators Work for Us*. Cambridge, MA: MIT Press.

Beattie, Peter. 2018. "Theory, Media, and Democracy for Realists." *Critical Review* 30(1–2): 13–36.

Bellamy, Edward. [1888] 1951. *Looking Backward: 2000–1887.* New York: Random House.

Bennett, Eileen. 2015. "Many Criticizing Teachers Have No Idea What Goes On." *Buffalo News,* February 4.

Bennett, Stephen E., and Jeffrey Friedman. 2008. "The Irrelevance of Economic Theory to Understanding Economic Ignorance." *Critical Review* 20: 195–258.

Bentham, Jeremy. [1817] 1969. "Parliamentary Reform Catechism." In *A Bentham Reader,* ed. Mary Peter Mach. New York: Pegasus.

Berelson, Bernard R. 1952. "Democratic Theory and Public Opinion." *Public Opinion Quarterly* 16(3): 313–330.

Berger, Brooke. 2013. "Don't Teach to the Test." *USNews.com,* April 11.

Berlin, Isaiah. [1958] 1969. "Two Concepts of Liberty." In idem, *Four Essays on Liberty.* Oxford: Oxford University Press.

Bernanke, Ben S. 2005. "Testimony before the Joint Economic Committee." October 20. https://www.federalreserve.gov/newsevents/testimony/bernanke20090603a.htm

Bernstein, David E. 2001. *Only One Place of Redress: African Americans, Labor Regulations, and the Courts from Reconstruction to the New Deal.* Durham, NC: Duke University Press.

Best, Joel. 2001. *Damned Lies and Statistics.* Berkeley: University of California Press.

Bevir, Mark. 1999. *The Logic of the History of Ideas.* Cambridge: Cambridge University Press.

Bhidé, Amar. 2017. "Constraining Knowledge: Traditions and Rules That Limit Medical Innovation." *Critical Review* 29(1): 1–33.

Blinder, Alan S. 2013. *After the Music Stopped: The Financial Crisis, the Response, and the Work Ahead.* New York: Penguin.

Blinder, Alan S., and Alan B. Krueger. 2004. "What Does the Public Know about Economic Policy, and How Does It Know It?" *Brookings Papers on Economic Activity,* no. 1.

Bloor, David. 1991. *Knowledge and Social Imagery.* 2nd ed. Chicago: University of Chicago Press.

Bohman, James. 2010. "Participation Through Publics: Did Dewey Answer Lippmann?" *Contemporary Pragmatism* 7(1): 49–68.

Brennan, Geoffrey, and Loren Lomasky. 1993. *Democracy and Decision.* New York: Cambridge University Press.

Brennan, Jason. 2011. *The Ethics of Voting.* Princeton, NJ: Princeton University Press.

Brennan, Jason. 2014. "How Smart Is Democracy? You Can't Answer That Question A Priori." *Critical Review* 26(1–2): 33–58.

Brennan, Jason. 2016. *Against Democracy.* Princeton, NJ: Princeton University Press.

Bronfenbrenner, Martin. 1991. "Economics as Dentistry." *Southern Economic Journal* 57(3): 599–605.

Brooks, David. 2018. "The Chaos after Trump." *New York Times,* March 5.

Bruni, Frank. 2014. "Toward Better Teachers." *New York Times,* November 1.

Bryant, Jennings, and Mary Beth Oliver. 2008. *Media Effects: Advances in Theory and Research.* 3rd ed. London: Routledge.

Buchanan, James M. 1996. "Minimum Wage Addendum." *Wall Street Journal,* April 25.

Buchanan, James M., and Gordon Tullock. 1962. *The Calculus of Consent.* Ann Arbor: University of Michigan Press.

Bullock, John G., and Robert C. Luskin. 2011. "'Don't Know' Means 'Don't Know': DK Responses and the Public's Level of Political Knowledge." *Journal of Politics* 73(2): 547–557.

References

Butler, Andrew C., Franklin M. Zaromb, Keith B. Lyle, and Henry L. Roediger. 2009. "Using Popular Films to Enhance Classroom Learning: The Good, the Bad, and the Interesting." *Psychological Science* 20(9): 1161–1168.

Buturovic, Zeljka. 2010. "Putting Political Experts to the Test." *Critical Review* 22(4): 389–396.

Buturovic, Zeljka. 2012. "Deep Down: Consequentialist Assumptions Underlying Policy Differences." *Critical Review* 24(2): 269–289.

Buturovic, Zeljka, and Slavisa Tasic. 2015. "Kahneman's Failed Revolution against Economic Orthodoxy." *Critical Review* 27:2: 127–145.

Caldwell, Bruce. 2004. *Hayek's Challenge: An Intellectual Biography of F. A. Hayek.* Chicago: University of Chicago Press.

Calomiris, Charles W., and Stephen H. Haber. 2014. *Fragile by Design: The Political Origins of Banking Crises and Scarce Credit.* Princeton, NJ: Princeton University Press.

Campbell, Angus, Philip E. Converse, Warren E. Miller, and Donald E. Stokes. 1960. *The American Voter.* Chicago: University of Chicago Press.

Campbell, David E. 2006. *Why We Vote.* Princeton, NJ: Princeton University Press.

Caplan, Bryan. 2007. *The Myth of the Rational Voter: Why Democracies Choose Bad Policies.* Princeton, NJ: Princeton University Press.

Caplan, Bryan. 2008. "Reply to My Critics." *Critical Review* 20(3): 377–413.

Card, David, and Alan B. Krueger. 1994. "Minimum Wages and Employment: A Case Study of the Fast-Food Industry in New Jersey and Pennsylvania." *American Economic Review* 84(4): 487–496.

Card, David, and Alan B. Krueger. 2000. "Minimum Wages and Employment: A Case Study of the Fast-Food Industry in New Jersey and Pennsylvania: Reply." *American Economic Review* 90(5): 1397–1420.

Carmines, Edward G., and Nicholas J. D'Amico. 2014. "The New Look in Political Ideology Research." *Annual Review of Political Science* 18: 205–216.

Carmines, Edward G., and James A. Stimson. 1980. "The Two Faces of Issue Voting." *American Political Science Review* 74: 78–91.

Carpenter, Jeffrey, Stephen Burs, and Eric Verhoogen. 2005. "Comparing Students to Workers: The Effect of Social Framing in Distribution Games." In *Field Experiments in Economics,* ed. Jeffrey Carpenter, Glenn Harrison, and John List. Amsterdam: Elsevier.

Cawelti, John G. 1973. "Blockbusters and Muckraking." In *Muckraking: Past, Present, and Future,* ed. John M. Harrison and Harry H. Stein. University Park: Pennsylvania State University Press.

Cherneski, JanaLee. 2018. "An Unacknowledged Adversary: Carl Schmitt, Joseph Schumpeter, and the Classical Doctrine of Democracy." *Critical Review* 29(4): 447–472.

Chinni, Dante. 2017. "Trump's Virginia Faithful." *Wall Street Journal,* February 21.

Chong, Dennis, and James N. Druckman. 2011. "Identifying Frames in Political News." In *Sourcebook for Political Communication Research,* ed. Erik P. Bucy and R. Lance Holbert. London: Routledge.

Christie, Richard, and Peggy Cook. 1958. "A Guide to the Published Literature Relating to the Authoritarian Personality Through 1956." *Journal of Psychology* 45: 171–199.

Citrin, Jack, and Donald Philip Green. 1990. "The Self-Interest Motive in American Public Opinion." In *Research in Micropolitics: Public Opinion, 1990: A Research Annual,* vol. 3, ed. Samuel Long. Greenwich, CT: JAI Press.

Cohan, William D. 2009. *House of Cards: A Tale of Hubris and Wretched Excess on Wall Street.* New York: Doubleday.

Cohen, Richard. 2009. "How Is Cramer to Know What Insiders Don't?" *Investor's Business Daily,* March 17.

Cohn, Jonathan. 2009. "Healthy Examples: Plenty of Countries Get Healthcare Right." *Boston Globe,* July 5.

Colander, David. 1991. *Why Aren't Economists as Important as Garbagemen? Essays on the State of Economics.* Armonk, NY: M. E. Sharpe.

Colander, David. 2007. *The Making of an Economist, Redux.* Princeton, NJ: Princeton University Press.

Colander, David, Richard P. F. Holt, and J. Barkley Rosser Jr. 2004. *The Changing Face of Economics: Conversations with Cutting Edge Economists.* Ann Arbor: University of Michigan Press.

Collingwood, R. G. [1946] 1993. *The Idea of History.* Rev. ed., ed. Jan van der Dussen. Oxford: Oxford University Press.

Converse, Philip E. 1964. "The Nature of Belief Systems in Mass Publics." In *Ideology and Discontent,* ed. David E. Apter. New York: Free Press.

Converse, Philip E. 1970. "Attitudes and Non-attitudes: Continuation of a Dialogue." In *The Quantitative Analysis of Social Problems,* ed. Edward R. Tufte. Reading, MA: Addison-Wesley.

Converse, Philip E. 2006. "Democratic Theory and Electoral Reality." *Critical Review* 18(1–3): 297–329.

Cooley, Thomas F., and Stephen F. LeRoy. 1981. "Identification and Estimation of Money Demand." *American Economic Review* 71(5): 825–844.

Cowley, Stacy. 2015. "Health Care Law Leads Business Owners to Rethink Plans for Growth." *New York Times,* November 19.

Crews, Clyde Wayne. 2016. "Ten Thousand Commandments: An Annual Snapshot of the Federal Regulatory State, 2016 Edition." Washington, DC: Heritage Foundation.

Dahl, Robert A. 1961. *Who Governs?* New Haven: Yale University Press.

Dahl, Robert A. 1989. *Democracy and Its Critics.* New Haven: Yale University Press.

Daley, Alan. 2014. "Getting Rid of Incompetent Teachers." *RealClearPolitics,* June 12.

Debreu, Gerard. 1991. "The Mathematization of Economic Theory." *American Economic Review* 81(1): 1–7.

DeCanio, Samuel. 2000. "Bringing the State Back In . . . Again." *Critical Review* 14: 139–146.

DeCanio, Samuel. 2005. "State Autonomy and American Political Development: How Mass Democracy Promoted State Power." *Studies in American Political Development* 19: 117–136.

DeCanio, Samuel. 2006. "Mass Opinion and American Political Development." *Critical Review* 18(1–3): 143–156.

DeCanio, Samuel. 2007. "The Autonomy of the Democratic State: Rejoinder to Carpenter, Ginsberg, and Shefter." *Critical Review* 19(1): 187–196.

Delli Carpini, Michael X., and Scott Keeter. 1996. *What Americans Know about Politics and Why It Matters.* New Haven: Yale University Press.

DeParle, Jason, Robert Gebeloff, and Sabrina Tavernise. 2011. "Experts Say Bleak Portrait of Poverty Missed the Mark." *New York Times,* November 4.

Dewan, Shaila. 2014. "Rent Asunder." *New York Times Magazine,* May 4.

Dewatripont, Mathias, Jean-Charles Rochet, and Jean Tirole. 2010. *Balancing the Banks: Global Lessons from the Financial Crisis*. Princeton, NJ: Princeton University Press.

Dewey, John. [1898] 1975. "Evolution and Ethics." In *John Dewey, The Middle Works, 1899–1924*, vol. 3, *1882–1898*, ed. Jo Ann Boydstun. Carbondale: Southern Illinois University Press.

Dewey, John. [1906] 1977. "Beliefs and Existences." In *John Dewey, The Middle Works, 1899–1924*, vol. 5, *1903–1906*, ed. Jo Ann Boydstun. Carbondale: Southern Illinois University Press.

Dewey, John. [1908] 1998. "Does Reality Possess Practical Character?" In *The Essential Dewey*, vol. 1: *Pragmatism, Education, Democracy*, ed. Larry A. Hickman and Thomas M. Alexander. Bloomington: Indiana University Press.

Dewey, John. 1910. *How We Think*. Boston: D. C. Heath and Co.

Dewey, John. [1917] 2011. "The Need for a Recovery of Philosophy." In *The Pragmatism Reader: From Peirce through the Present*, ed. Robert B. Talisse and Scott F. Aiken. Princeton, NJ: Princeton University Press.

Dewey, John. [1919] 1998. "Philosophy and Democracy." In *The Essential Dewey*, vol. 1: *Pragmatism, Education, Democracy*, ed. Larry A. Hickman and Thomas M. Alexander. Bloomington: Indiana University Press.

Dewey, John. [1920] 1948. *Reconstruction in Philosophy*. Boston: Beacon.

Dewey, John. 1921. *Human Nature and Conduct: An Introduction to Social Psychology*. New York: Henry Holt.

Dewey, John. 1922. "Public Opinion." *The New Republic*, May 3.

Dewey, John. 1925a. "The Development of American Pragmatism." In *The Essential Dewey*, vol. 1: *Pragmatism, Education, Democracy*, ed. Larry A. Hickman and Thomas M. Alexander. Bloomington: Indiana University Press.

Dewey, John. 1925b. "Practical Democracy." *The New Republic*, December 2.

Dewey, John. [1927] 1954. *The Public and Its Problems*. Athens: Ohio University Press.

Dewey, John. 1931. "Social Science and Social Control." *The New Republic*, July 29: 276–277.

Dewey, John. [1937] 1987. "Liberalism in a Vacuum: A Critique of Walter Lippmann's Social Philosophy." In *John Dewey: The Later Works, 1925–1953*, vol. 11, ed. Jo Ann Boydstun. Carbondale: Southern Illinois University Press.

Dewey, John. [1939] 1989. *Freedom and Culture*. Buffalo, NY: Prometheus.

Diamond, Jared. 2012. *The World until Yesterday: What Can We Learn from Traditional Societies?* New York: Viking.

Dilliard, Irving. 1973. Foreword to *Muckraking: Past, Present, and Future*, ed. John M. Harrison and Harry H. Stein. University Park: Pennsylvania State University Press.

Dougherty, Conor. 2011. "How to Accurately Measure the Poor Remains Elusive." *Wall Street Journal*, September 14.

Downs, Anthony. 1957. *An Economic Theory of Democracy*. New York: Harper & Row.

Druckman, James N., Jordan Fein, and Thomas J. Leeper. 2012. "A Source of Bias in Public Opinion Stability." *American Political Science Review* 106(2): 430–454.

Dryzek, John. 2006. *Deliberative Global Politics: Discourse and Democracy in a Divided World*. Cambridge: Polity.

Edlin, Aaron, Andrew Gelman, and Noah Kaplan. 2007. "Voting as a Rational Choice: Why and How People Vote to Improve the Well-Being of Others." *Rationality and Society* 19: 293–314.

Edwards, Kari, and Edward E. Smith. 1996. "A Disconfirmation Bias in the Evaluation of Arguments." *Journal of Personality and Social Psychology* 71(1): 5–24.

Eisenach, Eldon L. 1994. *The Lost Promise of Progressivism*. Lawrence: University Press of Kansas.

Ellis, Christopher, and James A. Stimson. 2012. *Ideology in America*. New York: Cambridge University Press.

Erel, Isil, Taylor Nadauld, and René M. Stulz. 2014. "Why Did Holdings of Highly Rated Securitization Tranches Differ So Much across Banks?" *Review of Financial Studies* 27 (2):404–453.

Erikson, Robert, Michael MacKuen, and James Stimson. 2002. *The Macro Polity*. Cambridge: Cambridge University Press.

Esbenshade, Jill. 2004. *Monitoring Sweatshops: Workers, Consumers, and the Global Apparel Industry*. Philadelphia: Temple University Press.

Estlund, David M. 2008. *Democratic Authority: A Philosophical Framework*. Princeton, NJ: Princeton University Press.

Evans, Anthony, and Jeffrey Friedman. 2011. "Search vs. Browse: A Theory of Error Grounded in Radical (Not Rational) Ignorance." *Critical Review* 23: 73–104.

Fay, Brian. [1983] 1994. "General Laws and Explaining Human Behavior." In *Readings in the Philosophy of Social Science*, ed. Michael Martin and Lee C. McIntyre. Cambridge, MA: MIT Press.

Feldman, Stanley, and Karen Stenner. 1997. "Perceived Threat and Authoritarianism." *Political Psychology* 18(4): 741–770.

Felin, Teppo. 2018. "The Fallacy of Obviousness." *Aeon*, July 5.

Ferejohn, John. 1986. "Incumbent Performance and Electoral Control." *Public Choice* 50(1): 5–25.

Ferejohn, John. 1990. "Information and the Electoral Process." In *Information and Democratic Processes*, ed. John Ferejohn and James Kuklinski. Urbana: University of Illinois Press.

Ferguson, Niall. 2013. "The Regulated States of America." *Wall Street Journal*, June 19.

Fernbach, Philip M., Todd Rogers, Craig R. Fox, and Steven A. Sloman. 2013. "Political Extremism Is Supported by an Illusion of Understanding." *Psychological Science* 24(6): 939–946.

Festenstein, Matthew. 1997. *Pragmatism and Political Theory: From Dewey to Rorty*. Chicago: University of Chicago Press.

Fiedler, Klaus. 1988. "The Dependence of the Conjunction Fallacy on Subtle Linguistic Factors." *Psychological Research* 50: 123–129.

Financial Crisis Inquiry Commission. 2011. *The Financial Crisis Inquiry Report*. New York: PublicAffairs.

Fiorina, Morris P. 1981. *Retrospective Voting in American National Elections*. New Haven: Yale University Press.

Fiorina, Morris P. 1990. "Information and Rationality in Elections." In *Information and Democratic Processes*, ed. John Ferejohn and James Kuklinski. Urbana: University of Illinois Press.

Fishkin, James L. 2009. *When the People Speak: Deliberative Democracy and Public Consultation*. New York: Oxford University Press.

Fletcher, Garth J. O. 1994. "Assessing Error in Social Judgment: Commentary on Koehler on Base-Rate." *Psycoloquy* 5(10): Base Rate (10).

Forcey, Charles. 1961. *The Crossroads of Liberalism: Croly, Weyl, Lippmann, and the Progressive Era, 1900–1925*. New York: Oxford University Press.

Fording, Richard C., and Sanford F. Schram. 2018. "The Cognitive and Emotional Sources of Trump Support: The Case of Low-Information Voters." *New Political Science* 39(4): 670–686.

Forrester, Jay. 1995. "Counterintuitive Behavior of Social Systems." Based on testimony before the Subcommittee on Urban Growth, Committee on Banking and Currency, U.S. House of Representatives, October 7, 1970.

Foucault, Michel. 1991. "Governmentality." In *The Foucault Effect: Studies in Governmentality*, ed. Graham Burchell, Colin Gordon, and Peter Miller. Chicago: University of Chicago Press.

Foucault, Michel. 2008. *The Birth of Biopolitics: Lectures at the Collège de France, 1978–1979*, trans. Graham Burchell. New York: Palgrave Macmillan.

Fourcade, Marion. 2009. *Economists and Societies: Discipline and Profession in the United States, Britain, and France, 1890s-1990s*. Princeton, NJ: Princeton University Press.

Freeder, Sean. 2018. "Malice and Stupidity: Outgroup Motive Attribution and Affective Polarization." Unpublished manuscript, Department of Political Science, University of California, Berkeley.

Freud, Sigmund. 1935. *An Autobiographical Study*. New York: Norton.

Friedman, Jeffrey. 1996. "Introduction." In idem, ed., *The Rational Choice Controversy: Economic Models of Politics Reconsidered*. New Haven: Yale University Press.

Friedman, Jeffrey. 2003. "Public Opinion: Bringing the Media Back In." *Critical Review* 15(3–4): 239–260.

Friedman, Jeffrey. 2006. "Democratic Competence in Normative and Positive Theory: Neglected Implications of 'The Nature of Belief Systems in Mass Publics.'" *Critical Review* 18(1–3): i–xlii.

Friedman, Jeffrey. 2007. "'A Weapon in the Hands of the People': The Rhetorical Presidency in Historical and Conceptual Context." *Critical Review* 19(2–3): 197–240.

Friedman, Jeffrey. 2011. "New Data on Bankers' Risk Aversion." causesofthecrisis.blogspot.com, October 15.

Friedman, Jeffrey. 2012a. "Beyond Cues and Political Elites: The Forgotten Zaller." *Critical Review* 24(4): 417–462.

Friedman, Jeffrey. 2012b. "Motivated Skepticism or Inevitable Conviction? Dogmatism and the Study of Politics." *Critical Review* 24(2): 131–156.

Friedman, Jeffrey. 2013a. "Freedom Has No Intrinsic Value." *Critical Review* 25(1): 13–85.

Friedman, Jeffrey. 2013b. "General Introduction." In *Political Knowledge* (4 vols.), ed. Jeffrey Friedman and Shterna Friedman. New York: Routledge.

Friedman, Jeffrey. 2014. "Political Epistemology." *Critical Review* 26(1–2): i–xvi.

Friedman, Jeffrey. 2017a. "The Legitimacy Crisis." Subtext.org, October 4.

Friedman, Jeffrey. 2017b. "Nationalism Isn't Xenophobia, But It's Just as Bad." Subtext.org, August 16.

Friedman, Jeffrey. 2017c. "The Problem of Epistocratic Identification and the (Possibly) Dysfunctional Division of Epistemic Labor." *Critical Review* 29(3): 293–327.

Friedman, Jeffrey, and Wladimir Kraus. 2011. *Engineering the Financial Crisis: Systemic Risk and the Failure of Regulation*. Philadelphia: University of Pennsylvania Press.

Frydl, Kathleen. 2013. *The Drug Wars in America, 1940–1973*. New York: Cambridge University Press.

Fuller, Dan, and Doris Geide-Stevenson. 2003. "Consensus Among Economists: Revisited." *Journal of Economic Education* 34(4): 369–387.

Funder, David C. 1987. "Errors and Mistakes: Evaluating the Accuracy of Social Judgment." *Psychological Bulletin* 101(1): 75–90.

Gaines, Brian J., James H. Kuklinski, Paul J. Quirk, Buddy Peyton, and Jay Verkuilen. 2007. "Same Facts, Different Interpretations: Partisan Motivation and Opinion in Iraq." *Journal of Politics* 69(4): 957–974.

Gardner, Walt. 2014. Letter to the Editor, *New York Times*, November 1.

Geanakoplos, John. 2010. "Solving the Present Crisis and Managing the Leverage Cycle." Paper presented to the Financial Crisis Inquiry Commission, Washington, DC, February 27–28.

Geertz, Clifford. [1983] 1994. "Thick Description: Toward an Interpretive Theory of Culture." In *Readings in the Philosophy of Social Science*, ed. Michael Martin and Lee C. McIntyre. Cambridge, MA: MIT Press.

Gigerenzer, Gerd. 1991. "How to Make Cognitive Illusions Disappear: Beyond 'Heuristics and Biases.'" *European Review of Social Psychology* 2: 83–115.

Gigerenzer, Gerd. 2005. "I Think, Therefore I Err." *Social Research* 72(1): 1–24.

Gilens, Martin. 2001. "Political Ignorance and Collective Policy Preferences." *American Political Science Review* 95: 379–96.

Gjerstad, Steven, and Vernon L. Smith. 2009. "Monetary Policy, Credit Extension, and Housing Bubbles: 2008 and 1929." *Critical Review* 21(2–3): 269–300.

Goldfarb, Zachary A. 2012. "Why August's Jobs Number Is Likely Wrong." *Washington Post*, September 7.

Gómez, Paz. 2018. "Minimum Wage a Win for Unions, Not the Poor." American Institute for Economic Research website, June 11.

Goodin, Robert E. 1995. *Utilitarianism as a Public Philosophy*. Cambridge: Cambridge University Press.

Goodman, John C. 2015. "How Obamacare Harms Low-Income Workers." *Wall Street Journal*, January 9.

Goodwin, Crauford D. W. 2014. *Walter Lippmann: Public Economist*. Cambridge, MA: Harvard University Press.

Gootman, Elissa, and David M. Herszenhorn. 2005. "Getting Smaller to Improve the Big Picture." *New York Times*, May 3.

Gopnik, Alison. 2010. *The Philosophical Baby*. New York: Farrar, Straus, and Giroux.

Gordon, Grey, and Aaron Hedlund. 2015. "Accounting for the Rise in College Tuition." Working Paper No. 21967. Cambridge, MA: National Bureau of Economic Research.

Goren, Paul. 2012. "Political Values and Political Awareness." *Critical Review* 24(4): 505–26.

Graber, Doris. 1988. *Processing the News: How People Tame the Information Tide*. 2nd ed. White Plains, NY: Longman.

Green, Donald P., Shang E. Ha, and John G. Bullock. 2010. "Enough Already about 'Black Box' Experiments: Studying Mediation Is More Difficult Than Most Scholars Suppose." *Annals of the American Academy of Political and Social Science* 628(1): 200–208.

Gunn, Paul. 2019. "Against Epistocracy." *Critical Review* 31(1): 26–82.

Gutmann, Amy, and Dennis Thompson. 1996. *Democracy and Disagreement*. Cambridge, MA: Belknap Press of Harvard University Press.

Habermas, Jürgen. [1967] 1988. *On the Logic of the Social Sciences*. Trans. Shierry Weber Nicholsen and Jerry A. Stark. Cambridge, MA: MIT Press.

Habermas, Jürgen. [1968] 1970. *Toward a Rational Society: Student Protest, Science, and Politics*. Trans. Jeremy J. Shapiro. Boston: Beacon.

Habermas, Jürgen. [1968] 1971. *Knowledge and Human Interests*. Trans. Jeremy J. Shapiro. Boston: Beacon.

Habermas, Jürgen. [1973] 1975. *Legitimation Crisis*. Trans. Thomas McCarthy. Boston: Beacon.

Habermas, Jürgen. 2006. "Political Communication in Media Society: Does Democracy Still Enjoy an Epistemic Dimension? The Impact of Normative Theory on Empirical Research." *Communication Theory* 16: 411–426.

Habermas, Jürgen. [2013] 2015. *The Lure of Technocracy*. Trans. Ciaran Cronin. Cambridge: Polity.

Hacohen, Malachi Haim. 2000. *Karl Popper: The Formative Years, 1902–1945*. Cambridge: Cambridge University Press.

Hardin, Russell. 2009. *How Do You Know? The Economics of Ordinary Knowledge*. Princeton, NJ: Princeton University Press.

Hargreaves Heap, Shaun P., and Yanis Varoufakis. 1995. *Game Theory: A Critical Introduction*. London: Routledge.

Harrison, John M., and Harry H. Stein. 1973. *Muckraking: Past, Present, and Future*. University Park: Pennsylvania State University Press.

Hart, H. L. A. 1961. *The Concept of Law*. Oxford: Clarendon.

Hart, Oliver, and Luigi Zingales. 2010. "Curbing Risk on Wall Street." *National Affairs* no. 3: 20–34.

Hausman, Daniel. 1992. *The Inexact and Separate Science of Economics*. Cambridge: Cambridge University Press.

Hayek, F. A., ed. [1935] 1975. *Collectivist Economic Planning: Critical Studies on the Possibilities of Socialism*. Clifton, NJ: Augustus M. Kelley.

Hayek, F. A. [1945] 1948. "The Use of Knowledge in Society." In idem, *Individualism and Economic Order*. Chicago: University of Chicago Press.

Heckman, James J. 2000. "Causal Parameters and Policy Analysis in Economics: A Twentieth Century Retrospective." *Quarterly Journal of Economics* 115: 45–97.

Hendry, David F., Edward E. Leamer, and Dale J. Poirier. 1990. "The ET Dialogue: A Conversation on Econometric Methodology." *Econometric Theory* 6: 171–261.

Henrich, Joseph, Steven J. Heine, and Ara Norenzayan. 2010. "The Weirdest People in the World?" *Behavioral and Brain Sciences* 33: 61–135.

Hetherington, Marc J. 1996. "The Media's Role in Forming Voters' National Economic Evaluations in 1992." *American Journal of Political Science* 40: 372–395.

Hibbing, John R., and Elizabeth Theiss-Morse. 1995. *Congress as Public Enemy: Public Attitudes toward American Political Institutions*. Cambridge: Cambridge University Press.

Hibbing, John R., and Elizabeth Theiss-Morse. 2002. *Stealth Democracy: Americans' Beliefs about How Government Should Work*. Cambridge: Cambridge University Press.

Hintikka, Jaakko. 2004. "A Fallacious Fallacy?" *Synthese* 140: 25–35.

Hirschman, Albert O. 1970. *Exit, Voice, and Loyalty: Responses to Decline in Firms, Organizations, and States*. Cambridge, MA: Harvard University Press.

Hirschman, Albert O. 1991. *The Rhetoric of Reaction: Perversity, Futility, Jeopardy*. Cambridge, MA: Harvard University Press.

Hochschild, Jennifer. 2013. "Should the Mass Public Follow Elite Opinion? It Depends . . ." *Critical Review* 24(4): 527–544.

Hochschild, Jennifer, and Katherine Levine Einstein. 2015a. *Do Facts Matter? Information and Misinformation in American Politics*. Norman: University of Oklahoma Press.

Hochschild, Jennifer, and Katherine Levine Einstein. 2015b. "Do Facts Matter? Information and Misinformation in American Politics." *Political Science Quarterly* 130(4): 585–624.

Hodgson, Geoffrey. 2001. *How Economics Forgot History: The Problem of Historical Specificity in Social Science*. London: Routledge.

Holbach, Baron d'. 1770. *The System of Nature*. Trans. Samuel Wilkinson. Teddington, Middlesex: Echo Library.

Holden, C., and R. Mace. 1997. "Phylogenetic Analysis of the Evolution of Lactose Digestion in Adults." *Human Biology* 69: 605–628.

Horkheimer, Max, and Theodor W. Adorno. [1944] 2002. *Dialectic of Enlightenment: Philosophical Fragments*, ed. Gunzelin Schmid Noerr. Trans. Edmund Jephcott. Stanford, CA: Stanford University Press.

House Budget Committee. 2014. "The War on Poverty: Fifty Years Later." Washington, DC: House Budget Committee Majority Staff.

Howard, Jennifer. 2018. "What We Lose by Reading 100,000 Words Every Day." *Washington Post*, October 4.

Huber, Peter W. 2013. *The Cure in the Code*. New York: Basic.

Hull, John, and Alan White. 2012. "Ratings, Mortgage Securitizations, and the Apparent Creation of Value." In *Rethinking the Financial Crisis*, ed. Alan S. Blinder, Andrew W. Lo, and Robert M. Solow. New York: Russell Sage Foundation.

Hume, David. [1772] 1999. *An Enquiry Concerning Human Understanding*, ed. Tom L. Beauchamp. Oxford: Oxford University Press.

Hyman, Herbert H., and Paul B. Sheatsley. 1954. "'The Authoritarian Personality'—a Methodological Critique." In *Studies in the Scope and Method of "The Authoritarian Personality,"* ed. Richard Christie and Marie Jahoda. Glencoe, IL: The Free Press.

Iannelli, Gerard. 2014. "What Makes the Best Teacher?" *New York Times*, November 1.

Ikeda, Sanford. 1996. *Dynamics of the Mixed Economy: Toward a Theory of Interventionism*. London: Routledge.

Inglehart, Ronald. 1990. *Culture Shift in Advanced Industrial Economies*. Princeton, NJ: Princeton University Press.

Inglehart, Ronald. 1996. "The Diminishing Utility of Economic Growth: From Maximizing Security toward Maximizing Subjective Satisfaction." *Critical Review* 10(4): 509–532.

International Monetary Fund. 2008. "Global Financial Stability Report: Containing Systemic Risks and Restoring Financial Soundness." April.

Isaac, William M. 2009. Testimony before the Subcommittee on Capital Markets, Insurance, and Government Sponsored Entities, US House of Representatives, Committee on Financial Services. March 12.

Isaac, William M. 2010. *Senseless Panic*. New York: Wiley.

James, William. 1890 [1918]. *Principles of Psychology*. Vol. 1. New York: Henry Holt.

Jarrow, Robert A. 2012. "The Role of ABSs, CDSs, and CDOs in the Credit Crisis and the Economy." In *Rethinking the Financial Crisis*, ed. Alan S. Blinder, Andrew W. Lo, and Robert M. Solow. New York: Russell Sage Foundation.

Jarvie, I. C. 1988. "Evolutionary Epistemology." *Critical Review* 2(1): 92–102.

Jennings, M. Kent. 1992. "Ideological Thinking among Mass Publics and Political Elites." *Public Opinion Quarterly* 56: 419–441.

Jervis, Robert. 2010. *Why Intelligence Fails*. Ithaca, NY: Cornell University Press.

Johnson, Marcia K. 1998. "Memory and Reality." *Trends in Cognitive Sciences* 2: 399–406.

Johnson, Simon, and James Kwak. 2010. *13 Bankers: The Wall Street Takeover and the Next Financial Meltdown*. New York: Pantheon.

Jones, Ward E. 2002. "Explaining Our Own Beliefs: Non-Epistemic Believing and Doxastic Instability." *Philosophical Studies* 111: 217–249.

Jost, John T., Arie W. Kruglanski, Jack Glaser, and Frank J. Sulloway. 2003. "Political Conservatism as Motivated Social Cognition." *Psychological Bulletin* 129(3): 339–375.

Junger, Sebastian. 2016. *Tribe: On Homecoming and Belonging*. New York: Twelve.

Kahneman, Daniel. 2011. *Thinking: Fast and Slow*. New York: Farrar, Straus, and Giroux.

Kahneman, Daniel, and Amos Tversky. 1973. "On the Psychology of Prediction." *Psychological Review* 80(4): 237–251.

Kearl, J. R., Clayne L. Pope, Gordon C. Whiting, and Larry T. Wimmer. 1979. "A Confusion of Economists?" *American Economic Review* 69(2): 28–37.

Key, V. O. 1961. *Public Opinion and American Democracy*. New York: Alfred A. Knopf.

Keynes, J. M. 1936. *The General Theory of Employment, Interest, and Money*. New York: Macmillan.

Kiewiet, D. Roderick. 1983. *Macroeconomics and Micropolitics*. Chicago: University of Chicago Press.

Kiewiet, D. Roderick, and Douglas Rivers. 2005. "A Retrospective on Retrospective Voting." *Political Behavior* 6(4): 369–393.

Kiewiet, D. Roderick, and Michael S. Lewis-Beck. 2011. "No Man Is an Island: Self-Interest, the Public Interest, and Sociotropic Voting." *Critical Review* 23(3): 303–320.

Kinder, Donald R. 1983. "Diversity and Complexity in American Public Opinion." In *Political Science: The State of the Discipline*, ed. Ada Finifter. Washington, DC: American Political Science Association.

Kinder, Donald R. 1998. "Opinion and Action in the Realm of Politics." In *The Handbook of Social Psychology*, 4th ed., ed. Daniel T. Gilbert, Susan T. Fiske, and Gardner Lindzey. New York: McGraw-Hill.

Kinder, Donald R., and D. Roderick Kiewiet. 1979. "Economic Discontent and Political Behavior: The Role of Personal Grievances and Collective Economic Judgments in Congressional Voting." *American Journal of Political Science* 23(3): 495–527.

Kinder, Donald R., and D. Roderick Kiewiet. 1981. "Sociotropic Politics: The American Case." *British Journal of Political Science* 11(2): 129–161.

Kleiner, Morris M., Alan B. Krueger, and Alex Mas. 2011. "A Proposal to Encourage States to Rationalize Occupational Licensing Practices." Manuscript, Department of Economics, Princeton University.

Kloppenberg, James T. 1986. *Uncertain Victory: Social Democracy and Progressivism in European and American Thought, 1870–1920*. New York: Oxford University Press.

Knight, Kathleen. 2006. "Transformations of the Concept of Ideology in the Twentieth Century." *American Political Science Review* 100(4): 619–626.

Koehler, Jonathan J. 1993. "The Base Rate Fallacy Myth." *Psycoloquy* 4(49): Base Rate (1).

Kolodny, Niko. 2014. "Rule Over None II: Social Equality and the Justification of Democracy." *Philosophy & Public Affairs* 42(4): 287–336.

Kristof, Nicholas D. 1998. "Asia's Crisis Upsets Rising Effort to Confront Blight of Sweatshops." *New York Times*, June 15.

Kristof, Nicholas D. 2009. "Where Sweatshops Are a Dream." *New York Times*, January 15.

Kuklinski, James H., and Paul J. Quirk. 2000. "Reconsidering the Rational Public: Cognition, Heuristics, and Public Opinion." In *Elements of Reason: Cognition, Choice, and the Bounds of Rationality*, ed. Arthur Lupia, Mathew D. McCubbins, and Samuel L. Popkin. New York: Cambridge University Press.

Kuklinski, James H., and Paul J. Quirk. 2001. "Conceptual Foundations of Citizen Competence." *Political Behavior* 23(3): 285–311.

Lahey, Jessica. 2012. "The Destructive 'Too Much Homework' Myth." *New York Times*, March 6.

Landemore, Hélène. 2013. *Democratic Reason: Politics, Collective Intelligence, and the Rule of the Many*. Princeton, NJ: Princeton University Press.

Landemore, Hélène. 2014. "Yes, We Can (Make It Up on Volume): Answers to Critics." *Critical Review* 26(1–2): 170–183.

Landemore, Hélène. 2017. "Beyond the Fact of Disagreement? The Epistemic Turn in Deliberative Democracy." *Social Epistemology* 31(3): 277–295.

Landemore, Hélène, and Scott E. Page. 2015. "Deliberation and Disagreement: Problem Solving, Prediction, and Positive Dissensus." *Politics, Philosophy, and Economics* 14(3): 229–254.

Lange, Oskar. 1936. "On the Economic Theory of Socialism, Part One." *Review of Economic Studies* 4(1): 53–71.

Lange, Oskar. 1937. "On the Economic Theory of Socialism, Part Two." *Review of Economic Studies* 4(2): 123–42.

Lange, Oskar. 1938. "On the Economic Theory of Socialism." In *On the Economic Theory of Socialism*, ed. Benjamin E. Lippincott. New York: McGraw-Hill.

Lau, Richard R., and Caroline Heldman. 2009. "Self-Interest, Symbolic Attitudes, and Support for Public Policy: A Multilevel Analysis." *Political Psychology* 30(4): 513–537.

Lau, Richard R., and David Redlawsk. 2001. "Advantages and Disadvantages of Cognitive Heuristics in Political Decision Making." *American Journal of Political Science* 45: 951–971.

Laudan, Larry. 1981. "A Confutation of Convergent Realism." *Philosophy of Science* 48: 19–48.

Lavoie, Don. 1985. *Rivalry and Central Planning: The Socialist Calculation Debate Reconsidered*. Cambridge: Cambridge University Press.

Lawson, Tony. 1997. *Economics and Reality*. London: Routledge.

Leamer, Edward. 1983. "Let's Take the Con Out of Econometrics." *American Economic Review* 73(1): 31–43.

Lenz, Gabriel S. 2012. *Follow the Leader? How Voters Respond to Politicians' Policies and Performance*. Chicago: University of Chicago Press.

Leontief, Wassily. 1971. "Theoretical Assumptions and Nonobservable Facts." *American Economic Review* 61(1): 1–7.

Levi, Isaac. 1985. "Illusions about Uncertainty." *British Journal of the Philosophy of Science* 36: 331–340.

Levine, Arthur. 2014. "What Makes the Best Teacher?" *New York Times*, November 1.

Levy, Helen, and David Meltzer. 2008. "The Impact of Health Insurance on Health." *Annual Review of Public Health* 29: 399–409.

Levy, Jill S. 2014. "What Makes the Best Teacher?" *New York Times*, November 1.

Levy, Philip I. 2011. "How Do Jobs Numbers Work?" *The American*, August 9.

Lewin, Leif. 1991. *Self-Interest and Public Interest in Western Democracies*. Oxford: Oxford University Press.

Lewis-Beck, Michael S. 1988. *Economics and Elections: The Major Western Democracies.* Ann Arbor: University of Michigan Press.

Lindblom, Charles E., and David K. Cohen. 1979. *Usable Knowledge: Social Science and Social Problem Solving.* New Haven: Yale University Press.

Lippmann, Walter. [1914] 1985. *Drift and Mastery: An Attempt to Diagnose the Current Unrest.* Madison: University of Wisconsin Press.

Lippmann, Walter. [1917] 1970. "In the Next Four Years." In idem, *Force and Ideas: The Early Writings.* New York: Liveright.

Lippmann, Walter. [1920] 2008. *Liberty and the News.* Princeton, NJ: Princeton University Press.

Lippmann, Walter. [1922] 1997. *Public Opinion.* New York: Free Press.

Lippmann, Walter. [1925] 1927. *The Phantom Public.* New York: Macmillan.

Lippmann, Walter. [1937] 2005. *The Good Society.* Boston: Little, Brown.

Lippmann, Walter. 1955. *The Public Philosophy.* Boston: Little, Brown.

Lippmann, Walter, and Charles Merz. 1920. "A Test of the News." *New Republic,* August 4: 1–42.

Lodge, Milton, and Ruth Hamill. 1986. "A Partisan Schema for Information Processing." *American Political Science Review* 80: 505–519.

Lodge, Milton, Kathleen M. McGraw, and Paul Stroh. 1989. "An Impression-Driven Model of Candidate Evaluation." *American Political Science Review* 87: 399–419.

Lodge, Milton, Marco R. Steenbergen, and Shawn Braun. 1995. "The Responsive Voter: Campaign Information and the Dynamics of Candidate Evaluation." *American Political Science Review* 89: 309–326.

Lordan, Grace, and David Neumark. 2017. "People versus Machines: The Impact of Minimum Wages on Automatable Jobs." Cambridge, MA: National Bureau of Economic Research Working Paper No. 23667.

Luca, Dara Lee, and Michael Luca. 2017. "Survival of the Fittest: The Impact of the Minimum Wage on Firm Exit." Cambridge, MA: Harvard Business School NOM Unit Working Paper No. 17-088.

Lupia, Arthur. 1994. "Shortcuts vs. Encyclopedias: Information and Voting Behavior in California's Insurance Reform Elections." *American Political Science Review* 88(1): 63–76.

Lupia, Arthur. 2006. "How Elitism Undermines the Study of Voter Competence." *Critical Review* 18(1–3): 217–232.

Lupia, Arthur, and Mathew D. McCubbins. 1998. *The Democratic Dilemma: Can Citizens Learn What They Need to Know?* New York: Cambridge University Press.

Lupia, Arthur, and Mathew D. McCubbins. 2000. "Foundations of Political Competence." In *Elements of Reason: Cognition, Choice, and the Bounds of Rationality,* ed. Arthur Lupia, Mathew D. McCubbins, and Samuel L Popkin. New York: Cambridge University Press.

Luskin, Robert C. 2002. "From Denial to Extenuation and (Finally) Beyond." In *Thinking about Political Psychology,* ed. James H. Kuklinski. Cambridge: Cambridge University Press.

Lynn, Lawrence E., Jr. 1987. "The Behavioral Foundations of Public Policy Making." In *Rational Choice: The Contrast between Economics and Psychology,* ed. Robin M. Hogarth and Melvin W. Reder. Chicago: University of Chicago Press.

MacAvoy, Paul W. 1987. "The Record of the Environmental Protection Agency in Controlling Industrial Air Pollution." In *Energy: Markets and Regulation, Essays in Honor of M. A. Adelman,* ed. Richard L. Gordon, Henry D. Jacoby, and Martin B. Zimmerman. Cambridge, MA: MIT Press.

MacGilvray, Eric A. 1999. "Experience as Experiment: Some Consequences of Pragmatism for Democratic Theory." *American Journal of Political Science* 43(2): 542–565.

MacGilvray, Eric A. 2010. "Dewey's Public." *Contemporary Pragmatism* 7(1): 31–47.

MacIntyre, Alasdair. 1988. *Whose Justice? Which Rationality?* Notre Dame: University of Notre Dame Press.

Madrian, Brigitte C., and Dennis F. Shea. 2001. "The Power of Suggestion: Inertia in 401(k) Participation and Savings Behavior." *Quarterly Journal of Economics* 116(4): 1149–1187.

Mameli, Matteo. 2007. "Evolution and Psychology in Philosophical Perspective." In *The Oxford Handbook of Evolutionary Psychology*, ed. R. I. M. Dunbar and Louise Barrett. New York: Oxford University Press.

Mandel, Michael. 2011. "How the FDA Impedes Innovation: A Case Study in Overregulation." Washington, DC: Progressive Policy Institute.

Mankiw, N. Gregory. 2013. "Politics Aside, a Common Bond." *New York Times*, June 30.

Manski, Charles. 2013. *Public Policy in an Uncertain World*. Cambridge, MA: Harvard University Press.

Martin, Jay. 1973. "The Literature of Argument and the Argument of Literature." In *Muckraking: Past, Present, and Future*, ed. John M. Harrison and Harry H. Stein. University Park: Pennsylvania State University Press.

Marx, Karl. [1837] 1975. "Letter from Marx to His Father." In *Karl Marx Frederick Engels Collected Works,* vol. 1. New York: International Publishers.

Mathews, Jay. 2014. "Parents Saying No to Too Much Homework." September 28. *WashingtonPost. com.*

Merton, Robert K. 1936. "The Unintended Consequences of Purposive Human Action." *American Sociological Review* 1(6): 894–904.

Mill, John Stuart. [1831] 2007. "On the Spirit of the Age." In *The Spirit of the Age: Victorian Essays,* ed. Gertrude Himmelfarb. New Haven: Yale University Press.

Miller, Claire Cain. 2015. "When Family-Friendly Rules Cost Women Too Much." *New York Times*, May 26.

Miller, Henry I. 2010. "Type I Errors." *Regulation*, Fall: 30–33.

Mirowski, Philip E. 1991. *More Heat Than Light: Economics as Social Physics, Physics as Nature's Economics*. Cambridge: Cambridge University Press.

Munz, Peter. 1985. *Our Knowledge of the Growth of Knowledge: Popper or Wittgenstein?* London: Routledge & Kegan Paul.

Murphy, Kevin J. 2012. "Pay, Politics, and the Financial Crisis." In *Rethinking the Financial Crisis*, ed. Alan S. Blinder, Andrew W. Lo, and Robert M. Solow. New York: Russell Sage Foundation.

Mutz, Diana. 2006. *Hearing the Other Side: Deliberative versus Participatory Democracy*. New York: Cambridge University Press.

Neumann, W. Russell. 1981. *The Paradox of Mass Politics: Knowledge and Opinion in the American Electorate*. Cambridge, MA: Harvard University Press.

Neumark, David, and William L. Wascher. 2007. "Minimum Wages and Employment." *Foundations and Trends in Microeconomics* 3(1–2): 1–182.

Neumark, David, and William L. Wascher. 2008. *Minimum Wages*. Cambridge, MA: MIT Press.

Ober, Josiah. 2015. "Democracy's Dignity." *American Political Science Review* 106(4): 827–846.

Oreskes, Naomi, and Erik M. Conway. 2008. "Challenging Knowledge." In *Agnotology: The Making and Unmaking of Ignorance*, ed. Robert N. Proctor and Londa Schiebinger. Stanford: Stanford University Press.

Page, Benjamin I. 2007. "Is Public Opinion an Illusion?" *Critical Review* 19(1): 35–45.

Page, Benjamin I., and Robert Y. Shapiro. 1992. *The Rational Public: Fifty Years of Trends in Americans' Policy Preferences*. Chicago: University of Chicago Press.

Page, Benjamin I., Robert Y. Shapiro, and Glenn R. Dempsey. 1987. "What Moves Public Opinion?" *American Political Science Review* 81: 23–43.

Palmer, Catherine. 2010. "Our Choice: How to Save the Schools." *New York Times*, October 17.

Pateman, Carole. 1970. *Participation and Democratic Theory*. Cambridge: Cambridge University Press.

Peltzman, Sam. 1973. "An Evaluation of Consumer Protection Legislation: The 1962 Drug Amendments." *Journal of Political Economy* 81(5): 1049–1091.

Peters, Jeremy W. 2014. "Democrats Assail G.O.P. after Filibuster of Proposal to Raise Minimum Wage." *New York Times*, May 1.

Pettit, Philip. 1997. *Republicanism*. Oxford: Clarendon Press.

Pincione, Guido, and Fernando Tesón. 2006. *Rational Choice and Democratic Deliberation: A Theory of Discourse Failure*. New York: Cambridge University Press.

Pinker, Stephen. 2002. *The Blank Slate: The Modern Denial of Human Nature*. New York: Viking.

Plott, Charles R., and Kathryn Zeiler. 2007. "Are Asymmetries in Exchange Behavior Incorrectly Interpreted as Evidence of Endowment Effect Theory and Prospect Theory?" *American Economic Review* 97: 1449–1471.

Popkin, Samuel L. 1991. *The Reasoning Voter*. Chicago: University of Chicago Press.

Popper, Karl R. [1945] 2013. *The Open Society and Its Enemies*. Princeton, NJ: Princeton University Press.

Popper, Karl R. 1957. *The Poverty of Historicism*. London: Routledge.

Popper, Karl R. 1963. *Conjectures and Refutations: The Growth of Scientific Knowledge*. New York: Harper and Row.

Popper, Karl R. 1988. "The Open Society and Its Enemies Revisited." *The Economist*, April 23.

Posner, Richard A. 2009. *A Failure of Capitalism*. Cambridge, MA: Harvard University Press.

Preiss, Raymond W., Barbara Mae Gayle, Nancy Burrell, Mike Allen, and Jennings Bryant. 2007. *Mass Media Effects Research: Advances through Meta-Analysis*. London: Routledge.

Puzder, Andrew. 2014. "Why Young People Can't Find Work." *Wall Street Journal*, June 10.

Quine, W. V. O. 1951. "Two Dogmas of Empiricism." *Philosophical Review* 60(1): 20–43.

Quine, W. V. O., and J. S. Ullian. 1978. *The Web of Belief*. 2nd ed. New York: Random House.

Radnitzky, Gerard, and W. W. Bartley, III. 1987. *Evolutionary Epistemology, Theory of Rationality, and the Sociology of Knowledge*. LaSalle, IL: Open Court.

Raeff, Marc. 1983. *The Well-Ordered Police State*. New Haven: Yale University Press.

Rahn, Wendy M. 1993. "The Role of Stereotypes in Information Processing about Political Candidates." *American Political Science Review* 37(2): 472–496.

Ralston, Shane J. 2005. "Hollowing Out the Dewey-Lippmann Debate." SSRN. DOI: 10.2139/ssrn.1503570.

Rasmussen Reports. 2016. "Voters Still Believe in Their Vote." September 7.

Rauch, Jonathan. 2015. "Political Realism: How Hacks, Machines, Big Money, and Backroom Deals Can Strengthen American Democracy." Washington, DC: Center for Effective Public Management at Brookings.

Rawls, John. 1993. "The Domain of the Political and Overlapping Consensus." In *The Idea of Democracy*, ed. David Copp, Jean Hampton, and John Roemer. Cambridge: Cambridge University Press.

Rawls, John. 2005. *Political Liberalism*. Expanded ed. New York: Columbia University Press.

Reich, Michael, and Ken Jacobs. 2014. "All Economics Is Local." *New York Times*, March 23.

Reid, T. R. 2009. "Five Myths about Health Care around the World." *Washington Post*, August 23.

Reiss, Julian. 2008. *Error in Economics: Towards a More Evidence-Based Methodology*. London: Routledge.

Riede, Paul. 2014. "How Can the Syracuse Schools Be Too Tough and Too Lax? What Both Sides Can Agree on about Discipline." *Syracuse.com*, July 15.

Rodgers, Daniel T. 1998. *Atlantic Crossings: Social Politics in a Progressive Age*. Cambridge, MA: Belknap Press of Harvard University Press.

Rogers, Melvin L. 2008. *The Undiscovered Dewey: Religion, Morality, and the Ethos of Democracy*. New York: Columbia University Press.

Roper Center for Public Opinion Research. 2001. *Public Perspective*, Special Issue on Polling and Democracy. July/August.

Roosevelt, Theodore. 1912a. "A Charter of Democracy." In idem, *Social Justice and Popular Rule: Essays, Addresses, and Public Statements Relating to the Progressive Movement (1910–1916)*. Vol. 17 of *The Works of Theodore Roosevelt: National Edition*, ed. Hermann Hagedorn. New York: Charles Scribner's Sons.

Roosevelt, Theodore. 1912b. "How I Became a Progressive." In idem, *Social Justice and Popular Rule: Essays, Addresses, and Public Statements Relating to the Progressive Movement (1910–1916)*. Vol. 17 of *The Works of Theodore Roosevelt: National Edition*, ed. Hermann Hagedorn. New York: Charles Scribner's Sons.

Roosevelt, Theodore. 1912c. "The Right of the People to Rule." In idem, *Social Justice and Popular Rule: Essays, Addresses, and Public Statements Relating to the Progressive Movement (1910–1916)*. Vol. 17 of *The Works of Theodore Roosevelt: National Edition*, ed. Hermann Hagedorn. New York: Charles Scribner's Sons.

Rosen, Michael. 1996. *On Voluntary Servitude: False Consciousness and the Theory of Ideology*. Cambridge: Polity Press.

Rosenberg, Alexander. 1992. *Economics—Mathematical Politics or Science of Diminishing Returns?* Chicago: University of Chicago Press.

Rosenberg, Alexander. 1994. "If Economics Isn't Science, What Is It?" In *Readings in the Philosophy of Social Science*, ed. Michael Martin and Lee C. McIntyre. Cambridge, MA: MIT Press.

Rosenberg, Shawn. 1995. "Against Neoclassical Political Economy: A Political Psychological Critique." *Political Psychology* 16(1): 99–136.

Ross, Lee. 2012. "Reflections on Biased Assimilation and Belief Polarization." *Critical Review* 24(2): 233–246.

Ross, Lee, and Andrew Ward. 1996. "Naïve Realism in Everyday Life." In *Values and Social Knowledge*, ed. Edward S. Reed, Elliot Turiel, and Terrance Brown. Mahwah, NJ: Lawrence Erlbaum Associates.

Roubini, Nouriel, and Stephen Mihm. 2010. *Crisis Economics: A Crash Course in the Future of Finance*. New York: Penguin.

Rumsey, Gary. 2006. "End Public Education." *WashingtonPost.com,* May 21.

Runciman, W. G. 1969. *Social Science and Political Theory*. 2nd ed. Cambridge: Cambridge University Press.

Ryan, Alan. 1995. *John Dewey and the High Tide of American Liberalism*. New York: Norton.

Sabl, Andrew. 2015. "The Two Cultures of Democratic Theory: Responsiveness, Democratic Quality, and the Empirical-Normative Divide." *Perspectives on Politics* 13(2): 345–365.

Saltsman, Michael. 2013. "The Record Is Clear: Minimum Wage Hikes Destroy Jobs." *Forbes Capital Flows,* April 17.

Samuels, Brett. 2018. "Trump: 'I Wouldn't Be Surprised' if Soros Were Paying for Migrant Caravan." *The Hill*, October 31.

Sartori, Giovanni. 1965. *Democratic Theory*. London: Frederick Praeger.

Schmidt, Peter. 2014. "What Makes the Best Teacher?" *New York Times*, November 1.

Schuck, Peter H. 2014. *Why Government Fails So Often*. Princeton, NJ: Princeton University Press.

Schudson, Michael. 1978. *Discovering the News: A Social History of American Newspapers*. New York: Basic Books.

Schudson, Michael. 2008. "The 'Lippmann-Dewey Debate' and the Invention of Walter Lippmann as an Anti-Democrat, 1986–1996." *International Journal of Communication* 2: 1–20.

Schumpeter, Joseph A. 1942. *Capitalism, Socialism, and Democracy*. New York: Harper & Row.

Scott, James C. 1998. *Seeing Like a State*. New Haven: Yale University Press.

Scott, James C. 2013. "Crops, Towns, Government." *London Review of Books*, November 21.

Scott, James C. 2017. *Against the Grain: A Deep History of the Earliest States*. New Haven: Yale University Press.

Scriven, Michael. [1956] 1994. "A Possible Distinction Between Traditional Scientific Disciplines and the Study of Human Behavior." In *Readings in the Philosophy of Social Science*, ed. Michael Martin and Lee C. McIntyre. Cambridge, MA: MIT Press.

Sears, David O., and Carolyn Funk. 1990. "Self-Interest in Americans' Political Opinions." In *Beyond Self-Interest*, ed. Jane J. Mansbridge. Chicago: University of Chicago Press.

Sears, David O., and Carolyn L. Funk. 1999. "Evidence of the Long-Term Persistence of Adults' Political Predispositions." *Journal of Politics* 61 (1): 1–28.

Sears, David O., Richard R. Lau, Tom R. Tyler, and Harris M. Allen Jr. 1980. "Self-Interest vs. Symbolic Politics in Policy Attitudes and Presidential Voting." *American Political Science Review* 74(3): 670–684.

Shackle, G. L. S. 1972. *Epistemics and Economics: A Critique of Economic Doctrines*. Cambridge: Cambridge University Press.

Shah, Dhavan V., Mark D. Watts, David Domke, and David P. Fan. 2002. "News Framing and Cueing of Issue Regimes: Explaining Clinton's Public Approval in Spite of Scandal." *Public Opinion Quarterly* 66: 339–370.

Shapiro, Ian. 1996. *Democracy's Place*. Ithaca, NY: Cornell University Press.

Shapiro, Ian. 2016. *Politics against Domination*. Cambridge, MA: Harvard University Press.

Shapiro, Robert Y., and Yaeli Bloch-Elkon. 2008. "Do the Facts Speak for Themselves? Partisan Disagreement as a Challenge to Democratic Competence." *Critical Review* 20(1–2): 115–140.

Shepardson, David. 2018. "FCC Reversal of Net Neutrality Rules Expected to Be Published Thursday: Sources." *Reuters.com*, February 20.

Shiller, Robert J. 2008. *The Subprime Solution*. Princeton, NJ: Princeton University Press.

Siebert, Horst. 1997. "Labor Market Rigidities: At the Root of Unemployment in Europe." *Journal of Economic Perspectives* 11(3): 37–54.

Simmel, Georg. [1910] 1950. *Hauptprobleme der Philosophier*. 7th ed. Berlin: de Gruyter.

Simon, Herbert L. 1976. "From Substantive to Procedural Rationality." In *Method and Appraisal in Economics*, ed. Spiro J. Latsis. Cambridge: Cambridge University Press.

Simon, Herbert L. 1985. "Human Nature in Politics: The Dialogue of Psychology with Political Science." *American Political Science Review* 79: 293–304.

Simon, Herbert L. 1987. "Rationality in Psychology and Economics." In *Rational Choice: The Contrast between Economics and Psychology*, ed. Robin M. Hogarth and Melvin W. Reder. Chicago: University of Chicago Press.

Shurter, Robert L. 1951. "Introduction" to Edward Bellamy, *Looking Backward: 2000–1887*. New York: Random House.

Skinner, Quentin. 2002. *Visions of Politics*. Vol. 1: *Regarding Method*. Cambridge: Cambridge University Press.

Smart, J. N. 1958. "Negative Utilitarianism." *Mind* 67(268): 542–543.

Sniderman, Paul M., Richard A. Brody, and Philip E. Tetlock. 1991. *Reasoning and Choice*. New York: Cambridge University Press.

Solomon, Miriam. 2001. *Social Empiricism*. Cambridge, MA: MIT Press.

Solow, Robert. 1985. "Economic History and Economics." *American Economic Review* 75(2): 328–331.

Somin, Ilya. 1998. "Voter Ignorance and the Democratic Ideal." *Critical Review* 12: 413–58.

Somin, Ilya. 2006. "Knowledge about Ignorance: New Directions in the Study of Political Information." *Critical Review* 18: 255–278.

Somin, Ilya. 2013. *Democracy and Political Ignorance*. Stanford, CA: Stanford University Press.

Somin, Ilya. 2014. "Why Political Ignorance Undermines the Wisdom of the Many." *Critical Review* 26(1–2): 151–169.

Somin, Ilya. 2015. "The Ongoing Debate over Public Ignorance: Reply to My Critics." *Critical Review* 27(3–4): 380–414.

Spence, Michael. 1973. "Job Market Signalling." *Quarterly Journal of Economics* 87: 355–374.

Stedman Jones, Gareth. 2016. *Karl Marx: Greatness and Illusion*. Cambridge, MA: Belknap Press of Harvard University Press.

Steel, Ronald. 1980. *Walter Lippmann and the American Century*. New York: Random House.

Steel, Ronald. 1997. "Foreword" to Lippmann [1922] 1997. New York: Free Press.

Stenner, Karen. 2005. *The Authoritarian Dynamic*. Cambridge: Cambridge University Press.

Stigler, George J. 1961. "The Economics of Information." *Journal of Political Economy* 69: 213–225.

Stiglitz, Joseph E. 2009. "Anatomy of a Murder." *Critical Review* 21(2–3): 329–340.

Stiglitz, Joseph E. 2010. *Freefall: America, Free Markets, and the Sinking of the World Economy*. New York: Norton.

Stimson, James A. 1975. "Belief Systems: Constraint, Complexity, and the 1972 Election." *American Journal of Political Science* 19(3): 393–417.

Stimson, James A. 1990. "A Macro Theory of Information Flow." In *Information and Democratic Processes*, ed. John Ferejohn and James Kuklinski. Urbana: University of Illinois Press.

Stokes, Donald E. 1966. "Some Dynamic Elements of Contests for the Presidency." *American Political Science Review* 60: 19–28.

Stokes, Susan. 2018. "Accountability for Realists." *Critical Review* 30(1–2): 133–142.

Stone, Deborah A. 1989. "Causal Stories and the Formation of Policy Agendas." *Political Science Quarterly* 104(2): 281–300.

Sunstein, Cass R. 1990. *After the Rights Revolution: Reconceiving the Regulatory State.* Cambridge, MA: Harvard University Press.

Sunstein, Cass R. 1998. "On Costs, Benefits, and Regulatory Success: Reply to Crandall." *Critical Review* 8(4): 623–633.

Sunstein, Cass R. 2000. "Cognition and Cost-Benefit Analysis." *Journal of Legal Studies* 29: 1059–1103.

Sunstein, Cass R. 2002. *The Cost-Benefit State: The Future of Regulatory Protection.* Chicago: American Bar Association.

Sunstein, Cass R. 2014. *Why Nudge: The Politics of Libertarian Paternalism.* New Haven: Yale University Press.

Sunstein, Cass R. 2018. *The Cost-Benefit Revolution.* Cambridge, MA: MIT Press.

Taber, Charles S., and Milton R. Lodge. 2006. "Motivated Skepticism in the Evaluation of Political Beliefs." *American Journal of Political Science* 50: 755–769.

Taylor, Charles. [1971] 1985. "Interpretation and the Sciences of Man." In idem, *Philosophical Papers*, vol. 2: *Philosophy and the Human Sciences.* Cambridge: Cambridge University Press.

Taylor, Charles. 1977. *Hegel.* Cambridge: Cambridge University Press.

Tetlock, Philip E. 2005. *Expert Political Judgment: How Good Is It? How Can We Know?* Princeton, NJ: Princeton University Press.

Tetlock, Philip E. 2010. "Second Thoughts about Expert Political Judgment." *Critical Review* 22(4): 467–88.

Thaler, Richard H., and Cass R. Sunstein. 2008. *Nudge: Improving Decisions about Health, Wealth, and Happiness.* New Haven: Yale University Press.

Time. 1992. "Perot the Front Runner," June 15.

Tribe, Keith. 1988. *Governing Economy: The Reformation of German Economic Discourse, 1750–1840.* Cambridge: Cambridge University Press.

Tuck, Richard. 2005. *The Sleeping Sovereign: The Invention of Modern Democracy.* Cambridge: Cambridge University Press.

Tuck, Richard. 2008. *Free Riding.* Cambridge, MA: Harvard University Press.

Tuckett, David, Antoine Mandel, Diana Mangalagiu, Allen Abramson, Jochen Hinkel, Konstantinos Katsikopoulos, Alan Kirman, Thierry Malleret, Igor Mozetic, Paul Ormerod, Robert Elliot Smith, Tommaso Venturini, and Angela Wilkinson. 2015. "Uncertainty, Decision Science, and Policy Making: A Manifesto for a Research Agenda." *Critical Review* 27(2): 213–242.

Tulis, Jeffrey K. 1987. *The Rhetorical Presidency.* Princeton, NJ: Princeton University Press.

Turner, Jonathan H., and Alexandra Maryanski. 2008. *On the Origin of Societies by Natural Selection.* Boulder, CO: Paradigm.

Tversky, Amos, and Daniel Kahneman. 1983. "Extensional versus Intuitive Reasoning: The Conjunction Fallacy in Probability Judgment." *Psychological Review* 90(4): 293–315.

Tyrrell, Martin. 1992. "Nation-States and States of Mind." *Critical Review* 10(2): 233–250.

Umanath, Sharda, Elizabeth J. Marsh, and Andrew C. Butler. 2012. "Positive and Negative Effects of Monitoring Popular Films for Historical Inaccuracies." *Applied Cognitive Psychology* 26(4): 556–567.

Uscinski, Joseph E., and Ryden W. Butler. 2013. "The Epistemology of Fact Checking." *Critical Review* 25(2): 162–180.

US Census Bureau. 2006. "Voting and Registration in the Election of November 2004." March.

Van der Dussen, Jan. 2013. "The Case for Historical Imagination: Defending the Human Factor and Narrative." In *The Sage Handbook of Historical Theory*, ed. Nancy Partner and Sarah Foot. Los Angeles: Sage.

Van Ijzendoorn, Marinus H. 1989. "Moral Judgment, Authoritarianism, and Ethnocentrism." *Journal of Social Psychology* 129: 37–45.

Wakefield, Andre. 2009. *The Disordered Police State: German Cameralism as Science and Practice.* Chicago: University of Chicago Press.

Waldron, Jeremy. 1999. *The Dignity of Legislation.* Oxford: Oxford University Press.

Walzer, Michael. 1981. "Philosophy and Democracy." *Political Theory* 9(3): 379–399.

Watts, Duncan J. 2011. *Everything Is Obvious.* New York: Random House.

Warren, Mark E. 2011. "Voting with Your Feet: Exit-Based Empowerment in Democratic Theory." *American Political Science Review* 105(4): 683–701.

Weber, Max. [1904] 1949. "'Objectivity' in Social Science and Social Policy." In *From Max Weber: Essays in Sociology,* ed. Hans Gerth and C. Wright Mills. New York: Oxford University Press.

Weber, Max. [1918] 1946. "Politics as a Vocation." In *From Max Weber: Essays in Sociology,* ed. Hans Gerth and C. Wright Mills. New York: Oxford University Press.

Weingarten, Randi. 2015. "The Teacher Shortage: Educators Cite Low Pay, Lack of Respect and Support, and High-Stakes Tests as Causes." *New York Times,* August 16.

Weingartner, Rudolph W. 1962. *Experience and Culture.* Middletown, CT: Wesleyan University Press.

Weinshall, Matthew. 2003. "Means, Ends, and Public Ignorance in Habermas's Theory of Democracy." *Critical Review* 15(1)-2: 23–58.

Westbrook, Robert B. 1991. *John Dewey and American Democracy.* Ithaca, NY: Cornell University Press.

Whaples, Robert. 2006. "Do Economists Agree on Anything? Yes!" *Economists' Voice,* November.

White, Lawrence J. 2009. "The Credit-Rating Agencies and the Subprime Debacle." *Critical Review* 21(2–3): 389–399.

White House. 2015. "Occupational Licensing: A Framework for Policymakers." Report Prepared by the Department of the Treasury Office of Economic Policy, the Council of Economic Advisers, and the Department of Labor.

Winston, Clifford. 2006. *Government Failure versus Market Failure: Microeconomics Policy Research and Government Performance.* Washington, DC: AEI-Brookings Joint Center for Regulatory Studies.

World Public Opinion. 2008. "World Publics See Government as Responsible for Ensuring Basic Healthcare, Food, and Education Needs." November 10.

Zaller, John R. 1992. *The Nature and Origins of Mass Opinion.* New York: Cambridge University Press.

Zaller, John. 2012. "What *Nature and Origins* Left Out." *Critical Review* 24(4): 573–644.

INDEX

For the benefit of digital users, indexed terms that span two pages (e.g., 52–53) may, on occasion, appear on only one of those pages.

Adorno, Theodor, 209–19, 220–21, 223, 228, 229, 236, 343, 345n.30

Affordable Care Act, 45, 56

Akerlof, George, 187n.17, 195, 196, 229

Almond, Gabriel, 150n.47

Altemeyer, Bob, 226–28, 229

American Economic Association, 183–84

American National Election Survey, 293–94

American Political Science Association, 191–92

American Political Science Review, 66

American Voter, The (1960), 238n.13, 265–66, 283–89, 293–94, 297, 312

Americans with Disabilities Act, 51–52, 53

Ann Arbor, Michigan, 105–6

anonymous others, 28, 30, 139, 143, 145–46, 147–48, 163, 165–66, 168, 172, 234, 279, 303–4, 330, 331, 334, 339, 341

anti-Semitism, 212–17, 228–29

Arrow, Kenneth J., 169

Atlas Shrugged, 143–44

authoritarian personality, theories of, 209–28

backfires, technocratic, 13, 53, 54–55, 57, 67, 75–76, 76n.115

Banerjee, Abhijit, 206–7, 220, 226, 227–28, 229

Bartels, Larry M., 14n.44, 18n.69, 264, 265n.11, 270, 298

Barth, James, 255–60

Bayesian updating, 237, 241–42

Bear Stearns, 254–55, 258–59

behavioral economics, 28, 59, 181–82, 196–200, 215, 298, 315, 343

behavioral norms. *See under* homogenizing factors

Bellamy, Edward, 84, 85–86, 88–89

Bentham, Jeremy, 18–19, 92

Berelson, Bernard, 7–10, 11, 12–13, 232

Berlin, Isaiah, 1–3, 5, 8, 9, 20, 35, 141–42, 168–69, 329–30